# THE top10★
## OF EVERYTHING
# 2002

# THE top10 OF EVERYTHING 2002

RUSSELL ASH

A Dorling Kindersley Book

# Contents

LONDON, NEW YORK, MUNICH, MELBOURNE, DELHI,

A PENGUIN COMPANY

**Senior Editor** Nicki Lampon
**Senior Art Editor** Kevin Ryan

**DTP Designer** Sonia Charbonnier
**Production** Louise Daly
**Picture Research** Anna Grapes

**Managing Editor** Sharon Lucas
**Senior Managing Art Editor** Derek Coombes

Produced for Dorling Kindersley by
**Cooling Brown**, 9–11 High Street,
Hampton, Middlesex TW12 2SA

**Senior Editor** Alison Bolus
**Art Editor** Tish Mills
**Creative Director** Arthur Brown

**Author's Project Manager** Aylla Macphail

First American Edition, 2001
01 02 03 04 05 10 9 8 7 6 5 4 3 2 1

Published in the United States by
DK Publishing Inc., 95 Madison Avenue,
New York, New York 10016

A Cataloging in Publication record is available from the Library of Congress

0-7894-8043-3 (pb)
0-7894-8042-5 (hc)

Reproduction by Colourscan, Singapore
Printed and bound by Printer Industria Grafica, S.A., Barcelona, Spain

See our complete catalog at
**www.dk.com**

# Introduction

## It's a Fact

If you have been buying *The Top 10 of Everything* every year since it was first published, you will now have 13 copies on your book shelf. Fortunately, I do not suffer from triskaidekaphobia (the fear of the number 13), but it is through researching and compiling Top 10 lists that I have discovered a wealth of unusual facts – such as the word triskaidekaphobia. In this year's volume, you too can discover facts, from the 10 places with the heaviest daily downpours to the Top 10 skateboarders, and from the first lie detector to the identity of the originals behind James Bond and Barbie.

## A Changing World

During recent years, certain lists have become widely featured in the press, among them lists of best-selling books and richest people, while the popularity of general knowledge is exemplified by the increasing number of TV game shows. Over the past 13 years, the information that this book presents has changed, and the nature of Top 10 lists has changed too. The Top 10 professions of cellular phone users was once of interest, but now that so many people in Western countries have cellular phones, such a list is synonymous with the Top 10 most common professions. Meanwhile, lists containing entries that have been valid for many centuries may alter: while work was in progress on this edition, the 5th tallest statue in the world, the 173-ft (53-m) Buddha at Bamian, Afghanistan, carved in the 3rd–4th centuries AD, was destroyed by the Taliban.

## Information Superhighway

In the past, it often took years for data to be processed and disseminated. Today, the use of computers and the Internet means that information is more quickly and more readily available. One of the problems with information is that it piles up. Only a few hundred years ago, an educated person could be well informed about almost every aspect of the arts and sciences, but as each generation adds to the sum total of knowledge, so the task of sifting through it for the items you require becomes an occupation in itself. I hope that *The Top 10 of Everything* offers some shortcuts through the information quagmire.

## In and Out

To newcomers to *The Top 10 of Everything* it is worth mentioning that there are no "bests," other than best-sellers, and no "worsts" (with the exception of lists about disasters and murders, which are measurable by numbers of victims). The book focuses on superlatives in numerous categories, and also contains a variety of "firsts" or "latests,"

which recognize the pioneers and most recent achievers in various fields of endeavor. Top 10 lists of films are based on worldwide box-office income, and those on such topics as recorded music, videos, DVDs, and books are based on sales, unless otherwise stated.

## Thanks for Everything

My ever-expanding network of experts has enabled me to ensure that certain lists are constantly updated as new data become available. As ever, I want to thank the many people who have supplied information, especially private individuals, experts, and enthusiasts, who provide some of the most fascinating and otherwise quite unobtainable information. If you have any list ideas or comments, please write to me c/o the publishers or email me directly at ash@pavilion.co.uk.

Other recent Dorling Kindersley books by Russell Ash:
*The Factastic Book of 1,001 Lists*
*The Factastic Book of Comparisons*
*Great Wonders of the World*

## Special Features

• More than 1,000 lists in many new categories make this the **most comprehensive** *Top 10 of Everything* ever.

• **Hundreds of new lists** are included, from the 10 countries with the most teenage brides to the Top 10 baked bean consumers.

• Interesting and unusual **2002 anniversaries** are celebrated throughout with "100 Years Ago" and "50 Years Ago" features.

• Numerous "Who Was…?" entries focus on the people behind **famous names**.

• "Did You Know?" entries offer **offbeat sidelights** on the subjects explored.

• **Quiz questions** with multichoice answers appear throughout the book.

# THE UNIVERSE & THE EARTH

# Star Gazing

## STARS NEAREST TO THE EARTH*

| | STAR | LIGHT-YEARS | MILES (MILLIONS) | KM (MILLIONS) |
|---|---|---|---|---|
| 1 | Proxima Centauri | 4.22 | 24,792,500 | 39,923,310 |
| 2 | Alpha Centauri | 4.35 | 25,556,250 | 41,153,175 |
| 3 | Barnard's Star | 5.98 | 35,132,500 | 56,573,790 |
| 4 | Wolf 359 | 7.75 | 45,531,250 | 73,318,875 |
| 5 | Lalande 21185 | 8.22 | 48,292,500 | 77,765,310 |
| 6 | Luyten 726-8 | 8.43 | 49,526,250 | 79,752,015 |
| 7 | Sirius | 8.65 | 50,818,750 | 81,833,325 |
| 8 | Ross 154 | 9.45 | 55,518,750 | 89,401,725 |
| 9 | Ross 248 | 10.40 | 61,100,000 | 98,389,200 |
| 10 | Epsilon Eridani | 10.80 | 63,450,000 | 102,173,400 |

*Excluding the Sun*

A spaceship traveling at 25,000 mph (40,237 km/h) – which is faster than any human has yet reached in space – would take more than 113,200 years to reach the Earth's closest star, Proxima Centauri. While the nearest stars in this list lie just over four light-years away from the Earth, others within the Milky Way lie at a distance of 2,500 light-years. Our own galaxy may span as much as 100,000 light-years from end to end, with the Sun some 25,000 to 30,000 light-years from its center.

**NEAR NEIGHBOR**

*Proxima Centauri, Earth's closest star beyond the Sun, was discovered in 1913 by Scottish astronomer Robert Thorburn Innes. It has 10 percent of the Sun's mass but only 0.006 percent of its luminosity.*

## BODIES IN THE SOLAR SYSTEM WITH THE GREATEST SURFACE GRAVITY*

| | BODY | SURFACE GRAVITY | WEIGHT (LB)[#] |
|---|---|---|---|
| 1 | Sun | 27.90 | 3,998.1 |
| 2 | Jupiter | 2.64 | 378.3 |
| 3 | Neptune | 1.20 | 172.0 |
| 4 | Uranus | 1.17 | 167.0 |
| 5 | Saturn | 1.16 | 166.2 |
| 6 | Earth | 1.00 | 143.3 |
| 7 | Venus | 0.90 | 129.0 |
| 8 = | Mars | 0.38 | 54.5 |
| = | Mercury | 0.38 | 54.5 |
| 10 | Pluto | 0.06 | 8.6 |

*Excluding satellites*

[#] *Of a 143 lb adult on the body's surface*

**SMALL WONDER**

*Pluto is less than a fifth of the size of the Earth. Not only is it the smallest of the solar system's planets, it also has the lowest gravity. It was discovered in 1930 by American astronomer Clyde Tombaugh.*

**THIN ICE**

*Saturn is the furthest planet that can be seen with the naked eye. Its rings, which are composed of ice, are up to 167,770 miles (270,000 km) in diameter, but only a few yards thick.*

## TOP 10 ★
## MOST MASSIVE BODIES IN THE SOLAR SYSTEM*

| | BODY | MASS# |
|---|---|---|
| 1 | Sun | 332,800.000 |
| 2 | Jupiter | 317.828 |
| 3 | Saturn | 95.161 |
| 4 | Neptune | 17.148 |
| 5 | Uranus | 14.536 |
| 6 | Earth | 1.000 |
| 7 | Venus | 0.815 |
| 8 | Mars | 0.10745 |
| 9 | Mercury | 0.05527 |
| 10 | Pluto | 0.0022 |

* Excluding satellites

# Compared with the Earth = 1; the mass of Earth is approximately 80 trillion tons

## TOP 10 ★
## GALAXIES NEAREST TO THE EARTH

| | GALAXY | DISTANCE (LIGHT-YEARS) |
|---|---|---|
| 1 | Large Cloud of Magellan | 169,000 |
| 2 | Small Cloud of Magellan | 190,000 |
| 3 | Ursa Minor dwarf | 250,000 |
| 4 | Draco dwarf | 260,000 |
| 5 | Sculptor dwarf | 280,000 |
| 6 | Fornax dwarf | 420,000 |
| 7 | =Leo I dwarf | 750,000 |
| | =Leo II dwarf | 750,000 |
| 9 | Barnard's Galaxy | 1,700,000 |
| 10 | Andromeda Spiral | 2,200,000 |

These, and other galaxies, are members of the so-called "Local Group," although with vast distances such as these, "local" is clearly a relative term.

## TOP 10 ★
## BODIES IN THE SOLAR SYSTEM WITH THE GREATEST ESCAPE VELOCITY*

| | BODY | ESCAPE VELOCITY (MILES/SEC) |
|---|---|---|
| 1 | Sun | 383.71 |
| 2 | Jupiter | 37.42 |
| 3 | Saturn | 20.04 |
| 4 | Neptune | 14.85 |
| 5 | Uranus | 13.98 |
| 6 | Earth | 6.94 |
| 7 | Venus | 6.44 |
| 8 | Mars | 3.13 |
| 9 | Mercury | 2.64 |
| 10 | Pluto | 0.73 |

* Excluding satellites

Escape velocity is the speed a rocket has to attain upon launching to overcome the gravitational pull of the body it is leaving. The escape velocity of the Moon is 1.48 miles/sec.

## TOP 10 ★
## LONGEST YEARS IN THE SOLAR SYSTEM

| | BODY | LENGTH OF YEAR* YEARS | DAYS |
|---|---|---|---|
| 1 | Pluto | 247 | 256 |
| 2 | Neptune | 164 | 298 |
| 3 | Uranus | 84 | 4 |
| 4 | Saturn | 29 | 168 |
| 5 | Jupiter | 11 | 314 |
| 6 | Mars | 1 | 322 |
| 7 | Earth | | 365 |
| 8 | Venus | | 225 |
| 9 | Mercury | | 88 |
| 10 | Sun | | 0 |

* Period of orbit around the Sun, in Earth years/days (based on a non-leap year of 365 days)

## TOP 10 ★
## LARGEST BODIES IN THE SOLAR SYSTEM

| | BODY | MAXIMUM DIAMETER MILES | KM |
|---|---|---|---|
| 1 | Sun | 865,036 | 1,392,140 |
| 2 | Jupiter | 88,846 | 142,984 |
| 3 | Saturn | 74,898 | 120,536 |
| 4 | Uranus | 31,763 | 51,118 |
| 5 | Neptune | 30,778 | 49,532 |
| 6 | Earth | 7,926 | 12,756 |
| 7 | Venus | 7,520 | 12,103 |
| 8 | Mars | 4,222 | 6,794 |
| 9 | Ganymede | 3,274 | 5,269 |
| 10 | Titan | 3,200 | 5,150 |

Most of the planets are visible from the Earth with the naked eye and have been observed since ancient times. The exceptions are Uranus, discovered on March 13, 1781, by the British astronomer Sir William Herschel; Neptune, found by German astronomer Johann Galle on September 23, 1846 (Galle was led to his discovery by the independent calculations of the French astronomer Urbain Leverrier and the British mathematician John Adams); and, outside the Top 10, Pluto, located using photographic techniques by American astronomer Clyde Tombaugh on March 13, 1930.

**Did You Know?** The name of the planet Pluto was suggested two days after its discovery by Venetia Burney, an 11-year-old English schoolgirl. Pluto is the Roman god of the underworld, but the name also begins with the initials of Percival Lowell, the astronomer who had suggested its existence.

# Asteroids, Meteorites & Comets

## MOST FREQUENTLY SEEN COMETS

| | COMET | YEARS BETWEEN APPEARANCES |
|---|---|---|
| 1 | Encke | 3.302 |
| 2 | Grigg-Skjellerup | 4.908 |
| 3 | Honda-Mrkós-Pajdusáková | 5.210 |
| 4 | Tempel 2 | 5.259 |
| 5 | Neujmin 2 | 5.437 |
| 6 | Brorsen | 5.463 |
| 7 | Tuttle-Giacobini-Kresák | 5.489 |
| 8 | Tempel-L. Swift | 5.681 |
| 9 | Tempel 1 | 5.982 |
| 10 | Pons-Winnecke | 6.125 |

These and several other comets return with regularity (although with some notable variations), while others have such long orbits that they may not be seen again for many thousands, or even millions, of years.

## OBJECTS COMING CLOSEST TO THE EARTH

| | NAME/DESIGNATION | DUE DATE* | DISTANCE# MILES | KM |
|---|---|---|---|---|
| 1 | 1999 RQ36 | Sep 23, 2080 | 130,130 | 209,440 |
| 2 | 1998 HH49 | Oct 17, 2023 | 232,393 | 374,000 |
| 3 | 1999 AN10 | Aug 7, 2027 | 241,689 | 388,960 |
| 4 | 1999 RQ36 | Sep 23, 2060 | 455,490 | 733,040 |
| 5 | 1999 MN | June 3, 2010 | 492,673 | 792,880 |
| 6 | Hathor (2340) | Oct 21, 2086 | 520,560 | 837,760 |
| 7 | 1999 RM45 | Mar 3, 2021 | 548,447 | 882,640 |
| 8 | 1997 XF11 | Oct 26, 2028 | 567,038 | 912,560 |
| 9 | 2000 LF3 | June 16, 2046 | 604,221 | 972,400 |
| 10 | Hathor (2340) | Oct 21, 2069 | 613,517 | 987,360 |

\* Of closest approach to the Earth

\# Closest distance from Earth

Source: *NASA*

It is believed that there are up to 2,000 "Near-Earth objects" (mostly asteroids and comets) over 0.6 miles (1 km) in diameter that approach the Earth's orbit.

## COMETS THAT HAVE COME CLOSEST TO THE EARTH

| | COMET | DATE* | DISTANCE# MILES | KM |
|---|---|---|---|---|
| 1 | Comet of 1491 | Feb 20, 1491 | 873,784 | 1,406,220 |
| 2 | Lexell | July 1, 1770 | 1,403,633 | 2,258,928 |
| 3 | Tempel-Tuttle | Oct 26, 1366 | 2,128,688 | 3,425,791 |
| 4 | IRAS-Araki-Alcock | May 11, 1983 | 2,909,516 | 4,682,413 |
| 5 | Halley | Apr 10, 837 | 3,104,724 | 4,996,569 |
| 6 | Biela | Dec 9, 1805 | 3,402,182 | 5,475,282 |
| 7 | Grischow | Feb 8, 1743 | 3,625,276 | 5,834,317 |
| 8 | Pons-Winnecke | June 26, 1927 | 3,662,458 | 5,894,156 |
| 9 | Comet of 1014 | Feb 24, 1014 | 3,783,301 | 6,088,633 |
| 10 | La Hire | Apr 20, 1702 | 4,062,168 | 6,537,427 |

\* Of closest approach to the Earth

\# Closest distance from the Earth

**HALLEY'S COMET**

*The predicted return of Halley's Comet, seen here during its most recent appearance in 1986, proved the theory that comets follow fixed orbits.*

# LARGEST METEORITES EVER FOUND

| LOCATION | ESTIMATED WEIGHT (TONS) |
|---|---|
| **1** **Hoba West**, Grootfontein, Namibia | more than 66.0 |
| **2** **Ahnighito** ("The Tent"), Cape York, West Greenland | 63.2 |
| **3** **Campo del Cielo**, Argentina | 45.3 |
| **4** **Canyon Diablo***, Arizona | 33.1 |
| **5** **Sikhote-Alin**, Russia | 29.8 |
| **6** **Chupaderos**, Mexico | 26.7 |
| **7** **Bacuberito**, Mexico | 24.3 |
| **8** **Armanty**, Western Mongolia | 22.0 |
| **9** **Mundrabilla**#, Western Australia | 18.7 |
| **10** **Mbosi**, Tanzania | 17.6 |

*\* Formed Meteor Crater; fragmented – total in public collections is around 12.7 tons*

*# In two parts*

---

## TOP 10 ★
## SOURCES OF ASTEROID NAMES

| SOURCE | ASTEROIDS* |
|---|---|
| **1** **Astronomers, astrophysicists, and planetary scientists** | 1,040 |
| **2** **Places and cultures** | 822 |
| **3** **Scientists other than astronomers** | 551 |
| **4** **Mythological characters** | 439 |
| **5** **Astronomers' families and friends** | 406 |
| **6** **Historical personalities** | 360 |
| **7** **Writers and editors** | 275 |
| **8** **Amateur astronomers** | 132 |
| **9** **Musicians, composers, and film and TV directors** | 130 |
| **10** **Literary characters** | 112 |

*\* Based on an analysis of 4,619 named asteroids within the first 6,000 discovered*

Source: *Jacob Schwartz,* Asteroid Name Encyclopedia, *1995*

Asteroid names have also been derived from individuals in fields such as singing and dancing, and art and architecture.

---

**EARTH IMPACT**

*The Canyon Diablo, or Barringer meteorite crater, in Arizona, the largest on the Earth, was caused by the impact of a meteorite weighing 69,500 tons, of which some 33 tons have been recovered.*

## TOP 10 ★
## LARGEST ASTEROIDS

| NAME | YEAR DISCOVERED | DIAMETER MILES | KM |
|---|---|---|---|
| **1** **Ceres** | 1801 | 582 | 936 |
| **2** **Pallas** | 1802 | 377 | 607 |
| **3** **Vesta** | 1807 | 322 | 519 |
| **4** **Hygeia** | 1849 | 279 | 450 |
| **5** **Euphrosyne** | 1854 | 229 | 370 |
| **6** **Interamnia** | 1910 | 217 | 349 |
| **7** **Davida** | 1903 | 200 | 322 |
| **8** **Cybele** | 1861 | 192 | 308 |
| **9** **Europa** | 1858 | 179 | 288 |
| **10** **Patientia** | 1899 | 171 | 275 |

Asteroids, sometimes known as "minor planets," are fragments of rock orbiting between Mars and Jupiter. There are perhaps 45,000 of them, but only about 10 percent have been named. The first and largest to be discovered was Ceres.

---

## TOP 10 ★
## LARGEST METEORITES EVER FOUND IN THE US

| LOCATION | ESTIMATED WEIGHT (TONS) |
|---|---|
| **1** **Canyon Diablo***, Arizona | 33.1 |
| **2** **Willamette**, Oregon | 16.5 |
| **3** **Old Woman**, California | 3.0 |
| **4** **Brenham**, Kansas | 2.6 |
| **5** **Navajo**, Arizona | 2.4 |
| **6** **Quinn Canyon**, Nevada | 1.6 |
| **7** **Goose Lake**, California | 1.3 |
| **8** **Norton County**, Kansas | 1.1 |
| **9** **Tucson**, Arizona | 1.0 |
| **10** **Sardis**#, Georgia | 0.9 |

*\* Formed Meteor Crater; fragmented – total in public collections is around 12.7 tons*

*# Now badly corroded*

It has been suggested that the weight of a meteorite discovered at Cosby's Creek, Tennesee, was 1.1 tons, but only 210 lb (95 kg) of it has been accounted for. There are approximately 1,200 meteorites known in the US.

---

**In which country is the world's highest waterfall?**
*see p.18 for the answer*
A Norway
B Venezuela
C Nepal

# Space Discoveries

## HUBBLE

American astronomer Edwin Powell Hubble (1889–1953) led a varied career, including heavyweight boxing and studying law at Oxford University, UK, before becoming a professional astronomer. After World War I, he worked at the Mount Wilson Observatory, home of the then most powerful telescope in the world. In 1923 he proved that the Universe extended beyond the Milky Way, and in 1929 that the universe is expanding. This became known as Hubble's Law. Named in his honor, the Hubble Telescope, launched in 1990 by Space Shuttle *Discovery*, has enabled exploration of distant galaxies without the atmospheric interference that is encountered on the Earth.

## TOP 10 MOST RECENT PLANETARY MOONS TO BE DISCOVERED

*(Moon/planet/year)*

❶ S/1999J1, Jupiter, 2000
❷ = Prospero, Uranus, 1999; = Setebos, Uranus, 1999; = Stephano, Uranus, 1999
❺ = Caliban, Uranus, 1997;
= Sycorax, Uranus, 1997 ❼ Pan, Saturn, 1990
❽ = Despina, Neptune, 1989; = Naiad, Neptune, 1989; = Thalassa, Neptune, 1989

Space probe *Voyager 2* discovered six moons of Neptune on the same day (Aug 25, 1989). Those listed in the Top 10 were the first, followed by Galatea, Larissa, and Proteus.

## TOP 10 ★ LARGEST REFLECTING TELESCOPES

| TELESCOPE/LOCATION | APERTURE FT | M |
|---|---|---|
| **1 Keck I & II Telescopes\***, Mauna Kea, Hawaii | 32.8 | 10.0 |
| **2 Hobby-Eberly Telescope**, Mount Fowlkes, Texas | 30.9 | 9.2 |
| **3 Subaru Telescope**, Mauna Kea, Hawaii | 27.2 | 8.3 |
| **4 Gemini North Telescope**, Mauna Kea, Hawaii | 25.6 | 8.0 |
| **5 MMT#**, Mount Hopkins, Arizona | 21.3 | 6.5 |
| **6 Bolshoi Teleskop Azimutalnyi**, Nizhny Arkhyz, Russia | 19.6 | 6.0 |
| **7 Hale Telescope**, Palomar Mountain, California | 16.4 | 5.0 |
| **8 William Herschel Telescope**, La Palma, Canary Islands, Spain | 13.8 | 4.2 |
| **9 Victor Blanco Telescope**, Gerro Tololo, Chile | 13.1 | 4.0 |
| **10 Anglo-Australian Telescope**, Coonabarabran, NSW, Australia | 12.8 | 3.9 |

\* *Identical telescopes that work in tandem to produce the largest reflecting surface*

# *Formerly the Multiple Mirror Telescope*

Antu, Kueyen, and Melipal, three telescopes located in Cerro Paranal, Chile, are soon to be combined to form the appropriately named Very Large Telescope, which will take first place in this list with an aperture of 53.8 ft (16.4 m). The Keck telescopes will combine with several smaller scopes to form the 47.9 ft (14.6 m) Keck Interferometer.

### GALILEAN DISCOVERY

*Ganymede, largest of Jupiter's satellites, was among the four to be discovered by Galileo, on January 7, 1610, using the newly invented telescope.*

## THE 10 ★ FIRST PLANETARY MOONS TO BE DISCOVERED

| MOON/DISCOVERER | PLANET | YEAR |
|---|---|---|
| **1 Moon** | Earth | Ancient |
| **2 =Callisto**, Galileo Galilei | Jupiter | 1610 |
| **=Europa**, Galileo Galilei | Jupiter | 1610 |
| **=Ganymede**, Galileo Galilei | Jupiter | 1610 |
| **=Io**, Galileo Galilei | Jupiter | 1610 |
| **6 Titan**, Christian Huygens | Saturn | 1655 |
| **7 Iapetus**, Giovanni Cassini | Saturn | 1671 |
| **8 Rhea**, Giovanni Cassini | Saturn | 1672 |
| **9 =Dione**, Giovanni Cassini | Saturn | 1684 |
| **=Tethys**, Giovanni Cassini | Saturn | 1684 |

While the Earth's moon has been observed since ancient times, it was not until the development of the telescope that Italian astronomer Galileo was able to discover (on January 7, 1610) the first moons of another planet. These, which are Jupiter's four largest, were named by German astronomer Simon Marius and are known as the Galileans.

### HEAVENLY TWINS

*Financed by US philanthropist W. M. Keck, twin telescopes Keck I (1993) and II (1996) on Mauna Kea, Hawaii, are the world's largest optical instruments.*

**Did You Know?** Until 1986, Uranus was believed to have only five moons, but in that year interplanetary probe *Voyager 2* discovered 10 more, all but one of which were named after Shakespearean characters.

## THE 10 ★
# FIRST PLANETARY PROBES

| | PROBE/COUNTRY | PLANET | ARRIVAL* |
|---|---|---|---|
| 1 | *Venera 4*, USSR | Venus | Oct 18, 1967 |
| 2 | *Venera 5*, USSR | Venus | May 16, 1969 |
| 3 | *Venera 6*, USSR | Venus | May 17, 1969 |
| 4 | *Venera 7*, USSR | Venus | Dec 15, 1970 |
| 5 | *Mariner 9*, US | Mars | Nov 13, 1971 |
| 6 | *Mars 2*, USSR | Mars | Nov 27, 1971 |
| 7 | *Mars 3*, USSR | Mars | Dec 2, 1971 |
| 8 | *Venera 8*, USSR | Venus | July 22, 1972 |
| 9 | *Venera 9*, USSR | Venus | Oct 22, 1975 |
| 10 | *Venera 10*, USSR | Venus | Oct 25, 1975 |

*\* Successfully entered orbit or landed*

This list excludes "flybys" – probes that passed by but did not land on the surface of the planet. The US's *Pioneer 10*, for example, flew past Jupiter on December 3, 1973, but did not land.

### VENUSIAN VOLCANOES

*Mapped by the Magellan probe, the volcanoes of Sif Mons (left) and Gula Mons (right) stand out above the lava surface of the Eistla Regio area of Venus.*

## THE 10 ★
# FIRST BODIES TO HAVE BEEN VISITED BY SPACECRAFT

| | BODY | SPACECRAFT/COUNTRY | DATE |
|---|---|---|---|
| 1 | Moon | *Luna 1*, USSR | Jan 2, 1959 |
| 2 | Venus | *Venera 1*, USSR | May 19, 1961 |
| 3 | Sun | *Pioneer 5*, US | Aug 10, 1961 |
| 4 | Mars | *Mariner 4*, US | July 14, 1965 |
| 5 | Jupiter | *Pioneer 10*, US | Dec 3, 1973 |
| 6 | Mercury | *Mariner 10*, US | Mar 29, 1974 |
| 7 | Saturn | *Pioneer 11*, US | Sep 1, 1979 |
| 8 | Comet Giacobini-Zinner | *International Sun–Earth Explorer 3 (International Cometary Explorer)* Europe/US | Sep 11, 1985 |
| 9 | Uranus | *Voyager 2*, US | Jan 30, 1986 |
| 10 | Halley's Comet | *Vega 1*, USSR | Mar 6, 1986 |

Only the first spacecraft successfully to approach or land on each body is included. Several of the bodies listed have since been visited on subsequent occasions, either by "flybys," orbiters, or landers. Other bodies also visited since the first 10 include Neptune (by *Voyager 2*, US, 1989).

## THE 10 ★
# FIRST UNMANNED MOON LANDINGS

| | NAME | COUNTRY | DATE (LAUNCH/IMPACT) |
|---|---|---|---|
| 1 | *Lunik 2* | USSR | Sep 12/14, 1959 |
| 2 | *Ranger 4** | US | Apr 23/26, 1962 |
| 3 | *Ranger 6* | US | Jan 30/Feb 2, 1964 |
| 4 | *Ranger 7* | US | July 28/31, 1964 |
| 5 | *Ranger 8* | US | Feb 17/20, 1965 |
| 6 | *Ranger 9* | US | Mar 21/24, 1965 |
| 7 | *Luna 5** | USSR | May 9/12, 1965 |
| 8 | *Luna 7** | USSR | Oct 4/8, 1965 |
| 9 | *Luna 8** | USSR | Dec 3/7, 1965 |
| 10 | *Luna 9* | USSR | Jan 31/Feb 3, 1966 |

*\* Crash landing*

In addition to these 10, debris left on the surface of the Moon includes the remains of several further *Luna* craft, including unmanned sample collectors and *Lunakhod 1* and *2* (1966–71; all Soviet), seven *Surveyors* (1966–68; all US), and five *Lunar Orbiters* (1966–67; all US).

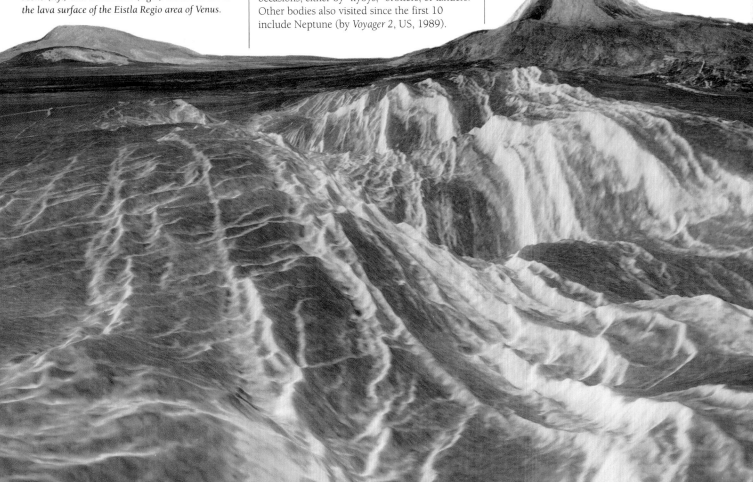

# Space Explorers

## THE 10 ★
### FIRST MOONWALKERS

| | ASTRONAUT | SPACECRAFT | TOTAL EVA* HR:MIN | MISSION DATES |
|---|---|---|---|---|
| 1 | Neil A. Armstrong | Apollo 11 | 2:32 | July 16–24, 1969 |
| 2 | Edwin E. ("Buzz") Aldrin | Apollo 11 | 2:15 | July 16–24, 1969 |
| 3 | Charles Conrad Jr. | Apollo 12 | 7:45 | Nov 14–24, 1969 |
| 4 | Alan L. Bean | Apollo 12 | 7:45 | Nov 14–24, 1969 |
| 5 | Alan B. Shepard | Apollo 14 | 9:23 | Jan 31–Feb 9, 1971 |
| 6 | Edgar D. Mitchell | Apollo 14 | 9:23 | Jan 31–Feb 9, 1971 |
| 7 | David R. Scott | Apollo 15 | 19:08 | July 26–Aug 7, 1971 |
| 8 | James B. Irwin | Apollo 15 | 18:35 | July 26–Aug 7, 1971 |
| 9 | John W. Young | Apollo 16 | 20:14 | Apr 16–27, 1972 |
| 10 | Charles M. Duke | Apollo 16 | 20:14 | Apr 16–27, 1972 |

* Extra Vehicular Activity (i.e. time spent out of the lunar module on the Moon's surface)

Six US Apollo missions resulted in successful Moon landings (Apollo 13, April 11–17, 1970, was aborted after an oxygen tank exploded). During the last of these (Apollo 17, December 7–19, 1972), Eugene A. Cernan and Harrison H. Schmitt became the only other astronauts to date who have walked on the surface of the Moon.

## TOP 10 ★
### LONGEST SPACE MISSIONS*

| | COSMONAUT | MISSION DATES | DAYS |
|---|---|---|---|
| 1 | Valeri V. Polyakov | Jan 8, 1994–Mar 22, 1995 | 437.7 |
| 2 | Sergei V. Avdeyev | Aug 13, 1998–Aug 28, 1999 | 379.6 |
| 3 = | Musa K. Manarov | Dec 21, 1987–Dec 21, 1988 | 365.9 |
| = | Vladimir G. Titov | Dec 21, 1987–Dec 21, 1988 | 365.9 |
| 5 | Yuri V. Romanenko | Feb 5–Dec 5, 1987 | 326.5 |
| 6 | Sergei K. Krikalyov | May 18, 1991–Mar 25, 1992 | 311.8 |
| 7 | Valeri V. Polyakov | Aug 31, 1988–Apr 27, 1989 | 240.9 |
| 8 = | Oleg Y. Atkov | Feb 8–Oct 2, 1984 | 237.0 |
| = | Leonid D. Kizim | Feb 8–Oct 2, 1984 | 237.0 |
| = | Anatoli Y. Solovyov | Feb 8–Oct 2, 1984 | 237.0 |

* To January 1, 2001

Space medicine specialist Valeri Vladimirovich Polyakov spent his 52nd birthday in space during his record-breaking mission aboard the Mir space station. One of the station's purposes was to study the effects on the human body of long-duration spaceflight.

**MAN ON THE MOON**
On April 21, 1972, Apollo 16 commander John W. Young (shown here), along with Charles M. Duke (who took this photograph), became the 9th and 10th of the 12 people ever to set foot on the Moon.

## TOP 10 ★
# YOUNGEST ASTRONAUTS AND COSMONAUTS

| ASTRONAUT OR COSMONAUT* | FIRST FLIGHT | AGE# |
|---|---|---|
| 1 Gherman S. Titov | June 17, 1970 | 25 |
| 2 Valentina V. Tereshkova | June 16, 1963 | 26 |
| 3 Boris B. Yegorov | Oct 15, 1964 | 26 |
| 4 Yuri A. Gagarin | Apr 12, 1961 | 27 |
| 5 Helen P. Sharman, UK | May 18, 1991 | 27 |
| 6 Dumitru D. Prunatiu, Romania | May 14, 1981 | 28 |
| 7 Valery F. Bykovsky | June 14, 1963 | 28 |
| 8 Salman Abdel Aziz Al-Saud, Saudi Arabia | June 17, 1985 | 28 |
| 9 Vladimir Remek, Czechoslovakia | Mar 2, 1978 | 29 |
| 10 Abdul Ahad Mohmand, Afghanistan | Aug 29, 1988 | 29 |

* All from Russia unless otherwise stated

# Those of apparently identical age have been ranked according to their precise age in days

## TOP 10 ★
# OLDEST ASTRONAUTS AND COSMONAUTS

| ASTRONAUT OR COSMONAUT* | LAST FLIGHT | AGE# |
|---|---|---|
| 1 John H. Glenn | Nov 6, 1998 | 77 |
| 2 F. Story Musgrave | Dec 7, 1996 | 61 |
| 3 Vance D. Brand | Dec 11, 1990 | 59 |
| 4 Jean-Loup Chrétien, France | Oct 6, 1997 | 59 |
| 5 Valery V. Ryumin, Russia | June 12, 1998 | 58 |
| 6 Karl G. Henize | Aug 6, 1985 | 58 |
| 7 Roger K. Crouch | July 17, 1997 | 56 |
| 8 William E. Thornton | May 6, 1985 | 56 |
| 9 Claude Nicollier, Switzerland | Dec 28, 1999 | 55 |
| 10 Don L. Lind | May 6, 1985 | 54 |

* All from the US unless otherwise stated

# Those of apparently identical age have been ranked according to their precise age in days

## THE 10 ★
# FIRST COUNTRIES TO HAVE ASTRONAUTS OR COSMONAUTS IN ORBIT

| COUNTRY/ASTRONAUT OR COSMONAUT | DATE* |
|---|---|
| 1 USSR, Yuri A. Gagarin | Apr 12, 1961 |
| 2 US, John H. Glenn | Feb 20, 1962 |
| 3 Czechoslovakia, Vladimir Remek | Mar 2, 1978 |
| 4 Poland, Miroslaw Hermaszewski | June 27, 1978 |
| 5 East Germany, Sigmund Jahn | Aug 26, 1978 |
| 6 Bulgaria, Georgi I. Ivanov | Apr 10, 1979 |
| 7 Hungary, Bertalan Farkas | May 26, 1980 |
| 8 Vietnam, Pham Tuan | July 23, 1980 |
| 9 Cuba, Arnaldo T. Mendez | Sep 18, 1980 |
| 10 Mongolia, Jugderdemidiyn Gurragcha | Mar 22, 1981 |

* Of first space entry of a national of that country

## THE 10 ★
# FIRST WOMEN IN SPACE

| ASTRONAUT OR COSMONAUT/ COUNTRY/SPACECRAFT | DATE |
|---|---|
| 1 Valentina V. Tereshkova, USSR, Vostok 6 | June 16–19, 1963 |
| 2 Svetlana Savitskaya, USSR, Soyuz T7 | Aug 19, 1982 |
| 3 Sally K. Ride, US, Challenger STS-7 | June 18–24, 1983 |
| 4 Judith A. Resnik, US, Discovery STS-41-D | Aug 30–Sep 5, 1984 |
| 5 Kathryn D. Sullivan, US, Challenger STS-41-G | Oct 5–13, 1984 |
| 6 Anna L. Fisher, US, Discovery STS-51-A | Nov 8–16, 1984 |
| 7 Margaret Rhea Seddon, US, Discovery STS-51-D | Apr 12–19, 1985 |
| 8 Shannon W. Lucid, US, Discovery STS-51-G | June 17–24, 1985 |
| 9 Bonnie J. Dunbar, US, Challenger STS-61-A | Oct 30–Nov 6, 1985 |
| 10 Mary L. Cleave, US, Atlantis STS-61-B | Nov 26–Dec 3, 1985 |

## THE 10 ★
# FIRST IN-FLIGHT SPACE FATALITIES

ASTRONAUT OR COSMONAUT(S)/INCIDENT

**1 Vladimir M. Komarov**
*Launched on April 24, 1967, Soviet spaceship Soyuz 1 experienced various technical problems during its 18th orbit. After a successful reentry, the capsule parachute was deployed at 23,000 ft (7,010 m), but its lines became tangled and it crash-landed near Orsk in the Urals, killing Komarov (the survivor of a previous one-day flight on October 12, 1964), who thus became the first-ever space fatality.*

**2 =Georgi T. Dobrovolsky**
**=Viktor I. Patsayev**
**=Vladislav N. Volkov**
*After a then-record 23 days in space, including a link-up with the Salyut space station, the Soviet Soyuz 9 mission ended in disaster on June 29, 1971, when the capsule depressurized during reentry. Although it landed intact, all three cosmonauts – who were not wearing spacesuits – were found to be dead. The ashes of the three men were buried, along with those of Yuri Gagarin and Vladimir Komarov, at the Kremlin, Moscow. Spacesuits have been worn during reentry on all subsequent missions.*

**5 =Gregory B. Jarvis**
**=Sharon C. McAuliffe**
**=Ronald E. McNair**
**=Ellison S. Onizuka**
**=Judith A. Resnik**
**=Francis R. Scobee**
**=Michael J. Smith**
*The Challenger STS-51-L, the 25th Space Shuttle mission, exploded on takeoff from Cape Canaveral, Florida, on January 28, 1986. The cause was determined to have been leakage of seals in the joint between rocket sections. The disaster, watched by thousands on the ground and millions on worldwide television, halted the US space program until a comprehensive review of the engineering problems and revision of the safety methods had been undertaken. It was not until September 29, 1988, that the next Space Shuttle, Discovery STS-26, was successfully launched.*

The 11 cosmonauts and astronauts in this list are, to date, the only inflight space fatalities. They are not, however, the only victims of accidents during the space programs of the former USSR and the US. On October 24, 1960, for example, five months before the first manned flight, Field Marshal Mitrofan Nedelin, the commander of the USSR's Strategic Rocket Forces, and an unknown number of other personnel (165 according to some authorities), were killed in the catastrophic launchpad explosion of an unmanned space rocket at the Baikonur cosmodrome.

**What is Manitoulin island's claim to fame?**
*see p.20 for the answer*
A It is the most densely inhabited island
B It is the largest island in a lake
C It has the highest island mountain

# Waterworld

## DEEPEST OCEANS AND SEAS

| OCEAN OR SEA | GREATEST DEPTH FT | M | AVERAGE DEPTH FT | M |
|---|---|---|---|---|
| 1 Pacific Ocean | 35,837 | 10,924 | 13,215 | 4,028 |
| 2 Indian Ocean | 24,460 | 7,455 | 13,002 | 3,963 |
| 3 Atlantic Ocean | 30,246 | 9,219 | 12,880 | 3,926 |
| 4 Caribbean Sea | 22,788 | 6,946 | 8,685 | 2,647 |
| 5 South China Sea | 16,456 | 5,016 | 5,419 | 1,652 |
| 6 Bering Sea | 15,659 | 4,773 | 5,075 | 1,547 |
| 7 Gulf of Mexico | 12,425 | 3,787 | 4,874 | 1,486 |
| 8 Mediterranean Sea | 15,197 | 4,632 | 4,688 | 1,429 |
| 9 Japan Sea | 12,276 | 3,742 | 4,429 | 1,350 |
| 10 Arctic Ocean | 18,456 | 5,625 | 3,953 | 1,205 |

The deepest point in the deepest ocean is the Marianas Trench in the Pacific Ocean, at a depth of 35,837 ft (10,924 m), according to a recent survey. The slightly lesser depth of 35,814 ft (10,916 m) was recorded on January 23, 1960, by Jacques Piccard and Donald Walsh in their 58-ft (17.7-m) long bathyscaphe *Trieste 2* during the deepest-ever ocean descent. Whichever is correct, it is close to 6.8 miles (11 km) down, or almost 29 times the height of the Empire State Building.

## HIGHEST WATERFALLS

| WATERFALL | RIVER | LOCATION | TOTAL DROP FT | M |
|---|---|---|---|---|
| 1 Angel | Carrao | Venezuela | 3,212 | 979* |
| 2 Tugela | Tugela | South Africa | 3,107 | 947 |
| 3 Utigård | Jostedal Glacier | Norway | 2,625 | 800 |
| 4 Mongefossen | Monge | Norway | 2,540 | 774 |
| 5 Yosemite | Yosemite Creek | US | 2,425 | 739 |
| 6 Østre Mardøla Foss | Mardals | Norway | 2,152 | 656 |
| 7 Tyssestrengane | Tysso | Norway | 2,120 | 646 |
| 8 Cuquenán | Arabopo | Venezuela | 2,000 | 610 |
| 9 Sutherland | Arthur | New Zealand | 1,904 | 580 |
| 10 Kjellfossen | Naero | Norway | 1,841 | 561 |

\* *Longest single drop 2,648 ft (807 m)*

**FALL AND ANGEL**

*On November 16, 1933, American adventurer James Angel wrote in his diary, "I found myself a waterfall." He had discovered the world's highest falls, later named Angel Falls.*

## TOP 10 ★
# DEEPEST DEEP-SEA TRENCHES*

| | TRENCH | DEEPEST POINT FT | M |
|---|---|---|---|
| 1 | Marianas | 35,837 | 10,924 |
| 2 | Tonga# | 35,430 | 10,800 |
| 3 | Philippine | 34,436 | 10,497 |
| 4 | Kermadec# | 32,960 | 10,047 |
| 5 | Bonin | 32,786 | 9,994 |
| 6 | New Britain | 32,609 | 9,940 |
| 7 | Kuril | 31,985 | 9,750 |
| 8 | Izu | 31,805 | 9,695 |
| 9 | Puerto Rico | 28,229 | 8,605 |
| 10 | Yap | 27,973 | 8,527 |

* With the exception of the Puerto Rico (Atlantic), all the trenches are in the Pacific

# Some authorities consider these to be parts of the same feature

Each of the eight deepest ocean trenches would be deep enough to submerge Mount Everest, which is 29,035 ft (8,850 m) above sea level.

**AMAZON v NILE**

*Although the Amazon is ranked second in length, it is possible to sail from it up the Rio Pará, a total of 4,195 miles (6,750 km), which is a greater distance than the length of the Nile.*

## TOP 10 ★
# COUNTRIES WITH THE GREATEST AREAS OF INLAND WATER

| | COUNTRY | PERCENTAGE OF TOTAL AREA | WATER AREA SQ MILES | SQ KM |
|---|---|---|---|---|
| 1 | US* | 4.88 | 292,125 | 756,600 |
| 2 | Canada | 7.60 | 291,573 | 755,170 |
| 3 | India | 9.56 | 121,391 | 314,400 |
| 4 | China | 2.82 | 104,460 | 270,550 |
| 5 | Ethiopia | 9.89 | 46,680 | 120,900 |
| 6 | Colombia | 8.80 | 38,691 | 100,210 |
| 7 | Indonesia | 4.88 | 35,908 | 93,000 |
| 8 | Russia | 0.47 | 30,657 | 79,400 |
| 9 | Australia | 0.90 | 26,610 | 68,920 |
| 10 | Tanzania | 6.25 | 22,799 | 59,050 |

* 50 states and District of Columbia

## TOP 10 ★
# GREATEST RIVERS*

| | RIVER | OUTFLOW/SEA | AV. FLOW (CU YD/SEC) |
|---|---|---|---|
| 1 | Amazon | Brazil/South Atlantic | 228,891 |
| 2 | Zaïre | Angola–Congo/ South Atlantic | 51,010 |
| 3 | Negro | Brazil/South Atlantic | 45,778 |
| 4 | Yangtze–Kiang | China/Yellow Sea | 42,103 |
| 5 | Orinoco | Venezuela/ South Atlantic | 32,960 |
| 6 | Plata–Paraná– Grande | Uruguay/ South Atlantic | 29,952 |
| 7 | Madeira–Mamoré– Grande | Brazil/ South Atlantic | 28,513 |
| 8 | Brahmaputra | Bangladesh/ Bay of Bengal | 25,113 |
| 9 | Yenisey–Angara– Selenga | Russia/ Kara Sea | 23,020 |
| 10 | Lena–Kirenga | Russia/ Arctic Ocean | 21,712 |

* Based on rate of discharge at mouth

## TOP 10 ★
# LONGEST RIVERS

| | RIVER/LOCATION | LENGTH MILES | KM |
|---|---|---|---|
| 1 | Nile, Tanzania/Uganda/ Sudan/Egypt | 4,145 | 6,670 |
| 2 | Amazon, Peru/Brazil | 4,007 | 6,448 |
| 3 | Yangtze–Kiang, China | 3,915 | 6,300 |
| 4 | Mississippi–Missouri– Red Rock, US | 3,710 | 5,971 |
| 5 | Yenisey–Angara– Selenga, Mongolia/Russia | 3,442 | 5,540 |
| 6 | Huang Ho (Yellow River), China | 3,395 | 5,464 |
| 7 | Ob'–Irtysh, Mongolia/ Kazakhstan/Russia | 3,362 | 5,410 |
| 8 | Congo, Angola/ Dem. Rep. of Congo | 2,920 | 4,700 |
| 9 | Lena–Kirenga, Russia | 2,734 | 4,400 |
| 10 | Mekong, Tibet/China/ Myanmar (Burma)/ Laos/Cambodia/Vietnam | 2,703 | 4,350 |

## TOP 10 ★
# LAKES WITH THE GREATEST VOLUME OF WATER

| | LAKE/LOCATION | VOLUME CU MILES | CU KM |
|---|---|---|---|
| 1 | Caspian Sea, Azerbaijan/ Iran/Kazakhstan/Russia/ Turkmenistan | 21,497 | 89,600 |
| 2 | Baikal, Russia | 5,517 | 22,995 |
| 3 | Tanganyika, Burundi/ Tanzania/Dem. Rep. of Congo/Zambia | 4,391 | 18,304 |
| 4 | Superior, Canada/US | 2,921 | 12,174 |
| 5 | Michigan/Huron, US/Canada | 2,642 | 8,449 |
| 6 | Nyasa (Malawi), Malawi/Mozambique/ Tanzania | 1,473 | 6,140 |
| 7 | Victoria, Kenya/ Tanzania/Uganda | 604 | 2,518 |
| 8 | Great Bear, Canada | 542 | 2,258 |
| 9 | Great Slave, Canada | 425 | 1,771 |
| 10 | Issyk, Kyrgyzstan | 420 | 1,752 |

**Did You Know?** Once the world's fourth largest lake, the Aral Sea has shrunk by over a third, as a result of feeder rivers being diverted for irrigation, and is in danger of disappearing completely.

# Islands of the World

## TOP 10 ★
## LARGEST VOLCANIC ISLANDS

| | ISLAND/LOCATION/TYPE | AREA SQ MILES | AREA SQ KM |
|---|---|---|---|
| 1 | **Sumatra**, Indonesia, Active volcanic | 171,069 | 443,066 |
| 2 | **Honshu**, Japan, Volcanic | 87,182 | 225,800 |
| 3 | **Java**, Indonesia, Volcanic | 53,589 | 138,794 |
| 4 | **North Island**, New Zealand, Volcanic | 43,082 | 111,583 |
| 5 | **Luzon**, Philippines, Active volcanic | 42,458 | 109,965 |
| 6 | **Iceland**, Active volcanic | 39,315 | 101,826 |
| 7 | **Mindanao**, Philippines, Active volcanic | 37,657 | 97,530 |
| 8 | **Hokkaido**, Japan, Active volcanic | 30,395 | 78,719 |
| 9 | **New Britain**, Papua New Guinea, Volcanic | 13,569 | 35,145 |
| 10 | **Halmahera**, Indonesia, Active volcanic | 6,965 | 18,040 |

Source: *United Nations*

## TOP 10 ★
## LARGEST ISLAND COUNTRIES

| | COUNTRY | AREA SQ MILES | AREA SQ KM |
|---|---|---|---|
| 1 | **Indonesia** | 735,358 | 1,904,569 |
| 2 | **Madagascar** | 226,917 | 587,713 |
| 3 | **Papua New Guinea** | 178,704 | 462,840 |
| 4 | **Japan** | 143,939 | 372,801 |
| 5 | **Malaysia** | 127,320 | 329,758 |
| 6 | **Philippines** | 115,831 | 300,000 |
| 7 | **New Zealand*** | 103,883 | 269,057 |
| 8 | **Great Britain** | 88,787 | 229,957 |
| 9 | **Cuba** | 42,804 | 110,861 |
| 10 | **Iceland** | 39,769 | 103,000 |

\* Total of all the islands

Greenland is not included in this Top 10 because it is part of Denmark.

## TOP 10 ★
## LARGEST LAKE ISLANDS

| | ISLAND/LAKE/LOCATION | AREA SQ MILES | AREA SQ KM |
|---|---|---|---|
| 1 | **Manitoulin**, Huron, Ontario, Canada | 1,068 | 2,766 |
| 2 | **Vozrozhdeniya**, Aral Sea, Uzbekistan/Kazakhstan | 888 | 2,300 |
| 3 | **René-Lavasseur**, Manicouagan Reservoir, Quebec, Canada | 780 | 2,020 |
| 4 | **Olkhon**, Baykal, Russia | 282 | 730 |
| 5 | **Samosir**, Toba, Sumatra, Indonesia | 243 | 630 |
| 6 | **Isle Royale**, Superior, Michigan, US | 209 | 541 |
| 7 | **Ukerewe**, Victoria, Tanzania | 205 | 530 |
| 8 | **St. Joseph**, Huron, Ontario, Canada | 141 | 365 |
| 9 | **Drummond**, Huron, Michigan, US | 134 | 347 |
| 10 | **Idjwi**, Kivu, Dem. Rep. of Congo | 110 | 285 |

Not all islands are surrounded by sea: many sizable islands are situated in lakes. The second largest in this list, Vozrozhdeniya, is growing as the Aral Sea contracts, and is set to link up with the surrounding land to become a peninsula.

## TOP 10 ★
## LARGEST ISLANDS IN THE US

| | ISLAND/LOCATION | AREA SQ MILES | AREA SQ KM |
|---|---|---|---|
| 1 | **Hawaii**, Hawaii | 4,037 | 10,456 |
| 2 | **Kodiak**, Alaska | 3,672 | 9,510 |
| 3 | **Prince of Wales**, Alaska | 2,587 | 6,700 |
| 4 | **Chicagof**, Alaska | 2,085 | 5,400 |
| 5 | **Saint Lawrence**, Alaska | 1,710 | 4,430 |
| 6 | **Admiralty**, Alaska | 1,649 | 4,270 |
| 7 | **Baranof**, Alaska | 1,636 | 4,237 |
| 8 | **Nunivak**, Alaska | 1,625 | 4,210 |
| 9 | **Unimak**, Alaska | 1,606 | 4,160 |
| 10 | **Long Island**, New York | 1,401 | 3,629 |

## TOP 10 ★
## LARGEST ISLANDS IN THE UK

| | ISLAND/LOCATION | POPULATION | AREA SQ MILES | AREA SQ KM |
|---|---|---|---|---|
| 1 | **Lewis and Harris**, Outer Hebrides | 23,390 | 859 | 2,225 |
| 2 | **Skye**, Hebrides | 8,139 | 643 | 1,666 |
| 3 | **Mainland**, Shetland | 22,184 | 373 | 967 |
| 4 | **Mull**, Inner Hebrides | 2,605 | 347 | 899 |
| 5 | **Ynys Môn** (Anglesey), Wales | 69,800 | 276 | 714 |
| 6 | **Islay**, Inner Hebrides | 3,997 | 247 | 639 |
| 7 | **Isle of Man**, England | 69,788 | 221 | 572 |
| 8 | **Mainland**, Orkney | 14,299 | 207 | 536 |
| 9 | **Arran**, Inner Hebrides | 4,726 | 168 | 435 |
| 10 | **Isle of Wight**, England | 126,600 | 147 | 381 |

**50TH STATE**

*Hawaii, the largest US island, is the largest of eight major and 124 smaller volcanic islands that make up the Hawaiian archipelago.*

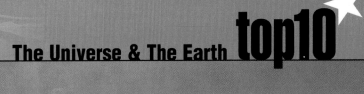

**UNDER THE VOLCANO**

*Indonesia's highest active volcano, Gunung Kerinci, rises to 12,484 ft (3,805 m). It lies in the Barisan Mountains of Sumatra, the world's largest volcanic island.*

## TOP 10 ★
# LARGEST ISLANDS

| ISLAND/LOCATION | APPROX. AREA* | |
|---|---|---|
| | SQ MILES | SQ KM |
| 1 **Greenland** (Kalaallit Nunaat) | 840,004 | 2,175,600 |
| 2 **New Guinea**, Papua New Guinea/Indonesia | 303,381 | 785,753 |
| 3 **Borneo**, Indonesia/ Malaysia/Brunei | 288,869 | 748,168 |
| 4 **Madagascar** | 226,917 | 587,713 |
| 5 **Baffin Island**, Canada | 194,574 | 503,944 |
| 6 **Sumatra**, Indonesia | 171,069 | 443,066 |
| 7 **Great Britain** | 88,787 | 229,957 |
| 8 **Honshu**, Japan | 87,182 | 225,800 |
| 9 **Victoria Island**, Canada | 85,154 | 220,548 |
| 10 **Ellesmere Island**, Canada | 71,029 | 183,965 |

\* *Mainlands, including areas of inland water, but excluding offshore islands*

Australia is regarded as a continental land mass rather than an island; otherwise it would rank first at 2,941,517 sq miles (7,618,493 sq km).

## TOP 10 ★
# LARGEST ISLANDS IN EUROPE

| ISLAND/LOCATION | AREA | |
|---|---|---|
| | SQ MILES | SQ KM |
| 1 **Great Britain**, North Atlantic | 88,787 | 229,957 |
| 2 **Iceland**, North Atlantic | 39,769 | 103,000 |
| 3 **Ireland**, North Atlantic | 32,342 | 83,766 |
| 4 **West Spitsbergen**, Arctic Ocean | 15,200 | 39,368 |
| 5 **Sicily**, Mediterranean Sea | 9,807 | 25,400 |
| 6 **Sardinia**, Mediterranean Sea | 9,189 | 23,800 |
| 7 **North East Land**, Barents Sea | 5,792 | 15,000 |
| 8 **Cyprus**, Mediterranean Sea | 3,572 | 9,251 |
| 9 **Corsica**, Mediterranean Sea | 3,367 | 8,720 |
| 10 **Crete**, Mediterranean Sea | 3,189 | 8,260 |

Great Britain became an island some 8,000 years ago, when the land bridge that had previously existed was inundated and the North Sea became connected with the English Channel.

## TOP 10 ★
# HIGHEST ISLANDS

| ISLAND/LOCATION | HIGHEST ELEVATION | |
|---|---|---|
| | FT | M |
| 1 **New Guinea**, Papua New Guinea/ Indonesia | 16,503 | 5,030 |
| 2 **Akutan**, Alaska, US | 14,026 | 4,275 |
| 3 **Hawaii**, US | 13,796 | 4,205 |
| 4 **Borneo**, Indonesia/ Malaysia/Brunei | 13,698 | 4,175 |
| 5 **Formosa**, China | 13,114 | 3,997 |
| 6 **Sumatra**, Indonesia | 12,484 | 3,805 |
| 7 **Ross**, Antarctica | 12,448 | 3,794 |
| 8 **Honshu**, Japan | 12,388 | 3,776 |
| 9 **South Island**, New Zealand | 12,349 | 3,764 |
| 10 **Lombok**, Lesser Sunda Islands, Indonesia | 12,224 | 3,726 |

Source: *United Nations*

The highest island peak is Puncak Jaya, Indonesia, which soars to 16,503 ft (5,030 m), making it also the highest mountain in the entire Pacific basin.

What is the most common element on Earth?
*see p.27 for the answer*

A Nitrogen
B Hydrogen
C Oxygen

TOP 10 ★

## DEEPEST DEPRESSIONS

| DEPRESSION/LOCATION | MAXIMUM DEPTH BELOW SEA LEVEL | |
|---|---|---|
| | FT | M |
| 1 Dead Sea, Israel/Jordan | 1,312 | 400 |
| 2 Lake Assal, Djibouti | 511 | 156 |
| 3 Turfan Depression, China | 505 | 154 |
| 4 Qattâra Depression, Egypt | 436 | 133 |
| 5 Mangyshlak Peninsula, Kazakhstan | 433 | 132 |
| 6 Danakil Depression, Ethiopia | 383 | 117 |
| 7 Death Valley, US | 282 | 86 |
| 8 Salton Sink, US | 235 | 72 |
| 9 Zapadny Chink Ustyurta, Kazakhstan | 230 | 70 |
| 10 Prikaspiyskaya Nizmennost', Kazakhstan/Russia | 220 | 67 |

### DEAD DEEP

*The Dead Sea is the world's deepest depression, with Ein Bokek alongside it the world's lowest inhabited place at 1,291 ft (393.5 m) below sea level.*

---

TOP 10 ★

## HIGHEST ACTIVE VOLCANOES

| VOLCANO/LOCATION | LATEST ACTIVITY | HEIGHT FT | M |
|---|---|---|---|
| 1 Ojos del Salado, Argentina/Chile | 1981 | 22,588 | 6,895 |
| 2 San Pedro, Chile | 1960 | 20,325 | 6,199 |
| 3 Guallatiri, Chile | 1993 | 19,918 | 6,071 |
| 4 Cotopaxi, Ecuador | 1975 | 19,347 | 5,897 |
| 5 Tupungatito, Chile | 1986 | 18,504 | 5,640 |
| 6 Láscar, Chile | 1995 | 18,346 | 5,591 |
| 7 Popocatépetl, Mexico | 1998 | 17,802 | 5,426 |
| 8 Nevado del Ruiz, Colombia | 1991 | 17,457 | 5,321 |
| 9 Sangay, Ecuador | 1998 | 17,159 | 5,230 |
| 10 Guagua Pichincha, Ecuador | 1993 | 15,696 | 4,784 |

This list includes only the volcanoes that were active at some time during the 20th century. The tallest currently active volcano in Europe is Mt. Etna, Sicily (10,855 ft/3,311 m), which has been responsible for numerous deaths.

TOP 10 ★

## LARGEST DESERTS

| DESERT/LOCATION | APPROX. AREA SQ MILES | SQ KM |
|---|---|---|
| 1 Sahara, Northern Africa | 3,500,000 | 9,100,000 |
| 2 Australian, Australia* | 1,300,000 | 3,400,000 |
| 3 Arabian Peninsula, Southwest Asia # | 1,000,000 | 2,600,000 |
| 4 Turkestan, Central Asia + | 750,000 | 1,900,000 |
| 5 =Gobi, Central Asia | 500,000 | 1,300,000 |
| =North American Desert, US/Mexico ★ | 500,000 | 1,300,000 |
| 7 Patagonia, Southern Argentina | 260,000 | 670,000 |
| 8 Thar, Northwest India/Pakistan | 230,000 | 600,000 |
| 9 Kalahari, Southwestern Africa | 220,000 | 570,000 |
| 10 Takla Makan, Northwestern China | 185,000 | 480,000 |

*\* Includes Gibson, Great Sandy, Great Victoria, and Simpson*
*# Includes an-Nafud and Rub alKhali   + Includes Kara-Kum and Kyzylkum*
*★ Includes Great Basin, Mojave, Sonora, and Chihuahuan*

## TOP 10 ★
## HIGHEST MOUNTAINS

| | MOUNTAIN/LOCATION | FIRST ASCENT/TEAM NATIONALITY | HEIGHT* FT | M |
|---|---|---|---|---|
| 1 | Everest, Nepal/China | May 29, 1953, British/New Zealand | 29,035 | 8,850 |
| 2 | K2 (Chogori), Pakistan/China | July 31, 1954, Italian | 28,238 | 8,607 |
| 3 | Kangchenjunga, Nepal/India | May 25, 1955, British | 28,208 | 8,598 |
| 4 | Lhotse, Nepal/China | May 18, 1956, Swiss | 27,923 | 8,511 |
| 5 | Makalu I, Nepal/China | May 15, 1955, French | 27,824 | 8,481 |
| 6 | Lhotse Shar (II), Nepal/China | May 12, 1970, Austrian | 27,504 | 8,383 |
| 7 | Dhaulagiri I, Nepal | May 13, 1960, Swiss/Austrian | 26,810 | 8,172 |
| 8 | Manaslu I (Kutang I), Nepal | May 9, 1956, Japanese | 26,760 | 8,156 |
| 9 | Cho Oyu, Nepal | Oct 19, 1954, Austrian | 26,750 | 8,153 |
| 10 | Nanga Parbat (Diamir), Pakistan | July 3, 1953, German/Austrian | 26,660 | 8,126 |

*Height of principal peak; lower peaks of the same mountain are excluded*

Dhaulagiri was once believed to be the world's tallest mountain, until Kangchenjunga was surveyed and declared to be even higher. When the results of the 19th-century Great Trigonometrical Survey of India were studied, however, it was realized that Everest was the tallest, its height being computed as 29,002 ft (8,840 m). Errors in measurement were corrected in 1955 to 29,029 ft (8,848 m), in April 1993 to 29,028 ft (8,847 m), and finally in November 1999 to its current record-breaking height.

## TOP 10 ★
## LONGEST CAVES

| | CAVE/LOCATION | TOTAL KNOWN LENGTH MILES | KM |
|---|---|---|---|
| 1 | Mammoth cave system, Kentucky, US | 352 | 567 |
| 2 | Optimisticheskaya, Ukraine | 130 | 208 |
| 3 | Jewel Cave, South Dakota, US | 122 | 195 |
| 4 | Hölloch, Switzerland | 103 | 166 |
| 5 | Lechuguilla Cave, New Mexico, US | 100 | 161 |
| 6 | Fisher Ridge cave system, Kentucky, US | 91 | 146 |
| 7 | Siebenhengstehohle, Switzerland | 87 | 140 |
| 8 | Wind Cave, South Dakota, US | 86 | 138 |
| 9 | Ozernaya, Ukraine | 69 | 111 |
| 10 | Gua Air Jernih, Malaysia | 68 | 109 |

Source: *Tony Waltham, BCRA*

## TOP 10 ★
## COUNTRIES WITH THE HIGHEST ELEVATIONS*

| | COUNTRY/PEAK | HEIGHT FT | M |
|---|---|---|---|
| 1 = | China, Everest | 29,035 | 8,850 |
| = | Nepal, Everest | 29,035 | 8,850 |
| 3 | Pakistan, K2 | 28,238 | 8,607 |
| 4 | India, Kangchenjunga | 28,208 | 8,598 |
| 5 | Bhutan, Khula Kangri | 24,784 | 7,554 |
| 6 | Tajikistan, Mt. Garmo (formerly Kommunizma) | 24,590 | 7,495 |
| 7 | Afghanistan, Noshaq | 24,581 | 7,490 |
| 8 | Kyrgyzstan, Pik Pobedy | 24,406 | 7,439 |
| 9 | Kazakhstan, Khan Tengri | 22,949 | 6,995 |
| 10 | Argentina, Cerro Aconcagua | 22,834 | 6,960 |

*Based on the tallest peak in each country*

An elevation of more than 1,000 ft (305 m) is commonly regarded as a mountain, and using this criterion almost every country in the world can claim to have at least one mountain. There are some 54 countries in the world with elevations of greater than 10,000 ft (3,048 m).

## TOP 10 ★
## LARGEST METEORITE CRATERS

| | CRATER/LOCATION | DIAMETER MILES | KM |
|---|---|---|---|
| 1 = | Sudbury, Ontario, Canada | 87 | 140 |
| = | Vredefort, South Africa | 87 | 140 |
| 3 = | Manicouagan, Quebec, Canada | 62 | 100 |
| = | Popigai, Russia | 62 | 100 |
| 5 | Puchezh-Katunki, Russia | 50 | 80 |
| 6 | Kara, Russia | 37 | 60 |
| 7 | Siljan, Sweden | 32 | 52 |
| 8 | Charlevoix, Quebec, Canada | 29 | 46 |
| 9 | Araguainha Dome, Brazil | 25 | 40 |
| 10 | Carswell, Saskatchewan, Canada | 23 | 37 |

Many astroblemes (collision sites) on the Earth have been weathered over time and obscured, unlike those on the solar system's other planets and moons. As a result of this weathering, one of the ongoing debates in geology is whether or not certain craterlike structures discovered on the Earth's surface are of meteoric origin or are the remnants of long-extinct volcanoes.

## TOP 10 ★
## DEEPEST CAVES

| | CAVE SYSTEM/LOCATION | DEPTH FT | M |
|---|---|---|---|
| 1 | Lamprechtsofen, Austria | 5,354 | 1,632 |
| 2 | Gouffre Mirolda, France | 5,282 | 1,610 |
| 3 | Réseau Jean Bernard, France | 5,256 | 1,602 |
| 4 | Torca del Cerro, Spain | 5,213 | 1,589 |
| 5 | Shakta Pantjukhina, Georgia | 4,948 | 1,508 |
| 6 | Ceki 2, Slovenia | 4,856 | 1,480 |
| 7 | Sistema Huautla, Mexico | 4,839 | 1,475 |
| 8 | Sistema de la Trave, Spain | 4,738 | 1,444 |
| 9 | Boj Bulok, Uzbekistan | 4,642 | 1,415 |
| 10 | Puerta di Illamina, Spain | 4,619 | 1,408 |

Source: *Tony Waltham, BCRA*

What was the nationality of Anders Celsius, after whom the Celsius temperature scale is named?
*see p.25 for the answer*

A Swedish
B Italian
C German

# World Weather

## PLACES WITH THE MOST RAINY DAYS

| | LOCATION* | RAINY DAYS PER ANNUM# |
|---|---|---|
| 1 | **Waialeale**, Hawaii | 335 |
| 2 | **Marion Island**, South Africa | 312 |
| 3 | **Pohnpei**, Federated States of Micronesia | 311 |
| 4 | **Andagoya**, Colombia | 306 |
| 5 | **Macquarie Island**, Australia | 299 |
| 6 | **Gough Island**, Tristan da Cunha group, South Atlantic | 291 |
| 7 | **Palau**, Federated States of Micronesia | 286 |
| 8 | **Heard Island**, Australia | 279 |
| 9 | **Camp Jacob**, Guadeloupe | 274 |
| 10 | **Atu Nau**, Alaska | 268 |

\* Maximum of two places per country listed
# Averaged over a period of many years
Source: *Philip Eden*

## TOP 10 ★
## WETTEST PLACES – AVERAGE

| | LOCATION* | AVERAGE ANNUAL RAINFALL# IN | MM |
|---|---|---|---|
| 1 | **Cherrapunji**, India | 498.0 | 12,649 |
| 2 | **Mawsynram**, India | 467.4 | 11,872 |
| 3 | **Waialeale**, Hawaii | 451.0 | 11,455 |
| 4 | **Debundscha**, Cameroon | 404.6 | 10,277 |
| 5 | **Quibdó**, Colombia | 353.9 | 8,989 |
| 6 | **Bellenden Ker Range**, Australia | 340.0 | 8,636 |
| 7 | **Andagoya**, Colombia | 281.0 | 7,137 |
| 8 | **Henderson Lake**, British Columbia, Canada | 256.0 | 6,502 |
| 9 | **Kikori**, Papua New Guinea | 232.9 | 5,916 |
| 10 | **Tavoy**, Myanmar (Burma) | 214.6 | 5,451 |

\* Maximum of two places per country listed
# Annual rainfall total, averaged over a period of many years
Source: *Philip Eden*

## TOP 10 PLACES WITH THE HEAVIEST DAILY DOWNPOURS*

*(Location#/highest rainfall in 24 hours in in/mm)*

1. **Chilaos**, Réunion, 73.6/1,870  2. **Baguio**, Philippines, 46.0/1,168
3. **Alvin**, Texas, 43.0/1,092  4. **Cherrapunji**, India, 41.0/1,041
5. **Smithport**, Pennsylvania, 39.9/1,013  6. **Crohamhurst**, Australia, 35.7/907
7. **Finch-Hatton**, Australia, 34.6/879  8. **Suva**, Fiji, 26.5/673
9. **Cayenne**, French Guiana, 23.5/597  10. **Aitutaki**, Cook Islands, 22.5/572

\* Based on limited data  # Maximum of two places per country listed
Source: *Philip Eden*

## TOP 10 ★
## PLACES WITH THE FEWEST RAINY DAYS

| | LOCATION* | NUMBER OF RAINY DAYS# |
|---|---|---|
| 1 | **Arica**, Chile | 1 day every 6 years |
| 2 | **Asyût**, Egypt | 1 day every 5 years |
| 3 | **Dakhla Oasis**, Egypt | 1 day every 4 years |
| 4 | **Al'Kufrah**, Libya | 1 day every 2 years |
| 5= | **Bender Qaasim**, Somalia | 1 day per year |
| = | **Wadi Halfa**, Sudan | 1 day per year |
| 7 | **Iquique**, Chile | 2 days per year |
| 8= | **Dongola**, Sudan | 3 days per year |
| = | **Faya-Largeau**, Chad | 3 days per year |
| = | **Masirāh Island**, Oman | 3 days per year |

\* Maximum of two places per country listed
# Lowest number of days with rain per year, averaged over a period of many years
Source: *Philip Eden*

## TOP 10 ★
## HOTTEST PLACES – EXTREMES*

| | LOCATION# | HIGHEST TEMPERATURE °F | °C |
|---|---|---|---|
| 1 | **Al'Azīzīyah**, Libya | 136.4 | 58.0 |
| 2 | **Greenland Ranch**, Death Valley, California | 134.0 | 56.7 |
| 3= | **Ghudamis**, Libya | 131.0 | 55.0 |
| = | **Kebili**, Tunisia | 131.0 | 55.0 |
| 5 | **Tombouctou**, Mali | 130.1 | 54.5 |
| 6 | **Araouane**, Mali | 130.0 | 54.4 |
| 7 | **Tirat Tavi**, Israel | 129.0 | 53.9 |
| 8 | **Ahwāz**, Iran | 128.3 | 53.5 |
| 9 | **Agha Jārī**, Iran | 128.0 | 53.3 |
| 10 | **Wadi Halfa**, Sudan | 127.0 | 52.8 |

\* Highest individual temperatures
# Maximum of two places per country listed
Source: *Philip Eden*

## TOP 10 ★
## DRIEST PLACES – AVERAGE

| | LOCATION* | AVERAGE ANNUAL RAINFALL# IN | MM | | LOCATION* | AVERAGE ANNUAL RAINFALL# IN | MM |
|---|---|---|---|---|---|---|---|
| 1 | **Arica**, Chile | 0.03 | 0.7 | 7 | **Iquique**, Chile | 0.20 | 5.0 |
| 2= | **Al'Kufrah**, Libya | 0.03 | 0.8 | 8 | **Pelican Point**, Namibia | 0.32 | 8.0 |
| = | **Aswân**, Egypt | 0.03 | 0.8 | 9= | **Aoulef**, Algeria | 0.48 | 12.0 |
| = | **Luxor**, Egypt | 0.03 | 0.8 | = | **Callao**, Peru | 0.48 | 12.0 |
| 5 | **Ica**, Peru | 0.09 | 2.3 | | | | |
| 6 | **Wadi Halfa**, Sudan | 0.10 | 2.6 | | | | |

\* Maximum of two places per country listed
# Annual total averaged over a period of many years
Source: *Philip Eden*

## TOP 10 ★
# PLACES WITH THE MOST CONTRASTING SEASONS*

| LOCATION # | WINTER °F | °C | SUMMER °F | °C | DIFFERENCE °F | °C |
|---|---|---|---|---|---|---|
| 1 **Verkhoyansk**, Russia | -58.5 | -50.3 | 56.5 | 13.6 | 115.0 | 63.9 |
| 2 **Yakutsk**, Russia | -49.0 | -45.0 | 63.5 | 17.5 | 112.5 | 62.5 |
| 3 **Manzhouli**, China | -15.0 | -26.1 | 69.0 | 20.6 | 84.0 | 46.7 |
| 4 **Fort Yukon**, Alaska | -20.2 | -29.0 | 61.4 | 16.3 | 81.6 | 45.3 |
| 5 **Fort Good Hope**, Northwest Territories, Canada | -21.8 | -29.9 | 59.5 | 15.3 | 81.3 | 45.2 |
| 6 **Brochet**, Manitoba, Canada | -20.5 | -29.2 | 59.7 | 15.4 | 80.2 | 44.6 |
| 7 **Tunka**, Mongolia | -16.0 | -26.7 | 61.0 | 16.1 | 77.0 | 42.8 |
| 8 **Fairbanks**, Alaska | -11.2 | -24.0 | 60.1 | 15.6 | 71.3 | 39.6 |
| 9 **Semipalatinsk**, Kazakhstan | 0.5 | -17.7 | 69.0 | 20.6 | 68.5 | 38.3 |
| 10 **Jorgen Bronlund Fjørd**, Greenland | -23.6 | -30.9 | 43.5 | 6.4 | 67.1 | 37.3 |

* Biggest differences between mean monthly temperatures in summer and winter

# Maximum of two places per country listed

Source: Philip Eden

## TOP 10 ★
# COLDEST PLACES – EXTREMES*

| LOCATION # | LOWEST TEMPERATURE °F | °C |
|---|---|---|
| 1 **Vostok+**, Antarctica | -128.6 | -89.2 |
| 2 **Plateau Station+**, Antarctica | -119.2 | -84.0 |
| 3 **Oymyakon**, Russia | -96.0 | -71.1 |
| 4 **Verkhoyansk**, Russia | -89.8 | -67.7 |
| 5 **Northice+**, Greenland | -86.8 | -66.0 |
| 6 **Eismitte+**, Greenland | -84.8 | -64.9 |
| 7 **Snag**, Yukon, Canada | -81.4 | -63.0 |
| 8 **Prospect Creek**, Alaska | -79.8 | -62.1 |
| 9 **Fort Selkirk**, Yukon, Canada | -74.0 | -58.9 |
| 10 **Rogers Pass**, Montana, US | -69.7 | -56.5 |

* Lowest individual temperatures

# Maximum of two places per country listed

+ Present or former scientific research base

Source: Philip Eden

## TOP 10 ★
# CLOUDIEST PLACES*

| LOCATION # | PERCENTAGE OF MAXIMUM POSSIBLE SUNSHINE | AVERAGE ANNUAL HOURS OF SUNSHINE |
|---|---|---|
| 1 **Ben Nevis**, Scotland | 16 | 736 |
| 2 **Hoyvik**, Faeroes, Denmark | 19 | 902 |
| 3 **Maam**, Ireland | 19 | 929 |
| 4 **Prince Rupert**, British Columbia, Canada | 20 | 955 |
| 5 **Riksgransen**, Sweden | 20 | 965 |
| 6 **Akureyri**, Iceland | 20 | 973 |
| 7 **Raufarhöfn**, Iceland | 21 | 995 |
| 8 **Nanortalik**, Greenland | 22 | 1,000 |
| 9 **Dalwhinnie**, Scotland | 22 | 1,032 |
| 10 **Karasjok**, Norway | 23 | 1,090 |

* Lowest annual sunshine total, averaged over a period of many years

# Maximum of two places per country listed

Source: Philip Eden

## TOP 10 ★
# SUNNIEST PLACES*

| LOCATION # | PERCENTAGE OF MAXIMUM POSSIBLE SUNSHINE | AVERAGE ANNUAL HOURS OF SUNSHINE |
|---|---|---|
| 1 **Yuma**, Arizona | 91 | 4,127 |
| 2 **Phoenix**, Arizona | 90 | 4,041 |
| 3 **Wadi Halfa**, Sudan | 89 | 3,964 |
| 4 **Bordj Omar Driss**, Algeria | 88 | 3,899 |
| 5 **Keetmanshoop**, Namibia | 88 | 3,876 |
| 6 **Aoulef**, Algeria | 86 | 3,784 |
| 7 **Upington**, South Africa | 86 | 3,766 |
| 8 **Atbara**, Sudan | 85 | 3,739 |
| 9 **Mariental**, Namibia | 84 | 3,707 |
| 10 **Bilma**, Niger | 84 | 3,699 |

* Highest yearly sunshine total, averaged over a period of many years

# Maximum of two places per country listed

Source: Philip Eden

## CELSIUS

Anders Celsius (1701–44) was a Swedish mathematician and, like his father before him, Professor of Astronomy at the University of Uppsala. While Celsius was on an expedition to Lapland, making measurements that proved that the Earth is flattened at the poles, he realized the need for an improved thermometer. In 1742 he devised a new temperature scale, taking two fixed points – 0° as the boiling point of water and 100° as the freezing point of water. It was not until 1750, after Celsius's death, that his pupil Martin Strömer proposed that the two be reversed. This scale became known as Centigrade, but was changed to Celsius in 1948 in honor of its inventor.

WHO WAS • WHO WAS • WHO WAS • WHO WAS

**What name was given to 1992's most devastating hurricane?**
*see p.29 for the answer*
A Andrew
B George
C Edward

# Out of This World

## HEAVIEST ELEMENTS

| | ELEMENT | DISCOVERER/COUNTRY | YEAR DISCOVERED | DENSITY* |
|---|---|---|---|---|
| 1 | Osmium | Smithson Tennant, UK | 1804 | 22.59 |
| 2 | Iridium | Smithson Tennant, UK | 1804 | 22.56 |
| 3 | Platinum | J. C. Scaliger[#], Italy/France; Charles Wood[+], UK | 1557 1741 | 21.45 |
| 4 | Rhenium | W. Noddack *et al.*, Germany | 1925 | 21.01 |
| 5 | Neptunium | Edwin M. McMillan and Philip H. Abelson, US | 1940 | 20.47 |
| 6 | Plutonium | Glenn T. Seaborg *et al.*, US | 1940 | 20.26 |
| 7 | Gold | – | Prehistoric | 19.29 |
| 8 | Tungsten | Juan José and Fausto de Elhuijar, Spain | 1783 | 19.26 |
| 9 | Uranium | Martin J. Klaproth, Germany | 1789 | 19.05 |
| 10 | Tantalum | Anders G. Ekeberg, Sweden | 1802 | 16.67 |

*\* Grams per cu cm at 20°C    # Made earliest reference to    + Discovered by*

The two heaviest elements, the metals osmium and iridium, were discovered at the same time by the British chemist Smithson Tennant (1761–1815), who was also the first to prove that diamonds are made of carbon. One cu ft (0.028317 cu m) of osmium weighs 1,410 lb (640 kg) – equivalent to 10 people each weighing 141 lb (64 kg).

## LIGHTEST ELEMENTS*

| | ELEMENT | DISCOVERER/COUNTRY | YEAR DISCOVERED | DENSITY[#] |
|---|---|---|---|---|
| 1 | Lithium | J. A. Arfvedson, Sweden | 1817 | 0.533 |
| 2 | Potassium | Sir Humphry Davy, UK | 1807 | 0.859 |
| 3 | Sodium | Sir Humphry Davy, UK | 1807 | 0.969 |
| 4 | Calcium | Sir Humphry Davy, UK | 1808 | 1.526 |
| 5 | Rubidium | Robert W. Bunsen and Gustav Kirchoff, Germany | 1861 | 1.534 |
| 6 | Magnesium | Sir Humphry Davy | 1808[+] | 1.737 |
| 7 | Phosphorus | Hennig Brandt, Germany | 1669 | 1.825 |
| 8 | Beryllium | Friedrich Wöhler, Germany; A.-A. B. Bussy, France | 1828[★] | 1.846 |
| 9 | Cesium | Robert W. Bunsen and Gustav Kirchoff, Germany | 1860 | 1.896 |
| 10 | Sulfur | – | Prehistoric | 2.070 |

*\* Solids only    # Grams per cu cm at 20°C    + Recognized by Joseph Black, 1755, but not isolated    ★ Recognized by Nicholas Vauquelin, 1797, but not isolated*

Osmium, the heaviest element, is over 42 times heavier than lithium, the lightest element. Lithium is not only extremely light, but it is also so soft that it can be easily cut with a knife. It is half as heavy as water, and even lighter than certain types of wood.

## TOP 10 PRINCIPAL COMPONENTS OF AIR

*(Component/volume percent)*

**1** Nitrogen, 78.110  **2** Oxygen, 20.953  **3** Argon, 0.934  **4** Carbon dioxide, 0.01–0.10
**5** Neon, 0.001818  **6** Helium, 0.000524  **7** Methane, 0.0002
**8** Krypton, 0.000114  **9** = Hydrogen, 0.00005; = Nitrous oxide, 0.00005

## METALLIC ELEMENTS WITH THE GREATEST RESERVES

| | ELEMENT | ESTIMATED GLOBAL RESERVES (TONS) |
|---|---|---|
| 1 | Iron | 121,254,342,000 |
| 2 | Magnesium | 22,046,244,000 |
| 3 | Potassium | 11,023,122,000 |
| 4 | Aluminum | 6,613,873,000 |
| 5 | Manganese | 3,968,324,000 |
| 6 | Zirconium | over 1,102,312,000 |
| 7 | Chromium | 1,102,312,000 |
| 8 | Barium | 496,040,000 |
| 9 | Titanium | 485,017,000 |
| 10 | Copper | 341,717,000 |

### COPPER BOTTOMED

*Over 14 million tons (12.7 million tonnes) of copper have been removed from the Bingham Copper Mine, Utah, which is an all-time record for a single mine. This is the world's largest manmade excavation.*

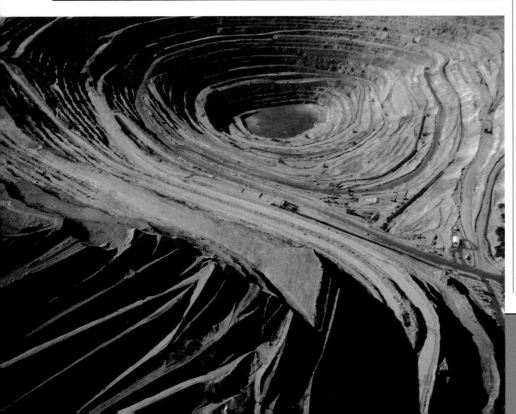

## TOP 10 MOST COMMON ELEMENTS IN SEAWATER

*(Element/tons per cu km)*

**1** Oxygen*, 944,681,600 **2** Hydrogen*, 118,829,300 **3** Chlorine, 21,902,900 **4** Sodium, 12,180,500 **5** Magnesium, 1,461,700 **6** Sulfur, 1,022,900 **7** Calcium, 465,200 **8** Potassium, 458,600 **9** Bromine, 74,200 **10** Carbon, 30,900

*\* Combined as water*

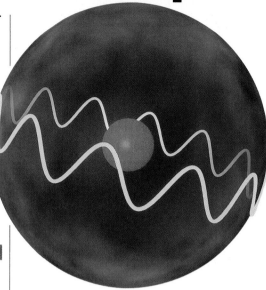

### TOP 10 ★
## MOST COMMON ELEMENTS IN THE EARTH'S CRUST

| ELEMENT | PARTS PER MILLION |
|---|---|
| 1 Oxygen | 474,000 |
| 2 Silicon | 277,100 |
| 3 Aluminum | 82,000 |
| 4 =Iron | 41,000 |
| =Calcium | 41,000 |
| 6 =Magnesium | 23,000 |
| =Sodium | 23,000 |
| 8 Potassium | 21,000 |
| 9 Titanium | 5,600 |
| 10 Hydrogen | 1,520 |

This Top 10 is based on the average percentages of the elements in igneous rock. At an atomic level, out of every million atoms, some 205,000 are silicon, 62,600 are aluminum, and 29,000 are hydrogen. In the universe as a whole, however, hydrogen is by far the most common element, comprising some 927,000 out of every million atoms. It is followed in second place by helium at 72,000 per million.

**LIGHT FANTASTIC**

*This computer-generated image shows a nucleus and orbiting electron, which make up a single atom of hydrogen, the lightest, simplest, most abundant, and most extracted of all elements.*

### TOP 10 ★
## MOST COMMON ELEMENTS ON THE MOON

| ELEMENT | PERCENTAGE |
|---|---|
| 1 Oxygen | 40.0 |
| 2 Silicon | 19.2 |
| 3 Iron | 14.3 |
| 4 Calcium | 8.0 |
| 5 Titanium | 5.9 |
| 6 Aluminum | 5.6 |
| 7 Magnesium | 4.5 |
| 8 Sodium | 0.33 |
| 9 Potassium | 0.14 |
| 10 Chromium | 0.002 |

This list is based on the chemical analysis of the 45.8 lb (20.77 kg) of rock samples brought back to the Earth by the three-man crew of the 1969 *Apollo 11* lunar mission.

## TOP 10 MOST COMMON ELEMENTS IN THE SUN

*(Element/parts per million)*

**1** Hydrogen, 745,000 **2** Helium, 237,000 **3** Oxygen, 8,990 **4** Carbon, 3,900 **5** Iron, 1,321 **6** Neon, 1,200 **7** Nitrogen, 870 **8** Silicon, 830 **9** Magnesium, 720 **10** Sulfur, 380

### TOP 10 ★
## ELEMENTS WITH THE HIGHEST MELTING POINTS

| ELEMENT | MELTING POINT °F | °C |
|---|---|---|
| 1 Carbon | 6,381 | 3,527 |
| 2 Tungsten | 6,192 | 3,422 |
| 3 Rhenium | 5,767 | 3,186 |
| 4 Osmium | 5,491 | 3,033 |
| 5 Tantalum | 5,463 | 3,017 |
| 6 Molybdenum | 4,753 | 2,623 |
| 7 Niobium | 4,491 | 2,477 |
| 8 Iridium | 4,471 | 2,466 |
| 9 Ruthenium | 4,233 | 2,334 |
| 10 Hafnium | 4,051 | 2,233 |

Other elements that melt at high temperatures include chromium (3,465°F/1,907°C), iron (2,800°F/1,538°C), and gold (1,947°F/1,064°C).

### THE DISCOVERY OF RADIUM

In 1898, Polish-born Marie Curie (1867–1934) and her French husband Pierre Curie detected radioactivity (a term Marie invented) in the mineral ore pitchblende, a waste product of mining. It took until 1902 before she had manually refined tons of ore to concentrate the radioactive content, producing about one tenth of a gram of radium chloride, an element that is a million times more radioactive than uranium. The following year, Marie and Pierre shared the Nobel Prize for Physics with Henry Becquerel. Marie eventually obtained pure radium in 1910. Marie was not only the first female Nobel winner, but also the first to achieve two Prizes, receiving the Chemistry Prize in 1911. Radium was subsequently used in the treatment of cancer, but, ironically, Marie died in 1934, from leukemia resulting from her prolonged contact with radium.

**100 YEARS AGO · YEARS AGO · YEARS AGO · YEARS**

**Did You Know?** Following the naming of the element Uranium after the planet Uranus, Neptunium and Plutonium were named after Neptune and Pluto, two more distant planets.

## THE 10 WORST YEARS FOR EPIDEMICS IN THE 1990s

*(Year/deaths due to epidemics)*

**1** 1991, 28,540 **2** 1996, 13,904 **3** 1998, 11,224 **4** 1997, 9,948 **5** 1992, 5,533
**6** 1999, 4,866 **7** 1995, 4,069 **8** 1990, 2,864 **9** 1994, 2,240 **10** 1993, 859

Source: *International Federation of Red Cross and Red Cross Societies*

Over two-thirds of those killed by epidemics in the 1990s were African. In 1991, 8,000 people died in Peru due to a diarrheal/enteric disease, and another 7,000 were killed by an epidemic of cholera in Nigeria.

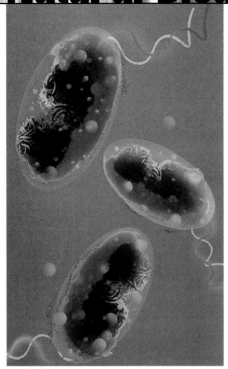

**CHOLERA KILLER**

*One of the scourges of the 19th century, when it killed millions, the cholera bacterium continues to cause illness and death in human communities that lack modern sanitation.*

## THE 10 ★ WORST EPIDEMICS OF ALL TIME

| EPIDEMIC/LOCATION | DATE | ESTIMATED NO. KILLED |
|---|---|---|
| **1** Black Death, Europe/Asia | 1347–51 | 75,000,000 |
| **2** Influenza, worldwide | 1918–20 | 21,640,000 |
| **3** AIDS, worldwide | 1981– | 16,300,000 |
| **4** Bubonic plague, India | 1896–1948 | 12,000,000 |
| **5** Typhus, Eastern Europe | 1914–15 | 3,000,000 |
| **6** ="Plague of Justinian," Europe/Asia | 541–90 | millions* |
| =Cholera, worldwide | 1846–60 | millions* |
| =Cholera, Europe | 1826–37 | millions* |
| =Cholera, worldwide | 1893–94 | millions* |
| **10** Smallpox, Mexico | 1530–45 | >1,000,000 |

\* *No precise figures available*

## THE 10 ★ WORST FLOODS OF ALL TIME

| | LOCATION | DATE | ESTIMATED NO. KILLED |
|---|---|---|---|
| **1** | Huang He River, China | Aug 1931 | 3,700,000 |
| **2** | Huang He River, China | Spring 1887 | 1,500,000 |
| **3** | Holland | Nov 1, 1530 | 400,000 |
| **4** | Kaifong, China | 1642 | 300,000 |
| **5** | Henan, China | Sep–Nov 1939 | over 200,000 |
| **6** | Bengal, India | 1876 | 200,000 |
| **7** | Yangtze River, China | Aug–Sep 1931 | 140,000 |
| **8** | Holland | 1646 | 110,000 |
| **9** | North Vietnam | Aug 30, 1971 | over 100,000 |
| **10** | =Friesland, Holland | 1228 | 100,000 |
| | =Dort, Holland | Apr 16, 1421 | 100,000 |
| | =Canton, China | June 12, 1915 | 100,000 |
| | =Yangtze River, China | Sep 1911 | 100,000 |

China's Huang He, or Yellow River, has flooded at least 1,500 times since records began in 2297 BC.

## THE 10 ★ COUNTRIES WITH MOST DEATHS DUE TO NATURAL DISASTERS

| | COUNTRY | ESTIMATED DEATHS DUE TO NATURAL DISASTERS (1999) |
|---|---|---|
| **1** | Venezuela | 30,021 |
| **2** | Turkey | 18,019 |
| **3** | India | 12,074 |
| **4** | China | 2,367 |
| **5** | Taiwan | 2,264 |
| **6** | Colombia | 1,284 |
| **7** | Nigeria | 1,190 |
| **8** | Mexico | 903 |
| **9** | Vietnam | 893 |
| **10** | US | 792 |
| | *World* | 212,544,647 |

Source: *International Federation of Red Cross and Red Cross Societies*

Deaths due to natural disasters in 1999 break down by continent to 6,294,514 in Africa, 13,494,780 in the Americas, 187,617,273 in Asia, 4,986,835 in Europe, and 151,245 in Oceania.

### THE ERUPTION OF MONT PELÉE

After lying dormant for centuries, Mont Pelée, a 4,430-ft (1,350-m) volcano on the West Indian island of Martinique, began to erupt in April 1902. Assured that the volcano presented no danger to them, the residents of the main city, St. Pierre, stayed in their homes instead of being evacuated. As a result of this catastrophic misreading of the volcano's activity, they were still there when, at 7.30 a.m. on May 8, the volcano burst apart and showered the port with molten lava, ash, and gas, destroying property, ships in the harbor, and virtually all life. A total of about 40,000 people were killed, which was more than twice as many as when Vesuvius engulfed Pompeii in AD 79. Raoul Sarteret, a prisoner in St. Pierre jail and the town's only survivor, provided a vivid eyewitness account of the event.

**100 YEARS AGO · YEARS AGO · YEARS AGO · YEARS**

**AFTER THE STORM**
*Hurricane Andrew, one of the costliest hurricanes ever, ravaged Miami, Florida, where it wrecked property and overturned vehicles to a cost of over $35.4 million dollars.*

## THE 10 ★
## MOST COSTLY HURRICANES TO STRIKE THE US

| | HURRICANE | YEAR | DAMAGE ($)* |
|---|---|---|---|
| 1 | Great Miami | 1926 | 77,490,000,000 |
| 2 | Andrew | 1992 | 35,468,000,000 |
| 3 | Southwest Florida | 1944 | 18,074,000,000 |
| 4 | New England | 1938 | 17,821,000,000 |
| 5 | Southeast Florida/ Lake Okeechobee | 1928 | 14,785,000,000 |
| 6 | Betsy | 1965 | 13,326,000,000 |
| 7 | Donna | 1960 | 12,913,000,000 |
| 8 | Camille | 1969 | 11,572,000,000 |
| 9 | Agnes | 1972 | 11,472,000,000 |
| 10 | Diane | 1955 | 10,966,000,000 |

\* Adjusted to 1998 dollars

Source: R. A. Pielke Jr. and C. W. Landsea, Normalized Atlantic Hurricane Damage, 1925–1995

## THE 10 ★
## MOST COSTLY TYPES OF DISASTER*

| | TYPE OF DISASTER | ESTIMATED DAMAGE 1990–99 ($) |
|---|---|---|
| 1 | Floods | 243,561,900,000 |
| 2 | Earthquakes | 215,023,211,000 |
| 3 | Wind storms | 179,391,693,000 |
| 4 | Forest/scrub fires | 36,975,436,000 |
| 5 | Non-natural disasters | 28,066,406,000 |
| 6 | Droughts | 21,941,064,000 |
| 7 | Extreme temperatures | 14,362,550,000 |
| 8 | Avalanches/landslides | 929,028,000 |
| 9 | Volcanoes | 672,628,000 |
| 10 | Other natural disasters (insect infestations, waves, and surges, etc.) | 109,467,000 |
| | World total | 741,033,383,000 |

\* Includes natural and non-natural

Source: *International Federation of Red Cross and Red Cross Societies*

## THE 10 ★
## MOST DEADLY TYPES OF NATURAL DISASTER IN THE 1990s

| | TYPE OF DISASTER | REPORTED DEATHS |
|---|---|---|
| 1 | Wind storms | 201,790 |
| 2 | Floods | 103,870 |
| 3 | Earthquakes | 98,678 |
| 4 | Epidemics* | 84,047 |
| 5 | Extreme temperatures | 9,055 |
| 6 | Avalanches/landslides | 8,658 |
| 7 | Droughts | 2,790 |
| 8 | Insect infestations, waves/surges | 2,686 |
| 9 | Volcanoes | 1,080 |
| 10 | Forest/scrub fires | 575 |

\* Excluding chronic public health disasters, such as the AIDS pandemic

Source: *International Federation of Red Cross and Red Cross Societies*

**Did You Know?** Since 1979, Atlantic hurricanes have been assigned men's and women's names, which alternate alphabetically and from year to year. Hurricane Bob, in July 1979, was the first.

# LIFE ON EARTH

# Land Animals

## HEAVIEST TERRESTRIAL MAMMALS

| MAMMAL | LENGTH | | WEIGHT | |
|---|---|---|---|---|
| | FT | M | LB | KG |
| 1 African elephant | 24 | 7.3 | 14,432 | 7,000 |
| 2 White rhinoceros | 14 | 4.2 | 7,937 | 3,600 |
| 3 Hippopotamus | 13 | 4.0 | 5,512 | 2,500 |
| 4 Giraffe | 19 | 5.8 | 3,527 | 1,600 |
| 5 American bison | 13 | 3.9 | 2,205 | 1,000 |
| 6 Arabian camel (dromedary) | 12 | 3.5 | 1,521 | 690 |
| 7 Polar bear | 8 | 2.6 | 1,323 | 600 |
| 8 Moose | 10 | 3.0 | 1,213 | 550 |
| 9 Siberian tiger | 11 | 3.3 | 661 | 300 |
| 10 Gorilla | 7 | 2.0 | 485 | 220 |

The list excludes domesticated cattle and horses. It also avoids comparing close kin such as the African and Indian elephants, highlighting instead the sumo stars within distinctive large mammal groups, such as the bears, big cats, primates, and bovines (ox-like mammals).

## MAMMALS WITH THE SHORTEST GESTATION PERIODS

| MAMMAL | AVERAGE GESTATION (DAYS) |
|---|---|
| 1 Short-nosed bandicoot | 12 |
| 2 Opossum | 13 |
| 3 Shrew | 14 |
| 4 Golden hamster | 16 |
| 5 Lemming | 20 |
| 6 Mouse | 21 |
| 7 Rat | 22 |
| 8 Gerbil | 24 |
| 9 Rabbit | 30 |
| 10 Mole | 38 |

The short-nosed bandicoot and the opossum are both marsupial mammals whose newborn young transfer to a pouch to complete their natal development. The babies of marsupials are minute when born.

## MOST ENDANGERED MAMMALS

| MAMMAL | ESTIMATED NO. |
|---|---|
| 1 =Ghana fat mouse | unknown |
| =Halcon fruit bat | unknown |
| =Tasmanian wolf | unknown |
| 4 Javan rhinoceros | 50 |
| 5 Iriomote cat | 60 |
| 6 Black lion tamarin | 130 |
| 7 Pygmy hog | 150 |
| 8 Kouprey | 100–200 |
| 9 Tamaraw | 200 |
| 10 Indus dolphin | 400 |

The first three mammals on the list have not been seen for many years and may well be extinct, but zoologists are hopeful of the possibility of their survival. The Tasmanian wolf, for example, has been technically extinct since the last specimen died in a zoo in 1936, but occasional unconfirmed sightings suggest that there may still be animals in the wild.

## HEAVIEST PRIMATES

| PRIMATE | LENGTH* | | WEIGHT | |
|---|---|---|---|---|
| | IN | CM | LB | KG |
| 1 Gorilla | 79 | 200 | 485 | 220 |
| 2 Man | 70 | 177 | 170 | 77 |
| 3 Orangutan | 54 | 137 | 165 | 75 |
| 4 Chimpanzee | 36 | 92 | 110 | 50 |
| 5 =Baboon | 39 | 100 | 99 | 45 |
| =Mandrill | 37 | 95 | 99 | 45 |
| 7 Gelada baboon | 30 | 75 | 55 | 25 |
| 8 Proboscis monkey | 30 | 76 | 53 | 24 |
| 9 Hanuman langur | 42 | 107 | 44 | 20 |
| 10 Siamung gibbon | 35 | 90 | 29 | 13 |

* Excluding tail

### ORANGUTAN

*Among the heaviest primates, and noted for its use of tools, the forest-dwelling orangutan gets its name from the Malay words for "man of the woods."*

TOP 10 ★

## LONGEST LAND ANIMALS

| | ANIMAL* | LENGTH FT | M |
|---|---|---|---|
| 1 | Reticulated python | 35 | 10.7 |
| 2 | Tapeworm | 33 | 10.0 |
| 3 | African elephant | 24 | 7.3 |
| 4 | Estuarine crocodile | 19 | 5.9 |
| 5 | Giraffe | 19 | 5.8 |
| 6 | White rhinoceros | 14 | 4.2 |
| 7 | Hippopotamus | 13 | 4.0 |
| 8 | American bison | 13 | 3.9 |
| 9 | Arabian camel (dromedary) | 12 | 3.5 |
| 10 | Siberian tiger | 11 | 3.3 |

\* *Longest representative of each species*

### NECK AND NECK

*The giraffe is the tallest of all living animals. In 1937 a calf giraffe that measured 5 ft 2 in (1.58 m) at birth was found to be growing at an astonishing ½ in (1.3 cm) per hour.*

## TOP 10 ★

## FASTEST MAMMALS

| | MAMMAL | MAXIMUM RECORDED SPEED MPH | KM/H |
|---|---|---|---|
| 1 | Cheetah | 65 | 105 |
| 2 | Pronghorn antelope | 55 | 89 |
| 3= | Mongolian gazelle | 50 | 80 |
| = | Springbok | 50 | 80 |
| 5= | Grant's gazelle | 47 | 76 |
| = | Thomson's gazelle | 47 | 76 |
| 7 | Brown hare | 45 | 72 |
| 8 | Horse | 43 | 69 |
| 9= | Greyhound | 42 | 68 |
| = | Red deer | 42 | 68 |

### QUICK OFF THE MARK

*The speedy cheetah can accelerate to 60 mph (96 km/h) in just three seconds.*

## TOP 10 ★

## LONGEST SNAKES

| | SNAKE | MAXIMUM LENGTH FT | M |
|---|---|---|---|
| 1 | Reticulated python | 35 | 10.7 |
| 2 | Anaconda | 28 | 8.5 |
| 3 | Indian python | 25 | 7.6 |
| 4 | Diamond python | 21 | 6.4 |
| 5 | King cobra | 19 | 5.8 |
| 6 | Boa constrictor | 16 | 4.9 |
| 7 | Bushmaster | 12 | 3.7 |
| 8 | Giant brown snake | 11 | 3.4 |
| 9 | Diamondback rattlesnake | 9 | 2.7 |
| 10 | Indigo or gopher snake | 8 | 2.4 |

**Did You Know?** "Old Bet," the first elephant ever seen in the US, arrived from Bengal, India, on April 13, 1796, and was exhibited in New York. She was known for her ability to draw corks from bottles using only her trunk.

# Marine Animals

## HEAVIEST MARINE MAMMALS

| MAMMAL | LENGTH FT | LENGTH M | WEIGHT (TONS) |
|---|---|---|---|
| 1 Blue whale | 110.0 | 33.5 | 151.0 |
| 2 Bowhead whale (Greenland right) | 65.0 | 20.0 | 95.0 |
| 3 Northern right whale (Black right) | 60.0 | 18.6 | 85.6 |
| 4 Fin whale (Common rorqual) | 82.0 | 25.0 | 69.9 |
| 5 Sperm whale | 59.0 | 18.0 | 48.2 |
| 6 Gray whale | 46.0 | 14.0 | 38.5 |
| 7 Humpback whale | 49.2 | 15.0 | 38.1 |
| 8 Sei whale | 60.0 | 18.5 | 32.4 |
| 9 Bryde's whale | 47.9 | 14.6 | 22.0 |
| 10 Baird's whale | 18.0 | 5.5 | 13.3 |

Source: *Lucy T. Verma*

Probably the largest animal that ever lived, the blue whale dwarfs even the other whales listed here, all but one of which far outweigh the biggest land animal, the elephant. The elephant seal, with a weight of 3.9 tons, is the heaviest marine mammal that is not a whale.

## HEAVIEST TURTLES

| TURTLE/TORTOISE | MAX. WEIGHT LB | KG |
|---|---|---|
| 1 Pacific leatherback turtle* | 1,552 | 704.4 |
| 2 Atlantic leatherback turtle* | 1,018 | 463.0 |
| 3 Green sea turtle | 783 | 355.3 |
| 4 Loggerhead turtle | 568 | 257.8 |
| 5 Alligator snapping turtle# | 220 | 100.0 |
| 6 Flatback (sea) turtle | 171 | 78.2 |
| 7 Hawksbill (sea) turtle | 138 | 62.7 |
| 8 Kemps ridley turtle | 133 | 60.5 |
| 9 Olive ridley turtle | 110 | 49.9 |
| 10 Common snapping turtle# | 85 | 38.5 |

\* *One species, differing in size according to where they live*

# *Freshwater species* Source: *Lucy T. Verma*

**MARINE MONSTER**

*There are several species of right whale, with larger examples of Greenland rights topping 65 ft (20 m) and weighing 95 tons. By contrast, the Pygmy right whale, found off New Zealand, rarely exceeds 20 ft (6 m).*

## TOP 10 LONGEST-LIVED MARINE MAMMALS

(*Marine mammal/lifespan in years*)

❶ Bowhead whale (*Balaena mysticetus*), 200
❷ Fin whale, 100 ❸ Orca (Killer whale), 90
❹ Baird's beaked whale, 82
❺ Sperm whale, 65 ❻ = Dugong, 60;
= Sei whale, 60 ❽ Bottlenose dolphin, 48
❾ Grey seal, 46 ❿ Blue whale, 45
Source: *Lucy T. Verma*

## TOP 10 ★

# SPECIES OF FISH MOST CAUGHT

| | SPECIES | TONS CAUGHT (1998) |
|---|---|---|
| 1 | Anchoveta (Peruvian anchovy) | 12,929,090 |
| 2 | Alaska pollock | 4,463,612 |
| 3 | Japanese anchovy | 2,308,118 |
| 4 | Chilean jack mackerel | 2,233,018 |
| 5 | Chubb mackerel | 2,105,696 |
| 6 | Skipjack tuna | 2,039,814 |
| 7 | Largehead hairtail | 1,338,725 |
| 8 | Atlantic cod | 1,313,057 |
| 9 | Yellowfin tuna | 1,270,510 |
| 10 | Capelin | 1,089,121 |
| | *World total all species* | 95,128,881 |

Source: *Food and Agriculture Organization of the United Nations*

The Food and Agriculture Organization of the United Nations estimates the volume of the world's fishing catch to be just over 95 million tons a year. Of this, about 83 million tons is estimated to be destined for human consumption – equivalent to approximately 29 lb (13 kg) a year for every inhabitant. The foremost species, anchoveta, are small anchovies used principally as bait to catch tuna.

## TOP 10 ★

# HEAVIEST SPECIES OF FRESHWATER FISH CAUGHT

| | SPECIES | ANGLER/LOCATION/DATE | LB | OZ | KG | G |
|---|---|---|---|---|---|---|
| | | | | WEIGHT | | |
| 1 | White sturgeon | Joey Pallotta III, Benicia, California, July 9, 1983 | 468 | 0 | 212 | 28 |
| 2 | Alligator gar | Bill Valverde, Rio Grande, Texas, Dec 2, 1951 | 279 | 0 | 126 | 55 |
| 3 | Beluga sturgeon | Merete Lehne, Guryev, Kazakhstan, May 3, 1993 | 224 | 13 | 102 | 00 |
| 4 | Nile perch | Adrian Brayshaw, Lake Nasser, Egypt, Dec 18, 1997 | 213 | 0 | 96 | 62 |
| 5 | Flathead catfish | Ken Paulie, Withlacoochee River, Florida, May 14, 1998 | 123 | 9 | 55 | 79 |
| 6 | Blue catfish | William P. McKinley, Wheeler Reservoir, Tennessee, July 5, 1996 | 111 | 0 | 50 | 35 |
| 7 | Redtailed catfish | Gilberto Fernandes, Amazon River, Amazonia, Brazil, July 16, 1988 | 97 | 7 | 44 | 20 |
| 8 | Chinook salmon | Les Anderson, Kenai River, Alaska, May 17, 1985 | 97 | 4 | 44 | 11 |
| 9 | Giant tigerfish | Raymond Houtmans, Zaïre River, Kinshasa, Zaïre, July 9, 1988 | 97 | 0 | 44 | 00 |
| 10 | Guilded catfish | Gilberto Fernandes, Amazon River, Amazonia Brazil, Nov 15, 1986 | 85 | 8 | 38 | 80 |

Source: *International Game Fish Association, World Record Game Fishes 2000*

## TOP 10 ★

# HEAVIEST SHARKS

| | SHARK | MAXIMUM WEIGHT LB | KG |
|---|---|---|---|
| 1 | Whale shark | 67,240 | 30,500 |
| 2 | Basking shark | 20,410 | 9,258 |
| 3 | Great white shark | 7,731 | 3,507 |
| 4 | Greenland shark | 2,224 | 1,009 |
| 5 | Tiger shark | 2,043 | 927 |
| 6 | Great hammerhead shark | 1,889 | 857 |
| 7 | Six-gill shark | 1,327 | 602 |
| 8 | Gray nurse shark | 1,243 | 564 |
| 9 | Mako shark | 1,221 | 554 |
| 10 | Thresher shark | 1,097 | 498 |

Source: *Lucy T. Verma*

**SPEEDY SWIMMER**

*The highly streamlined sailfish is acknowledged as the fastest over short distances, with anglers reporting them capable of unreeling 300 ft (91 m) of line in three seconds.*

# TOP 10 FASTEST FISH

*(Fish/maximum recorded speed in mph/km/h)*

❶ Sailfish, 69/112  ❷ Marlin, 50/80  ❸ Wahoo, 48/77  ❹ Bluefin tuna, 47/76
❺ Yellowfin tuna, 46/74  ❻ Blue shark, 43/69  ❼ = Bonefish, 40/64;
= Swordfish, 40/64  ❾ Tarpon, 35/56  ❿ Tiger shark, 33/53

Source: *Lucy T. Verma*

**Did You Know?** In a survey of recorded shark attacks from 1580 to 2000, the Great white shark was alone responsible for 348 out of a total of 980, resulting in 67 fatalities.

# Flying Animals

## FASTEST BIRDS

| BIRD | SPEED MPH | KM/H |
|------|-----|------|
| 1 Common eider | 47 | 76 |
| 2 Bewick's swan | 44 | 72 |
| 3 = Barnacle goose | 42 | 68 |
| = Common crane | 42 | 68 |
| 5 Mallard | 40 | 65 |
| 6 = Red-throated diver | 38 | 61 |
| = Wood pigeon | 38 | 61 |
| 8 Oyster catcher | 36 | 58 |
| 9 = Pheasant | 33 | 54 |
| = White-fronted goose | 33 | 54 |

Source: *Chris Mead*

Recent research reveals that, contrary to popular belief, swifts are not fast fliers but very efficient ones, with long, thin wings like gliders and low wing-loading. Fast fliers generally have high wing-loading and fast wing beats.

## OLDEST RINGED WILD BIRDS

| BIRD | AGE* YEARS | MONTHS |
|------|-------|--------|
| 1 Royal albatross | 50 | 0 |
| 2 Fulmar | 40 | 11 |
| 3 Manx shearwater | 37 | 0 |
| 4 Gannet | 36 | 4 |
| 5 Oystercatcher | 36 | 0 |
| 6 White (Fairy) tern | 35 | 11 |
| 7 Common eider | 35 | 0 |
| 8 Lesser black-backed gull | 34 | 10 |
| 9 Pink-footed goose | 34 | 2 |
| 10 Great frigate bird | 33 | 9 |

* *Elapsed time between marking and report*

Source: *Chris Mead*

Hard rings, likely to last as long as the bird, started to be used about 50 years ago. Land-based songbirds do not live as long as the slow-breeding seabirds. In general, big birds live longer than small ones, so the tiny White (Fairy) tern is especially noteworthy.

## FURTHEST BIRD MIGRATIONS

| SPECIES | APPROXIMATE DISTANCE MILES | KM |
|---------|-------|------|
| 1 Pectoral sandpiper | 11,806* | 19,000 |
| 2 Wheatear | 11,184 | 18,000 |
| 3 Slender-billed shearwater | 10,874* | 17,500 |
| 4 Ruff | 10,314 | 16,600 |
| 5 Willow warbler | 10,128 | 16,300 |
| 6 Arctic tern | 10,066 | 16,200 |
| 7 Parasitic jaeger | 9,693 | 15,600 |
| 8 Swainson's hawk | 9,445 | 15,200 |
| 9 Knot | 9,320 | 15,000 |
| 10 Barn swallow | 9,258 | 14,900 |

* *Thought to be only half of the path taken during a whole year*

Source: *Chris Mead*

This list is of the likely extremes for a normal migrant, not one that has gotten lost and wandered into new territory. All migrant birds fly much farther than is indicated by the direct route.

## LARGEST FLIGHTLESS BIRDS

| BIRD* | HEIGHT IN | CM | WEIGHT LB | OZ | KG |
|-------|-----|------|-----|-----|------|
| 1 Ostrich (male) | 100.4 | 255.0 | 343 | 9 | 156.0 |
| 2 Northern cassowary | 59.1 | 150.0 | 127 | 9 | 58.0 |
| 3 Emu (female) | 61.0 | 155.0 | 121 | 6 | 55.0 |
| 4 Emperor penguin (female) | 45.3 | 115.0 | 101 | 4 | 46.0 |
| 5 Greater rhea | 55.1 | 140.0 | 55 | 2 | 25.0 |
| 6 Flightless steamer# (duck) | 33.1 | 84.0 | 13 | 7 | 6.2 |
| 7 Flightless cormorant | 39.4 | 100.0 | 9 | 15 | 4.5 |
| 8 Kiwi (female) | 25.6 | 65.0 | 8 | 4 | 3.8 |
| 9 Takahe (rail) | 19.7 | 50.0 | 7 | 2 | 3.2 |
| 10 Kakapo (parrot) | 25.2 | 64.0 | 7 | 1 | 3.2 |

* *By species*

# *The Flightless steamer is 33 in (84 cm) long, but does not stand upright*

Source: *Chris Mead*

### EMPEROR RULES

*The Emperor penguin is the largest of all penguins, with females as much as twice as heavy as males. There are estimated to be 220,000 breeding pairs in the Antarctic.*

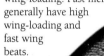

| BAT/HABITAT | LENGTH | | WEIGHT | |
|---|---|---|---|---|
| | IN | CM | OZ | GM |
| 1 Kitti's hognosed bat (*Craseonycteris thonglongyai*), Thailand | 1.10 | 2.9 | 0.07 | 2.0 |
| 2 Proboscis bat (*Rhynchonycteris naso*), Central and South America | 1.50 | 3.8 | 0.09 | 2.5 |
| 3 =Banana bat (*Pipistrellus nanus*), Africa | 1.50 | 3.8 | 0.11 | 3.0 |
| =Smoky bat (*Furipterus horrens*), Central and South America | 1.50 | 3.8 | 0.11 | 3.0 |
| 5 =Little yellow bat (*Rhogeessa mira*), Central America | 1.57 | 4.0 | 0.12 | 3.5 |
| =Lesser bamboo bat (*Tylonycteris pachypus*), Southeast Asia | 1.57 | 4.0 | 0.12 | 3.5 |
| 7 Disc-winged bat (*Thyroptera tricolor*), Central and South America | 1.42 | 3.6 | 0.14 | 4.0 |
| 8 =Lesser horseshoe bat (*Rhinolophus hipposideros*), Europe and Western Asia | 1.46 | 3.7 | 0.18 | 5.0 |
| =California myotis (*Myotis californienses*), North America | 1.69 | 4.3 | 0.18 | 5.0 |
| 10 Northern blossom bat (*Macroglossus minimus*), Southeast Asia to Australia | 2.52 | 6.4 | 0.53 | 15.0 |

This list focuses on the smallest example of 10 different bat families. The weights shown are typical, rather than extreme – and as a bat can eat more than half its own weight, the weights of individual examples may vary considerably. Length is of head and body only, since tail lengths vary from zero (Kitti's hognosed bat and the Northern blossom bat) to long (Proboscis bat and Lesser horseshoe bat).

**JUST HANGING AROUND**
*The Banana bat, the smallest found in Africa, roosts in small groups among the leaves of banana plants, using sucker pads to cling to the slippery leaf surfaces.*

# TOP 10 ⭐
## LARGEST BIRDS OF PREY (BY LENGTH)

| BIRD* | LENGTH | |
|---|---|---|
| | IN | CM |
| 1 Himalayan griffon vulture | 59 | 150 |
| 2 Californian condor | 53 | 134 |
| 3 Andean condor | 51 | 130 |
| 4 =Lammergeier | 45 | 115 |
| =Lappet-faced vulture | 45 | 115 |
| 6 Eurasian griffon vulture | 43 | 110 |
| 7 European black vulture | 42 | 107 |
| 8 Harpy eagle | 41 | 105 |
| 9 Wedge-tailed eagle | 41 | 104 |
| 10 Ruppell's griffon | 40 | 101 |

*\* Diurnal only – hence excluding owls*

The entrants in this Top 10 all measure more than 39 in (1 m) from beak to tail. In all but the vultures, the female will be larger than the male. All these raptors, or aerial hunters, have remarkable eyesight and can spot their victims from great distances. If they kill animals heavier than themselves, they are generally unable to take wing with them, unless they take advantage of a powerful updraft of air to soar up.

# TOP 10 ⭐
## BIRDS WITH THE LARGEST WINGSPANS

| BIRD* | MAXIMUM WINGSPAN | |
|---|---|---|
| | IN | CM |
| 1 Great white pelican | 141 | 360 |
| 2 Wandering albatross# | 138 | 351 |
| 3 Andean condor | 126 | 320 |
| 4 Himalayan griffon (vulture) | 122 | 310 |
| 5 Black vulture (Old World) | 116 | 295 |
| 6 Marabou stork | 113 | 287 |
| 7 Lammergeier | 111 | 282 |
| 8 Sarus crane | 110 | 280 |
| 9 Kori bustard | 106 | 270 |
| 10 Stellers Sea eagle | 104 | 265 |

*\* By species*

*# The royal albatross, a close relative, is the same size*

Source: *Chris Mead*

Very much bigger wingspans have been claimed for many species, but dead specimens of some species may easily be stretched by as much as 15 to 20 percent. The measurements given are, as far as can be ascertained, for wingtip to wingtip for live birds measured in a natural position.

# TOP 10 ⭐
## RAREST BIRDS

| BIRD/COUNTRY | ESTIMATED NO.* |
|---|---|
| 1 =Cebu flower pecker, Philippines | 1 |
| =Spix's macaw, Brazil | 1 |
| 3 Hawaiian crow, Hawaii | 5 |
| 4 Black stilt, New Zealand | 12 |
| 5 Echo parakeet, Mauritius | 13 |
| 6 Imperial Amazon parrot, Dominica | 15 |
| 7 Magpie robin, Seychelles | 20 |
| 8 Kakapo, New Zealand | 24 |
| 9 Pink pigeon, Mauritius | 70 |
| 10 Mauritius kestrel, Mauritius | 100 |

*\* Of breeding pairs reported since 1986*

Several rare bird species are known from old records or from only one specimen, but must be assumed to be extinct in the absence of recent sightings or records of breeding pairs.

**Did You Know?** On June 5, 1932, near Trondheim, Norway, a white-tailed sea eagle lifted 4-year-old Svanhild Hansen 800 ft (244 m) to its mountain eyrie. She was recovered unharmed.

# Popular Pets

## PEDIGREE CAT BREEDS IN THE US

| | BREED | NO. REGISTERED* |
|---|---|---|
| 1 | Persian | 25,524 |
| 2 | Maine coon | 4,539 |
| 3 | Siamese | 2,131 |
| 4 | Exotic | 2,094 |
| 5 | Abyssinian | 1,683 |
| 6 | Oriental | 1,085 |
| 7 | Birman | 998 |
| 8 | American shorthair | 885 |
| 9 | Scottish fold | 851 |
| 10 | Burmese | 846 |

\* Year ending December 31, 2000

Source: Cat Fancier's Association

## CAT POPULATIONS

| | COUNTRY | ESTIMATED CAT POPULATION (1999) |
|---|---|---|
| 1 | US | 72,600,000 |
| 2 | China | 46,800,000 |
| 3 | Russia | 12,500,000 |
| 4 | Brazil | 10,000,000 |
| 5 | France | 8,700,000 |
| 6 | UK | 7,700,000 |
| 7 | Japan | 7,540,000 |
| 8 | Ukraine | 7,150,000 |
| 9 | Italy | 7,000,000 |
| 10 | Germany | 6,500,000 |

Source: Euromonitor

Estimates of the number of domestic cats in the 20 leading countries reveal a total of 221 million, with the greatest increases experienced in China and other Asian countries.

## PETS IN THE US

| | PET | ESTIMATED NUMBER |
|---|---|---|
| 1 | Cats | 72,600,000 |
| 2 | Dogs | 58,500,000 |
| 3 | Small animal pets* | 13,080,000 |
| 4 | Parakeets | 11,000,000 |
| 5 | Freshwater fish | 10,800,000# |
| 6 | Reptiles | 7,680,000 |
| 7 | Finches | 7,350,000 |
| 8 | Cockatiels | 6,320,000 |
| 9 | Canaries | 2,580,000 |
| 10 | Parrots | 1,550,000 |

\* Includes small rodents – rabbits, ferrets, hamsters, guinea pigs, and gerbils

\# Number of households owning, rather than individual specimens

Source: Pet Industry Joint Advisory Council/ Euromonitor

The size of the US pet population is mirrored in the sales of dog food ($6,169 million in 1999) and cat food ($4,922 million), and total expenditure on pet food and care products ($15,707,200,000).

## TOP 10 CATS' NAMES IN THE US

❶ Tigger ❷ Tiger ❸ Smokey ❹ Shadow ❺ Sam ❻ Max ❼ Kitty ❽ Oreo ❾ Buddy ❿ Misty

Source: American Pet Classics

## DOG POPULATIONS

| | COUNTRY | ESTIMATED DOG POPULATION (1999) |
|---|---|---|
| 1 | US | 58,500,000 |
| 2 | Brazil | 23,000,000 |
| 3 | China | 19,380,000 |
| 4 | Japan | 9,567,000 |
| 5 | Russia | 9,375,000 |
| 6 | France | 8,100,000 |
| 7 | South Africa | 7,800,000 |
| 8 | Poland | 7,400,000 |
| 9 | UK | 6,700,000 |
| 10 | Italy | 6,300,000 |

Source: Euromonitor

### WHAT'S NEW PUSSYCAT?

*Although their role as household mouse exterminators is less significant today, cats maintain their place among the world's favorite animals.*

## TOP 10 DOGS' NAMES IN THE US

**1** Max **2** Buddy **3** Maggie **4** Molly **5** Jake **6** Bailey **7** Lucy
**8** Daisy **9** Lucky **10** Sadie

*Source: American Pet Classics*

---

### TOP 10 ★
## DOG BREEDS IN THE US

| | BREED | NO. REGISTERED BY AMERICAN KENNEL CLUB, INC. (2000) |
|---|---|---|
| 1 | Labrador retriever | 172,841 |
| 2 | Golden retriever | 66,300 |
| 3 | German shepherd | 57,660 |
| 4 | Dachshund | 54,773 |
| 5 | Beagle | 52,026 |
| 6 | Poodle | 45,868 |
| 7 | Yorkshire terrier | 43,574 |
| 8 | Chihuahua | 43,096 |
| 9 | Boxer | 38,803 |
| 10 | Shih tzu | 37,599 |

*Source: The American Kennel Club*

---

### TOP 10 ★
## FILMS STARRING DOGS

| | FILM | YEAR |
|---|---|---|
| 1 | *101 Dalmatians* | 1996 |
| 2 | *One Hundred and One Dalmatians** | 1961 |
| 3 | *102 Dalmatians* | 2000 |
| 4 | *Lady and the Tramp** | 1955 |
| 5 | *Oliver & Company* | 1988 |
| 6 | *Turner & Hooch* | 1989 |
| 7 | *The Fox and the Hound** | 1981 |
| 8 | *Beethoven* | 1992 |
| 9 | *Homeward Bound II: Lost in San Francisco* | 1996 |
| 10 | *Beethoven's 2nd* | 1993 |

\* Animated

Man's best friend has been stealing scenes since the earliest years of filmmaking, with the 1905 low-budget *Rescued by Rover* outstanding as one of the most successful productions of the pioneer period. The numerous silent-era films starring Rin Tin Tin, an ex-German army dog who emigrated to the US, and his successor Lassie, whose long series of feature and TV films dates from the 1940s onward, are among the most enduring in cinematic history.

---

### JACK RUSSELL

In 1819, according to legend, John "Jack" Russell (1795–1883) spotted a milkman accompanied by a distinctive-looking dog, which he persuaded its owner to sell to him and which he named Trump. Russell later became Curate of Swimbridge near Barnstaple, Devon, UK, where he devoted himself to breeding a type of fox terrier with short legs and a short white, black, and tan coat, ideally suited for hunting and able to follow animals into burrows. These dogs are today known in his honor as Jack Russell terriers.

WHO WAS • WHO WAS • WHO WAS • WHO WAS • ?

---

### THE 10 ★
## LATEST BEST IN SHOW WINNERS AT THE WESTMINSTER KENNEL CLUB DOG SHOW

| YEAR | BREED/CHAMPION |
|---|---|
| 2001 | Bichons Frises, Special Times Just Right |
| 2000 | English springer spaniel, Salilyn 'N Erin's Shameless |
| 1999 | Papillon, Loteki Supernatural Being |
| 1998 | Norwich terrier, Fairewood Frolic |
| 1997 | Standard schnauzer, Parsifal Di Casa Netzer |
| 1996 | Clumber spaniel, Clussexx Country Sunrise |
| 1995 | Scottish terrier, Gaelforce Post Script |
| 1994 | Norwich terrier, Chidley Willum The Conqueror |
| 1993 | English springer spaniel, Salilyn's Condor |
| 1992 | Wire fox terrier, Registry's Lonesome Dove |

*Source: Westminster Kennel Club*

**TOP DOGS**
*Labrador retrievers are the most popular dogs in both the US and the UK, where they were first bred as gundogs in the 19th century.*

# Creepy Crawlies

## TOP 10 ★
### FASTEST INSECT FLYERS

| INSECT | MPH | KM/H |
|---|---|---|
| 1 Hawkmoth (*Sphingidaei*) | 33.3 | 53.6 |
| 2 =West Indian butterfly (*Nymphalidae prepona*) | 30.0 | 48.0 |
| =Deer bot fly (*Cephenemyia pratti*) | 30.0 | 48.0 |
| 4 Deer bot fly (*Chrysops*) | 25.0 | 40.0 |
| 5 West Indian butterfly (*Hesperiidae sp.*) | 18.6 | 30.0 |
| 6 Dragonfly (*Anax parthenope*) | 17.8 | 28.6 |
| 7 Hornet (*Vespa crabro*) | 13.3 | 21.4 |
| 8 Bumble bee (*Bombus lapidarius*) | 11.1 | 17.9 |
| 9 Horsefly (*Tabanus bovinus*) | 8.9 | 14.3 |
| 10 Honey bee (*Apis millefera*) | 7.2 | 11.6 |

Few accurate assessments of insect flying speeds have ever been attempted, and this Top 10 represents the results of only the handful of scientific studies that are widely recognized by entomologists. Some experts have also suggested that the male *Hybomitra linei wrighti* (*Diptera tabanidae*) is capable of traveling at 90 mph (145 km/h) when in pursuit of a female, while there are exceptional, one-time examples such as that of a dragonfly (*Austophlebia costalis*) allegedly recorded as flying at a speed of 61 mph (98 km/h).

## TOP 10 ★
### LARGEST BUTTERFLIES

| BUTTERFLY | AVERAGE WINGSPAN IN | MM |
|---|---|---|
| 1 Queen Alexandra's birdwing | 11.0 | 280 |
| 2 African giant swallowtail | 9.1 | 230 |
| 3 Goliath birdwing | 8.3 | 210 |
| 4 =Buru opalescent birdwing | 7.9 | 200 |
| =*Trogonoptera trojana* | 7.9 | 200 |
| =*Troides hypolitus* | 7.9 | 200 |
| 7 =*Chimaera birdwing* | 7.5 | 190 |
| =*Ornithoptera lydius* | 7.5 | 190 |
| =*Troides magellanus* | 7.5 | 190 |
| =*Troides miranda* | 7.5 | 190 |

## TOP 10 ★
### CREATURES WITH THE MOST LEGS

| CREATURE | AVERAGE LEGS |
|---|---|
| 1 Millipede *Illacme plenipes* | 750 |
| 2 Centipede *Himantarum gabrielis* | 354 |
| 3 Centipede *Haplophilus subterraneus* | 178 |
| 4 Millipedes* | 30 |
| 5 Symphylans | 24 |
| 6 Caterpillars* | 16 |
| 7 Woodlice | 14 |
| 8 Crabs, shrimps | 10 |
| 9 Spiders | 8 |
| 10 Insects | 6 |

\* Most species

Despite their names, centipedes, depending on their species, have anything from 28 to 354 legs and millipedes have up to 400 legs, with the record standing at around 750.

## TOP 10 ★
### LARGEST MOLLUSCS

| SPECIES/CLASS | AVERAGE LENGTH* IN | MM |
|---|---|---|
| 1 Giant squid (*Architeuthis sp.*), Cephalopod | 660 | 16,764# |
| 2 Giant clam (*Tridacna gigas*), Marine bivalve | 51 | 1,300 |
| 3 Australian trumpet, Marine snail | 30 | 770 |
| 4 *Hexabranchus sanguineus*, Sea slug | 20 | 520 |
| 5 *Carinaria cristata*, Heteropod | 19 | 500 |
| 6 Steller's coat of mail shell (*Cryptochiton stelleri*), Chiton | 18 | 470 |
| 7 Freshwater mussel (*Cristaria plicata*), Freshwater bivalve | 11 | 300 |
| 8 Giant African snail (*Achatina achatina*), Land snail | 7 | 200 |
| 9 Tusk shell (*Dentalium vernedi*), Scaphopod | 5 | 138 |
| 10 Apple snail (*Pila werneri*), Freshwater snail | 4 | 125 |

\* Largest species within each class
\# Estimated; actual length unknown

## THE 10 ★
### COUNTRIES WITH THE MOST THREATENED INVERTEBRATES

| COUNTRY | THREATENED INVERTEBRATE SPECIES |
|---|---|
| 1 US | 594 |
| 2 Australia | 281 |
| 3 South Africa | 101 |
| 4 Portugal | 67 |
| 5 France | 61 |
| 6 Spain | 57 |
| 7 Tanzania | 46 |
| 8 =Dem. Rep. of Congo | 45 |
| =Japan | 45 |
| 10 =Austria | 41 |
| =Italy | 41 |

Source: *International Union for the Conservation of Nature*

## TOP 10 ★
### LARGEST MOTHS

| MOTH | AVERAGE WINGSPAN IN | MM |
|---|---|---|
| 1 Atlas moth (*Attacus atlas*) | 11.8 | 300 |
| 2 Owlet moth (*Thysania agrippina*)* | 11.4 | 290 |
| 3 *Haematopis grataria* | 10.2 | 260 |
| 4 Hercules emperor moth (*Coscinocera hercules*) | 8.3 | 210 |
| 5 Malagasy silk moth (*Argema mitraei*) | 7.1 | 180 |
| 6 *Eacles imperialis* | 6.9 | 175 |
| 7 = Common emperor moth (*Bunaea alcinoe*) | 6.3 | 160 |
| =Giant peacock moth (*Saturnia pyri*) | 6.3 | 160 |
| 9 Gray moth (*Brahmaea wallichii*) | 6.1 | 155 |
| 10 =Black witch (*Ascalapha odorata*) | 5.9 | 150 |
| =Regal moth (*Citheronia regalis*) | 5.9 | 150 |
| =Polyphemus moth (*Antheraea polyphemus*) | 5.9 | 150 |

\* Exceptional specimen measured at 12¼ in (308 mm)

## TOP 10 ★
# DEADLIEST SPIDERS
SPIDER/LOCATION

1 **Banana spider** (*Phonenutria nigriventer*), Central and South America

2 **Sydney funnel web** (*Atrax robustus*), Australia

3 **Wolf spider** (*Lycosa raptoria/erythrognatha*), Central and South America

4 **Black widow** (*Latrodectus species*), Widespread

5 **Violin spider/Recluse spider**, Widespread

6 **Sac spider**, Southern Europe

7 **Tarantula** (*Eurypelma rubropilosum*), Neotropics

8 **Tarantula** (*Acanthoscurria atrox*), Neotropics

9 **Tarantula** (*Lasiodora klugi*), Neotropics

10 **Tarantula** (*Pamphobeteus species*), Neotropics

This list ranks spiders according to their "lethal potential" – their venom yield divided by their venom potency. The Banana spider, for example, yields 6 mg of venom, with 1 mg the estimated lethal dose in man.

## THE 10 MOST ENDANGERED SPIDERS
*(Spider/country)*

❶ **Kauai cave wolf spider**, US ❷ **Doloff cave spider**, US ❸ **Empire cave pseudoscorpion**, US ❹ **Glacier Bay wolf spider**, US ❺ **Great raft spider**, Europe ❻ **Kocevje subterranean spider** (*Troglohyphantes gracilis*), Slovenia ❼ **Kocevje subterranean spider** (*Troglohyphantes similis*), Slovenia ❽ **Kocevje subterranean spider** (*Troglohyphantes spinipes*), Slovenia ❾ **Lake Placid funnel wolf spider**, US ❿ **Melones cave harvestman**, US

Source: *International Union for the Conservation of Nature*

**THE FLY**
*The 120,000 known species of flies include houseflies, mosquitoes, midges, and gnats, all of which number among the insects human beings consider the most irritating.*

## TOP 10 ★
# MOST COMMON INSECTS*

| SPECIES | APPROX. NO. OF KNOWN SPECIES |
|---|---|
| 1 **Beetles** (*Coleoptera*) | 400,000 |
| 2 **Butterflies and moths** (*Lepidoptera*) | 165,000 |
| 3 **Ants, bees, and wasps** (*Hymenoptera*) | 140,000 |
| 4 **True flies** (*Diptera*) | 120,000 |
| 5 **Bugs** (*Hemiptera*) | 90,000 |
| 6 **Crickets, grasshoppers, and locusts** (*Orthoptera*) | 20,000 |
| 7 **Caddisflies** (*Trichoptera*) | 10,000 |
| 8 **Lice** (*Phthiraptera/Psocoptera*) | 7,000 |
| 9 **Dragonflies and damselflies** (*Odonata*) | 5,500 |
| 10 **Lacewings** (*Neuroptera*) | 4,700 |

* By number of known species

This list includes only species that have been discovered and named. It is surmised that many thousands of species still await discovery. It takes no account of the truly colossal numbers of each species: there are at least 1 million insects for each of the Earth's 6.1 billion human beings.

The UK has over 44 million and the US less than 5 million. What are they?
see p.42 for the answer

A Houses over 100 years old
B Sheep
C Oak trees

# Livestock

## CATTLE COUNTRIES

| | COUNTRY | CATTLE (2000) |
|---|---|---|
| 1 | India | 218,800,000 |
| 2 | Brazil | 167,471,000 |
| 3 | China | 104,169,000 |
| 4 | US | 98,048,000 |
| 5 | Argentina | 55,000,000 |
| 6 | Sudan | 35,300,000 |
| 7 | Ethiopia | 35,100,000 |
| 8 | Mexico | 30,293,000 |
| 9 | Russian Federation | 27,500,000 |
| 10 | Colombia | 26,000,000 |
| | *World* | 1,343,794,190 |

Source: *Food and Agriculture Organization of the United Nations*

US cattle numbers have declined from their 1970 peak of 112 million, and now stand at the level they held in 1961.

## SHEEP COUNTRIES

| | COUNTRY | SHEEP (2000) |
|---|---|---|
| 1 | China | 131,095,000 |
| 2 | Australia | 116,900,000 |
| 3 | India | 57,900,000 |
| 4 | Iran | 55,000,000 |
| 5 | New Zealand | 45,497,000 |
| 6 | UK | 44,656,000 |
| 7 | Sudan | 42,800,000 |
| 8 | Turkey | 30,238,000 |
| 9 | South Africa | 28,700,000 |
| 10 | Pakistan | 24,084,000 |
| | *US* | 7,215,000 |
| | *World* | 1,064,377,000 |

Source: *Food and Agriculture Organization of the United Nations*

The 1900 Census put the US's sheep stocks at an all-time level of over 61 million.

## CHICKEN COUNTRIES

| | COUNTRY | CHICKENS (2000) |
|---|---|---|
| 1 | China | 3,625,012,000 |
| 2 | US | 1,720,000,000 |
| 3 | Indonesia | 1,000,000,000 |
| 4 | Brazil | 950,000,000 |
| 5 | Mexico | 476,000,000 |
| 6 | India | 402,000,000 |
| 7 | Russia | 340,000,000 |
| 8 | Japan | 298,000,000 |
| 9 | France | 232,970,000 |
| 10 | Iran | 230,000,000 |
| | *World* | 14,525,381,000 |

Source: *Food and Agriculture Organization of the United Nations*

The Top 10 countries have 65 percent of the world's chicken population, with almost half the world total being reared in Asian countries. The US's estimated chicken population outnumbers the human population by a factor of over six.

## TOP 10 MILK-PRODUCING COUNTRIES

*(Country/production in tons\*, 2000)*

**1** US, 84,100,000 **2** Russia, 34,789,000 **3** India, 34,061,000 **4** Germany, 31,085,000 **5** France, 27,437,000 **6** Brazil, 24,797,000 **7** UK, 16,227,100 **8** Ukraine, 13,669,000 **9** New Zealand, 13,243,200 **10** Poland, 12,660,000

World 534,342,000

\* *Fresh cow's milk*   Source: *Food and Agriculture Organization of the United Nations*

## GEESE COUNTRIES

| | COUNTRY | GEESE (2000) |
|---|---|---|
| 1 | China | 203,225,000 |
| 2 | Egypt | 9,100,000 |
| 3 | Romania | 4,000,000 |
| 4 | Russia | 3,300,000 |
| 5 | Madagascar | 3,100,000 |
| 6 | Turkey | 1,650,000 |
| 7 | Hungary | 1,226,000 |
| 8 | Iran | 1,200,000 |
| 9 | Israel | 1,100,000 |
| 10 | France | 1,000,000 |
| | *World* | 235,087,000 |

Source: *Food and Agriculture Organization of the United Nations*

**GOLDEN EGG**

*Some 86 percent of the world's geese reside in China, where they play an important part in culture and cuisine. China is also the top producer of goose down.*

## TOP 10 ★
## GOAT COUNTRIES

| | COUNTRY | GOATS (2000) |
|---|---|---|
| 1 | China | 148,400,500 |
| 2 | India | 123,000,000 |
| 3 | Pakistan | 47,475,000 |
| 4 | Sudan | 37,800,000 |
| 5 | Bangladesh | 33,500,000 |
| 6 | Iran | 26,000,000 |
| 7 | Nigeria | 24,300,000 |
| 8 | Ethiopia | 17,000,000 |
| 9 | Indonesia | 15,198,000 |
| 10 | Brazil | 12,600,000 |
| | US | 1,350,000 |
| | World | 715,247,550 |

Source: *Food and Agriculture Organization of the United Nations*

The goat is one of the most widely distributed of all domesticated animals. Its resilience to diseases, such as the tuberculosis that affects cattle, and its adaptability to harsh conditions make it ideally suited to the environments encountered in some of the less-developed parts of the world. Goat meat and milk figures in the national diets of many countries, with even some of the smaller African nations having a million or more goats.

**BUFFALO**

More than 95 percent of the world's buffalo population resides in the Top 10 countries. Only one European country has a significant herd: Italy, with 170,000.

## TOP 10 ★
## BUFFALO COUNTRIES

| | COUNTRY | BUFFALOES (2000) |
|---|---|---|
| 1 | India | 93,772,000 |
| 2 | Pakistan | 22,670,000 |
| 3 | China | 22,599,000 |
| 4 | Nepal | 3,471,000 |
| 5 | Egypt | 3,200,000 |
| 6 | Indonesia | 3,145,000 |
| 7 | Philippines | 3,018,000 |
| 8 | Vietnam | 3,000,000 |
| 9 | Myanmar (Burma) | 2,400,000 |
| 10 | Thailand | 2,100,000 |
| | World | 165,804,000 |

Source: *Food and Agriculture Organization of the United Nations*

## TOP 10 ★
## PIG COUNTRIES

| | COUNTRY | PIGS (2000) |
|---|---|---|
| 1 | China | 437,551,000 |
| 2 | US | 59,337,000 |
| 3 | Brazil | 27,320,000 |
| 4 | Germany | 27,049,000 |
| 5 | Spain | 23,682,000 |
| 6 | Vietnam | 19,584,000 |
| 7 | Russia | 18,300,000 |
| 8 | Poland | 18,200,000 |
| 9 | India | 16,005,000 |
| 10 | France | 14,635,000 |
| | World | 909,486,000 |

Source: *Food and Agriculture Organization of the United Nations*

The distribution of the world's pig population is determined by cultural, religious, and dietary factors, with the result that there are few pigs in African and Islamic countries, and a disproportionate concentration of pigs in those countries that do not have such prohibitions.

## TOP 10 ★
## DONKEY COUNTRIES

| | COUNTRY | DONKEYS (2000) |
|---|---|---|
| 1 | China | 9,348,000 |
| 2 | Ethiopia | 5,200,000 |
| 3 | Pakistan | 4,500,000 |
| 4 | Mexico | 3,250,000 |
| 5 | Egypt | 3,050,000 |
| 6 | Iran | 1,600,000 |
| 7 | Brazil | 1,350,000 |
| 8 | Afghanistan | 1,160,000 |
| 9 = | India | 1,000,000 |
| = | Nigeria | 1,000,000 |
| | World | 43,564,000 |

Source: *Food and Agriculture Organization of the United Nations*

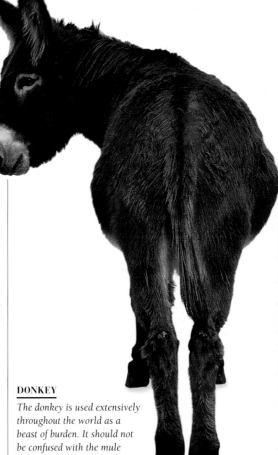

**DONKEY**

*The donkey is used extensively throughout the world as a beast of burden. It should not be confused with the mule (the offspring of a horse and a donkey).*

**Did You Know?** The first pig to fly took to the air on November 4, 1909, the passenger of Claude Moore- (later Lord) Brabazon, in a wicker basket attached to his Voisin biplane.

43

**TAPPING RUBBER**

*In the 20th century, world demand for natural rubber, especially for the automotive industry, increased from under 50,000 to over 6 million tons.*

## TOP 10 ★
## RUBBER-PRODUCING COUNTRIES

| | COUNTRY | 1999 PRODUCTION (TONS) |
|---|---|---|
| 1 | Thailand | 2,423,334 |
| 2 | Indonesia | 1,724,373 |
| 3 | Malaysia | 976,318 |
| 4 | India | 606,272 |
| 5 | China | 485,017 |
| 6 | Vietnam | 236,806 |
| 7 | Côte d'Ivoire | 131,021 |
| 8 | Sri Lanka | 105,502 |
| 9 | Nigeria | 99,208 |
| 10 | Philippines | 70,548 |
| | *World total* | 7,197,810 |

Source: *Food and Agriculture Organization of the United Nations*

## TOP 10 ★
## MOST FORESTED COUNTRIES

| | COUNTRY | PERCENTAGE FOREST COVER |
|---|---|---|
| 1 | French Guiana | 90.0 |
| 2 | Solomon Islands | 87.8 |
| 3 | Surinam | 86.4 |
| 4 | Gabon | 81.5 |
| 5 | Guyana | 78.5 |
| 6 | Brunei | 76.6 |
| 7 | Palau | 76.1 |
| 8 | Finland | 72.0 |
| 9 | North Korea | 68.1 |
| 10 | Sweden | 66.8 |
| | *US* | 24.7 |

Source: *Food and Agriculture Organization of the United Nations*

These are the 10 countries with the greatest area of forest and woodland as a percentage of their total land area. With increasing deforestation, the world average has fallen from about 32 percent in 1972 to its present 29 percent. The least forested large countries in the world are the desert lands of the Middle East and North Africa, such as Oman, which has no forests, and Egypt with just 0.1 percent forested land.

## TOP 10 ★
## COUNTRIES WITH THE LARGEST AREAS OF FOREST

| | COUNTRY | AREA SQ MILES | AREA SQ KM |
|---|---|---|---|
| 1 | Russia | 3,287,243 | 8,513,920 |
| 2 | Brazil | 2,055,921 | 5,324,810 |
| 3 | Canada | 944,294 | 2,445,710 |
| 4 | US | 872,564 | 2,259,930 |
| 5 | China | 631,200 | 1,634,800 |
| 6 | Australia | 610,350 | 1,580,800 |
| 7 | Dem. Rep. of Congo | 522,037 | 1,352,070 |
| 8 | Indonesia | 405,353 | 1,049,860 |
| 9 | Angola | 269,329 | 697,560 |
| 10 | Peru | 251,796 | 652,150 |
| | *World total* | 14,888,715 | 38,561,590 |

## TOP 10 ★
## LARGEST NATIONAL FORESTS IN THE US

| | FOREST/LOCATION | AREA SQ MILES | SQ KM |
|---|---|---|---|
| 1 | **Tongass National Forest,** Sitka, Alaska | 25,920 | 67,133 |
| 2 | **Chugach National Forest,** Anchorage, Alaska | 8,439 | 21,856 |
| 3 | **Toiyabe National Forest,** Sparks, Nevada | 5,053 | 13,087 |
| 4 | **Tonto National Forest,** Phoenix, Arizona | 4,489 | 11,627 |
| 5 | **Gila National Forest,** Silver City, New Mexico | 4,231 | 10,961 |
| 6 | **Boise National Forest,** Boise, Idaho | 4,145 | 10,734 |
| 7 | **Humboldt National Forest,** Elko, Nevada | 3,878 | 10,044 |
| 8 | **Challis National Forest,** Challis, Idaho | 3,851 | 9,974 |
| 9 | **Shoshone National Forest,** Cody, Wyoming | 3,808 | 9,862 |
| 10 | **Flathead National Forest,** Kalispess, Montana | 3,681 | 9,533 |

Source: *Land Areas of the National Forest System*

**TREE TOPS**

*The US leads the world in timber production, supplying the requirements of industries such as construction and paper manufacture.*

## TOP 10 ✴
## TIMBER-PRODUCING COUNTRIES

| | COUNTRY | CU FT | 1999 PRODUCTION CU M |
|---|---|---|---|
| 1 | China | 20,576,445,622 | 582,660,000 |
| 2 | US | 17,683,644,429 | 500,745,000 |
| 3 | India | 10,693,069,905 | 302,793,992 |
| 4 | Brazil | 6,988,667,249 | 197,897,000 |
| 5 | Indonesia | 6,730,994,042 | 190,600,508 |
| 6 | Canada | 6,556,480,455 | 185,658,834 |
| 7 | Russia | 3,919,928,370 | 111,000,000 |
| 8 | Nigeria | 3,553,962,445 | 100,637,000 |
| 9 | Sweden | 2,072,971,129 | 58,700,000 |
| 10 | Finland | 1,901,715,074 | 53,850,569 |
| | *World total* | 115,658,445,703 | 3,275,082,160 |

Source: *Food and Agriculture Organization of the United Nations*

## TOP 10 ✴
## MOST COMMON TREES IN THE US

1 Silver maple

2 Black cherry

3 Boxelder

4 Eastern cottonwood

5 Black willow

6 Northern red oak

7 Flowering dogwood

8 Black oak

9 Ponderosa pine

10 Coast Douglas fir

Source: *American Forests*

Hardwood trees native to the Eastern and Southern states prevail in this list, while the Ponderosa pine and Douglas fir are softwoods most typical of the Northwest coast forests.

## TOP 10 ✴
## TALLEST TREES IN THE US*

| | TREE/LOCATION | HEIGHT FT | M |
|---|---|---|---|
| 1 | **Coast redwood**, Jedidiah Smith State Park, California | 321 | 97.8 |
| 2 | **Coast Douglas fir**, Olympic National Forest, Washington | 281 | 85.6 |
| 3 | **General Sherman giant sequoia**, Sequoia National Park, California | 275 | 83.8 |
| 4 | **Noble fir**, Mount St. Helens National Monument, Washington | 272 | 82.9 |
| 5 | **Sugar pine**, Dorrington, California | 232 | 70.7 |
| 6 | **Ponderosa pine**, Plumas National Forest, California | 227 | 69.1 |
| 7 | **Port-Orford cedar**, Siskiyou National Forest, Oregon | 219 | 66.8 |
| 8 | **Sitka spruce**, Seaside, Oregon | 206 | 62.8 |
| 9 | **Western hemlock**, Olympic National Park, Washington | 194 | 59.1 |
| 10 | **Western redcedar**, Forks, Washington | 178 | 54.3 |

* By species (i.e. the tallest known example of each of the 10 tallest species)

Source: *American Forests*

A Coast redwood known as the Dyerville Giant (from Dyerville, California), which stood 362 ft (110.3 m) high, fell in a storm on March 27, 1991, and a slightly taller (363-ft/110.6-m) Coast redwood, which formerly topped this list, fell during the winter of 1992.

*Achatina achatina* **is the scientific name for what?**

*see p.40 for the answer*

A The giant African snail

B The gorilla

C The common toad

# THE HUMAN WORLD

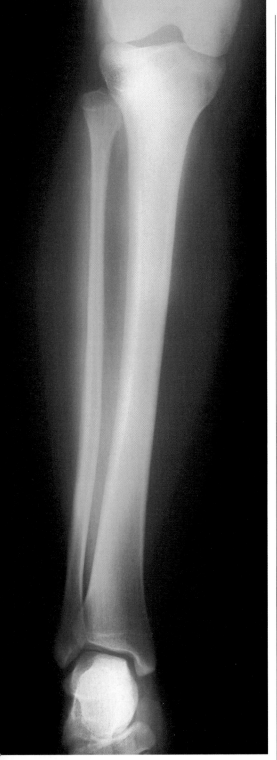

**THE WINNING LEG**

*The second longest bone, the tibia is named after the Latin word for a flute, which it resembles in shape and length. The three longest bones are all in the leg.*

## TOP 10 ★
## LONGEST BONES IN THE HUMAN BODY

| BONE | AVERAGE LENGTH IN | CM |
|---|---|---|
| **1 Femur** (thighbone – upper leg) | 19.88 | 50.50 |
| **2 Tibia** (shinbone – inner lower leg) | 16.94 | 43.03 |
| **3 Fibula** (outer lower leg) | 15.94 | 40.50 |
| **4 Humerus** (upper arm) | 14.35 | 36.46 |
| **5 Ulna** (inner lower arm) | 11.10 | 28.20 |
| **6 Radius** (outer lower arm) | 10.40 | 26.42 |
| **7 7th rib** | 9.45 | 24.00 |
| **8 8th rib** | 9.06 | 23.00 |
| **9 Innominate bone** (hipbone – half pelvis) | 7.28 | 18.50 |
| **10 Sternum** (breastbone) | 6.69 | 17.00 |

## THE 10 MOST COMMON HOSPITAL ER CASES

*(Reason for visit/visits, 1998)*

❶ **Stomach and abdominal pain, cramps, and spasms,** 5,958,000 ❷ **Chest pain and related symptoms,** 5,329,000 ❸ **Fever,** 4,419,000 ❹ **Headache, pain in head,** 2,867,000 ❺ **Cough,** 2,471,000 ❻ **Laceration and cuts – upper extremity,** 2,293,000 ❼ **Back symptoms,** 2,284,000 ❽ **Shortness of breath,** 2,283,000 ❾ **Symptoms referable to throat,** 2,205,000 ❿ **Pain, site not referable to a specific body system,** 1,990,000

Source: *National Ambulatory Medical Care Survey/Center for Disease Control/National Center for Health Statistics*

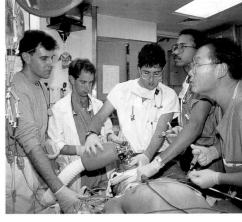

**ER, US**

*The world's hospital emergency rooms are equipped to treat victims of everything from minor injuries to major traumas from vehicle accidents and disasters.*

## THE 10 ★
## COUNTRIES WITH THE MOST PATIENTS PER DOCTOR

| COUNTRY | PATIENTS PER DOCTOR |
|---|---|
| **1 Malawi** | 49,118 |
| **2 Eritrea** | 46,200 |
| **3 Mozambique** | 36,320 |
| **4 Niger** | 35,141 |
| **5 Ethiopia** | 30,195 |
| **6 Chad** | 27,765 |
| **7 Burkina Faso** | 27,158 |
| **8 Rwanda** | 24,697 |
| **9 Liberia** | 24,600 |
| **10 Ghana** | 22,970 |
| US | 365 |

Source: *World Bank*

### THE FIRST INJECTABLE ANESTHETIC

The first anesthetics – ether, chloroform, and nitrous oxide ("laughing gas") – came into use in the mid-19th century. All were administered by the patient breathing in the vapors or gases, but all had their drawbacks, in particular the difficulty of safely controlling the precise quantity that was being administered. In 1902, German chemist Emil Fischer and pathologist Joseph Freiherr von Mering introduced the hypnotic drugs known as barbiturates, including Veronal, the first injectable anesthetic. This enabled the anesthetist to control the patient's breathing. It is said that von Mering proposed that the new substance be called "Veronal," since the most peaceful place he knew was the Italian city of Verona.

**100 YEARS AGO · YEARS AGO · YEARS AGO · YEARS**

How many cigarettes does the average Iraqi smoker consume annually?
*see p.50 for the answer*
A 3,777
B 5,751
C 18,902

# COUNTRIES THAT SPEND THE MOST ON HEALTH CARE

| COUNTRY | HEALTH SPENDING PER CAPITA ($) |
|---|---|
| 1 US | 4,080 |
| 2 Switzerland | 3,616 |
| 3 Germany | 2,727 |
| 4 Norway | 2,616 |
| 5 Denmark | 2,576 |
| 6 Japan | 2,379 |
| 7 France | 2,287 |
| 8 Sweden | 2,220 |
| 9 Austria | 2,108 |
| 10 Netherlands | 1,988 |

Source: *World Bank*, World Development Indicators 2000

# GLOBAL DISEASES THAT CAUSE THE HIGHEST LEVEL OF DISABILITY

| DISEASE | PERCENTAGE OF TOTAL BURDEN OF DISEASE * # |
|---|---|
| 1 Neuropsychiatric disorders | 11.0 |
| 2 Cardiovascular diseases | 10.9 |
| 3 Respiratory infections | 7.0 |
| 4 =HIV/AIDS | 6.2 |
| =Perinatal conditions | 6.2 |
| 6 Malignant neoplasms (cancers) | 5.9 |
| 7 Diarrheal diseases | 5.0 |
| 8 Respiratory diseases (noncommunicable) | 4.9 |
| 9 Childhood diseases | 3.8 |
| 10 Malaria | 3.1 |

\* *Measured in Disability-Adjusted Life Years (DALYs): a measure of the difference between a population's actual level of health and a normative goal of living in full health*

\# *Total percentage includes injuries at 13.9 percent*

Source: *World Health Organisation*, World Health Report 2000

# LARGEST HUMAN ORGANS

| ORGAN | | AVERAGE WEIGHT OZ | G |
|---|---|---|---|
| 1 Skin | | 384.0 | 10,886 |
| 2 Liver | | 55.0 | 1,560 |
| 3 Brain | male | 49.7 | 1,408 |
| | female | 44.6 | 1,263 |
| 4 Lungs | right | 20.5 | 580 |
| | left | 18.0 | 510 |
| | total | 38.5 | 1,090 |
| 5 Heart | male | 11.1 | 315 |
| | female | 9.3 | 265 |
| 6 Kidneys | right | 4.9 | 140 |
| | left | 5.3 | 150 |
| | total | 10.2 | 290 |
| 7 Spleen | | 6.0 | 170 |
| 8 Pancreas | | 3.5 | 98 |
| 9 Thyroid | | 1.2 | 35 |
| 10 Prostate | male only | 0.7 | 20 |

This list is based on average immediate post-mortem weights, as recorded by St. Bartholemew's Hospital, London, England, and other sources during a 10-year period.

**BRAIN WAVE**

*The modern technique of Magnetic Resonance Imaging (MRI) enables us to view the human brain, the human body's third-largest organ.*

# MOST COMMON PHOBIAS

| OBJECT OF PHOBIA | MEDICAL TERM |
|---|---|
| 1 Spiders | Arachnephobia or arachnophobia |
| 2 People and social situations | Anthropophobia or sociophobia |
| 3 Flying | Aerophobia or aviatophobia |
| 4 Open spaces | Agoraphobia, cenophobia, or kenophobia |
| 5 Confined spaces | Claustrophobia, cleisiophobia, cleithrophobia, or clithrophobia |
| 6 =Vomiting | Emetophobia or emitophobia |
| =Heights | Acrophobia, altophobia, hypsophobia, or hypsiphobia |
| 8 Cancer | Carcinomaphobia, carcinophobia, carcinomatophobia, cancerphobia, or cancerophobia |
| 9 Thunderstorms | Brontophobia or keraunophobia |
| 10 =Death | Necrophobia or thanatophobia |
| =Heart disease | Cardiophobia |

A phobia is a morbid fear that is out of all proportion to the object of the fear. Many people would admit to being uncomfortable about the objects of these principal phobias, as well as about others, such as snakes (ophiophobia) or ghosts (phasmophobia).

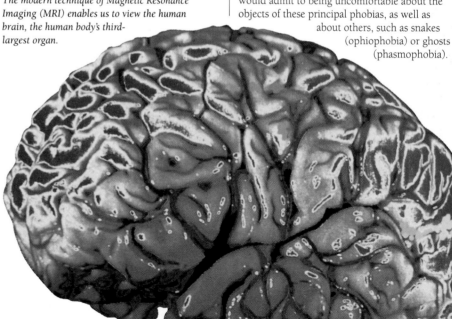

# Lifestyle

## COUNTRIES WITH THE HEAVIEST SMOKERS

| | COUNTRY | AVERAGE ANNUAL CIGARETTE CONSUMPTION PER SMOKER (1988–98)* |
|---|---|---|
| 1 | Iraq | 5,751 |
| 2 | Belgium | 5,300 |
| 3 | Australia | 4,951 |
| 4 | Hungary | 4,949 |
| 5 | US | 4,938 |
| 6 | Greece | 4,877 |
| 7 | Switzerland | 4,618 |
| 8 | Poland | 4,544 |
| 9 | Singapore | 4,250 |
| 10 | Japan | 4,126 |

* Smokers aged over 15, in those countries for which data available

Source: World Bank, World Development Indicators 2000

## MOST UNDERNOURISHED COUNTRIES

| | COUNTRY | APPROXIMATE PERCENTAGE UNDERNOURISHED*, 1995–97 |
|---|---|---|
| 1 | Somalia | 73 |
| 2 | Eritrea | 67 |
| 3 = | Burundi | 63 |
| = | Mozambique | 63 |
| 5 | Afghanistan | 62 |
| 6 | Haiti | 61 |
| 7 | Dem. Rep. of Congo | 55 |
| 8 | Ethiopia | 51 |
| 9 = | Mongolia | 49 |
| = | North Korea | 49 |

* Food intake that is insufficient to meet dietary requirements continuously

Source: Food and Agriculture Organization of the United Nations

## FAT CONSUMERS

| | COUNTRY | DAILY CONSUMPTION PER CAPITA OZ | G |
|---|---|---|---|
| 1 | France | 5.80 | 164.7 |
| 2 | Austria | 5.64 | 159.9 |
| 3 | Belgium and Luxembourg | 5.58 | 158.6 |
| 4 | Italy | 5.37 | 152.3 |
| 5 | Greece | 5.35 | 151.7 |
| 6 | Switzerland | 5.19 | 147.3 |
| 7 | Germany | 5.18 | 147.0 |
| 8 | Spain | 5.17 | 146.8 |
| 9 | US | 5.16 | 146.4 |
| 10 | UK | 5.06 | 143.7 |
| | World | 2.59 | 73.5 |

Source: Food and Agriculture Organization of the United Nations

## CALORIE CONSUMERS

| | COUNTRY | AVERAGE DAILY CONSUMPTION PER CAPITA |
|---|---|---|
| 1 | US | 3,756.8 |
| 2 | Portugal | 3,691.1 |
| 3 | Greece | 3,629.9 |
| 4 | Ireland | 3,622.0 |
| 5 | Italy | 3,608.3 |
| 6 | Belgium and Luxembourg | 3,606.3 |
| 7 | Turkey | 3,554.1 |
| 8 | France | 3,541.2 |
| 9 | Austria | 3,530.8 |
| 10 | Cyprus | 3,473.8 |
| | World | 2,791.8 |

Source: Food and Agriculture Organization of the United Nations

The calorie requirement of the average man is 2,700 and that of a woman 2,500. Inactive people need less, while those engaged in heavy labor might need even to double these figures.

**FAT OF THE LAND**

*The ubiquitous burger and fries contribute to the US's place at the top of the table of high calorie consumers.*

# TOP 10 MOST EFFECTIVE FITNESS ACTIVITIES

❶ Swimming ❷ Cycling ❸ Rowing ❹ Gymnastics ❺ Judo ❻ Dancing
❼ Soccer ❽ Jogging ❾ Walking (briskly!) ❿ Squash

These are the sports and activities recommended by fitness experts as the best means of acquiring all-around fitness, building stamina and strength, and increasing suppleness.

## TOP 10 ★ MULTIVITAMIN CONSUMERS

| COUNTRY | PERCENTAGE OF HEALTH SUPPLEMENT MARKET |
|---|---|
| 1 Mexico | 34.8 |
| 2 =Brazil | 30.9 |
| =Spain | 30.9 |
| 4 Switzerland | 30.5 |
| 5 UK | 30.4 |
| 6 Canada | 27.1 |
| 7 Italy | 24.8 |
| 8 US | 24.0 |
| 9 Finland | 22.0 |
| 10 Germany | 20.5 |

Source: *Euromonitor*

## TOP 10 ★ CAUSES OF STRESS-RELATED ILLNESS

| EVENT | VALUE |
|---|---|
| 1 Death of spouse | 100 |
| 2 Divorce | 73 |
| 3 Marital separation | 65 |
| 4 =Death of close family member | 63 |
| =Detention in prison or other institution | 63 |
| 6 Major personal injury or illness | 53 |
| 7 Marriage | 50 |
| 8 Losing one's job | 47 |
| 9 =Marital reconciliation | 45 |
| =Retirement | 45 |

Psychiatrists Dr. Thomas Holmes and Dr. Richard Rahe devised what they called the "Social Readjustment Rating Scale" to place a value on the likelihood of illness occurring as a result of stress caused by various "life events." The cumulative effect of several incidents increases the risk factor.

## TOP 10 ★ COUNTRIES SPENDING THE MOST ON WEIGHT MANAGEMENT PRODUCTS

| COUNTRY | VALUE OF SALES IN 1999 ($) |
|---|---|
| 1 US | 3,546,300,000 |
| 2 Japan | 896,000,000 |
| 3 France | 142,700,000 |
| 4 UK | 126,800,000 |
| 5 Italy | 114,400,000 |
| 6 China | 102,400,000 |
| 7 Canada | 84,000,000 |
| 8 Australia | 56,700,000 |
| 9 Brazil | 56,600,000 |
| 10 Germany | 44,200,000 |

Source: *Euromonitor*

## TOP 10 ★ SPENDERS ON VITAMINS AND DIETARY SUPPLEMENTS

| COUNTRY | VALUE OF SALES IN 1999 ($) |
|---|---|
| 1 US | 11,430,200,000 |
| 2 Japan | 10,733,400,000 |
| 3 Germany | 795,500,000 |
| 4 UK | 630,500,000 |
| 5 China | 523,300,000 |
| 6 France | 511,700,000 |
| 7 Italy | 510,400,000 |
| 8 Brazil | 465,200,000 |
| 9 Canada | 430,400,000 |
| 10 Russia | 230,400,000 |

Source: *Euromonitor*

**TWO WHEELS GOOD**
*Cycling's popularity has increased since the invention of the mountain bike. It is ranked second only to swimming as one of the most effective fitness activities.*

## TOP 10 ★ COSMETIC SURGERY PROCEDURES

1 Body reshaping by liposuction/liposculpture
2 Nose reshaping (rhinoplasty)
3 Upper or lower eye bag removal (blepharoplasty)
4 Face lift
5 Breast augmentation
6 Breast reduction
7 Ear reshaping (otoplasty)
8 Laser treatment for the removal of lines and wrinkles
9 Laser treatment for snoring problems
10 Varicose veins/thread vein removal

Source: *The Harley Medical Group*

**Did You Know?** Soon after the press identified 54-year-old Chao Boonchu as Thailand's champion chain-smoker (120 cigarettes a day for 30 years), he collapsed with severe breathing difficulties and heart problems and went into a coma.

# Cradle to the Grave

## COUNTRIES WITH THE HIGHEST BIRTH RATE

| COUNTRY | EST. LIVE BIRTH RATE PER 1,000 POPULATION, 2002 |
|---|---|
| 1 Niger | 50.5 |
| 2 Mali | 48.4 |
| 3 Chad | 47.7 |
| 4 Uganda | 47.1 |
| 5 Somalia | 46.8 |
| 6 Angola | 46.2 |
| 7 Liberia | 46.0 |
| 8 Dem. Rep of Congo | 45.5 |
| 9 Marshall Islands | 45.0 |
| 10 Sierra Leone | 44.6 |
| US | 14.1 |

Source: *US Census Bureau, International Data Base*

The countries with the highest birth rates are among the poorest countries in the world. In these countries, people often want to have large families so that the children can help earn income for the family when they are older.

### CHILDREN FROM MALI

*Mali is one of only a handful of countries with a birth rate of more than 45 per 1,000. The country also has the ninth highest fertility rate (the average number of children born to each woman) of 6.6.*

## TOP 10 COUNTRIES WITH THE LOWEST BIRTH RATE

*(Country/est. live birth rate per 1,000 population, 2002)*

❶ Bulgaria, 8.1  ❷ Latvia, 8.3  ❸ Italy, 8.9  ❹ = Estonia, 9.0; = Germany, 9.0  ❻ Czech Republic, 9.1  ❼ = Hungary, 9.3;  = Slovenia, 9.3; = Spain, 9.3  ❿ = Austria, 9.6;  = Monaco, 9.6;  = Ukraine, 9.6

Source: *US Census Bureau, International Data Base*

## COUNTRIES WITH THE HIGHEST UNDER-5 MORTALITY RATE

| COUNTRY | MORTALITY RATE PER 1,000 LIVE BIRTHS (1998) |
|---|---|
| 1 Sierra Leone | 316 |
| 2 Angola | 292 |
| 3 Niger | 280 |
| 4 Afghanistan | 257 |
| 5 Mali | 237 |
| 6 Liberia | 235 |
| 7 Malawi | 213 |
| 8 Somalia | 211 |
| 9 Dem. Rep. of Congo | 207 |
| 10 Mozambique | 206 |

Source: *UNICEF, The State of the World's Children 2000*

## COUNTRIES WITH THE HIGHEST DEATH RATE

| COUNTRY | DEATH RATE PER 1,000 POPULATION |
|---|---|
| 1 Angola | 25.01 |
| 2 Mozambique | 23.29 |
| 3 Niger | 23.17 |
| 4 Malawi | 22.44 |
| 5 Zimbabwe | 22.43 |
| 6 = Botswana | 22.08 |
| = Zambia | 22.08 |
| 8 Rwanda | 20.95 |
| 9 Swaziland | 20.40 |
| 10 Sierra Leone | 19.58 |

Source: *Central Intelligence Agency*

The 15 countries with the highest death rate are all in the African continent; the highest outside Africa is Afghanistan, with a rate of 18.01. Ukraine's 16.48 is the highest of any European country, and Haiti's 15.12 the highest of any in the Western hemisphere.

## THE 10 MOST COMMON CAUSES OF DEATH

*(Cause/approximate no. of deaths per annum)*

❶ Ischemic heart disease, 7,089,000  ❷ Cancers*, 7,065,000  ❸ Cerebrovascular disease, 5,544,000  ❹ Acute lower respiratory infection, 3,963,000  ❺ HIV/AIDS, 2,673,000  ❻ Chronic obstructive pulmonary disease, 2,660,000  ❼ Diarrhea, including dysentery, 2,213,000  ❽ Tuberculosis, 1,669,000  ❾ Childhood diseases#, 1,554,000  ❿ Traffic accidents, 1,230,000

*\* Lung cancer deaths alone number 1,193,000*
*# Childhood diseases include pertussis, polio, diphtheria, measles, and tetanus*
Source: *WHO, World Health Report 2000*

**GREEK GIFT**

*The country's traditional Mediterranean diet, high in olive oil, fruits and vegetables, and fish, may partly explain why Greek men enjoy one of the world's highest life expectancies.*

## TOP 10 ★
# COUNTRIES WITH THE HIGHEST MALE LIFE EXPECTANCY

| | COUNTRY | LIFE EXPECTANCY AT BIRTH, 2002 (YEARS) |
|---|---|---|
| 1 | Andorra | 80.6 |
| 2 | San Marino | 77.8 |
| 3 | Japan | 77.7 |
| 4 | Iceland | 77.4 |
| 5 | Singapore | 77.3 |
| 6 = | Australia | 77.2 |
| = | Sweden | 77.2 |
| 8 | Switzerland | 77.0 |
| 9 | Israel | 76.8 |
| 10 | Canada | 76.3 |
| | US | 74.3 |

Source: *US Census Bureau, International Data Base*

## TOP 10 ★
# COUNTRIES WITH THE HIGHEST FEMALE LIFE EXPECTANCY

| | COUNTRY | LIFE EXPECTANCY AT BIRTH, 2002 (YEARS) |
|---|---|---|
| 1 | Andorra | 86.6 |
| 2 | San Marino | 85.2 |
| 3 | Japan | 84.2 |
| 4 | Singapore | 83.5 |
| 5 = | Canada | 83.2 |
| = | Monaco | 83.2 |
| 7 | France | 83.1 |
| 8 | Australia | 83.0 |
| 9 | Switzerland | 82.9 |
| 10 | Spain | 82.8 |
| | US | 80.2 |

Source: *US Census Bureau, International Data Base*

## THE 10 ★
# COUNTRIES WITH THE MOST CASES OF AIDS

| | COUNTRY | DEATHS | NO. OF CASES |
|---|---|---|---|
| 1 | South Africa | 250,000 | 4,200,000 |
| 2 | India | 310,000 | 3,700,000 |
| 3 | Ethiopia | 280,000 | 3,000,000 |
| 4 | Nigeria | 250,000 | 2,700,000 |
| 5 | Kenya | 180,000 | 2,100,000 |
| 6 | Zimbabwe | 160,000 | 1,500,000 |
| 7 | Tanzania | 140,000 | 1,300,000 |
| 8 | Mozambique | 98,000 | 1,200,000 |
| 9 | Dem. Rep. of Congo | 95,000 | 1,100,000 |
| 10 | Zambia | 99,000 | 870,000 |
| | US | 20,000 | 850,000 |
| | World | 2,800,000 | 34,300,000 |

Source: *UNAIDS*, Report on the Global HIV/AIDS Epidemic, June 2000

## THE 10 ★
# MOST COMMON TYPES OF CANCER

| | TYPE | ANNUAL DEATHS |
|---|---|---|
| 1 | Trachea, bronchus, and lung | 1,193,000 |
| 2 | Stomach | 801,000 |
| 3 | Liver | 589,000 |
| 4 | Colon and rectum | 509,000 |
| 5 | Breast | 467,000 |
| 6 | Esophagus | 381,000 |
| 7 | Lymphomas | 295,000 |
| 8 | Mouth and pharynx | 282,000 |
| 9 | Leukemias | 268,000 |
| 10 | Prostate | 255,000 |

Source: *WHO, World Health Report 2000*

Globally, a clear trend is emerging: the gradual elimination of other fatal diseases, combined with rising life expectancy, means that the risks of developing cancer are steadily growing. One of the most noticeable changes in the ranking compared with 10 years ago is the increase in lung cancer.

# THE 10 MOST SUICIDAL COUNTRIES

*(Country/suicides per 100,000 population\*)*

❶ **Lithuania**, 42.0 ❷ **Russia**, 37.4 ❸ **Belarus**, 35.0 ❹ **Latvia**, 34.3 ❺ **Estonia**, 33.2
❻ **Hungary**, 32.1 ❼ **Slovenia**, 30.9 ❽ **Ukraine**, 29.4 ❾ **Kazakhstan**, 28.7
❿ **Finland**, 24.3 *US*, 11.4

*\* In those countries/latest year for which data available*
It is perhaps surprising that the highest suicide rates are not generally recorded in the poorest countries in the world. Source: United Nations

---

**In what did New Zealand lead the world in 1893?**
*see p.60 for the answer*

A  Granting women the vote
B  Abolishing capital punishment
C  Making firearms illegal

# Marriage & Divorce

## COUNTRIES WITH THE MOST MARRIAGES

| COUNTRY | MARRIAGES PER ANNUM* |
|---|---|
| 1 US | 2,384,000 |
| 2 Bangladesh | 1,181,000 |
| 3 Russia | 848,306 |
| 4 Japan | 784,580 |
| 5 Brazil | 734,045 |
| 6 Mexico | 707,840 |
| 7 Turkey | 519,216 |
| 8 Egypt | 493,787 |
| 9 Iran | 479,263 |
| 10 Thailand | 470,751 |

* In those countries/latest year for which data available

Source: United Nations

This list regrettably excludes certain large countries such as Indonesia, India, and Pakistan, which fail to provide accurate data.

## COUNTRIES WITH THE HIGHEST PROPORTION OF TEENAGE BRIDES

| COUNTRY | PERCENTAGE OF 15–19-YEAR-OLD GIRLS WHO HAVE EVER BEEN MARRIED* |
|---|---|
| 1 Dem. Rep. of Congo | 74.2 |
| 2 Congo | 55.0 |
| 3 Afghanistan | 53.7 |
| 4 Bangladesh | 51.3 |
| 5 Uganda | 49.8 |
| 6 Mali | 49.7 |
| 7 Guinea | 49.0 |
| 8 Chad | 48.6 |
| 9 Mozambique | 47.1 |
| 10 Senegal | 43.8 |
| US | 3.9 |

* In latest year for which data available

Source: United Nations

## COUNTRIES WITH THE HIGHEST PROPORTION OF TEENAGE HUSBANDS

| COUNTRY | PERCENTAGE OF 15–19-YEAR-OLD BOYS WHO HAVE EVER BEEN MARRIED* |
|---|---|
| 1 Iraq | 14.9 |
| 2 Nepal | 13.5 |
| 3 Congo | 11.8 |
| 4 Uganda | 11.4 |
| 5 India | 9.5 |
| 6 Afghanistan | 9.2 |
| 7 Guinea | 8.2 |
| 8 Central African Republic | 8.1 |
| 9 Guatemala | 7.8 |
| 10 Columbia | 7.7 |
| US | 1.3 |

* In latest year for which data available

Source: United Nations

## COUNTRIES WITH THE LOWEST MARRIAGE RATE

| COUNTRY | ANNUAL MARRIAGES PER 1,000* |
|---|---|
| 1 United Arab Emirates | 2.5 |
| 2 =Andorra | 2.9 |
| =Bolivia | 2.9 |
| 4 =Dominica | 3.1 |
| =Marshall Islands | 3.1 |
| =Qatar | 3.1 |
| 7 Cape Verde | 3.2 |
| 8 St. Lucia | 3.3 |
| 9 =Dominican Republic | 3.5 |
| =Sweden | 3.5 |

* In those countries/latest year for which data available

Source: United Nations

Marriage rates around the world vary according to a variety of religious and cultural factors.

## COUNTRIES WHERE MOST WOMEN MARRY

| COUNTRY | PERCENTAGE OF WOMEN MARRIED BY AGE 50* |
|---|---|
| 1 =Comoros | 100.0 |
| =The Gambia | 100.0 |
| =Ghana | 100.0 |
| =Nauru | 100.0 |
| 5 Chad | 99.9 |
| 6 =China | 99.8 |
| =Guinea | 99.8 |
| =Mali | 99.8 |
| =Papua New Guinea | 99.8 |
| 10 Benin | 99.7 |
| US | 93.9 |

* In latest year for which data available

Source: United Nations

Marriage in these countries can be considered the norm, contrasting with others where almost half the female population opts never to marry.

## COUNTRIES WHERE MOST MEN MARRY

| COUNTRY | PERCENTAGE OF MEN MARRIED BY AGE 50* |
|---|---|
| 1 =Chad | 100.0 |
| =The Gambia | 100.0 |
| 3 Guinea | 99.7 |
| 4 =Mali | 99.6 |
| =Niger | 99.6 |
| 6 =Bangladesh | 99.3 |
| =Mozambique | 99.3 |
| 8 Cameroon | 99.2 |
| 9 Nepal | 99.1 |
| 10 =Central African Republic | 99.0 |
| =Eritrea | 99.0 |
| =Tajikistan | 99.0 |
| US | 91.9 |

* In latest year for which data available

Source: United Nations

What invention earned Nobel Prize founder Alfred Nobel his fortune?

see p.64 for the answer

A Dynamite
B The typewriter
C Aspirin

## TOP 10 ★

# COUNTRIES WHERE WOMEN MARRY THE LATEST

| COUNTRY | AVERAGE AGE AT FIRST MARRIAGE |
|---|---|
| 1 Jamaica | 33.1 |
| 2 =Barbados | 31.8 |
| =Sweden | 31.8 |
| 4 Iceland | 31.7 |
| 5 =Antigua and Barbuda | 31.5 |
| =Dominica | 31.5 |
| =Greenland | 31.5 |
| 8 St. Kitts and Nevis | 31.3 |
| 9 Martinique | 31.0 |
| 10 =Grenada | 30.9 |
| =St. Vincent and the Grenadines | 30.9 |
| US | 26.0 |

Source: United Nations

This list is based on the "singulate mean age at marriage" (SMAM), or average age for first marriage among those who ever marry by the age of 50, after which first marriages are so rare as to be statistically insignificant

# COUNTRIES WITH THE LOWEST DIVORCE RATES

| COUNTRY | DIVORCE RATE PER 1,000* |
|---|---|
| 1 Colombia | 0.11 |
| 2 Libya | 0.24 |
| 3 Mongolia | 0.38 |
| 4 Georgia | 0.42 |
| 5 =Mexico | 0.43 |
| =Chile | 0.43 |
| 7 Italy | 0.47 |
| 8 El Salvador | 0.49 |
| 9 Macedonia | 0.51 |
| 10 Turkey | 0.52 |

* In those countries/latest year for which data available

Source: United Nations

The UN data on divorce rates omit a number of countries and ones that we might expect to have a very low divorce rate, such as Ireland. The data are difficult to collect, given the different laws relating to divorce in each country. In some, no legal document has to be signed for a divorce.

# COUNTRIES WITH THE HIGHEST DIVORCE RATES

| COUNTRY | DIVORCE RATE PER 1,000* |
|---|---|
| 1 Maldives | 10.97 |
| 2 Belarus | 4.63 |
| 3 US | 4.34 |
| 4 Cuba | 3.72 |
| 5 Estonia | 3.65 |
| 6 =Panama | 3.61 |
| =Puerto Rico | 3.61 |
| 8 Ukraine | 3.56 |
| 9 Russia | 3.42 |
| 10 Antigua and Barbuda | 3.40 |

* In those countries/latest year for which data available

Source: United Nations

The UK has the highest divorce rate in Europe (excluding republics of the former Soviet Union) at 2.89 per 1,000. According the UN, Britain's Isle of Man, if it were independent, would appear in seventh place, with a rate of 4.04 per 1,000.

# COUNTRIES WHERE MEN MARRY THE LATEST

| COUNTRY | AVERAGE AGE AT FIRST MARRIAGE |
|---|---|
| 1 Dominica | 35.4 |
| 2 Jamaica | 34.6 |
| 3 St. Vincent and the Grenadines | 34.5 |
| 4 Grenada | 34.4 |
| 5 Barbados | 34.3 |
| 6 Sweden | 34.0 |
| 7 Greenland | 33.7 |
| 8 Iceland | 33.3 |
| 9 Antigua and Barbuda | 33.2 |
| 10 Martinique | 33.0 |
| US | 28.7 |

Source: United Nations

# COUNTRIES WHERE THE FEWEST WOMEN MARRY

| COUNTRY | PERCENTAGE OF WOMEN MARRIED BY AGE 50* |
|---|---|
| 1 =French Guiana | 54.2 |
| =Jamaica | 54.2 |
| 3 Grenada | 57.4 |
| 4 St. Vincent and the Grenadines | 58.3 |
| 5 Dominica | 59.7 |
| 6 Barbados | 59.8 |
| 7 St. Kitts and Nevis | 62.1 |
| 8 Antigua and Barbuda | 62.6 |
| 9 Martinique | 67.1 |
| 10 Netherlands Antilles | 72.4 |

* In latest year for which data available

Source: United Nations

# COUNTRIES WHERE THE FEWEST MEN MARRY

| COUNTRY | PERCENTAGE OF MEN MARRIED BY AGE 50* |
|---|---|
| 1 St. Kitts and Nevis | 51.1 |
| 2 Jamaica | 51.8 |
| 3 French Guiana | 53.9 |
| 4 Grenada | 59.8 |
| 5 =Montserrat | 60.7 |
| =St. Vincent and the Grenadines | 60.7 |
| 7 Barbados | 62.8 |
| 8 =Dominica | 63.4 |
| =Greenland | 63.4 |
| 10 Antigua and Barbuda | 68.1 |

* In latest year for which data available

Source: United Nations

# People on the Move

## PLACES RECEIVING THE MOST REFUGEES AND ASYLUM SEEKERS

| | COUNTRY OR TERRITORY | REFUGEES/ASYLUM SEEKERS, 1999 |
|---|---|---|
| 1 | Iran | 1,980,000 |
| 2 | Jordan | 1,518,000 |
| 3 | Pakistan | 1,125,000 |
| 4 | Gaza Strip | 798,000 |
| 5 | West Bank | 570,000 |
| 6 | US | 505,000 |
| 7 | Yugoslavia | 480,000 |
| 8 | Guinea | 450,000 |
| 9 | Tanzania | 400,000 |
| 10 | Syria | 379,200 |

Source: *US Committee for Refugees*

**SEEKING REFUGE**

*Refugees displaced during the 1990 Iraq–Kuwait War are among the millions who fled from the many conflicts that beset the 1990s.*

## COUNTRIES WITH THE MOST INTERNALLY DISPLACED PEOPLE

| | COUNTRY | INTERNALLY DISPLACED PEOPLE, 1999 |
|---|---|---|
| 1 | Sudan | 4,000,000 |
| 2 | Colombia | 1,800,000 |
| 3 | Angola | 1,500,000 |
| 4 | Russia | 1,000,000 |
| 5 | Iraq | 900,000 |
| 6 | Bosnia and Herzegovina | 830,000 |
| 7 | Dem. Rep. of Congo | 800,000 |
| 8 | Afghanistan | 750,000 |
| 9 | Yugoslavia | 640,000 |
| 10= | Burundi | 600,000 |
| = | Myanmar (Burma) | 600,000 |
| = | Rwanda | 600,000 |
| = | Turkey | 600,000 |

Source: *US Committee for Refugees*

## COUNTRIES OF ORIGIN OF US IMMIGRANTS, 1820–1998

| | COUNTRY OF LAST RESIDENCE | IMMIGRANTS |
|---|---|---|
| 1 | Germany | 7,156,257 |
| 2 | Mexico* | 5,819,966 |
| 3 | Italy | 5,431,454 |
| 4 | UK | 5,247,821 |
| 5 | Ireland | 4,779,998 |
| 6 | Canada | 4,453,149 |
| 7 | USSR# | 3,830,033 |
| 8 | Austria+ | 1,842,722 |
| 9 | Hungary+ | 1,675,324 |
| 10 | Philippines | 1,460,421 |

\* *Unreported 1886–93*

\# *Russia before 1917*

\+ *Unreported before 1861; combined 1862–1904; separately 1905; Austria included with Germany 1938–45*

## TOP 10 ★
## ANCESTRIES OF THE US POPULATION

| | ANCESTRY GROUP | NUMBER |
|---|---|---|
| 1 | German | 57,947,873 |
| 2 | Irish | 38,735,539 |
| 3 | English | 32,651,788 |
| 4 | Afro-American | 23,777,098 |
| 5 | Italian | 14,664,550 |
| 6 | American | 12,395,999 |
| 7 | Mexican | 11,586,983 |
| 8 | French | 10,320,935 |
| 9 | Polish | 9,366,106 |
| 10 | Native Americans | 8,708,220 |

The 1990 US Census asked people to identify the ancestry group to which they believed themselves to belong. Five percent were unable to define their family origin more precisely than "American," while many claimed multiple ancestry.

## TOP 10 ★
## STATES WITH THE MOST FOREIGN-BORN RESIDENTS

| | STATE | FOREIGN-BORN RESIDENTS* |
|---|---|---|
| 1 | California | 6,458,825 |
| 2 | New York | 2,851,861 |
| 3 | Florida | 1,662,601 |
| 4 | Texas | 1,524,436 |
| 5 | New Jersey | 966,610 |
| 6 | Illinois | 952,272 |
| 7 | Massachusetts | 573,733 |
| 8 | Pennsylvania | 369,316 |
| 9 | Michigan | 355,393 |
| 10 | Washington | 322,144 |
| | Total of all states | 19,767,316 |

* US Bureau of the Census 1990 figures

Source: US Census Bureau

At the time of the 1990 Census, California had the greatest proportion of foreign-born residents of any state at 21.7 percent, compared with just 7.9 percent for the US as a whole.

**HEADING DOWN UNDER**
*A young British emigrant waits to embark for Australia in 1950. The two countries' longstanding links have been maintained over the decades.*

## TOP 10 ★
## COUNTRIES OF ORIGIN OF UK IMMIGRANTS

| | COUNTRY | IMMIGRANTS, 1999 |
|---|---|---|
| 1 | Pakistan | 11,860 |
| 2 | Former Yugoslavia | 6,650 |
| 3 | India | 6,290 |
| 4 | Sri Lanka | 5,370 |
| 5 | Turkey | 5,220 |
| 6 | US | 3,760 |
| 7 | Ghana | 3,480 |
| 8 | Bangladesh | 3,280 |
| 9 = | Nigeria | 3,180 |
| = | Somalia | 3,180 |

Source: British Home Office

## TOP 10 ★
## COUNTRIES OF ORIGIN OF IMMIGRANTS TO AUSTRALIA

| | COUNTRY OF BIRTH | IMMIGRANTS, 1999 |
|---|---|---|
| 1 | UK | 8,876 |
| 2 | China* | 5,982 |
| 3 | South Africa | 5,558 |
| 4 | Philippines | 3,409 |
| 5 | Indonesia | 3,313 |
| 6 | India | 3,156 |
| 7 | Iraq | 2,307 |
| 8 | Former Yugoslavia | 1,998 |
| 9 | Vietnam | 1,889 |
| 10 | Fiji | 1,554 |

* Excluding Taiwan and Special Administrative Regions

Source: *Australian Department of Immigration and Multicultural Affairs*

Since the era of the first settlement of Australia the UK has always been the principal country of origin of immigrants, and it still provides 13.5 percent of the total. In 1999, a further 27,911 immigrants were recorded as having arrived from other countries not listed in the Top 10, together with 1,272 whose birthplace was unknown, making an overall total of 67,215.

## TOP 10 ★
## FOREIGN BIRTHPLACES OF THE US POPULATION

| | BIRTHPLACE | NUMBER* |
|---|---|---|
| 1 | Mexico | 4,298,014 |
| 2 | Philippines | 912,674 |
| 3 | Canada | 744,830 |
| 4 | Cuba | 736,971 |
| 5 | Germany | 711,929 |
| 6 | UK | 640,145 |
| 7 | Italy | 580,592 |
| 8 | Korea | 568,397 |
| 9 | Vietnam | 543,262 |
| 10 | China | 529,837 |

* US Census figures, 1990

**Did You Know?** The top single year for immigration to the US was 1907, with 1,285,349 arrivals; Italy was the leading country of origin, with 285,731 emigrants.

# What's in a Name?

## BOYS' NAMES
## IN THE US, 1990–2000

| 1990 | | 2000 |
|------|---|------|
| Michael | 1 | Michael |
| Christopher | 2 | Jacob |
| Joshua | 3 | Matthew |
| Matthew | 4 | Joseph |
| David | 5 | Nicholas |
| Daniel | 6 | Christopher |
| Andrew | 7 | Andrew |
| Joseph | 8 | William |
| Justin | 9 | Joshua |
| James | 10 | Daniel |

## TOP 10 MOST COMMON
## FEMALE FIRST NAMES
## IN THE US

*(Name/% of all first names)*

❶ **Mary**, 2.629  ❷ **Patricia**, 1.073
❸ **Linda**, 1.035  ❹ **Barbara**, 0.980
❺ **Elizabeth**, 0.937  ❻ **Jennifer**, 0.932
❼ **Maria**, 0.828  ❽ **Susan**, 0.794
❾ **Margaret**, 0.768  ❿ **Dorothy**, 0.727

Source: *US Census Bureau*

According to an analysis of the 1990 US Census, the Top 10 female names account for 10.703 percent of all names, while the male names (listed below) account for 23.185 percent. It should be noted that these lists represent names of people of all age groups enumerated, and not the current popularity of first names.

## TOP 10 MOST COMMON
## MALE FIRST NAMES
## IN THE US

*(Name/% of all first names)*

❶ **James**, 3.318  ❷ **John**, 3.271
❸ **Robert**, 3.143  ❹ **Michael**, 2.629
❺ **William**, 2.451  ❻ **David**, 2.363
❼ **Richard**, 1.703  ❽ **Charles**, 1.523
❾ **Joseph**, 1.404  ❿ **Thomas**, 1.380

Source: *US Census Bureau*

## GIRLS' NAMES
## IN THE US, 1990–2000

| 1990 | | 2000 |
|------|---|------|
| Jessica | 1 | Hannah |
| Ashley | 2 | Emily |
| Brittany | 3 | Madison |
| Amanda | 4 | Elizabeth |
| Stephanie | 5 | Alexis |
| Jennifer | 6 | Sarah |
| Samantha | 7 | Taylor |
| Sarah | 8 | Lauren |
| Megan | 9 | Jessica |
| Lauren | 10 | Ashley |

## MOST COMMON
## SURNAMES IN THE US

| | NAME | PERCENTAGE OF ALL US NAMES |
|---|------|-----|
| 1 | Smith | 1.006 |
| 2 | Johnson | 0.810 |
| 3 | Williams | 0.699 |
| 4 =| Brown | 0.621 |
| = | Jones | 0.621 |
| 6 | Davis | 0.480 |
| 7 | Miller | 0.424 |
| 8 | Wilson | 0.339 |
| 9 | Moore | 0.312 |
| 10 =| Anderson | 0.311 |
| = | Taylor | 0.311 |
| = | Thomas | 0.311 |

The Top 10 (or, in view of those in equal 10th place, 12) US surnames together make up over 6 percent of the entire US population – in other words, one American in every 16 bears one of these names. Extending the list, some 28 different names comprise 10 percent of the entire population, 115 names 20 percent, 315 names 30 percent, 755 names 40 percent, 1,712 names 50 percent, and 3,820 names 60 percent. Beyond this, large numbers of less common – and in some instances, unique – names make up the remainder.

## TOP 10 SURNAMES
## IN SCOTLAND*

❶ Smith  ❷ Brown  ❸ Wilson
❹ Thomson  ❺ Robertson  ❻ Campbell
❼ Stewart  ❽ Anderson
❾ Macdonald  ❿ Scott

*\* Based on a survey of names appearing on birth and death registers, and both names on marriage registers*

## FIRST NAMES
## IN SCOTLAND, 2000

| GIRLS/RISE OR FALL | | BOYS/RISE OR FALL |
|------|---|------|
| Chloe | 1 | Jack |
| Amy (+3) | =2/2 | Lewis |
| Lauren (+2) | =/3 | Ryan |
| Emma (–1) | 4 | Cameron |
| Rebecca (–3) | 5 | James (+2) |
| Megan | 6 | Andrew |
| Caitlin | 7 | Matthew (+6) |
| Rachel | 8 | Liam |
| Erin | 9 | Callum (+3) |
| Hannah (+2) | 10 | Jamie (+6) |

+ Indicates rise in popularity since previous year
– Represents decline in popularity since previous year

## FIRST NAMES
## IN AUSTRALIA*

| GIRLS | | BOYS |
|-------|---|------|
| Jessica | 1 | Joshua |
| Emily | 2 | Jack |
| Sarah | 3 | Thomas |
| Georgia | 4 | Lachlan |
| Olivia | 5 | Matthew |
| Chloe | 6 | James |
| Emma | 7 | Daniel |
| Sophie | 8 | Benjamin |
| Hannah | 9 | Nicholas |
| Isabella | 10 | William |

*\* Based on births registered in New South Wales*

## TOP 10 ★
# FIRST NAMES
# IN IRELAND

| GIRLS | | BOYS |
|---|---|---|
| Chloe | 1 | Conor |
| Aoife | 2 | Sean |
| Sarah | 3 | Jack |
| Ciara | 4 | James |
| Niamh | 5 | Adam |
| Emma | 6 | Michael |
| Rachel | 7 | David |
| Rebecca | 8 | Aaron |
| Lauren | 9 | Daniel |
| Megan | 10 | Dylan |

While these were the Top 10 girls' and boys' names among the total of 53,354 births registered in Ireland in 1999, there are certain regional variations: Rachel was the most popular girls' name in the West, and Sean was the most popular boy's name in the West and Dublin. As with other first name lists, boys' names remain more static than girls': the top five are identical to the previous year.

## TOP 10 ★
# FIRST NAMES
# IN CANADA*

| GIRLS | | BOYS |
|---|---|---|
| Emily | 1 | Matthew |
| Sarah | 2 | Joshua |
| Emma | 3 | Jacob |
| Hannah | 4 | Nicholas |
| Taylor | 5 | Ryan |
| Jessica | 6 | Brandon |
| Megan | 7 | Michael |
| Samantha | 8 | Jordan |
| Ashley | 9 | Alexander |
| Madison | 10 | Liam |

*Based on births in British Columbia*

## TOP 10 ★
# FIRST NAMES
# IN WALES, 2000

| GIRLS/RISE OR FALL | | BOYS/RISE OR FALL |
|---|---|---|
| Chloe | 1 | Thomas |
| Megan | 2 | Jack |
| Emily | 3 | Joshua |
| Sophie | 4 | Callum (+1) |
| Lauren | 5 | Rhys (+8) |
| Hannah (+3) | 6 | Daniel (−2) |
| Jessica (−1) | 7 | Jordan (+5) |
| Georgina (−1) | 8 | Ryan (+1) |
| Ffion (−1) | 9 | Liam (−2) |
| Olivia (+1) | 10 | James (−4) |

+ *Indicates rise in popularity since previous year*

− *Represents decline in popularity since previous year*

Among girls' names, all those in the Top 10 also appear, though in different order of popularity, in a combined England and Wales Top 10, with the exception of Georgina (No. 11 in England and Wales) and Ffion, which does not even appear in the Top 50.

## TOP 10 ★
# NAMES IN THE US
# 100 YEARS AGO

| GIRLS | | BOYS |
|---|---|---|
| Mary | 1 | John |
| Helen | 2 | William |
| Anna | 3 | James |
| Margaret | 4 | George |
| Ruth | 5 | Joseph |
| Elizabeth | 6 | Charles |
| Marie | 7 | Robert |
| Lillian | 8 | Frank |
| Florence | 9 | Edward |
| Alice | =10/10 | Walter |
| Rose | = | |

# TOP 10 SURNAMES IN CHINA
❶ Zhang ❷ Whang ❸ Li ❹ Zhao ❺ Chen ❻ Yang ❼ Wu ❽ Liu
❾ Huang ❿ Zhou

It has been estimated that there are more than 100 million people with the surname Zhang in China.

## THE JONESES

San Diego-born artist Arthur R. "Pop" Momand (1886–1987) settled in Cedarhurst, New York, where he rubbed shoulders with a group of wealthy people, each of whom he noticed was competing with those with even more money. After moving to Manhattan, he devised a comic strip featuring the exploits of such people, which he called "Keeping up with the Joneses" – perhaps named after American novelist Edith Wharton's wealthy aunt Elizabeth Schermerhorn Jones, the owner of a large New York estate. The strip ran for many years, and the phrase entered the language.

WHO WAS • WHO WAS • WHO WAS • WHO WAS ?

## TOP 10 ★
# MOST COMMON
# SURNAMES IN THE UK

| | SURNAME | NUMBER |
|---|---|---|
| 1 | Smith | 538,369 |
| 2 | Jones | 402,489 |
| 3 | Williams | 279,150 |
| 4 | Brown | 260,652 |
| 5 | Taylor | 251,058 |
| 6 | Davies/Davis | 209,584 |
| 7 | Wilson | 191,006 |
| 8 | Evans | 170,391 |
| 9 | Thomas | 152,945 |
| 10 | Johnson | 146,535 |

This survey of British surnames is based on an analysis of almost 50 million appearing in the British electoral rolls – hence enumerating only those aged over 18 and eligible to vote. Some 10.77 people out of every 1,000 in the UK are called Smith, compared with 14.55 per 1,000 of names appearing in a sample from the 1851 census. This decline may be accounted for by considering the diluting effect of immigrant names, the same survey indicating, for example, that 66,663 people, or 1.33 per 1,000, now bear the name Patel, whereas none with that name was listed in 1851.

**Did You Know?** Although it is often claimed that J. M. Barrie invented the name Wendy in his 1904 play *Peter Pan*, researchers have uncovered a record of a 21-year-old woman and two girls with this name in the 1851 British census.

# World Leaders & Politics

## FIRST COUNTRIES TO GIVE WOMEN THE VOTE

| | COUNTRY | YEAR |
|---|---|---|
| 1 | New Zealand | 1893 |
| 2 | Australia (South Australia 1894; Western Australia 1898) | 1902 |
| 3 | Finland (then a Grand Duchy under the Russian Crown) | 1906 |
| 4 | Norway (restricted franchise; all women over 25 in 1913) | 1907 |
| 5 | Denmark and Iceland (a Danish dependency until 1918) | 1915 |
| 6 = | Netherlands | 1917 |
| = | USSR | 1917 |
| 8 = | Austria | 1918 |
| = | Canada | 1918 |
| = | Germany | 1918 |
| = | Great Britain and Ireland (Ireland part of the UK until 1921; women over 30 only – lowered to 21 in 1928) | 1918 |
| = | Poland | 1918 |

Until 1920, the only other European countries to enfranchise women were Sweden in 1919 and Czechoslovakia in 1920.

---

## TOP 10 BEST-PAID MEMBERS OF THE ROYAL FAMILY

*(Member/annual payment in $)*

❶ The Queen, 11,536,370
❷ The Queen Mother, 938,973
❸ The Duke of Edinburgh, 524,248
❹ The Duke of York, 363,615 ❺ The Duke of Kent, 344,631 ❻ The Princess Royal, 332,948 ❼ Princess Alexandra, 328,568 ❽ Princess Margaret, 319,806
❾ The Duke of Gloucester, 256,283
❿ Prince Edward, 149,189

The Civil List is not technically the Royal Family's "pay" but is the allowance made by the government for their staff and costs incurred while performing their public duties. The Prince of Wales receives nothing from the Civil List, his income deriving from the Duchy of Cornwall.

**VOTES FOR WOMEN**
*The women of New Zealand, granted suffrage on September 19, 1893, were able to cast their votes at the country's general election on November 28.*

## PARLIAMENTS WITH THE HIGHEST PERCENTAGE OF WOMEN MEMBERS*

| | PARLIAMENT/ ELECTION DATE | WOMEN MEMBERS | TOTAL MEMBERS | % WOMEN | | PARLIAMENT/ ELECTION DATE | WOMEN MEMBERS | TOTAL MEMBERS | % WOMEN |
|---|---|---|---|---|---|---|---|---|---|
| 1 | Sweden, 1998 | 149 | 349 | 42.7 | 7 | Germany, 1998 | 207 | 669 | 30.9 |
| 2 | Denmark, 1998 | 67 | 179 | 37.4 | 8 | New Zealand, 1999 | 37 | 120 | 30.8 |
| 3 | Finland, 1999 | 73 | 200 | 36.5 | 9 | Mozambique, 1999 | 75 | 250 | 30.0 |
| 4 | Norway, 1997 | 60 | 165 | 36.4 | 10 | South Africa, 1999 | 119 | 399 | 29.8 |
| 5 | Netherlands, 1998 | 54 | 150 | 36.0 | | | | | |
| 6 | Iceland, 1999 | 22 | 63 | 34.9 | | | | | |

\* As at April 25, 2001
Source: *Inter-Parliamentary Union*

---

### AUSTRALIAN WOMEN GET THE VOTE

Following pressure exerted by the Womanhood Suffrage League, Australia followed the lead of New Zealand (the first country to grant women suffrage) when, on June 12, 1902, Melbourne Governor-General Lord Hopetoun signed the Uniform Franchise Act. Although a major advance, it still imposed a number of limitations: it was restricted to federal elections and was granted only to British subjects aged over 21 and with a minimum of six months' residence; "Aboriginal natives of Australia, Asia, Africa, or the Islands of the Pacific" were excluded. Over the next few years, all women aged over 21 were progressively granted the vote, though it was not until 1962 that aboriginal women (and men) were given the vote.

· YEARS AGO · YEARS AGO · 100 · YEARS AGO · YEARS AGO ·

## TOP 10 ⭐
# LONGEST-SERVING PRESIDENTS TODAY

| | PRESIDENT/COUNTRY | TOOK OFFICE |
|---|---|---|
| 1 | General Gnassingbé Eyadéma, Togo | Apr 14, 1967 |
| 2 | El Hadj Omar Bongo, Gabon | Dec 2, 1967 |
| 3 | Colonel Mu'ammar Gadhafi, Libya* | Sep 1, 1969 |
| 4 | Zayid ibn Sultan al-Nuhayyan, United Arab Emirates | Dec 2, 1971 |
| 5 | Fidel Castro, Cuba | Nov 2, 1976 |
| 6 | France-Albert René, Seychelles | June 5, 1977 |
| 7 | Ali Abdullah Saleh, Yemen | July 17, 1978 |
| 8 | Daniel Teroitich arap Moi, Kenya | Oct 14, 1978 |
| 9 | Maumoon Abdul Gayoom, Maldives | Nov 11, 1978 |
| 10 | Saddam Hussein, Iraq | July 16, 1979 |

* Since a reorganization in 1979, Colonel Gadhafi has held no formal position, but continues to rule under the ceremonial title of "Leader of the Revolution"

All the presidents in this list have been in power for more than 20 years, some for over 30. Fidel Castro was Prime Minister of Cuba from February 1959. As he was also chief of the army, and there was no opposition party, he effectively ruled as dictator from then, but he was not technically President until the Cuban constitution was revised in 1976. Among those no longer in office, Abu Sulayman Hafiz al-Assad, President of Syria, died on June 10, 2000 after serving as leader of his country since February 22, 1971.

## TOP 10 ⭐
# LONGEST-REIGNING LIVING MONARCHS*

| | MONARCH/COUNTRY | DATE OF BIRTH | ACCESSION |
|---|---|---|---|
| 1 | Bhumibol Adulyadej, Thailand | Dec 5, 1927 | June 9, 1946 |
| 2 | Prince Rainier III, Monaco | May 31, 1923 | May 9, 1949 |
| 3 | Elizabeth II, UK | Apr 21, 1926 | Feb 6, 1952 |
| 4 | Malietoa Tanumafili II, Western Samoa | Jan 4, 1913 | Jan 1, 1962# |
| 5 | Taufa'ahau Tupou IV, Tonga | July 4, 1918 | Dec 16, 1965+ |
| 6 | Haji Hassanal Bolkiah, Brunei | July 15, 1946 | Oct 5, 1967 |
| 7 | Sayyid Qaboos ibn Said al-Said, Oman | Nov 18, 1942 | July 23, 1970 |
| 8 | Margrethe II, Denmark | Apr 16, 1940 | Jan 14, 1972 |
| 9 | Birendra Bir Bikram Shah Dev, Nepal | Dec 28, 1945 | Jan 31, 1972 |
| 10 | Jigme Singye Wangchuk, Bhutan | Nov 11, 1955 | July 24, 1972 |

* Including hereditary rulers of principalities, dukedoms, etc.

# Sole ruler since April 15, 1963

+ Full sovereignty from June 5, 1970 when British protectorate ended

There are 28 countries that have emperors, kings, queens, princes, dukes, sultans, or other hereditary rulers as their heads of state. Earlier lists included Grand Duke Jean of Luxembourg, who abdicated on September 28, 2000.

## THE 10 ⭐
# FIRST COUNTRIES TO RATIFY THE UN CHARTER

| | COUNTRY | DATE |
|---|---|---|
| 1 | Nicaragua | July 6, 1945 |
| 2 | US | Aug 8, 1945 |
| 3 | France | Aug 31, 1945 |
| 4 | Dominican Republic | Sep 4, 1945 |
| 5 | New Zealand | Sep 19, 1945 |
| 6 | Brazil | Sep 21, 1945 |
| 7 | Argentina | Sep 24, 1945 |
| 8 | China | Sep 28, 1945 |
| 9 | Denmark | Oct 9, 1945 |
| 10 | Chile | Oct 11, 1945 |

In New York on June 26, 1945, 50 nations signed the World Security Charter, thus establishing the UN as an international peacekeeping organization.

**WORLD PEACE**
While World War II still raged in the Far East, delegates signed the charter that inaugurated the United Nations as the world's peacekeepers.

**What was unusual about the transatlantic balloon crossing reported in 1844?**
see p.63 for the answer
A It was kept secret for over 100 years
B It was the first
C It was a hoax

# Human Achievements

## FIRST MOUNTAINEERS TO CLIMB EVEREST

| MOUNTAINEER/NATIONALITY | DATE |
|---|---|
| 1 Edmund Hillary, New Zealander | May 29, 1953 |
| 2 Tenzing Norgay, Nepalese | May 29, 1953 |
| 3 Jürg Marmet, Swiss | May 23, 1956 |
| 4 Ernst Schmied, Swiss | May 23, 1956 |
| 5 Hans-Rudolf von Gunten, Swiss | May 24, 1956 |
| 6 Adolf Reist, Swiss | May 24, 1956 |
| 7 Wang Fu-chou, Chinese | May 25, 1960 |
| 8 Chu Ying-hua, Chinese | May 25, 1960 |
| 9 Konbu, Tibetan | May 25, 1960 |
| 10 =Nawang Gombu, Indian | May 1, 1963 |
| =James Whittaker, American | May 1, 1963 |

Nawang Gombu and James Whittaker are 10th equal because, neither wishing to deny the other the privilege of being first, they ascended the last feet to the summit side by side.

## FIRST PEOPLE TO REACH THE SOUTH POLE

| NAME/NATIONALITY | DATE |
|---|---|
| 1 =Roald Amundsen*, Norwegian | Dec 14, 1911 |
| =Olav Olavsen Bjaaland, Norwegian | Dec 14, 1911 |
| =Helmer Julius Hanssen, Norwegian | Dec 14, 1911 |
| =Helge Sverre Hassel, Norwegian | Dec 14, 1911 |
| =Oscar Wisting, Norwegian | Dec 14, 1911 |
| 6 = Robert Falcon Scott*, British | Jan 17, 1912 |
| =Henry Robertson Bowers, British | Jan 17, 1912 |
| =Edgar Evans, British | Jan 17, 1912 |
| =Lawrence Edward Grace Oates, British | Jan 17, 1912 |
| =Edward Adrian Wilson, British | Jan 17, 1912 |

* Expedition leader

## FIRST EXPEDITIONS TO REACH THE NORTH POLE OVERLAND

| NAME*/NATIONALITY | DATE |
|---|---|
| 1 Ralph S. Plaisted, American | Apr 19, 1968 |
| 2 Wally W. Herbert, British | Apr 5, 1969 |
| 3 Naomi Uemura, Japanese | May 1, 1978 |
| 4 Dmitri Shparo, Soviet | May 31, 1979 |
| 5 Sir Ranulph Fiennes/ Charles Burton, British | Apr 11, 1982 |
| 6 Will Steger/Paul Schurke, American | May 1, 1986 |
| 7 Jean-Louis Etienne, French | May 11, 1986 |
| 8 Fukashi Kazami, Japanese | Apr 20, 1987 |
| 9 Helen Thayer, American | Apr 20, 1988 |
| 10 Robert Swan, British | May 14, 1989 |

* Expedition leader or co-leader

## LATEST WINNERS OF *TIME MAGAZINE*'S "PERSON OF THE YEAR" AWARD

| RECIPIENT | YEAR |
|---|---|
| 1 George W. Bush (1946– ), 43rd US President | 2000 |
| 2 Jeffrey T. Bezos (1964– ), Entrepreneur, founder of Amazon.com | 1999 |
| 3 Bill Clinton (1946– ), US President, Kenneth Starr (1946– ), Independent Counsel | 1998 |
| 4 Andrew S. Grove (1936– ), CEO of Intel microchip company | 1997 |
| 5 David Ho (1952– ), AIDS researcher | 1996 |
| 6 Newt Gingrich (1943– ), US politician | 1995 |
| 7 Pope John Paul II (1920– ) | 1994 |
| 8 Yasser Arafat (1929– ), F. W. de Klerk (1936– ), Nelson Mandela (1918– ), Yitzhak Rabin (1922–95), "Peacemakers" | 1993 |
| 9 Bill Clinton (1946– ), US President | 1992 |
| 10 George Bush (1924– ), US President | 1991 |

## FASTEST CROSS-CHANNEL SWIMMERS

| SWIMMER/NATIONALITY | YEAR | TIME HR:MIN | SWIMMER/NATIONALITY | YEAR | TIME HR:MIN |
|---|---|---|---|---|---|
| 1 Chad Hundeby, American | 1994 | 7:17 | 6 Richard Davey, British | 1988 | 8:05 |
| 2 Penny Lee Dean, American | 1978 | 7:40 | 7 Irene van der Laan, Dutch | 1982 | 8:06 |
| 3 Tamara Bruce, Australian | 1994 | 7:53 | 8 =Paul Asmuth, American | 1985 | 8:12 |
| 4 Philip Rush, New Zealander | 1987 | 7:55 | =Gail Rice, American | 1999 | 8:12 |
| 5 Hans Van Goor, Dutch | 1995 | 8:02 | 10 Anita Sood, Indian | 1987 | 8:15 |

Source: *Channel Swimming Association*

### FIRST US LANDING AT THE NORTH POLE

The first US landing at the Pole was that of Lt.-Col. William Pershing Benedict, with a team of 10 US Air Force scientists. They flew in a C-47 fitted with skis, landing on May 3, 1952. Co-pilot Lt.-Col. Joseph Otis Fletcher became the first American undisputedly to set foot on the North Pole. (This achievement had previously been claimed by American Robert Peary and his companions, who were reported to have reached the Pole in 1909. This claim has since been widely discredited.) Dr. Albert Paddock Crary, one of the scientists on the American expedition, later trekked to the South Pole, arriving there on February 12, 1961, thus becoming the first man to set foot on both North and South Poles.

50 YEARS AGO · YEARS AGO · YEARS AGO · YEARS

## TOP 10 ★
## CIRCUMNAVIGATION FIRSTS

| CIRCUMNAVIGATION | CRAFT | CAPTAIN(S) | RETURN DATE |
|---|---|---|---|
| 1 First voyage | *Vittoria* | Juan Sebastian de Elcano | Sep 6, 1522 |
| 2 First in less than 80 days | Various | "Nellie Bly" (Elizabeth Cochrane) | Jan 25, 1890 |
| 3 First solo voyage | *Spray* | Capt. Joshua Slocum | July 3, 1898 |
| 4 First by air | *Chicago* and *New Orleans* | Lt. Lowell Smith and Lt. Leslie P. Arnold | Sep 28, 1924 |
| 5 First nonstop by air | *Lucky Lady I* | Capt. James Gallagher | Mar 2, 1949 |
| 6 First underwater voyage | *Triton* | Capt. Edward Latimer Beach | Apr 25, 1960 |
| 7 First nonstop solo voyage | *Suhaili* | Robin Knox-Johnston | Apr 22, 1969 |
| 8 First helicopter | *Spirit of Texas* | H. Ross Perot Jr. and Jay Coburn | Sep 30, 1982 |
| 9 First air without refueling | *Voyager* | Richard Rutan and Jeana Yeager | Dec 23, 1986 |
| 10 First by balloon | *Breitling Orbiter 3* | Brian Jones and Bertrand Piccard | Mar 21, 1999 |

The first ever circumnavigation, by Juan Sebastian de Elcano and his crew of 17, sailed from Spain, returning to Italy. US journalist "Nellie Bly" (Elizabeth Cochrane) set out to beat the fictitious "record" established in Jules Verne's novel *Around the World in 80 Days*, traveling from New York and returning on January 25, 1890 – a record circumnavigation of 72 days, 6 hours, 11 minutes, and 14 seconds.

**AROUND THE WORLD IN 19 DAYS**

*In 1999, traveling from Switzerland to Egypt, the 180-ft (55-m) tall Breitling Orbiter 3 achieved the first balloon circumnavigation of the Earth.*

## THE 10 ★
## FIRST SUCCESSFUL HUMAN DESCENTS OVER NIAGARA FALLS

| NAME/METHOD | DATE |
|---|---|
| 1 **Annie Edson Taylor**, Wooden barrel | Oct 24, 1901 |
| 2 **Bobby Leach**, Steel barrel | July 25, 1911 |
| 3 **Jean Lussier**, Steel and rubber ball fitted with oxygen cylinders | July 4, 1928 |
| 4 **William Fitzgerald** (aka Nathan Boya), Steel and rubber ball fitted with oxygen cylinders | July 15, 1961 |
| 5 **Karel Soucek**, Barrel | July 3, 1984 |
| 6 **Steven Trotter**, Barrel | Aug 18, 1985 |
| 7 **Dave Mundy**, Barrel | Oct 5, 1985 |
| 8 = **Peter deBernardi**, Metal container | Sep 28, 1989 |
| = **Jeffrey Petkovich**, Metal container | Sep 28, 1989 |
| 10 **Dave Mundy**, Diving bell | Sep 26, 1993 |

Source: *Niagara Falls Museum*

WITH KIND AUTHORIZATION OF BREITLING SA

**Did You Know?** The first transatlantic crossing by balloon, reported in the *New York Sun* of April 13, 1844, was a hoax perpetrated by novelist Edgar Allan Poe. It was another 134 years before balloonists truly achieved the feat.

# The Nobel Prize

## THE 10 ★
### LATEST WINNERS OF THE NOBEL PRIZE FOR ECONOMIC SCIENCES

| WINNER | COUNTRY | YEAR |
|---|---|---|
| 1 =James J. Heckman | US | 2000 |
| =Daniel L. McFadden | US | 2000 |
| 3 Robert A. Mundell | Canada | 1999 |
| 4 Amartya Sen | India | 1998 |
| 5 =Robert C. Merton | US | 1997 |
| =Myron S. Scholes | US | 1997 |
| 7 =James A. Mirrlees | UK | 1996 |
| =William Vickrey | Canada | 1996 |
| 9 Robert E. Lucas | US | 1995 |
| 10 =John C. Harsanyi | Hungary/US | 1994 |
| =Reinhard Selten | Germany | 1994 |
| =John F. Nash | US | 1994 |

Correctly called the Bank of Sweden Prize in Economic Sciences in Memory of Alfred Nobel, this is a recent addition to the Nobel Prizes. It is presented annually by the Royal Swedish Academy of Sciences and consists of a gold medal, a diploma, and a sum of money. The presentation of this and the other Prizes is made on December 10, the anniversary of Alfred Nobel's death.

### NOBEL

Swedish scientist Alfred Bernhard Nobel (1833–96) studied widely in Europe and the US. He perfected a way of stabilizing nitroglycerine, a dangerous explosive. The result was dynamite, which Nobel patented in 1866. It was used extensively in quarrying and railway construction. At his death in 1896, the unmarried Nobel left a will establishing a trust fund, which is now estimated to be worth over $420 million. Interest earned from this has enabled annual prizes to be awarded to those who have achieved the greatest common good in the fields of Physics, Chemistry, Literature, Physiology or Medicine, Peace, and, since 1969, Economic Sciences.

WHO WAS • WHO WAS • WHO WAS • WHO WAS • ?

## TOP 10 ★
### NOBEL LITERATURE PRIZE-WINNING COUNTRIES

| COUNTRY | LITERATURE PRIZES |
|---|---|
| 1 France | 12 |
| 2 US | 10 |
| 3 UK | 8 |
| 4 =Germany | 7 |
| =Sweden | 7 |
| 6 Italy | 6 |
| 7 Spain | 5 |
| 8 =Denmark | 3 |
| =Ireland | 3 |
| =Norway | 3 |
| =Poland | 3 |
| =USSR | 3 |

## TOP 10 ★
### NOBEL PHYSIOLOGY OR MEDICINE PRIZE-WINNING COUNTRIES

| COUNTRY | PHYSIOLOGY OR MEDICINE PRIZES |
|---|---|
| 1 US | 80 |
| 2 UK | 24 |
| 3 Germany | 16 |
| 4 Sweden | 8 |
| 5 France | 7 |
| 6 Switzerland | 6 |
| 7 Denmark | 5 |
| 8 =Austria | 4 |
| =Belgium | 4 |
| 10 =Italy | 3 |
| =Australia | 3 |

## THE 10 ★
### LATEST WINNERS OF THE NOBEL PRIZE FOR LITERATURE

| WINNER | COUNTRY | YEAR |
|---|---|---|
| 1 Gao Xingjian | China | 2000 |
| 2 Günter Grass | Germany | 1999 |
| 3 José Saramago | Portugal | 1998 |
| 4 Dario Fo | Italy | 1997 |
| 5 Wislawa Szymborska | Poland | 1996 |
| 6 Seamus Heaney | Ireland | 1995 |
| 7 Kenzaburo Oe | Japan | 1994 |
| 8 Toni Morrison | US | 1993 |
| 9 Derek Walcott | Saint Lucia | 1992 |
| 10 Nadine Gordimer | South Africa | 1991 |

## THE 10 ★
### LATEST WINNERS OF THE NOBEL PRIZE FOR PHYSICS

| WINNER | COUNTRY | YEAR |
|---|---|---|
| 1 =Zhores I. Alferov | Russia | 2000 |
| =Herbert Kroemer | US | 2000 |
| =Jack S. Kilby | US | 2000 |
| 4 =Gerardus 't Hooft | Netherlands | 1999 |
| =Martinus J.G. Veltman | Netherlands | 1999 |
| 6 =Robert B. Laughlin | US | 1998 |
| =Horst L. Störmer | Germany | 1998 |
| =Daniel C. Tsui | US | 1998 |
| 9 = Steven Chu | US | 1997 |
| =William D. Phillips | US | 1997 |
| =Claude Cohen-Tannoudji | France | 1997 |

## TOP 10 NOBEL PHYSICS PRIZE-WINNING COUNTRIES
### (Country/physics prizes)

❶ US, 69 ❷ UK, 21 ❸ Germany, 20 ❹ France, 12 ❺ Netherlands, 8 ❻ USSR, 7
❼ Sweden, 4 ❽ = Austria, 3; = Denmark, 3; = Italy, 3; = Japan, 3

Which country does not appear among the Top 10 largest armed forces?
*see p.72 for the answer*

A Israel
B Turkey
C India

# TOP 10 ★

## NOBEL PRIZE-WINNING COUNTRIES

| | COUNTRY | PHY | CHE | PH/MED | LIT | PCE | ECO | TOTAL |
|---|---|---|---|---|---|---|---|---|
| 1 | US | 69 | 45 | 80 | 10 | 18 | 27 | 249 |
| 2 | UK | 21 | 25 | 24 | 8 | 13 | 7 | 98 |
| 3 | Germany* | 20 | 27 | 16 | 7 | 4 | 1 | 75 |
| 4 | France | 12 | 7 | 7 | 12 | 9 | 1 | 48 |
| 5 | Sweden | 4 | 4 | 8 | 7 | 5 | 2 | 30 |
| 6 | Switzerland | 2 | 5 | 6 | 2 | 3 | – | 18 |
| 7 | =USSR | 7 | 1 | 2 | 3 | 2 | 1 | 16 |
| | =Institutions | – | – | – | – | 16 | – | 16 |
| 9 | Netherlands | 8 | 3 | 2 | – | 1 | 1 | 15 |
| 10 | Italy | 3 | 1 | 3 | 6 | 1 | – | 14 |

*Phy – Physics; Che – Chemistry; Ph/Med – Physiology or Medicine; Lit – Literature; Pce – Peace; Eco – Economic Sciences.*

*\* Includes the united country before 1948, West Germany to 1990, and the united country since 1990*

**PEACE OF MIND**
*Selected from a record 150 nominees, South Korean president Kim Dae Jung was awarded the first Nobel Peace Prize of the 21st century for his work in forging ties with North Korea.*

## TOP 10 NOBEL PEACE PRIZE-WINNING COUNTRIES

*(Country/peace prizes)*

**1** US, 18 **2** International institutions, 16 **3** UK, 13 **4** France, 9 **5** Sweden, 5
**6** = Belgium, 4; = Germany, 4; = South Africa, 4 **9** = Israel, 3; = Switzerland, 3

# THE 10 ★

## LATEST WINNERS OF THE NOBEL PRIZE FOR CHEMISTRY

| | WINNER | COUNTRY | YEAR |
|---|---|---|---|
| 1 | =Alan J. Heeger | US | 2000 |
| | =Alan G. MacDiarmid | US | 2000 |
| | =Hideki Shirakawa | Japan | 2000 |
| 4 | Ahmed Zewail | Egypt | 1999 |
| 5 | =Walter Kohn | US | 1998 |
| | =John A. Pople | UK | 1998 |
| 7 | =Paul D. Boyer | US | 1997 |
| | =Jens C. Skou | Denmark | 1997 |
| | =John E. Walker | UK | 1997 |
| 10 | =Sir Harold W. Kroto | UK | 1996 |
| | =Richard E. Smalley | US | 1996 |

# THE 10 ★

## LATEST WINNERS OF THE NOBEL PRIZE FOR PHYSIOLOGY OR MEDICINE

| | WINNER | COUNTRY | YEAR |
|---|---|---|---|
| 1 | =Arvid Carlsson | Sweden | 2000 |
| | =Paul Greengard | US | 2000 |
| | =Eric Kandel | US | 2000 |
| 4 | Günter Blobel | Germany | 1999 |
| 5 | =Robert F. Furchgott | US | 1998 |
| | =Louis J. Ignarro | US | 1998 |
| | =Ferid Murad | US | 1998 |
| 8 | Stanley B. Prusiner | US | 1997 |
| 9 | =Peter C. Doherty | Australia | 1996 |
| | =Rolf M. Zinkernagel | Switzerland | 1996 |

# THE 10 ★

## LATEST WINNERS OF THE NOBEL PEACE PRIZE

| | WINNER | COUNTRY | YEAR |
|---|---|---|---|
| 1 | Kim Dae Jung | South Korea | 2000 |
| 2 | Médecins Sans Frontières | Belgium | 1999 |
| 3 | =John Hume | UK | 1998 |
| | =David Trimble | UK | 1998 |
| 5 | =International Campaign to Ban Landmines | – | 1997 |
| | =Jody Williams | US | 1997 |
| 7 | =Carlos Filipe Ximenes Belo | East Timor | 1996 |
| | =José Ramos-Horta | East Timor | 1996 |
| 9 | Joseph Rotblat | UK | 1995 |
| 10 | =Yasir Arafat | Palestine | 1994 |
| | =Shimon Peres | Israel | 1994 |
| | =Itzhak Rabin | Israel | 1994 |

# Criminal Records

## COUNTRIES WITH THE HIGHEST PRISON POPULATION RATES

| COUNTRY | TOTAL PRISON POPULATION* | PRISONERS PER 100,000# |
|---|---|---|
| 1 Russia | 1,060,085 | 730 |
| 2 US | 1,860,520 | 680 |
| 3 Belarus | 58,879 | 575 |
| 4 Kazakhstan | 82,945 | 495 |
| 5 Bahamas | 1,401 | 485 |
| 6 Belize | 1,097 | 460 |
| 7 Kyrgyzstan | 19,857 | 440 |
| 8 Surinam | 1,933 | 435 |
| 9 Ukraine | 217,400 | 430 |
| 10 Dominica | 298 | 420 |

\* Including pretrial detainees

# In latest year for which figures are available

Source: British Home Office

## COUNTRIES WITH THE MOST PRISONERS

| COUNTRY | PRISONERS* |
|---|---|
| 1 US | 1,860,520 |
| 2 China | 1,408,860 |
| 3 Russia | 1,060,085 |
| 4 India | 381,147 |
| 5 Ukraine | 217,400 |
| 6 Thailand | 197,214 |
| 7 Brazil | 194,074 |
| 8 South Africa | 161,163 |
| 9 Rwanda | 143,021# |
| 10 Mexico | 139,707 |

\* In latest year for which figures are available

# Includes 135,000 held on suspicion of participation in genocide

Source: British Home Office

## TYPES OF OFFENSE FOR WHICH MOST PEOPLE ARE IMPRISONED IN THE US

| TYPE OF OFFENSE | NO. OF PRISONERS* | PERCENTAGE OF PRISON POPULATION |
|---|---|---|
| 1 Drug offenses | 63,448 | 58.0 |
| 2 Firearms, explosives, and arson | 10,398 | 9.5 |
| 3 Robbery | 8,306 | 7.6 |
| 4 Immigration offenses | 7,695 | 7.0 |
| 5 Property offenses | 6,241 | 5.7 |
| 6 Extortion, fraud, and bribery | 5,423 | 5.0 |
| 7 Homicide, aggravated assault, and kidnapping | 2,444 | 2.2 |
| 8 Disorderly conduct | 1,404 | 1.3 |
| 9 Sex offenses | 888 | 0.8 |
| 10 White collar offenses | 776 | 0.7 |

\* As of May 30, 2000

Source: US Department of Justice Federal Bureau of Prisons

## THE 10 COUNTRIES WITH THE HIGHEST CRIME RATES

*(Country/crime rate\*)*

**1** Gibraltar, 18,316 **2** Surinam, 17,819 **3** St. Kitts and Nevis, 15,468
**4** Finland, 14,799 **5** Rwanda, 14,550 **6** New Zealand, 13,854 **7** Sweden, 12,982
**8** Denmark, 10,525 **9** Canada, 10,451 **10** US Virgin Islands, 10,441

*US, 5,374*
*\* Reported crime per 100,000 population*

## US CITIES WITH THE MOST POLICE OFFICERS

| CITY/STATE | OFFICERS* |
|---|---|
| 1 New York, New York | 41,791 |
| 2 Chicago, Illinois | 13,366 |
| 3 Los Angeles, California | 9,525 |
| 4 Philadelphia, Pennsylvania | 6,935 |
| 5 Houston, Texas | 5,443 |
| 6 Detroit, Michigan | 3,988 |
| 7 Washington, DC | 3,488 |
| 8 Baltimore, Maryland | 3,000 |
| 9 Dallas, Texas | 2,873 |
| 10 Suffolk, New York | 2,605 |

\* As of October 31, 1999

Source: FBI Uniform Crime Reports

### THE FIRST MECHANICAL LIE DETECTOR

Italian criminologist Cesare Lombroso first described using blood pressure changes to measure the reactions of suspects during questioning in 1895, but it was not until 1902 that this proposal was put into practice. Working in Burnley, UK, Scottish doctor James MacKenzie (1853–1925) published a book, *The Study of the Pulse*, and, with the aid of a local watchmaker, invented the polygraph, a machine to record the rhythms of the heart. Although MacKenzie's instrument, which was later produced commercially, was primarily designed for medical purposes, its principles were used by subsequent researchers to develop increasingly sophisticated devices to relate such phenomena as blood pressure, respiratory changes, and even voice frequencies to lying, and thus to create lie detectors. However, since the results of tests using such devices can be literally a matter of life or death, to this day few jurisdictions accept their results.

*100 YEARS AGO · YEARS AGO · YEARS AGO · YEARS*

## THE 10 ★
## METROPOLITAN AREAS WITH THE MOST VIOLENT CRIMES*

| METROPOLITAN AREA# | VIOLENT CRIMES PER 100,000 PEOPLE |
|---|---|
| 1 Pine Bluff, Arkansas | 1,446.8 |
| 2 Miami, Florida | 1,251.4 |
| 3 Tallahassee, Florida | 1,153.0 |
| 4 Lubbock, Texas | 1,081.8 |
| 5 Springfield, Massachusetts | 1,052.9 |
| 6 Jackson, Tennessee | 1,039.0 |
| 7 Gainesville, Florida | 1,021.1 |
| 8 Albuquerque, New Mexico | 1,020.0 |
| 9 Florence, South Carolina | 1,014.8 |
| 10 Orlando+, Florida | 989.3 |

\* Murder, forcible rape, aggravated assault, and robbery

\# Metropolitan Statistical Area

\+ Includes Lake, Orange, Osceola, and Seminole Counties

Source: FBI Uniform Crime Reports

## THE 10 ★
## MOST COMMON REASONS FOR ARREST IN THE US

| OFFENCE | RATE* | ARRESTS (1999) |
|---|---|---|
| 1 Drug abuse violations | 586.0 | 1,007,002 |
| 2 Driving under the influence | 551.0 | 931,235 |
| 3 Larceny-theft | 462.2 | 794,201 |
| 4 Drunkenness | 254.4 | 437,153 |
| 5 Contravention of liquor laws | 249.0 | 427,873 |
| 6 Disorderly conduct | 245.4 | 421,662 |
| 7 Aggravated assault | 185.1 | 318,051 |
| 8 Fraud | 131.5 | 225,934 |
| 9 Burglary | 112.1 | 192,570 |
| 10 Vandalism | 105.9 | 182,043 |

\* Per 100,000 inhabitants

Source: FBI Uniform Crime Reports

## TOP 10 US STATES WITH THE LOWEST CRIME RATES
*(State/crimes per 100,000 in 1999)*

**1** New Hampshire, 2,281.9　**2** North Dakota, 2,393.1　**3** South Dakota, 2,644.7　**4** West Virginia, 2,720.6　**5** Vermont, 2,817.3　**6** Maine, 2,875.0　**7** Kentucky, 2,878.1　**8** Pennsylvania, 3,113.7　**9** Idaho, 3,149.3　**10** Iowa, 3,224.0

Source: FBI Uniform Crime Reports

## THE 10 ★
## CARS MOST STOLEN IN THE US

| CAR | NO. STOLEN (1998) |
|---|---|
| 1 Chrysler Jeep Grand Cherokee | 1,085 |
| 2 Ford Escort | 995 |
| 3 Ford Taurus | 943 |
| 4 Ford Contour | 866 |
| 5 GM Chevrolet Cavalier | 844 |
| 6 Honda Civic | 838 |
| 7 Ford F-150 Pickup Truck | 805 |
| 8 Toyota Camry | 790 |
| 9 GM Chevrolet Blazer | 759 |
| 10 Chrysler Dodge Stratus | 750 |

Source: *Department of Transportation - National Highway Traffic Safety Administration*

## THE 10 ★
## US STATES WITH THE HIGHEST CRIME RATES

| STATE | CRIMES PER 100,000 (1999) |
|---|---|
| 1 Florida | 6,205.5 |
| 2 New Mexico | 5,962.1 |
| 3 Arizona | 5,896.5 |
| 4 Louisiana | 5,746.8 |
| 5 South Carolina | 5,324.4 |
| 6 Washington | 5,255.5 |
| 7 North Carolina | 5,175.4 |
| 8 Georgia | 5,148.5 |
| 9 Texas | 5,031.8 |
| 10 Oregon | 5,002.0 |

Source: FBI Uniform Crime Reports

## THE 10 ★
## PRISONS IN THE US WITH THE HIGHEST OCCUPANCY

| INSTITUTION/LOCATION | CURRENT OCCUPANCY* |
|---|---|
| 1 Federal Correctional Institution, Fort Dix, New Jersey | 3,755 |
| 2 Metropolitan Detention Center, Brooklyn, New York | 2,041 |
| 3 Federal Correctional Institution (Low Security), Coleman, Florida | 2,009 |
| 4 Federal Correctional Institution (Low Security), Beaumont, Texas | 1,926 |
| 5 Federal Correctional Institution, Elkton, Ohio | 1,887 |
| 6 Federal Medical Center, Lexington, Kentucky | 1,880 |
| 7 Federal Correctional Institution, Yazoo City, Mississippi | 1,835 |
| 8 Correctional Institution#, Taft, California | 1,824 |
| 9 Federal Correctional Institution, Forrest City, Arizona | 1,737 |
| 10 US Penitentiary, Atlanta, Georgia | 1,708 |

\* As of March 23, 2001

\# Privately managed

Source: *Bureau of Federal Prisons*

**Did You Know?** Although regarded as "priceless," Leonardo da Vinci's *Mona Lisa* is believed to be the most valuable single object ever stolen. It was taken from the Louvre Museum on August 21, 1911, and returned on January 4, 1914.

# Capital Punishment

## THE 10 ★
### LAST PUBLIC HANGINGS IN THE UK

| | HANGED/CRIME | DATE |
|---|---|---|
| 1 | Michael Barrett *Murder of Sarah Ann Hodgkinson, one of 12 victims of bombing in Clerkenwell, London* | May 26, 1868 |
| 2 | Robert Smith *Murder of a girl (the last public hanging in Scotland)* | May 12, 1868 |
| 3 | Richard Bishop *Stabbing of Alfred Cartwright* | Apr 30, 1868 |
| 4 | John Mapp *Murder of a girl* | Apr 9, 1868 |
| 5 | Frederick Parker *Murder of Daniel Driscoll* | Apr 4, 1868 |
| 6 | Timothy Faherty *Murder of Mary Hanmer* | Apr 4, 1868 |
| 7 | Miles Wetherill or Weatherill *Murder of Rev. Plow and his maid* | Apr 4, 1868 |
| 8 | Frances Kidder *Murder of 12-year-old Louise Kidder-Staple (the last public hanging of a woman)* | Apr 2, 1868 |
| 9 | William Worsley *Murder of William Bradbury* | Mar 31, 1868 |
| 10 | Frederick Baker *Murder and mutilation of 8-year-old Fanny Adams* | Dec 24, 1867 |

## THE 10 ★
### FIRST COUNTRIES TO ABOLISH CAPITAL PUNISHMENT

| | COUNTRY | ABOLISHED |
|---|---|---|
| 1 | Russia | 1826 |
| 2 | Venezuela | 1863 |
| 3 | Portugal | 1867 |
| 4 = | Brazil | 1882 |
| = | Costa Rica | 1882 |
| 6 | Ecuador | 1897 |
| 7 | Panama | 1903 |
| 8 | Norway | 1905 |
| 9 | Uruguay | 1907 |
| 10 | Colombia | 1910 |

## THE 10 ★
### PRISONS WITH THE MOST HANGINGS IN ENGLAND AND WALES, 1868–1964

| | PRISON | HANGINGS 1868–99 | 1900–64 | TOTAL |
|---|---|---|---|---|
| 1 | Wandsworth, London | 18 | 98 | 116 |
| 2 | Pentonville, London | – | 105 | 105 |
| 3 | Manchester (Strangeways) | 28 | 71 | 99 |
| 4 | Liverpool (Walton) | 39 | 52 | 91 |
| 5 | Leeds (Armley) | 23 | 66 | 89 |
| 6 | Durham | 21 | 54 | 75 |
| 7 | Newgate, London | 50 | 9 | 59 |
| 8 | Birmingham (Winson Green) | 6 | 34 | 40 |
| 9 | Lincoln | 12 | 18 | 30 |
| 10 = | Maidstone | 17 | 11 | 28 |
| = | Winchester | 14 | 14 | 28 |

## THE 10 ★
### WORST YEARS FOR LYNCHINGS IN THE US*

| | YEAR | LYNCHING VICTIMS WHITE | BLACK | TOTAL |
|---|---|---|---|---|
| 1 | 1892 | 69 | 161 | 230 |
| 2 | 1884 | 160 | 51 | 211 |
| 3 | 1894 | 58 | 134 | 192 |
| 4 = | 1885 | 110 | 74 | 184 |
| = | 1891 | 71 | 113 | 184 |
| 6 | 1895 | 66 | 113 | 179 |
| 7 | 1889 | 76 | 94 | 170 |
| 8 | 1897 | 35 | 123 | 158 |
| 9 | 1893 | 34 | 118 | 152 |
| 10 | 1886 | 64 | 74 | 138 |

*\* Since 1882*

Lynching is the "rough justice" of a mob seizing a crime suspect and hanging him or her (92 women were lynched between 1882 and 1927) without trial. Although lynching progressively became a racial crime, in its early years white victims actually outnumbered black.

## THE 10 ★
### FIRST EXECUTIONS BY LETHAL INJECTION IN THE US

| | NAME | EXECUTION |
|---|---|---|
| 1 | Charles Brooks | Dec 7, 1982 |
| 2 | James Autry | Mar 14, 1984 |
| 3 | Ronald O'Bryan | Mar 31, 1984 |
| 4 | Thomas Barefoot | Oct 30, 1984 |
| 5 | Dovle Skillem | Jan 16, 1985 |
| 6 | Stephen Morin | Mar 13, 1985 |
| 7 | Jesse de la Rosa | May 15, 1985 |
| 8 | Charles Milton | June 25, 1985 |
| 9 | Henry M. Porter | July 9, 1985 |
| 10 | Charles Rumbaugh | Sep 11, 1985 |

Source: *Death Penalty Information Center*

Although Oklahoma was the first State to legalize execution by lethal injection, the option was not taken there until 1990. All of the above were executed in Texas (where, curiously, death row inmates with the first name of Charles figure prominently). It is now the most commonly used form of execution in the US.

## THE 10 ★
### COUNTRIES WITH THE MOST EXECUTIONS

| | COUNTRY | EXECUTIONS (1998) |
|---|---|---|
| 1 | China | 1,067 |
| 2 | Dem. Rep. of Congo | 100 |
| 3 | US | 68 |
| 4 | Iran | 66 |
| 5 | Egypt | 48 |
| 6 | Belarus | 33 |
| 7 | Taiwan | 32 |
| 8 | Saudi Arabia | 29 |
| 9 | Singapore | 28 |
| 10 = | Rwanda | 24 |
| = | Sierra Leone | 24 |

Source: *Amnesty International*

Although unconfirmed, Amnesty International also received reports of many hundreds of executions in Iraq.

## THE 10 ★
# STATES WITH THE MOST PRISONERS ON DEATH ROW

| STATE | PRISONERS UNDER DEATH SENTENCE* |
|---|---|
| 1 California | 582 |
| 2 Texas | 448 |
| 3 Florida | 385 |
| 4 Pennsylvania | 238 |
| 5 North Carolina | 237 |
| 6 Ohio | 202 |
| 7 Alabama | 185 |
| 8 Illinois | 172 |
| 9 Oklahoma | 137 |
| 10 Georgia | 136 |

* As at October 1, 2000

Source: *Death Penalty Information Center*

A total of 3,703 prisoners were on death row at the end of 2000. Some were sentenced in more than one state, causing a higher total to be achieved than by adding individual state figures together.

## THE 10 ★
# STATES WITH THE MOST EXECUTIONS, 1977–2000*

| STATE | EXECUTIONS |
|---|---|
| 1 Texas | 239 |
| 2 Virginia | 81 |
| 3 Florida | 50 |
| 4 Missouri | 46 |
| 5 Oklahoma | 30 |
| 6 Louisiana | 26 |
| 7 South Carolina | 25 |
| 8 =Alabama | 23 |
| =Arkansas | 23 |
| =Georgia | 23 |

* To December 19, 2000

Source: *Death Penalty Information Center*

A total of 557 people have been executed since 1977, when the death penalty was reintroduced after a 10-year moratorium. During this period, 20 states have not carried out any executions.

## THE 10 ★
# FIRST ELECTROCUTIONS AT SING SING

| PERSON ELECTROCUTED | AGE | ELECTROCUTED |
|---|---|---|
| 1 Harris A. Smiler | 32 | July 7, 1891 |
| 2 James Slocum | 22 | July 7, 1891 |
| 3 Joseph Wood | 21 | July 7, 1891 |
| 4 Schihick Judigo | 35 | July 7, 1891 |
| 5 Martin D. Loppy | 51 | Dec 7, 1891 |
| 6 Charles McElvaine | 20 | Feb 8, 1892 |
| 7 Jeremiah Cotte | 40 | Mar 28, 1892 |
| 8 Fred McGuire | 24 | Dec 19, 1892 |
| 9 James L. Hamilton | 40 | Apr 3, 1893 |
| 10 Carlyle Harris | 23 | May 8, 1893 |

The electric chair was installed in Sing Sing Prison, Ossining, New York, in 1891, just a year after it was first used to execute William Kemmler at Auburn Prison, also in New York State. By the end of the 19th century, 29 inmates had been executed by this means.

## THE 10 ★
# STATES WITH THE MOST WOMEN ON DEATH ROW

| STATE | WOMEN UNDER DEATH SENTENCE* |
|---|---|
| 1 California | 12 |
| 2 Texas | 7 |
| 3 North Carolina | 6 |
| 4 =Illinois | 4 |
| =Pennsylvania | 4 |
| 6 =Alabama | 3 |
| =Florida | 3 |
| 8 =Arizona | 2 |
| =Tennessee | 2 |
| 10 =Georgia | 1 |
| =Idaho | 1 |
| =Indiana | 1 |
| =Kentucky | 1 |
| =Louisiana | 1 |
| =Mississipi | 1 |
| =Nevada | 1 |
| =Oklahoma | 1 |

* As at May 2, 2001, when a total of 51 women were on death row

Source: *Death Penalty Information Center*

At the beginning of 2001, women represented only 1.4 per cent of death row prisoners. Since 1973, California, Florida, North Carolina, and Texas have accounted for more than 40 per cent of the death sentences passed on women.

## THE 10 ★
# STATES WITH THE MOST WOMEN SENTENCED TO DEATH, 1973–2000

| STATE | WOMEN SENTENCED TO DEATH* |
|---|---|
| 1 North Carolina | 16 |
| 2 Florida | 15 |
| 3 California | 14 |
| 4 Texas | 13 |
| 5 Ohio | 9 |
| 6 Alabama | 8 |
| 7 =Illinois | 7 |
| =Mississippi | 7 |
| =Oklahoma | 7 |
| 10 Georgia | 6 |

* As at June 30, 2000

Source: *Death Penalty Information Center*

In the US, the sentencing of women to death is comparatively rare, and occasions when the sentence is actually carried are even rarer. In fact, there are only 561 known instances since 1632 out of a massive total of some 19,200 executions. A total of 45 executions of women have been carried out since 1900. Of these, seven have been executed since May 2, 1962, when Elizabeth Ann Duncan was executed, the most recent was Wanda Jean Allen in Oklahoma on Jan 11, 2001.

# Murder File

## WORST GUN MASSACRES*

PERPETRATOR/LOCATION/DATE/CIRCUMSTANCES     VICTIMS

**1 Woo Bum Kong**, Sang-Namdo, South Korea, Apr 28, 1982    57
*Off-duty policeman Woo Bum Kong (or Wou Bom-Kon), 27, went on a drunken rampage with rifles and hand grenades, killing 57 and injuring 38 before blowing himself up with a grenade.*

**2 Martin Bryant**, Port Arthur, Tasmania, Australia, Apr 28, 1996    35
*Bryant, a 28-year-old Hobart resident, used a rifle in a horrific spree that began in a restaurant and ended with a siege in a guesthouse in which he held hostages. He set the building on fire before being captured by police.*

**3 Baruch Goldstein**, Hebron, occupied West Bank, Israel, Feb 25, 1994    29
*Goldstein, a 42-year-old US immigrant doctor, carried out a gun massacre of Palestinians at prayer at the Tomb of the Patriarchs before being beaten to death by the crowd.*

**4 Campo Elias Delgado**, Bogota, Colombia, Dec 4, 1986    28
*Delgado, a Vietnamese war veteran and electronics engineer, stabbed two and shot a further 26 people before being killed by police.*

**5 =James Oliver Huberty**, San Ysidro, California, July 18, 1984    22
*Huberty, aged 41, opened fire in a McDonald's restaurant, killing 21 before being shot dead by a SWAT marksman. A further 19 were wounded, including a victim who died the following day.*

**=George Jo Hennard**, Killeen, Texas, Oct 16, 1991    22
*Hennard drove his pickup truck through the window of Luby's Cafeteria and, in 11 minutes, killed 22 with semiautomatic pistols before shooting himself.*

**7 Thomas Hamilton**, Dunblane, Stirling, UK, Mar 13, 1996    17
*Hamilton, 43, shot 16 children and a teacher in Dunblane Primary School before killing himself in the UK's worst-ever shooting incident.*

**8 =Charles Joseph Whitman**, Austin, Texas, July 31–Aug 1, 1966    16
*25-year-old ex-Marine marksman Whitman killed his mother and wife; the following day he shot 14 and wounded 34 from the observation deck at the University of Texas at Austin, before being shot dead by police.*

**=Michael Ryan**, Hungerford, Berkshire, UK, Aug 19, 1987    16
*Ryan, 26, shot 14 dead and wounded 16 others (two of whom died later) before shooting himself.*

**=Ronald Gene Simmons**, Russellville, Arkansas, Dec 28, 1987    16
*47-year-old Simmons killed 16, including 14 members of his own family, by shooting or strangling. He was caught and then sentenced to death on Feb 10, 1989.*

* By individuals, excluding terrorist and military actions; totals exclude perpetrator

Gun massacres at workplaces in the US have attracted considerable attention in recent years, with post offices being especially notable: on August 20, 1986, in Edmond, Oklahoma, 44-year-old postal worker Patrick Henry Sherrill shot 14 dead and wounded six others at the post office where he worked, before killing himself. Since then, there have been some 15 such incidents perpetrated by postal workers, in which 40 victims have been killed. Equally distressing have been a number of shootings at schools and other educational establishments, among the worst of which – and Canada's worst gun massacre – was that committed by Marc Lépine, a student at the Université de Montreal, Quebec, Canada. On December 6, 1989 he went on an armed rampage, shooting 14 women before killing himself.

## MOST PROLIFIC SERIAL KILLERS OF THE 20TH CENTURY

KILLER/COUNTRY/CRIME     VICTIMS*

**1 Pedro Alonso López**, Colombia    300
*Captured in 1980, López, nicknamed the "Monster of the Andes," led police to 53 graves, but probably murdered at least 300 in Colombia, Ecuador, and Peru. He was sentenced to life imprisonment.*

**2 Dr. Harold Shipman**, UK    236
*In January 2000, Manchester doctor Shipman was found guilty of the murder of 15 women patients, but an official report published in January 2001 suggested that the potential figure could be at least 236 and perhaps as high as 345.*

**3 Henry Lee Lucas**, US    200
*Lucas confessed in 1983 to 360 murders, although the number of murder sites to which he led police was "only" 200. He committed many crimes with his partner-in-crime Ottis Toole, who died in jail in 1996. He remains on death row in Huntsville Prison, Texas.*

**4 Hu Wanlin**, China    196
*Posing as a doctor specializing in ancient Chinese medicine, Hu Wanlin was sentenced on October 1, 2000 to 15 years imprisonment for three deaths, but authorities believe he was responsible for considerably more, an estimated 20 in Taiyuan, 146 in Shanxi, and 30 in Shangqiu.*

**5 Luis Alfredo Gavarito**, Colombia    140
*Gavarito confessed in 1999 to a spate of murders that are still the subject of investigation.*

**6 Dr. Jack Kevorkian**, US    130
*In 1999 Kevorkian, who admitted to assisting in 130 suicides since 1990, was convicted of second-degree murder. His 10- to 25-year prison sentence is subject to appeal.*

**7 =Donald Henry "Pee Wee" Gaskins**, US    100
*Gaskins was executed in 1991 for a series of murders that may have reached 200.*

**=Javed Iqbal**, Pakistan    100
*Iqbal and two accomplices were found guilty in March 2000 of murdering boys in Lahore. Iqbal was sentenced to be publicly strangled, dismembered, and his body dissolved in acid.*

**9 Delfina and Maria de Jesús Gonzales**, Mexico    91
*In 1964 the Gonzales sisters were sentenced to 40 years imprisonment after the remains of 80 women and 11 men were discovered on their property.*

**10 Bruno Lüdke**, Germany    86
*Lüdke confessed to murdering 86 women between 1928 and 1943. He died in the hospital in 1944 after a lethal injection.*

* Estimated minimum; includes only individual and partnership murderers; excludes "mercy killings" by doctors, murders by bandits, those carried out by groups, such as political and military atrocities, and gangland slayings

Serial killers are mass murderers who kill repeatedly, often over long periods, in contrast to the so-called "spree killers" who have been responsible for single-occasion massacres, usually with guns, and other perpetrators of single outrages, often by means of bombs, resulting in multiple deaths. Because of the secrecy surrounding their horrific crimes, and the time spans involved, it is almost impossible to calculate the precise numbers of their victims.

## THE 10 ★
# MOST COMMON CIRCUMSTANCES FOR MURDER IN THE US

| | CIRCUMSTANCE | MURDERS (1999) |
|---|---|---|
| 1 | **Argument** (unspecified) | 3,391 |
| 2 | **Robbery** | 1,010 |
| 3 | **Juvenile gang killing** | 579 |
| 4 | **Contravention of narcotic drug laws** | 564 |
| 5 | **Argument over money or property** | 211 |
| 6 | **Brawl due to influence of alcohol** | 187 |
| 7 | **Romantic triangle** | 133 |
| 8 | **Gangland killing** | 116 |
| 9 | **Brawl due to influence of narcotics** | 111 |
| 10 | **Burglary** | 79 |

Source: FBI Uniform Crime Reports

A total of 12,658 murders were reported in 1999, including 1,903 without a specified reason, and 3,779 for which the reasons were unknown.

## THE 10 ★
# MOST COMMON MURDER WEAPONS AND METHODS IN THE US

| | WEAPON OR METHOD | VICTIMS (1999) |
|---|---|---|
| 1 | **Handguns** | 6,498 |
| 2 | **Knives or cutting instruments** | 1,667 |
| 3 | **"Personal weapons"** (hands, feet, fists, etc.) | 855 |
| 4 | **Blunt objects** (hammers, clubs, etc.) | 736 |
| 5 | **Shotguns** | 503 |
| 6 | **Rifles** | 387 |
| 7 | **Strangulation** | 190 |
| 8 | **Fire** | 125 |
| 9 | **Asphyxiation** | 103 |
| 10 | **Drowning** | 26 |

Source: FBI Uniform Crime Reports

In 1999 "other weapons or weapons not stated" were used in 863 murders, and a further 871 murders involved unspecified firearms. Relatively less common methods included narcotics (23 cases) and poison (11).

**FIREPOWER**
*While handguns are the most common murder weapons in the US and certain other countries, restrictions on their use elsewhere relegates them to a less significant position.*

## THE 10 ★
# WORST STATES FOR MURDER IN THE US

| | STATE | FIREARMS USED | TOTAL MURDERS |
|---|---|---|---|
| 1 | **California** | 1,338 | 2,005 |
| 2 | **Texas** | 746 | 1,210 |
| 3 | **New York** | 487 | 864 |
| 4 | **Michigan** | 485 | 714 |
| 5 | **Illinois** | 458 | 640 |
| 6 | **Pennsylvania** | 407 | 560 |
| 7 | **North Carolina** | 362 | 539 |
| 8 | **Georgia** | 360 | 516 |
| 9 | **Louisiana** | 315 | 453 |
| 10 | **Maryland** | 293 | 394 |

Source: FBI Uniform Crime Reports

Of the 7,895 murders committed in the Top 10 states in 1999, 5,241 involved firearms. North Dakota had the fewest murders, at just eight.

## THE 10 ★
# WORST CITIES FOR MURDER IN THE US

| | CITY/STATE | MURDERS, 1999* |
|---|---|---|
| 1 | **New York**, New York | 671 |
| 2 | **Chicago**, Illinois | 642 |
| 3 | **Los Angeles**, California | 425 |
| 4 | **Detroit**, Michigan | 415 |
| 5 | **Philadelphia**, Pennsylvania | 292 |
| 6 | =**Houston**, Texas | 241 |
| | =**Washington**, DC | 241 |
| 8 | **Dallas**, Texas | 191 |
| 9 | **New Orleans**, Louisiana | 158 |
| 10 | **Atlanta**, Georgia | 143 |

*\* Murders and non-negligent manslaughter*

Source: FBI Uniform Crime Reports

New York's status as the murder capital of the US improved during the 1990s.

**Did You Know?** The peak year for murder in the US was 1994, when 22,084 cases were recorded, 14,463 of them, or 65 percent, involving firearms.

# Military Matters

**CHINESE ARMED FORCES**
*Members of the Chinese army, the largest military force in the world, parade in the now infamous Tiananmen Square, Beijing.*

## THE 10 YEARS WITH THE MOST NUCLEAR EXPLOSIONS

*(Year/explosions)*

**❶** 1962, 178 **❷** 1958, 116 **❸** 1968, 79 **❹** 1966, 76 **❺** 1961, 71 **❻** 1969, 67 **❼** 1978, 66 **❽** = 1967, 64; = 1970, 64 **❿** 1964, 60

---

**TOP 10** ★

## COUNTRIES WITH THE LARGEST DEFENSE BUDGETS

| | COUNTRY | BUDGET ($) |
|---|---|---|
| 1 | US | 291,200,000,000 |
| 2 | Japan | 45,600,000,000 |
| 3 | UK | 34,500,000,000 |
| 4 | Russia | 29,000,000,000 |
| 5 | France | 27,000,000,000 |
| 6 | Germany | 23,300,000,000 |
| 7 | Saudi Arabia | 18,700,000,000 |
| 8 | Italy | 16,000,000,000 |
| 9 | India | 15,900,000,000 |
| 10 | China | 14,500,000,000 |

The savings made as a consequence of the end of the Cold War between the West and the former Soviet Union mean that both the numbers of personnel and the defense budgets of many countries have been cut.

---

**TOP 10** ★

## LARGEST ARMED FORCES

| | COUNTRY | ESTIMATED ACTIVE FORCES ARMY | NAVY | AIR | TOTAL |
|---|---|---|---|---|---|
| 1 | China | 1,700,000 | 220,000 | 420,000 | 2,340,000 |
| 2 | US | 471,700 | 370,700 | 353,600 | 1,365,800* |
| 3 | India | 1,100,000 | 53,000 | 150,000 | 1,303,000 |
| 4 | North Korea | 950,000 | 46,000 | 86,000 | 1,082,000 |
| 5 | Russia | 348,000 | 171,500 | 184,600 | 1,004,100# |
| 6 | South Korea | 560,000 | 60,000 | 63,000 | 683,000 |
| 7 | Pakistan | 550,000 | 22,000 | 40,000 | 612,000 |
| 8 | Turkey | 495,000 | 54,600 | 60,100 | 609,700 |
| 9 | Iran | 325,000 | 18,000 | 45,000 | 513,000+ |
| 10 | Vietnam | 412,000 | 42,000 | 30,000 | 484,000 |

\* Includes 169,800 Marine Corps
\# Includes Strategic Deterrent Forces, Paramilitary, National Guard, etc.
\+ Includes 125,000 Revolutionary Guards

# TOP 10 COUNTRIES WITH THE HIGHEST MILITARY/CIVILIAN RATIO

*(Country/ratio\* in 2000)*

**1** North Korea, 503 **2** Israel, 278 **3** United Arab Emirates, 240 **4** Jordan, 201
**5** Iraq, 192 **6** Oman, 189 **7** Syria, 187 **8** Qatar, 178
**9** Bahrain, 172 **10** Taiwan, 168 *US, 50*

*\* Military personnel per 10,000 population*

## TOP 10 ⭐
# COUNTRIES WITH THE HIGHEST PER CAPITA DEFENSE EXPENDITURE

| | COUNTRY | EXPENDITURE PER CAPITA, 1999 ($) |
|---|---|---|
| 1 | Qatar | 2,026 |
| 2 | Israel | 1,435 |
| 3 | Kuwait | 1,407 |
| 4 | Brunei | 1,211 |
| 5 | United Arab Emirates | 1,185 |
| 6 | Singapore | 1,138 |
| 7 | Saudi Arabia | 1,006 |
| 8 | US | 1,000 |
| 9 | Norway | 743 |
| 10 | Oman | 696 |

## TOP 10 ⭐
# COUNTRIES WITH THE LARGEST NAVIES

| | COUNTRY | MANPOWER, 2000\* |
|---|---|---|
| 1 | US | 370,700 |
| 2 | China | 220,000 |
| 3 | Russia | 171,500 |
| 4 | Taiwan | 62,000 |
| 5 | South Korea | 60,000 |
| 6 | Turkey | 54,600 |
| 7 | India | 53,000 |
| 8 | France | 49,490 |
| 9 | North Korea | 46,000 |
| 10 | UK | 43,770 |

*\* Including naval air forces and marines*

**CRUISE SHIP**

*The US Navy is the world's largest. Here, the destroyer USS Merrill launches a Tomahawk cruise missile.*

### THOMPSON OF THE TOMMY GUN

The "Tommy gun," or Thompson sub-machine gun, was originally produced as a military weapon. It takes its name from US Army ordnance officer John Taliaferro Thompson (1860–1940), but the operating mechanism of the .45-caliber weapon was the brainchild of naval officer John N. Blish, from whom John Thompson acquired the patent. The gun was manufactured by Thompson's Auto-Ordnance Company from 1919, but was not widely used until World War II, when over 2 million were made. Unusually, the nickname "Tommy Gun" was registered as a trademark.

**WHO WAS • WHO WAS • WHO WAS • WHO WAS •**
**?**

## TOP 10 ⭐
# ARMS IMPORTERS

| | COUNTRY | ANNUAL IMPORTS ($) |
|---|---|---|
| 1 | Saudi Arabia | 6,103,000,000 |
| 2 | Taiwan | 2,604,000,000 |
| 3 | Japan | 1,866,000,000 |
| 4 | South Korea | 1,847,000,000 |
| 5 | Israel | 1,504,000,000 |
| 6 | Egypt | 800,000,000 |
| 7 | Indonesia | 767,000,000 |
| 8 | China | 500,000,000 |
| 9 | Thailand | 410,000,000 |
| 10 | Kuwait | 314,000,000 |

## TOP 10 ⭐
# COUNTRIES WITH THE MOST COMBAT AIRCRAFT\*

| | COUNTRY | COMBAT AIRCRAFT |
|---|---|---|
| 1 | China | 3,000 |
| 2 | Russia | 2,733 |
| 3 | US | 2,529 |
| 4 | Ukraine | 911 |
| 5 | India | 774 |
| 6 | North Korea | 621 |
| 7 | Egypt | 580 |
| 8 | Taiwan | 570 |
| 9 | South Korea | 555 |
| 10 | France | 517 |

*\* Air force only, excluding long-range strike/attack aircraft*

**Which country has the largest Muslim population?**  *see p.77 for the answer*   A India   B Egypt   C Indonesia

# The World at War

## TOP 10 ★
### LARGEST ARMED FORCES OF WORLD WAR I

| COUNTRY | PERSONNEL* |
|---|---|
| 1 Russia | 12,000,000 |
| 2 Germany | 11,000,000 |
| 3 British Empire# | 8,904,000 |
| 4 France | 8,410,000 |
| 5 Austria–Hungary | 7,800,000 |
| 6 Italy | 5,615,000 |
| 7 US | 4,355,000 |
| 8 Turkey | 2,850,000 |
| 9 Bulgaria | 1,200,000 |
| 10 Japan | 800,000 |

*Total at peak strength
# Inc. Australia, Canada, India, New Zealand, etc.

Russia's armed forces were relatively small in relation to the country's population – some 6 percent, compared with 17 percent in Germany. Several other European nations had forces that were similarly sized in relation to their populations: Serbia's army was equivalent to 4 percent of its population. In total, more than 65 million combatants were involved in fighting some of the costliest battles, in terms of numbers killed, that the world has ever known.

## TOP 10 ★
### SMALLEST ARMED FORCES OF WORLD WAR I

| COUNTRY | PERSONNEL* |
|---|---|
| 1 Montenegro | 50,000 |
| 2 Portugal | 100,000 |
| 3 Greece | 230,000 |
| 4 Belgium | 267,000 |
| 5 Serbia | 707,000 |
| 6 Romania | 750,000 |
| 7 Japan | 800,000 |
| 8 Bulgaria | 1,200,000 |
| 9 Turkey | 2,850,000 |
| 10 US | 4,355,000 |

* Total at peak strength

## THE 10 COUNTRIES WITH THE MOST PRISONERS OF WAR, 1914–18
*(Country/captured)*

1 Russia, 2,500,000  2 Austria–Hungary, 2,200,000  3 Germany, 1,152,800  4 Italy, 600,000  5 France, 537,000  6 Turkey, 250,000  7 British Empire, 191,652  8 Serbia, 152,958  9 Romania, 80,000  10 Belgium, 34,659

## THE 10 ★
### COUNTRIES SUFFERING THE GREATEST MILITARY LOSSES IN WORLD WAR I

| COUNTRY | KILLED |
|---|---|
| 1 Germany | 1,773,700 |
| 2 Russia | 1,700,000 |
| 3 France | 1,357,800 |
| 4 Austria–Hungary | 1,200,000 |
| 5 British Empire* | 908,371 |
| 6 Italy | 650,000 |
| 7 Romania | 335,706 |
| 8 Turkey | 325,000 |
| 9 US | 116,516 |
| 10 Bulgaria | 87,500 |

* Inc. Australia, Canada, India, New Zealand, etc.

The number of battle fatalities and deaths from other causes among military personnel varied enormously from country to country. Romania's death rate was highest, at 45 percent of its total mobilized forces; Germany's was 16 percent, Austria–Hungary's and Russia's 15 percent, and the British Empire's 10 percent, with the US's 2 percent and Japan's 0.04 percent among the lowest. Japan's forces totalled only 800,000, of which an estimated 300 were killed, 907 wounded, and just three taken prisoner or reported missing.

**WAR GRAVES**
*The first Battle of the Somme (July 1 to November 18, 1916) resulted in some 1,265,000 casualties, with no significant territorial gain.*

## THE 10 ★ COUNTRIES SUFFERING THE GREATEST MILITARY LOSSES IN WORLD WAR II

| | COUNTRY | KILLED |
|---|---|---|
| 1 | USSR | 13,600,000* |
| 2 | Germany | 3,300,000 |
| 3 | China | 1,324,516 |
| 4 | Japan | 1,140,429 |
| 5 | British Empire# | 357,116 |
| 6 | Romania | 350,000 |
| 7 | Poland | 320,000 |
| 8 | Yugoslavia | 305,000 |
| 9 | US | 292,131 |
| 10 | Italy | 279,800 |
| | Total | 21,268,992 |

\* Total, of which 7,800,000 battlefield deaths

# Inc. Australia, Canada, India, New Zealand, etc.

The actual numbers killed in World War II have been the subject of intense argument for over 50 years. Most authorities now agree that of the 30 million Soviets who bore arms, there were 13.6 million military deaths.

## TOP 10 ★ LARGEST ARMED FORCES OF WORLD WAR II

| | COUNTRY | PERSONNEL* |
|---|---|---|
| 1 | USSR | 12,500,000 |
| 2 | US | 12,364,000 |
| 3 | Germany | 10,000,000 |
| 4 | Japan | 6,095,000 |
| 5 | France | 5,700,000 |
| 6 | UK | 4,683,000 |
| 7 | Italy | 4,500,000 |
| 8 | China | 3,800,000 |
| 9 | India | 2,150,000 |
| 10 | Poland | 1,000,000 |

\* Total at peak strength

## THE 10 ★ COUNTRIES SUFFERING THE GREATEST CIVILIAN LOSSES IN WORLD WAR II

| | COUNTRY | KILLED |
|---|---|---|
| 1 | China | 8,000,000 |
| 2 | USSR | 6,500,000 |
| 3 | Poland | 5,300,000 |
| 4 | Germany | 2,350,000 |
| 5 | Yugoslavia | 1,500,000 |
| 6 | France | 470,000 |
| 7 | Greece | 415,000 |
| 8 | Japan | 393,400 |
| 9 | Romania | 340,000 |
| 10 | Hungary | 300,000 |

Deaths among civilians during this war – many resulting from famine and internal purges, such as those in China and the USSR – were colossal, but they were less well documented than those among fighting forces. Although the figures are the best available from authoritative sources, and present a broad picture of the scale of civilian losses, the precise numbers will never be known.

## TOP 10 ★ LARGEST SUBMARINE FLEETS OF WORLD WAR II

| | COUNTRY | SUBMARINES |
|---|---|---|
| 1 | Japan* | 163 |
| 2 | US* | 112 |
| 3 | France | 77 |
| 4 | USSR | 75 |
| 5 | Germany | 57 |
| 6 | UK | 38 |
| 7 | Netherlands | 21 |
| 8 | Italy | 15 |
| 9 | Denmark | 12 |
| 10 | Greece | 6 |

\* Strength at December 1941

These show submarine strengths at the outbreak of the war. During hostilities, production rose sharply.

## THE 10 ★ COUNTRIES SUFFERING THE GREATEST NUMBER OF WARSHIP LOSSES IN WORLD WAR II

| | COUNTRY | WARSHIPS SUNK |
|---|---|---|
| 1 | UK | 213 |
| 2 | Japan | 198 |
| 3 | US | 105 |
| 4 | Italy | 97 |
| 5 | Germany | 60 |
| 6 | USSR | 37 |
| 7 | Canada | 17 |
| 8 | France | 11 |
| 9 | Australia | 9 |
| 10 | Norway | 2 |

## TOP 10 ★ TANKS OF WORLD WAR II

| | TANK | COUNTRY | WEIGHT TONS | NO. PRODUCED |
|---|---|---|---|---|
| 1 | M4A3 Sherman | US | 34.7 | 41,530 |
| 2 | T34 Model 42 | USSR | 31.9 | 35,120 |
| 3 | T34/85 | USSR | 35.8 | 29,430 |
| 4 | M3 General Stuart | US | 13.7 | 14,000 |
| 5 | Valentine II | UK | 19.6 | 8,280 |
| 6 | M3A1 Lee/Grant | US | 30.0 | 7,400 |
| 7 | Churchill VII | UK | 44.8 | 5,640 |
| 8 =| Panzer IVD | Germany | 22.4 | 5,500 |
| =| Panzer VG | Germany | 50.2 | 5,500 |
| 10 | Crusader I | UK | 21.3 | 4,750 |

The tank named after US Civil War General William Tecumseh Sherman was used in large numbers by both US and British troops during World War II. It carried a crew of five and could cruise over a distance of 143 miles (230 km) at up to 25 mph (40 km/h). Its weaponry comprised two machine guns and, originally, a 75-mm cannon, but after 1944 about half the Shermans in operation had their cannons replaced by one capable of firing a powerful 7.7-kg shell or a 5.5-kg armor-piercing shell.

**Did You Know?** Argentina, the 53rd country to enter World War II, did not declare war on Germany and Japan until March 27, 1945 – just six weeks before Germany was defeated.

# World Religions

## TOP 10 ★
## RELIGIOUS GROUPS IN THE US

| | RELIGIOUS GROUP | MEMBERS (MID-2000) |
|---|---|---|
| 1 | Protestant | 88,800,000 |
| 2 | Roman Catholic | 58,000,000 |
| 3 | Black Christian | 37,200,000 |
| 4 | Christian (unaffiliated) | 36,255,000 |
| 5 | Christian Orthodox | 6,260,000 |
| 6 | Jewish | 5,621,000 |
| 7 | Muslim | 4,132,000 |
| 8 | Buddhist | 2,450,000 |
| 9 | Anglican | 2,400,000 |
| 10 | Hindu | 1,032,000 |

In 2000, Christians were considered to represent 84.7 percent of the US population, with Protestant groups encompassing 31.9 percent and Roman Catholics 20.8 percent. Followers of the Jewish faith were estimated to comprise 2.0 percent and Muslims 1.5 percent. It should be noted, however, that in the US, as in other countries, Census and other surveys regularly report much higher nominal affiliation to particular religious groups – individual claims to belong to a religion – than actual membership, on which this Top 10 is based.

## TOP 10 ★
## COUNTRIES WITH THE HIGHEST PROPORTION OF HINDUS

| | COUNTRY | HINDU PERCENTAGE OF POPULATION |
|---|---|---|
| 1 | Nepal | 89 |
| 2 | India | 79 |
| 3 | Mauritius | 52 |
| 4 | Guyana | 40 |
| 5 | Fiji | 38 |
| 6 | Suriname | 30 |
| 7 | Bhutan | 25 |
| 8 | Trinidad and Tobago | 24 |
| 9 | Sri Lanka | 15 |
| 10 | Bangladesh | 11 |

Source: *Adherents.com*

## THE 10 LATEST DALAI LAMAS
*(Dalai Lama/lifespan)*

❶ Tenzin Gyatso, 1935–  ❷ Thupten Gyatso, 1876–1933
❸ Trinley Gyatso, 1856–1875  ❹ Khendrup Gyatso, 1838–1856
❺ Tsultrim Gyatso, 1816–1837  ❻ Luntok Gyatso, 1806–1815  ❼ Jampel Gyatso, 1758–1804  ❽ Kesang Gyatso, 1708–1757  ❾ Tsangyang Gyatso, 1683–1706
❿ Ngawang Lobsang Gyatso, 1617–1682

The current Dalai Lama is the fourteenth in line since the first head of the "Yellow Hat Order" of Tibetan Buddhists (1391–1475).

## TOP 10 ★
## LARGEST CHRISTIAN POPULATIONS

| | COUNTRY | CHRISTIAN POPULATION (2000) |
|---|---|---|
| 1 | US | 189,983,000 |
| 2 | Brazil | 170,405,000 |
| 3 | Mexico | 96,614,000 |
| 4 | China | 86,801,000 |
| 5 | Philippines | 72,255,000 |
| 6 | Germany | 60,712,000 |
| 7 | Nigeria | 54,012,000 |
| 8 | Italy | 47,704,000 |
| 9 | France | 45,505,000 |
| 10 | Dem. Rep. of Congo | 42,283,000 |
| | *World total* | 2,094,371,000 |

Source: *Christian Research*

## TOP 10 ★
## CHRISTIAN DENOMINATIONS

| | DENOMINATION | MEMBERS |
|---|---|---|
| 1 | Roman Catholic | 936,192,000 |
| 2 | Orthodox | 139,469,000 |
| 3 | Pentecostal | 122,096,000 |
| 4 | Lutheran | 82,943,000 |
| 5 | Anglican | 78,395,000 |
| 6 | Baptist | 71,590,000 |
| 7 | Presbyterian | 49,286,000 |
| 8 | Methodist | 26,374,000 |
| 9 | Seventh Day Adventist | 11,589,000 |
| 10 | Churches of Christ | 6,759,000 |

Source: *Christian Research*

## TOP 10 ★
## RELIGIOUS BELIEFS

| | RELIGION | FOLLOWERS (2000) |
|---|---|---|
| 1 | Christianity | 2,094,371,000 |
| 2 | Islam | 1,188,242,000 |
| 3 | Hinduism | 811,337,000 |
| 4 | Non-religions | 768,158,000 |
| 5 | Buddhism | 359,981,000 |
| 6 | Ethnic religions | 228,366,000 |
| 7 | Atheism | 150,089,000 |
| 8 | New religions | 102,356,000 |
| 9 | Sikhism | 23,259,000 |
| 10 | Judaism | 13,191,500 |

## TOP 10 ★
## LARGEST JEWISH POPULATIONS

| | COUNTRY | JEWISH POPULATION (2000) |
|---|---|---|
| 1 | US | 5,700,000 |
| 2 | Israel | 4,882,000 |
| 3 | France | 521,000 |
| 4 | Canada | 362,000 |
| 5 | Russia | 290,000 |
| 6 | UK | 276,000 |
| 7 | Argentina | 200,000 |
| 8 | Ukraine | 100,000 |
| 9 | Brazil | 98,000 |
| 10 | Australia | 97,000 |
| | *World total* | 13,191,500 |

Source: *American Jewish Year Book, Vol. 100*

Jewish communities are found in virtually every country in the world.

**Did You Know?** Completed in 1989, the world's largest church, Our Lady of Peace Basilica in Yamoussoukro, Côte d'Ivoire, is taller than and has double the floor area of St. Peter's, Rome, the previous record holder.

## TOP 10 ★
## LARGEST MUSLIM POPULATIONS

| | COUNTRY | MUSLIM POPULATION (2000) |
|---|---|---|
| 1 | Indonesia | 182,570,000 |
| 2 | Pakistan | 134,480,000 |
| 3 | India | 121,000,000 |
| 4 | Bangladesh | 114,080,000 |
| 5 | Turkey | 65,510,000 |
| 6 | Iran | 62,430,000 |
| 7 | Egypt | 58,630,000 |
| 8 | Nigeria | 53,000,000 |
| 9 | Algeria | 30,530,000 |
| 10 | Morocco | 28,780,000 |
| | World total | 1,188,242,000 |

There are at least 15 countries where the population is 95 percent Muslim, including Bahrain, Kuwait, Somalia, and Yemen. Historically, Islam spread both as a result of missionary activity and through contacts with Muslim traders.

### BOWING TO MECCA

*Islam places many strictures on its female members but is nonetheless the world's fastest-growing religion. Here, hundreds of Muslim women unite in prayer.*

## TOP 10 ★
## COUNTRIES WITH THE HIGHEST PROPORTION OF BUDDHISTS

| | COUNTRY | BUDDHIST PERCENTAGE OF POPULATION |
|---|---|---|
| 1 | Thailand | 95 |
| 2 | Cambodia | 90 |
| 3 | Myanmar (Burma) | 88 |
| 4 | Bhutan | 75 |
| 5 | Sri Lanka | 70 |
| 6 | Tibet* | 65 |
| 7 | Laos | 60 |
| 8 | Vietnam | 55 |
| 9 | Japan* | 50 |
| 10 | Macau | 45 |

*\* No accurate figures available*
Source: *Adherents.com*

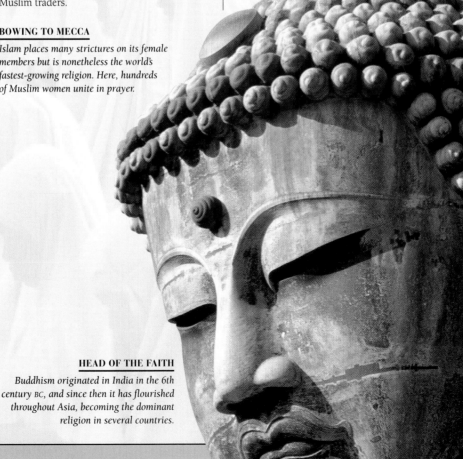

### HEAD OF THE FAITH

*Buddhism originated in India in the 6th century BC, and since then it has flourished throughout Asia, becoming the dominant religion in several countries.*

# TOWN & COUNTRY

# Country Matters

## LARGEST COUNTRIES IN EUROPE

| | COUNTRY | AREA SQ MILES | SQ KM |
|---|---|---|---|
| 1 | **Russia** (in Europe) | 1,818,629 | 4,710,227 |
| 2 | **Ukraine** | 233,090 | 603,700 |
| 3 | **France** | 212,935 | 551,500 |
| 4 | **Spain*** | 194,897 | 504,781 |
| 5 | **Sweden** | 173,732 | 449,964 |
| 6 | **Germany** | 137,735 | 356,733 |
| 7 | **Finland** | 130,559 | 338,145 |
| 8 | **Norway** | 125,050 | 323,877 |
| 9 | **Poland** | 124,808 | 323,250 |
| 10 | **Italy** | 116,320 | 301,268 |

*\* Including offshore islands*

The UK falls just outside the Top 10 at 94,247 sq miles (244,101 sq km). Excluding the Isle of Man and Channel Islands, its area comprises: England (50,351 sq miles/130,410 sq km), Scotland (30,420 sq miles/78,789 sq km), Wales (8,015 sq miles/20,758 sq km), and Northern Ireland (5,461 sq miles1/4,144 sq km).

### SPANISH MAIN STREET

*Spain covers most of the Iberian Peninsula in southwestern Europe. At its center lies Madrid, which has been Spain's capital city since 1561.*

## LARGEST COUNTRIES

| | COUNTRY | AREA SQ MILES | SQ KM | PERCENTAGE OF WORLD TOTAL |
|---|---|---|---|---|
| 1 | **Russia** | 6,590,876 | 17,070,289 | 11.46 |
| 2 | **Canada** | 3,849,670 | 9,970,599 | 6.69 |
| 3 | **US** | 3,717,813 | 9,629,091 | 6.46 |
| 4 | **China** | 3,705,408 | 9,596,961 | 6.44 |
| 5 | **Brazil** | 3,286,488 | 8,511,965 | 5.71 |
| 6 | **Australia** | 2,967,909 | 7,686,848 | 5.16 |
| 7 | **India** | 1,269,346 | 3,287,590 | 2.20 |
| 8 | **Argentina** | 1,068,302 | 2,766,890 | 1.85 |
| 9 | **Kazakhstan** | 1,049,156 | 2,717,300 | 1.82 |
| 10 | **Sudan** | 967,500 | 2,505,813 | 1.68 |
| | *World total* | 57,506,061 | 148,940,000 | 100.00 |

The world's largest countries, the Top 10 of which comprise more than 50 percent of the Earth's land, have undergone substantial revision lately. The breakup of the former Soviet Union has effectively introduced two new countries into the list, with Russia taking preeminent position (since it occupies a vast 76 percent of the area of the old USSR, which it replaces, and, for comparison, is 70 times the size of the UK), while Kazakhstan, which enters in 9th position, ousts Algeria from the bottom of the previous list.

### WESTWARD EXPANSION

*The land area of the United States 200 years ago, at 864,746 sq miles (2,239,682 sq km), was less than a quarter of its present extent.*

## COUNTRIES WITH THE LONGEST COASTLINES

| | COUNTRY | TOTAL COASTLINE LENGTH MILES | KM |
|---|---|---|---|
| 1 | **Canada** | 151,485 | 243,791 |
| 2 | **Indonesia** | 33,999 | 54,716 |
| 3 | **Russia** | 23,396 | 37,653 |
| 4 | **Philippines** | 22,559 | 36,289 |
| 5 | **Japan** | 18,486 | 29,751 |
| 6 | **Australia** | 16,007 | 25,760 |
| 7 | **Norway** | 13,624 | 21,925 |
| 8 | **US** | 12,380 | 19,924 |
| 9 | **New Zealand** | 9,404 | 15,134 |
| 10 | **China** | 9,010 | 14,500 |

Including all of its islands, the coastline of Canada is more than six times as long as the distance around the Earth at the equator (24,902 miles/40,076 km). The coastline of the UK (7,723 miles/12,429 km – greater than the distance from London to Honolulu) puts it in 13th place after Greece (8,498 miles/13,676 km). Were it included as a country, Greenland (27,394 miles/44,087 km) would be in 3rd place.

## TOP 10 ★
# COUNTRIES WITH THE MOST NEIGHBORS

| COUNTRY/NEIGHBORS | NO. |
|---|---|

**1 China** — 15
*Afghanistan, Bhutan, India, Kazakhstan, Kyrgyzstan, Laos, Mongolia, Myanmar (Burma), Nepal, North Korea, Pakistan, Russia, Tajikistan, Thailand, Vietnam*

**2 Russia** — 14
*Azerbaijan, Belarus, China, Estonia, Finland, Georgia, Kazakhstan, Latvia, Lithuania, Mongolia, North Korea, Norway, Poland, Ukraine*

**3 Brazil** — 10
*Argentina, Bolivia, Colombia, French Guiana, Guyana, Paraguay, Peru, Surinam, Uruguay, Venezuela*

**4 =Dem. Rep. of Congo** — 9
*Angola, Burundi, Central African Republic, Congo, Rwanda, Sudan, Tanzania, Uganda, Zambia*

**=Germany** — 9
*Austria, Belgium, Czech Republic, Denmark, France, Luxembourg, Netherlands, Poland, Switzerland*

**=Sudan** — 9
*Central African Republic, Chad, Dem. Rep. of Congo, Egypt, Eritrea, Ethiopia, Kenya, Libya, Uganda*

**7 =Austria** — 8
*Czech Republic, Germany, Hungary, Italy, Liechtenstein, Slovac Republic, Slovenia, Switzerland*

**=France** — 8
*Andorra, Belgium, Germany, Italy, Luxembourg, Monaco, Spain, Switzerland*

**=Saudi Arabia** — 8
*Iraq, Jordan, Kuwait, Oman, People's Democratic Republic of Yemen, Qatar, United Arab Emirates, Yemen Arab Republic*

**=Tanzania** — 8
*Burundi, Dem. Rep. of Congo, Kenya, Malawi, Mozambique, Rwanda, Uganda, Zambia*

**=Turkey** — 8
*Armenia, Azerbaijan, Bulgaria, Georgia, Greece, Iran, Iraq, Syria*

Some countries have more than one discontinuous border with the same country; this has been counted only once. Outside the Top 10, five countries – Mali, Niger, the Ukraine, Zambia, and Yugoslavia – each have seven neighbors. Political changes make this a volatile list: the former Soviet Union had 12 neighbors, but since its breakup Russia has 14, while Eritrea's separation from Ethiopia in 1993 increased Sudan's total.

## TOP 10 ★
# LARGEST LANDLOCKED COUNTRIES

| COUNTRY | AREA | |
|---|---|---|
| | SQ MILES | SQ KM |
| **1** Kazakhstan | 1,049,156 | 2,717,300 |
| **2** Mongolia | 604,829 | 1,566,500 |
| **3** Chad | 495,755 | 1,284,000 |
| **4** Niger | 489,191 | 1,267,000 |
| **5** Mali | 478,841 | 1,240,192 |
| **6** Ethiopia | 426,373 | 1,104,300 |
| **7** Bolivia | 424,165 | 1,098,581 |
| **8** Zambia | 290,587 | 752,618 |
| **9** Afghanistan | 251,773 | 652,090 |
| **10** Central African Republic | 240,535 | 622,984 |

There are more than 40 landlocked countries, although the largest, Kazakhstan, and the 12th largest, Turkmenistan, both have coasts on the Caspian Sea – which is itself landlocked. The largest landlocked state in Europe is Hungary (35,919 sq miles/93,030 sq km). Europe contains the world's smallest landlocked states: Andorra, Liechtenstein, San Marino, and Vatican City.

**MONACO GRAND PRIX**
*An enclave within France, Monaco's wealth, from tourism, gambling, and other sources, is out of proportion to its status as one of the world's smallest sovereign states.*

# TOP 10 SMALLEST COUNTRIES
*(Country/area in sq miles/sq km)*

**1** Vatican City, 0.17/0.44  **2** Monaco, 0.38/1.00  **3** Gibraltar, 2.49/6.47
**4** Nauru, 8.19/21.23  **5** Tuvalu, 10.00/25.90  **6** Bermuda, 20.59/53.35
**7** San Marino, 23.00/59.57  **8** Liechtenstein, 61.00/157.99
**9** Marshall Islands, 70.00/181.00  **10** Antigua, 108.00/279.72

The "country" status of several of these microstates is questionable, since their government, defense, currency, and other features are often intricately linked with those of larger countries – the Vatican City with Italy, and Monaco with France, for example, while Gibraltar and Bermuda are dependent territories of the UK.

## THE FOUNDATION OF SAUDI ARABIA

One of the largest and, through its oil wealth, richest countries in the world, Saudi Arabia has a history that dates back just 100 years. The territory had long been subject to rule by Egypt, the Ottoman Empire, and competing Arab families, with the head of one, Abdul Aziz Bin Abdul Rahman Al-Saud (known in the West as Ibn Saud), living in exile in Kuwait. At the age of just 21, he became the leader of a small group that in 1902 captured the city of Riyadh from the rival Al-Rashid family. This conquest marks the beginning of the formation of the modern state, but it took 30 years to incorporate all the regions into one kingdom, which, in honor of its founder, was named Saudi Arabia. Oil was discovered in 1938, and Ibn Saud ruled until 1953, fathering 45 sons and over 200 daughters.

**100 YEARS AGO**

**Did You Know?** Greenland is part of Danish territory, but if regarded as a country, its 840,004 sq miles (2,175,600 sq km) would make it the 12th largest in the world.

# World & Country Populations

## FASTEST GROWING COUNTRIES

| COUNTRY | ANNUAL GROWTH RATE, 1998–2015 (%) |
|---|---|
| 1 Yemen | 3.4 |
| 2 Oman | 3.2 |
| 3 Niger | 3.0 |
| 4 =Angola | 2.9 |
| =Dem. Rep. of Congo | 2.9 |
| =Saudi Arabia | 2.9 |
| 7 =Burkina Faso | 2.8 |
| =Rwanda | 2.8 |
| =Solomon Islands | 2.8 |
| 10 =Congo | 2.7 |
| =Iraq | 2.7 |
| =Jordan | 2.7 |
| US | 0.7 |

Source: *UN, Human Development Report 2000*

## FASTEST SHRINKING COUNTRIES

| COUNTRY | ANNUAL GROWTH RATE, 1998–2015 (%) |
|---|---|
| 1 =Estonia | -0.9 |
| =Latvia | -0.9 |
| 3 Bulgaria | -0.6 |
| 4 St. Kitts and Nevis | -0.5 |
| 5 =Hungary | -0.4 |
| =Romania | -0.4 |
| =Ukraine | -0.4 |
| 8 =Belarus | -0.3 |
| =Italy | -0.3 |
| =Lithuania | -0.3 |

Source: *UN, Human Development Report 2000*

Many of the countries in the Top 10 are in the former Soviet Union or Eastern Europe. They have a negative population growth rate, which means that their populations are actually shrinking, in some cases at a rate of almost 1 percent a year. This is probably related to the rapid social and economic changes that these countries experienced in the final years of the 20th century.

## COUNTRIES WITH THE YOUNGEST POPULATIONS

| COUNTRY | PERCENTAGE UNDER 15, 2002 |
|---|---|
| 1 Uganda | 50.9 |
| 2 Marshall Islands | 49.1 |
| 3 Dem. Rep. of Congo | 48.2 |
| 4 Niger | 47.9 |
| 5 Chad | 47.8 |
| 6 São Tomé and Principe | 47.7 |
| 7 Burkina Faso | 47.4 |
| 8 Ethiopia | 47.3 |
| 9 Benin | 47.2 |
| 10 =Zambia | 47.1 |
| =Mali | 47.1 |
| UK | 18.7 |

Source: *US Census Bureau International Data Base*

Countries with high proportions of their population under the age of 15 are usually characterized by high birth rates and high death rates.

## COUNTRIES WITH THE OLDEST POPULATIONS

| COUNTRY | PERCENTAGE OVER 65, 2002 |
|---|---|
| 1 Monaco | 22.4 |
| 2 Italy | 18.6 |
| 3 =Greece | 18.0 |
| =Japan | 18.0 |
| 5 Spain | 17,4 |
| 6 Sweden | 17.3 |
| 7 Belgium | 17.1 |
| 8 Germany | 17.0 |
| 9 Bulgaria | 16.9 |
| 10 San Marino | 16.4 |

Source: *US Census Bureau International Data Base*

Nine of the 10 countries with the oldest populations are in Europe, implying that this region has lower death rates and a higher life expectancy than the rest of the world. On average, one in every 6.6 people (15.2 percent) in Europe is over the age of 65.

## COUNTRIES IN WHICH MEN MOST OUTNUMBER WOMEN

| COUNTRY | MEN PER 100 WOMEN (2000) |
|---|---|
| 1 Qatar | 187 |
| 2 United Arab Emirates | 172 |
| 3 Bahrain | 132 |
| 4 Saudi Arabia | 123 |
| 5 Oman | 113 |
| 6 =Cook Islands | 111 |
| =Guam | 111 |
| =Kuwait | 111 |
| 9 =Brunei | 110 |
| =Northern Mariana Islands | 110 |

Source: *United Nations*

The world male/female ratio is balanced virtually 50:50, although in many Western countries male births slightly outnumber female by a very small percentage. There are certain countries, however, where one sex dominates more obviously. No one knows why these imbalances occur, or even if such apparent differentials represent a true picture.

## COUNTRIES IN WHICH WOMEN MOST OUTNUMBER MEN

| COUNTRY | WOMEN PER 100 MEN (2000) |
|---|---|
| 1 Latvia | 120 |
| 2 Ukraine | 115 |
| 3 =Cape Verde | 114 |
| =Russia | 114 |
| 5 =Belarus | 112 |
| =Estonia | 112 |
| =Lithuania | 112 |
| 8 =Georgia | 109 |
| =Hungary | 109 |
| =Moldova | 109 |
| US | 103 |

Source: *United Nations*

## TOP 10 ★
# MOST DENSELY POPULATED COUNTRIES

| | COUNTRY | AREA (SQ MILES) | ESTIMATED POPULATION (2002) | POPULATION PER SQ MILE |
|---|---|---|---|---|
| 1 | Monaco | 0.75 | 31,987 | 42,649.3 |
| 2 | Singapore | 241 | 4,452,732 | 18,476.1 |
| 3 | Malta | 124 | 397,499 | 3,205.6 |
| 4 | Maldives | 116 | 320,165 | 2,760.0 |
| 5 | Bahrain | 239 | 656,397 | 2,746.4 |
| 6 | Bangladesh | 51,703 | 133,376,684 | 2,579.7 |
| 7 | Taiwan | 12,456 | 22,548,009 | 1,810.2 |
| 8 | Mauritius | 714 | 1,196,172 | 1,675.3 |
| 9 | Barbados | 166 | 276,607 | 1,666.3 |
| 10 | Nauru | 8 | 12,329 | 1,541.1 |
| | US | 3,539,245 | 280,562,489 | 79.3 |
| | World | 50,580,568 | 6,234,250,387 | 123.1 |

Source: *US Census Bureau International Data Base*

## TOP 10 ★
# MOST HIGHLY POPULATED COUNTRIES

| | COUNTRY | 1980 | 1990 | 2000* |
|---|---|---|---|---|
| 1 | China | 984,736,000 | 1,138,895,000 | 1,256,168,000 |
| 2 | India | 690,462,000 | 850,558,000 | 1,017,645,000 |
| 3 | US | 227,726,000 | 249,949,000 | 274,943,000 |
| 4 | Indonesia | 154,936,000 | 187,728,000 | 219,267,000 |
| 5 | Brazil | 122,936,000 | 151,040,000 | 173,791,000 |
| 6 | Russia | 139,045,000 | 148,088,000 | 145,905,000 |
| 7 | Pakistan | 85,219,000 | 113,914,000 | 141,145,000 |
| 8 | Bangladesh | 88,077,000 | 110,118,000 | 129,147,000 |
| 9 | Japan | 116,807,000 | 123,537,000 | 126,434,000 |
| 10 | Nigeria | 65,699,000 | 86,530,000 | 117,171,000 |
| | World | 4,453,778,000 | 5,276,992,000 | 6,073,099,000 |

* Estimated

Source: *US Census Bureau*

According to estimates prepared by the US Census Bureau, the world entered the 21st century with a total population topping 6 billion. In 1999, India joined China as the second country to achieve a population in excess of 1 billion, while Mexico ascended to the 100-million-plus club in 11th place, with a population of 102,027,000. In contrast, the populations of certain countries, such as Russia and (in 22nd place in the world) Italy, actually declined during the 1990s as their birth rates fell.

## TOP 10 ★
# MOST POPULOUS ISLAND COUNTRIES

| | ISLAND COUNTRY | POPULATION PER SQ MILE | POPULATION PER SQ KM | POPULATION |
|---|---|---|---|---|
| 1 | Indonesia | 305.6 | 118.0 | 224,784,210 |
| 2 | Japan | 879.1 | 339.4 | 126,549,976 |
| 3 | Philippines | 700.6 | 270.5 | 81,159,644 |
| 4 | UK | 631.4 | 243.7 | 59,508,382 |
| 5 | Taiwan | 1,608.0 | 620.8 | 22,191,087 |
| 6 | Sri Lanka | 759.4 | 293.2 | 19,238,575 |
| 7 | Madagascar | 68.4 | 26.4 | 15,506,472 |
| 8 | Cuba | 260.3 | 100.5 | 11,141,997 |
| 9 | Dominican Republic | 448.6 | 173.2 | 8,442,533 |
| 10 | Haiti | 641.0 | 247.4 | 6,867,995 |

## TOP 10 ★
# LEAST DENSELY POPULATED COUNTRIES

| | COUNTRY | AREA (SQ MILES) | ESTIMATED POPULATION (2002) | POPULATION PER SQ MILE |
|---|---|---|---|---|
| 1 | Mongolia | 604,250 | 2,694,432 | 4.5 |
| 2 | Namibia | 317,874 | 1,820,916 | 5.7 |
| 3 | Australia | 2,941,300 | 19,546,792 | 6.6 |
| 4 =| Botswana | 226,013 | 1,591,232 | 7.0 |
| = | Surinam | 62,344 | 436,494 | 7.0 |
| 6 | Mauritania | 397,840 | 2,828,858 | 7.1 |
| 7 | Iceland | 38,707 | 279,384 | 7.2 |
| 8 | Libya | 679,362 | 5,368,585 | 7.9 |
| 9 =| Canada | 3,560,237 | 31,902,268 | 9.0 |
| = | Guyana | 76,004 | 698,209 | 9.2 |

Source: *US Census Bureau International Data Base*

# TOP 10 MOST HIGHLY POPULATED COUNTRIES 100 YEARS AGO
*(Country/population)*

**1** China, 372,563,000 **2** India, 287,223,431 **3** Russia, 147,277,000 **4** US, 76,356,000 **5** Germany, 56,345,014 **6** Austro-Hungarian Empire, 47,013,835 **7** Japan, 43,759,577 **8** UK, 41,605,220 **9** France, 38,641,333 **10** Italy, 32,100,000

The extensive Austro-Hungarian Empire included all its territories in its census, the largest being Austria, with a population of 26,150,708.

**Did You Know?** China has led the world as the most highly populated country since ancient times: as early as 1393 a figure of 60 million was recorded.

# Future Shock

## TOP 10 ★
## MOST POPULATED COUNTRIES IN EUROPE IN 2050

| COUNTRY | EST. POPULATION IN 2050 |
|---|---|
| 1 Russia (including in Asia) | 118,233,243 |
| 2 Germany | 79,702,511 |
| 3 France | 58,967,418 |
| 4 UK | 58,210,627 |
| 5 Italy | 45,016,465 |
| 6 Ukraine | 37,726,401 |
| 7 Poland | 33,779,568 |
| 8 Spain | 32,562,163 |
| 9 Romania | 18,340,400 |
| 10 Netherlands | 16,721,036 |

Source: US Census Bureau, International Data Base

## THE 10 ★
## DECADES OF WORLD POPULATION, 1960–2050

| YEAR | WORLD POPULATION |
|---|---|
| 1960 | 3,039,332,401 |
| 1970 | 3,707,610,112 |
| 1980 | 4,456,705,217 |
| 1990 | 5,283,755,345 |
| 2000 | 6,080,141,683 |
| 2010 | 6,823,634,553 |
| 2020 | 7,518,010,600 |
| 2030 | 8,140,344,240 |
| 2040 | 8,668,391,454 |
| 2050 | 9,104,205,830 |

Source: US Census Bureau, International Data Base

## TOP 10 ★
## MOST POPULATED METROPOLITAN AREAS IN THE US IN 2010

| METRO AREA*/STATE | ESTIMATED POPULATION IN 2010 |
|---|---|
| 1 New York, New York | 8,635,700 |
| 2 Chicago, Illinois | 8,626,300 |
| 3 Philadelphia, Pennsylvania | 5,396,200 |
| 4 Houston, Texas | 4,491,500 |
| 5 Detroit, Michigan | 4,408,000 |
| 6 Atlanta, Georgia | 4,231,300 |
| 7 Riverside–San Bernardino, California | 4,130,200 |
| 8 Los Angeles–Long Beach, California | 3,597,556 |
| 9 Dallas, Texas | 3,538,100 |
| 10 San Diego, California | 3,434,900 |

* Primary and Metropolitan Statistical Areas only, hence not comparable to city populations

Source: US Bureau of Economic Analysis

The greatest population increases in the coming decade – in some instances approaching a million new inhabitants – are focused in the "sun belt," with major northern centers of population experiencing relatively slower growth.

## TOP 10 MOST POPULATED US STATES IN 2025

(State/estimated population in 2025)

**1** California, 49,285,000 **2** Texas, 27,183,000 **3** Florida, 20,710,000 **4** New York, 19,830,000 **5** Illinois, 13,440,000 **6** Pennsylvania, 12,683,000 **7** Ohio, 11,744,000 **8** Michigan, 10,078,000 **9** Georgia, 9,869,000 **10** New Jersey, 9,558,000

Source: US Census Bureau

## TOP 10 ★
## MOST POPULATED WORLD CITIES IN 2015

| CITY | COUNTRY | % GROWTH 2000–15 | ESTIMATED POPULATION IN 2015 |
|---|---|---|---|
| 1 Tokyo | Japan | 0.0 | 26,400,000 |
| 2 Bombay | India | 2.4 | 26,100,000 |
| 3 Lagos | Nigeria | 3.7 | 23,200,000 |
| 4 Dhaka | Bangladesh | 3.6 | 21,100,000 |
| 5 São Paulo | Brazil | 0.9 | 20,400,000 |
| 6 =Karachi | Pakistan | 3.2 | 19,200,000 |
| =Mexico City | Mexico | 0.4 | 19,200,000 |
| 8 New York | US | 0.3 | 17,400,000 |
| 9 =Calcutta | India | 1.9 | 17,300,000 |
| =Jakarta | Indonesia | 3.0 | 17,300,000 |

Source: United Nations, World Urbanization Prospects: The 1999 Revision

## TOP 10 ★
## FASTEST-GROWING CITIES*

| CITY | COUNTRY | INCREASE (%) 1975–95 | ESTIMATED INCREASE (%) 1995–2010 |
|---|---|---|---|
| 1 Hangzhou | China | 283.5 | 171.1 |
| 2 Addis Ababa | Ethiopia | 161.6 | 170.7 |
| 3 Kabul | Afghanistan | 200.9 | 156.3 |
| 4 Handan | China | 245.9 | 141.6 |
| 5 Isfahan | Iran | 150.9 | 141.3 |
| 6 Maputo | Mozambique | 318.6 | 139.9 |
| 7 Lagos | Nigeria | 211.7 | 139.5 |
| 8 Luanda | Angola | 210.9 | 138.8 |
| 9 Nairobi | Kenya | 167.4 | 133.6 |
| 10 Qingdao | China | 183.8 | 132.4 |

* Urban agglomerations of over 1 million population only

Source: United Nations

**TEEMING MILLIONS**
*China began the 20th century with a population of some 400 million and ended it with 1.2 billion – about one-fifth of the world's population.*

## TOP 10 ★

# MOST POPULATED COUNTRIES IN 2005

| | COUNTRY | ESTIMATED POPULATION IN 2005 |
|---|---|---|
| 1 | China | 1,315,507,068 |
| 2 | India | 1,092,502,123 |
| 3 | US | 287,972,263 |
| 4 | Indonesia | 242,799,696 |
| 5 | Brazil | 180,395,927 |
| 6 | Pakistan | 156,689,148 |
| 7 | Russia | 143,736,793 |
| 8 | Bangladesh | 139,794,159 |
| 9 | Nigeria | 139,779,647 |
| 10 | Japan | 127,404,212 |
| | *UK* | *60,129,050* |

Source: *US Census Bureau, International Data Base*
China and India entered the 21st century as the first countries ever with billion-plus populations.

## TOP 10 ★

# MOST POPULATED COUNTRIES IN 2025

| | COUNTRY | ESTIMATED POPULATION IN 2025 |
|---|---|---|
| 1 | China | 1,464,028,860 |
| 2 | India | 1,377,264,176 |
| 3 | US | 338,070,951 |
| 4 | Indonesia | 301,461,556 |
| 5 | Pakistan | 213,338,252 |
| 6 | Nigeria | 204,453,333 |
| 7 | Brazil | 200,606,553 |
| 8 | Bangladesh | 177,499,122 |
| 9 | Russia | 135,951,626 |
| 10 | Mexico | 133,834,712 |
| | *UK* | *60,613,482* |

Source: *US Census Bureau, International Data Base*
In a single generation (2000–25), Nigeria's population is set to increase by almost 75 percent.

## TOP 10 ★

# MOST POPULATED COUNTRIES IN 2050

| | COUNTRY | ESTIMATED POPULATION IN 2050 |
|---|---|---|
| 1 | India | 1,619,582,271 |
| 2 | China | 1,470,468,924 |
| 3 | US | 403,943,147 |
| 4 | Indonesia | 337,807,011 |
| 5 | Nigeria | 303,586,770 |
| 6 | Pakistan | 267,813,495 |
| 7 | Brazil | 206,751,477 |
| 8 | Bangladesh | 205,093,861 |
| 9 | Ethiopia | 187,892,174 |
| 10 | Dem. Rep. of Congo | 181,922,656 |
| | *UK* | *58,210,627* |

Source: *US Census Bureau, International Data Base*
Estimates of populations in 2050 present a striking change: China should be eclipsed by India in 2036.

**Which country has the longest coastline?**
*see p.80 for the answer*
A Russia
B Canada
C USA

# Parks & Reserves

## THE 10 FIRST UNESCO HERITAGE SITES IN THE US

*(Site/year)*

**1** = Mesa Verde National Park, Colorado, 1978; = Yellowstone National Park, Wyoming/Idaho/Montana, 1978 **3** = Everglades National Park, Florida, 1979; = Grand Canyon National Park, Arizona, 1979; = Independence Hall, Pennsylvania, 1979 **6** Redwood National Park, California, 1980 **7** = Mammoth Cave National Park, Kentucky, 1981; = Olympic National Park, Washington State, 1981 **9** Cahokia Mounds State Historic Site, Illinois, 1982 **10** Great Smoky Mountains National Park, North Carolina/Tennessee, 1983

## THE 10 ★ FIRST NATIONAL MONUMENTS IN THE US

| NATIONAL MONUMENT/LOCATION | ESTABLISHED |
|---|---|
| 1 Little Big Horn Battlefield, Montana | Jan 29, 1879 |
| 2 Casa Grande Ruins, Arizona | Mar 2, 1889 |
| 3 Devils Tower, Wyoming | Sep 24, 1906 |
| 4 =El Morro, New Mexico | Dec 8, 1906 |
| =Montezuma Castle, Arizona | Dec 8, 1906 |
| 6 Gila Cliff Dwellings, New Mexico | Nov 16, 1907 |
| 7 Tonto, Arizona | Dec 19, 1907 |
| 8 Muir Woods, California | Jan 9, 1908 |
| 9 Grand Canyon, Arizona | Jan 11, 1908 |
| 10 Pinnacles, California | Jan 16, 1908 |

There are some 73 national monuments in the US, covering a total of 2,064,446 acres. Some sites were identified as of special historical importance earlier than those in the Top 10 but were not officially designated as national monuments until later dates, among them the Custer Battlefield, Montana (the site of the Battle of Little Big Horn).

## THE 10 ★ FIRST NATIONAL MEMORIALS IN THE US

| NATIONAL MEMORIAL/LOCATION | ESTABLISHED |
|---|---|
| 1 Washington Monument, Washington, DC | Jan 31, 1848 |
| 2 Lincoln Memorial, Washington, DC | Feb 9, 1911 |
| 3 Mount Rushmore, South Dakota | Mar 3, 1925 |
| 4 Arlington House, The Robert E. Lee Memorial, Virginia | Mar 4, 1925 |
| 5 Wright Brothers, North Carolina | Mar 2, 1927 |
| 6 Theodore Roosevelt Island, Washington, DC | May 21, 1932 |
| 7 Thomas Jefferson Memorial, Washington, DC | June 26, 1934 |
| 8 Perry's Victory and International Peace Memorial, Ohio | June 2, 1936 |
| 9 Federal Hall, New York | May 26, 1939 |
| 10 Coronado, Arizona | Aug 18, 1941 |

## TOP 10 ★ MOST VISITED NATIONAL PARKS IN THE US

| NATIONAL PARK/LOCATION | VISITORS (1999) |
|---|---|
| 1 Great Smoky Mountains National Park, North Carolina/Tennessee | 10,467,875 |
| 2 Grand Canyon National Park, Arizona | 4,493,629 |
| 3 Olympic National Park, Washington | 3,736,214 |
| 4 Yosemite National Park, California | 3,589,245 |
| 5 Rocky Mountain National Park, Colorado | 3,020,589 |
| 6 Yellowstone National Park, Wyoming | 3,012,969 |
| 7 Grand Teton National Park, Wyoming | 2,792,336 |
| 8 Acadia National Park, Maine | 2,627,879 |
| 9 Zion National Park, Utah | 2,467,041 |
| 10 Mammoth Cave, Kentucky | 2,071,844 |

## THE 10 ★ FIRST NATIONAL PARKS IN THE US

| NATIONAL PARK/LOCATION | ESTABLISHED |
|---|---|
| 1 Yellowstone, Wyoming/Montana/Idaho | Mar 1, 1872 |
| 2 Sequoia, California | Sep 25, 1890 |
| 3 =Yosemite, California | Oct 1, 1890 |
| =General Grant, California* | Oct 1, 1890 |
| 5 Mount Rainier, Washington | Mar 2, 1899 |
| 6 Crater Lake, Oregon | May 22, 1902 |
| 7 Wind Cave, South Dakota | Jan 9, 1903 |
| 8 Mesa Verde, Colorado | June 29, 1906 |
| 9 Glacier, Montana | May 11, 1910 |
| 10 Rocky Mountain, Colorado | Jan 26, 1915 |

*\* Name changed to Kings Canyon National Park on Mar 4, 1940*

Several other national parks may claim a place in this list by virtue of having been founded under different appellations (such as a public park or a national monument) at earlier dates.

### CRATER LAKE BECOMES A NATIONAL PARK

According to Native American legend, the collapse of Mount Mazama and the creation of Crater Lake, Oregon, resulted from a battle between rival chiefs: Llao of the Below World and Skell of the Above World. Revered as a sacred place, it lay undiscovered by outsiders until 1853, when three gold prospectors, John Wesley Hillman, Henry Klippel, and Isaac Skeeters, stumbled upon it, naming it Deep Blue Lake. In 1886, it was explored by Captain Clarence Dutton, who carried the survey ship *Cleetwood* overland and took soundings that established the lake to be the world's sixth deepest. Crater Lake became a popular tourist attraction and, following the efforts of William Gladstone Steel, who named many of its features, achieved national park status on May 22, 1902.

*100 YEARS AGO • YEARS AGO • YEARS AGO • YEARS*

# TOP 10 ★
## LARGEST NATIONAL PARKS IN THE US

| | NATIONAL PARK/LOCATION | ESTABLISHED | ACREAGE |
|---|---|---|---|
| 1 | **Wrangell-St. Elias**, Alaska | Dec 2, 1980 | 8,323,618 |
| 2 | **Gates of the Arctic**, Alaska | Dec 2, 1980 | 7,523,898 |
| 3 | **Denali** (formerly Mt. McKinley), Alaska | Feb 26, 1917 | 4,740,912 |
| 4 | **Katmai**, Alaska | Dec 2, 1980 | 3,674,530 |
| 5 | **Death Valley**, California/Nevada | Oct 31, 1994 | 3,286,242 |
| 6 | **Glacier Bay**, Alaska | Dec 2, 1980 | 3,224,840 |
| 7 | **Lake Clark**, Alaska | Dec 2, 1980 | 2,619,733 |
| 8 | **Yellowstone**, Wyoming/Montana/Idaho | Mar 1, 1872 | 2,219,791 |
| 9 | **Kobuk Valley**, Alaska | Dec 2, 1980 | 1,750,737 |
| 10 | **Everglades**, Florida | May 30, 1934 | 1,508,571* |

*\* Includes Everglades Expansion*

Source: *Land Resources Division, Washington, D.C.*

Yellowstone National Park was established as the first national park in the world with its role "as a public park or pleasuring ground for the benefit and enjoyment of the people." There are now some 1,200 national parks in more than 100 countries. There are 54 national parks in the US, with a total area of 51,914,773 acres (more than double their area before 1980, when large tracts of Alaska were added). With the addition of various national monuments, national historic parks, national preserves, and other specially designated areas, the total area is 84,327,466 acres

# TOP 10 ★
## COUNTRIES WITH THE LARGEST PROTECTED AREAS

| | COUNTRY | PERCENTAGE OF TOTAL AREA | DESIGNATED AREA SQ MILES | SQ KM |
|---|---|---|---|---|
| 1 | US | 24.9 | 902,091 | 2,336,406 |
| 2 | Australia | 13.4 | 395,911 | 1,025,405 |
| 3 | Greenland | 45.2 | 379,345 | 982,500 |
| 4 | Canada | 9.3 | 357,231 | 925,226 |
| 5 | Saudi Arabia | 34.4 | 318,811 | 825,717 |
| 6 | China | 7.1 | 263,480 | 682,410 |
| 7 | Venezuela | 61.7 | 217,397 | 563,056 |
| 8 | Brazil | 6.6 | 215,312 | 557,656 |
| 9 | Russia | 3.1 | 204,273 | 529,067 |
| 10 | Indonesia | 18.6 | 138,002 | 357,425 |

"Protected Areas" encompass national parks, nature reserves, national monuments, and other sites. There are at least 44,300 protected areas around the world, covering more than 10 percent of the total land area. In the case of some islands, such as Easter Island, almost 100 percent of the land is designated a protected area.

**JOSHUA TREE NATIONAL PARK**
*Over 20 percent of the US land area is protected. National parks, such as that of the Biosphere Reserve of Joshua Tree National Monument in the Californian desert, comprise some 80 percent of the total.*

---

**What is the name of the legendary character associated with two of the world's longest place names?**
*see p.93 for the answer*

A  Tannhäuser
B  Tamberlane
C  Tamatea

# World Cities

## TOP 10 ★

## LARGEST NONCAPITAL CITIES

| | CITY/COUNTRY/CAPITAL CITY | POPULATIONS* |
|---|---|---|
| 1 | **Bombay**, India <br> *New Delhi* | 15,138,000 <br> *8,419,000* |
| 2 | **Shanghai**, China <br> *Beijing* | 13,584,000 <br> *11,299,000* |
| 3 | **Calcutta**#, India <br> *New Delhi* | 11,923,000 <br> *8,419,000* |
| 4 | **Lagos**#, Nigeria <br> *Abuja* | 10,287,000 <br> *378,671* |
| 5 | **São Paulo**, Brazil <br> *Brasília* | 10,017,821 <br> *1,864,000* |
| 6 | **Karachi**#, Pakistan <br> *Islamabad* | 9,733,000 <br> *350,000* |
| 7 | **Tianjin**, China <br> *Beijing* | 9,415,000 <br> *11,299,000* |
| 8 | **Istanbul**#, Turkey <br> *Ankara* | 8,274,921 <br> *2,937,524* |
| 9 | **New York**, US <br> *Washington, DC* | 7,420,166 <br> *523,124* |
| 10 | **Madras**, India <br> *New Delhi* | 6,002,000 <br> *8,419,000* |

\* Based on comparison of population within administrative boundaries

\# Former capital

## TOP 10 ★

## MOST CROWDED CITIES

| | CITY/COUNTRY | AVERAGE FLOOR SPACE PER PERSON* | |
|---|---|---|---|
| | | SQ FT | SQ M |
| 1 = | **Lahore**, Pakistan | 12.9 | 1.2 |
| = | **Tangail**, Bangladesh | 12.9 | 1.2 |
| 3 | **Bhiwandi**, India | 25.8 | 2.4 |
| 4 | **Dhaka**, Bangladesh | 29.1 | 2.7 |
| 5 | **Kano**, Nigeria | 30.1 | 2.8 |
| 6 | **Bamako**, Mali | 34.4 | 3.2 |
| 7 | **Bombay**, India | 37.7 | 3.5 |
| 8 = | **Mwanza**, Tanzania | 43.1 | 4.0 |
| = | **Kampala**, Uganda | 43.1 | 4.0 |
| = | **Sana'a**, Yemen | 43.1 | 4.0 |

\* In those countries for which data available

Source: *World Bank*, World Development Indicators 2000

## TOP 10 ★

## MOST DECLINED CITIES

| | CITY/COUNTRY | PEAK | LATEST | % DECLINE FROM PEAK |
|---|---|---|---|---|
| 1 | **St. Louis**, US | 875,000 | 334,000 | -61.0 |
| 2 | **Pittsburgh**, US | 677,000 | 341,000 | -49.6 |
| 3 | **Buffalo**, US | 580,000 | 301,000 | -48.1 |
| 4 | **Detroit**, US | 1,850,000 | 970,000 | -47.6 |
| 5 | **Manchester**, UK | 766,000 | 403,000 | -47.4 |
| 6 | **Cleveland**, US | 915,000 | 496,000 | -45.8 |
| 7 | **Liverpool**, UK | 857,000 | 479,000 | -44.1 |
| 8 | **Copenhagen**, Denmark | 768,000 | 456,000 | -39.5 |
| 9 | **Newark**, US | 442,000 | 268,000 | -39.4 |
| 10 | **Glasgow**, UK | 1,088,000 | 681,000 | -37.4 |

## THE 10 FIRST CITIES WITH POPULATIONS OF MORE THAN ONE MILLION

*(City/country)*

**1** Rome, Italy **2** Alexandria, Egypt
**3** Angkor, Cambodia **4** Hangchow, China
**5** London, UK **6** Paris, France
**7** Peking, China **8** Canton, China
**9** Berlin, Prussia **10** New York, US

Rome's population is believed to have exceeded 1 million some time in the 2nd century BC. Alexandria was soon after.

In its first 10 years, how many times was the Empire State Building struck by lightning?

*see p.95 for the answer*

A None
B 68
C 1,002

## TOP 10 ★
# HIGHEST CITIES

| | CITY/COUNTRY | HEIGHT FT | M |
|---|---|---|---|
| 1 | **Wenchuan**, China | 16,730 | 5,099 |
| 2 | **Potosí**, Bolivia | 13,045 | 3,976 |
| 3 | **Oruro**, Bolivia | 12,146 | 3,702 |
| 4 | **Lhasa**, Tibet | 12,087 | 3,684 |
| 5 | **La Paz**, Bolivia | 11,916 | 3,632 |
| 6 | **Cuzco**, Peru | 11,152 | 3,399 |
| 7 | **Huancayo**, Peru | 10,660 | 3,249 |
| 8 | **Sucre**, Bolivia | 9,301 | 2,835 |
| 9 | **Tunja**, Colombia | 9,252 | 2,820 |
| 10 | **Quito**, Ecuador | 9,249 | 2,819 |

Lhasa was formerly the highest capital city in the world, a role now occupied by La Paz, the capital of Bolivia. Wenchuan is situated at more than half the elevation of Everest, and even the cities at the bottom of this list are more than one-third as high as Everest.

## TOP 10 ★
# LARGEST CITIES IN THE US*

| | CITY/STATE | POPULATION |
|---|---|---|
| 1 | **New York**, New York | 7,420,166 |
| 2 | **Los Angeles**, California | 3,597,556 |
| 3 | **Chicago**, Illinois | 2,802,079 |
| 4 | **Houston**, Texas | 1,786,691 |
| 5 | **Philadelphia**, Pennsylvania | 1,436,287 |
| 6 | **San Diego**, California | 1,220,666 |
| 7 | **Phoenix**, Arizona | 1,198,064 |
| 8 | **San Antonio**, Texas | 1,114,130 |
| 9 | **Dallas**, Texas | 1,075,894 |
| 10 | **Detroit**, Michigan | 970,196 |

*\* Estimated figures up to July 1, 1998*

Source: *US Bureau of the Census*

These are estimates for central city areas only, not for the total metropolitan areas that surround them, which may be several times as large. In 1996, for the first time, all the cities in the Top 10 had populations of more than 1 million; but in 1998 the population of Detroit declined to just below that figure. The population of Philadelphia also fell. In recent years there has been a general shift toward the southern and western "sun belt" states.

## TOP 10 ★
# MOST URBANIZED COUNTRIES

| | COUNTRY | % OF POPULATION LIVING IN URBAN AREAS, 1998 |
|---|---|---|
| 1 | **Singapore** | 100.0 |
| 2 | **Kuwait** | 97.4 |
| 3 | **Belgium** | 97.2 |
| 4 | **Qatar** | 92.1 |
| 5 | **Iceland** | 92.0 |
| 6 | **Uruguay** | 90.9 |
| 7 | **Luxembourg** | 90.4 |
| 8 | **Malta** | 90.1 |
| 9 = | **Argentina** | 88.9 |
| | **=Lebanon** | 88.9 |

Source: *UN, Human Development Report 2000*

The last few decades have brought about a world that is far more urbanized, with a much higher proportion of the world's population living in large cities and metropolitan areas. There are also tens of millions of "rural-urban dwellers," who live in rural settlements but work in urban areas.

## TOP 10 ★
# LEAST URBANIZED COUNTRIES

| | COUNTRY | % OF POPULATION LIVING IN URBAN AREAS, 1998 |
|---|---|---|
| 1 | **Rwanda** | 5.9 |
| 2 | **Bhutan** | 6.7 |
| 3 | **Burundi** | 8.4 |
| 4 | **Nepal** | 11.2 |
| 5 | **Uganda** | 13.5 |
| 6 | **Malawi** | 14.6 |
| 7 | **Ethiopia** | 16.7 |
| 8 | **Papua New Guinea** | 16.8 |
| 9 | **Burkino Faso** | 17.4 |
| 10 | **Eritrea** | 18.0 |

Source: *United Nations*

**CAPITAL CITY**

*Paris grew from 2.7 million at the turn of the 20th century to just over 10 million in 2000, making it Europe's third largest city.*

## TOP 10 ★
# LARGEST CITIES IN EUROPE, 2000

| | CITY/COUNTRY | EST. POPULATION, 2000* |
|---|---|---|
| 1 | **Moscow**, Russia | 13,200,000 |
| 2 | **London**, UK | 11,800,000 |
| 3 | **Paris**, France | 10,150,000 |
| 4 | **Essen**, Germany | 6,050,000 |
| 5 | **St. Petersburg**, Russia | 5,550,000 |
| 6 | **Madrid**, Spain | 5,050,000 |
| 7 | **Barcelona**, Spain | 4,200,000 |
| 8 | **Berlin**, Germany | 4,150,000 |
| 9 | **Milan**, Italy | 3,800,000 |
| 10 | **Athens**, Greece | 3,500,000 |

*\* Of urban agglomeration*

Source: *Th. Brinkhoff: Principal Agglomerations and Cities of the World, www.citypopulation.de, 4.6.00*

# States of the US

## MOST DENSELY POPULATED STATES IN THE US

| | STATE | POPULATION PER SQ MILE OF LAND AREA* |
|---|---|---|
| 1 | New Jersey | 1,134.2 |
| 2 | Rhode Island | 1,003.2 |
| 3 | Massachusetts | 810.0 |
| 4 | Connecticut | 702.9 |
| 5 | Maryland | 541.8 |
| 6 | New York | 401.8 |
| 7 | Delaware | 400.8 |
| 8 | Florida | 296.3 |
| 9 | Ohio | 277.2 |
| 10 | Pennsylvania | 274.0 |

* Based on 2000 Census

Source: *US Census Bureau*

Population densities of the states have increased dramatically over the past 200 years: that of New Jersey, for example, was 250.7 per square mile in 1900, and just 28.1 in 1800. Most remarkably, in 1900 Florida had a density of only 9.6, while Ohio's in 1800 was a sparse 1.1.

## LEAST DENSELY POPULATED STATES IN THE US

| | STATE | POPULATION PER SQ MILE OF LAND AREA* |
|---|---|---|
| 1 | Alaska | 1.1 |
| 2 | Wyoming | 5.1 |
| 3 | Montana | 6.2 |
| 4 | North Dakota | 9.3 |
| 5 | South Dakota | 10.0 |
| 6 | New Mexico | 15.0 |
| 7 | Idaho | 15.6 |
| 8 | Nevada | 18.2 |
| 9 | Nebraska | 22.3 |
| 10 | Utah | 27.2 |

* Based on 2000 Census

Source: *US Census Bureau*

## LARGEST STATES IN THE US

| | STATE | LAND AREA SQ MILES | LAND AREA SQ KM |
|---|---|---|---|
| 1 | Alaska | 570,374 | 1,477,262 |
| 2 | Texas | 261,914 | 678,354 |
| 3 | California | 155,973 | 403,968 |
| 4 | Montana | 145,556 | 376,988 |
| 5 | New Mexico | 121,364 | 314,331 |
| 6 | Arizona | 113,642 | 294,331 |
| 7 | Nevada | 109,806 | 284,396 |
| 8 | Colorado | 103,729 | 268,657 |
| 9 | Wyoming | 97,105 | 251,501 |
| 10 | Oregon | 96,002 | 248,644 |

The total land area of the US has grown progressively: in 1800 it was 867,980 sq miles (2,248,058 sq km), and in 1900 2,974,159 sq miles (7,703,036 sq km). The admission of Alaska to the Union on January 3 and Hawaii on August 20, 1959, increased the total by almost 20 percent.

## SMALLEST STATES IN THE US

| | STATE | LAND AREA SQ MILES | LAND AREA SQ KM |
|---|---|---|---|
| 1 | Rhode Island | 1,045 | 2,706 |
| 2 | Delaware | 1,955 | 5,063 |
| 3 | Connecticut | 4,845 | 12,548 |
| 4 | Hawaii | 6,423 | 16,635 |
| 5 | New Jersey | 7,419 | 19,215 |
| 6 | Massachusetts | 7,838 | 20,300 |
| 7 | New Hampshire | 8,969 | 23,229 |
| 8 | Vermont | 9,249 | 23,955 |
| 9 | Maryland | 9,775 | 25,317 |
| 10 | West Virginia | 24,087 | 62,385 |

## MOST HIGHLY POPULATED STATES IN THE US

| | STATE | POPULATION 1900 | POPULATION 2000 |
|---|---|---|---|
| 1 | California | 1,485,053 | 33,871,648 |
| 2 | Texas | 3,048,710 | 20,851,820 |
| 3 | New York | 7,268,894 | 18,976,457 |
| 4 | Florida | 528,542 | 15,982,378 |
| 5 | Illinois | 4,821,550 | 12,419,293 |
| 6 | Pennsylvania | 6,302,115 | 12,281,054 |
| 7 | Ohio | 4,157,545 | 11,353,140 |
| 8 | Michigan | 2,420,982 | 9,938,444 |
| 9 | New Jersey | 1,883,669 | 8,414,350 |
| 10 | Georgia | 2,216,231 | 8,186,453 |

Source: *US Census Bureau*

The total population of the US according to the 1900 Census was 76,212,168, compared to the preliminary results of the April 1, 2000 Census, which put the total at 281,421,906.

## LEAST POPULATED STATES IN THE US

| | STATE | POPULATION (2000) |
|---|---|---|
| 1 | Wyoming | 493,782 |
| 2 | Vermont | 608,827 |
| 3 | Alaska | 626,932 |
| 4 | North Dakota | 642,200 |
| 5 | South Dakota | 754,844 |
| 6 | Delaware | 783,600 |
| 7 | Montana | 902,195 |
| 8 | Rhode Island | 1,048,319 |
| 9 | Hawaii | 1,211,537 |
| 10 | New Hampshire | 1,235,786 |

Source: *US Census Bureau*

## TOP 10 US STATES WITH THE MOST COUNTIES

*(State/counties)*

**1** Texas, 254 **2** Georgia, 159 **3** Kentucky, 120 **4** Missouri, 114 **5** Kansas, 105 **6** Illinois, 102 **7** North Carolina, 100 **8** Iowa, 99 **9** = Tennessee, 95; = Virginia, 95

## TOP 10 ⭐
# US STATES WITH THE LONGEST SHORELINES

| | STATE | SHORELINE MILES | KM |
|---|---|---|---|
| 1 | Alaska | 33,904 | 54,563 |
| 2 | Florida | 8,426 | 13,560 |
| 3 | Louisiana | 7,721 | 12,426 |
| 4 | Maine | 3,478 | 5,597 |
| 5 | California | 3,427 | 5,515 |
| 6 | North Carolina | 3,375 | 5,432 |
| 7 | Texas | 3,359 | 5,406 |
| 8 | Virginia | 3,315 | 5,335 |
| 9 | Maryland | 3,190 | 5,134 |
| 10 | Washington | 3,026 | 4,870 |

Pennsylvania's 89-mile (143-km) shoreline is the shortest among states that have one – 26 states, plus the District of Columbia, have no shoreline at all.

## TOP 10 ⭐
# US STATES WITH THE GREATEST AREAS OF INLAND WATER

| | STATE | SQ MILES | SQ KM |
|---|---|---|---|
| 1 | Alaska | 44,856 | 116,177 |
| 2 | Michigan | 39,895 | 103,328 |
| 3 | Wisconsin | 11,186 | 28,972 |
| 4 | Minnesota | 7,326 | 18,974 |
| 5 | New York | 6,766 | 17,524 |
| 6 | Louisiana | 6,085 | 15,760 |
| 7 | Florida | 5,991 | 15,571 |
| 8 | Texas | 5,363 | 13,890 |
| 9 | Washington | 4,055 | 10,502 |
| 10 | North Carolina | 3,954 | 10,241 |

Areas include those of rivers, lakes, and other inland water, as well as coastal waters, but exclude territorial water. A further seven states have totals of more than 2,000 sq miles (5,180 sq km), and 12 have over 1,000 sq miles (2,590 sq km), while at the other end of the scale, states with the least are Hawaii (36 sq miles/93 sq km) and West Virginia (145 sq miles/376 sq km). The Great Lakes within the US comprise some 60,052 sq miles (1,000,867 sq km).

## THE 10 ⭐
# FIRST STATES OF THE US

| | STATE | ENTERED UNION |
|---|---|---|
| 1 | Delaware | Dec 7, 1787 |
| 2 | Pennsylvania | Dec 12, 1787 |
| 3 | New Jersey | Dec 18, 1787 |
| 4 | Georgia | Jan 2, 1788 |
| 5 | Connecticut | Jan 9, 1788 |
| 6 | Massachusetts | Feb 6, 1788 |
| 7 | Maryland | Apr 28, 1788 |
| 8 | South Carolina | May 23, 1788 |
| 9 | New Hampshire | June 21, 1788 |
| 10 | Virginia | June 25, 1788 |

The names of two of the first 10 American states commemorate early colonists. Delaware Bay (and hence the river, and later the state) was named after Thomas West, Lord De La Warr, a governor of Virginia. Pennsylvania was called "Pensilvania," or "Penn's woodland," in its original charter, issued in 1681 to the Quaker leader William Penn. He had acquired the territory as part settlement of a debt of £16,000 owed to his father, Admiral William Penn, by King Charles II. Two states were named after places with which their founders had associations: New Jersey was the subject of a deed issued in 1644 by the Duke of York to John Berkeley and Sir George Carteret, who came from Jersey in the Channel Islands, and New Hampshire was called after the English county by settler Captain John Mason.

## THE 10 ⭐
# LATEST STATES OF THE US

| | STATE | ENTERED UNION |
|---|---|---|
| 1 | Hawaii | Aug 21, 1959 |
| 2 | Alaska | Jan 3, 1959 |
| 3 | Arizona | Feb 14, 1912 |
| 4 | New Mexico | Jan 6, 1912 |
| 5 | Oklahoma | Nov 16, 1907 |
| 6 | Utah | Jan 4, 1896 |
| 7 | Wyoming | July 10, 1890 |
| 8 | Idaho | July 3, 1890 |
| 9 | Washington | Nov 11, 1889 |
| 10 | Montana | Nov 8, 1889 |

## THE 10 ⭐
# FIRST OFFICIAL STATE FLOWERS IN THE US

| | STATE | FLOWER | ADOPTED |
|---|---|---|---|
| 1 | Oklahoma | Mistletoe | Feb 11, 1893 |
| 2 | Vermont | Red clover | Nov 9, 1894 |
| 3 | Nebraska | Goldenrod | Apr 4, 1895 |
| 4 | Delaware | Peach blossom | May 9, 1895 |
| 5 | Michigan | Apple blossom | Apr 28, 1897 |
| 6 | Iowa | Wild rose | May 5, 1897 |
| 7 | Oregon | Oregon grape | Jan 30/31, 1899 |
| 8 | Colorado | Rocky Mountain columbine | Apr 4, 1899 |
| 9 | Louisiana | Magnolia | July 12, 1900 |
| 10 | Texas | Bluebonnet | Mar 7, 1901 |

## THE 10 ⭐
# FIRST OFFICIAL STATE ANIMALS IN THE US

| | STATE | ANIMAL | ADOPTED |
|---|---|---|---|
| 1 | South Dakota | Coyote | 1949 |
| 2 | California | California grizzly bear | 1953 |
| 3 | Kansas | American buffalo | 1955 |
| 4 | Wisconsin | Badger/ White-tailed deer* | 1957 |
| 5 | Pennsylvania | White-tailed deer | 1959 |
| 6 | Vermont | Morgan horse | 1961 |
| 7 | Colorado | Rocky mountain bighorn sheep | 1961 |
| 8 | Oregon | Beaver | 1969 |
| 9 | North Carolina | Gray squirrel | 1969 |
| 10 | Utah | Elk | 1971 |

*Distinction made between "animal" and "wild animal"*

Many states have followed South Dakota's lead, several of them adopting the same animal. The white-tailed deer has proved the most popular. This list is restricted to land mammals in general. In addition to their chosen animal, several states have chosen to adopt specific breeds, such as particular cats and dogs, as well as marine mammals.

**Where is the world's longest cantilever bridge?**
see p.96 for the answer

A  Quebec, Canada
B  San Francisco, CA
C  The Firth of Forth, Scotland

# Place Names

## TOP 10 MOST COMMON STREET NAMES IN THE US

*(Street/occurrences)*

**1** 2nd/Second Street, 10,866 **2** 3rd/Third Street, 10,131 **3** 1st/First Street, 9,898 **4** 4th/Fourth Street, 9,190 **5** Park Street, 8,926 **6** 5th/Fifth Street, 8,186 **7** Main Street, 7,664 **8** 6th/Sixth Street, 7,283 **9** Oak Street, 6,946 **10** 7th/Seventh Street, 6,377

Source: *US Census Bureau*

## TOP 10 ★
## COUNTRIES WITH THE LONGEST OFFICIAL NAMES

| | OFFICIAL NAME* | COMMON ENGLISH NAME | LETTERS |
|---|---|---|---|
| 1 | al-Jamāhīrīyah al-'Arabīyah al-Lībīyah ash-Sha'bīyah al-Ishtirākīyah | Libya | 59 |
| 2 | al-Jumhūrīyah al-Jazā'irīyah ad-Dīmuqrātīyah ash-Sha'bīyah | Algeria | 51 |
| 3 | United Kingdom of Great Britain and Northern Ireland | United Kingdom | 45 |
| 4= | Śrī Lankā Prajātāntrika Samājavādī Janarajaya | Sri Lanka | 41 |
| = | Jumhurīyat al-Qumur al-Ittihādīyah al-Islāmīyah | The Comoros | 41 |
| 6 | República Democrática de São Tomé e Príncipe | São Tomé and Príncipe | 38 |
| 7 | al-Jūmhurīyah al-Islāmīyah al-Mūrītānīyah | Mauritania | 36 |
| 8= | al-Mamlakah al-Urdunnīyah al-Hāshimīyah | Jordan | 34 |
| = | Sathalanalat Paxathipatai Paxaxôn Lao | Laos | 34 |
| 10 | Federation of St. Christopher and Nevis | St. Kitts and Nevis | 33 |

\* *Some official names have been transliterated from languages that do not use the Roman alphabet; their length may vary according to the method used*

There is no connection between the length of names and the longevity of the nation-states that bear them, for since this list was first published in 1991, three have ceased to exist: Socijalisticka Federativna Republika Jugoslavija (Yugoslavia, 45 letters), Soyuz Sovetskikh Sotsialisticheskikh Respublik (USSR, 43), and Ceskoslovenská Socialistická Republika (Czechoslovakia, 36).

## TOP 10 MOST COMMON CITY NAMES IN THE US

*(Name/occurrences*)*

**1** Fairview, 66 **2** Midway, 52 **3** Oak Grove, 44 **4** = Franklin, 40; = Riverside, 40 **6** Centerville, 39 **7** Mount Pleasant, 38 **8** Georgetown, 37 **9** Salem, 36 **10** Greenwood, 34

*\* Incorporated city status only*

## TOP 10 ★
## LARGEST COUNTRIES THAT CHANGED THEIR NAMES IN THE 20TH CENTURY

| | FORMER NAME | CURRENT NAME | YEAR CHANGED | SQ MILES | AREA SQ KM |
|---|---|---|---|---|---|
| 1 | Zaïre | Dem. Rep. of Congo | 1997 | 905,567 | 2,345,409 |
| 2 | Persia | Iran | 1935 | 630,577 | 1,633,188 |
| 3 | Tanganyika/Zanzibar | Tanzania | 1964 | 364,900 | 945,087 |
| 4 | South West Africa | Namibia | 1990 | 318,261 | 824,292 |
| 5 | Northern Rhodesia | Zambia | 1964 | 290,586 | 752,614 |
| 6 | Burma | Myanmar | 1989 | 261,218 | 676,552 |
| 7 | Ubanghi Shari | Central African Republic | 1960 | 240,535 | 622,984 |
| 8 | Bechuanaland | Botswana | 1966 | 224,607 | 581,730 |
| 9 | Siam | Thailand | 1939 | 198,115 | 513,115 |
| 10 | Mesopotamia | Iraq | 1921 | 169,235 | 438,317 |

Although not a country, Greenland (840,004 sq miles/2,175,600 sq km) has been officially known as Kalaallit Nunaat since 1979. Some old names die hard: it is still common for Myanmar to be written as "Myanmar (Burma)".

## TOP 10 ★
## LARGEST COUNTRIES NAMED AFTER REAL PEOPLE

| | COUNTRY | NAMED AFTER | SQ MILES | AREA SQ KM |
|---|---|---|---|---|
| 1 | United States of America | Amerigo Vespucci (Italy; 1451–1512) | 3,717,813 | 9,629,091 |
| 2 | Saudi Arabia | Abdul Aziz Ibn Saud (Nejd; 1882–1953) | 830,000 | 2,149,690 |
| 3 | Colombia | Christopher Columbus (Italy; 1451–1506) | 439,737 | 1,138,914 |
| 4 | Bolivia | Simon Bolivar (Venezuela; 1783–1830) | 424,165 | 1,098,581 |
| 5 | Philippines | Philip II (Spain; 1527–98) | 115,831 | 300,000 |
| 6 | Falkland Islands | Lucius Cary, 2nd Viscount Falkland (UK; c.1610–43) | 4,700 | 12,173 |
| 7 | Northern Mariana | Maria Theresa (Austria; 1717–80) | 179 | 464 |
| 8 | Cook Islands | Capt. James Cook (UK; 1728–79) | 91 | 236 |
| 9 | Wallis & Futuna | Samuel Wallis (UK; 1728–95) | 77 | 200 |
| 10 | Marshall Islands | Capt. John Marshall (UK; 1748–after 1818) | 70 | 181 |

## TOP 10 ★
## LONGEST PLACE NAMES*

| NAME | LETTERS |
| --- | --- |

**1** Krung thep mahanakhon bovorn ratanakosin mahintharayutthaya mahadilok pop noparatratchathani burirom udomratchanivetmahasathan amornpiman avatarnsathit sakkathattiyavisnukarmprasit — **167**

*When the poetic name of Bangkok, capital of Thailand, is used, it is usually abbreviated to "Krung Thep" (city of angels).*

**2** Taumatawhakatangihangakoauauotamateaturipukakapiki-maungahoronukupokaiwhenuakitanatahu — **85**

*This is the longer version (the other has a mere 83 letters) of the Māori name of a hill in New Zealand. It translates as "The place where Tamatea, the man with the big knees, who slid, climbed, and swallowed mountains, known as land-eater, played on the flute to his loved one."*

**3** Gorsafawddachaidraigddanheddogleddollônpenrhynareurdraethceredigion — **67**

*A name contrived by the Fairbourne Steam Railway, Gwynedd, North Wales, for publicity purposes and in order to outdo its rival, No. 4. It means "The Mawddach station and its dragon teeth at the Northern Penrhyn Road on the golden beach of Cardigan Bay."*

**4** Llanfairpwllgwyngyllgogerychwyrndrobwllllantysiliogogogoch — **58**

*This is the place in Gwynedd famed especially for the length of its railroad tickets. It means "St. Mary's Church in the hollow of the white hazel near to the rapid whirlpool of the church of St. Tysilo near the Red Cave." Questions have been raised about its authenticity, since its official name comprises only the first 20 letters and the full name appears to have been invented as a hoax in the 19th century by a local tailor.*

**5** El Pueblo de Nuestra Señora la Reina de los Ángeles de la Porciúncula — **57**

*The site of a Franciscan mission and the full Spanish name of Los Angeles; it means "The town of Our Lady the Queen of the Angels of the Little Portion." Nowadays it is customarily known by its initial letters, "LA," making it also one of the shortest-named cities in the world.*

**6** Chargoggagoggmanchaugagoggchaubunagungamaug — **43**

*America's second longest place name is that of a lake near Webster, Massachusetts. Its Indian name, loosely translated, means "You fish on your side, I'll fish on mine, and no one fishes in the middle." It is said to be pronounced "Char-gogg-a-gogg (pause) man-chaugg-a-gog (pause) chau-bun-a-gung-a-maug." It is, however, an invented extension of its real name (Chabunagungamaug, or "boundary fishing place"), devised in the 1920s by Larry Daly, the editor of the Webster Times.*

**7 =** Lower North Branch Little Southwest Miramichi — **40**

*Canada's longest place name – a short river in New Brunswick.*

**=** Villa Real de la Santa Fé de San Francisco de Asis — **40**

*The full Spanish name of Santa Fe, New Mexico, translates as "Royal city of the holy faith of St. Francis of Assisi."*

**9** Te Whakatakanga-o-te-ngarehu-o-te-ahi-a-Tamatea — **38**

*The Māori name of Hammer Springs, New Zealand; like the second name in this list, it refers to a legend of Tamatea, explaining how the springs were warmed by "the falling of the cinders of the fire of Tamatea." Its name is variously written either hyphenated or as a single word.*

**10** Meallan Liath Coire Mhic Dhubhghaill — **32**

*The longest multiple name in Scotland, a place near Aultanrynie, Highland, alternatively spelled Meallan Liath Coire Mhic Dhughaill (30 letters).*

\* *Including single-word, hyphenated, and multiple names*

**THE LONG AND THE SHORT OF IT**

*The original 57-letter Spanish name of Los Angeles contrasts with its more common designation as "LA."*

**What is special about the Rôve tunnel?**
*see p.97 for the answer*

**A** It is the world's longest canal tunnel
**B** It is the first undersea tunnel
**C** It is the highest rail tunnel

# The Tallest Buildings

## TALLEST APARTMENT BUILDINGS

| BUILDING/LOCATION/ YEAR COMPLETED | STORIES | HEIGHT FT | M |
|---|---|---|---|
| **1** Trump World Tower, New York City, US, 2000 | 72 | 863 | 263 |
| **2** Tregunter Tower III, Hong Kong, China, 1994 | 70 | 656 | 200 |
| **3** Lake Point Tower, Chicago, US, 1968 | 70 | 645 | 197 |
| **4** Central Park Place, New York City, US, 1988 | 56 | 628 | 191 |
| **5** Huron Plaza Apartments, Chicago, US, 1983 | 61 | 599 | 183 |
| **6** 3 Lincoln Center, New York City, US, 1993 | 60 | 593 | 181 |
| **7 =** May Road Apartments, Hong Kong, China, 1993 | 58 | 590 | 180 |
| **=** 1000 Lake Shore Plaza, Chicago, US, 1964 | 55 | 590 | 180 |
| **9** Marina City Apartments, Chicago, US, 1968 | 61 | 588 | 179 |
| **10** North Pier Apartments, Chicago, US, 1990 | 61 | 581 | 177 |

These towers are all purely residential, rather than office buildings with a proportion given over to residential use. Above its 50 levels of office suites, the 1,127-ft (343-m) John Hancock Center, Chicago, built in 1968, has 48 levels of apartments (floors 44 through to 92 at 509 ft/155 m to 1,033 ft/315 m above street level), which are thus the "highest" apartments in the world.

## TALLEST BUILDINGS ERECTED MORE THAN 100 YEARS AGO

| BUILDING/LOCATION/ YEAR COMPLETED | HEIGHT FT | M |
|---|---|---|
| **1** Eiffel Tower, Paris, France, 1889 | 984 | 300 |
| **2** Washington Monument, Washington, DC, US, 1885 | 555 | 169 |
| **3** Ulm Cathedral, Ulm, Germany, 1890 | 528 | 161 |
| **4** Lincoln Cathedral, Lincoln, England, c.1307 (destroyed 1548) | 525 | 160 |
| **5** Cologne Cathedral, Cologne, Germany, 1880 | 513 | 156 |
| **6** Rouen Cathedral I, Rouen, France, 1530 (destroyed 1822) | 512 | 156 |
| **7** St. Pierre Church, Beauvais, France, 1568 (collapsed 1573) | 502 | 153 |
| **8** St. Paul's Cathedral, London, England, 1315 (destroyed 1561) | 489 | 149 |
| **9** Rouen Cathedral II, Rouen, France, 1876 | 485 | 148 |
| **10** Great Pyramid, Giza, Egypt, c.2580 BC | 480 | 146 |

The height of the Washington Monument is less than it was when it was erected because it has steadily sunk into the ground.

## TALLEST MASTS

| MAST/LOCATION | HEIGHT FT | M |
|---|---|---|
| **1** KVLY* Channel 11 TV tower, Blanchard/Fargo, North Dakota | 2,063 | 629 |
| **2** KSLA-TV Mast, Shreveport, Louisiana | 1,898 | 579 |
| **3 =** WBIR-TV Mast, Knoxville, Tennessee | 1,749 | 533 |
| **=** WTVM & WRBL Television Mast, Columbus, Georgia | 1,749 | 533 |
| **5** KFVS Television Mast, Cape Girardeau, Missouri | 1,676 | 511 |
| **6** WPSD-TV Mast, Paducah, Kentucky | 1,638 | 499 |
| **7** WGAN Television Mast, Portland, Maine | 1,619 | 493 |
| **8** KWTV Television Mast, Oklahoma City, Oklahoma | 1,572 | 479 |
| **9** BREN Tower, Area 25, Nevada Test Site, Nevada | 1,530 | 465 |
| **10** Omega Base Navigational Mast, Gippsland, Victoria, Australia | 1,400 | 426 |

*\* Formerly KTHI-TV*

## WORLD CITIES WITH MOST SKYSCRAPERS

| CITY/LOCATION | SKYSCRAPERS* |
|---|---|
| **1** New York City, US | 162 |
| **2** Chicago, US | 75 |
| **3** Hong Kong, China | 42 |
| **4** Shanghai, China | 38 |
| **5 =** Houston, US | 30 |
| **=** Tokyo, Japan | 30 |
| **7** Singapore City, Singapore | 26 |
| **8** Los Angeles, US | 22 |
| **9** Dallas, US | 20 |
| **10 =** Melbourne, Australia | 18 |
| **=** Sydney, Australia | 18 |

*\* Habitable buildings of more than 500 ft (152 m)*

**SKY HIGH**
*Despite the ever-attendant earthquake threat to tall buildings, Tokyo boasts one of the world's highest city skylines.*

## EIFFEL

French engineer Alexandre Gustave Eiffel (1832–1923) is one of the few people after whom a world famous structure has been named. Drawing on his experience as a bridge designer, Eiffel built the Eiffel Tower as a temporary structure for the 1889 Universal Exhibition. It proved so popular that it was decided to retain it. It remained the world's tallest structure until 1930, when it was overtaken by New York's Chrysler Building. Eiffel also designed the iron framework that supports the Statue of Liberty. In 1893, when a project to build a Panama Canal collapsed, Eiffel was implicated in a scandal and was sent to prison for two years.

WHO WAS • WHO WAS • WHO WAS • WHO WAS

# TOP 10 ★
# TALLEST HOTELS

| # | BUILDING/LOCATION/YEAR COMPLETED | STORIES | HEIGHT FT | M |
|---|---|---|---|---|
| 1 | **Baiyoke II Tower**, Bangkok, Thailand, 1997 | 89 | 1,046 | 319 |
| 2 | **Yu Kyong**, Pyong Yang, North Korea, 1993 | 105 | 985 | 300 |
| 3 | **Emirates Tower 2**, Dubai, United Arab Emirates, 1999 with spire | 50 | 858 1,010 | 262 308 |
| 4 | **Shangri-la**, Hong Kong, China, 1990 | 60 | 748 | 228 |
| 5 | **Raffles Western Hotel**, Singapore, 1986 | 73 | 742 | 226 |
| 6 | **Westin Peachtree Hotel**, Atlanta, US, 1973 | 71 | 723 | 220 |
| 7 | **Westin Hotel**, Detroit, US, 1973 | 71 | 720 | 219 |
| 8 | **Four Seasons Hotel**, New York City, US, 1993 | 52 | 682 | 208 |
| 9 | **Trump International Hotel**, New York City, US, 1995 | 45 | 679 | 207 |
| 10 | **Trump Tower**, New York City, US, 1983 | 68 | 664 | 202 |

# TOP 10 ★
# TALLEST HABITABLE BUILDINGS

| # | BUILDING/LOCATION/YEAR COMPLETED | STORIES | HEIGHT FT | M |
|---|---|---|---|---|
| 1 | **Petronas Towers**, Kuala Lumpur, Malaysia, 1996 | 96 | 1,482 | 452 |
| 2 | **Taipei Financial Center**, Taipei, China, 2003* with spire | 101 | 1,460 1,666 | 445 508 |
| 3 | **Sears Tower**, Chicago, US, 1974 with spires | 110 | 1,454 1,730 | 443 527 |
| 4 | **World Trade Center**[#], New York, US, 1972 | 110 | 1,368 | 417 |
| 5 | **Jin Mao Building**, Shanghai, China, 1997 with spire | 93 | 1,255 1,378 | 382 420 |
| 6 | **Empire State Building**, New York, US, 1931 with spire | 102 | 1,250 1,472 | 381 449 |
| 7 | **T & C Tower**, Kao-hsiung, Taiwan, 1997 | 85 | 1,142 | 348 |
| 8 | **Amoco Building**, Chicago, US, 1973 | 80 | 1,136 | 346 |
| 9 | **John Hancock Center**, Chicago, US, 1969 with spires | 100 | 1,127 1,470 | 343 449 |
| 10 | **Shun Hing Square**, Shenzen, China, 1996 with spires | 80 | 1,082 1,260 | 330 384 |

*\* Under construction; scheduled completion date*

*# Twin towers; the second tower, completed in 1973, has the same number of stories but is slightly smaller at 1,362 ft (415 m) – although its spire takes it up to 1,710 ft (521 m)*

Heights do not include television and radio antennas and uninhabited extensions. Although the twin Petronas Towers are now officially accepted as the world's tallest, their completion generated a controversy when it became clear that their overall measurement includes their spires, and that their roof height (at the point where the two towers are connected) is "only" 1,244 ft (379 m).

### EMPIRE BUILDING

*Over 70 years old and still going strong, the majestic 102-story Empire State Building has become a symbol of New York, dominating its skyline.*

**Did You Know?** Lightning does strike (at least) twice: the lightning conductor on the Empire State Building was struck 68 times in the structure's first 10 years.

# Bridges & Other Structures

## TOP 10 ★
## LONGEST SUSPENSION BRIDGES

| | BRIDGE/LOCATION | YEAR COMPLETED | LENGTH OF MAIN SPAN FT | M |
|---|---|---|---|---|
| 1 | **Akashi-Kaiko**, Kobe–Naruto, Japan | 1998 | 6,532 | 1,991 |
| 2 | **Great Belt**, Denmark | 1997 | 5,328 | 1,624 |
| 3 | **Humber Estuary**, UK | 1980 | 4,626 | 1,410 |
| 4 | **Jiangyin**, China | 1998 | 4,544 | 1,385 |
| 5 | **Tsing Ma**, Hong Kong, China | 1997 | 4,518 | 1,377 |
| 6 | **Verrazano Narrows**, New York, NY | 1964 | 4,260 | 1,298 |
| 7 | **Golden Gate**, San Francisco, CA | 1937 | 4,200 | 1,280 |
| 8 | **Höga Kusten** (High Coast), Veda, Sweden | 1997 | 3,970 | 1,210 |
| 9 | **Mackinac Straits**, Michigan | 1957 | 3,800 | 1,158 |
| 10 | **Minami Bisan-seto**, Kojima–Sakaide, Japan | 1988 | 3,609 | 1,100 |

The Messina Strait Bridge between Sicily and Calabria, Italy, remains a speculative project but, if constructed according to plan, it will have by far the longest center span of any bridge at 10,827 ft (3,300 m).

## TOP 10 ★
## LONGEST CANTILEVER BRIDGES

| | BRIDGE/LOCATION | YEAR COMPLETED | LONGEST SPAN FT | M |
|---|---|---|---|---|
| 1 | **Pont de Quebec**, Quebec, Canada | 1917 | 1,800 | 549 |
| 2 | **Firth of Forth**, Scotland, UK | 1890 | 1,710 | 521 |
| 3 | **Minato**, Osaka, Japan | 1974 | 1,673 | 510 |
| 4 | **Commodore John Barry**, New Jersey/Pennsylvania | 1974 | 1,622 | 494 |
| 5 = | **Greater New Orleans 1**, Louisiana | 1958 | 1,575 | 480 |
| = | **Greater New Orleans 2**, Louisiana | 1988 | 1,575 | 480 |
| 7 | **Howrah**, Calcutta, India | 1943 | 1,500 | 457 |
| 8 | **Gramercy**, Louisiana | 1995 | 1,460 | 445 |
| 9 | **Transbay**, San Francisco, California | 1936 | 1,400 | 427 |
| 10 | **Baton Rouge**, Louisiana | 1969 | 1,235 | 376 |

**SHANGHAI SURPRISE**

*One of the world's longest cable-stayed bridges, Shanghai's Yang Pu was built to ease traffic congestion on the city's busy inner ring road.*

## TOP 10 ★
## LONGEST BRIDGES IN THE US

| | BRIDGE/LOCATION | YEAR COMPLETED | LENGTH OF MAIN SPAN FT | M |
|---|---|---|---|---|
| 1 | **Verrazona Narrows**, New York, NY | 1964 | 4,260 | 1,298 |
| 2 | **Golden Gate**, San Francisco, CA | 1937 | 4,200 | 1,280 |
| 3 | **Mackinac Straits**, MI | 1957 | 3,800 | 1,158 |
| 4 | **George Washington**, New York, NY | 1931/62* | 3,500 | 1,067 |
| 5 | **Tacoma Narrows II**, Washington, DC | 1950 | 2,800 | 853 |
| 6 | **Transbay**, San Francisco, CA# | 1936 | 2,310 | 704 |
| 7 | **Bronx–Whitestone**, New York, NY | 1939 | 2,300 | 701 |
| 8 | **Delaware Memorial**, Wilmington, DE# | 1951/68 | 2,150 | 655 |
| 9 | **Walt Whitman**, Philadelphia, PA | 1957 | 2,000 | 610 |
| 10 | **Ambassador**, Detroit, MI | 1929 | 1,850 | 564 |

\* *Lower deck added*

\# *Twin spans*

All these are suspension bridges. The US also has the longest steel-arch bridges in the world: the New River Gorge Bridge, Fayetteville, West Virginia (1,700 ft/518 m) and the Bayonne at Bayonne, New Jersey (1,675 ft/511 m).

## TOP 10 ★
## LONGEST CABLE-STAYED BRIDGES

| | BRIDGE/LOCATION | YEAR COMPLETED | LENGTH OF MAIN SPAN FT | M |
|---|---|---|---|---|
| 1 | **Tatara**, Onomichi–Imabari, Japan | 1999 | 2,920 | 890 |
| 2 | **Pont de Normandie**, Le Havre, France | 1994 | 2,808 | 856 |
| 3 | **Qinghzhou Minjiang**, Fozhou, China | 1996 | 1,985 | 605 |
| 4 | **Yang Pu**, Shanghai, China | 1993 | 1,975 | 602 |
| 5 = | **Meiko-chuo**, Nagoya, Japan | 1997 | 1,936 | 590 |
| = | **Xu Pu**, Shanghai, China | 1997 | 1,936 | 590 |
| 7 | **Skarnsundet**, Trondheim Fjord, Norway | 1991 | 1,739 | 530 |
| 8 | **Tsurumi Tsubasa**, Yokohama, Japan | 1994 | 1,673 | 510 |
| 9 = | **Ikuchi**, Onomichi–Imabari, Japan | 1994 | 1,608 | 490 |
| = | **Öresund**, Copenhagen–Malmö, Denmark/Sweden | 2000 | 1,608 | 490 |

## TOP 10 ⭐
# LONGEST CANAL TUNNELS

| TUNNEL/CANAL/LOCATION | LENGTH FT | M |
|---|---|---|
| **1 Rôve**, Canal de Marseille au Rhône, France | 23,360 | 7,120 |
| **2 Bony** ("Le Grand Souterrain"), Canal de St. Quentin, France | 18,625 | 5,677 |
| **3 Standedge**, Huddersfield Narrow, UK | 17,093 | 5,210 |
| **4 Mauvages**, Canal de la Marne et Rhin, France | 16,306 | 4,970 |
| **5 Balesmes**, Canal Marne à la Saône, France | 15,748 | 4,800 |
| **6 Ruyaulcourt**, Canal du Nord, France | 14,764 | 4,500 |
| **7 Strood***, Thames and Medway, UK | 11,837 | 3,608 |
| **8 Lapal**, Birmingham, UK | 11,713 | 3,570 |
| **9 Sapperton**, Thames and Severn, UK | 11,444 | 3,488 |
| **10 Pouilly-en-Auxois**, Canal de Bourgogne, France | 10,935 | 3,333 |

*\* Later converted to a rail tunnel*

## TOP 10 ⭐
# LONGEST RAIL TUNNELS

| TUNNEL/LOCATION/ YEAR COMPLETED* | LENGTH MILES | KM |
|---|---|---|
| **1 Seikan**, Japan, 1988 | 33.49 | 53.90 |
| **2 Channel Tunnel**, France–England, 1994 | 31.03 | 49.94 |
| **3 Moscow Metro** (Medvedkovo/ Belyaevo section), Russia, 1979 | 19.07 | 30.70 |
| **4 London Underground** (East Finchley–Morden, Northern Line), UK, 1939 | 17.30 | 27.84 |
| **5 Hakkoda**, Japan, U/C | 16.44 | 26.46 |
| **6 Iwate**, Japan, U/C | 16.04 | 25.81 |
| **7 Iiyama**, Japan, U/C | 13.98 | 22.50 |
| **8 Dai-Shimizu**, Japan, 1982 | 13.78 | 22.17 |
| **9 Simplon II**, Italy– Switzerland, 1922 | 12.31 | 19.82 |
| **10 Simplon I**, Italy– Switzerland, 1906 | 12.30 | 19.80 |

*\* U/C = under construction*

The longest railroad tunnel in the US is the 7.8-mile (12.6-km) Cascade, to the east of Seattle, Washington, completed on January 12, 1929.

## TOP 10 ⭐
# LARGEST SPORTS STADIUMS

| STADIUM/LOCATION | CAPACITY |
|---|---|
| **1 Strahov Stadium**, Prague, Czech Republic | 240,000 |
| **2 Maracaña Municipal Stadium**, Rio de Janeiro, Brazil | 220,000 |
| **3 Rungnado Stadium**, Pyongyang, North Korea | 150,000 |
| **4 Mineiro Stadium**, Belo Horizonte, Brazil | 130,000 |
| **5 National Stadium of Iran**, Azadi, Iran | 128,000 |
| **6 Estádio Maghalaes Pinto**, Belo Horizonte, Brazil | 125,000 |
| **7= Estádio da Luz**, Lisbon, Portugal | 120,000 |
| **= Estádio Morumbi**, São Paulo, Brazil | 120,000 |
| **= Saltlake Stadium**, Calcutta, India | 120,000 |
| **= Senayan Main Stadium**, Jakarta, Indonesia | 120,000 |
| **= Yuba Bharati Krirangan**, Nr. Calcutta, India | 120,000 |

## TOP 10 ⭐
# HIGHEST DAMS

| DAM/RIVER/LOCATION | YEAR COMPLETED* | HEIGHT FT | M |
|---|---|---|---|
| **1 Rogun**, Vakhsh, Tajikistan | U/C | 1,099 | 335 |
| **2 Nurek**, Vakhsh, Tajikistan | 1980 | 984 | 300 |
| **3 Grande Dixence**, Dixence, Switzerland | 1961 | 935 | 285 |
| **4 Inguri**, Inguri, Georgia | 1980 | 892 | 272 |
| **5 Vajont**, Vajont, Italy | 1960 | 860 | 262 |
| **6= Manuel M. Torres**, Chicoasén, Grijalva, Mexico | 1980 | 856 | 261 |
| **= Tehri**, Bhagirathi, India | U/C | 856 | 261 |
| **8 Alvaro Obregon**, El Gallinero, Tenasco, Mexico | 1946 | 853 | 260 |
| **9 Mauvoisin**, Drance de Bagnes, Switzerland | 1957 | 820 | 250 |
| **10 Alberto Lleras C.**, Guavio, Colombia | 1989 | 797 | 243 |

*\* U/C = under construction*

Source: *International Commission on Large Dams (ICOLD)*

**DAM RECORD BUSTER**

*An incongruous mural depicting Lenin celebrates this Soviet engineering accomplishment, the building of the world's second highest dam, the Nurek in Tajikistan.*

**Did You Know?** So vast is the 3,250,000 cu yd (2,484,800 cu m) volume of concrete in the Hoover Dam (1936), Colorado River, on the Arizona/Nevada border, that it will take until the year 2030 for it to set completely.

Lasorda's

8, '94, '95)

ames,
3).

VINCE COMPAGNONE / Los Angeles Times

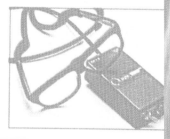

TECHNOLOGY

DGETS
FOR SPIES
products are
popularity
▶ See Page C4

San Fran

NORTHERN CAL

T

g a        Olympic He
nt

Atlanta 1996.

s basketball
gold, respect

ael Wilbon
ington Post

esn't feel the dominance,
U.S. women's basketball
mpic games by an average
art of the Summer Games
like the so-called Dream
't a certainty to win a gold
in fact of winning

# CULTURE & LEARNING

# Word Power

## TOP 10 ★
## MOST WIDELY SPOKEN LANGUAGES

| | LANGUAGE | APPROXIMATE NO. OF SPEAKERS |
|---|---|---|
| 1 | Chinese (Mandarin) | 1,075,000,000 |
| 2 | Hindustani* | 602,000,000 |
| 3 | English | 514,000,000 |
| 4 | Spanish | 425,000,000 |
| 5 | Russian | 275,000,000 |
| 6 | Arabic | 256,000,000 |
| 7 | Bengali | 215,000,000 |
| 8 | Portuguese | 194,000,000 |
| 9 | Malay-Indonesian | 176,000,000 |
| 10 | French | 129,000,000 |

*Hindi and Urdu are essentially the same language, Hindustani. As the official language of Pakistan, it is written in modified Arabic script and called Urdu. As the official language of India, it is written in the Devanagari script and called Hindi*

According to mid-1999 estimates by Emeritus Professor Sidney S. Culbert of the University of Washington, Seattle, in addition to those languages appearing in the Top 10, there are two further languages that are spoken by more than 100 million individuals: German and Japanese.

## TOP 10 ★
## MOST SPOKEN LANGUAGES IN THE US

| | LANGUAGE | SPEAKERS |
|---|---|---|
| 1 | English | 198,601,000 |
| 2 | Spanish | 17,339,172 |
| 3 | French | 1,702,176 |
| 4 | German | 1,547,099 |
| 5 | Italian | 1,308,648 |
| 6 | Chinese | 1,249,213 |
| 7 | Tagalog | 843,251 |
| 8 | Polish | 723,483 |
| 9 | Korean | 626,478 |
| 10 | Vietnamese | 507,069 |

Source: *US Census Bureau*

Census statistics indicated a total of 27 different languages spoken at home by more than 100,000 individuals aged 5 and over.

## TOP 10 ★
## LANGUAGES OFFICIALLY SPOKEN IN THE MOST COUNTRIES

| | LANGUAGE | COUNTRIES |
|---|---|---|
| 1 | English | 57 |
| 2 | French | 33 |
| 3 | Arabic | 23 |
| 4 | Spanish | 21 |
| 5 | Portuguese | 7 |
| 6 | =Dutch | 5 |
| | =German | 5 |
| 8 | =Chinese (Mandarin) | 3 |
| | =Danish | 3 |
| | =Italian | 3 |
| | =Malay | 3 |

## TOP 10 ★
## COUNTRIES WITH THE MOST ENGLISH-LANGUAGE SPEAKERS*

| | COUNTRY | APPROX. NO. OF SPEAKERS |
|---|---|---|
| 1 | US | 237,320,000 |
| 2 | UK | 58,090,000 |
| 3 | Canada | 18,218,000 |
| 4 | Australia | 15,561,000 |
| 5 | Ireland | 3,720,000 |
| 6 | South Africa | 3,700,000 |
| 7 | New Zealand | 3,338,000 |
| 8 | Jamaica# | 2,460,000 |
| 9 | Trinidad and Tobago#+ | 1,245,000 |
| 10 | Guyana# | 764,000 |

* Inhabitants for whom English is their mother tongue
# Includes English Creole
+ Trinidad English

This Top 10 represents the countries with the greatest numbers of inhabitants who speak English as their mother-tongue. After the 10th entry, the figures dive to around or under 260,000. In addition to these, there are perhaps as many as 1 billion who speak English as a second language.

## TOP 10 ★
## MOST COMMON WORDS IN ENGLISH

| SPOKEN ENGLISH | | WRITTEN ENGLISH |
|---|---|---|
| the | 1 | the |
| and | 2 | of |
| I | 3 | to |
| to | 4 | in |
| of | 5 | and |
| a | 6 | a |
| you | 7 | for |
| that | 8 | was |
| in | 9 | is |
| it | 10 | that |

Various surveys have been conducted to establish the most common words in spoken English, from telephone conversations to broadcast commentaries.

## THE 10 ★
## EARLIEST DATED WORDS IN THE *OXFORD ENGLISH DICTIONARY*

| | WORD | SOURCE | DATE |
|---|---|---|---|
| 1 | =priest | Laws of Ethelbert | 601–4 |
| | =town | Laws of Ethelbert | 601–4 |
| 3 | earl | Laws of Ethelbert | 616 |
| 4 | this | Bewcastle Column | c.670 |
| 5 | streale | Ruthwell Cross | c.680 |
| 6 | ward | Caedmon, *Hymn* | 680 |
| 7 | thing | Laws of Hlothaer and Eadric | 685–6 |
| 8 | theft | Laws of Ine | 688–95 |
| 9 | worth | Laws of Ine | 695 |
| 10 | then | Laws of King Wihtraed | 695–6 |

The 10 earliest citations in the *Oxford English Dictionary* (OED) come from 7th-century Anglo-Saxon documents and stone inscriptions. All have survived as commonly used English words, with the exception of "streale," which is another name for an arrow. A few other English words can be definitely dated to before 700, among them "church," which, like "then," appears in a law of King Wihtraed.

# MOST STUDIED LANGUAGES IN THE US*

| | LANGUAGE | REGISTRATIONS |
|---|---|---|
| 1 | Spanish | 656,590 |
| 2 | French | 199,064 |
| 3 | German | 89,020 |
| 4 | Italian | 49,287 |
| 5 | Japanese | 43,141 |
| 6 | Chinese | 28,456 |
| 7 | Latin | 26,145 |
| 8 | Russian | 23,791 |
| 9 | Ancient Greek | 16,402 |
| 10 | American Sign Language | 11,420 |

* In US institutions of higher education

Source: *Modern Language Association of America*

These figures are from a 1999 survey of colleges and universities, which indicated a total of 1,193,830 foreign language registrations.

# MOST USED LETTERS IN WRITTEN ENGLISH

| SURVEY* | | MORSE # |
|---|---|---|
| e | 1 | e |
| t | 2 | t |
| a | 3 | a |
| o | 4 | i |
| i | 5 | n |
| n | 6 | o |
| s | 7 | s |
| r | 8 | h |
| h | 9 | r |
| l | 10 | d |

* The order as indicated by a survey across approximately 1 million words appearing in a wide variety of printed texts, ranging from newspapers to novels

# The order estimated by Samuel Morse, the inventor in the 1830s of Morse Code, based on his calculations of the respective quantities of type used by a printer. The number of letters in the printer's type trays ranged from 12,000 for "e" to 4,400 for "d," with only 200 for "z"

# LONGEST WORDS IN THE ENGLISH LANGUAGE*

| WORD/MEANING | LETTERS |
|---|---|

**1** Ornicopytheobibliopsychocrystarroscioaerogenethliometeoroaustrohiero-anthropoichthyopyrosiderochpnomyoalectryoophiobotanopegohydrorhab-docrithoaleuroalphitohalomolybdoclerobeloaxinocoscinodactyliogeolitho-pessopsephocatoptrotephraoneirochiroonychodactyloarithstichooxogelo-scogastrogyrocerobletonooenoscapulinaniac — **310**

*Medieval scribes used this word to refer to "A deluded human who practises divination or forecasting by means of phenomena, interpretation of acts, or other manifestations related to the following animate or inanimate objects and appearances: birds, oracles, Bible, ghosts, crystal gazing, shadows, air appearances, birth stars, meteors, winds, sacrificial appearances, entrails of humans and fishes, fire, red-hot irons, altar smoke, mice, grain picking by rooster, snakes, herbs, fountains, water, wands, dough, meal, barley, salt, lead, dice, arrows, hatchet balance, sieve, ring suspension, random dots, precious stones, pebbles, pebble heaps, mirrors, ash writing, dreams, palmistry, nail rays, finger rings, numbers, book passages, name letterings, laughing manners, ventriloquism, circle walking, wax, susceptibility to hidden springs, wine, and shoulder blades."*

**2** Lopadotemachoselachogaleokranioleipsanodrimhypotrimmatosilphioparao-melitokatakechymenokichlepikossyphophattoperisteralektryonoptekephall-iokigklopeleiolagoiosiraiobaphetraganopterygon — **182**

*The English transliteration of a 170-letter Greek word that appears in The Ecclesiazusae (a comedy by the Greek playwright Aristophanes, c.448–380 BC). It is used as a description of a 17-ingredient dish.*

**3** Aequeosalinocalcalinosetaceoaluminosocupreovitriolic — **52**

*Invented by a medical writer, Dr. Edward Strother (1675–1737), to describe the spa waters at Bath.*

**4** Osseocarnisanguineoviscericartilaginonervomedullary — **51**

*Coined by writer and East India Company official Thomas Love Peacock (1785–1866), and used in his satire Headlong Hall (1816) as a description of the structure of the human body.*

**5** Pneumonoultramicroscopicsilicovolcanoconiosis — **45**

*It first appeared in print (though ending in "-koniosis") in F. Scully's Bedside Manna [sic] (1936), then found its way into Webster's Dictionary and is now in the Oxford English Dictionary. It is said to mean a lung disease caused by breathing fine dust.*

**6** Hepaticocholecystostcholecystenterostomies — **42**

*Surgical operations to create channels of communication between gall bladders and hepatic ducts or intestines.*

**7** Praetertranssubstantiationalistically — **37**

*The adverb describing the act of surpassing the act of transubstantiation; the word is found in Mark McShane's novel Untimely Ripped (1963).*

**8 =** Pseudoantidisestablishmentarianism — **34**

*A word meaning "false opposition to the withdrawal of state support from a Church," derived from that perennial favorite long word, antidisestablishmentarianism (a mere 28 letters).*

**=** Supercalifragilisticexpialidocious — **34**

*An invented word, but perhaps now eligible since it has appeared in the Oxford English Dictionary. It was popularized by the song of this title in the film Mary Poppins (1964), where it is used to mean "wonderful," but it was originally written in 1949 in an unpublished song by Parker and Young who spelled it "supercalafajalistickespialadojus" (32 letters).*

**10 =** Encephalomyeloradiculoneuritis — **30**

*Inflammation of the whole nervous system.*

**=** Hippopotomonstrosesquipedalian — **30**

*Appropriately, the word that means "pertaining to an extremely long word."*

**=** Pseudopseudohypoparathyroidism — **30**

*First used (hyphenated) in the US in 1952 and (unhyphenated) in Great Britain in The Lancet in 1962 to describe a medical case in which a patient appeared to have symptoms of pseudohypoparathyroidism, but with "no manifestations suggesting hypoparathyroidism."*

* Excluding names of chemical compounds

---

**Harvard University was named after whom?**
*see p.105 for the answer*

A John Harvard, a British preacher
B Johannes Harvard, a Dutch trader
C Harvard Hawkins, an American actor

# Children at School

Italo Calvino

## EASTERN PROMISE

*China has the most children in school and the world's longest school year, but spends just 2 percent of its GNP on education – less than half that of Western countries.*

### TOP 10 ★
## COUNTRIES WITH THE HIGHEST NUMBER OF PRIMARY SCHOOL PUPILS PER TEACHER

| COUNTRY | PUPIL/TEACHER RATIO IN PRIMARY SCHOOLS* |
|---|---|
| 1 Central African Republic | 77 |
| 2 Congo | 70 |
| 3 Chad | 67 |
| 4 Bangladesh | 63 |
| 5 Malawi | 59 |
| 6 =Afghanistan | 58 |
| =Mozambique | 58 |
| =Rwanda | 58 |
| 9 =Benin | 56 |
| =Senegal | 56 |

*\* In latest year for which figures are available*
Source: *UNESCO*

### TOP 10 ★
## COUNTRIES SPENDING THE MOST ON EDUCATION

| COUNTRY | EXPENDITURE AS PERCENTAGE OF GNP* |
|---|---|
| 1 Kiribati | 11.4 |
| 2 Moldova | 10.3 |
| 3 Namibia | 8.5 |
| 4 Denmark | 7.7 |
| 5 Sweden | 7.6 |
| 6 =South Africa | 7.5 |
| =Zimbabwe | 7.5 |
| 8 Uzbekistan | 7.4 |
| 9 Barbados | 7.3 |
| 10 Saudi Arabia | 7.2 |
| *US* | 4.7 |

*\* GNP in latest year for which data available*
Source: *UNESCO*

### TOP 10 ★
## COUNTRIES WITH THE MOST PRIMARY SCHOOLS

| COUNTRY | PRIMARY SCHOOLS |
|---|---|
| 1 China | 628,840 |
| 2 India | 598,354 |
| 3 Brazil | 196,479 |
| 4 Indonesia | 173,893 |
| 5 Mexico | 95,855 |
| 6 Pakistan | 77,207 |
| 7 US | 72,000 |
| 8 Russia | 66,235 |
| 9 Iran | 63,101 |
| 10 Colombia | 48,933 |

Source: *UNESCO*

The European country with the most primary schools is France, with some 41,000.

### TOP 10 ★
## OLDEST SECONDARY SCHOOLS IN THE US

| SCHOOL/LOCATION | YEAR FOUNDED |
|---|---|
| 1 Roxbury Latin School, West Roxbury, MA | 1645 |
| 2 Hopkins School, New Haven, CT | 1660 |
| 3 =Friends Select School, Philadelphia, PA | 1689 |
| =William Penn Charter School, Philadelphia, PA | 1689 |
| 5 Abington Friends School, Jenkinton, PA | 1697 |
| 6 Trinity School, New York, NY | 1709 |
| 7 Moravian Academy, Bethlehem, PA | 1742 |
| 8 Linden Hall School, Lititz, PA | 1746 |
| 9 Governor Dummer Academy, Byfield, MA | 1763 |
| 10 Columbia Grammar & Preparatory School, New York, NY | 1764 |

Source: The Handbook of Private Schools

## TOP 10 COUNTRIES WITH THE LONGEST SCHOOL YEARS
*(Country/school year in days)*

❶ China, 251 ❷ Japan, 243 ❸ South Korea, 220 ❹ Israel, 215 ❺ = Germany, 210;
= Russia, 210 ❼ Switzerland, 207 ❽ = Netherlands, 200;
= Scotland, 200; = Thailand, 200
*US, 180*

**EDUCATING THE MASSES**

*Indian culture places a high value on education, and consequently some 7 percent of the country's entire population attends secondary school.*

## COUNTRIES WITH THE MOST SECONDARY SCHOOL PUPILS

| COUNTRY | PERCENTAGE FEMALE | SECONDARY SCHOOL PUPILS |
|---|---|---|
| 1 China | 45 | 71,883,000 |
| 2 India | 38 | 68,872,393 |
| 3 US | 49 | 21,473,692 |
| 4 Indonesia | 46 | 14,209,974 |
| 5 Russia | 50 | 13,732,000 |
| 6 Japan | 49 | 9,878,568 |
| 7 Iran | 46 | 8,776,792 |
| 8 Germany | 48 | 8,382,335 |
| 9 Mexico | 49 | 7,914,165 |
| 10 UK | 52 | 6,548,786 |

Source: *UNESCO*

The number of pupils enrolled at secondary schools as a percentage of the total population in those countries in this Top 10 list varies from 6 percent in China to 14 percent in both Iran and Germany. The figures for the US and UK are 8 percent and 11 percent respectively.

## STATES SPENDING THE MOST PER ELEMENTARY AND SECONDARY DAY SCHOOL PUPIL

| STATE | SPENDING PER PUPIL, 1998 ($) |
|---|---|
| 1 New Jersey | 9,703 |
| 2 Connecticut | 9,184 |
| 3 New York | 8,860 |
| 4 Alaska | 8,842 |
| 5 Delaware | 8,055 |
| 6 Rhode Island | 7,607 |
| 7 Michigan | 7,488 |
| 8 Massachusetts | 7,306 |
| 9 Wisconsin | 7,264 |
| 10 Pennsylvania | 7,152 |

Source: *National Center for Education Statistics, US Department of Education*

## STATES WITH THE HIGHEST HIGH SCHOOL GRADUATION RATES

| STATE | PERCENTAGE RATE |
|---|---|
| 1 Washington | 92.0 |
| 2 Alaska | 90.6 |
| 3 Wyoming | 90.0 |
| 4 Colorado | 89.6 |
| 5 Minnesota | 89.4 |
| 6 Utah | 89.3 |
| 7 Kansas | 89.2 |
| 8 =Montana | 89.1 |
| =Nevada | 89.1 |
| 10 Wisconsin | 88.0 |

This Top 10 represents the percentages of the population aged 25 or over who have attained a high school diploma or higher educational qualification. The average was 82.8 percent.

## COUNTRIES WITH THE HIGHEST ILLITERACY RATES

| COUNTRY | PERCENTAGE ADULT ILLITERACY RATE* |
|---|---|
| 1 Niger | 84.3 |
| 2 Burkina Faso | 77.0 |
| 3 =Afghanistan | 63.7 |
| =Sierra Leone | 63.7 |
| 5 Gambia | 63.5 |
| 6 Guinea-Bissau | 63.2 |
| 7 Senegal | 62.7 |
| 8 Benin | 62.5 |
| 9 Ethiopia | 61.3 |
| 10 Mauritania | 60.1 |

* Age over 15; estimates for 2000

Source: *UNESCO*

**Did You Know?** The first blackboards used in schools were invented in Skippack, Pennsylvania, in 1714 by Christopher Dock (1698–1771), a German immigrant schoolmaster who also wrote the first teaching manual published in America.

# Higher Education

**CRÈME DE LA CRÈME**

*Between the late 1960s and 1970, the University of Paris was split into 13 separate establishments, which comprise the world's largest higher education body.*

## TOP 10 ★
## LARGEST UNIVERSITIES

| | UNIVERSITY | STUDENTS |
|---|---|---|
| 1 | University of Paris, France | 311,163 |
| 2 | University of Calcutta, India | 300,000 |
| 3 | University of Mexico, Mexico | 269,000 |
| 4 | University of Bombay, India | 262,350 |
| 5 | University of Guadalajara, Mexico | 214,986 |
| 6 | University of Rome, Italy | 189,000 |
| 7 | University of Buenos Aires, Argentina | 183,397 |
| 8 | University of Rajasthan, India | 175,000 |
| 9 | University of California, US | 157,331 |
| 10 | University if Wisconsin, US | 153,379 |

Several other universities in India, Egypt, Italy, and the US have more than 100,000 students. It should be noted, however, that certain universities listed are divided into numerous separate centers – the University of Wisconsin, for example, comprises some 14 campuses, with Madison's enrollment of over 40,000 the largest.

## TOP 10 ★
## COUNTRIES WITH THE HIGHEST PERCENTAGE OF FEMALE UNIVERSITY STUDENTS

| | COUNTRY | % OF FEMALE STUDENTS* |
|---|---|---|
| 1 | Cyprus | 75 |
| 2 | US Virgin Islands | 74 |
| 3 | Qatar | 73 |
| 4 = | St. Lucia | 72 |
| = | United Arab Emirates | 72 |
| 6 | Kuwait | 67 |
| 7 | Myanmar (Burma) | 64 |
| 8 | Barbados | 62 |
| 9 | Namibia | 61 |
| 10 = | Bulgaria | 60 |
| = | Cuba | 60 |
| = | Latvia | 60 |
| = | Lesotho | 60 |
| = | Mongolia | 60 |
| = | Panama | 60 |
| | US | 56 |

*\* In latest year for which data available*

Source: *UNESCO*

## TOP 10 ★
## COUNTRIES WITH THE LOWEST PERCENTAGE OF FEMALE UNIVERSITY STUDENTS

| | COUNTRY | % OF FEMALE STUDENTS* |
|---|---|---|
| 1 | Samoa | 3 |
| 2 | Equatorial Guinea | 4 |
| 3 | Central African Republic | 9 |
| 4 | Somalia | 10 |
| 5 | Guinea | 11 |
| 6 | Chad | 12 |
| 7 | Yemen | 13 |
| 8 | Eritrea | 14 |
| 9 | Rwanda | 15 |
| 10 | Cambodia | 16 |

*\* In latest year for which data available*

Source: *UNESCO*

**WOMAN'S WORK**

*Women study separately but in large numbers at the United Arab Emirates University in Al-Ain, which was founded in 1976.*

## HARVARD

Harvard, the first college founded in the US, takes its name from John Harvard (1607–38). Born in Southwark, London, he graduated from Emmanuel College, Cambridge, in 1631, and in 1637 married Ann Sadler, a clergyman's daughter, in Lewes, England. He later emigrated to Charlestown, Massachusetts, where he worked as a preacher. Barely a year after his arrival, he died of consumption. In his will he bequeathed his library of 300 books and a sum of £779 to Cambridge College, which had been founded in 1636. Two years later, it was renamed as Harvard College in honor of its benefactor.

WHO WAS • WHO WAS • WHO WAS • WHO WAS • WHO WAS

### TOP 10 ★
## COUNTRIES WITH THE MOST UNIVERSITY STUDENTS

| | COUNTRY | PERCENTAGE FEMALE | UNIVERSITY STUDENTS* |
|---|---|---|---|
| 1 | US | 56 | 14,261,778 |
| 2 | India | 36 | 6,060,418 |
| 3 | Japan | 44 | 3,917,709 |
| 4 | China | 36 | 3,350,715 |
| 5 | Russia | 53 | 2,587,510 |
| 6 | France | 55 | 2,062,495 |
| 7 | Philippines | 57 | 2,017,972 |
| 8 | Italy | 54 | 1,892,542 |
| 9 | Indonesia | 31 | 1,889,408 |
| 10 | Brazil | 52 | 1,868,529 |

\* In latest year for which data available
Source: UNESCO

### TOP 10 ★
## COUNTRIES WITH THE MOST UNIVERSITIES

| | COUNTRY | UNIVERSITIES |
|---|---|---|
| 1 | India | 8,407 |
| 2 | US | 5,758 |
| 3 | Argentina | 1,705 |
| 4 | Spain | 1,415 |
| 5 | Mexico | 1,341 |
| 6 | Bangladesh | 1,268 |
| 7 | Indonesia | 1,236 |
| 8 | Japan | 1,223 |
| 9 | France | 1,062 |
| 10 | China | 1,054 |

The huge number of university institutions in India reflects not only the country's population and the high value placed on education in Indian culture but also the inclusion of many "Affiliating and Teaching" colleges attached to universities.

### TOP 10 ★
## COUNTRIES WITH THE HIGHEST PROPORTION OF ADULTS IN HIGHER EDUCATION

| | COUNTRY | TOTAL | STUDENTS PER 100,000* |
|---|---|---|---|
| 1 | Canada | 1,763,105 | 5,997 |
| 2 | South Korea | 2,541,659 | 5,609 |
| 3 | Australia | 1,002,476 | 5,552 |
| 4 | US | 14,261,778 | 5,339 |
| 5 | New Zealand | 162,350 | 4,508 |
| 6 | Finland | 213,995 | 4,190 |
| 7 | Norway | 180,383 | 4,164 |
| 8 | Spain | 1,591,863 | 4,017 |
| 9 | Ireland | 47,955 | 3,618 |
| 10 | France | 2,091,688 | 3,600 |

\* In latest year for which data available
Source: UNESCO

### GRADUATION DAY

*Decked in their traditional tasseled mortar boards and gowns, more students graduate from US universities than from those of any other country.*

# Libraries of the World

## THE 10 ★
## FIRST PUBLIC LIBRARIES IN THE US

| LIBRARY/LOCATION | FOUNDED |
|---|---|
| 1 Peterboro Public Library, Peterboro, NH | 1833 |
| 2 New Orleans Public Library, New Orleans, LA | 1843 |
| 3 Boston Public Library, Boston, MA | 1852 |
| 4 Public Library of Cincinnati and Hamilton County, Cincinnati, OH | 1853 |
| 5 Springfield City Library, Springfield, MA | 1857 |
| 6 Worcester Public Library, Worcester, MA | 1859 |
| 7 Multnomah County Library, Portland, OR | 1864 |
| 8 =Detroit Public Library, Detroit, MI | 1865 |
| =St. Louis Public Library, St. Louis, MO | 1865 |
| 10 Atlanta-Fulton Public Library, Atlanta, GA | 1867 |

Source: *Public Library Association*

Although Medford Public Library in Medford, MA, claims to have been founded as early as 1825, evidence exists that Peterboro Public Library, founded on April 9, 1833, with 700 volumes, was the first public library (in that it was the first supported by local taxes) in the US.

### DEWEY

Any visitor to a library will have noticed the system by which books are organized into 10 subject groups and a series of sub-groups, each bearing a decimal number. This was the brainchild of Melville Louis Kossuth Dewey (1851–1931). At the age of 21, Dewey devised the system that bears his name. Published in 1876, it became adopted throughout the world and still remains the most widely used classification system. Dewey also helped to establish the American Library Association (ALA).

WHO WAS • WHO WAS • WHO WAS • WHO WAS • ?

## TOP 10 ★
## OLDEST NATIONAL LIBRARIES

| | LIBRARY | LOCATION | FOUNDED |
|---|---|---|---|
| 1 | National Library of the Czech Republic | Prague, Czech Republic | 1366 |
| 2 | National Library of Austria | Vienna, Austria | 1368 |
| 3 | Biblioteca Nazionale Marciana | Venice, Italy | 1468 |
| 4 | Bibliothèque Nationale de France | Paris, France | 1480 |
| 5 | National Library of Malta | Valetta, Malta | 1555 |
| 6 | Bayericsche Staatsbibliothek | Munich, Germany | 1558 |
| 7 | National Library of Belgium | Brussels, Belgium | 1559 |
| 8 | Zagreb National and University Library | Zagreb, Croatia | 1606 |
| 9 | National Library of Finland | Helsinki, Finland | 1640 |
| 10 | National Library of Denmark | Copenhagen, Denmark | 1653 |

What may claim to be the world's first national library was that in Alexandria, Egypt, founded in about 307 BC by King Ptolemy I Soter. The library assembled the world's largest collection of scrolls, which were partly destroyed during Julius Caesar's invasion of 47 BC, and totally by Arab invaders in 642 AD, an event that is considered one of the greatest ever losses to scholarship. Among national libraries in the English-speaking world, Scotland's dates from 1682 (thus predating the British Library, part of the British Museum, established in 1753). The US Library of Congress was founded in 1800.

## TOP 10 ★
## LARGEST PUBLIC LIBRARIES IN THE US

| | LIBRARY/NO. OF BRANCHES | LOCATION | FOUNDED | BOOKS |
|---|---|---|---|---|
| 1 | New York Public Library (The Branch Libraries), 85 | New York, NY | 1895* | 10,421,691# |
| 2 | Public Library of Cincinnati and Hamilton County, 41 | Cincinnati, OH | 1853 | 9,608,333 |
| 3 | Chicago Public Library, 79 | Chicago, IL | 1872 | 9,238,328 |
| 4 | Queens Borough Public Library, 62 | Jamaica, NY | 1896 | 9,143,760 |
| 5 | Free Library of Philadelphia, 52 | Philadelphia, PA | 1891 | 8,144,478 |
| 6 | Boston Public Library, 25 | Boston, MA | 1852 | 7,438,880 |
| 7 | County of Los Angeles Public Library, 85 | Los Angeles, CA | 1872 | 7,289,562 |
| 8 | Brooklyn Public Library, 58 | Brooklyn, NY | 1896 | 6,809,959 |
| 9 | Carnegie Library of Pittsburgh, 19 | Pittsburgh, PA | 1895 | 6,303,408 |
| 10 | Los Angeles Public Library, 66 | Los Angeles, CA | 1872 | 5,722,733 |

* Astor Library founded 1848; consolidated with Lenox Library and Tilden Trust to form New York Public Library, 1895

# Lending library and reference library holdings available for loan   Source: *American Library Association*

## TOP 10 COUNTRIES WITH THE MOST PUBLIC LIBRARIES
*(Country/public libraries)*

1 Russia, 33,200  2 UK, 23,678  3 Germany, 20,448  4 US, 9,097
5 Czech Republic, 8,398  6 Romania, 7,181  7 Bulgaria, 5,591  8 Hungary, 4,765
9 Brazil, 3,600  10 China, 2,406

## TOP 10 ★
# LARGEST LIBRARIES

| | LIBRARY | LOCATION | FOUNDED | BOOKS |
|---|---|---|---|---|
| 1 | Library of Congress | Washington, DC | 1800 | 24,616,867 |
| 2 | National Library of China | Beijing, China | 1909 | 20,000,000 |
| 3 | National Library of Canada | Ottawa, Canada | 1953 | 16,000,000 |
| 4 | Deutsche Bibliothek* | Frankfurt, Germany | 1990 | 15,997,000 |
| 5 | British Library# | London, UK | 1753 | 15,000,000 |
| 6 | Harvard University Library | Cambridge, Massachusetts | 1638 | 14,190,704 |
| 7 | Vernadsky Central Scientific Library of the National Academy of Sciences | Kiev, Ukraine | 1919 | 13,000,000 |
| 8 | Russian State Library+ | Moscow, Russia | 1862 | 11,750,000 |
| 9 | Bibliothèque Nationale de Paris | Paris, France | 1400 | 11,000,000 |
| 10 | New York Public Library★ | New York | 1895 | 10,421,691 |

\* Formed in 1990 through the unification of the Deutsche Bibliothek, Frankfurt (founded 1947) and the Deutsche Bucherei, Leipzig

# Founded as part of the British Museum, 1753; became an independent body in 1973

+ Founded 1862 as Rumyantsev Library, formerly State V. I. Lenin Library

★ Astor Library founded 1848, consolidated with Lenox Library and Tilden Trust to form New York Public Library in 1895

The figures for books in such vast collections as held by these libraries represent only a fraction of the total collections, which include manuscripts, microfilms, maps, prints, and records. The Library of Congress has perhaps more than 100 million cataloged items.

### DEUTSCHE BIBLIOTHEK

*Formed in October 1990 through the merging of West and East German libraries, the Deutsche Bibliothek contains unified Germany's largest collection of books and other printed and recorded material.*

## TOP 10 ★
# LARGEST UNIVERSITY LIBRARIES IN THE US

| | LIBRARY | BOOKS |
|---|---|---|
| 1 | Harvard University | 14,190,704 |
| 2 | Yale University | 10,294,792 |
| 3 | University of Illinois-Urbana | 9,302,203 |
| 4 | University of California-Berkeley | 8,946,754 |
| 5 | Temple University | 7,783,847 |
| 6 | University of California-Los Angeles | 7,401,780 |
| 7 | University of Michigan | 7,195,097 |
| 8 | Stanford University | 7,151,546 |
| 9 | Columbia University | 7,144,703 |
| 10 | Cornell University | 6,448,496 |

Source: *American Library Association*

**Whose valuable notebooks are known as the Codex Hammer?**
*see p.109 for the answer*

A Leonardo da Vinci
B William Shakespeare
C Albert Einstein

# Book Firsts & Records

## TOP 10 ★
### MOST-PUBLISHED AUTHORS OF ALL TIME

AUTHOR/NATIONALITY

| | |
|---|---|
| 1 | **William Shakespeare** (British; 1564–1616) |
| 2 | **Charles Dickens** (British; 1812–70) |
| 3 | **Sir Walter Scott** (British; 1771–1832) |
| 4 | **Johann Goethe** (German; 1749–1832) |
| 5 | **Aristotle** (Greek; 384–322 BC) |
| 6 | **Alexandre Dumas** (père) (French; 1802–70) |
| 7 | **Robert Louis Stevenson** (British; 1850–94) |
| 8 | **Mark Twain** (American; 1835–1910) |
| 9 | **Marcus Tullius Cicero** (Roman; 106–43 BC) |
| 10 | **Honoré de Balzac** (French; 1799–1850) |

## TOP 10 ★
### BOOK-PRODUCING COUNTRIES

| | COUNTRY | TITLES PUBLISHED* |
|---|---|---|
| 1 | UK | 110,155 |
| 2 | China | 73,923 |
| 3 | Germany | 62,277 |
| 4 | US | 49,276 |
| 5 | France | 45,379 |
| 6 | Japan | 42,245 |
| 7 | Spain | 37,325 |
| 8 | Italy | 26,620 |
| 9 | South Korea | 25,017 |
| 10 | Russia | 22,028 |

\* Total of new titles, new editions, and reprints in latest year for which figures are available

## TOP 10 ★
### BOOK MARKETS

| | COUNTRY | EST. BOOK SALES, 2001 ($) |
|---|---|---|
| 1 | US | 28,379,200,000 |
| 2 | Japan | 10,872,400,000 |
| 3 | Germany | 9,764,400,000 |
| 4 | UK | 4,870,100,000 |
| 5 | China | 2,771,400,000 |
| 6 | Italy | 2,760,400,000 |
| 7 | Brazil | 2,735,500,000 |
| 8 | Spain | 2,733,300,000 |
| 9 | France | 2,733,000,000 |
| 10 | South Korea | 1,805,200,000 |

## TOP 10 ★
### BOOK BUYING COUNTRIES

| | COUNTRY | BOOK SALES PER CAPITA, 2001 ($)* |
|---|---|---|
| 1 | Norway | 134.40 |
| 2 | Germany | 119.20 |
| 3 | US | 102.60 |
| 4 | Finland | 101.30 |
| 5 | Switzerland | 100.70 |
| 6 | Belgium | 98.40 |
| 7 | Japan | 85.60 |
| 8 | UK | 81.80 |
| 9 | Singapore | 76.50 |
| 10 | Denmark | 73.00 |

\* Estimate based on 1999 prices

Source: *Euromonitor*

## TOP 10 ★
### BESTSELLING PAPERBACKS PUBLISHED OVER 50 YEARS AGO

| | BOOK/AUTHOR/YEAR | US SALES ($)* |
|---|---|---|
| 1 | *The Common Sense Book of Baby and Child Care*, Benjamin Spock, 1946 | 23,285,000 |
| 2 | *The Merriam-Webster Pocket Dictionary*, 1947 | 15,500,000 |
| 3 | *English–Spanish, Spanish–English Dictionary*, Carlos Castillo and Otto F. Bond, 1948 | 10,187,000 |
| 4 | *Gone With the Wind*, Margaret Mitchell, 1936 | 8,630,000 |
| 5 | *God's Little Acre*, Erskine Caldwell, 1946 | 8,258,400 |
| 6 | *1984*, George Orwell, 1949 | 8,147,629 |
| 7 | *Animal Farm*, George Orwell, 1946 | 7,070,892 |
| 8 | *Roget's Pocket Thesaurus*, 1946 | 7,020,000 |
| 9 | *How to Win Friends and Influence People*, Dale Carnegie, 1940 | 6,578,314 |
| 10 | *Lady Chatterley's Lover*, D. H. Lawrence, 1932 | 6,326,470 |

\* Includes hardback sales where relevant, estimated to 1975

### DR. SPOCK

Dr. Benjamin McLane Spock (1903–98) was the eldest of six children. He became a pediatric specialist and studied psychoanalysis, but his chief celebrity came from his *The Common Sense Book of Baby and Child Care*, which was published in 1946. Originally sold for 25 cents, this manual became the bestselling paperback of all time in the US. Translated into some 40 languages, it also sold more than 50 million copies worldwide, making Dr. Spock the most famous of all childcare experts.

**UNDER THE HAMMER**
The Codex Hammer, *a collection of Leonardo da Vinci's scientific writings, was compiled c.1508–10. It contains over 350 drawings illustrating the artist's scientific theories. In 1994 it achieved a record price at auction when bought by Bill Gates.*

**BEST RED BOOK**

*During the Cultural Revolution, Chinese Communist leader Mao Tse-tung (Zedong) became the subject of a personality cult, with his bestselling* Quotations ... *(Little Red Book) its most potent symbol.*

## THE 10 ★ FIRST POCKET BOOKS

BOOK/AUTHOR

1 *Lost Horizon*, James Hilton

2 *Wake Up and Live!*, Dorothea Brande

3 *Five Great Tragedies*, William Shakespeare

4 *Topper*, Thorne Smith

5 *The Murder of Roger Ackroyd*, Agatha Christie

6 *Enough Rope*, Dorothy Parker

7 *Wuthering Heights*, Emily Brontë

8 *The Way of All Flesh*, Samuel Butler

9 *The Bridge of San Luis Rey*, Thornton Wilder

10 *Bambi*, Felix Saltern

All 10 Pocket Books were published in the US in 1939 (a single title, Pearl S. Buck's Nobel Prize-winning *The Good Earth* had been test-marketed the previous year, but only in New York). When a survey of sales was conducted 18 years later, it was discovered that of the first 10, Shakespeare was the bestselling title with over 2 million copies in print, followed by James Hilton's *Lost Horizon* (1,750,000), and Thorne Smith's *Topper* (1,500,000).

## TOP 10 ★ BESTSELLING BOOKS OF ALL TIME

| BOOK/AUTHOR | FIRST PUBLISHED | APPROX. SALES |
|---|---|---|
| 1 The Bible | c.1451–55 | more than 6,000,000,000 |
| 2 Quotations from the Works of Mao Tse-tung (dubbed *Little Red Book* by the Western press) | 1966 | 900,000,000 |
| 3 American Spelling Book, Noah Webster | 1783 | up to 100,000,000 |
| 4 The Guinness Book of Records (now *Guinness World Records*) | 1955 | more than 90,000,000* |
| 5 World Almanac | 1868 | 73,500,000* |
| 6 The McGuffey Readers, William Holmes McGuffey | 1836 | 60,000,000 |
| 7 The Common Sense Book of Baby and Child Care, Benjamin Spock | 1946 | more than 50,000,000 |
| 8 A Message to Garcia, Elbert Hubbard | 1899 | up to 40,000,000 |
| 9 =In His Steps: "What Would Jesus Do?", Rev. Charles Monroe Sheldon | 1896 | more than 30,000,000 |
| =Valley of the Dolls, Jacqueline Susann | 1966 | more than 30,000,000 |

* Aggregate sales of annual publication

## TOP 10 ★ MOST EXPENSIVE BOOKS AND MANUSCRIPTS EVER SOLD AT AUCTION

| BOOK OR MANUSCRIPT/SALE | PRICE ($)* |
|---|---|
| 1 *The Codex Hammer*, c.1508–10, Christie's, New York, Nov 11, 1994 | 28,800,000 |

*Leonardo da Vinci notebook purchased by Bill Gates, the billionaire founder of Microsoft.*

| 2 *The Rothschild Prayerbook*, c.1505, Christie's, London, July 8, 1999 | 12,557,220 |

*The world record price for an illuminated manuscript.*

| 3 *The Gospels of Henry the Lion*, c.1173–75, Sotheby's, London, Dec 6, 1983 | 10,841,000 |

*At the time of sale, the most expensive manuscript or book ever sold.*

| 4 *The Birds of America*, John James Audubon, 1827–38, Christie's, New York, Mar 10, 2000 | 8,000,000 |

*The record for any natural history book.*

| 5 *The Canterbury Tales*, Geoffrey Chaucer, c.1476–77, Christie's, London, July 8, 1998 | 7,696,720 |

*Printed by William Caxton and bought by Paul Getty.*

| 6 The Gutenberg Bible, 1455, Christie's, New York, Oct 22, 1987 | 5,390,000 |

*One of the first books ever printed, by Johann Gutenberg and Johann Fust in 1455.*

| 7 *The Northumberland Bestiary*, c.1250–60, Sotheby's, London, Nov 29, 1990 | 5,049,000 |

*The highest price ever paid for an English manuscript.*

| 8 *The Burdett Psalter and Hours*, 1282–86, Sotheby's, London, June 23, 1998 | 4,517,640 |

*The third most expensive illuminated manuscript.*

| 9 *The Cornaro Missal*, c.1503, Christie's, London, July 8, 1999 | 4,185,740 |

*The world record price for an Italian manuscript.*

| 10 Autographed manuscript of nine symphonies by Wolfgang Amadeus Mozart, c.1773–74, Sotheby's, London, May 22, 1987 | 3,854,000 |

*The record for a music manuscript.*

* Excluding premiums

**Did You Know?** Audubon's *The Birds of America* is not only one of the most expensive books ever published, but it is also one of the largest: its pages measure 25 x 38 in (63.5 x 96.5 cm).

# Best-Sellers & Literary Awards

## PULITZER

Joseph Pulitzer (1847–1911) was born in Makó, Hungary. He settled in St. Louis, US, where he became a journalist and within a few years publisher of the *St. Louis Post-Dispatch*. He then purchased the *New York World*, which became America's largest circulation newspaper. In his publications, he waged war against corruption in business and government and promoted freedom of the press and journalistic professionalism. He left a $2 million endowment to establish the Columbia School of Journalism, which since 1917 has administered the Pulitzer Prizes in a range of categories for journalism, literature, music, and drama.

---

## TOP 10 ★
### CHILDREN'S BOOKS IN THE US, 2000

| AUTHOR/TITLE | SALES |
|---|---|
| 1 J. K. Rowling, *Harry Potter and the Goblet of Fire* | 7,900,000 |
| 2 Jack Canfield, *et al.*, *Chicken Soup for the Teenage Soul* | 5,250,566 |
| 3 J. K. Rowling, *Harry Potter and the Chamber of Secrets* (pb) | 4,500,000 |
| 4 J. K. Rowling, *Harry Potter and the Sorcerer's Stone* (pb) | 3,400,000 |
| 5 Jack Canfield, *et al.*, *Chicken Soup for the Teenage Soul II* | 3,036,879 |
| 6 J. K. Rowling, *Harry Potter and the Chamber of Secrets* (hb) | 2,900,000 |
| 7 J. K. Rowling, *Harry Potter and the Prisoner of Azkaban* | 2,700,000 |
| 8 Jack Canfield, *et al.*, *Chicken Soup for the Kid's Soul* | 2,053,897 |
| 9 J. K. Rowling, *Harry Potter and the Sorcerer's Stone* (hb) | 1,800,000 |
| 10 Jack Canfield, *et al.*, *Chicken Soup for the Teenage Soul III* | 1,326,652 |

Source: Publishers Weekly

---

## TOP 10 ★
### US HARDBACK NONFICTION, 2000

| AUTHOR/TITLE | SALES |
|---|---|
| 1 Spencer Johnson, *Who Moved My Cheese?* | 3,095,675 |
| 2 *Guinness World Records 2001* | 1,938,699 |
| 3 Bill Phillips, *Body for Life* | 1,265,750 |
| 4 Mitch Alborn, *Tuesdays with Morrie* | 1,265,501 |
| 5 The Beatles, *The Beatles Anthology* | 1,038,666 |
| 6 Bill O'Reilly, *The O'Reilly Factor* | 975,000 |
| 7 Philip C. McGraw, *Relationship Rescue* | 767,609 |
| 8 Thomas J. Stanley, *The Millionaire Mind* | 752,000 |
| 9 Maria Shriver, *Ten Things I Wish I'd Known – Before I Went Out Into the Real World* | 650,957 |
| 10 Andrew Weil, *Eating Well for Optimum Health* | 623,329 |

Source: Publishers Weekly

---

## TOP 10 ★
### US HARDBACK FICTION, 2000

| AUTHOR/TITLE | SALES |
|---|---|
| 1 John Grisham, *The Brethren* | 2,875,000 |
| 2 Jerry B. Jenkins and Tim LaHaye, *The Mark: The Beast Rules the World* | 2,613,087 |
| 3 Tom Clancy, *The Bear and the Dragon* | 2,130,793 |
| 4 Jerry B. Jenkins and Tim LaHaye, *The Indwelling: The Beast Takes Possession* | 1,993,694 |
| 5 Patricia Cornwell, *The Last Precinct* | 1,144,105 |
| 6 Danielle Steel, *Journey* | 975,000 |
| 7 Nicholas Sparks, *The Rescue* | 909,597 |
| 8 James Patterson, *Roses Are Red* | 854,906 |
| 9 James Patterson, *Cradle and All* | 763,321 |
| 10 Danielle Steel, *The House on Hope Street* | 750,000 |

Source: Publishers Weekly

---

## THE 10 ★
### LATEST WINNERS OF THE JOHN NEWBERY MEDAL

| YEAR | AUTHOR/BOOK |
|---|---|
| 2001 | Richard Peck, *A Year Down Yonder* |
| 2000 | Christopher Paul Curtis, *Bud, Not Buddy* |
| 1999 | Louis Sachar, *Holes* |
| 1998 | Karen Hesse, *Out of the Dust* |
| 1997 | E. L. Konigsburg, *The View from Saturday* |
| 1996 | Karen Cushman, *The Midwife's Apprentice* |
| 1995 | Sharon Creech, *Walk Two Moons* |
| 1994 | Lois Lowry, *The Giver* |
| 1993 | Cynthia Rylant, *Missing May* |
| 1992 | Phyllis Reynolds Naylor, *Shiloh* |

The John Newbery Medal is awarded annually for "the most distinguished contribution to American literature for children." Its first winner in 1923 was Hugh Lofting's *The Voyages of Doctor Dolittle*.

---

## THE 10 ★
### LATEST WINNERS OF THE NATIONAL BOOK AWARD FOR FICTION

| YEAR | AUTHOR/TITLE |
|---|---|
| 2000 | Susan Sontag, *In America* |
| 1999 | Ha Jin, *Waiting* |
| 1998 | Alice McDermott, *Charming Billy* |
| 1997 | Charles Frazier, *Cold Mountain* |
| 1996 | Andrea Barrett, *Ship Fever and Other Stories* |
| 1995 | Philip Roth, *Sabbath's Theater* |
| 1994 | William Gaddis, *A Frolic of His Own* |
| 1993 | E. Annie Proulx, *The Shipping News* |
| 1992 | Cormac McCarthy, *All the Pretty Horses* |
| 1991 | Norman Rush, *Mating* |

The National Book Award is presented by the National Book Foundation as part of its program to foster reading in the US through author events and literacy campaigns.

---

With what product is the German company Steiff associated?

*see p.114 for the answer*

A Guns
B Camera lenses
C Teddy bears

## THE 10 ★

## LATEST WINNERS OF THE PULITZER PRIZE FOR FICTION

| YEAR | AUTHOR/TITLE |
| --- | --- |
| 2001 | Michael Chabon, *The Amazing Adventures of Kavalier & Clay* |
| 2000 | Jhumpa Lhiri, *Interpreter of Maladies* |
| 1999 | Michael Cunningham, *The Hours* |
| 1998 | Philip Roth, *American Pastoral* |
| 1997 | Steven Millhauser, *Martin Dressler: The Tale of an American Dreamer* |
| 1996 | Richard Ford, *Independence Day* |
| 1995 | Carol Shields, *The Stone Diaries* |
| 1994 | E. Annie Proulx, *The Shipping News* |
| 1993 | Robert Olen Butler, *A Good Scent From a Strange Mountain: Stories* |
| 1992 | Jane Smiley, *A Thousand Acres* |

## THE 10 ★

## LATEST WINNERS OF HUGO AWARDS FOR THE BEST SCIENCE FICTION NOVEL

| YEAR | AUTHOR/TITLE |
| --- | --- |
| 2000 | Vernor Vinge, *A Deepness in the Sky* |
| 1999 | Connie Willis, *To Say Nothing of the Dog* |
| 1998 | Joe Haldeman, *Forever Peace* |
| 1997 | Kim Stanley Robinson, *Blue Mars* |
| 1996 | Neal Stephenson, *The Diamond Age* |
| 1995 | Lois McMaster Bujold, *Mirror Dance* |
| 1994 | Kim Stanley Robinson, *Green Mars* |
| 1993 = | Vernor Vinge, *A Fire Upon the Deep* |
| = | Connie Willis, *Doomsday Book* |
| 1992 | Lois McMaster Bujold, *Barrayar* |

## THE 10 ★

## LATEST WINNERS OF THE RANDOLPH CALDECOTT MEDAL

| YEAR | AUTHOR/BOOK |
| --- | --- |
| 2001 | Judith St. George (illustrated by David Small), *So You Want to be President?* |
| 2000 | Simms Taback, *Joseph Had a Little Overcoat* |
| 1999 | Jacqueline Briggs Martin (illustrated by Mary Azarian), *Snowflake Bentley* |
| 1998 | Paul O. Zelinsky, *Rapunzel* |
| 1997 | David Wisniewski, *Golem* |
| 1996 | Peggy Rathman, *Officer Buckle and Gloria* |
| 1995 | Eve Bunting (illustrated by David Diaz), *Smoky Night* |
| 1994 | Allen Say, *Grandfather's Journey* |
| 1993 | Emily Arnold McCully, *Mirette on the High Wire* |
| 1992 | David Wiesner, *Tuesday* |

## THE 10 ★

## LATEST BOOKER PRIZE WINNERS

| YEAR | AUTHOR/TITLE |
| --- | --- |
| 2000 | Margaret Atwood, *The Blind Assassin* |
| 1999 | J. M. Coetzee, *Disgrace* |
| 1998 | Ian McEwan, *Amsterdam* |
| 1997 | Arundhati Roy, *The God of Small Things* |
| 1996 | Graham Swift, *Last Orders* |
| 1995 | Pat Barker, *The Ghost Road* |
| 1994 | James Kelman, *How Late It Was, How Late* |
| 1993 | Roddy Doyle, *Paddy Clarke Ha Ha Ha* |
| 1992 = | Michael Ondaatje, *The English Patient* |
| = | Barry Unsworth, *Sacred Hunger* |

J. M. Coetzee is the only person to have won the Booker prize twice, in 1999 with *Disgrace* and in 1983 with *Life and Times of Michael K*.

#### MARGARET ATWOOD

*Canadian poet and novelist Margaret Atwood joins the list of Booker Prize winners for her tenth novel,* The Blind Assassin. *Two of her previous books,* The Handmaid's Tale *and* Cat's Eye, *were shortlisted.*

# The Press

## TOP 10 ★
### NON-ENGLISH-LANGUAGE DAILY NEWSPAPERS

| | NEWSPAPER | COUNTRY | AVERAGE DAILY CIRCULATION |
|---|---|---|---|
| 1 | Yomiuri Shimbun | Japan | 14,476,000 |
| 2 | Asahi Shimbun | Japan | 12,475,000 |
| 3 | Mainichi Shimbun | Japan | 5,785,000 |
| 4 | Nihon Keizai Shimbun | Japan | 4,674,000 |
| 5 | Chunichi Shimbun | Japan | 4,667,000 |
| 6 | Bild-Zeitung | Germany | 4,256,000 |
| 7 | Sankei Shimbun | Japan | 2,890,000 |
| 8 | Reference News | China | 2,800,000 |
| 9 | Chosen Ilbo | South Korea | 2,348,000 |
| 10 | People's Daily | China | 2,300,000 |

Source: *World Association of Newspapers*

## TOP 10 ★
### ENGLISH-LANGUAGE DAILY NEWSPAPERS

| | NEWSPAPER | COUNTRY | AVERAGE DAILY CIRCULATION |
|---|---|---|---|
| 1 | The Sun | UK | 3,554,000 |
| 2 | Daily Mail | UK | 2,367,000 |
| 3 | The Mirror | UK | 2,262,000 |
| 4 | Wall Street Journal | US | 1,753,000 |
| 5 | USA Today | US | 1,672,000 |
| 6 | Times of India | India | 1,479,000 |
| 7 | The New York Times | US | 1,086,000 |
| 8 | Los Angeles Times | US | 1,078,000 |
| 9 | Daily Express | UK | 1,044,000 |
| 10 | The Daily Telegraph | UK | 1,033,000 |

Source: *World Association of Newspapers*

## TOP 10 ★
### MAGAZINES IN THE US

| | MAGAZINE/ISSUES PER YEAR | CIRCULATION* |
|---|---|---|
| 1 | NRTA/AARP Bulletin, 10 | 20,826,083 |
| 2 | Modern Maturity, 36 | 20,824,815 |
| 3 | Reader's Digest, 12 | 12,613,790 |
| 4 | TV Guide, 52 | 10,844,269 |
| 5 | National Geographic Magazine, 12 | 7,957,062 |
| 6 | Better Homes and Gardens, 12 | 7,627,977 |
| 7 | Family Circle, 17 | 5,002,383 |
| 8 | Good Housekeeping, 12 | 4,507,306 |
| 9 | McCall's, 12 | 4,204,022 |
| 10 | Ladies Home Journal, 12 | 4,173,295 |

* Average for the first six months of 2000

Source: *Magazine Publishers of America*

## TOP 10 ★
### NEWSPAPER-READING COUNTRIES

| | COUNTRY | DAILY COPIES PER 1,000 PEOPLE | | COUNTRY | DAILY COPIES PER 1,000 PEOPLE |
|---|---|---|---|---|---|
| 1 | Norway | 583 | 6 | Austria | 356 |
| 2 | Japan | 574 | 7 | Iceland | 341 |
| 3 | Finland | 452 | 8 | Singapore | 334 |
| 4 | Sweden | 420 | 9 | UK | 321 |
| 5 | Switzerland | 376 | 10 | Germany | 300 |

Source: *World Association of Newspapers*

## TOP 10 COUNTRIES WITH THE HIGHEST NEWSPAPER CIRCULATIONS
*(Country/average daily circulation)*

❶ Japan, 72,218,000 ❷ US, 55,979,000 ❸ China, 50,000,000 ❹ India, 25,587,000 ❺ Germany, 24,565,000 ❻ Russia, 23,800,000 ❼ UK, 18,939,000 ❽ France, 8,799,000 ❾ Brazil, 7,245,000 ❿ Italy, 5,937,000

Source: *World Association of Newspapers*

### HOLD THE FRONT PAGE

*The US is well served by its local press, but few US newspapers can claim national readership. The circulations of the three major publications shown here tend to be as regionally based as their titles imply.*

## TOP 10 ★
# DAILY NEWSPAPERS IN THE US

| NEWSPAPER | AVERAGE DAILY CIRCULATION* |
|---|---|
| 1 Wall Street Journal | 1,762,751 |
| 2 USA Today | 1,692,666 |
| 3 The New York Times | 1,097,180 |
| 4 Los Angeles Times | 1,033,399 |
| 5 Washington Post | 762,009 |
| 6 New York Daily News | 704,463 |
| 7 Chicago Tribune | 661,699 |
| 8 Long Island Newsday | 576,345 |
| 9 Houston Chronicle | 546,699 |
| 10 Dallas Morning News | 495,597 |

*\* Through September 30, 2000*

Source: *Audit Bureau of Circulations*

Apart from the *Wall Street Journal*, which focuses mainly on financial news, *USA Today* remains the US's only true national daily newspaper. Historically, America's press has been regionally based, and in consequence the top four listed are the only newspapers with million-plus circulations.

## TOP 10 ★
# SUNDAY NEWSPAPERS IN THE US

| NEWSPAPER | AVERAGE SUNDAY CIRCULATION* |
|---|---|
| 1 The New York Times | 1,682,208 |
| 2 Los Angeles Times | 1,379,564 |
| 3 Washington Post | 1,065,011 |
| 4 Chicago Tribune | 1,007,236 |
| 5 Philadelphia Inquirer | 798,252 |
| 6 New York Sunday News | 790,935 |
| 7 Dallas News | 785,758 |
| 8 Detroit News & Free Press | 748,383 |
| 9 Houston Chronicle | 743,009 |
| 10 Boston Globe | 721,859 |

*\* Through September 30, 2000*

Source: *Audit Bureau of Circulations*

America's first-ever Sunday newspaper was the Baltimore, MD, *Sunday Monitor*. Its first issue appeared on December 18, 1796, and comprised just four pages measuring 10.25 x 17 inches. Of those in the Top 10, the oldest-established is the *Philadelphia Inquirer*, founded in 1830 by printer Jasper Harding as the *Pennsylvania Inquirer*.

## TOP 10 ★
# OLDEST NEWSPAPERS IN THE US

| NEWSPAPER | YEAR ESTABLISHED |
|---|---|
| 1 The Hartford Courant, Hartford, CT | 1764 |
| 2 = Poughkeepsie Journal, Poughkeepsie, NY | 1785 |
| = The Augusta Chronicle, Augusta, GA | 1785 |
| = Register Star, Hudson, NY | 1785 |
| 5 = Pittsburgh Post Gazette, Pittsburgh, PA | 1786 |
| = Daily Hampshire Gazette, Northampton, MA | 1786 |
| 7 The Berkshire Eagle, Pittsfield, MA | 1789 |
| 8 Norwich Bulletin, Norwich, CT | 1791 |
| 9 The Recorder, Greenfield, MA | 1792 |
| 10 Intelligencer Journal, Lancaster, PA | 1794 |

Source: *Editor & Publisher Year Book*

## TOP 10 ★
# COUNTRIES WITH THE MOST NEWSPAPER TITLES PER CAPITA

| COUNTRY | DAILY TITLES PER 1,000,000 PEOPLE |
|---|---|
| 1 Uruguay | 24.79 |
| 2 Norway | 18.67 |
| 3 Russia | 18.00 |
| 4 Switzerland | 14.74 |
| 5 Cyprus | 12.27 |
| 6 Estonia | 11.76 |
| 7 Luxembourg | 11.48 |
| 8 = Iceland | 10.87 |
| = Sweden | 10.87 |
| 10 Finland | 10.85 |
| US | 5.36 |

Source: *World Association of Newspapers*

## TOP 10 ★
# WOMEN'S MAGAZINES IN THE US

| MAGAZINE/ISSUES PER YEAR | CIRCULATION* |
|---|---|
| 1 Better Homes and Gardens, 12 | 7,627,977 |
| 2 Family Circle, 17 | 5,002,383 |
| 3 Good Housekeeping, 12 | 4,507,306 |
| 4 McCall's, 12 | 4,204,022 |
| 5 Ladies Home Journal, 12 | 4,173,295 |
| 6 Woman's Day, 17 | 4,151,481 |
| 7 Cosmopolitan, 12 | 2,709,496 |
| 8 Redbook, 12 | 2,338,941 |
| 9 Martha Stewart Living, 12 | 2,310,692 |
| 10 Glamour, 12 | 2,207,914 |

*\* Average for the first six months of 2000*

Source: *Magazine Publishers of America*

The earliest women's magazine in this list is *McCall's*, originally founded (as *The Queen*) in New York by Scots-American James McCall.

## TOP 10 ★
# LONGEST-RUNNING MAGAZINES IN THE US

| MAGAZINE | FIRST PUBLISHED |
|---|---|
| 1 Scientific American | 1845 |
| 2 Town & Country | 1846 |
| 3 Harper's* | 1850 |
| 4 The Moravian | 1856 |
| 5 The Atlantic# | 1857 |
| 6 Armed Forces Journal+ | 1863 |
| 7 The Nation | 1865 |
| 8 American Naturalist | 1867 |
| 9 Harper's Bazaar | 1867 |
| 10 Animals★ | 1868 |

*\* Originally Harper's New Monthly Magazine*
*# Originally The Atlantic Monthly*
*+ Originally Army and Navy Journal*
*★ Originally Our Dumb Animals*

Source: *Magazine Publishers of America*

**Did You Know?** British writer Rudyard Kipling was fired as a reporter on the *San Francisco Examiner*, which told him "You just don't know how to use the English language." In 1907, he won the Nobel Prize for Literature.

# Toys & Games

## TOY-BUYING COUNTRIES

| | COUNTRY* | SPENDING ON TOYS, 2000 ($) |
|---|---|---|
| 1 | US | 34,554,900,000 |
| 2 | Japan | 9,190,600,000 |
| 3 | UK | 5,348,100,000 |
| 4 | France | 3,397,200,000 |
| 5 | Germany | 3,117,900,000 |
| 6 | Canada | 2,689,500,000 |
| 7 | Italy | 1,941,000,000 |
| 8 | Australia | 937,100,000 |
| 9 | Spain | 933,600,000 |
| 10 | Belgium | 754,700,000 |

\* Of those covered by survey

Source: *Euromonitor*

## TOYS INTRODUCED IN THE US IN 2000*

| | TOY/INTRODUCED | MANUFACTURER |
|---|---|---|
| 1 | Poo-chi robotic dog, April | Tiger Electronics |
| 2 | Tekno robot dog, June | Manley Toy Quest |
| 3 | Celebration Barbie, June | Mattel |
| 4 | Who Wants to Be a Millionaire, February | Pressman |
| 5 | Pokémon Rocket Booster, April | Wizards of the Coast |
| 6 | Barbie Wizard of Oz assistant, February | Mattel |
| 7 | Diva Starz doll assistant, August | Mattel |
| 8 | Barbie and Krissy mermaids, July | Mattel |
| 9 | Razor scooter, July | Razor USA |
| 10 | Gooze assistant, January | Flying Colors |

\* Ranked by dollar sales, excluding video games

Source: *NPD TRSTS Toys Tracking Service*

## TOYS IN THE US BY DOLLAR SALES, 2000

| | TOY | MANUFACTURER |
|---|---|---|
| 1 | Hot Wheels basic cars | Mattel |
| 2 | Poo-chi robotic dog | Tiger Electronics |
| 3 | Leap pad | Leapfrog |
| 4 | Barbie cruisin' jeep | Fisher-Price |
| 5 | Tekno robot dog | Manley Toy Quest |
| 6 | Celebration Barbie | Mattel |
| 7 | Pokémon series number 2 | Wizards of the Coast |
| 8 | Who Wants to Be a Millionaire | Pressman |
| 9 | Pokémon Rocket Booster pack | Wizards of the Coast |
| 10 | Barbie cash register | Kid Designs |

Source: *NPD TRSTS Toys Tracking Service*

## MOST LANDED-ON SQUARES IN MONOPOLY®*

| US GAME | | UK GAME |
|---|---|---|
| Illinois Avenue | 1 | Trafalgar Square |
| Go | 2 | Go |
| B. & O. Railroad | 3 | Fenchurch Street Station |
| Free Parking | 4 | Free Parking |
| Tennessee Avenue | 5 | Marlborough Street |
| New York Avenue | 6 | Vine Street |
| Reading Railroad | 7 | King's Cross Station |
| St. James Place | 8 | Bow Street |
| Water Works | 9 | Water Works |
| Pennsylvania Railroad | 10 | Marylebone Station |

Monopoly® is a registered trade mark of Parker Brothers division of Tonka Corporation, US.

\* Based on a computer analysis of the probability of landing on each square

## MOST EXPENSIVE TEDDY BEARS SOLD AT AUCTION IN THE UK

| | BEAR/SALE | PRICE ($)* |
|---|---|---|
| 1 | "Teddy Girl," Steiff cinnamon teddy bear, 1904, Christie's, London, Dec 5, 1994 (£110,000) | 169,928 |

*Formerly owned by Lt.-Col. Bob Henderson, this sale precisely doubled the previous world record for a teddy bear when it was acquired by Yoshiro Sekiguchi for display at his teddy bear museum near Tokyo.*

| 2 | Black mohair Steiff teddy bear, c.1912, Christie's, London, Dec 4, 2000 (£91,750) | 132,157 |

*One of a number of black Steiff teddy bears brought out in the UK after of the sinking of the Titanic; these have since become known as "mourning" teddies.*

| 3 | "Happy," dual-plush Steiff teddy bear, 1926, Sotheby's, London, Sep 19, 1989 (£55,000) | 85,470 |

*Although estimated at £700–900, competitive bidding pushed the price up to the then world record, when it was acquired by collector Paul Volpp.*

| 4 | "Elliot," blue Steiff bear, 1908, Christie's, London, Dec 6, 1993 (£49,500) | 74,275 |

*Produced as a sample for Harrods but never manufactured commercially.*

| 5 | "Teddy Edward," golden mohair teddy bear, Christie's, London, Dec 9, 1996 (£38,500) | 60,176 |
| 6 | Black mohair Steiff teddy bear, c.1912, Sotheby's, London, May 18, 1990 (£24,200) | 45,327 |

*See entry no. 2.*

| 7 | Blank button, brown Steiff teddy bear, c.1905, Christie's, London, Dec 8, 1997 (£23,000) | 35,948 |
| 8 | Black mohair Steiff teddy bear, c.1912, Christie's, London, Dec 5, 1994 (£22,000) | 34,331 |

*See entry no. 2.*

| 9 | "Albert," Steiff teddy bear, c.1910, Christie's, London, Dec 9, 1996 (£18,400) | 28,759 |
| 10 | Steiff teddy bear, Christie's, London, Dec 9, 1996 (£17,250) | 26,962 |

\* Prices include buyer's premium where appropriate

It is said that, while on a hunting trip, US President Theodore ("Teddy") Roosevelt refused to shoot a young bear. A New York shopkeeper made some stuffed bears and sold them as "Teddy's Bears."

## TOP 10 ★
# MOST EXPENSIVE TOYS EVER SOLD BY CHRISTIE'S EAST, NY

| TOY/SALE | PRICE ($)* |
|---|---|
| **1 The Charles**, a fire hose-reel made by American manufacturer George Brown & Co, c.1875, Dec 1991 | 231,000 |
| **2 Märklin fire station**, Dec 1991 | 79,200 |
| **3 Horse-drawn double-decker tram**, Dec 1991 | 71,500 |
| **4 Mikado mechanical bank**, Dec 1993 | 63,000 |
| **5 Märklin Ferris wheel**, June 1994 | 55,200 |
| **6 Girl skipping rope mechanical bank**, June 1994 | 48,300 |
| **7 Märklin battleship**, June 1994 | 33,350 |
| **8 Märklin battleship**, June 1994 | 32,200 |
| **9 =Bing keywind open phaeton tinplate automobile**, Dec 1991 | 24,200 |
| **=Märklin fire pumper**, Dec 1991 | 24,200 |

* *Including 10 percent buyer's premium*

The fire hose-reel at No. 1 in this list is the record price paid at auction for a toy other than a doll. Models by the German tinplate maker Märklin, regarded by collectors as the Rolls-Royce of toys, similarly feature among the record prices of auction houses in the UK and other countries, where high prices have also been attained. On both sides of the Atlantic, pristine examples of high-quality mechanical toys (ideally in their original boxes, and unplayed with by the children for whom they were designed) command top dollar.

# TOP 10 TRADITIONAL TOY RETAILERS IN THE US
*(Retailer/type/market share percentage, 1999)*

**1** Wal-Mart, discount, 17.4 **2** Toys R Us, toy, 15.6 **3** Kmart, discount, 7.2 **4** Target, discount, 6.8 **5** KB Toys/Toy Works, toy, 5.1 **6** Ames, discount, 1.6 **7** J. C. Penney, department, 1.2 **8** Hallmark, card, 1.1 **9** Meijer, discount, 1.0 **10** Shopko, discount, 0.8

Source: *NPD Toy Market Index Service*

## TOP 10 ★
# INTERACTIVE ENTERTAINMENT SOFTWARE TITLES IN THE US, 2000*

| GAME/FORMAT | PUBLISHER |
|---|---|
| **1 Pokémon Silver**, Gameboy Color | Nintendo of America |
| **2 Pokémon Gold**, Gameboy Color | Nintendo of America |
| **3 Pokémon Yellow**, Gameboy | Nintendo of America |
| **4 Pokémon Stadium**, Nintendo 64 | Nintendo of America |
| **5 Tony Hawks Pro Skater 2**, Playstation | Activision |
| **6 Legend Zelda: Majora's Mask**, Nintendo 64 | Nintendo of America |
| **7 Tony Hawks Pro Skater**, Playstation | Activision |
| **8 Gran Turismo 2**, Playstation | Sony Computer Entertainment |
| **9 Pokémon Blue**, Gameboy | Nintendo of America |
| **10 Pokémon Red**, Gameboy | Nintendo of America |

* *Ranked by units sold*

Source: *NPD TRSTS Toys Tracking Service*

## TOP 10 ★
# BOARD GAMES IN THE US

| GAME* | MANUFACTURER |
|---|---|
| **1 Who Wants to Be a Millionaire** | Pressman |
| **2 Monopoly** | Hasbro Games |
| **3 The Game of Life** | Hasbro Games |
| **4 Trouble** | Hasbro Games |
| **5 Sorry** | Hasbro Games |
| **6 Clue** | Hasbro Games |
| **7 Pokémon Monopoly** | Hasbro Games |
| **8 Guess Who** | Hasbro Games |
| **9 Taboo** | Hasbro Games |
| **10 Pokémon Master Trainer** | Hasbro Games |

* *Including children's, family, and adult board games*

Source: *NPD TRSTS Standard Service*

### BARBIE

Ruth and Elliot Handler, cofounders of American toy manufacturers Mattel, introduced the first Barbie doll in February 1959. Previously, most dolls were babies, but Ruth Handler had seen her daughter Barbara – who provided the doll's name – playing with paper dolls with adult attributes and realized that there would be a market for a grown-up doll, complete with an extensive wardrobe of clothes and accessories. The first Barbie was dressed in a striped swimsuit, with high heels, sunglasses, and gold hoop earrings. Sold at $3.00 each, 351,000 Barbies were sold in the first year.

WHO WAS · WHO WAS · WHO WAS · WHO WAS

# TOP 10 MOST POPULAR TYPES OF TOY
*(Type of toy/market share percentage, 1998)*

**1** Video games, 21.5 **2** Activity toys, 13.0 **3** Infant/pre-school toys, 11.0 **4** = Dolls, 10.5; = Games/puzzles, 10.5; = Other toys, 10.5 **7** Toy vehicles, 9.0 **8** = Action figures, 5.0; = Plushes, 5.0 **10** Ride-on toys, 4.0

Source: *Eurotoys/The NPD Group Worldwide*

This list is based on a survey of toy consumption in the European Union and can be taken as a reliable guide to the most popular types of toy in the developed world.

# Art on Show

## ART EXHIBITIONS, 2000

| | EXHIBITION/ART GALLERY/LOCATION | DATES | ATTENDANCE TOTAL | DAILY |
|---|---|---|---|---|
| 1 | *Earthly Art – Heavenly Beauty*, State Hermitage, St. Petersburg, Russia | June 13–Sep 17 | 570,000* | 5,876 |
| 2 | *Sinai: Byzantium, Russia*, State Hermitage, St. Petersburg, Russia | June 20–Sep 18 | 500,000* | 5,495 |
| 3 | *Seeing Salvation: Image of Christ*, National Gallery, London, UK | Feb 26–May 7 | 355,175 | 5,002 |
| 4 | *Picasso's World of Children*, National Museum of Western Art, Tokyo, Japan | Mar 14–June 18 | 386,086 | 4,290 |
| 5 | *Dutch Art: Rembrandt and Vermeer*, National Museum of Western Art, Tokyo, Japan | July 4–Sep 24 | 280,259 | 3,892 |
| 6 | *Amazons of the Avant-Garde*, Guggenheim Museum, Bilbao, Spain | June 13–Aug 27 | 283,181 | 3,879 |
| 7 | *The Glory of the Golden Age*, Rijksmuseum, Amsterdam, Netherlands | Apr 15–Sep 17 | 594,122 | 3,808 |
| 8 | *Van Gogh: Face to Face*, Museum of Fine Arts, Boston, US | July 2–Sep 24 | 316,049 | 3,762 |
| 9 | *Van Gogh: Face to Face*, Detroit Institute of Arts, Detroit, US | Mar 12–June 4 | 315,000* | 3,706 |
| 10 | *Triumph of the Baroque*, National Gallery of Art, Washington, DC, US | May 21–Oct 9 | 526,050 | 3,705 |

\* *Approximate total provided by museum*          Source: *The Art Newspaper*

## BEST ATTENDED EXHIBITIONS AT THE MUSEUM OF FINE ARTS, BOSTON

| | EXHIBITION/YEAR | ATTENDANCE |
|---|---|---|
| 1 | *Monet in the 20th Century*, 1998 | 565,992 |
| 2 | *Monet in the Nineties*, 1990 | 537,502 |
| 3 | *Renoir*, 1985–86 | 515,795 |
| 4 | *John Singer Sargent*, 1999 | 318,707 |
| 5 | *Van Gogh: Face to Face*, 2000 | 316,049 |
| 6 | *Picasso: The Early Years*, 1892–1906, 1997–98 | 283,423 |
| 7 | *Winslow Homer*, 1996 | 276,922 |
| 8 | *A New World: Masterpieces of American Painting 1760–1910*, 1983 | 264,640 |
| 9 | *Herb Ritts: Work*, 1996–97 | 253,649 |
| 10 | *Mary Cassatt Modern Woman*, 1999 | 230,750 |

Source: *Museum of Fine Arts, Boston*

## EXHIBITIONS IN NEW YORK, 2000

| | EXHIBITION/VENUE | ATTENDANCE TOTAL | DAILY |
|---|---|---|---|
| 1 | *Egyptian Art in the Age of the Pyramids*, Metropolitan Museum of Art | 462,757 | 3,560 |
| 2 | *World of Nam June Paik*, Solomon R. Guggenheim | 22,078 | 3,154 |
| 3 | *Walker Evans*, Metropolitan Museum of Art | 212,487 | 2,951 |
| 4 | *1900: Art at the Crossroads*, Solomon R. Guggenheim | 20,290 | 2,899 |
| 5 | *Chardin*, Metropolitan Museum of Art | 182,040 | 2,638 |
| 6 | *Portraits by Ingres: Image of an Epoch*, Metropolitan Museum of Art | 232,191 | 2,580 |
| 7 | *Rock Style*, Metropolitan Museum of Art | 248,145 | 2,457 |
| 8 | *Ancient Faces: Mummy Portraits from Roman Egypt*, Metropolitan Museum of Art | 186,272 | 2,272 |
| 9 | *American Century Part II*, Whitney Museum | 274,714 | 2,270 |
| 10 | *Barbara Kruger*, Whitney Museum | 184,395 | 2,095 |

Source: The Art Newspaper

The impressive attendance figures achieved by New York's Guggenheim were actually lower than those of the relatively new (1997) Guggenheim in Bilbao, Spain. This list of Manhattan's most popular shows excludes two staged by the Museum of Modern Art, *Modern Starts* and *Making Choices*, which each attracted over 4,000 visitors a day, since both were based on the Museum's own collections, and thus do not constitute temporary exhibitions.

## EXHIBITIONS AT THE NATIONAL GALLERY OF ART, WASHINGTON, DC

| | EXHIBITION/YEAR | ATTENDANCE |
|---|---|---|
| 1 | *Rodin Rediscovered*, 1981–82 | 1,053,223 |
| 2 | *Treasure Houses of Britain*, 1985–86 | 990,474 |
| 3 | *The Treasures of Tutankhamun*, 1976–77 | 835,924 |
| 4 | *Archaeological Finds of the People's Republic of China*, 1974–75 | 684,238 |
| 5 | *Ansel Adams: Classic Images*, 1985–86 | 651,652 |
| 6 | *The Splendor of Dresden*, 1978 | 620,089 |
| 7 | *The Art of Paul Gauguin*, 1988 | 596,058 |
| 8 | *Circa 1492: Art in the Age of Exploration*, 1991–92 | 568,192 |
| 9 | *Andrew Wyeth: The Helga Pictures*, 1987 | 558,433 |
| 10 | *Post Impressionism: Cross Currents in European & American Painting*, 1980 | 557,533 |

Source: *National Gallery of Art*

In which year was Dr. Spock's baby and child care book published?   A 1952
*see p.108 for the answer*   B 1946
C 1943

# TOP 10 ★
## TALLEST FREESTANDING STATUES

| STATUE/LOCATION | HEIGHT FT | M |
|---|---|---|
| **1 Chief Crazy Horse**, Thunderhead Mountain, South Dakota | 563 | 172 |

*Started in 1948 by Polish–American sculptor Korczak Ziolkowski, and continued after his death in 1982 by his widow and eight of his children, this gigantic equestrian statue is even longer (641 ft/195 m) than it is high. It is being carved out of the granite mountain by dynamiting and drilling, and is not expected to be completed for several years.*

| | | |
|---|---|---|
| **2 Buddha**, Tokyo, Japan | 394 | 120 |

*This Japanese–Taiwanese project, unveiled in 1993, took seven years to complete and weighs 1,100 tons.*

| | | |
|---|---|---|
| **3 The Indian Rope Trick**, Riddersberg Säteri, Jönköping, Sweden | 337 | 103 |

*Sculptor Calle Örnemark's 159-ton wooden sculpture depicts a long strand of "rope" held by a fakir, while another figure ascends.*

| | | |
|---|---|---|
| **4 Motherland**, Volgograd, Russia | 270 | 82 |

*This concrete statue of a woman with a raised sword, designed by Yevgeniy Vuchetich, commemorates the Soviet victory at the Battle of Stalingrad (1942–43).*

| | | |
|---|---|---|
| **5 Kannon**, Otsubo-yama, near Tokyo, Japan | 170 | 52 |

*The immense statue of the goddess of mercy was unveiled in 1961 in honor of the dead of World War II.*

| | | |
|---|---|---|
| **6 Statue of Liberty**, New York | 151 | 46 |

*Designed by Auguste Bartholdi and presented to the US by the people of France, the statue was shipped in sections to Liberty (formerly Bedloes) Island, where it was assembled before being unveiled on October 28, 1886.*

| | | |
|---|---|---|
| **7 Christ**, Rio de Janeiro, Brazil | 125 | 38 |

*The work of sculptor Paul Landowski and engineer Heitor da Silva Costa, the figure of Christ was unveiled in 1931.*

| | | |
|---|---|---|
| **8 Tian Tan (Temple of Heaven) Buddha**, Po Lin Monastery, Lantau Island, Hong Kong, China | 112 | 34 |

*This was completed after 20 years' work and was unveiled on December 29, 1993.*

| | | |
|---|---|---|
| **9 Quantum Cloud**, Greenwich, London, UK | 95 | 29 |

*A gigantic steel human figure surrounded by a matrix of steel struts, it was created in 1999 by Antony Gormley, the sculptor of the similarly gigantic 66-ft (20-m) Angel of the North, Gateshead, UK.*

| | | |
|---|---|---|
| **10 Colossi of Memnon**, Karnak, Egypt | 70 | 21 |

*This statue portrays two seated sandstone figures of Pharaoh Amenhotep III.*

Various projects are in the planning stages, including a 555-ft (169-m) statue of a woman, the Spirit of Houston, and even taller statues of Buddha. If realized, these will enter this Top 10 in the future.

**STATUE OF LIBERTY**
*Originally called "Liberty Enlightening the World," the Statue of Liberty was a gift to the people of the United States of America from the French nation.*

# Art on Sale

## MOST EXPENSIVE PAINTINGS EVER SOLD AT AUCTION

| PAINTING/ARTIST/SALE | PRICE ($) |
|---|---|
| 1 *Portrait of Dr. Gachet*, **Vincent van Gogh** (Dutch; 1853–90), Christie's, New York, May 15, 1990 | 75,000,000 |
| 2 *Au Moulin de la Galette*, **Pierre-Auguste Renoir** (French; 1841–1919), Sotheby's, New York, May 17, 1990 | 71,000,000 |
| 3 *Portrait de l'Artiste sans Barbe*, **Vincent van Gogh**, Christie's, New York, Nov 19, 1998 | 65,000,000 |
| 4 *Rideau, Cruchon et Compotier*, **Paul Cézanne** (French; 1839–1906), Sotheby's, New York, May 10, 1999 | 55,000,000 |
| 5 *Les Noces de Pierrette, 1905*, **Pablo Picasso** (Spanish; 1881–1973), Binoche et Godeau, Paris, Nov 30, 1989 | 51,671,920 (F.Fr315,000,000) |
| 6 *Femme aux Bras Croisés*, **Pablo Picasso**, Christie's Rockefeller, New York, Nov 8, 2000 | 50,000,000 |
| 7 *Irises*, **Vincent van Gogh**, Sotheby's, New York, Nov 11, 1987 | 49,000,000 |
| 8 *Femme Assise dans un Jardin*, **Pablo Picasso**, Sotheby's, New York, Nov 10, 1999 | 45,000,000 |
| 9 *Le Rêve*, **Pablo Picasso**, Christie's, New York, Nov 10, 1997 | 44,000,000 |
| 10 *Self Portrait: Yo Picasso*, **Pablo Picasso**, Sotheby's, New York, May 9, 1989 | 43,500,000 |

## ARTISTS WITH THE MOST WORKS SOLD AT AUCTION FOR MORE THAN $1 MILLION

| ARTIST | TOTAL VALUE OF WORKS SOLD ($) | NO. OF WORKS SOLD |
|---|---|---|
| 1 **Pablo Picasso** (Spanish; 1881–1973) | 1,313,943,108 | 272 |
| 2 **Claude Monet** (French; 1840–1926) | 945,249,016 | 218 |
| 3 **Pierre Auguste Renoir** (French; 1841–1919) | 633,928,714 | 196 |
| 4 **Edgar Degas** (French; 1834–1917) | 299,862,103 | 100 |
| 5 **Paul Cézanne** (French; 1839–1906) | 417,550,573 | 80 |
| 6 **Camille Pissaro** (French; 1830–1903) | 136,504,994 | 74 |
| 7 **Marc Chagall** (Russian; 1887–1985) | 164,486,200 | 73 |
| 8 **Henri Matisse** (French; 1869–1954) | 249,980,445 | 68 |
| 9 **Amedeo Modigliani** (Italian; 1884–1920) | 272,613,301 | 61 |
| 10 **Vincent van Gogh** (Dutch; 1853–90) | 542,660,639 | 57 |

**RAGS TO RICHES**

*The impoverished van Gogh painted this self-portrait,* Portrait de l'Artiste sans Barbe, *at Arles in September 1888. Just over a century later, it realized $65 million, making it the third most expensive painting ever sold at auction.*

## MOST EXPENSIVE PIECES OF SCULPTURE EVER SOLD AT AUCTION

| SCULPTURE/ARTIST/SALE | PRICE ($) |
|---|---|
| 1 *Grande Femme Debout I*, **Alberto Giacometti** (Swiss; 1901–66), Christie's Rockefeller, New York, Nov 8, 2000 | 13,000,000 |
| 2 *La Serpentine Femme à la Stèle – l'Araignée*, **Henri Matisse** (French; 1869–1954), Sotheby's, New York, May 10, 2000 | 12,750,000 |
| 3 *Petite Danseuse de Quatorze Ans*, **Edgar Degas**, Sotheby's, New York, Nov 11, 1999 | 11,250,000 |
| 4 *Petite Danseuse de Quatorze Ans*, **Edgar Degas**, Sotheby's, New York, Nov 12, 1996 | 10,800,000 |
| 5 *Petite Danseuse de Quatorze Ans*, **Edgar Degas**, (French; 1834–1917), Sotheby's, London, June 27, 2000 | 10,222,100 (£7,000,000) |
| 6 *The Dancing Faun*, **Adriaen de Vries**, (Dutch; c.1550–1626), Sotheby's, London, Dec 7, 1989 | 9,634,800 (£6,200,000) |
| 7 *Petite Danseuse de Quatorze Ans*, **Edgar Degas**, Christie's, New York, Nov 14, 1988 | 9,250,000 |
| 8 *Petite Danseuse de Quatorze Ans*, **Edgar Degas**, Sotheby's, New York, May 10, 1988 | 9,200,000 |
| 9 *Nu Couché, Aurore*, **Henri Matisse**, Christie's Rockefeller, New York, Nov 9, 1999 | 8,400,000 |
| 10 *La Muse Endormie III*, **Constantin Brancusi** (Romanian; 1876–1957), Christie's, New York, Nov 14, 1989 | 7,500,000 |

**What is the most expensive item of pop memorabilia ever sold at auction?**
*see p.125 for the answer*

A  A guitar
B  A dress
C  A car

## TOP 10 ★
# MOST EXPENSIVE OLD MASTER PAINTINGS EVER SOLD AT AUCTION

PAINTING/ARTIST/SALE      PRICE ($)

**1** *Portrait of Duke Cosimo I de Medici*, **Jacopo da Carucci (Pontormo)**
(Italian; 1493–1558), Christie's, New York, May 31, 1989    32,000,000

**2** *The Old Horse Guards, London, from St. James's Park*, **Canaletto**
(Italian; 1697–1768), Christie's, London, Apr 15, 1992    16,008,000 (£9,200,000)

**3** *Vue de la Giudecca et du Zattere à Venise*, **Francesco Guardi**
(Italian; 1712–93), Sotheby's, Monaco, Dec 1, 1989    13,943,218 (F.Fr85,000,000)

**4** *Venus and Adonis*, **Titian**
(Italian; c.1488–1576), Christie's, London, Dec 13, 1991    12,376,000 (£6,800,000)

**5** *Tieleman Roosterman in Black Doublet, White Ruff*, **Frans Hals the Elder**
(Dutch; c.1580–1666), Christie's, London, July 8, 1999    11,625,001 (£7,500,000)

**6** *Le Retour du Bucentaure le Jour de l'Ascension*, **Canaletto**, Ader Tajan, Paris, Dec 15, 1993    11,316,457 (F.Fr66,000,000)

**7** *The Risen Christ*, **Michelangelo**
(Italian; 1475–1564), Christie's, London, July 4, 2000    11,174,001 (£7,400,000)

**8** *View of Molo from Bacino di San Marco, Venice* and *View of the Grand Canal Facing East from Campo di Santi, Venice* (pair), **Canaletto**, Sotheby's, New York, June 1, 1990    10,000,000

**9** *Adoration of the Magi*, **Andrea Mantegna**
(Italian; 1431–1506), Christie's, London, Apr 18, 1985    9,525,000 (£7,500,000)

**10** *Portrait of a Girl Wearing a Gold-trimmed Cloak*, **Rembrandt**
(Dutch; 1606–69), Sotheby's, London, Dec 10, 1986    9,372,000 (£6,600,000)

### PRICEY PRE-RAPHAELITE

*Although popular in their day, the Pre-Raphaelites fell out of favor until the late 20th century, when works such as* Sleeping *by Sir John Everett Millais began to command record prices.*

## TOP 10 ★
# MOST EXPENSIVE PRE-RAPHAELITE PAINTINGS EVER SOLD AT AUCTION

| PAINTING/ARTIST*/SALE | PRICE ($) |
|---|---|
| **1** *St. Cecilia*, **John William Waterhouse** (1849–1917), Christie's, London, June 14, 2000 (£6,000,000) | 9,060,001 |
| **2** *Pandora*, **Dante Gabriel Rossetti** (1828–82), Christie's, London, June 14, 2000 (£2,400,000) | 3,624,000 |
| **3** *Sleeping*, **Sir John Everett Millais** (1829–96), Christie's, London, June 10, 1999 (£1,900,000) | 3,040,000 |
| **4** *The Shadow of Death*, **William Holman Hunt**, (1827–1910), Sotheby's, London, Nov 2, 1994 (£1,700,000) | 2,720,000 |
| **5** *Proserpine*, **Dante Gabriel Rossetti**, Christie's, London, Nov 27, 1987 (£1,300,000) | 2,366,000 |

| PAINTING/ARTIST*/SALE | PRICE ($) |
|---|---|
| **6** *Ophelia*, **John William Waterhouse**, Phillips, London, June 14, 2000 (£1,500,000) | 2,265,000 |
| **7** *The Awakening of Adonis*, **John William Waterhouse**, Sotheby's, New York, Nov 10, 1998 | 2,125,000 |
| **8=** *Val d'Aosta*, **John Brett** (1830–1902), Sotheby's, London, June 20, 1989 (£1,200,000) | 1,932,000 |
| **=** *Joan of Arc*, **Sir John Everett Millais**, Sotheby's, London, Nov 10, 1999 (£1,200,000) | 1,848,000 |
| **10** *Master Hilary – The Tracer*, **William Holman Hunt**, Christie's, London, June 3, 1994 (£880,000) | 1,320,000 |

*\* All British*

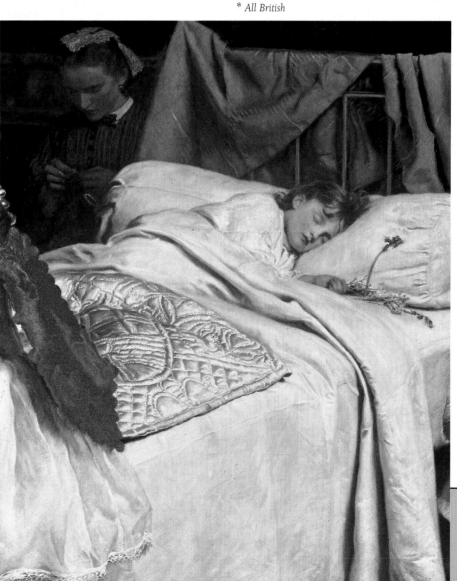

# 20th-Century Artists

## MOST EXPENSIVE WORKS BY ALEXANDER CALDER

| MOBILE OR SCULPTURE/SALE | PRICE ($) |
|---|---|
| **1** *Brazilian Fish*, Sotheby's, New York, Nov 17, 1999 | 3,550,000 |
| **2** *The Tree*, Selkirks, St. Louis, May 22, 1989 | 1,900,000 |
| **3** *Constellation*, Sotheby's, New York, May 18, 1999 | 1,800,000 |
| **4** *Constellation*, Sotheby's, New York, Nov 10, 1993 | 1,650,000 |
| **5** *Trépied*, Sotheby's, New York, May 18, 1999 | 1,400,000 |
| **6** *Eighteen Numbered Black*, Sotheby's, New York, Nov 17, 1998 | 1,150,000 |
| **7** *Mobile au Plomb*, Christie's, London, June 28, 2000 | 1,087,000 (£720,000) |
| **8** *Haverford Monster*, Sotheby's, New York, May 4, 1994 | 980,000 |
| **9** =*Laocoon*, Christie's, New York, Nov 14, 1995 | 900,000 |
| =*Hanging Apricot*, Christie's Rockefeller, New York, May 13, 1999 | 900,000 |

## MOST EXPENSIVE PAINTINGS BY LUCIAN FREUD

| PAINTING/SALE | PRICE ($) |
|---|---|
| **1** *Large Interior, W11*, Sotheby's, New York, May 14, 1998 | 5,300,000 |
| **2** *Naked Portrait with Reflection*, Sotheby's, London, Dec 9, 1998 | 4,284,000 (£2,550,000) |
| **3** *Painter's Mother*, Sotheby's, New York, May 18, 1999 | 3,000,000 |
| **4** *Evening in the Studio*, Sotheby's, New York, Nov 17, 1999 | 2,200,000 |
| **5** *Man in Headscarf*, Christie's, London, June 30, 1999 | 1,659,000 (£1,050,000) |
| **6** *Portrait of Frank Auerbach*, Sotheby's, London, Dec 3, 1998 | 1,377,800 (£830,000) |
| **7** *John Deakin*, Christie's, London, June 25, 1997 | 1,344,600 (£810,000) |
| **8** *Man Smoking*, Sotheby's, London, June 28, 1990 | 1,056,000 (£600,000) |
| **9** *The Painter's Room*, Sotheby's, London, June 29, 1994 | 703,800 (£460,000) |
| **10** *Naked Man on Bed*, Sotheby's, New York, Nov 17, 1998 | 600,000 |

## MOST EXPENSIVE PAINTINGS BY PABLO PICASSO

| PAINTING/SALE | PRICE ($) |
|---|---|
| **1** *Les Noces de Pierrette, 1905*, Binoche et Godeau, Paris, Nov 30, 1989 | 51,671,920 (F.Fr315,000,000) |
| **2** *Femme aux Bras Croisés*, Christie's Rockefeller, New York, Nov 8, 2000 | 50,000,000 |
| **3** *Femme Assise dans un Jardin*, Sotheby's, New York, Nov 10, 1999 | 45,000,000 |
| **4** *Le Rêve*, Christie's, New York, Nov 10, 1997 | 44,000,000 |
| **5** *Self Portrait: Yo Picasso*, Sotheby's, New York, May 9, 1989 | 43,500,000 |
| **6** *Nu au Fauteuil Noir*, Christie's Rockefeller, New York, Nov 9, 1999 | 41,000,000 |
| **7** *Au Lapin Agile*, Sotheby's, New York, Nov 15, 1989 | 37,000,000 |
| **8** *Acrobate et Jeune Arlequin*, Christie's, London, Nov 28, 1988 | 35,530,000 (£19,000,000) |
| **9** *Les Femmes d'Alger, Version O*, Christie's, New York, Nov 10, 1997 | 29,000,000 |
| **10** *Angel Fernandez de Soto*, Sotheby's, New York, May 8, 1995 | 26,500,000 |

## MOST EXPENSIVE PAINTINGS BY MARC CHAGALL

| PAINTING/SALE | PRICE ($) |
|---|---|
| **1** *Anniversaire*, Sotheby's, New York, May 17, 1990 | 13,500,000 |
| **2** *Au Dessus de la Ville*, Christie's, New York, May 15, 1990 | 9,000,000 |
| **3** *Le Village Russe de la Lune*, Sotheby's, New York, Nov 11, 1999 | 7,500,000 |
| **4** *La Mariée sous le Baldaquin*, Sotheby's, London, Apr 3, 1990 | 5,542,000 (£3,400,000) |
| **5** =*Le Buveur – Le Saoul*, Christie's, New York, Nov 14, 1990 | 5,000,000 |
| =*La Chambre Jaune*, Christie's Rockefeller, New York, Nov 9, 1999 | 5,000,000 |
| **7** *Le Bouquet des Fermiers*, Sotheby's, London, Apr 3, 1990 | 4,564,000 (£2,800,000) |
| **8** *Two Bouquets*, Sotheby's, New York, May 17, 1990 | 4,400,000 |
| **9** *Le Violoniste au Monde Renversé*, Habsburg, New York, May 8, 1989 | 4,200,000 |
| **10** *Les Amoureux*, Sotheby's, London, June 24, 1996 | 3,850,000 (£2,500,000) |

**Did You Know?** Alexander Calder's *White Cascade* mobile, installed in Philadelphia, Pennsylvania, in 1976, is one of the biggest works of art ever constructed: it is 100 ft (30.5 m) tall and weighs 8.8 tons.

## TOP 10 ★
# MOST EXPENSIVE PAINTINGS BY FRANCIS BACON

| PAINTING/SALE | PRICE ($) |
|---|---|
| **1** *Triptych May–June*, Sotheby's, New York, May 2, 1989 | 5,700,000 |
| **2** *Study for Portrait of van Gogh II*, Sotheby's, New York, May 2, 1989 | 5,300,000 |
| **3** *Study for Pope*, Christie's, New York, Nov 7, 1989 | 5,200,000 |
| **4** *Study for Portrait*, Sotheby's, New York, May 8, 1990 | 5,000,000 |
| **5** *Study for a Portrait – Man Screaming*, Christie's, London, June 28, 2000 | 4,077,000 (£2,700,000) |
| **6** *Portrait of George Dyer Staring into Mirror*, Christie's, New York, Nov 7, 1990 | 3,500,000 |
| **7** *Portrait of Lucian Freud*, Sotheby's, New York, Nov 8, 1989 | 3,300,000 |
| **8** *Study for Portrait VIII, 1953*, Sotheby's, London, Dec 5, 1991 | 3,258,000 (£1,800,000) |
| **9** *Turning Figure*, Sotheby's, New York, Nov 8, 1989 | 3,000,000 |
| **10** *Studies for Self-Portrait*, Christie's, London, June 30, 1999 | 2,686,000 (£1,700,000) |

## TOP 10 ★
# MOST EXPENSIVE WORKS BY JASPER JOHNS

| WORK/SALE | PRICE ($) |
|---|---|
| **1** *False Start*, Sotheby's, New York, Nov 10, 1988 | 15,500,000 |
| **2** *Two Flags*, Christie's Rockefeller, New York, May 13, 1999 | 6,500,000 |
| **3** *Jubilee*, Sotheby's, New York, Nov 13, 1991 | 4,500,000 |
| **4** *Device Circle*, Christie's, New York, Nov 12, 1991 | 4,000,000 |
| **5** *Alphabets*, Sotheby's, New York, May 2, 1989 | 2,600,000 |
| **6** *0 Through 9*, Christie's, New York, Nov 18, 1992 | 2,100,000 |
| **7** *Double Flag*, Sotheby's, New York, Dec 11, 1986 | 1,600,000 |
| **8** *Screen Piece II*, Sotheby's, New York, Nov 10, 1988 | 1,250,000 |
| **9** *Screen Piece No. 3, The Sonnets*, Sotheby's, New York, Nov 1, 1994 | 600,000 |
| **10** *Untitled*, Christie's, New York, May 4, 1993 | 550,000 |

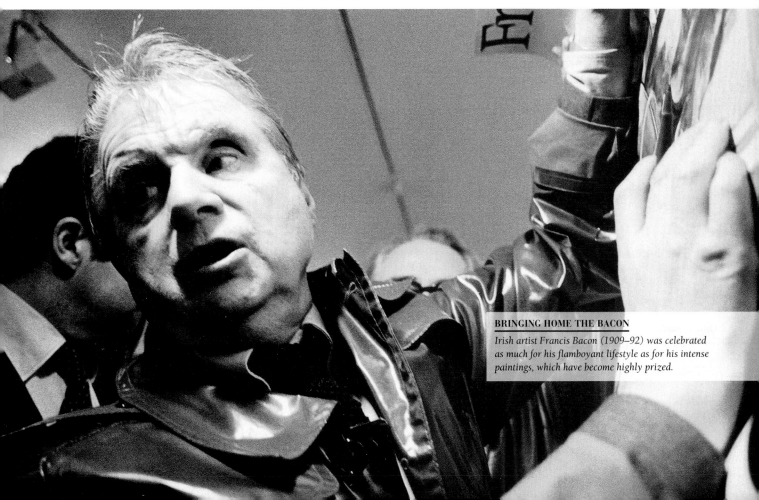

**BRINGING HOME THE BACON**
*Irish artist Francis Bacon (1909–92) was celebrated as much for his flamboyant lifestyle as for his intense paintings, which have become highly prized.*

# Women Artists

**GEORGIA ON MY MIND**

*Georgia O'Keeffe (1887–1986), who specialized in richly colored paintings of plants and natural forms, is ranked high in the pantheon of 20th-century American painters.*

## TOP 10 ★ MOST EXPENSIVE PAINTINGS BY FRIDA KAHLO

| PAINTING/SALE | PRICE ($) |
|---|---|
| 1 *Autoretrato con Chango y Loro*, Sotheby's, New York, May 17, 1995 | 2,900,000 |
| 2 *Autorretrato con Pelo Suelto*, Christie's, New York, May 15, 1991 | 1,500,000 |
| 3 *Diego and I*, Sotheby's, New York, May 2, 1990 | 1,300,000 |
| 4 *Recuerdo*, Christie's, New York, May 18, 1992 | 850,000 |
| 5 *Los Cuatro Habitantes de Mexico*, Sotheby's, New York, May 14, 1996 | 800,000 |
| 6 *Parade in a Street in Detroit*, Gary Nader, Miami, Jan 23, 2000 | 750,000 |
| 7 *La Tierra Misma o Dos Desnudos en la Jungla*, Christie's, New York, Nov 21, 1989 | 460,000 |
| 8 *What the Water Gave Me*, Sotheby's, New York, Nov 29, 1983 | 235,000 |
| 9 *Ella Juega Sola o Nina con Mascara de la Muerte*, Christie's, New York, Nov 21, 1989 | 220,000 |
| 10 *Moses*, Sotheby's, New York, Nov 26, 1985 | 210,000 |

Mexican painter Frida Kahlo (1907–54) overcame disabilities resulting from childhood polio and a car accident to become a talented artist whose work was much revered by the Surrealists. She was married to the artist Diego Rivera, and their turbulent life together (they divorced in 1939 and married again the following year) and Kahlo's personal joys and suffering are revealed in her vivid, often autobiographical paintings.

## TOP 10 ★ MOST EXPENSIVE PAINTINGS BY GEORGIA O'KEEFFE

| PAINTING/SALE | PRICE ($) |
|---|---|
| 1 *From the Plains*, Sotheby's, New York, Dec 3, 1997 | 3,300,000 |
| 2 *Calla Lily with Red Roses*, Sotheby's, New York, May 20, 1998 | 2,400,000 |
| 3 *Black Hollyhocks with Blue Larkspur*, Sotheby's, New York, Dec 3, 1987 | 1,800,000 |
| 4 *Dark Iris, No. 2*, Sotheby's, New York, May 24, 1989 | 1,500,000 |
| 5 *At the Rodeo, New Mexico*, Sotheby's, New York, Dec 3, 1987 | 1,430,000 |
| 6 *Yellow Cactus Flowers*, Sotheby's, New York, May 24, 1989 | 1,200,000 |
| 7 *White Rose, New Mexico*, Sotheby's, New York, Dec 5, 1985 | 1,150,000 |
| 8 = *Ritz Tower, Night*, Christie's, New York, Dec 4, 1992 | 1,100,000 |
| = *Two Jimson Weeds*, Sotheby's, New York, Dec 3, 1987 | 1,100,000 |
| 10 = *Black Iris II – Black Iris VI*, Christie's, New York, May 21, 1998 | 1,000,000 |
| = *Cow's Skull on Red*, Christie's, New York, Nov 30, 1994 | 1,000,000 |
| = *Red Poppy, No. VI*, Christie's, New York, May 23, 1990 | 1,000,000 |
| = *Slightly Open Clam Shell*, Christie's, New York, Dec 4, 1997 | 1,000,000 |

## TOP 10 ★ MOST EXPENSIVE SCULPTURES BY DAME BARBARA HEPWORTH

| SCULPTURE/SALE | PRICE ($) |
|---|---|
| 1 *Family of Man, Ultimate Form*, Sotheby's, New York, May 11, 2000 | 420,000 |
| 2 *Concoid, Sphere and Hollow II*, Sotheby's, London, June 25, 1997 | 340,300 (£205,000) |
| 3 *Musician*, Christie's, London, Oct 23, 1996 | 296,000 (£185,000) |
| 4 = *Sculpture with Colour, Oval Form, Pale Blue and Red*, Christie's, London, July 1, 1998 | 262,400 (£160,000) |
| = *Sunlon*, Christie's, London, July 1, 1998 | 262,400 (£160,000) |
| 6 *Two Segments and Sphere*, Sotheby's, New York, Nov 11, 1999 | 260,000 |
| 7 *The Family of Man, Figure 1, Ancestor 1*, Sotheby's, New York, May 14, 1992 | 250,000 |
| 8 *Sea Form, Atlantic*, Christie's, New York, May 13, 1998 | 230,000 |
| 9 *Rock Form – Porthcurno*, Sotheby's, New York, May 12, 1993 | 185,000 |
| 10 *Three Part Vertical*, Sotheby's, London, Mar 31, 1987 | 152,950 (£95,000) |

**Did You Know?** In 1947, Madame Claude Latour was convicted of producing forgeries of paintings by Pablo Picasso and Maurice Utrillo that were so skillful that Utrillo himself could not tell which were his and which she had painted.

## TOP 10 ★
# MOST EXPENSIVE PAINTINGS BY BERTHE MORISOT

| PAINTING/SALE | PRICE ($) |
|---|---|
| **1** *Cache-cache*, Sotheby's, New York, Nov 9, 2000 | 4,000,000 |
| **2** *Cache-cache*, Sotheby's, New York, May 10, 1999 | 3,500,000 |
| **3** *Après le Déjeuner*, Christie's, New York, May 14, 1997 | 3,250,000 |
| **4** *La Femme au Gant, ou La Parisienne*, Sotheby's, New York, Nov 16, 1998 | 1,500,000 |
| **5** *Derrière la Jalousie*, Sotheby's, New York, May 10, 2000 | 1,200,000 |
| **6** *Le Thé*, Sotheby's, New York, May 9, 1995 | 1,150,000 |
| **7** =*Derrière la Jalousie*, Christie's, New York, May 5, 1998 | 1,100,000 |
| =*Fillettes à la Fenêtre, Jeanne et Edma Bodeau*, Christie's, New York, Nov 11, 1997 | 1,100,000 |
| **9** *Julie Manet à la Perruche*, Sotheby's, New York, May 17, 1990 | 950,000 |
| **10** *La Leçon au Jardin*, Christie's, New York, May 10, 1989 | 900,000 |

Berthe Morisot (1841–95) was a French Impressionist painter who was closely associated with the leading figures in the movement (and married to Manet's brother). Landscapes and women and children chiefly feature in her work, which has commanded escalating prices in the world's salesrooms.

**THERE'S SOMETHING ABOUT MARY**

*Five paintings by Mary Cassatt, including her Mother, Sara and the Baby, are numbered among the 10 highest-priced paintings by a woman.*

## TOP 10 ★
# MOST EXPENSIVE PAINTINGS BY WOMEN ARTISTS EVER SOLD AT AUCTION

| PAINTING/ARTIST/SALE | PRICE ($) |
|---|---|
| **1** *The Conversation*, Mary Cassatt (American; 1844–1926), Christie's, New York, May 11, 1988 | 4,100,000 |
| **2** *Cache-cache*, Berthe Morisot (French; 1841–95), Sotheby's, New York, Nov 9, 2000 | 4,000,000 |
| **3** *In the Box*, Mary Cassatt, Christie's, New York, May 23, 1996 | 3,700,000 |
| **4** =*Cache-cache*, Berthe Morisot, Sotheby's, New York, May 10, 1999 | 3,500,000 |
| =*Mother, Sara and the Baby*, Mary Cassatt, Christie's, New York, May 10, 1989 | 3,500,000 |
| **6** *From the Plains*, Georgia O'Keeffe (American; 1887–1986), Sotheby's, New York, Dec 3, 1997 | 3,300,000 |
| **7** *Après le Déjeuner*, Berthe Morisot, Christie's, New York, May 14, 1997 | 3,250,000 |
| **8** *Autoretrato con Chango y Loro*, Frida Kahlo (Mexican; 1907–54), Sotheby's, New York, May 17, 1995 | 2,900,000 |
| **9** *Augusta Reading to Her Daughter*, Mary Cassatt, Sotheby's, New York, May 9, 1989 | 2,800,000 |
| **10** *Children Playing with Cat*, Mary Cassatt, Sotheby's, New York, Dec 3, 1998 | 2,700,000 |

# Objects of Desire

## TOP 10 ★

## MOST EXPENSIVE ITEMS OF AMERICAN FURNITURE

| ITEM/SALE | PRICE ($) |
|---|---|
| **1 The Nicholas Brown Chippendale mahogany block and shell desk and bookcase**, c.1760–70, attributed to John Goddard, Christie's, New York, June 3, 1989 | 12,100,000 |
| **2 Richard Edwards Chippendale carved mahogany pier table**, by Thomas Tufft, c.1775–76, Christie's, New York, Jan 20, 1990 | 4,620,000 |
| **3 The Samuel Whitehorne Queen Anne block-and-shell carved mahogany kneehole desk**, attributed to Edmund Townsend, c.1780, Sotheby's, New York, Jan 20, 1996 | 3,632,500 |
| **4 Chippendale carved mahogany tea table**, c.1760–80, Christie's, New York, May 28, 1987 | 2,422,500 |
| **5 The Edwards-Harrison family Chippendale carved mahogany high chest-of-drawers, dressing table, and pair of side chairs**, by Thomas Tufft, c. 1775–76, Christie's, New York, May 28, 1987 | 1,760,000 |
| **6 The Edward Jackson parcel gilt inlaid and figured mahogany mirrored bonnet-top secretary bookcase**, c.1738–48, Sotheby's, New York, Jan 20, 1996 | 1,432,500 |
| **7 Cornelius Stevenson Chippendale carved mahogany tea table**, attributed to Thomas Affleck, carving attributed to Nicholas Bernard & Martin Jugiez, c.1760–80, Christie's, New York, Jan 20, 1990 | 1,210,000 |
| **8 Chippendale carved mahogany tea table**, c. 1760–80, Christie's, New York, Jan 25, 1986 | 1,045,000 |
| **9 Chipppendale carved mahogany tea table**, c.1770, Christie's, New York, Jan 26, 1995 | 695,500 |
| **10 Chippendale mahogany block front and shell-carved kneehole desk**, c.1760–85, Christie's, New York, June 2, 1983 | 627,000 |

## TOP 10 ★

## MOST EXPENSIVE PRINTS

| PRINT/ARTIST/SALE | PRICE ($) |
|---|---|
| **1 Diehard, Robert Rauschenberg** (American; 1925– ), Sotheby's, New York, May 2, 1989 | 1,600,000 |
| **2 Mao, Andy Warhol** (American; 1928–87), Sotheby's, London, June 26, 1996 | 939,400 (£610,000) |
| **3 Famille Tahitienne, Paul Gauguin** (French; 1848–1903), Francis Briest, Paris, Dec 4, 1998 | 806,922 (F.Fr4,545,010) |
| **4 Elles\*, Henri de Toulouse-Lautrec** (French; 1864–1901), Sotheby's, New York, May 10, 1999 | 800,000 |
| **5 Glider, Robert Rauschenberg**, Christie's, New York, Nov 14, 1995 | 750,000 |
| **6 The Kiss – Bela Lugosi, Andy Warhol**, Christies Rockefeller, New York, May 9, 2000 | 720,000 |
| **7 Elles\*, Henri de Toulouse-Lautrec**, Sotheby's, New York, Nov 7, 1997 | 695,000 |
| **8 =La Suite Vollard, Pablo Picasso** (Spanish; 1881–1973), Christie's, New York, Nov 2, 1999 | 650,000 |
| **=Suicide, Andy Warhol**, Sotheby's, New York, May 18, 1999 | 650,000 |
| **10 Head of Marilyn Monroe, Andy Warhol**, Beijers, Stockholm, May 21, 1990 | 640,525 (SKR 3,900,000) |

*\* A collection of 10 lithographs*

Included within the classification of prints are silkscreens, lithographs, monotypes, aquatints, woodcuts, engravings, and etchings.

## TOP 10 ★

## MOST EXPENSIVE PHOTOGRAPHS

| PHOTOGRAPH/PHOTOGRAPHER/SALE | PRICE ($) |
|---|---|
| **1 Egypte et Nubie: Sites et monuments les plus intéressants pour l'étude de l'art et de l'histoire\*** (1858), **Félix Teynard** (French; 1817–92), Laurin Guilloux Buffetaud Tailleur, Paris, Dec 21, 1990 | 707,000 (F.Fr3,700,000) |
| **2 The North American Indian\*** (1907–30), **Edward S. Curtis** (American; 1868–1952), Sotheby's, New York, Oct 7, 1993 | 662,500 |
| **3 Noire et Blanche** (1926), **Man Ray** (American; 1890–1976), Christie's, New York, Oct 4, 1998 | 607,500 |
| **4 Light Trap for Henry Moore No. 1, Bruce Nauman** (American; 1941–), Sotheby's, New York, May 17, 2000 | 480,000 |
| **5 The North American Indian\*** (1907–30), **Edward S. Curtis**, Christie's, New York, Apr 6, 1995 | 464,500 |
| **6 Georgia O'Keeffe: A Portrait – Hands with Thimble** (1930), **Alfred Stieglitz** (American; 1864–1946), Christie's, New York, Oct 8, 1993 | 398,500 |
| **7 =Equivalents (21)\*** (1920s), **Alfred Stieglitz**, Christie's, New York, Oct 30, 1989 | 396,000 |
| **=The North American Indian\*** (1907–30), **Edward S. Curtis**, Christie's, New York, Oct 13, 1992 | 396,000 |
| **9 Arrival of the Body of Admiral Bruat and Flagship Montebello at Toulon** (1855), **Gustave le Gray** (French; 1820–82), Bearnes, Exeter, May 6, 2000 | 380,000 (£250,000) |
| **10 Mondrian's Pipe and Glasses** (1926), **André Kertész** (Hungarian–American; 1894–1985), Christie's, New York, Apr 17, 1997 | 376,500 |

*\* Collections; all others are single prints*

**LENNON'S LIMO**
*Repainted in 1967, John Lennon's Rolls-Royce was eventually donated to Queen Elizabeth and is preserved by the Royal British Columbia Museum in Victoria, British Columbia, Canada.*

# MOST EXPENSIVE MUSICAL INSTRUMENTS

| INSTRUMENT*/SALE | PRICE ($) |
|---|---|
| **1** John Lennon's Steinway Model Z upright piano (on which he composed *Imagine*), teak veneered, complete with cigarette burns, Fleetwood-Owen online auction, Hard Rock Café, London and New York, Oct 17, 2000 | 2,150,000 |
| **2** "Kreutzer" violin by Antonio Stradivari, Christie's, London, Apr 1, 1998 | 1,582,847 (£946,000) |
| **3** "Cholmondeley" violincello by Antonio Stradivari, Sotheby's, London, June 22, 1998 | 1,141,122 (£682,000) |
| **4** "Brownie", one of Eric Clapton's favourite guitars, Christie's, New York, June 24, 1999 | 497,500 |

*Clapton used the 1956 sunburst Fender to record his definitive guitar track, Layla. It was sold to an anonymous telephone bidder for double the expected price, making it the most expensive guitar ever bought at auction.*

| | |
|---|---|
| **5** Jimi Hendrix's Fender *Stratocaster* electric guitar, Sotheby's, London, Apr 25, 1990 | 370,854 (£198,000) |
| **6** Double bass by Domenico Montagnana, Sotheby's, London, Mar 16, 1999 | 250,339 (£155,500) |
| **7** Verne Powell's platinum flute, Christie's, New York, Oct 18, 1986 | 187,000 |
| **8** English double-manual harpsichord by Burkat Shudi and John Broadwood, Sotheby's, London, Oct 27, 1999 | 170,649 (£106,000) |
| **9** Viola by Giovanni Paolo Maggini, Christie's, London, Nov 20, 1984 | 161,121 (£129,000) |
| **10** Bundfrei clavichord by Marcus Gabriel Sondermann, late 18th/early 19th century, Sotheby's, London, Nov 16, 2000 | 29,370 (£20,625) |

\* *Most expensive example only for each category of instrument*

# MOST EXPENSIVE ITEMS OF POP MEMORABILIA

| ITEM/SALE | PRICE ($)* |
|---|---|
| **1** John Lennon's 1965 Rolls-Royce Phantom V touring limousine, finished in psychedelic paintwork, Sotheby's, New York, June 29, 1985 | 2,299,000 |
| **2** John Lennon's Steinway Model Z upright piano (on which he composed *Imagine*), teak veneered, complete with cigarette burns, Fleetwood-Owen online auction, Hard Rock Café, London and New York, Oct 17, 2000 | 2,150,000 |
| **3** "Brownie," one of Eric Clapton's favorite guitars (on which he recorded *Layla*), Christie's, New York, June 24, 1999 | 497,500 |
| **4** Bernie Taupin's handwritten lyrics for the rewritten *Candle in the Wind*, Christie's, Los Angeles, Feb 11, 1998 | 400,000 |
| **5** Jimi Hendrix's Fender *Stratocaster* electric guitar, which he played at Woodstock in 1969, Sotheby's, London, Apr 25, 1990 | 370,260 (£198,000) |
| **6** Paul McCartney's handwritten lyrics for *Getting Better*, 1967, Sotheby's, London, Sep 14, 1995 | 251,643 (£161,000) |
| **7** Buddy Holly's Gibson acoustic guitar, c.1945, in a tooled leather case made by Holly, Sotheby's, New York, June 23, 1990 | 242,000 |
| **8** John Lennon's 1970 Mercedes-Benz 600 Pullman four-door limousine, Christie's, London, Apr 27, 1989 | 213,125 (£137,500) |
| **9** John Lennon's 1965 Ferrari 330 GT 2+2 two-door coupe, right-hand drive, Fleetwood-Owen online auction, Hard Rock Café, London and New York, Oct 17, 2000 | 190,750 |
| **10** Mal Evan's notebook, compiled 1967–68, which includes a draft by Paul McCartney of the lyrics for *Hey Jude*, Sotheby's, London, Sep 15, 1998 | 185,202 (£111,500) |

\* *Including 10 percent buyer's premium, where appropriate*

What was the nationality of the painter Frida Kahlo?
*see p.122 for the answer*

**A** Russian
**B** Mexican
**C** Swedish

# MUSIC & MUSICIANS

# Popular Songs

## US HITS COMPOSED BY BOB DYLAN

| | TITLE | CHARTING ARTIST(S) |
|---|---|---|
| 1 | Blowin' in the Wind | Peter, Paul & Mary, Stevie Wonder |
| 2 | Mr. Tambourine Man | The Byrds |
| 3 | Lay Lady Lay | Bob Dylan, Ferrante & Teicher, Isley Brothers |
| 4 | Like a Rolling Stone | Bob Dylan |
| 5 | Rainy Day Women Nos. 12 & 35 | Bob Dylan |
| 6 | Don't Think Twice | Peter, Paul & Mary, Wonder Who? |
| 7 | It Ain't Me Babe | Johnny Cash, Turtles |
| 8 | Mighty Quinn (Quinn the Eskimo) | Manfred Mann |
| 9 | Knockin' on Heaven's Door | Bob Dylan |
| 10 | All I Really Want to Do | The Byrds, Cher |

A much-covered songwriter, with hundreds of his titles recorded by other artists, often as album tracks, Bob Dylan's material has also proved successful for the likes of Jimi Hendrix (*All Along the Watchtower*), Rod Stewart (*Forever Young*), and even Olivia Newton-John (*If Not For You*).

## US HITS COMPOSED BY BRUCE SPRINGSTEEN

| | TITLE | CHARTING ARTIST(S) |
|---|---|---|
| 1 | Dancing in the Dark | Bruce Springsteen |
| 2 | Fire | The Pointer Sisters, Bruce Springsteen |
| 3 | Blinded by the Light | Manfred Mann's Earth Band |
| 4 | Born in the USA/ Banned in the USA | Bruce Springsteen, Luke & The 2 Live Crew |
| 5 | Streets of Philadelphia | Bruce Springsteen |
| 6 | Because the Night* | Patti Smith Group, 10,000 Maniacs |
| 7 | Hungry Heart | Bruce Springsteen |
| 8 | Glory Days | Bruce Springsteen |
| 9 | Pink Cadillac | Natalie Cole |
| 10 | I'm on Fire | Bruce Springsteen |

* Cowritten with Patti Smith

## US HITS COMPOSED BY PRINCE

| | TITLE | CHARTING ARTIST(S) |
|---|---|---|
| 1 | When Doves Cry/Pray* | Prince, MC Hammer |
| 2 | Nothing Compares 2 U | Sinead O'Connor |
| 3 | Batdance | Prince |
| 4 | Cream | Prince & the New Power Generation |
| 5 | Kiss | Prince & the Revolution, Art of Noise |
| 6 | Let's Go Crazy | Prince & the Revolution |
| 7 | The Most Beautiful Girl in the World | Prince |
| 8 | I Feel For You | Chaka Khan |
| 9 | Purple Rain | Prince & the Revolution |
| 10 | I Wanna Be Your Lover | Prince |

* MC Hammer's hit Pray used the rhythm track from When Doves Cry

The first three songs in this list all sold over 1 million copies, while the first six have all peaked at No. 1 in the US. Prince is a prolific writer – with 74 hits to his credit, constantly penning material for his stable of artists at Paisley Park, his Minneapolis recording empire.

## US HITS COMPOSED BY GEORGE MICHAEL

| | TITLE | CHARTING ARTIST(S) |
|---|---|---|
| 1 | I Want Your Sex | George Michael |
| 2 | Careless Whisper | Wham! featuring George Michael |
| 3 | Wake Me Up Before You Go-Go | Wham! |
| 4 | Everything She Wants | Wham! |
| 5 | Faith | George Michael |
| 6 | One More Try | George Michael |
| 7 | Freedom | Wham! |
| 8 | Too Funky | George Michael |
| 9 | Fast Love | George Michael |
| 10 | Jesus to a Child | George Michael |

It is ironic that George Michael's only 2 million-selling single in the US (*I Want Your Sex*) is his only composition in the Top 10 listed here not to make it to No. 1 (it peaked at No. 2 in 1987).

## US HITS COMPOSED BY JOHN LENNON AND PAUL McCARTNEY

| | TITLE | CHARTING ARTIST(S) |
|---|---|---|
| 1 | I Want to Hold Your Hand | The Beatles, Boston Pops Orchestra |
| 2 | Hey Jude | The Beatles, Wilson Pickett |
| 3 | She Loves You | The Beatles |
| 4 | Can't Buy Me Love | The Beatles |
| 5 | Come Together | Aerosmith, The Beatles, Ike & Tina Turner |
| 6 | Get Back | The Beatles with Billy Preston, Billy Preston* |
| 7 | I Feel Fine | The Beatles |
| 8 | Help! | The Beatles |
| 9 | A Hard Day's Night | The Beatles, Ramsey Lewis Trio |
| 10 | Let It Be | Joan Baez, The Beatles |

* In addition to accompanying the Beatles on the original version, Preston also charted with a solo version in 1978

*I Want to Hold Your Hand* remains the biggest-selling Lennon and McCartney composition in the US, selling just under 5 million copies in 1964, the year of the Beatles' first public appearances in America. It was also their first American hit – the first of three holding the US No. 1 slot in that year – and the first No. 1 by a UK group since the Tornados' *Telstar* in 1962. Including solo hits, Paul McCartney has secured more Hot 100 hits than any other writer (169), while John Lennon has penned 141.

## TOP 10 SINGER-SONGWRITERS IN THE US

1 Paul McCartney  2 James Brown
3 Stevie Wonder  4 Elton John
5 Fats Domino  6 Neil Diamond
7 Prince  8 Paul Anka  9 Sam Cooke
10 Chuck Berry

Based on an analysis of consistent US singles success during the period 1955–99, these are the acts whose hits were largely, or entirely, self-penned. Paul McCartney's solo placing excludes his success as half of Lennon/McCartney on the Beatles' records, but he still comfortably tops the list.

## TOP 10 ★
# US HITS COMPOSED BY DOC POMUS

| | TITLE | CHARTING ARTIST(S) |
|---|---|---|
| 1 | Save the Last Dance for Me | DeFranco Family, Drifters, Dolly Parton |
| 2 | Young Blood | Bad Company, Coasters, Bruce Willis |
| 3 | Surrender | Elvis Presley |
| 4 | Can't Get Used to Losing You | Andy Williams |
| 5 | This Magic Moment | Drifters, Jay & the Americans |
| 6 | Suspicion | Terry Stafford |
| 7 | Marie's the Name (His Latest Flame) | Elvis Presley |
| 8 | A Teenager in Love | Dion & the Belmonts |
| 9 | She's Not You | Elvis Presley |
| 10 | Go, Jimmy, Go | Jimmy Clanton |

Legendary American songwriter Doc Pomus wrote many of his hits, particularly those for Elvis Presley, with Mort Shuman. The pair joined Hill & Range Publishing as staff writers through another Presley hit composer, Otis Blackwell. Even though they wrote hits with other partners, coincidentally they both have 59 Hot 100 hits to their credit.

## THE 10 ★
# LATEST GRAMMY SONGS OF THE YEAR

| YEAR | SONG/SONGWRITER(S) |
|---|---|
| 2000 | Beautiful Day, U2 |
| 1999 | Smooth, Itaal Shur and Rob Thomas |
| 1998 | My Heart Will Go On, James Horner and Will Jennings |
| 1997 | Sunny Came Home, Shawn Colvin |
| 1996 | Change the World, Gordon Kennedy, Wayne Kirkpatrick, and Tommy Sims |
| 1995 | Kiss From a Rose, Seal |
| 1994 | Streets of Philadelphia, Bruce Springsteen |
| 1993 | A Whole New World, Alan Menken and Tim Rice |
| 1992 | Tears in Heaven, Eric Clapton |
| 1991 | Unforgettable, Irving Gordon |

## THE 10 ★
# LATEST RECIPIENTS OF THE SONGWRITERS HALL OF FAME SAMMY CAHN LIFETIME ACHIEVEMENT AWARD

| YEAR | ARTIST |
|---|---|
| 2000 | Neil Diamond |
| 1999 | Kenny Rogers |
| 1998 | Berry Gordy |
| 1997 | Vic Damone |
| 1996 | Frankie Laine |
| 1995 | Steve Lawrence and Eydie Gorme |
| 1994 | Lena Horne |
| 1993 | Ray Charles |
| 1992 | Nat "King" Cole |
| 1991 | Gene Autry |

Source: *National Academy of Popular Music*

The National Academy of Popular Music was founded in 1969. Its most prestigious award is named after Sammy Cahn, who served for 20 years as the Academy's president.

## THE 10 ★
# LASTEST WINNERS OF THE ASCAP SONGWRITER OF THE YEAR (POP CATEGORY)

| YEAR | ARTIST |
|---|---|
| 2000 | Max Martin |
| 1999 | Diane Warren and Max Martin |
| 1998 | Diane Warren |
| 1997 | Glen Ballard |
| 1996 | Melissa Etheridge/Hootie and the Blowfish |
| 1995 | Robert John "Mutt" Lange |
| 1994 | Elton John and Bernie Taupin |
| 1993 | Diane Warren |
| 1992 | Jimmy Jam and Terry Lewis |
| 1991 | Diane Warren |

Source: *American Society of Composers, Authors, and Publishers*

## TOP 10 ★
# ROCK SONGS OF ALL TIME*

| | SONG | ARTIST OR GROUP |
|---|---|---|
| 1 | (I Can't Get No) Satisfaction | The Rolling Stones |
| 2 | Respect | Aretha Franklin |
| 3 | Stairway to Heaven | Led Zeppelin |
| 4 | Like a Rolling Stone | Bob Dylan |
| 5 | Born to Run | Bruce Springsteen |
| 6 | Hotel California | The Eagles |
| 7 | Light My Fire | The Doors |
| 8 | Good Vibrations | The Beach Boys |
| 9 | Hey Jude | The Beatles |
| 10 | Imagine | John Lennon |

* Determined by a panel of 700 voters assembled by the music network VH1

The all-time Top 100 list, from which this Top 10 is taken, is dominated by songs dating from the 1960s. Within it, there are no fewer than nine Beatles songs, as well as five by the Rolling Stones and three by Bob Dylan.

## TOP 10 ★
# MOST COVERED BEATLES SONGS

| | SONG | YEAR WRITTEN |
|---|---|---|
| 1 | Yesterday | 1965 |
| 2 | Eleanor Rigby | 1966 |
| 3 | Something | 1969 |
| 4 | Hey Jude | 1968 |
| 5 | Let It Be | 1969 |
| 6 | Michelle | 1965 |
| 7 | With a Little Help from My Friends | 1967 |
| 8 | Day Tripper | 1965 |
| 9 | Come Together | 1969 |
| 10 | The Long and Winding Road | 1969 |

*Yesterday* is one of the most-covered songs of all time, with the number of recorded versions now in four figures. Although most of these songs are Lennon and McCartney compositions, the No. 3 song, *Something*, was written by George Harrison. *Hey Jude* and *Day Tripper* were both No. 1 hits.

Who recorded the two "greatest hits" albums that are among the bestselling of all time?
*see p.130 for the answer*
A The Beatles and the Rolling Stones
B Michael Jackson and Elvis Presley
C The Eagles and Elton John

# Chart Hits

## ALBUMS OF ALL TIME IN THE US

| ALBUM/ARTIST OR GROUP/YEAR | SALES ($) |
|---|---|
| **1** *Their Greatest Hits 1971–1975*, The Eagles, 1976 | 27,000,000 |
| **2** *Thriller*, Michael Jackson, 1982 | 26,000,000 |
| **3** *Led Zeppelin IV*, Led Zeppelin, 1971 | 22,000,000 |
| **4** *AC/DC*, Back In Black, 1980 | 19,000,000 |
| **5** =*Come On Over*, Shania Twain, 1997 | 18,000,000 |
| =*Rumours*, Fleetwood Mac, 1977 | 18,000,000 |
| **7** *The Bodyguard*, Soundtrack, 1992 | 17,000,000 |
| **8** =*Back In Black*, AC/DC, 1980 | 16,000,000 |
| =*Boston*, Boston, 1976 | 16,000,000 |
| =*Cracked Rear View*, Hootie & the Blowfish, 1994 | 16,000,000 |
| =*Jagged Little Pill*, Alanis Morissette, 1995 | 16,000,000 |
| =*No Fences*, Garth Brooks, 1990 | 16,000,000 |

Source: *RIAA*

## ALBUMS OF ALL TIME

| ALBUM/ARTIST OR GROUP | YEAR |
|---|---|
| **1** *Thriller*, Michael Jackson | 1982 |
| **2** *Dark Side of the Moon*, Pink Floyd | 1973 |
| **3** *Their Greatest Hits 1971–1975*, The Eagles | 1976 |
| **4** *The Bodyguard*, Soundtrack | 1992 |
| **5** *Rumours*, Fleetwood Mac | 1977 |
| **6** *Sgt. Pepper's Lonely Hearts Club Band*, The Beatles | 1967 |
| **7** *Led Zeppelin IV*, Led Zeppelin | 1971 |
| **8** *Greatest Hits*, Elton John | 1974 |
| **9** *Jagged Little Pill*, Alanis Morissette | 1995 |
| **10** *Bat Out of Hell*, Meat Loaf | 1977 |

**BEAT ALL**

*Although disbanded over 30 years ago, the Beatles remain prominent in many all-time Top 10 lists and continue to achieve chart success in the 21st century.*

## ARTISTS WITH THE MOST CONSECUTIVE US TOP 10 ALBUMS

| ARTIST/PERIOD | CONSECUTIVE TOP 10 ALBUMS |
|---|---|
| **1** The Rolling Stones, Nov 1964–July 1980 | 26 |
| **2** Johnny Mathis, Sep 1957–Dec 1960 | 14 |
| **3** =Frank Sinatra, Feb 1958–Mar 1962 | 12 |
| =Garth Brooks, Mar 1991–Dec 1999 | 12 |
| **5** =The Beatles, June 1965–Mar 1970 | 11 |
| =Elton John, Nov 1971–Nov 1976 | 11 |
| =Van Halen, Apr 1979–Nov 1996 | 11 |
| **8** =Led Zeppelin, Feb 1969–Dec 1982 | 10 |
| =Chicago, Feb 1970–Oct 1977 | 10 |
| =Bruce Springsteen, Sep 1975–Mar 1995 | 10 |

Source: *The Popular Music Database*

## ARTISTS WITH THE MOST CONSECUTIVE US TOP 10 SINGLES

| ARTIST/PERIOD | CONSECUTIVE TOP 10 SINGLES |
|---|---|
| **1** Elvis Presley, Mar 1956–May 62 | 30 |
| **2** The Beatles, Dec 1964–Aug 76 | 20 |
| **3** Janet Jackson, Sep 1989–Mar 98 | 18 |
| **4** =Michael Jackson, July 1979–July 1988 | 17 |
| =Madonna, Mar 1984–Oct 1989 | 17 |
| **6** Pat Boone, Feb 1956–May 58 | 14 |
| **7** =Phil Collins, Feb 1984–Oct 90 | 13 |
| =Whitney Houston, May 1985–June 91 | 13 |
| =Lionel Richie, July 1981–Feb 1987 | 13 |
| **10** Mariah Carey, June 1990–Apr 94 | 11 |

Source: *The Popular Music Database*

## TOP 10 ARTISTS WITH MOST WEEKS ON THE US SINGLES CHART*

*(Artist/total weeks)*

**1** Elvis Presley, 1,586　**2** Elton John, 1,021　**3** Stevie Wonder, 766　**4** Madonna, 757　**5** Rod Stewart, 731　**6** James Brown, 706　**7** Pat Boone, 697　**8** Michael Jackson, 661　**9** Beatles, 629　**10** Fats Domino, 605

*\* As at January 1, 2001*
Source: *The Popular Music Database*

**CANDLE POWER**

*Elton John's Candle in the Wind 1997 tribute to Princess Diana overtook* White Christmas, *the world's best-selling single for over 50 years.*

## TOP 10 ⭐

# SINGLES WITH THE MOST CONSECUTIVE WEEKS ON THE US SINGLES CHART

| | SINGLE/ARTIST OR GROUP/YEAR | WEEKS |
|---|---|---|
| 1 | *How Do I Live*, LeAnn Rimes, 1997 | 69 |
| 2 | *Foolish Games/You Were Meant for Me*, Jewel, 1996 | 65 |
| 3 | *I Don't Want To Wait*, Paula Cole, 1997 | 56 |
| 4 = | *Missing*, Everything But the Girl, 1996 | 55 |
| = | *Barely Breathing*, Duncan Sheik, 1996 | 55 |
| 6 | *Too Close*, Next, 1998 | 53 |
| 7 = | *Truly Madly Deeply*, Savage Garden, 1997 | 52 |
| = | *How's it Going to Be*, Third Eye Blind, 1997 | 52 |
| 9 | *Run-Around*, Blues Traveler, 1995 | 49 |
| 10 | *Counting Blue Cars*, Dishwalla, 1996 | 48 |

Source: *The Popular Music Database*

## TOP 10 ⭐

# OLDEST ARTISTS TO HAVE A N0. 1 HIT SINGLE IN THE US

| | ARTIST/SINGLE | AGE* YRS | MTHS |
|---|---|---|---|
| 1 | **Louis Armstrong**, *Hello Dolly!* | 63 | 10 |
| 2 | **Lawrence Welk**, *Calcutta* | 57 | 11 |
| 3 | **Morris Stoloff**, *Moonglow and Theme from* Picnic on Hanging Rock | 57 | 10 |
| 4 | **Cher**, *Believe* | 52 | 7 |
| 5 | **Frank Sinatra**#, *Somethin' Stupid* | 51 | 4 |
| 6 | **Elton John**, *Candle in The Wind (1997)/Something About the Way You Look Tonight* | 50 | 6 |
| 7 | **Lorne Greene**, *Ringo* | 49 | 9 |
| 8 | **Dean Martin**, *Everybody Loves Somebody* | 47 | 2 |
| 9 | **Bill Medley**+, *(I've Had), The Time of My Life* | 47 | 2 |
| 10 | **Sammy Davis Jr.**, *The Candy Man* | 46 | 6 |

\* *During first week of No.1 US single*

# *Duet with Nancy Sinatra*

+ *Duet with Jennifer Warnes*

Source: *The Popular Music Database*

## TOP 10 ⭐

# SINGLES OF ALL TIME

| | SINGLE/ARTIST OR GROUP/YEAR | SALES EXCEED |
|---|---|---|
| 1 | *Candle in the Wind (1997)/ Something About the Way You Look Tonight*, Elton John, 1997 | 37,000,000 |
| 2 | *White Christmas*, Bing Crosby, 1945 | 30,000,000 |
| 3 | *Rock Around the Clock*, Bill Haley and His Comets, 1954 | 17,000,000 |
| 4 | *I Want to Hold Your Hand*, The Beatles, 1963 | 12,000,000 |
| 5 = | *Hey Jude*, The Beatles, 1968 | 10,000,000 |
| = | *It's Now or Never*, Elvis Presley, 1960 | 10,000,000 |
| = | *I Will Always Love You*, Whitney Houston, 1993 | 10,000,000 |
| 8 = | *Hound Dog/Don't Be Cruel*, Elvis Presley, 1956 | 9,000,000 |
| = | *Diana*, Paul Anka, 1957 | 9,000,000 |
| 10 = | *I'm a Believer*, The Monkees, 1966 | 8,000,000 |
| = | *(Everything I Do) I Do It for You*, Bryan Adams, 1991 | 8,000,000 |

Source: *The Popular Music Database*

**FENDER**

Californian-born Leo Fender (1909–91) set up the Fender Electrical Instrument Company in 1946, launching the Broadcaster (later Telecaster) electric guitar in 1948. He then developed the solid-bodied, contoured, double cutaway *Stratocaster* (the "Strat"), with his patented tremolo, which first went on sale in 1954. It was immediately and enduringly popular with rock musicians from Buddy Holly to Eric Clapton and Jimi Hendrix. The Fender Company was sold for $13 million to CBS in 1965, but Fender continued designing guitars until his death.

**After Elvis Presley, who has achieved the most weeks at US No. 1?**

*see p.135 for the answer*

A Madonna
B The Beatles
C Michael Jackson

# Record Firsts

THE KING

*Only the third US single ever certified with sales of over 1 million, ELvis Presley's Hard Headed Woman was released in 1958, the year he joined the army.*

## THE 10 ★
### FIRST MILLION-SELLING US SINGLES

| | SINGLE/ARTIST OR GROUP | CERTIFICATION DATE |
|---|---|---|
| 1 | *Catch a Falling Star,* Perry Como | Mar 14, 1958 |
| 2 | *He's Got the Whole World in His Hands,* Laurie London | July 18, 1958 |
| 3 | *Hard Headed Woman,* Elvis Presley | Aug 11, 1958 |
| 4 | *Patricia,* Perez Prado | Aug 18, 1958 |
| 5 | *Tom Dooley,* Kingston Trio | Jan 21, 1959 |
| 6 | *Calcutta,* Lawrence Welk | Feb 14, 1961 |
| 7 | *Big Bad John,* Jimmy Dean | Dec 14, 1961 |
| 8 | *The Lion Sleeps Tonight,* Tokens | Jan 19, 1962 |
| 9 | *Can't Help Falling in Love,* Elvis Presley | Mar 30, 1962 |
| 10 | *I Can't Stop Loving You,* Ray Charles | July 19, 1962 |

Source: *RIAA*

## THE 10 ★
### FIRST US CHART SINGLES

| | SINGLE | ARTIST OR GROUP |
|---|---|---|
| 1 | *I'll Never Smile Again* | Tommy Dorsey |
| 2 | *The Breeze and I* | Jimmy Dorsey |
| 3 | *Imagination* | Glenn Miller |
| 4 | *Playmates* | Kay Kyser |
| 5 | *Fools Rush in* | Glenn Miller |
| 6 | *Where Was I* | Charlie Barnet |
| 7 | *Pennsylvania 6-5000* | Glenn Miller |
| 8 | *Imagination* | Tommy Dorsey |
| 9 | *Sierra Sue* | Bing Crosby |
| 10 | *Make-believe Island* | Mitchell Ayres |

Source: Billboard

This was the first singles Top 10 compiled by *Billboard* magazine, issued on July 20, 1940.

## THE 10 ★
### FIRST US CHART ALBUMS

| | ALBUM | ARTIST OR GROUP |
|---|---|---|
| 1 | *Al Jolson (Volume III)* | Al Jolson |
| 2 | *A Presentation of Progressive Jazz* | Stan Kenton |
| 3 | *Emperor's Waltz* | Bing Crosby |
| 4 | *Songs of Our Times* | Carmen Cavallaro |
| 5 | *Wizard at the Organ* | Ken Griffin |
| 6 | *Glenn Miller Masterpieces* | Glenn Miller |
| 7 | *Busy Fingers* | Three Suns |
| 8 | *Songs of Our Times* | B. Grant Orchestra |
| 9 | *Glenn Miller* | Glenn Miller |
| 10 | *Theme Songs* | Various artists |

Source: Billboard

This was the first albums Top 10 compiled by *Billboard* magazine, issued on September 3, 1948.

## THE 10 ★
### FIRST FEMALE SINGERS TO HAVE A US NO. 1

| | ARTIST/SINGLE | DATE AT NO. 1 |
|---|---|---|
| 1 | **Joan Weber,** *Let Me Go Lover* | Jan 1, 1955 |
| 2 | **Georgia Gibbs,** *Dance With Henry (Wallflower)* | May 14, 1955 |
| 3 | **Kay Starr,** *Rock and Roll Waltz* | Feb 18, 1956 |
| 4 | **Gogi Grant,** *The Wayward Wind* | June 16, 1956 |
| 5 | **Debbie Reynolds,** *Tammy* | Aug 19, 1957 |
| 6 | **Connie Francis,** *Everybody's Somebody's Fool* | June 27, 1960 |
| 7 | **Brenda Lee,** *I'm Sorry* | July 18, 1960 |
| 8 | **Shelley Fabares,** *Johnny Angel* | Apr 7, 1962 |
| 9 | **Little Eva,** *The Loco-motion* | Aug 25, 1962 |
| 10 | **Little Peggy March,** *I Will Follow Him* | Apr 27, 1963 |

Source: *The Popular Music Database*

**Before his solo career, in what group did Lionel Richie perform?**
*see p.138 for the answer*

A The Temptations
B The Commodores
C The Four Tops

## THE 10 ★
## FIRST SINGLES RELEASED ON THE TAMLA LABEL

| | SINGLE/B SIDE/ARTIST OR GROUP | DATE |
|---|---|---|
| 1 | *Come to Me/Whisper*, Marv Johnson | Jan 1959 |
| 2 | *Merry Go Round/It Moves Me*, Eddie Holland | Jan 1959 |
| 3 | *Ich-I-Bon-I/Cool & Crazy*, Nick & The Jaguars | May 1959 |
| 4 | *Solid Sender/I'll Never Love Again*, Chico Leverette | June 1959 |
| 5 | *Snake Walk (Part I)/Snake Walk (Part II)*, Swinging Tigers | June 1959 |
| 6 | *It/Don't Say Bye Bye*, Ron & Bill | Aug 1959 |
| 7 | *Money (That's What I Want)/ Oh I Apologise*, Barrett Strong | Aug 1959 |
| 8 | *Going to the Hop/ Motor City*, Satintones | Oct 1959 |
| 9 | *The Feeling Is So Fine/You Can Depend on Me*, Miracles | Mar 1960 |
| 10 | *The Feeling Is So Fine/You Can Depend on Me* (2nd version), Miracles | Apr 1960 |

## THE 10 ★
## FIRST AMERICAN GROUPS TO HAVE A NO. 1 SINGLE IN THE UK

| | GROUP/SINGLE | DATE AT NO. 1 |
|---|---|---|
| 1 | Bill Haley & His Comets, *Rock Around the Clock* | Nov 25, 1955 |
| 2 | Dream Weavers, *It's Almost Tomorrow* | Mar 16, 1956 |
| 3 | Teenagers featuring Frankie Lymon, *Why Do Fools Fall in Love?* | July 20, 1956 |
| 4 | Crickets, *That'll Be the Day* | Nov 1, 1957 |
| 5 | Platters, *Smoke Gets in Your Eyes* | Mar 20, 1959 |
| 6 | Marcels, *Blue Moon* | May 4, 1961 |
| 7 | Highwaymen, *Michael* | Oct 12, 1961 |
| 8 | B. Bumble & the Stingers, *Nut Rocker* | May 17, 1962 |
| 9 | The Supremes, *Baby Love* | Nov 19, 1964 |
| 10 | The Byrds, *Mr. Tambourine Man* | July 22, 1965 |

Source: *The Popular Music Database*

## THE 10 ★
## FIRST MILLION-SELLING ROCK 'N' ROLL SINGLES IN THE US

| | SINGLE/ARTIST OR GROUP | YEAR |
|---|---|---|
| 1 | *Rock Around the Clock*, Bill Haley & His Comets | 1954 |
| 2 | *Shake Rattle and Roll*, Bill Haley & His Comets | 1954 |
| 3 | *Maybelline*, Chuck Berry | 1955 |
| 4 | *Ain't That a Shame*, Fats Domino | 1955 |
| 5 | *Ain't That a Shame*, Pat Boone | 1955 |
| 6 | *Seventeen*, Boyd Bennett | 1955 |
| 7 | *I Hear You Knocking*, Gale Storm | 1955 |
| 8 | *See You Later Alligator*, Bill Haley & His Comets | 1955 |
| 9 | *Tutti Frutti*, Little Richard | 1955 |
| 10 | *Heartbreak Hotel*, Elvis Presley | 1956 |

Widely regarded as the first Rock 'n' Roll hit, *Rock Around The Clock* saw the dawn of a new musical era, a hybrid of R & B and Country that would explode as its own genre in the mid-1950s.

## THE 10 ★
## FIRST BRITISH SOLO ARTISTS TO HAVE A NO. 1 HIT IN THE US

| | ARTIST | SINGLE | DATE AT NO. 1 |
|---|---|---|---|
| 1 | Mr. Acker Bilk | *Stranger on the Shore* | May 26, 1962 |
| 2 | Petula Clark | *Downtown* | Jan 23, 1965 |
| 3 | Donovan | *Sunshine Superman* | Sep 3, 1966 |
| 4 | Lulu | *To Sir With Love* | Oct 21, 1967 |
| 5 | George Harrison | *My Sweet Lord* | Dec 26, 1970 |
| 6 | Rod Stewart | *Maggie May* | Oct 2, 1971 |
| 7 | Gilbert O'Sullivan | *Alone Again Naturally* | July 29, 1972 |
| 8 | Elton John | *Crocodile Rock* | Feb 3, 1973 |
| 9 | Ringo Starr | *Photograph* | Nov 24, 1973 |
| 10 | Eric Clapton | *I Shot the Sheriff* | Sep 14, 1974 |

Source: *The Popular Music Database*

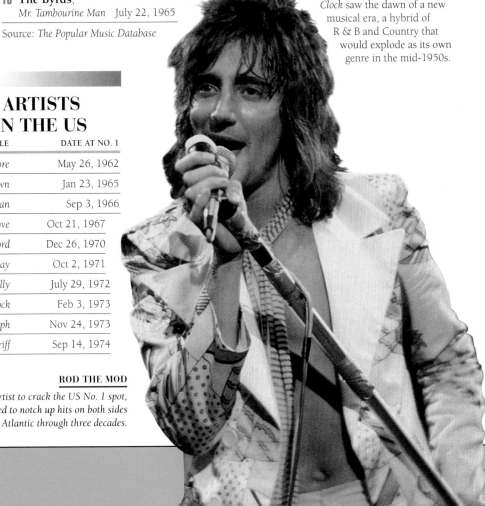

**ROD THE MOD**

*Only the sixth British solo artist to crack the US No. 1 spot, Rod Stewart has continued to notch up hits on both sides of the Atlantic through three decades.*

## TOP 10 ARTISTS WITH THE MOST US NO. 1 SINGLES

*(Artist or group/No. 1 singles)*

**1** The Beatles, 20  **2** Elvis Presley, 17  **3** Mariah Carey, 15*
**4** Michael Jackson, 13  **5** = Madonna, 12;  = The Supremes, 12
**7** Whitney Houston, 11  **8** Stevie Wonder, 10  **9** = Bee Gees, 9;
= Elton John, 9;  = Paul McCartney/Wings, 9

*\* Including duets with Boyz II Men, Joe & 98 Degrees, and Jay-Z*
*Source: The Popular Music Database*

## TOP 10 ★

## SINGLES WITH THE MOST WEEKS AT NO. 1 IN THE US*

| SINGLE/ARTIST OR GROUP/YEAR | WEEKS AT NO. 1 |
|---|---|
| **1** *One Sweet Day*, Mariah Carey & Boyz II Men, 1995 | 16 |
| **2** = *I Will Always Love You*, Whitney Houston, 1992 | 14 |
| = *I'll Make Love to You*, Boyz II Men, 1994 | 14 |
| = *Macarena (Bayside Boys Mix)*, Los Del Rio, 1995 | 14 |
| = *Candle in the Wind (1997)/ Something About the Way You Look Tonight*, Elton John, 1997 | 14 |
| **6** = *End of the Road*, Boyz II Men, 1992 | 13 |
| = *The Boy Is Mine*, Brandy & Monica, 1998 | 13 |
| **8** = *Don't Be Cruel/Hound Dog*, Elvis Presley, 1956 | 11 |
| = *I Swear*, All-4-One, 1994 | 11 |
| = *Un-break My Heart*, Toni Braxton, 1996 | 11 |
| = *Independent Women Part 1*, Destiny's Child, 2000 | 11 |

*\* Based on Billboard charts*

**HOUSTON LIFTS OFF**

*Whitney Houston's long-running No. 1 single* I Will Always Love You, *from the film* The Bodyguard, *in which she also starred, was written by Dolly Parton.*

# TOP 10 ARTISTS WITH THE MOST WEEKS AT NO. 1 IN THE US

*(Artist or group/weeks at No. 1)*

❶ Elvis Presley, 80  ❷ The Beatles, 59
❸ Mariah Carey, 58*  ❹ Boyz II Men, 50*
❺ Michael Jackson, 37  ❻ Elton John, 32;
= Madonna, 32  ❽ Whitney Houston, 31
❾ Paul McCartney/ Wings, 30
❿ The Bee Gees, 27

*\* Boyz II Men and Mariah Carey share a
16-week run with a duet*
Source: *The Popular Music Database*

---

## TOP 10 ★
# YOUNGEST ARTISTS TO HAVE A NO. 1 SINGLE IN THE US*

| ARTIST/TITLE/YEAR | AGE# YRS | MTHS |
|---|---|---|
| 1 Jimmy Boyd, *I Saw Mommy Kissing Santa Claus*, 1952 | 12 | 11 |
| 2 Stevie Wonder, *Fingertips*, 1963 | 13 | 1 |
| 3 Donny Osmond, *Go Away Little Girl*, 1971 | 13 | 7 |
| 4 Michael Jackson, *Ben*, 1972 | 13 | 11 |
| 5 Laurie London, *He's Got the Whole World in His Hands*, 1958 | 14 | 2 |
| 6 Little Peggy March, *I Will Follow Him*, 1963 | 15 | 0 |
| 7 Brenda Lee, *I'm Sorry*, 1960 | 15 | 5 |
| 8 Paul Anka, *Diana*, 1957 | 16 | 0 |
| 9 Tiffany, *I Think We're Alone Now*, 1987 | 16 | 10 |
| 10 Lesley Gore, *It's My Party*, 1963 | 17 | 0 |

*\* Up to Jan 1, 2001*
*# During first week of debut No. 1 US single*
Source: *The Popular Music Database*

If group members were eligible for the list, all three Hanson brothers would be in the Top 10. Isaac was 16 years and 6 months, Taylor 14 years and 2 months, and Zachary 11 years and 7 months when *Mmmbop* topped the charts in 1997.

---

## TOP 10 ★
# TOP 10 LONGEST GAPS BETWEEN NO. 1 HIT SINGLES IN THE US

| ARTIST OR GROUP/PERIOD | GAP YRS | MTHS |
|---|---|---|
| 1 Cher, Mar 23, 1974–Mar 19, 1999 | 24 | 11 |
| 2 Elton John, Nov 11, 1975–Oct 11, 1997 | 21 | 11 |
| 3 The Beach Boys, Dec 10, 1966–Nov 5, 1988 | 21 | 11 |
| 4 Paul Anka, July 13, 1959–Aug 24, 1974 | 15 | 1 |
| 5 George Harrison, June 30, 1973–Jan 16, 1988 | 14 | 7 |
| 6 Neil Sedaka, Aug 11, 1962–Feb 1, 1975 | 12 | 6 |
| 7 Four Seasons, July 18, 1964–Mar 13, 1976 | 11 | 8 |
| 8 Herb Alpert, June 22, 1968–Oct 20, 1979 | 11 | 4 |
| 9 Frank Sinatra, July 9, 1955–July 2, 1966 | 11 | 0 |
| 10 Stevie Wonder, Aug 10, 1963–Jan 27, 1973 | 10 | 5 |

Source: *The Popular Music Database*

---

## TOP 10 ★
# ALBUMS WITH THE SLOWEST RISE TO NO. 1

| ALBUM/ ARTIST OR GROUP | WEEKS TO REACH NO. 1 |
|---|---|
| 1 *First Take*, Roberta Flack | 118 |
| 2 *You Don't Mess Around With Jim*, Jim Croce | 81 |
| 3 *Forever Your Girl*, Paula Abdul | 64 |
| 4 *Film Encores*, Mantovani & His Orchestra | 59 |
| 5 *Fleetwood Mac*, Fleetwood Mac | 58 |
| 6 *Hangin' Tough*, New Kids on the Block | 55 |
| 7 = *Nick of Time*, Bonnie Raitt | 52 |
| = *Throwing Copper*, Live | 52 |
| 9 = *Appetite for Destruction*, Guns 'N Roses | 50 |
| = *Whitney Houston*, Whitney Houston | 50 |

Source: *The Popular Music Database*

---

## TOP 10 ★
# ARTISTS WITH THE MOST CONSECUTIVE NO. 1 SINGLES IN THE US*

| ARTIST OR GROUP | CONSECUTIVE PERIOD | NO. 1s |
|---|---|---|
| 1 Elvis Presley | 1956–58 | 9 |
| 2 Whitney Houston | 1985–88 | 7 |
| 3 = The Beatles | 1964–66 | 6 |
| = The Bee Gees | 1977–79 | 6 |
| = Paula Abdul | 1988–91 | 6 |
| 6 = Michael Jackson | 1987–88 | 5 |
| = The Supremes | 1964–65 | 5 |
| = Mariah Carey | 1990–91 | 5 |
| = Mariah Carey | 1995–98 | 5 |
| 10 = Jackson 5 | 1970 | 4 |
| = George Michael | 1987–88 | 4 |

*\* Up to Jan 1, 2001*
Source: *The Popular Music Database*

---

## TOP 10 ★
# ALBUMS WITH THE MOST CONSECUTIVE WEEKS AT NO. 1 IN THE US CHARTS*

| ALBUM/ARTIST OR GROUP | WEEKS AT NO. 1 |
|---|---|
| 1 *Love Me or Leave Me* (Soundtrack), Doris Day | 25 |
| 2 = *Calypso*, Harry Belafonte | 24 |
| = *Purple Rain* (Soundtrack), Prince | 24 |
| = *Saturday Night Fever*, Soundtrack | 24 |
| 5 *Blue Hawaii* (Soundtrack), Elvis Presley | 20 |
| 6 *Rumours*, Fleetwood Mac | 19 |
| 7 = *More of the Monkees*, The Monkees | 18 |
| = *Please Hammer Don't Hurt 'Em*, MC Hammer | 18 |
| 9 = *Thriller*, Michael Jackson (1st entry) | 17 |
| = *Thriller*, Michael Jackson (2nd entry) | 17 |
| = *Some Gave All*, Billy Ray Cyrus | 17 |

*\* Based on Billboard charts, up to Jan 1, 2001*

---

**Did You Know?** Canadian-born Paul Anka wrote *Diana* at the age of 14 and released it aged 16. He became the first Canadian soloist to sell more than 1 million.

# Hit Singles of the Decades

## SINGLES OF THE 1960s IN THE US

| SINGLE/ARTIST OR GROUP | YEAR RELEASED |
|---|---|
| 1 *I Want to Hold Your Hand*, The Beatles | 1964 |
| 2 *It's Now or Never*, Elvis Presley | 1960 |
| 3 *Hey Jude*, The Beatles | 1968 |
| 4 *The Ballad of the Green Berets*, Sgt. Barry Sadler | 1966 |
| 5 *Love Is Blue*, Paul Mauriat | 1968 |
| 6 *I'm a Believer*, The Monkees | 1966 |
| 7 *Can't Buy Me Love*, The Beatles | 1964 |
| 8 *She Loves You*, The Beatles | 1964 |
| 9 *Sugar Sugar*, The Archies | 1969 |
| 10 *The Twist*, Chubby Checker | 1960 |

Though the 1960s are recalled as the decade in which British music invaded America, the only UK representatives among the decade's 10 biggest sellers in the US are by the leaders of that invasion, the Beatles – although they do completely dominate the list. Elvis Presley's *It's Now or Never*, with sales of around 5 million, almost equaled his total on *Hound Dog/Don't be Cruel*, which had been the previous decade's biggest-selling single.

TOP 10 ★

## SINGLES OF THE 1970s IN THE US

| SINGLE/ARTIST OR GROUP | YEAR RELEASED |
|---|---|
| 1 *You Light up My Life*, Debby Boone | 1977 |
| 2 *Night Fever*, The Bee Gees | 1978 |
| 3 *(I Will Be Your) Shadow Dancing*, Andy Gibb | 1978 |
| 4 *Le Freak*, Chic | 1978 |
| 5 *Bad Girls*, Donna Summer | 1979 |
| 6 *Stayin' Alive*, The Bee Gees | 1978 |
| 7 *Da Ya Think I'm Sexy?*, Rod Stewart | 1978 |
| 8 *Disco Lady*, Johnnie Taylor | 1976 |
| 9 *Reunited*, Peaches & Herb | 1979 |
| 10 *I Will Survive*, Gloria Gaynor | 1978 |

During the last four years of the 1970s, singles sales rose to their highest-ever level, and chart-toppers were routinely selling over 2 million copies.

TOP 10 ★

## SINGLES OF THE 1980s IN THE US

| SINGLE/ARTIST OR GROUP | YEAR RELEASED |
|---|---|
| 1 *We Are the World*, USA for Africa | 1985 |
| 2 *Physical*, Olivia Newton-John | 1981 |
| 3 *Endless Love*, Diana Ross and Lionel Richie | 1981 |
| 4 *Eye of the Tiger*, Survivor | 1982 |
| 5 *I Love Rock 'n' Roll*, Joan Jett and The Blackhearts | 1982 |
| 6 *When Doves Cry*, Prince | 1984 |
| 7 *Celebration*, Kool and The Gang | 1981 |
| 8 *Another One Bites the Dust*, Queen | 1980 |
| 9 *Wild Thing*, Tone Loc | 1989 |
| 10 *Islands in the Stream*, Kenny Rogers and Dolly Parton | 1983 |

America's top-selling single of the 1980s was a record that included contributions from many of those artists who had become the recording élite during the decade – the charity single for Africa's famine victims, *We Are the World*. Meanwhile, three of the close runners-up, *Endless Love* (from the movie of the same name), *Eye of the Tiger* (from *Rocky III*), and *When Doves Cry* (from Prince's *Purple Rain*) were all taken from movies.

**OUT OF PUFF**

*I'll Be Missing You, by Sean Combs, aka Puff Daddy, is the world's most successful rap single. It was written as a tribute to Notorious B.I.G.*

TOP 10 ★

## SINGLES OF EACH YEAR OF THE 1980s IN THE US

| YEAR | SINGLE/ARTIST OR GROUP |
|---|---|
| 1980 | *Another One Bites the Dust*, Queen |
| 1981 | *Endless Love*, Diana Ross and Lionel Richie |
| 1982 | *Eye of the Tiger*, Survivor |
| 1983 | *Islands in the Stream*, Kenny Rogers and Dolly Parton |
| 1984 | *When Doves Cry*, Prince |
| 1985 | *We Are the World*, USA for Africa |
| 1986 | *That's What Friends Are For*, Dionne Warwick and Friends |
| 1987 | *I Wanna Dance with Somebody (Who Loves Me)*, Whitney Houston |
| 1988 | *Kokomo*, The Beach Boys |
| 1989 | *Wild Thing*, Tone Loc |

## TOP 10 ★
### SINGLES OF THE 1990s IN THE US

| | SINGLE/ARTIST OR GROUP | YEAR RELEASED |
|---|---|---|
| 1 | *Candle in the Wind (1997)/ Something About the Way You Look Tonight*, Elton John | 1997 |
| 2 | *I Will Always Love You*, Whitney Houston | 1992 |
| 3 | *Whoomp! (There It Is)*, Tag Team | 1993 |
| 4 | *Macarena*, Los Del Rio | 1995 |
| 5 | *(Everything I Do) I Do It for You*, Bryan Adams | 1991 |
| 6 | *I'll Be Missing You*, Puff Daddy & Faith Evans (featuring 112) | 1997 |
| 7 | *How Do I Live*, LeAnn Rimes | 1997 |
| 8 | *Gangsta's Paradise*, Coolio featuring L.V. | 1995 |
| 9 | *Dazzey Duks*, Duice | 1993 |
| 10 | *The Boy Is Mine*, Brandy & Monica | 1995 |

## TOP 10 ★
### SINGLES OF EACH YEAR OF THE 1990s IN THE US

| YEAR | SINGLE/ARTIST OR GROUP |
|---|---|
| 1990 | *Vogue*, Madonna |
| 1991 | *(Everything I Do) I Do It for You*, Bryan Adams |
| 1992 | *I Will Always Love You*, Whitney Houston |
| 1993 | *Rump Shaker*, Wreckx 'N' Effects |
| 1994 | *Whoomp! (There It Is)*, Tag Team |
| 1995 | *Gangsta's Paradise*, Coolio featuring L.V. |
| 1996 | *Macarena (Bayside Boys Mix)*, Los Del Rio |
| 1997 | *Candle in the Wind (1997)/ Something About the Way You Look Tonight*, Elton John |
| 1998 | *The Boy Is Mine*, Brandy & Monica |
| 1999 | *Believe*, Cher |

Source: *RIAA*

## TOP 10 ★
### SINGLES OF THE 1990s IN THE US (MALE)

| | SINGLE/ARTIST | YEAR RELEASED |
|---|---|---|
| 1 | *Candle in the Wind (1997)/ Something About the Way You Look Tonight*, Elton John | 1997 |
| 2 | *(Everything I Do) I Do It for You*, Bryan Adams | 1991 |
| 3 | *Gangsta's Paradise*, Coolio featuring L.V. | 1995 |
| 4 | *How Do U Want It*, 2-Pac | 1996 |
| 5 | *I Believe I Can Fly*, R. Kelly | 1996 |
| 6 | *You Make Me Wanna*, Usher | 1997 |
| 7 | *Livin' La Vida Loca*, Ricky Martin | 1999 |
| 8 | *Here Comes the Hotstepper*, Ini Kamoze | 1994 |
| 9 | *Ice Ice Baby*, Vanilla Ice | 1990 |
| 10 | *This Is How We Do It*, Montell Jordan | 1995 |

## TOP 10 ★
### SINGLES OF THE 1990s IN THE US (FEMALE)

| | SINGLE/ARTIST | YEAR RELEASED |
|---|---|---|
| 1 | *I Will Always Love You*, Whitney Houston | 1992 |
| 2 | *How Do I Live*, LeAnn Rimes | 1997 |
| 3 | *The Boy Is Mine*, Brandy & Monica | 1998 |
| 4 | *Fantasy*, Mariah Carey | 1995 |
| 5 | *Vogue*, Madonna | 1990 |
| 6 | *You Were Meant for Me/ Foolish Games*, Jewel | 1996 |
| 7 | *The Power of Love*, Celine Dion | 1993 |
| 8 | *Believe*, Cher | 1999 |
| 9 | *Hero*, Mariah Carey | 1993 |
| 10 | *You're Still the One*, Shania Twain | 1998 |

**CHER SUCCESS**

*Now into her fifth decade of chart successes, both in partnership with Sonny Bono and solo, Cher has also carved out an Oscar-winning film career.*

**What is unusual about John Lennon's single *Imagine*?**
*see p.143 for the answer*
A It was a posthumous hit
B It has the shortest title of a No. 1 single
C It was the first-ever CD single

# Hit Albums of the Decades

## ALBUMS OF THE 1960s IN THE US

| ALBUM/ARTIST OR GROUP | YEAR RELEASED |
|---|---|
| 1 *West Side Story* (Soundtrack), Various | 1961 |
| 2 *Blue Hawaii* (Soundtrack), Elvis Presley | 1961 |
| 3 *The Sound of Music* (Soundtrack), Various | 1965 |
| 4 *Sgt. Pepper's Lonely Hearts Club Band*, The Beatles | 1967 |
| 5 *More of The Monkees*, The Monkees | 1967 |
| 6 *Days of Wine and Roses*, Andy Williams | 1963 |
| 7 *G.I. Blues*, Elvis Presley | 1960 |
| 8 *The Button-Down Mind of Bob Newhart*, Bob Newhart | 1960 |
| 9 *Whipped Cream and Other Delights*, Herb Alpert & The Tijuana Brass | 1965 |
| 10 *A Hard Day's Night* (Soundtrack), The Beatles | 1964 |

## ALBUMS OF EACH YEAR OF THE 1970s IN THE US

| YEAR | ALBUM/ARTIST OR GROUP |
|---|---|
| 1970 | *Bridge Over Troubled Water*, Simon and Garfunkel |
| 1971 | *Tapestry*, Carole King |
| 1972 | *American Pie*, Don McLean |
| 1973 | *Dark Side of the Moon*, Pink Floyd |
| 1974 | *John Denver's Greatest Hits*, John Denver |
| 1975 | *Captain Fantastic and the Brown Dirt Cowboy*, Elton John |
| 1976 | *Frampton Comes Alive!*, Peter Frampton |
| 1977 | *Rumours*, Fleetwood Mac |
| 1978 | *Saturday Night Fever*, Soundtrack |
| 1979 | *Breakfast in America*, Supertramp |

## ALBUMS OF EACH YEAR OF THE 1980s IN THE US

| YEAR | ALBUM/ARTIST OR GROUP |
|---|---|
| 1980 | *The Wall*, Pink Floyd |
| 1981 | *Hi Infidelity*, REO Speedwagon |
| 1982 | *Asia*, Asia |
| 1983 | *Thriller*, Michael Jackson |
| 1984 | *Purple Rain*, Prince |
| 1985 | *Like a Virgin*, Madonna |
| 1986 | *Whitney Houston*, Whitney Houston |
| 1987 | *Slippery When Wet*, Bon Jovi |
| 1988 | *Faith*, George Michael |
| 1989 | *Girl You Know It's True*, Milli Vanilli |

The 1980s opened with Pink Floyd's *The Wall* spending three and a half months at No. 1, approaching their former triumph with *Dark Side of the Moon*. *The Wall* eventually sold over 7 million copies in the US.

### RICH REWARDS

*Formerly a member of the Commodores, Lionel Richie began a successful solo career in the 1980s, with* Can't Slow Down *selling 8 million copies in the US alone within a year of its release.*

## ALBUMS OF THE 1970s IN THE US

| ALBUM/ARTIST OR GROUP | YEAR RELEASED |
|---|---|
| 1 *Rumours*, Fleetwood Mac | 1977 |
| 2 *Their Greatest Hits 1971–1975*, The Eagles | 1976 |
| 3 *Dark Side of the Moon*, Pink Floyd | 1973 |
| 4 *Tapestry*, Carole King | 1971 |
| 5 *Saturday Night Fever* (Soundtrack), Various | 1977 |
| 6 *Led Zeppelin IV*, Led Zeppelin | 1971 |
| 7 *Boston*, Boston | 1976 |
| 8 *Grease* (Soundtrack), Various | 1978 |
| 9 *Frampton Comes Alive!*, Peter Frampton | 1976 |
| 10 *Songs in the Key of Life*, Stevie Wonder | 1976 |

## ALBUMS OF THE 1980s IN THE US

| ALBUM/ARTIST OR GROUP | YEAR RELEASED |
|---|---|
| 1 *Thriller*, Michael Jackson | 1982 |
| 2 *Born in the U.S.A.*, Bruce Springsteen | 1984 |
| 3 *Dirty Dancing* (Soundtrack), Various | 1987 |
| 4 *Purple Rain* (Soundtrack), Prince & The Revolution, | 1984 |
| 5 *Can't Slow Down*, Lionel Richie | 1983 |
| 6 *Whitney Houston*, Whitney Houston | 1985 |
| 7 *Hysteria*, Def Leppard | 1987 |
| 8 *Slippery When Wet*, Bon Jovi | 1986 |
| 9 *Appetite For Destruction*, Guns N' Roses | 1988 |
| 10 *The Wall*, Pink Floyd | 1979 |

On Oct 30, 1984, *Thriller* became the first album to receive its 20th platinum sales certificate, for sales of 20 million copies in the US alone.

## TOP 10 ⭐
### ALBUMS OF EACH YEAR IN THE 1990s IN THE US

| YEAR | ALBUM/ARTIST OR GROUP |
|------|------------------------|
| 1990 | *Please Hammer Don't Hurt 'Em*, MC Hammer |
| 1991 | *Ropin' the Wind*, Garth Brooks |
| 1992 | *Some Gave All*, Billy Ray Cyrus |
| 1993 | *The Bodyguard*, Soundtrack |
| 1994 | *The Sign*, Ace of Base |
| 1995 | *Cracked Rear View*, Hootie & the Blowfish |
| 1996 | *Jagged Little Pill*, Alanis Morissette |
| 1997 | *Spice*, Spice Girls |
| 1998 | *Titanic*, Soundtrack |
| 1999 | *Millennium*, Backstreet Boys |

Source: *RIAA*

## TOP 10 ⭐
### ALBUMS OF THE 1990s IN THE US

| | ALBUM/ARTIST OR GROUP | YEAR RELEASED | SALES (1990s) |
|---|------------------------|---------------|---------------|
| 1 | *The Bodyguard*, Soundtrack | 1992 | 17,000,000 |
| 2 | =*Come on Over*, Shania Twain | 1990 | 16,000,000 |
| | =*Cracked Rear View*, Hootie & the Blowfish | 1995 | 16,000,000 |
| | =*Jagged Little Pill*, Alanis Morissette | 1994 | 16,000,000 |
| | =*No Fences*, Garth Brooks | 1991 | 16,000,000 |
| 6 | =*Ropin' the Wind*, Garth Brooks | 1997 | 14,000,000 |
| | =*Their Greatest Hits 1971–1975*, The Eagles | 1992 | 14,000,000 |
| 8 | =*Backstreet Boys*, Backstreet Boys | 1994 | 12,000,000 |
| | =*Breathless*, Kenny G | 1995 | 12,000,000 |
| | =*II*, Boyz II Men | 1995 | 12,000,000 |
| | =*Led Zeppelin IV*, Led Zeppelin | 1995 | 12,000,000 |
| | =*Metallica*, Metallica | 1995 | 12,000,000 |

Source: *RIAA*

Each of the Top 10 albums of the 1990s sold in excess of 10 million units in the US, thus qualifying them all for RIAA Diamond Awards.

**TWAIN MAKES HER MARK**

*After achieving her first chart success in 1993, Canadian-born country singer Shania Twain has rapidly become one of the bestselling female artistes of all time.*

**Did You Know?** Shania Twain was born Eilleen Regina Edwards. Her new name, adopted in 1990, comes from the Native American Chippewa (Ojibway) phrase for "I'm on my way."

# Female Singers

## TOP 10 ★
## SINGLES BY FEMALE GROUPS IN THE US

| | SINGLE/GROUP | YEAR |
|---|---|---|
| 1 | *Don't Let Go*, En Vogue | 1996 |
| 2 | *Hold On*, En Vogue | 1990 |
| 3 | *Wannabe*, Spice Girls | 1997 |
| 4 | *Whatta Man*, Salt-n-Pepa | 1994 |
| 5 | *Expressions*, Salt-n-Pepa | 1990 |
| 6 | *Push It*, Salt-n-Pepa | 1987 |
| 7 | *Waterfall*, TLC | 1995 |
| 8 | *Creep*, TLC | 1994 |
| 9 | *Weak*, SWV | 1993 |
| 10 | *Unpretty*, TLC | 1999 |

Source: *The Popular Music Database*

## TOP 10 ★
## FEMALE SINGERS WITH THE MOST TOP 10 HITS IN THE US

| | SINGER | TOP 10 HITS* |
|---|---|---|
| 1 | Madonna | 33 |
| 2 | Janet Jackson (including one duet with Michael Jackson and one with Busta Rhymes) | 25 |
| 3 = | Whitney Houston (including one duet with CeCe Winans and one with Faith Evans) | 20 |
| = | Mariah Carey (including one duet with Boyz II Men, one with Luther Vandross, and one with Jay-Z) | 20 |
| 5 | Aretha Franklin (including one duet with George Michael) | 17 |
| 6 | Connie Francis | 16 |
| 7 | Olivia Newton-John (including two duets with John Travolta and one with the Electric Light Orchestra) | 15 |
| 8 | Donna Summer | 14 |
| 9 = | Brenda Lee | 12 |
| = | Diana Ross (including one duet with Marvin Gaye and one with Lionel Richie) | 12 |
| = | Dionne Warwick (including one duet with the Detroit Spinners and one with Stevie Wonder, Gladys Knight, and Elton John) | 12 |

* up to January 1, 2001

**GIRL POWER**

*In a relatively short period, the Spice Girls set new records for best-sellers and single and album chart entries on both sides of the Atlantic.*

## TOP 10 ★
## ALBUMS BY FEMALE GROUPS IN THE US

| | ALBUM/GROUP | YEAR |
|---|---|---|
| 1 | *Wide Open Spaces*, Dixie Chicks | 1998 |
| 2 | *Crazysexycool*, TLC | 1994 |
| 3 | *Spice*, Spice Girls | 1997 |
| 4 | *The Writing's on the Wall*, Destiny's Child | 1999 |
| 5 | *Fanmail*, TLC | 1999 |
| 6 | *Fly*, Dixie Chicks | 1999 |
| 7 | *Wilson Phillips*, Wilson Phillips | 1990 |
| 8 | *Very Necessary*, Salt-n-Pepa | 1993 |
| 9 | *Oooooohhh ... On the TLC Tip*, TLC | 1992 |
| 10 | *Spiceworld*, Spice Girls | 1997 |

Source: *The Popular Music Database*

As this list exemplifies, the 1990s saw a huge surge in the popularity of all-girl groups, with sales eclipsing those of such predecessors as the Supremes and the Bangles.

## TOP 10 ★
## FEMALE GROUPS IN THE US

| | GROUP* | NO. 1 | TOP 10 | TOP 20 |
|---|---|---|---|---|
| 1 | The Supremes | 12 | 20 | 24 |
| 2 | The Pointer Sisters | – | 7 | 13 |
| 3 | TLC | 2 | 9 | 11 |
| 4 = | Expose | 1 | 8 | 9 |
| = | The McGuire Sisters | 2 | 4 | 9 |
| 6 | The Fontane Sisters | 2 | 2 | 8 |
| 7 = | The Shirelles | 2 | 6 | 7 |
| = | Martha & the Vandellas | – | 6 | 7 |
| = | En Vogue | – | 5 | 7 |
| = | Spice Girls | – | 4 | 7 |

* *Ranked according to total number of Top 20 singles*

Source: *The Popular Music Database*

Coincidentally, two groups in this list – the McGuire Sisters and the Fontane Sisters (real name Rosse) – each consisted of three sisters. Both groups achieved their chart hits in the 1950s. The McGuires' 1955 version of *Sincerely* was a million seller, remaining a US No. 1 for 10 weeks. The Fontanes reached No. 1 in 1954 with *Hearts of Stone*.

**What was the name of Cher's 1999 smash hit?**
*see p.137 for the answer*

A Strong Enough
B Believe
C Walking in Memphis

## TOP 10 ★

# SINGLES BY FEMALE SINGERS IN THE US

| | SINGLE/ARTIST | YEAR |
|---|---|---|
| 1 | *I Will Always Love You*, Whitney Houston | 1992 |
| 2 | *How Do I Live*, LeAnn Rimes | 1997 |
| 3 | *The Boy Is Mine*, Brandy & Monica | 1998 |
| 4 | *Fantasy*, Mariah Carey | 1995 |
| 5 | *Vogue*, Madonna | 1990 |
| 6 | *Mr. Big Stuff*, Jean Knight | 1971 |
| 7 | *You Were Meant for Me/Foolish Games*, Jewel | 1996 |
| 8 | *You Light up My Life*, Debby Boone | 1977 |
| 9 | *The Power of Love*, Celine Dion | 1993 |
| 10 | *Believe*, Cher | 1999 |

Among these blockbusters, all of them platinum sellers, it is fitting that Whitney Houston's multi-platinum success from *The Bodyguard* (original soundtrack) was also written by a woman – Dolly Parton – whose original version of *I Will Always Love You* peaked in 1982 at a lowly No. 53. Jean Knight's *Mr. Big Stuff*, an R&B No. 1, took 25 years to reach certified sales of 2 million copies.

## TOP 10 ★

# ALBUMS BY FEMALE SINGERS IN THE US

| | ALBUM/ARTIST | YEAR | ESTIMATED COPIES SOLD |
|---|---|---|---|
| 1 = | *The Bodyguard* (Soundtrack), Whitney Houston | 1992 | 17,000,000 |
| = | *Come on Over*, Shania Twain | 1997 | 17,000,000 |
| 3 | *Jagged Little Pill*, Alanis Morissette | 1995 | 16,000,000 |
| 4 | *Whitney Houston*, Whitney Houston | 1985 | 13,000,000 |
| 5 | *...Baby One More Time*, Britney Spears | 1999 | 12,000,000 |
| 6 = | *The Woman in Me*, Shania Twain | 1995 | 11,000,000 |
| = | *Pieces of You*, Jewel | 1997 | 11,000,000 |
| 8 = | *Tapestry*, Carole King | 1971 | 10,000,000 |
| = | *Let's Talk About Love*, Celine Dion | 1997 | 10,000,000 |
| = | *Falling into You*, Celine Dion | 1996 | 10,000,000 |
| = | *Music Box*, Mariah Carey | 1993 | 10,000,000 |
| = | *Like a Virgin*, Madonna | 1984 | 10,000,000 |

Source: *The Popular Music Database*

## TOP 10 ★

# YOUNGEST FEMALE SINGERS TO HAVE A NO. 1 SINGLE IN THE US

| | SINGER/SINGLE/YEAR | YEARS | AGE MTHS | DAYS |
|---|---|---|---|---|
| 1 | Little Peggy March, *I Will Follow Him*, 1963 | 15 | 1 | 20 |
| 2 | Brenda Lee, *I'm Sorry*, 1960 | 15 | 7 | 7 |
| 3 | Tiffany, *I Think We're Alone*, 1987 | 16 | 1 | 5 |
| 4 | Lesley Gore, *It's My Party*, 1963 | 17 | 0 | 30 |
| 5 | Little Eva, *The Loco-Motion*, 1962 | 17 | 1 | 27 |
| 6 | Britney Spears, *...Baby One More Time*, 1999 | 17 | 1 | 29 |
| 7 | Monica, *The First Night*, 1998 | 17 | 11 | 9 |
| 8 | Shelley Fabares, *Johnny Angel*, 1962 | 18 | 2 | 19 |
| 9 | Debbie Gibson, *Foolish Beat*, 1988 | 18 | 6 | 4 |
| 10 | Christina Aguilera, *Genie in a Bottle*, 1999 | 18 | 7 | 13 |

Source: *The Popular Music Database*

**CHRISTINA AGUILERA**

*Within a year of her professional debut, Christina Aguilera became one of only a handful of teenage girls to achieve a No. 1 single. She also sold over 8 million copies of her first album and won a Grammy award.*

# All-Time Greats

TOP 10

## COUNTRY MUSIC AWARDS WINNERS

| | ARTIST | AWARDS |
|---|---|---|
| 1 | Vince Gill | 18 |
| 2 | George Strait | 12 |
| 3 | Garth Brooks | 11 |
| 4 | =Roy Clark | 10 |
| | =Brooks & Dunn | 10 |
| 6 | =Alabama | 9 |
| | =Chet Atkins | 9 |
| | =Judds | 9 |
| 9 | =Loretta Lynn | 8 |
| | =Ronnie Milsap | 8 |
| | =Willie Nelson | 8 |
| | = Dolly Parton | 8 |
| | =Ricky Skaggs | 8 |

The Country Music Awards are the most prestigious Country awards, held as an annual ceremony since 1967. Veteran Country instrumentalist Roy Clark netted the Instrumentalist of the Year award for seven consecutive years (1974–1980).

## TOP 10 — PRINCE ALBUMS IN THE US

| | ALBUM | YEAR |
|---|---|---|
| 1 | *Purple Rain* | 1984 |
| 2 | *1999* | 1982 |
| 3 | *Around the World in a Day* | 1985 |
| 4 | *Batman* | 1989 |
| 5 | *Diamonds and Pearls* | 1991 |
| 6 | ⚥ | 1992 |
| 7 | *The Hits I* | 1993 |
| 8 | *The Hits II* | 1993 |
| 9 | *Sign O' the Times* | 1987 |
| 10 | *The Hits/B Sides* | 1993 |

Source: *The Popular Music Database*

## TOP 10 — BRUCE SPRINGSTEEN ALBUMS IN THE US

| | ALBUM | YEAR |
|---|---|---|
| 1 | *Born in the USA* | 1984 |
| 2 | *Born to Run* | 1975 |
| 3 | *Greatest Hits* | 1995 |
| 4 | *Tunnel of Love* | 1986 |
| 5 | *The River* | 1980 |
| 6 | *Bruce Springsteen & the E Street Band Live/1975–85* | 1986 |
| 7 | *Darkness on the Edge of Town* | 1978 |
| 8 | *Greetings from Asbury Park, NJ* | 1975 |
| 9 | *Human Touch* | 1992 |
| 10 | *Lucky Town* | 1992 |

Source: *The Popular Music Database*

## TOP 10 GROUPS OF THE 1970s IN THE US*

❶ The Bee Gees ❷ Carpenters ❸ Chicago ❹ Jackson 5/Jacksons
❺ Three Dog Night ❻ Gladys Knight & The Pips ❼ Dawn ❽ Earth, Wind & Fire
❾ The Eagles ❿ Fleetwood Mac

*\* Based on comparative US singles chart performance*

**PRINCE, CHARMING**

*Although he achieved a string of hit singles and albums throughout the 1980s, and picked up six BRIT awards, Prince did not gain a UK No. 1 – his only chart-topper to date – until 1994.*

# TOP 10 ★
## JOHN LENNON SINGLES IN THE US

| SINGLE | YEAR |
| --- | --- |
| 1 (Just Like) Starting Over | 1980 |
| 2 Woman | 1981 |
| 3 Instant Karma | 1970 |
| 4 Whatever Gets You Thru the Night | 1974 |
| 5 Imagine | 1971 |
| 6 #9 Dream | 1974 |
| 7 Nobody Told Me | 1984 |
| 8 Watching the Wheels | 1981 |
| 9 Power to the People | 1971 |
| 10 Mind Games | 1973 |

Source: MRIB

**KEY PLAYER**
*The most charismatic of the Beatles, John Lennon achieved a run of hits before and after his 1980 murder, including his anthemic US No. 1 Imagine.*

# TOP 10 ★
## JUKEBOX SINGLES OF ALL TIME IN THE US*

| SINGLE/ARTIST OR GROUP | YEAR |
| --- | --- |
| 1 Crazy, Patsy Cline | 1962 |
| 2 Old Time Rock 'n' Roll, Bob Seger | 1979 |
| 3 Hound Dog/Don't be Cruel, Elvis Presley | 1956 |
| 4 Mack the Knife, Bobby Darin | 1959 |
| 5 Born to Be Wild, Steppenwolf | 1968 |
| 6 New York, New York, Frank Sinatra | 1980 |
| 7 Rock Around the Clock, Bill Haley & His Comets | 1955 |
| 8 I Heard It Through the Grapevine, Marvin Gaye | 1968 |
| 9 (Sittin' on) The Dock of the Bay, Otis Redding | 1968 |
| 10 Light My Fire, Doors | 1967 |

* From 1950 to 1996

This list, which is updated every three or four years, was compiled by the Amusement & Music Operators Association, whose members service and operate over 250,000 jukeboxes in the US. The 1989 list's chart-topper was the double A-side *Hound Dog/Don't Be Cruel*, while the Righteous Brothers' *Unchained Melody* was the highest new entry into the Top 40 in 1992 (at No. 12).

# TOP 10 ★
## BOB DYLAN SINGLES IN THE US

| SINGLE | YEAR |
| --- | --- |
| 1 Like a Rolling Stone | 1965 |
| 2 Rainy Day Women, Nos. 12 & 35 | 1966 |
| 3 Positively 4th Street | 1965 |
| 4 Lay Lady Lay | 1969 |
| 5 Knockin' on Heaven's Door | 1973 |
| 6 I Want You | 1966 |
| 7 Just Like a Woman | 1966 |
| 8 Gotta Serve Somebody | 1979 |
| 9 Hurricane | 1976 |
| 10 Subterranean Homesick Blues | 1965 |

Source: MRIB

*Like a Rolling Stone*, which hit US No. 2 in December 1965, became Dylan's first million-selling single. It was also noteworthy for its length, which, at six minutes, was double that of most chart singles of the day.

# TOP 10 ★
## ARTISTS WITH THE MOST GRAMMY AWARDS

| ARTIST | AWARDS |
| --- | --- |
| 1 Sir Georg Solti | 31 |
| 2 Quincy Jones | 26 |
| 3 Vladimir Horowitz | 25 |
| 4 Pierre Boulez | 23 |
| 5 Stevie Wonder | 21 |
| 6 Henry Mancini | 20 |
| 7 =John T. Williams | 17 |
| =Leonard Bernstein | 17 |
| 9 =Aretha Franklin | 15 |
| =Itzhak Perlman | 15 |

The Grammy Awards ceremony has been held annually in the US since its inauguration on May 4, 1959, and the awards are considered to be the most prestigious in the music industry. The proliferation of classical artists in this Top 10 is largely attributable to the large number of classical award categories at the Grammys, which have been latterly overshadowed by the rise of pop and rock. Grammy winners are selected annually by the voting membership of NARAS (the National Academy of Recording Arts & Sciences).

## TOP 10 GROUPS OF THE 1980s IN THE US*

**①** Wham! **②** Kool & The Gang **③** Huey Lewis & The News **④** Journey **⑤** Duran Duran **⑥** U2 **⑦** Rolling Stones **⑧** Alabama **⑨** Pointer Sisters **⑩** Jefferson Airplane/Starship

*\* Based on comparative US single and album chart performance* Source: MRIB

**Did You Know?** John Lennon's single *Imagine* was released in the US in 1971. Its UK release was delayed until 1975, and it made No. 1 only after his death in 1980.

# Top of the Pops

## TOP 10 ★
### JANET JACKSON SINGLES IN THE US

| SINGLE | YEAR |
|---|---|
| 1 Again | 1993 |
| 2 That's the Way Love Goes | 1993 |
| 3 Miss You Again | 1989 |
| 4 Together Again | 1997 |
| 5 Love Will Never Do Without You | 1990 |
| 6 Doesn't Really Matter | 2000 |
| 7 Escapade | 1990 |
| 8 Black Cat | 1990 |
| 9 Runaway | 1995 |
| 10 If | 1993 |

## TOP 10 ★
### MARIAH CAREY SINGLES IN THE US

| SINGLE | YEAR |
|---|---|
| 1 Fantasy | 1995 |
| 2 One Sweet Day* | 1995 |
| 3 Hero | 1993 |
| 4 Always Be My Baby | 1996 |
| 5 My All | 1997 |
| 6 Honey | 1997 |
| 7 Dreamlover | 1993 |
| 8 I Still Believe | 1999 |
| 9 Love Takes Time | 1990 |
| 10 Vision of Love | 1990 |

* Featuring Boyz II Men

### THE 10 LATEST GRAMMY NEW ARTISTS OF THE YEAR
(Year/artist or group)

❶ 2000, Shelby Lynne
❷ 1999, Christina Aguilera ❸ 1998, Lauryn Hill ❹ 1997, Paula Cole
❺ 1996, LeeAnn Rimes ❻ 1995, Hootie & The Blowfish ❼ 1994, Sheryl Crow
❽ 1993, Toni Braxton ❾ 1992, Arrested Development ❿ 1991, Mark Cohn

## TOP 10 BACKSTREET BOYS SINGLES IN THE US
(Single/year)

❶ Quit Playing Games (With My Heart) 1997 ❷ Everybody (Backstreet's Back) 1998
❸ All I Have to Give 1999 ❹ I Want It That Way 1999 ❺ Show Me the Meaning of Being Lonely 2000 ❻ Larger than Life 1999 ❼ Shape of My Heart 2000
❽ The One 2000 ❾ We've Got It Goin' On 1995 ❿ I'll Never Break Your Heart 1998

## TOP 10 ★
### WHITNEY HOUSTON SINGLES IN THE US

| SINGLE | YEAR |
|---|---|
| 1 I Will Always Love You | 1992 |
| 2 Exhale (Shoop Shoop) | 1995 |
| 3 I Believe in You and Me | 1996 |
| 4 Heartbreak Hotel* | 1999 |
| 5 I Wanna Dance with Somebody (Who Loves Me) | 1987 |
| 6 My Love is Your Love | 1999 |
| 7 I'm Your Baby Tonight | 1990 |
| 8 All the Man that I Need | 1990 |
| 9 I'm Every Woman | 1993 |
| 10 It's Not Right But It's Okay | 1999 |

* With Faith Evans and Kelly Price

## TOP 10 ★
### 'N SYNC SINGLES IN THE US

| SINGLE | YEAR |
|---|---|
| 1 It's Gonna Be Me | 2000 |
| 2 Music of My Heart* | 1999 |
| 3 I Want You Back | 1998 |
| 4 Bring It All to Me# | 1999 |
| 5 Bye Bye Bye | 2000 |
| 6 (God Must Have Spent) A Little More Time on You | 1998 |
| 7 This I Promise You | 2000 |
| 8 (God Must Have Spent) A Little More Time on You+ | 1999 |
| 9 I Drive Myself Crazy | 1999 |
| 10 Tearin' up My Heart | 1998 |

* With Gloria Estefan   # With Blaque
+ With Alabama

## TOP 10 ★
### LATEST GRAMMY POP VOCAL PERFORMANCES OF THE YEAR

| MALE VOCALIST/SONG | YEAR | FEMALE VOCALIST/SONG |
|---|---|---|
| Sting, She Walks This Earth (Soberana Rosa) | 2000 | Macy Gray, I Try |
| Sting, Brand New Day | 1999 | Sarah McLachlan, I Will Remember You |
| Eric Clapton, My Father's Eyes | 1998 | Celine Dion, My Heart Will Go On |
| Elton John, Candle in the Wind (1997) | 1997 | Sarah McLachlan, Building a Mystery |
| Eric Clapton, Change the World | 1996 | Toni Braxton, Un-Break My Heart |
| Seal, Kiss From a Rose | 1995 | Annie Lennox, No More "I Love You"s |
| Elton John, Can You Feel the Love Tonight | 1994 | Sheryl Crow, All I Wanna Do |
| Sting, If I Ever Lose My Faith in You | 1993 | Whitney Houston, I Will Always Love You |
| Eric Clapton, Tears in Heaven | 1992 | k.d. lang, Constant Craving |
| Michael Bolton, When a Man Loves a Woman | 1991 | Bonnie Raitt, Something to Talk About |

The first male winner of this award was Perry Como in 1958, for his million-selling Catch a Falling Star. It was not introduced as a separate category for female singers until 1976, when it was won by Carole King for her single Tapestry.

What is the title of Bon Jovi's bestselling 1986 album?
see p.138 for the answer
A Slippery When Wet
B Slipping and Sliding
C Many a Slip...

## TOP 10 ★

### LATEST INDUCTEES INTO THE COUNTRY MUSIC HALL OF FAME

| | ARTIST | YEAR |
|---|---|---|
| 1= | Charley Pride | 2000 |
| = | Faron Young | 2000 |
| 3= | Johnny Bond | 1999 |
| = | Dolly Parton | 1999 |
| = | Conway Twitty | 1999 |
| 6= | George Morgan | 1998 |
| = | Elvis Presley | 1998 |
| = | E. W. "Bud" Wendell | 1998 |
| = | Tammy Wynette | 1998 |
| 10= | Harlan Howard | 1997 |
| = | Brenda Lee | 1997 |
| = | Cindy Walker | 1997 |

Source: *Country Music Association*

Founded in 1961 by the Country Music Association in Nashville, the Country Music Hall of Fame recognizes outstanding contributions to the world of Country.

## TOP 10 ★

### MADONNA SINGLES IN THE US

| | SINGLE | YEAR |
|---|---|---|
| 1 | Vogue | 1990 |
| 2 | Justify My Love | 1990 |
| 3 | Music | 2000 |
| 4 | Like a Prayer | 1989 |
| 5 | Take a Bow | 1994 |
| 6 | This Used to be My Playground | 1992 |
| 7 | Like a Virgin | 1984 |
| 8 | Crazy for You | 1985 |
| 9 | Papa Don't Preach | 1986 |
| 10 | Erotica | 1992 |

#### MATERIAL GIRL

*Madonna's hit singles span three decades. Her marriage in 2000 to British film director Guy Ritchie generated media frenzy, despite being an unusually private celebrity event.*

# Music Genres

TAKING THE RAP

*On his rapid rise to rap superstardom, Marshall Mathers, aka Eminem, aka Slim Shady, has attracted both praise for the quality of his lyrics and notoriety for their offensive content.*

## TOP 10 ★
### R&B/HIP-HOP ALBUMS IN THE US, 2000
ALBUM/ARTIST OR GROUP

| | |
|---|---|
| 1 | *Dr. Dre – 2001*, Dr. Dre |
| 2 | *The Marshall Mathers LP*, Eminem |
| 3 | *…And Then There Was X*, DMX |
| 4 | *Unleash the Dragon*, Sisqo |
| 5 | *Vol. 3 … Life and Times of S. Carter*, Jay-Z |
| 6 | *Country Grammar*, Nelly |
| 7 | *Voodoo*, D'Angelo |
| 8 | *My Name is Joe*, Joe |
| 9 | *Born Again*, Notorious B.I.G. |
| 10 | *J.E. Heartbreak*, Jagged Edge |

Source: Billboard

## TOP 10 ★
### COUNTRY ALBUMS OF ALL TIME IN THE US

| | TITLE/ARTIST/YEAR | APPROX. SALES |
|---|---|---|
| 1 | *Come On Over*, Shania Twain, 2000 | 18,000,000 |
| 2 | *No Fences*, Garth Brooks, 1990 | 16,000,000 |
| 3 | *Ropin' the Wind*, Garth Brooks, 1991 | 14,000,000 |
| 4 = | *Greatest Hits*, Kenny Rogers, 1997 | 12,000,000 |
| = | *The Woman in Me*, Shania Twain, 1998 | 12,000,000 |
| 6 = | *The Hits*, Garth Brooks, 1994 | 10,000,000 |
| = | *Wide Open Spaces*, Dixie Chicks, 1999 | 10,000,000 |
| 8 = | *Garth Brooks*, Garth Brooks, 1994 | 9,000,000 |
| = | *Greatest Hits*, Patsy Cline, 1998 | 9,000,000 |
| = | *Some Gave All*, Billy Ray Cyrus, 1996 | 9,000,000 |

Source: *RIAA*

## TOP 10 ★
### DANCE MAXI-SINGLES IN THE US, 2000
MAXI-SINGLE/ARTIST OR GROUP

| | |
|---|---|
| 1 | *Music*, Madonna |
| 2 | *Desert Rose*, Sting featuring Cheb Mami |
| 3 | *Say My Name*, Destiny's Child |
| 4 | *Jumpin', Jumpin'*, Destiny's Child |
| 5 | *Let's Get Married*, Jagged Edge |
| 6 | *Maria Maria*, Santana featuring the Product |
| 7 | *Sexual (Li Da Di)*, Amber |
| 8 | *I Will Love Again*, Lara Fabian |
| 9 | *What a Girl Wants*, Christina Aguilera |
| 10 | *Most Girls*, Pink |

Source: Billboard

*Billboard* publishes two dance charts: Maxi-Single (sales of extended mixes of dance tracks) and Club Play (those most played in clubs). In 1999, Cher headed both lists with *Believe*, while in 2000 Madonna emulated the feat by leading the two charts with *Music*.

## TOP 10 ★
### RAP SINGLES IN THE US

| | TITLE/ARTIST/YEAR | APPROX. SALES |
|---|---|---|
| 1 | *Whoomp! (There It Is)*, Tag Team, 1994 | 4,000,000 |
| 2 | *I'll Be Missing You*, Puff Daddy & Faith Evans (featuring 112), 1997 | 3,000,000 |
| 3 = | *How Do U Want It*, 2Pac, 1996 | 2,000,000 |
| = | *Tha Crossroads*, Bone Thugs-N-Harmony, 1996 | 2,000,000 |
| = | *Gangsta's Paradise*, Coolio featuring L. V., 1995 | 2,000,000 |
| = | *Dazzey Duks*, Duice, 1994 | 2,000,000 |
| = | *O.P.P.*, Naughty By Nature, 1992 | 2,000,000 |
| = | *Baby Got Back*, Sir Mix-A-Lot, 1992 | 2,000,000 |
| = | *Wild Thing*, Tone Loc, 1989 | 2,000,000 |
| = | *Jump*, Kris Kross, 1992 | 2,000,000 |
| = | *Rump Shaker*, Wreckx-N-Effect, 1993 | 2,000,000 |
| = | *Can't Nobody Hold Me Down*, Puff Daddy, 1997 | 2,000,000 |

Source: *RIAA*

# TOP 10 LATIN POP ALBUMS IN THE US, 2000

*(Album/artist or group)*

**1** *Mi Reflejo*, Christina Aguilera **2** *Amor, Familia y Respeto …*, A. B. Quintanilla y Los Kumbia Kings **3** *MTV Unplugged*, Shakira **4** *Donde Estan los Ladrones?*, Shakira **5** *MTV Unplugged*, Maná **6** *The Best Hits*, Enrique Iglesias **7** *Amarte es un Placer*, Luis Miguel **8** *Trovos de mi Alma*, Marco Antonio Solis **9** *Llegar a Ti*, Jaci Velasquez **10** *Entre tus Brazos*, Alejandro Fernandez

Source: Billboard

## TOP 10 ★ REGGAE ALBUMS IN THE US, 2000

ALBUM/ARTIST OR GROUP

| 1 | *Chant Down Babylon*, Bob Marley |
|---|---|
| 2 | *Art and Life*, Beenie Man |
| 3 | *Reggae Gold 2000*, Various Artists |
| 4 | *Stage One*, Sean Paul |
| 5 | *Reggae Party*, Various Artists |
| 6 | *Reggae Gold 1999*, Various Artists |
| 7 | *Scrolls of the Prophet – The Best of Peter Tosh*, Peter Tosh |
| 8 | *Unchained Spirit*, Buju Banton |
| 9 | *1999 Biggest Ragga Dancehall Anthems*, Various Artists |
| 10 | *More Fire*, Capleton |

Source: Billboard

## TOP 10 ★ HEAVY METAL ALBUMS IN THE US

| ALBUM/ARTIST OR GROUP/YEAR | APPROX. SALES |
|---|---|
| 1 = *Back in Black*, AC/DC, 1997 | 16,000,000 |
| = *Boston*, Boston, 1997 | 16,000,000 |
| 3 *Bat Out of Hell*, Meat Loaf, 1997 | 13,000,000 |
| 4 = *Hysteria*, Def Leppard, 1998 | 12,000,000 |
| = *Metallica*, Metallica, 1999 | 12,000,000 |
| 6 = *Eliminator*, ZZ Top, 1996 | 10,000,000 |
| = *1984*, Van Halen, 1999 | 10,000,000 |
| = *Van Halen*, Van Halen, 1996 | 10,000,000 |
| 9 *Pyromania*, Def Leppard, 1994 | 9,000,000 |
| 10 *Whitesnake*, Whitesnake, 1987 | 8,000,000 |

Source: RIAA

## TOP 10 ★ JAZZ ALBUMS IN THE US

| | ALBUM/ARTIST OR GROUP | YEAR |
|---|---|---|
| 1 | *Time Out Featuring Take Five*, Dave Brubeck Quartet | 1960 |
| 2 | *Hello Dolly*, Louis Armstrong | 1964 |
| 3 | *Getz & Gilberto*, Stan Getz and Joao Gilberto | 1964 |
| 4 | *Sun Goddess*, Ramsey Lewis | 1975 |
| 5 | *Jazz Samba*, Stan Getz and Charlie Byrd | 1962 |
| 6 | *Bitches Brew*, Miles Davis | 1970 |
| 7 | *The In Crowd*, Ramsey Lewis Trio | 1965 |
| 8 | *Time Further Out*, Dave Brubeck Quartet | 1961 |
| 9 | *Mack The Knife – Ella In Berlin*, Ella Fitzgerald | 1960 |
| 10 | *Exodus To Jazz*, Eddie Harris | 1961 |

Dave Brubeck's *Time Out* album spent 86 weeks in the American Top 40 between 1960 and 1962, an unprecedented achievement for a jazz album during that era and due, not least, to the huge popularity of the track featured in its full title, *Take Five*, which hit No. 25 on the US pop chart. The quartet comprised Brubeck (b. David Warren) on piano, Joe Morello (drums), Eugene Wright (bass), and Paul Desmond (alto sax).

**BON JOVI**
*Born John Francis Bongiovi, Jon Bon Jovi and his band Bon Jovi have won chart success and global acclaim since their first recordings in 1984, with Slippery When Wet one of the best-selling albums of the 1980s.*

# Gold & Platinum Disks

## GROUPS WITH THE MOST GOLD ALBUMS IN THE US

| GROUP | GOLD ALBUM AWARDS |
| --- | --- |
| 1 The Beatles | 40 |
| 2 The Rolling Stones | 38 |
| 3 Kiss | 23 |
| 4 =Rush | 22 |
| =Alabama | 22 |
| 6 =Aerosmith | 21 |
| =Chicago | 21 |
| 8 =Jefferson Airplane/Starship | 20 |
| =Beach Boys | 20 |
| 10 AC/DC | 18 |

Source: *RIAA*

The RIAA's Gold Awards have been presented since 1958 to artists who have sold 500,000 units of a single, album, or multidisc set. The first album to be so honored was the soundtrack to *Oklahoma*. To date, more than 8,000 titles have gone gold.

## FEMALE ARTISTS WITH THE MOST GOLD ALBUMS IN THE US

| ARTIST | GOLD ALBUM AWARDS |
| --- | --- |
| 1 Barbra Streisand | 41 |
| 2 Reba McEntire | 20 |
| 3 Linda Ronstadt | 16 |
| 4 Madonna | 14 |
| 5 =Aretha Franklin | 13 |
| =Anne Murray | 13 |
| 7 =Natalie Cole | 12 |
| =Tanya Tucker | 12 |
| =Amy Grant | 12 |
| =Olivia Newton-John | 12 |

Source: *RIAA*

## FEMALE ARTISTS WITH THE MOST PLATINUM AND MULTI-PLATINUM ALBUMS IN THE UK

| ARTIST | PLATINUM AND MULTI-PLATINUM ALBUM AWARDS |
| --- | --- |
| 1 Madonna | 38 |
| 2 =Celine Dion | 21 |
| =Tina Turner | 21 |
| 4 Whitney Houston* | 16 |
| 5 =Enya | 12 |
| =Gloria Estefan | 12 |
| 7 =Kylie Minogue | 10 |
| =Mariah Carey | 10 |
| =Alanis Morissette | 10 |
| =Kate Bush | 10 |

* *Not including the album* The Bodyguard

Source: *BPI*

### MARIAH CAREY

*Mariah Carey has sold over 100 million albums since 1990, and her singles success ranks her third for most weeks at US No. 1.*

## MALE ARTISTS WITH THE MOST GOLD ALBUMS IN THE US

| ARTIST | GOLD ALBUM AWARDS |
| --- | --- |
| 1 Elvis Presley | 81 |
| 2 Neil Diamond | 35 |
| 3 Elton John | 32 |
| 4 =Bob Dylan | 26 |
| =Frank Sinatra | 26 |
| 6 =Kenny Rogers | 25 |
| =George Strait | 25 |
| 8 Hank Williams Jr. | 21 |
| 9 Rod Stewart | 20 |
| 10 Eric Clapton | 19 |

Source: *RIAA*

## MALE ARTISTS WITH THE MOST PLATINUM AND MULTI-PLATINUM ALBUMS IN THE US

| ARTIST | PLATINUM AND MULTI-PLATINUM ALBUM AWARDS |
| --- | --- |
| 1 Garth Brooks | 97 |
| 2 Elvis Presley | 75 |
| 3 Billy Joel | 74 |
| 4 Elton John | 58 |
| 5 =Michael Jackson | 53 |
| =Bruce Springsteen | 53 |
| 7 George Strait | 46 |
| 8 Kenny Rogers | 44 |
| 9 Kenny G | 41 |
| 10 Neil Diamond | 35 |

Source: *RIAA*

Platinum singles and albums in the US are those that have achieved sales of 1 million units. The award has been made by the Recording Industry Association of America (RIAA) since 1976, when it was introduced in response to escalating music sales, as a result of which many discs were outselling the 500,000 required to achieve a gold award. In 1984, the RIAA introduced multi-platinum awards for certified sales of 2 million or more units.

**TWO OF U2**
Formed in Ireland in 1976, supergroup U2 has enjoyed two decades of chart hits and sell-out international tours. The band still retains its original lineup.

## TOP 10 ⭐
### FEMALE ARTISTS WITH THE MOST PLATINUM AND MULTI-PLATINUM ALBUMS IN THE US

| ARTIST | PLATINUM AND MULTI-PLATINUM ALBUM AWARDS |
|---|---|
| 1 Barbra Streisand | 55 |
| 2 =Madonna | 51 |
| =Whitney Houston | 51 |
| =Mariah Carey | 51 |
| 5 Celine Dion | 39 |
| 6 Reba McEntire | 32 |
| 7 Shania Twain | 29 |
| 8 Linda Ronstadt | 24 |
| 9 Janet Jackson | 20 |
| 10 =Sade | 19 |
| =Gloria Estefan | 19 |

Source: *RIAA*

## TOP 10 ⭐
### GROUPS WITH THE MOST PLATINUM AND MULTI-PLATINUM ALBUMS IN THE US

| GROUP | PLATINUM AND MULTI-PLATINUM ALBUM AWARDS |
|---|---|
| 1 The Beatles | 118 |
| 2 Led Zeppelin | 97 |
| 3 Pink Floyd | 66 |
| 4 The Eagles | 63 |
| 5 Aerosmith | 53 |
| 6 Van Halen | 50 |
| 7 Fleetwood Mac | 43 |
| 8 =Alabama | 42 |
| =AC/DC | 42 |
| =U2 | 42 |

Source: *RIAA*

## TOP 10 ⭐
### GROUPS WITH THE MOST PLATINUM AND MULTI-PLATINUM ALBUMS IN THE UK

| GROUP | PLATINUM AND MULTI-PLATINUM ALBUM AWARDS |
|---|---|
| 1 Simply Red | 38 |
| 2 Queen | 33 |
| 3 Oasis | 28 |
| 4 Dire Straits | 27 |
| 5 U2 | 25 |
| 6 Fleetwood Mac | 23 |
| 7 Abba | 21 |
| 8 =R.E.M. | 17 |
| =UB40 | 17 |
| =Wet Wet Wet | 17 |

Source: *BPI*

Who composed Sinead O'Connor's hit *Nothing Compares 2 U*?
*see p.128 for the answer*

A George Michael
B Dolly Parton
C Prince

# Classical & Opera

## TOP 10 CITIES WITH THE MOST OPERAS

(City/performances*)

**1** Vienna, Austria, 32 **2** Berlin, Germany, 21 **3** Prague, Czech Republic, 20 **4** Paris, France, 16 **5** Hamburg, Germany, 13 **6** = London, UK, 12; = Zurich, Switzerland, 12 **8** = New York, US, 11; = Munich, Germany, 11 **10** Hanover, Germany, 10

*\* Sample during a 12-month period*

---

## TOP 10 ★ LONGEST OPERAS PERFORMED AT THE METROPOLITAN OPERA HOUSE*

| OPERA/COMPOSER | RUNNING TIME# HR:MIN |
|---|---|
| **1** *Götterdämmerung*, Richard Wagner | 4:27 |
| **2** *Die Meistersinger von Nürnberg*, Richard Wagner | 4:21 |
| **3** *Parsifal*, Richard Wagner | 4:17 |
| **4** =*Les Troyens*, Hector Berlioz | 4:02 |
| =*Siegfried*, Richard Wagner | 4:02 |
| **6** *Tristan und Isolde*, Richard Wagner | 4:00 |
| **7** *Die Walküre*, Richard Wagner | 3:41 |
| **8** *Don Carlo*, Giuseppe Verdi | 3:33 |
| **9** *Semiramide*, Gioachino Rossini | 3:30 |
| **10** *Lohengrin*, Richard Wagner | 3:28 |

*\* In current repertory*
*# Excluding intervals*
Source: *Metropolitan Opera House*

---

**ANDREA BOCELLI**

*Despite his blindness, Italian opera singer Andrea Bocelli has achieved remarkable success both in performance and through his internationally best-selling albums.*

## TOP 10 ★ MOST PROLIFIC CLASSICAL COMPOSERS

| COMPOSER | HOURS OF MUSIC |
|---|---|
| **1** Joseph Haydn (1732–1809, Austrian) | 340 |
| **2** George Handel (1685–1759, German–English) | 303 |
| **3** Wolfgang Amadeus Mozart (1756–91, Austrian) | 202 |
| **4** Johann Sebastian Bach (1685–1750, German) | 175 |
| **5** Franz Schubert (1797–1828, German) | 134 |
| **6** Ludwig van Beethoven (1770–1827, German) | 120 |
| **7** Henry Purcell (1659–95, English) | 116 |
| **8** Giuseppe Verdi (1813–1901, Italian) | 87 |
| **9** Anton Dvorák (1841–1904, Czech) | 79 |
| **10** =Franz Liszt (1811–86, Hungarian) | 76 |
| =Peter Tchaikovsky (1840–93, Russian) | 76 |

This list is based on a survey conducted by *Classical Music* magazine, which ranked classical composers by the total number of hours of music each composed. If the length of the composer's working life is brought into the calculation, Schubert wins: his 134 hours were composed in a career of 18 years, giving an average of 7 hours 27 minutes per annum.

---

## TOP 10 ★ CLASSICAL ALBUMS IN THE US

| ALBUM/PERFORMER(S)/ORCHESTRA | YEAR |
|---|---|
| **1** *The Three Tenors in Concert*, Carreras, Domingo, Pavarotti | 1990 |
| **2** *Romanza*, Andrea Bocelli | 1997 |
| **3** *Sogno*, Andrea Bocelli | 1999 |
| **4** *Voice of an Angel*, Charlotte Church | 1999 |
| **5** *Chant*, Benedictine Monks of Santo Domingo De Silos | 1994 |
| **6** *The Three Tenors in Concert 1994*, Carreras, Domingo, Pavarotti | 1994 |
| **7** *Sacred Arias*, Andrea Bocelli | 1999 |
| **8** *Tchaikovsky: Piano Concerto No. 1*, Van Cliburn | 1958 |
| **9** *Fantasia (50th Anniversary Edition)*, Soundtrack (Philadelphia Orchestra) | 1990 |
| **10** *Perhaps Love*, Placido Domingo | 1981 |

Classical recordings held far greater sway in the early years of the US album chart than they have in subsequent decades.

---

### ENRICO CARUSO'S FIRST MILLION-SELLING RECORDINGS

Opera singer Enrico Caruso (1873–1921) was born in Naples, Italy, and made his first public appearance in 1895, playing the role of Faust. Performing in opera houses as far afield as Russia and Argentina, he rapidly established an international reputation. On November 12, 1902, he recorded the aria "Vesti la Giubba" ("On with the Motley") from *I Pagliacci* for the Gramophone Co. By now regarded as the world's greatest operatic tenor, Caruso appeared in this year at the Royal Opera House, Covent Garden, London, and then at the Metropolitan Opera House, New York. "Vesti la Giubba" was later rerecorded with orchestral accompaniment for recording company Victor. The cumulative sales of the two versions easily passed the million mark, perhaps the first record ever to do so.

• YEARS AGO • 100 YEARS AGO • YEARS AGO •

## THE 10 ★
# LATEST WINNERS OF THE "BEST SOLOIST PERFORMANCE"* GRAMMY AWARD

| YEAR | SOLOIST/INSTRUMENT[#] | COMPOSER/WORK |
|---|---|---|
| 2000 | Sharon Isbin, guitar | Lauro, Ruiz-Pipo, Duarte, etc., *Dreams of a World* |
| 1999 | Vladimir Ashkenazy | Shostakovich, *24 Preludes and Fugues, Op. 87* |
| 1998 | Murray Perahia | Bach, *English Suites Nos. 1, 3, and 6* |
| 1997 | Janos Starker, cello | Bach, *Suites for Solo Cello Nos. 1–6* |
| 1996 | Earl Wild | Saint-Saens, Handel, etc., *The Romantic Master* |
| 1995 | Radu Lupu | Schubert, *Piano Sonatas (B Flat Maj. and A Maj.)* |
| 1994 | Emanuel Ax | Haydn, *Piano Sonatas Nos. 32, 47, 53, and 59* |
| 1993 | John Browning | Barber, *The Complete Solo Piano Music* |
| 1992 | Vladimir Horowitz | Chopin, Liszt, Scarlatti, Scriabin, Clementi, *Discovered Treasures* |
| 1991 | Alicia de Larrocha | Granados, *Goyescas; Allegro de Concierto; Danza Lenta* |

*Without orchestra  #Piano unless otherwise stated

## TOP 10 ★
# LARGEST OPERA THEATERS

| | THEATER | LOCATION | CAPACITY* |
|---|---|---|---|
| 1 | Arena di Verona[#] | Verona, Italy | 16,663 |
| 2 | Municipal Opera Theater[#] | St. Louis, US | 11,745 |
| 3 | Teatro alla Scala | Milan, Italy | 3,600 |
| 4 | Civic Opera House | Chicago, US | 3,563 |
| 5 = | The Metropolitan | New York, US | 3,500 |
| = | Teatro San Carlo | Naples, Italy | 3,500 |
| 7 | Music Hall | Cincinnati, US | 3,417 |
| 8 = | Teatro Massimo | Palermo, Italy | 3,200 |
| = | The Hummingbird Centre | Toronto, Canada | 3,200 |
| 10 | Halle aux Grains | Toulouse, France | 3,000 |

* For indoor venues seating capacity only is given, although capacity is often larger when standing capacity is included

# Open-air venue

Although there are many more venues in the world where opera is regularly performed, the above list is limited to those venues whose principal performances are opera.

**CLASSIC CONDUCTOR**

*Leonard Bernstein's posthumous Grammy Award for Candide was one of the 16 Grammys he won, including a Lifetime Achievement Award.*

## THE 10 ★
# LATEST WINNERS OF THE "BEST CLASSICAL ALBUM" GRAMMY AWARD

| YEAR | COMPOSER/WORK | CONDUCTOR/SOLOIST/ORCHESTRA |
|---|---|---|
| 2000 | Shostakovich, *The String Quartets* | Emerson String Quartet |
| 1999 | Stravinsky, *Firebird; The Right of Spring; Perséphone* | Michael Tilson Thomas, Stuart Neill, San Francisco Symphony Orchestra |
| 1998 | Barber, *Prayers of Kierkegaard/* Vaughan Williams, *Dona Nobis Pacem/* Bartok, *Cantata Profana* | Robert Shaw, Richard Clement, Nathan Gunn, Atlanta Symphony Orchestra and Chorus |
| 1997 | Danielpour, Kirchner, Rouse, *Premieres – Cello Concertos* | Yo-Yo Ma, David Zinman, Philadelphia Orchestra |
| 1996 | Corigliano, *Of Rage and Remembrance* | Leonard Slatkin, National Symphony Orchestra |
| 1995 | Claude Debussy, *La Mer* | Pierre Boulez, Cleveland Orchestra |
| 1994 | Béla Bartók, *Concerto for Orchestra; Four Orchestral Pieces, Op. 12* | Pierre Boulez, Chicago Symphony Orchestra |
| 1993 | Béla Bartók, *The Wooden Prince* | Pierre Boulez, Chicago Symphony Orchestra and Chorus |
| 1992 | Gustav Mahler, *Symphony No. 9* | Leonard Bernstein, Berlin Philharmonic Orchestra |
| 1991 | Leonard Bernstein, *Candide* | Leonard Bernstein, London Symphony Orchestra |

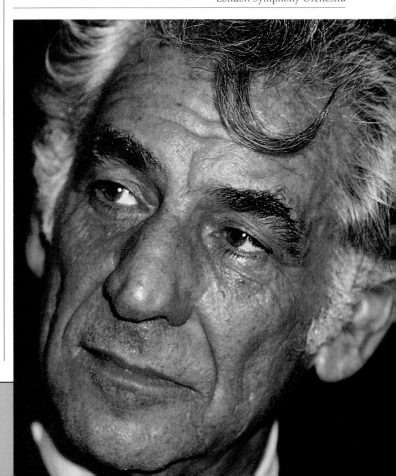

# STAGE & SCREEN

# All the World's a Stage

MONEY FOR NOTHING

Much Ado About Nothing, *starring Emma Thompson and Kenneth Branagh (who also directed it), achieved both critical and commercial success.*

## THE 10 ★
## LATEST TONY AWARDS FOR AN ACTOR*

| YEAR | ACTOR/PLAY |
|------|-----------|
| 2000 | Stephen Dillane, *The Real Thing* |
| 1999 | Brian Dennehy, *Death of a Salesman* |
| 1998 | Anthony LaPaglia, *A View From the Bridge* |
| 1997 | Christopher Plummer, *Barrymore* |
| 1996 | George Grizzard, *A Delicate Balance* |
| 1995 | Ralph Fiennes, *Hamlet* |
| 1994 | Stephen Spinella, *Angels in America Part II: Perestroika* |
| 1993 | Ron Leibman, *Angels in America Part I: Millennium Approaches* |
| 1992 | Judd Hirsch, *Conversations with My Father* |
| 1991 | Nigel Hawthorne, *Shadowlands* |

\* *In a play*

The Tony Awards, established in 1947 by the American Theater Wing, honor outstanding Broadway plays and musicals, actors and actresses, music, costume, and other contributions.

## THE 10 ★
## LATEST TONY AWARDS FOR AN ACTRESS*

| YEAR | ACTRESS/PLAY |
|------|-----------|
| 2000 | Jennifer Ehle, *The Real Thing* |
| 1999 | Judi Dench, *Amy's View* |
| 1998 | Marie Mullen, *The Beauty Queen of Leenane* |
| 1997 | Janet McTeer, *A Doll's House* |
| 1996 | Zoë Caldwell, *Master Class* |
| 1995 | Cherry Jones, *The Heiress* |
| 1994 | Diana Rigg, *Medea* |
| 1993 | Madeline Kahn, *The Sisters Rosensweig* |
| 1992 | Glenn Close, *Death and the Maiden* |
| 1991 | Mercedes Ruehl, *Lost in Yonkers* |

\* *In a play*

## TOP 10 ★
## FILMS OF SHAKESPEARE PLAYS

| | FILM | YEAR |
|---|------|------|
| 1 | *William Shakespeare's Romeo + Juliet* | 1996 |
| 2 | *Romeo and Juliet* | 1968 |
| 3 | *Much Ado About Nothing* | 1993 |
| 4 | *Hamlet* | 1990 |
| 5 | *Henry V* | 1989 |
| 6 | *Hamlet* | 1996 |
| 7 | *Richard III* | 1995 |
| 8 | *Othello* | 1995 |
| 9 | *The Taming of the Shrew* | 1967 |
| 10 | *Hamlet* | 1948 |

The romantic appeal of *Romeo and Juliet* has ensured its place in first and second positions.

## THE 10 ★
## FIRST PLAYS WRITTEN BY SHAKESPEARE

| | PLAY | YEAR WRITTEN (APPROX.) |
|---|------|------|
| 1 | *Titus Andronicus* | 1588–90 |
| 2 | *Love's Labour's Lost* | 1590 |
| 3 | *Henry VI, Parts I–III* | 1590–91 |
| 4 = | *The Comedy of Errors* | 1591 |
| = | *Richard III* | 1591 |
| = | *Romeo and Juliet* | 1591 |
| 7 | *The Two Gentlemen of Verona* | 1592–93 |
| 8 | *A Midsummer Night's Dream* | 1593–94 |
| 9 | *Richard II* | 1594 |
| 10 | *King John* | 1595 |

There are only scant contemporary records of Shakespeare's plays' early performances, and only half of them appeared in print in his lifetime.

## THE 10 LATEST DRAMA DESK AWARDS FOR A MUSICAL
*(Year/play)*

❶ 2000 *Contact* ❷ 1999 *Parade* ❸ 1998 *Ragtime* ❹ 1997 *The Life* ❺ 1996 *Rent*
❻ 1995 *Showboat* ❼ 1994 *Passion* ❽ 1993 *Kiss of the Spider Woman*
❾ 1992 *Crazy for You* ❿ 1991 *The Will Rogers Follies*

# THE 10 ★
## LATEST DRAMA DESK AWARDS FOR AN ACTOR

| YEAR | ACTOR/PLAY |
|---|---|
| 2000 | Stephen Dillane, *The Real Thing* |
| 1999 | Brian Dennehy, *Death of a Salesman* |
| 1998 | Anthony LaPaglia, *A View From the Bridge* |
| 1997 | = David Morse, *How I Learned to Drive* |
| | = Christopher Plummer, *Barrymore* |
| 1996 | Frank Langella, *The Father* |
| 1995 | Ralph Fiennes, *Hamlet* |
| 1994 | Stephen Spinella, *Angels in America Part II: Perestroika* |
| 1993 | Ron Leibman, *Angels in America Part I: Millennium Approaches* |
| 1992 | Brian Bedford, *Two Shakespearean Actors* |

Source: *New York Drama Desk*

# THE 10 ★
## LATEST DRAMA DESK AWARDS FOR AN ACTRESS

| YEAR | ACTRESS/PLAY |
|---|---|
| 2000 | Eileen Heckart, *The Waverly Gallery* |
| 1999 | Kathleen Chalfant, *Wit* |
| 1998 | Cherry Jones, *Pride's Crossing* |
| 1997 | Janet McTeer, *A Doll's House* |
| 1996 | Zoë Caldwell, *Master Class* |
| 1995 | Glenn Close, *Sunset Boulevard* |
| 1994 | Myra Carter, *Three Tall Women* |
| 1993 | Jane Alexander, *The Sisters Rosensweig* |
| 1992 | Laura Esterman, *Marvin's Room* |
| 1991 | Irene Worth, *Lost in Yonkers* |

Source: *New York Drama Desk*

Founded in 1949 by New York drama reporters, editors, and critics, the Drama Desk has presented awards since the 1954–55 season. The 1991 winner of this award presents the unusual event of an actress receiving a Drama Desk Award for the same play in which a different actress received a Tony Award.

# TOP 10 ★
## LONGEST-RUNNING SHOWS ON BROADWAY

| | SHOW | PERFORMANCES* |
|---|---|---|
| 1 | *Cats*, 1982–2000 | 7,485 |
| 2 | *A Chorus Line*, 1975–90 | 6,137 |
| 3 | *Oh! Calcutta!*, 1976–89 | 5,962 |
| 4 | *Les Misérables*, 1987– | 5,698# |
| 5 | *The Phantom of the Opera*, 1988– | 5,398# |
| 6 | *Miss Saigon*, 1991-2001 | 4,095 |
| 7 | *42nd Street*, 1980–89 | 3,486 |
| 8 | *Grease*, 1972–80 | 3,388 |
| 9 | *Fiddler on the Roof*, 1964–72 | 3,242 |
| 10 | *Life with Father*, 1939–47 | 3,224 |

\* As of January 1, 2001

\# Still running

Source: *The League of American Theaters and Producers*

*Cats*, which finally closed on September 10, 2000, became the longest-running Broadway show of all time on June 19, 1997 when it notched up its 6,138th performance. *Life with Father*, the earliest show to be listed here and the only non-musical, was a roaring success from the moment it opened. Its popularity had not been predicted and after the lead parts were refused by major actors and actresses, the author, Howard Lindsay, and his wife, Dorothy Stickney, decided to play the roles themselves. They continued to do so, amid rave reviews, for the next five years.

# TOP 10 ★
## LONGEST-RUNNING THRILLERS OF ALL TIME ON BROADWAY

| | THRILLER | PERFORMANCES |
|---|---|---|
| 1 | *Deathtrap*, 1978–82 | 1,793 |
| 2 | *Arsenic and Old Lace*, 1941–44 | 1,444 |
| 3 | *Angel Street*, 1941–1944 | 1,295 |
| 4 | *Sleuth*, 1970–73 | 1,222 |
| 5 | *Dracula*, 1977–80 | 925 |
| 6 | *Witness for the Prosecution*, 1954–56 | 644 |
| 7 | *Dial M for Murder*, 1952–54 | 552 |
| 8 | *Sherlock Holmes*, 1975–76 | 479 |
| 9 | *An Inspector Calls*, 1994–95 | 454 |
| 10 | *Ten Little Indians*, 1944–45 | 424 |

Source: Theatre World

**OUT OF THEIR MISERY**

*Les Misérables has achieved the dual feat of being one of the longest-running musicals both in London and on Broadway.*

# Film Hits

## FILMS SHOWN AT THE MOST CINEMAS IN THE US

| FILM | OPENING WEEKEND | CINEMAS |
|---|---|---|
| 1 Mission: Impossible 2 | May 24, 2000 | 3,653 |
| 2 Scream 3 | Feb 4, 2000 | 3,467 |
| 3 The Perfect Storm | June 30, 2000 | 3,407 |
| 4 Wild Wild West | June 30, 1999 | 3,342 |
| 5 Book of Shadows: Blair Witch 2 | Oct 27, 2000 | 3,317 |
| 6 Austin Powers: The Spy Who Shagged Me | June 11, 1999 | 3,312 |
| 7 Godzilla | May 20, 1998 | 3,310 |
| 8 Battlefield Earth | May 12, 2000 | 3,307 |
| 9 Lost in Space | Apr 3, 1998 | 3,306 |
| 10 The Lost World: Jurassic Park | May 23, 1997 | 3,281 |

## FILMS BY ATTENDANCE

| FILM | YEAR | ATTENDANCE |
|---|---|---|
| 1 Gone With the Wind | 1939 | 208,100,000 |
| 2 Star Wars | 1977 | 198,600,000 |
| 3 The Sound of Music | 1965 | 170,600,000 |
| 4 E.T.: The Extra-Terrestrial | 1982 | 151,600,000 |
| 5 The Ten Commandments | 1956 | 132,800,000 |
| 6 The Jungle Book | 1967 | 126,300,000 |
| 7 Titanic | 1997 | 124,300,000 |
| 8 Jaws | 1975 | 123,300,000 |
| 9 Doctor Zhivago | 1965 | 122,700,000 |
| 10 101 Dalmatians | 1961 | 119,600,000 |

This list is based on the actual number of people buying tickets at the US box office. Because it takes account of the large numbers of tickets sold to children and other discounted sales, it differs both from lists that present total box office receipts and those that are adjusted for inflation.

## FILM SERIES OF ALL TIME

| FILM SERIES | DATES |
|---|---|
| 1 Star Wars / The Empire Strikes Back / Return of the Jedi / Episode I – The Phantom Menace | 1977–99 |
| 2 Jurassic Park / The Lost World: Jurassic Park | 1993–97 |
| 3 Batman / Batman Returns / Batman Forever / Batman & Robin | 1989–97 |
| 4 Raiders of the Lost Ark / Indiana Jones and the Temple of Doom / Indiana Jones and the Last Crusade | 1981–89 |
| 5 Mission: Impossible / Mission: Impossible 2 | 1996–2000 |
| 6 Star Trek: The Motion Picture / II / III / IV / V / VI / Generations / First Contact / Insurrection | 1979–98 |
| 7 Back to the Future / II / III | 1985–90 |
| 8 Lethal Weapon / 2 / 3 / 4 | 1987–98 |
| 9 Toy Story / Toy Story 2 | 1995–99 |
| 10 Home Alone / 2: Lost in NY | 1990–92 |

## HIGHEST-GROSSING FILMS OF ALL TIME

| FILM | YEAR | GROSS INCOME ($) US | GROSS INCOME ($) WORLD TOTAL |
|---|---|---|---|
| 1 Titanic | 1997 | 600,800,000 | 1,835,400,000 |
| 2 Star Wars: Episode I – The Phantom Menace | 1999 | 431,100,000 | 922,600,000 |
| 3 Jurassic Park | 1993 | 357,100,000 | 920,100,000 |
| 4 Independence Day | 1996 | 306,200,000 | 811,200,000 |
| 5 Star Wars | 1977/97 | 461,000,000 | 798,000,000 |
| 6 The Lion King | 1994 | 312,900,000 | 771,900,000 |
| 7 E.T.: The Extra-Terrestrial | 1982 | 399,800,000 | 704,800,000 |
| 8 Forrest Gump | 1994 | 329,700,000 | 679,700,000 |
| 9 The Sixth Sense | 1999 | 293,500,000 | 660,700,000 |
| 10 The Lost World: Jurassic Park | 1997 | 229,100,000 | 614,400,000 |

## FILMS OF 2000 IN THE US

| FILM | GROSS INCOME ($) |
|---|---|
| 1 How the Grinch Stole Christmas | 253,400,000* |
| 2 Mission: Impossible 2 | 215,400,000 |
| 3 Gladiator | 186,600,000 |
| 4 The Perfect Storm | 182,600,000 |
| 5 Meet the Parents | 161,300,000 |
| 6 X-Men | 157,300,000 |
| 7 Scary Movie | 156,300,000 |
| 8 What Lies Beneath | 155,400,000 |
| 9 Dinosaur | 137,700,000 |
| 10 Erin Brockovich | 125,500,000 |

\* To December 31, 2000, only, although film remained on release

**TITANIC RISES**

*All-time highest grossing film Titanic has earned almost twice as much at the global box office as its closest rival, Star Wars: Episode I.*

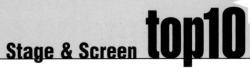
# OPENING WEEKENDS OF ALL TIME IN THE US

| | FILM | RELEASE DATE | OPENING WEEKEND GROSS INCOME ($) |
|---|---|---|---|
| 1 | The Lost World: Jurassic Park | May 23, 1997 | 72,132,785 |
| 2 | Star Wars: Episode I – The Phantom Menace | May 21, 1999 | 64,820,970 |
| 3 | Mission: Impossible 2 | May 24, 2000 | 57,845,297 |
| 4 | Toy Story 2 | Nov 24, 1999 | 57,388,839 |
| 5 | Austin Powers: The Spy Who Shagged Me | June 11, 1999 | 54,917,604 |
| 6 | X-Men | July 14, 2000 | 54,471,475 |
| 7 | Batman Forever | June 16, 1995 | 52,784,433 |
| 8 | Men in Black | July 2, 1997 | 51,068,455 |
| 9 | Independence Day | July 3, 1996 | 50,228,264 |
| 10 | Jurassic Park | June 11, 1993 | 47,059,560 |

A high-earning opening weekend (generally three days, Friday to Sunday, but sometimes a four-day holiday weekend) in the US is usually a pointer to the ongoing success of a film, but does not guarantee it.

# HIGHEST-GROSSING FILMS OF ALL TIME IN THE US

| | FILM | YEAR | US GROSS ($) |
|---|---|---|---|
| 1 | Titanic | 1998 | 600,800,000 |
| 2 | Star Wars | 1977 | 461,000,000 |
| 3 | Star Wars: Episode I – The Phantom Menace | 1999 | 431,100,000 |
| 4 | E.T.: The Extra-Terrestrial | 1982 | 399,800,000 |
| 5 | Jurassic Park | 1993 | 357,100,000 |
| 6 | Forrest Gump | 1994 | 329,700,000 |
| 7 | The Lion King | 1994 | 312,900,000 |
| 8 | Return of the Jedi | 1983 | 309,100,000 |
| 9 | Independence Day | 1996 | 306,200,000 |
| 10 | The Sixth Sense | 1999 | 293,500,000 |

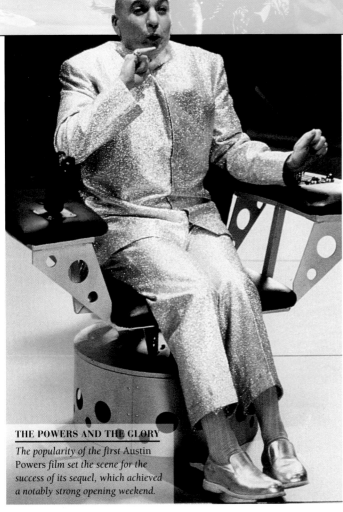

**THE POWERS AND THE GLORY**

*The popularity of the first Austin Powers film set the scene for the success of its sequel, which achieved a notably strong opening weekend.*

# FILMS OF 2000

| | FILM | GROSS INCOME ($) US | WORLD TOTAL |
|---|---|---|---|
| 1 | Mission: Impossible 2 | 215,400,000 | 545,400,000 |
| 2 | Gladiator | 186,600,000 | 445,000,000 |
| 3 | The Perfect Storm | 182,600,000 | 325,800,000 |
| 4 | How the Grinch Stole Christmas | 253,400,000 | 320,400,000 |
| 5 | Dinosaur | 137,700,000 | 317,800,000 |
| 6 | X-Men | 157,300,000 | 291,300,000 |
| 7 | Scary Movie | 156,300,000 | 277,000,000 |
| 8 | What Lies Beneath | 154,400,000 | 269,400,000 |
| 9 | Erin Brockovich | 125,500,000 | 253,900,000 |
| 10 | Charlie's Angels | 122,800,000 | 235,800,000 |

**GLAD TO SEE YOU**

*One of the most successful films of 2000, Gladiator echoes the epics of the past, a genre that many believed had been consigned to movie history.*

# Films of the Decades

## FILMS OF THE 1930s

| | | |
|---|---|---|
| 1 | Gone With the Wind* | 1939 |
| 2 | Snow White and the Seven Dwarfs | 1937 |
| 3 | The Wizard of Oz | 1939 |
| 4 | The Woman in Red | 1935 |
| 5 | King Kong | 1933 |
| 6 | San Francisco | 1936 |
| 7 =| Hell's Angels | 1930 |
| =| Lost Horizon | 1937 |
| =| Mr. Smith Goes to Washington | 1939 |
| 10 | Maytime | 1937 |

* Winner of "Best Picture" Academy Award

Gone With the Wind and Snow White and the Seven Dwarfs have generated more income than any other prewar film. If the income of Gone With the Wind is adjusted to allow for inflation in the period since its release, it could also be regarded as the most successful film ever, earning some $885 million in the US alone.

## FILMS OF THE 1940s

| | | |
|---|---|---|
| 1 | Bambi | 1942 |
| 2 | Pinocchio | 1940 |
| 3 | Fantasia | 1940 |
| 4 | Cinderella | 1949 |
| 5 | Song of the South | 1946 |
| 6 | The Best Years of Our Lives* | 1946 |
| 7 | The Bells of St. Mary's | 1945 |
| 8 | Duel in the Sun | 1946 |
| 9 | Mom and Dad | 1948 |
| 10 | Samson and Delilah | 1949 |

* Winner of "Best Picture" Academy Award

With the top four films of the decade classic Disney cartoons, the 1940s may be regarded as the "golden age" of the animated film. This colorful genre was especially appealing during and after the drabness of the war years.

### MONKEY BUSINESS

*In an iconic scene from King Kong, one of the 1930s' highest-earning films, the giant ape fights off his attackers while perched atop the newly opened Empire State Building.*

## FILMS OF THE 1950s

| | | |
|---|---|---|
| 1 | Lady and the Tramp | 1955 |
| 2 | Peter Pan | 1953 |
| 3 | Ben-Hur* | 1959 |
| 4 | The Ten Commandments | 1956 |
| 5 | Sleeping Beauty | 1959 |
| 6 | Around the World in 80 Days* | 1956 |
| 7 =| The Greatest Show on Earth* | 1952 |
| =| The Robe | 1953 |
| 9 | The Bridge on the River Kwai* | 1957 |
| 10 | Peyton Place | 1957 |

* Winner of "Best Picture" Academy Award

While the popularity of animated films continued, the 1950s was outstanding as the decade of the "big" picture (in cast and scale).

## TOP 10 FILMS OF THE 1960s

❶ *101 Dalmatians*, 1961 ❷ *The Jungle Book*, 1967 ❸ *The Sound of Music**, 1965 ❹ *Thunderball*, 1965 ❺ *Goldfinger*, 1964 ❻ *Doctor Zhivago*, 1965 ❼ *You Only Live Twice*, 1967 ❽ *The Graduate*, 1968 ❾ *Mary Poppins*, 1964 ❿ *Butch Cassidy and the Sundance Kid*, 1969

* Winner of "Best Picture" Academy Award

## FILMS OF THE LAST 10 YEARS

| | | |
|---|---|---|
| 1 | *Titanic\** | 1997 |
| 2 | *Star Wars: Episode I – The Phantom Menace* | 1999 |
| 3 | *Jurassic Park* | 1993 |
| 4 | *Independence Day* | 1996 |
| 5 | *The Lion King* | 1994 |
| 6 | *Forrest Gump\** | 1994 |
| 7 | *The Sixth Sense* | 1999 |
| 8 | *The Lost World: Jurassic Park* | 1997 |
| 9 | *Men in Black* | 1997 |
| 10 | *Armageddon* | 1998 |

\* *Winner of "Best Picture" Academy Award*

**BRINGING THE HOUSE DOWN**

*The White House sustains a direct hit from an invading spacecraft in a scene from* Independence Day, *one of the top films of the last 10 years.*

## FILMS OF THE 1970s

| | | |
|---|---|---|
| 1 | *Star Wars* | 1977/97\* |
| 2 | *Jaws* | 1975 |
| 3 | *Close Encounters of the Third Kind* | 1977/80\* |
| 4 | *The Exorcist* | 1973/98\* |
| 5 | *Moonraker* | 1979 |
| 6 | *The Spy Who Loved Me* | 1977 |
| 7 | *The Sting\#* | 1973 |
| 8 | *Grease* | 1978 |
| 9 | *The Godfather\#* | 1972 |
| 10 | *Saturday Night Fever* | 1977 |

\* *Date of re-release*

\# *Winner of "Best Picture" Academy Award*

In the 1970s the arrival of two prodigies, Steven Spielberg and George Lucas, set the scene for the high-adventure blockbusters whose domination has continued ever since.

**JAWS OF DEATH**

*After holding the record as the world's highest-earning film,* Jaws *was overtaken before the decade was out by* Star Wars.

## TOP 10 FILMS OF THE 1980s

**①** *E.T.: The Extra-Terrestrial*, 1982 **②** *Indiana Jones and the Last Crusade*, 1989 **③** *Batman*, 1989 **④** *Rain Man*, 1988 **⑤** *Return of the Jedi*, 1983 **⑥** *Raiders of the Lost Ark*, 1981 **⑦** *The Empire Strikes Back*, 1980 **⑧** *Who Framed Roger Rabbit?*, 1988 **⑨** *Back to the Future*, 1985 **⑩** *Top Gun*, 1986

**Did You Know?** In *Independence Day*, the American flag left on the Moon in 1969 by *Apollo 11* astronauts is seen standing proudly on the surface. In reality, the flag fell over when Neil Armstrong and "Buzz" Aldrin blasted off from the surface.

# Film Genres

## TOP 10 ★ WESTERNS

| 1 | *Dances With Wolves* | 1990 |
|---|---|---|
| 2 | *Wild Wild West* | 1999 |
| 3 | *Maverick* | 1994 |
| 4 | *Unforgiven* | 1992 |
| 5 | *Butch Cassidy and the Sundance Kid* | 1969 |
| 6 | *Jeremiah Johnson* | 1972 |
| 7 | *How the West Was Won* | 1962 |
| 8 | *Young Guns* | 1988 |
| 9 | *Young Guns II* | 1990 |
| 10 | *Pale Rider* | 1985 |

## TOP 10 ★ GHOST FILMS

| 1 | *The Sixth Sense* | 1999 |
|---|---|---|
| 2 | *Ghost* | 1990 |
| 3 | *Ghostbusters* | 1984 |
| 4 | *Casper* | 1995 |
| 5 | *What Lies Beneath* | 2000 |
| 6 | *Ghostbusters II* | 1989 |
| 7 | *Sleepy Hollow* | 1999 |
| 8 | *The Haunting* | 1999 |
| 9 | *Beetlejuice* | 1988 |
| 10 | *The Nightmare Before Christmas* | 1993 |

## TOP 10 ★ WEDDING FILMS

| 1 | *My Best Friend's Wedding* | 1997 |
|---|---|---|
| 2 | *Runaway Bride* | 1999 |
| 3 | *Four Weddings and a Funeral* | 1994 |
| 4 | *The Wedding Singer* | 1998 |
| 5 | *Father of the Bride* | 1991 |
| 6 | *Father of the Bride Part II* | 1995 |
| 7 | *Muriel's Wedding* | 1994 |
| 8 | *The Princess Bride* | 1987 |
| 9 | *Betsy's Wedding* | 1990 |
| 10 | *A Wedding* | 1978 |

## TOP 10 ★ HORROR FILMS

| 1 | *Jurassic Park* | 1993 |
|---|---|---|
| 2 | *The Sixth Sense* | 1999 |
| 3 | *The Lost World: Jurassic Park* | 1997 |
| 4 | *Jaws* | 1975 |
| 5 | *The Mummy* | 1999 |
| 6 | *Godzilla* | 1998 |
| 7 | *The Exorcist* | 1973 |
| 8 | *Scary Movie* | 2000 |
| 9 | *The Blair Witch Project* | 1999 |
| 10 | *Interview With the Vampire* | 1994 |

## TOP 10 ★ JAMES BOND FILMS

| | FILM/YEAR | BOND ACTOR |
|---|---|---|
| 1 | *The World Is Not Enough*, 1999 | Pierce Brosnan |
| 2 | *GoldenEye*, 1995 | Pierce Brosnan |
| 3 | *Tomorrow Never Dies*, 1997 | Pierce Brosnan |
| 4 | *Moonraker*, 1979 | Roger Moore |
| 5 | *For Your Eyes Only*, 1981 | Roger Moore |
| 6 | *The Living Daylights*, 1987 | Timothy Dalton |
| 7 | *The Spy Who Loved Me*, 1977 | Roger Moore |
| 8 | *Octopussy*, 1983 | Roger Moore |
| 9 | *Licence to Kill*, 1990 | Timothy Dalton |
| 10 | *A View to a Kill*, 1985 | Roger Moore |

## TOP 10 ★ FILMS FEATURING DINOSAURS

| 1 | *Jurassic Park* | 1993 |
|---|---|---|
| 2 | *The Lost World: Jurassic Park* | 1997 |
| 3 | *Godzilla* | 1998 |
| 4 | *Dinosaur** | 2000 |
| 5 | *Mission to Mars* | 2000 |
| 6 | *Fantasia** | 1940 |
| 7 | *T-Rex: Back to the Cretaceous* | 1998 |
| 8 | *The Flintstones in Viva Rock Vegas* | 2000 |
| 9 | *The Land Before Time** | 1988 |
| 10 | *Super Mario Bros.* | 1993 |

*\* Animated; others live-action with mechanical or computer-generated sequences*

**BLOCKBUSTERS**
*Ghostbusters starred Bill Murray alongside Dan Aykroyd and Harold Ramis, both of whom also cowrote the first film and its sequel.*

**FUTURE PERFECT**

*Schoolkid Marty McFly (Michael J. Fox) and scientist Dr. Emmett "Doc" L. Brown (Christopher Lloyd) test the Doc's time machine DeLorean.*

## TOP 10 ★
### TIME TRAVEL FILMS

| | | |
|---|---|---|
| 1 | Terminator II: Judgment Day | 1991 |
| 2 | Back to the Future | 1985 |
| 3 | Austin Powers: The Spy Who Shagged Me | 2000 |
| 4 | Back to the Future III | 1990 |
| 5 | Back to the Future II | 1989 |
| 6 | Twelve Monkeys | 1995 |
| 7 | Timecop | 1994 |
| 8 | The Terminator | 1984 |
| 9 | Austin Powers: International Man of Mystery | 1997 |
| 10 | Pleasantville | 1998 |

### JAMES BOND

In 1952, at his Jamaican house, Goldeneye, former Royal Navy intelligence officer-turned-journalist Ian Fleming (1908–64) was working on a spy story and searching for a suitable name for his hero, when his eye fell on a book, *Field Guide of Birds of the West Indies* by American ornithologist James Bond (1900–89). As Fleming later commented, "It struck me that this name, brief, unromantic, and yet very masculine, was just what I needed," and thus an internationally popular fictitious character and, later, a huge cinema industry, was born. The fictional James Bond's first appearance in print was in *Casino Royale*, published in Britain in 1953 and in the US a year later.

WHO WAS · WHO WAS · WHO WAS · WHO WAS ?

## TOP 10 MAFIA FILMS

**❶** *The Untouchables*, 1987 **❷** *Analyze This*, 1999
**❸** *The Godfather, Part III*, 1990 **❹** *The Godfather*, 1972
**❺** *L.A. Confidential*, 1997 **❻** *Donnie Brasco*, 1997
**❼** *The Client*, 1994 **❽** *The Godfather, Part II*, 1974
**❾** *The Firm*, 1993 **❿** *The Whole Nine Yards*, 2000

## TOP 10 ★
### COP FILMS

| | | |
|---|---|---|
| 1 | The Fugitive | 1993 |
| 2 | Die Hard: With a Vengeance | 1995 |
| 3 | Basic Instinct | 1992 |
| 4 | Se7en | 1995 |
| 5 | Lethal Weapon 3 | 1993 |
| 6 | Beverly Hills Cop | 1984 |
| 7 | Beverly Hills Cop II | 1987 |
| 8 | Lethal Weapon 4 | 1998 |
| 9 | Speed | 1994 |
| 10 | Die Hard 2 | 1990 |

Although films in which one of the central characters is a policeman have never been among the most successful films of all time, many have earned respectable amounts at the box office. Both within and outside the Top 10, they are divided between those with a comic slant, such as the two *Beverly Hills Cop* films, and darker police thrillers, such as *Basic Instinct*. Films featuring FBI and CIA agents have been excluded from the reckoning, hence eliminating blockbusters such as *Mission: Impossible* and *The Silence of the Lambs*.

## TOP 10 ★
### COMEDY FILMS

| | | |
|---|---|---|
| 1 | Forrest Gump | 1994 |
| 2 | Home Alone | 1990 |
| 3 | Ghost | 1990 |
| 4 | Pretty Woman | 1990 |
| 5 | Mrs. Doubtfire | 1993 |
| 6 | There's Something About Mary | 1998 |
| 7 | The Flintstones | 1994 |
| 8 | Notting Hill | 1999 |
| 9 | Who Framed Roger Rabbit | 1988 |
| 10 | How the Grinch Stole Christmas | 1999 |

**"LIFE IS LIKE A BOX OF CHOCOLATES ..."**

*As Forrest Gump, Tom Hanks plays a man whose simple, homespun philosophy enables him to succeed against all odds.*

From what 1968 film did the Oscar-winning song *The Windmills of Your Mind* come?
*see p.179 for the answer*

A *The Graduate*
B *Funny Girl*
C *The Thomas Crown Affair*

# Oscar-Winning Films

## FILMS NOMINATED FOR THE MOST OSCARS

| FILM/YEAR | AWARDS | NOMINATIONS |
|---|---|---|
| 1 =*All About Eve*, 1950 | 6 | 14 |
| =*Titanic*, 1997 | 11 | 14 |
| 3 =*Gone With the Wind*, 1939 | 8* | 13 |
| =*From Here to Eternity*, 1953 | 8 | 13 |
| =*Mary Poppins*, 1964 | 5 | 13 |
| =*Who's Afraid of Virginia Woolf?*, 1966 | 5 | 13 |
| =*Forrest Gump*, 1994 | 6 | 13 |
| =*Shakespeare in Love*, 1998 | 7 | 13 |
| 9 =*Mrs. Miniver*, 1942 | 6 | 12 |
| =*The Song of Bernadette*, 1943 | 4 | 12 |
| =*Johnny Belinda*, 1948 | 1 | 12 |
| =*A Streetcar Named Desire*, 1951 | 4 | 12 |
| =*On the Waterfront*, 1954 | 8 | 12 |
| =*Ben-Hur*, 1959 | 11 | 12 |
| =*Becket*, 1964 | 1 | 12 |
| =*My Fair Lady*, 1964 | 8 | 12 |
| =*Reds*, 1981 | 3 | 12 |
| =*Dances With Wolves*, 1990 | 7 | 12 |
| =*Schindler's List*, 1993 | 7 | 12 |
| =*The English Patient*, 1996 | 9 | 12 |
| =*Gladiator*, 2000 | 5 | 12 |

* Plus two special awards

While *Johnny Belinda* and *Becket* at least had the consolation of winning once out of their 12 nominations each, both *The Turning Point* (1977) and *The Color Purple* (1985) suffered the ignominy of receiving 11 nominations without a single win.

## FILMS TO WIN THE MOST OSCARS

| FILM/YEAR | NOMINATIONS | AWARDS |
|---|---|---|
| 1 =*Ben-Hur*, 1959 | 12 | 11 |
| =*Titanic*, 1997 | 14 | 11 |
| 3 *West Side Story*, 1961 | 11 | 10 |
| 4 =*Gigi*, 1958 | 9 | 9 |
| =*The Last Emperor*, 1987 | 9 | 9 |
| =*The English Patient*, 1996 | 12 | 9 |
| 7 =*Gone With the Wind*, 1939 | 13 | 8* |
| =*From Here to Eternity*, 1953 | 13 | 8 |
| =*On the Waterfront*, 1954 | 12 | 8 |
| =*My Fair Lady*, 1964 | 12 | 8 |
| =*Cabaret*, 1972 | 10 | 8 |
| =*Gandhi*, 1982 | 11 | 8 |
| =*Amadeus*, 1984 | 11 | 8 |

* Plus two special awards

## FIRST "BEST PICTURE" OSCAR-WINNING FILMS

| YEAR | FILM |
|---|---|
| 1927/28 | *Wings* |
| 1928/29 | *Broadway Melody* |
| 1930 | *All Quiet on the Western Front* |
| 1931 | *Cimarron* |
| 1932 | *Grand Hotel* |
| 1933 | *Cavalcade* |
| 1934 | *It Happened One Night** |
| 1935 | *Mutiny on the Bounty* |
| 1936 | *The Great Ziegfeld* |
| 1937 | *The Life of Emile Zola* |

* Winner of Oscars for "Best Director," "Best Actor," "Best Actress," and "Best Screenplay"

The first Academy Awards, popularly known as Oscars, were presented at a ceremony at the Hollywood Roosevelt Hotel on May 16, 1929, and were for films released in the period 1927–28. *Wings*, the first film to be honored as "Best Picture," was silent. A second ceremony, held at the Ambassador Hotel on October 31 of the same year, was for films released in 1928–29, and was won by *Broadway Melody*.

## HIGHEST-EARNING "BEST PICTURE" OSCAR WINNERS

| | FILM | YEAR |
|---|---|---|
| 1 | *Titanic* | 1997 |
| 2 | *Forrest Gump* | 1994 |
| 3 | *Gladiator* | 2000 |
| 4 | *Dances With Wolves* | 1990 |
| 5 | *Rain Man* | 1988 |
| 6 | *Schindler's List* | 1993 |
| 7 | *Shakespeare in Love* | 1998 |
| 8 | *The English Patient* | 1996 |
| 9 | *American Beauty* | 1999 |
| 10 | *Braveheart* | 1995 |

Winning the Academy Award for "Best Picture" is no guarantee of box-office success: the award is given for a picture released the previous year, and by the time the Oscar ceremony takes place, the film-going public has already effectively decided on the winning picture's fate. Receiving the Oscar may enhance a successful picture's continuing earnings, but it is generally too late to revive a film that may already have been judged mediocre.

## "BEST PICTURE" OSCAR WINNERS OF THE 1950s

| YEAR | FILM |
|---|---|
| 1950 | *All About Eve* |
| 1951 | *An American in Paris* |
| 1952 | *The Greatest Show on Earth* |
| 1953 | *From Here to Eternity* |
| 1954 | *On the Waterfront* |
| 1955 | *Marty* |
| 1956 | *Around the World in 80 Days* |
| 1957 | *The Bridge on the River Kwai* |
| 1958 | *Gigi* |
| 1959 | *Ben-Hur* |

The first winning film of the 1950s, *All About Eve*, received the most Oscar nominations (14), while the last, *Ben-Hur*, won the most (11).

**SWORD PLAY**

*Michelle Yeoh stars in* Crouching Tiger, Hidden Dragon, *which crowned its international success and host of awards with the "Best Foreign Language Film" Oscar.*

 **THE 10** ★

# LATEST "BEST FOREIGN LANGUAGE FILM" OSCAR WINNERS

| YEAR | ENGLISH TITLE/LANGUAGE |
|------|------------------------|
| 2000 | *Crouching Tiger, Hidden Dragon*, Mandarin |
| 1999 | *All About My Mother*, Spanish |
| 1998 | *Life is Beautiful*, Italian |
| 1997 | *Character*, Dutch/English/ German/French |
| 1996 | *Kolya*, Czech/Russsian |
| 1995 | *Antonia's Line*, Dutch |
| 1994 | *Burnt by the Sun*, Russian |
| 1993 | *The Age of Beauty*, Spanish |
| 1992 | *Indochine*, French/Vietnamese |
| 1991 | *Mediterraneo*, Italian |

**THE 10** ★

# "BEST PICTURE" OSCAR WINNERS OF THE 1960s

| YEAR | FILM |
|------|------|
| 1960 | *The Apartment* |
| 1961 | *West Side Story* |
| 1962 | *Lawrence of Arabia* |
| 1963 | *Tom Jones* |
| 1964 | *My Fair Lady* |
| 1965 | *The Sound of Music* |
| 1966 | *A Man for All Seasons* |
| 1967 | *In the Heat of the Night* |
| 1968 | *Oliver!* |
| 1969 | *Midnight Cowboy* |

The 1960 winner, *The Apartment*, was the last black-and-white winner until *Schindler's List*, which was released in 1993.

# THE 10 "BEST PICTURE" OSCAR WINNERS OF THE 1970s
(Year/film)

❶ 1970 *Patton*  ❷ 1971 *The French Connection*  ❸ 1972 *The Godfather*
❹ 1973 *The Sting*  ❺ 1974 *The Godfather Part II*  ❻ 1975 *One Flew Over the Cuckoo's Nest*
❼ 1976 *Rocky*  ❽ 1977 *Annie Hall*  ❾ 1978 *The Deer Hunter*
❿ 1979 *Kramer vs. Kramer*

**THE 10** ★

# "BEST PICTURE" OSCAR WINNERS OF THE 1980s

| YEAR | FILM |
|------|------|
| 1980 | *Ordinary People* |
| 1981 | *Chariots of Fire* |
| 1982 | *Gandhi* |
| 1983 | *Terms of Endearment* |
| 1984 | *Amadeus* |
| 1985 | *Out of Africa* |
| 1986 | *Platoon* |
| 1987 | *The Last Emperor* |
| 1988 | *Rain Man* |
| 1989 | *Driving Miss Daisy* |

**THE 10** ★

# LATEST "BEST PICTURE" OSCAR WINNERS

| YEAR | FILM |
|------|------|
| 2000 | *Gladiator* |
| 1999 | *American Beauty* |
| 1998 | *Shakespeare in Love* |
| 1997 | *Titanic* |
| 1996 | *The English Patient* |
| 1995 | *Braveheart* |
| 1994 | *Forrest Gump* |
| 1993 | *Schindler's List* |
| 1992 | *Unforgiven* |
| 1991 | *The Silence of the Lambs* |

**Which actor supplied the voice of Mushu in the animated film *Mulan*?**
*see p.169 for the answer*

A Bruce Willis
B Eddie Murphy
C Jim Carrey

# Oscar-Winning Stars

## YOUNGEST OSCAR-WINNING ACTORS AND ACTRESSES

| | ACTOR OR ACTRESS | AWARD/FILM (WHERE SPECIFIED) | YEAR | AGE* |
|---|---|---|---|---|
| 1 | Shirley Temple | Special Award – outstanding contribution during 1934 | 1934 | 6 |
| 2 | Margaret O' Brien | Special Award (*Meet Me in St. Louis*) | 1944 | 8 |
| 3 | Vincent Winter | Special Award (*The Little Kidnappers*) | 1954 | 8 |
| 4 | Ivan Jandl | Special Award (*The Search*) | 1948 | 9 |
| 5 | Jon Whiteley | Special Award (*The Little Kidnappers*) | 1954 | 10 |
| 6 | Tatum O'Neal | "Best Supporting Actress" (*Paper Moon*) | 1973 | 10 |
| 7 | Anna Paquin | "Best Supporting Actress" (*The Piano*) | 1993 | 11 |
| 8 | Claude Jarman, Jr. | Special Award (*The Yearling*) | 1946 | 12 |
| 9 | Bobby Driscoll | Special Award (*The Window*) | 1949 | 13 |
| 10 | Hayley Mills | Special Award (*Pollyanna*) | 1960 | 13 |

* At the time of the Award ceremony; those of apparently identical age have been ranked according to their precise age in days at the time of the ceremony

The Academy Awards ceremony usually takes place at the end of March in the year following that in which the film was released in the US, so the winners are generally at least a year older when they receive their Oscars than when they acted in their award-winning films.

## THE 10 "BEST ACTRESS" OSCAR WINNERS OF THE 1970s

*(Year/actress/film)*

**1** 1970 Glenda Jackson, *Women in Love*   **2** 1971 Jane Fonda, *Klute*
**3** 1972 Liza Minnelli, *Cabaret*   **4** 1973 Glenda Jackson, *A Touch of Class*
**5** 1974 Ellen Burstyn, *Alice Doesn't Live Here Any More*   **6** 1975 Louise Fletcher, *One Flew Over the Cuckoo's Nest*\*#   **7** 1976 Faye Dunaway, *Network*   **8** 1977 Diane Keaton, *Annie Hall*\*
**9** 1978 Jane Fonda, *Coming Home*   **10** 1979 Sally Field, *Norma Rae*
* Winner of "Best Picture" Oscar
# Winner of "Best Director," "Best Actor," and "Best Screenplay" Oscars

## OSCAR

Founded on May 4, 1927, the Hollywood-based Academy of Motion Picture Arts and Sciences proposed improving the image of the film industry by issuing "awards for merit or distinction" in various categories. The award itself, a statuette designed by Cedric Gibbons, was modeled by a young artist, George Stanley. The gold-plated naked male figure holds a sword and stands on a reel of film. It was simply called "the statuette" up until 1931, when Academy librarian Mrs. Margaret Herrick said, "It looks like my Uncle Oscar!" – and the name stuck until this day.

## "BEST ACTOR" OSCAR WINNERS OF THE 1970s

| YEAR | ACTOR/FILM |
|---|---|
| 1970 | George C. Scott, *Patton*\* |
| 1971 | Gene Hackman, *The French Connection*\* |
| 1972 | Marlon Brando, *The Godfather*\* |
| 1973 | Jack Lemmon, *Save the Tiger* |
| 1974 | Art Carney, *Harry and Tonto* |
| 1975 | Jack Nicholson, *One Flew Over the Cuckoo's Nest*\*# |
| 1976 | Peter Finch, *Network* |
| 1977 | Richard Dreyfuss, *The Goodbye Girl* |
| 1978 | John Voight, *Coming Home* |
| 1979 | Dustin Hoffman, *Kramer vs. Kramer*\* |

* Winner of "Best Picture" Oscar
# Winner of "Best Director," "Best Actress," and "Best Screenplay" Oscars

## FIRST CUCKOO

*Winner of five Oscars,* One Flew Over the Cuckoo's Nest *established the movie careers of both its star, Jack Nicholson, and producer, Michael Douglas.*

## THE 10 ★
## "BEST ACTOR" OSCAR WINNERS OF THE 1980s

| YEAR | ACTOR/FILM |
|------|------------|
| 1980 | Robert De Niro, *Raging Bull* |
| 1981 | Henry Fonda, *On Golden Pond** |
| 1982 | Ben Kingsley, *Gandhi*# |
| 1983 | Robert Duvall, *Tender Mercies* |
| 1984 | F. Murray Abraham, *Amadeus*# |
| 1985 | William Hurt, *Kiss of the Spider Woman* |
| 1986 | Paul Newman, *The Color of Money* |
| 1987 | Michael Douglas, *Wall Street* |
| 1988 | Dustin Hoffman, *Rain Man*# |
| 1989 | Daniel Day-Lewis, *My Left Foot* |

\* *Winner of "Best Actress" Oscar*
\# *Winner of "Best Picture" Oscar*

## THE 10 ★
## "BEST ACTRESS" OSCAR WINNERS OF THE 1980s

| YEAR | ACTRESS/FILM |
|------|--------------|
| 1980 | Sissy Spacek, *Coal Miner's Daughter* |
| 1981 | Katharine Hepburn, *On Golden Pond** |
| 1982 | Meryl Streep, *Sophie's Choice* |
| 1983 | Shirley MacLaine, *Terms of Endearment*# |
| 1984 | Sally Field, *Places in the Heart* |
| 1985 | Geraldine Page, *The Trip to Bountiful* |
| 1986 | Marlee Matlin, *Children of a Lesser God* |
| 1987 | Cher, *Moonstruck* |
| 1988 | Jodie Foster, *The Accused* |
| 1989 | Jessica Tandy, *Driving Miss Daisy*# |

\* *Winner of "Best Actor" Oscar*
\# *Winner of "Best Picture" Oscar*

## THE 10 ★
## LATEST "BEST ACTOR" OSCAR WINNERS

| YEAR | ACTOR/FILM |
|------|------------|
| 2000 | Russell Crowe, *Gladiator** |
| 1999 | Kevin Spacey, *American Beauty** |
| 1998 | Roberto Benigni, *La vita é bella* (*Life Is Beautiful*) |
| 1997 | Jack Nicholson, *As Good as It Gets*# |
| 1996 | Geoffrey Rush, *Shine* |
| 1995 | Nicolas Cage, *Leaving Las Vegas* |
| 1994 | Tom Hanks, *Forrest Gump** |
| 1993 | Tom Hanks, *Philadelphia* |
| 1992 | Al Pacino, *Scent of a Woman* |
| 1991 | Anthony Hopkins, *The Silence of the Lambs**# |

\* *Winner of "Best Picture" Oscar*
\# *Winner of "Best Actress" Oscar*

Tom Hanks shares the honor of two consecutive wins with Spencer Tracy (1937: *Captains Courageous* and 1938: *Boys Town*). Only four other actors have won twice: Marlon Brando (1954; 1972), Gary Cooper (1941; 1952), Dustin Hoffman (1979; 1988), and Jack Nicholson (1975; 1997).

## THE 10 ★
## LATEST "BEST ACTRESS" OSCAR WINNERS

| YEAR | ACTRESS/FILM |
|------|--------------|
| 2000 | Julia Roberts, *Erin Brockovich* |
| 1999 | Hilary Swank, *Boys Don't Cry* |
| 1998 | Gwyneth Paltrow, *Shakespeare in Love** |
| 1997 | Helen Hunt, *As Good as It Gets*# |
| 1996 | Frances McDormand, *Fargo* |
| 1995 | Susan Sarandon, *Dead Man Walking* |
| 1994 | Jessica Lange, *Blue Sky* |
| 1993 | Holly Hunter, *The Piano* |
| 1992 | Emma Thompson, *Howard's End* |
| 1991 | Jodie Foster, *The Silence of the Lambs**# |

\* *Winner of "Best Picture" Oscar*
\# *Winner of "Best Actor" Oscar*

### FARGO

*Frances McDormand's performance as policewoman Marge Gunderson in Fargo, directed by her husband Joel Cohen, gained her the 1996 "Best Actress" Oscar.*

# And the Winner Is ...

## THE 10 ★
### LATEST WINNERS OF THE CANNES PALME D'OR FOR "BEST FILM"

| YEAR | FILM/COUNTRY |
|------|--------------|
| 2000 | *Dancer in the Dark*, Denmark |
| 1999 | *Rosetta*, France |
| 1998 | *Eternity and a Day*, Greece |
| 1997 | *The Eel*, Japan/ *The Taste of Cherries*, Iran |
| 1996 | *Secrets and Lies*, UK |
| 1995 | *Underground*, Yugoslavia |
| 1994 | *Pulp Fiction*, US |
| 1993 | *Farewell My Concubine*, China/ *The Piano*, Australia |
| 1992 | *Best Intentions*, Denmark |
| 1991 | *Barton Fink*, US |

In its early years, there was no single "Best Film" award at the Cannes Film Festival, several films being honored jointly. A "Grand Prize," first awarded in 1949, has been known since 1955 as the "Palme d'Or."

## THE 10 ★
### LATEST ENGLISH-LANGUAGE FILMS TO WIN THE CANNES PALME D'OR

| | FILM/DIRECTOR/COUNTRY | YEAR |
|--|----------------------|------|
| 1 | *Secrets and Lies*, Mike Leigh, UK | 1996 |
| 2 | *Pulp Fiction*, Quentin Tarantino, US | 1994 |
| 3 | *The Piano**, Jane Campion, Australia | 1993 |
| 4 | *Barton Fink*, Joel Coen, US | 1991 |
| 5 | *Wild at Heart*, David Lynch, US | 1990 |
| 6 | *sex, lies, and videotape*, Steven Soderbergh, US | 1989 |
| 7 | *The Mission*, Roland Joffé, UK | 1986 |
| 8 | *Paris, Texas*, Wim Wenders, US | 1984 |
| 9 | *Missing#*, Constantin Costa-Gavras, US | 1982 |
| 10 | *All that Jazz+*, Bob Fosse, US | 1980 |

* *Shared with Farewell My Concubine (Chen Kaige, China)*

\# *Shared with Yol (Serif Goren, Turkey)*

+ *Shared with Kagemusha (Akira Kurosawa, Japan)*

## THE 10 ★
### LATEST RECIPIENTS OF THE AMERICAN FILM INSTITUTE LIFETIME ACHIEVEMENT AWARD

| YEAR | RECIPIENT |
|------|-----------|
| 2001 | Barbra Streisand |
| 2000 | Harrison Ford |
| 1999 | Dustin Hoffman |
| 1998 | Robert Wise |
| 1997 | Martin Scorsese |
| 1996 | Clint Eastwood |
| 1995 | Steven Spielberg |
| 1994 | Jack Nicholson |
| 1993 | Elizabeth Taylor |
| 1992 | Sidney Poitier |

## THE 10 ★
### LATEST WINNERS OF THE GOLDEN GLOBE "BEST DIRECTOR" AWARD

| YEAR | DIRECTOR/FILM |
|------|---------------|
| 2001 | Ang Lee, *Crouching Tiger, Hidden Dragon* |
| 2000 | Sam Mendes, *American Beauty* |
| 1999 | Steven Spielberg, *Saving Private Ryan* |
| 1998 | James Cameron, *Titanic* |
| 1997 | Milos Foreman, *The People vs. Larry Flynt* |
| 1996 | Mel Gibson, *Braveheart* |
| 1995 | Robert Zemeckis, *Forrest Gump* |
| 1994 | Steven Spielberg, *Schindler's List* |
| 1993 | Clint Eastwood, *Unforgiven* |
| 1992 | Oliver Stone, *JFK* |

### SONG AND DANCE

*Winner of the 2000 Palme d'Or, Dancer in the Dark also won the "Best Actress" award for Icelandic singer Björk. She had previously appeared in Juniper Tree (1987) and in a cameo role in Prêt-à-Porter (1994).*

## THE 10 ★
## LATEST WINNERS OF THE GOLDEN GLOBE "BEST MOTION PICTURE – MUSICAL OR COMEDY" AWARD

| YEAR | FILM |
| --- | --- |
| 2001 | *Almost Famous* |
| 2000 | *Toy Story 2* |
| 1999 | *Shakespeare in Love* |
| 1998 | *As Good as It Gets* |
| 1997 | *Evita* |
| 1996 | *Babe* |
| 1995 | *The Lion King* |
| 1994 | *Mrs. Doubtfire* |
| 1993 | *The Player* |
| 1992 | *Beauty and the Beast* |

The Golden Globes are awarded retrospectively, the 2001 award being presented for productions during 2000, and so on.

## THE 10 ★
## LATEST WINNERS OF THE GOLDEN GLOBE "BEST PERFORMANCE BY AN ACTOR IN A MOTION PICTURE – DRAMA" AWARD

| YEAR | ACTOR/FILM |
| --- | --- |
| 2001 | Tom Hanks, *Cast Away* |
| 2000 | Denzel Washington, *The Hurricane* |
| 1999 | Jim Carrey, *The Truman Show* |
| 1998 | Peter Fonda, *Ulee's Gold* |
| 1997 | Geoffrey Rush, *Shine* |
| 1996 | Nicolas Cage, *Leaving Las Vegas* |
| 1995 | Tom Hanks, *Forrest Gump* |
| 1994 | Tom Hanks, *Philadelphia* |
| 1993 | Al Pacino, *Scent of a Woman* |
| 1992 | Nick Nolte, *The Prince of Tides* |

## THE 10 ★
## LATEST WINNERS OF THE GOLDEN GLOBE "BEST MOTION PICTURE – DRAMA" AWARDS

| YEAR | FILM |
| --- | --- |
| 2001 | *Billy Elliott* |
| 2000 | *American Beauty* |
| 1999 | *Saving Private Ryan* |
| 1998 | *Titanic* |
| 1997 | *The English Patient* |
| 1996 | *Sense and Sensibility* |
| 1995 | *Forrest Gump* |
| 1994 | *Schindler's List* |
| 1993 | *Scent of a Woman* |
| 1992 | *Bugsy* |

## THE 10 ★
## LATEST WINNERS OF THE GOLDEN GLOBE "BEST PERFORMANCE BY AN ACTRESS IN A MOTION PICTURE – DRAMA" AWARDS

| YEAR | ACTRESS/FILM |
| --- | --- |
| 2001 | Julia Roberts, *Erin Brockovich* |
| 2000 | Hilary Swank, *Boys Don't Cry* |
| 1999 | Cate Blanchett, *Elizabeth* |
| 1998 | Judi Dench, *Mrs. Brown* |
| 1997 | Brenda Blethyn, *Secrets and Lies* |
| 1996 | Sharon Stone, *Casino* |
| 1995 | Jessica Lange, *Blue Sky* |
| 1994 | Holly Hunter, *The Piano* |
| 1993 | Emma Thompson, *Howard's End* |
| 1992 | Jodie Foster, *The Silence of the Lambs* |

**ERIN BROCKOVICH**

*Julia Roberts's BAFTA and Golden Globe Award for her eponymous role in Erin Brockovich foreshadowed her "Best Actress" Oscar. The real Erin Brockovich appears in the film as a waitress called Julia.*

**Whose debut screen role was billed as "Pretty girl on train"?**
*see p.171 for the answer*

A  Glenn Close
B  Marilyn Monroe
C  Sharon Stone

# Leading Men

## TOP 10 ★
## NICOLAS CAGE FILMS

| | | |
|---|---|---|
| 1 | The Rock | 1996 |
| 2 | Face/Off | 1997 |
| 3 | Gone in Sixty Seconds | 2000 |
| 4 | Con Air | 1997 |
| 5 | City of Angels | 1998 |
| 6 | Snake Eyes | 1998 |
| 7 | 8MM | 1999 |
| 8 | Moonstruck | 1987 |
| 9 | Leaving Las Vegas | 1995 |
| 10 | Peggy Sue Got Married | 1986 |

**RATTLING THE CAGE**

*Nicolas Cage stars as FBI biochemist Dr. Stanley Goodspeed in the 1996 film The Rock, which is his highest-earning film to date.*

## TOP 10 ★
## PIERCE BROSNAN FILMS

| | | |
|---|---|---|
| 1 | Mrs. Doubtfire | 1993 |
| 2 | The World Is Not Enough | 1999 |
| 3 | GoldenEye | 1995 |
| 4 | Tomorrow Never Dies | 1997 |
| 5 | Dante's Peak | 1997 |
| 6 | The Thomas Crown Affair | 1999 |
| 7 | Mars Attacks! | 1996 |
| 8 | The Mirror Has Two Faces | 1996 |
| 9 | The Lawnmower Man | 1992 |
| 10 | Love Affair | 1994 |

Pierce Brosnan, now best known as James Bond, provided the voice of King Arthur in the animated film *Quest for Camelot* (1998). If included, it would be ranked ninth.

## TOP 10 ★
## TOM CRUISE FILMS

| | | |
|---|---|---|
| 1 | Mission: Impossible 2 | 2000 |
| 2 | Mission: Impossible | 1996 |
| 3 | Rain Man | 1988 |
| 4 | Top Gun | 1986 |
| 5 | Jerry Maguire | 1996 |
| 6 | The Firm | 1993 |
| 7 | A Few Good Men | 1992 |
| 8 | Interview With the Vampire | 1994 |
| 9 | Days of Thunder | 1990 |
| 10 | Eyes Wide Shut | 1999 |

## TOP 10 ★
## KEVIN SPACEY FILMS

| | | |
|---|---|---|
| 1 | American Beauty | 1999 |
| 2 | Se7en | 1995 |
| 3 | Outbreak | 1995 |
| 4 | A Time to Kill | 1996 |
| 5 | L.A. Confidential | 1997 |
| 6 | The Negotiator | 1998 |
| 7 | The Usual Suspects | 1995 |
| 8 | Pay it Forward | 2000 |
| 9 | See No Evil, Hear No Evil | 1989 |
| 10 | Heartburn | 1986 |

Kevin Spacey provided the voice of Hopper in the animated film *A Bug's Life* (1998). If included, this would be his No. 1 film.

**PIERCING LOOK**

*Irish-born Pierce Brosnan took over the role of James Bond with GoldenEye. This, along with Tomorrow Never Dies and The World Is Not Enough, are the highest earning of all the Bond movies.*

## TOP 10 ★
### $100 MILLION FILM ACTORS

| | ACTOR* | FILMS# | TOTAL ($)+ |
|---|---|---|---|
| 1 | Harrison Ford | 16 | 5,090,800,000 |
| 2 | Samuel L. Jackson | 10 | 3,426,000,000 |
| 3 | Bruce Willis | 13 | 3,420,100,000 |
| 4 | Tom Cruise | 10 | 3,055,300,000 |
| 5 | James Earl Jones | 9 | 3,001,200,000 |
| 6 | Robin Williams | 11 | 2,749,800,000 |
| 7 | Mel Gibson | 14 | 2,595,700,000 |
| 8 | Tommy Lee Jones | 11 | 2,405,800,000 |
| 9 | Eddie Murphy | 10 | 2,366,000,000 |
| 10 | Leonardo DiCaprio | 4 | 2,293,500,000 |

\* Appeared in or provided voice in film

\# Earning over $100 million worldwide as of the end of 2000

\+ Of all $100-million-plus films

## TOP 10 ★
### BRAD PITT FILMS

| 1 | Se7en | 1995 |
|---|---|---|
| 2 | Interview With the Vampire | 1994 |
| 3 | Sleepers | 1996 |
| 4 | Legends of the Fall | 1994 |
| 5 | Twelve Monkeys | 1995 |
| 6 | The Devil's Own | 1997 |
| 7 | Meet Joe Black | 1998 |
| 8 | Seven Years in Tibet | 1997 |
| 9 | Fight Club | 1999 |
| 10 | Thelma & Louise | 1991 |

**PITT STOPPER**

Brad (William Bradley) Pitt plays Detective David Mills in Se7en, his most successful film to date. Pitt appeared in more than 20 films during the 1990s.

## TOP 10 EDDIE MURPHY FILMS

❶ Beverly Hills Cop, 1984 ❷ Beverly Hills Cop II, 1987 ❸ Doctor Dolittle, 1998
❹ Coming to America, 1988 ❺ The Nutty Professor, 1996
❻ Nutty Professor II: The Klumps, 2000 ❼ Another 48 Hrs., 1990
❽ The Golden Child, 1986 ❾ Boomerang, 1992 ❿ Harlem Nights*, 1989

*Also director*

Eddie Murphy also provided the voice of Mushu in the animated film *Mulan* (1998), which, if included, would rank second in his Top 10.

## TOP 10 ★
### SAMUEL L. JACKSON FILMS

| 1 | Star Wars: Episode I – The Phantom Menace | 1999 |
|---|---|---|
| 2 | Jurassic Park | 1993 |
| 3 | Die Hard: With a Vengeance | 1995 |
| 4 | Coming to America | 1988 |
| 5 | Pulp Fiction | 1994 |
| 6 | Patriot Games | 1992 |
| 7 | Deep Blue Sea | 1999 |
| 8 | A Time to Kill | 1996 |
| 9 | Unbreakable | 2000 |
| 10 | Sea of Love | 1989 |

## TOP 10 ★
### JOHN CUSACK FILMS

| 1 | Con Air | 1997 |
|---|---|---|
| 2 | The Thin Red Line | 1998 |
| 3 | Stand by Me | 1986 |
| 4 | Broadcast News | 1987 |
| 5 | Being John Malkovich | 1999 |
| 6 | High Fidelity | 2000 |
| 7 | City Hall | 1996 |
| 8 | Grosse Pointe Blank | 1997 |
| 9 | Midnight in the Garden of Good and Evil | 1997 |
| 10 | The Player | 1992 |

John Cusack supplied the voice of Dimitri in the animated film *Anastasia* (1997). Were it included here, it would rank in second place.

## TOP 10 ★
### BRUCE WILLIS FILMS

| 1 | The Sixth Sense | 1999 |
|---|---|---|
| 2 | Armageddon | 1998 |
| 3 | Die Hard: With a Vengeance | 1995 |
| 4 | The Fifth Element | 1997 |
| 5 | Die Hard 2 | 1990 |
| 6 | Pulp Fiction | 1994 |
| 7 | Twelve Monkeys | 1995 |
| 8 | The Jackal | 1997 |
| 9 | Death Becomes Her | 1992 |
| 10 | Die Hard | 1988 |

*Look Who's Talking* (1989), in which typically tough-guy Willis took the role of a baby, is discounted here because the role consisted only of Willis's dubbed voice.

## TOP 10 KEANU REEVES FILMS

❶ The Matrix, 1999 ❷ Speed, 1994
❸ Bram Stoker's Dracula, 1992 ❹ The Devil's Advocate, 1997 ❺ Parenthood, 1989 ❻ A Walk in the Clouds, 1995 ❼ Chain Reaction, 1996 ❽ Johnny Mnemonic, 1995 ❾ The Replacements, 2000 ❿ Point Break, 1991

**Did You Know?** The first actor to receive a movie contract was prizefighter James John Corbett. In August 1894, he signed with the Kinetoscope Exhibition Company to appear in a film of a six-round fight against Pete Courtney.

# Leading Ladies

**RYAN'S DAUGHTER**

*Born Margaret Mary Emily Anne Hyra, Meg Ryan took her mother's maiden name before her film debut in 1981. She has gone on to enjoy huge success in a range of romantic comedies.*

## TOP 10 ★
## MICHELLE PFEIFFER FILMS

| | | |
|---|---|---|
| 1 | *Batman Returns* | 1992 |
| 2 | *What Lies Beneath* | 2000 |
| 3 | *Dangerous Minds* | 1995 |
| 4 | *Wolf* | 1994 |
| 5 | *Up Close and Personal* | 1996 |
| 6 | *One Fine Day* | 1996 |
| 7 | *The Witches of Eastwick* | 1987 |
| 8 | *The Story of Us* | 1999 |
| 9 | *Tequila Sunrise* | 1988 |
| 10 | *Scarface* | 1983 |

Michelle Pfeiffer also provided the voice of Tzipporah in the animated film *The Prince of Egypt* (1998). If included in her Top 10, this would feature in third place.

**CATWOMAN**

*Batman Returns is Michelle Pfeiffer's most successful film to date, but half the films in her Top 10 have earned a healthy $100 million-plus.*

## TOP 10 ★
## MEG RYAN FILMS

| | | |
|---|---|---|
| 1 | *Top Gun* | 1986 |
| 2 | *You've Got M@il* | 1998 |
| 3 | *Sleepless in Seattle* | 1993 |
| 4 | *City of Angels* | 1998 |
| 5 | *French Kiss* | 1995 |
| 6 | *Courage under Fire* | 1996 |
| 7 | *When Harry Met Sally* | 1989 |
| 8 | *Addicted to Love* | 1997 |
| 9 | *When a Man Loves a Woman* | 1994 |
| 10 | *Hanging Up* | 2000 |

Meg Ryan provided the voice of Anastasia in the 1997 film of that title. If included, it would appear in ninth place.

## TOP 10 ★
## BETTE MIDLER FILMS

| | | |
|---|---|---|
| 1 | *The First Wives Club* | 1996 |
| 2 | *What Women Want* | 2000 |
| 3 | *Get Shorty* | 1995 |
| 4 | *Ruthless People* | 1986 |
| 5 | *Down and Out in Beverly Hills* | 1986 |
| 6 | *Beaches** | 1988 |
| 7 | *Outrageous Fortune* | 1987 |
| 8 | *The Rose* | 1979 |
| 9 | *Big Business* | 1988 |
| 10 | *Hocus Pocus* | 1993 |

\* *Also producer*

Bette Midler's role in *Get Shorty* is no more than a cameo. If this were excluded, *Hawaii* (1966) would join the list in 10th place.

## TOP 10
## JUDI DENCH FILMS

**1** *The World is Not Enough*, 1999 **2** *GoldenEye*, 1995 **3** *Tomorrow Never Dies*, 1997 **4** *Shakespeare in Love*, 1998 **5** *Tea with Mussolini*, 1999 **6** *A Room with a View*, 1986 **7** *Mrs. Brown*, 1997 **8** *Henry V*, 1989 **9** *Chocolat*, 2000 **10** *Hamlet*, 1996

## TOP 10 ★
## MINNIE DRIVER FILMS

| | | |
|---|---|---|
| 1 | *GoldenEye* | 1995 |
| 2 | *Good Will Hunting* | 1997 |
| 3 | *Sleepers* | 1996 |
| 4 | *Circle of Friends* | 1995 |
| 5 | *Return to Me* | 2000 |
| 6 | *Grosse Pointe Blank* | 1997 |
| 7 | *Hard Rain* | 1998 |
| 8 | *An Ideal Husband* | 1999 |
| 9 | *Big Night* | 1996 |
| 10 | *The Governess* | 1998 |

Minnie Driver has also had three successful voice-only roles: Jane Porter in *Tarzan* (1999), Lady Eboshi in *Mononoke Hime* (1997), and Brooke Shields in *South Park: Bigger, Longer and Uncut* (1999).

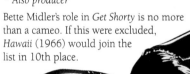

**PRETTY WOMAN**

*Julia Roberts became the first Hollywood actress to be paid $10 million (for her role in the 1996 film* Mary Reilly*). She now commands almost $20 million.*

## TOP 10 ⭐
### JULIA ROBERTS FILMS

| 1 | Pretty Woman* | 1990 |
|---|---|---|
| 2 | Notting Hill | 1999 |
| 3 | Hook | 1991 |
| 4 | My Best Friend's Wedding | 1997 |
| 5 | Runaway Bride | 1999 |
| 6 | Erin Brockovich# | 2000 |
| 7 | The Pelican Brief | 1993 |
| 8 | Sleeping with the Enemy | 1991 |
| 9 | Stepmom | 1998 |
| 10 | Conspiracy Theory | 1997 |

\* *Academy Award nomination for "Best Actress"*

\# *Winner of "Best Actress" Oscar*

## TOP 10 ⭐
### $100 MILLION FILM ACTRESSES

| | ACTRESS* | FILMS# | TOTAL ($)+ |
|---|---|---|---|
| 1 | Julia Roberts | 10 | 2,602,300,000 |
| 2 | Carrie Fisher | 4 | 2,047,700,000 |
| 3 | Whoopi Goldberg | 7 | 2,027,200,000 |
| 4 | Glenn Close | 6 | 1,777,700,000 |
| 5 | Demi Moore | 6 | 1,672,200,000 |
| 6 | Bonnie Hunt | 5 | 1,577,800,000 |
| 7 | Drew Barrymore | 5 | 1,561,800,000 |
| 8 | Rene Russo | 7 | 1,524,900,000 |
| 9 | Annie Potts | 4 | 1,351,600,000 |
| 10 | Minnie Driver | 5 | 1,337,400,000 |

\* *Appeared in or provided voice in film*

\# *Earning over $100 million worldwide to end of 2000*

\+ *Of all $100-million-plus films*

Among well-known high-earning stars, this list contains several surprising names of less familiar or prolific artists who have appeared in or provided voices for some of the most successful films of all time. One such is Annie Potts, who appeared in both *Ghostbusters* films and supplied the voice of Bo Peep for both *Toy Story* films.

## TOP 10 ⭐
### SHARON STONE FILMS

| 1 | Basic Instinct | 1992 |
|---|---|---|
| 2 | Total Recall | 1990 |
| 3 | The Specialist | 1995 |
| 4 | Last Action Hero | 1993 |
| 5 | Sliver | 1993 |
| 6 | Casino* | 1995 |
| 7 | Sphere | 1998 |
| 8 | Diabolique | 1996 |
| 9 | Police Academy 4: Citizens on Patrol | 1987 |
| 10 | Gloria | 1999 |

\* *Academy Award nomination for "Best Actress"*

Sharon Stone's first film role was a fleeting appearance in Woody Allen's *Stardust Memories* (1980), where she appears credited only as "Pretty girl on train."

## TOP 10 ⭐
### DREW BARRYMORE FILMS

| 1 | E.T.: The Extra-Terrestrial | 1982 |
|---|---|---|
| 2 | Batman Forever | 1995 |
| 3 | Charlie's Angels | 2000 |
| 4 | Scream | 1996 |
| 5 | The Wedding Singer | 1998 |
| 6 | Never Been Kissed | 1999 |
| 7 | Ever After | 1998 |
| 8 | Wayne's World 2 | 1993 |
| 9 | Everyone Says I Love You | 1996 |
| 10 | Boys on the Side | 1995 |

Drew Barrymore also provided the voice of Akima in the animated *Titan A.E.* (2000), which would be in 10th place in her Top 10.

## TOP 10 ⭐
### GWYNETH PALTROW FILMS

| 1 | Se7en | 1995 |
|---|---|---|
| 2 | Hook | 1991 |
| 3 | Shakespeare in Love* | 1998 |
| 4 | A Perfect Murder | 1998 |
| 5 | The Talented Mr. Ripley | 1999 |
| 6 | Sliding Doors | 1998 |
| 7 | Great Expectations | 1998 |
| 8 | Malice | 1993 |
| 9 | Emma | 1996 |
| 10 | Bounce | 2000 |

\* *Winner of "Best Actress" Oscar*

## TOP 10 UMA THURMAN FILMS

❶ *Batman & Robin*, 1997 ❷ *Pulp Fiction*, 1994 ❸ *The Truth About Cats and Dogs*, 1996 ❹ *The Avengers*, 1998 ❺ *Dangerous Liaisons*, 1988 ❻ *Final Analysis*, 1992 ❼ *Beautiful Girls*, 1996 ❽ *Les Misérables*, 1998 ❾ *Johnny Be Good*, 1988 ❿ *Gattaca*, 1997

**Did You Know?** One of the most prolific actresses in movie history was Bess Flowers (1898–1984). In the period from 1923 to 1964 she appeared, often uncredited, in at least 371 films.

# The Directors & Writers

## FILMS DIRECTED BY ACTORS

| | FILM/YEAR | DIRECTOR |
|---|---|---|
| 1 | *Pretty Woman*, 1990 | Garry Marshall |
| 2 | *Dances With Wolves*, 1990 | Kevin Costner |
| 3 | *The Bodyguard*, 1992 | Kevin Costner |
| 4 | *How the Grinch Stole Christmas*, 2000 | Ron Howard |
| 5 | *Apollo 13*, 1995 | Ron Howard |
| 6 | *Ransom*, 1996 | Ron Howard |
| 7 | *Rocky IV*, 1985 | Sylvester Stallone |
| 8 | *Doctor Dolittle*, 1998 | Betty Thomas |
| 9 | *Runaway Bride*, 1999 | Garry Marshall |
| 10 | *Waterworld*, 1995 | Kevin Costner |

## FILMS DIRECTED BY WOMEN

| | FILM/YEAR | DIRECTOR |
|---|---|---|
| 1 | *Look Who's Talking*, 1989 | Amy Heckerling |
| 2 | *Doctor Dolittle*, 1998 | Betty Thomas |
| 3 | *Sleepless in Seattle*, 1993 | Nora Ephron |
| 4 | *What Women Want*, 2000 | Nancy Meyers |
| 5 | *The Birdcage*, 1996 | Elaine May |
| 6 | *You've Got M@il*, 1998 | Nora Ephron |
| 7 | *Wayne's World*, 1992 | Penelope Spheeris |
| 8 | *Big*, 1988 | Penny Marshall |
| 9 | *Michael*, 1996 | Nora Ephron |
| 10 | *A League of Their Own*, 1992 | Penny Marshall |

## DIRECTORS, 2000

| | DIRECTOR* | FILM(S)# |
|---|---|---|
| 1 | Ron Howard | *How the Grinch Stole Christmas* |
| 2 | John Woo | *Mission: Impossible 2* |
| 3 | Robert Zemeckis | *What Lies Beneath*, *Cast Away* |
| 4 | Ridley Scott | *Gladiator* |
| 5 | Wolfgang Petersen | *The Perfect Storm* |
| 6 | Jay Roach | *Meet the Parents* |
| 7 | Bryan Singer | *X-Men* |
| 8 | Keenan Ivory Wayans | *Scary Movie* |
| 9 | Eric Leighton, Ralph Zondag | *Dinosaur* |
| 10 | Steven Soderbergh | *Erin Brockovich*, *The Limey* |

\* *Including codirectors*

\# *Ranking based on total domestic (US) gross of all films released in 2000*

**WOOING THE AUDIENCES**

Mission: Impossible 2 *director John Woo moved from Hong Kong to Hollywood to become a thriller specialist. He was the first Asian director to make a mainstream Hollywood film, Hard Target, in 1993.*

## FILMS DIRECTED BY RON HOWARD

| 1 | *How the Grinch Stole Christmas* | 2000 |
|---|---|---|
| 2 | *Apollo 13* | 1995 |
| 3 | *Ransom* | 1996 |
| 4 | *Backdraft* | 1991 |
| 5 | *Parenthood* | 1989 |
| 6 | *Cocoon* | 1985 |
| 7 | *Splash* | 1984 |
| 8 | *Far and Away* | 1992 |
| 9 | *Willow* | 1988 |
| 10 | *The Paper* | 1994 |

## FILMS DIRECTED BY STEVEN SPIELBERG

| 1 | *Jurassic Park* | 1993 |
|---|---|---|
| 2 | *E.T.: The Extra-Terrestrial* | 1982 |
| 3 | *The Lost World: Jurassic Park* | 1997 |
| 4 | *Indiana Jones and the Last Crusade* | 1989 |
| 5 | *Saving Private Ryan* | 1998 |
| 6 | *Jaws* | 1975 |
| 7 | *Raiders of the Lost Ark* | 1981 |
| 8 | *Indiana Jones and the Temple of Doom* | 1984 |
| 9 | *Schindler's List* | 1993 |
| 10 | *Hook* | 1991 |

## TOP 10 FILMS DIRECTED BY STANLEY KUBRICK

❶ *Eyes Wide Shut*, 1999 ❷ *The Shining*, 1980 ❸ *2001: A Space Odyssey*, 1968 ❹ *Full Metal Jacket*, 1987 ❺ *A Clockwork Orange*, 1971 ❻ *Spartacus*, 1960 ❼ *Barry Lyndon*, 1975 ❽ *Dr. Strangelove*, 1964 ❾ *Lolita*, 1962 ❿ *Paths of Glory*, 1957

# TOP 10 FILMS WRITTEN BY STEPHEN KING

**1** *The Green Mile*, 1999 **2** *The Shining*, 1980 **3** *Misery*, 1990 **4** *The Shawshank Redemption*, 1994 **5** *Pet Sematary*, 1989 **6** *Stand by Me*, 1986 **7** *Dolores Claiborne*, 1995 **8** *The Running Man*, 1987 **9** *Carrie*, 1976 **10** *Sleepwalkers*, 1992

## TOP 10 ★

# FILMS BASED ON CLASSIC ENGLISH NOVELS

| FILM/YEAR | NOVELIST/PUBLISHED |
|---|---|
| **1** *Bram Stoker's Dracula*, 1992 | Bram Stoker, 1897 |
| **2** *Sense and Sensibility*, 1995 | Jane Austen, 1811 |
| **3** *Mary Shelley's Frankenstein*, 1994 | Mary Shelley, 1818 |
| **4** *Emma*, 1996 | Jane Austen, 1816 |
| **5** *The Age of Innocence*, 1993 | Edith Wharton, 1920 |
| **6** *A Passage to India*, 1984 | E. M. Forster, 1924 |
| **7** *Howard's End*, 1992 | E. M. Forster, 1910 |
| **8** *A Room with a View*, 1986 | E. M. Forster, 1908 |
| **9** *The Portrait of a Lady*, 1996 | Henry James, 1881 |
| **10** *The Wings of the Dove*, 1997 | Henry James, 1902 |

This Top 10 excludes films inspired by novels but not following the text and storyline.

# TOP 10 FILMS WRITTEN BY RON BASS

**1** *Rain Man*, 1988 **2** *My Best Friend's Wedding*, 1997 **3** *Entrapment*, 1999 **4** *Dangerous Minds*, 1995 **5** *Sleeping With the Enemy*, 1991 **6** *Stepmom*, 1998 **7** *What Dreams May Come*, 1998 **8** *Waiting to Exhale*, 1995 **9** *How Stella Got Her Groove Back*, 1998 **10** *When a Man Loves a Woman*, 1994

## TOP 10 ★

# WRITERS, 2000

| WRITER* | FILM(S)# |
|---|---|
| **1** William Goldman | *Mission: Impossible 2, Hollow Man* |
| **2** Ed Solomon | *X-Men, Charlie's Angels* |
| **3** Zak Penn | *Nutty Professor II: The Klumps, Charlie's Angels* |
| **4** John Logan | *Gladiator, Any Given Sunday* |
| **5** Jeffrey Price, Peter S. Seaman, Dr. Seuss | *How the Grinch Stole Christmas* |
| **6** Brannon Braga, David Marconi, Ronald D. Moore, Michael Tolkin, Robert Towne | *Mission: Impossible 2* |
| **7** David H. Franzoni, William Nicholson | *Gladiator* |
| **8** Bo Goldman, Sebastian Junger, William D. Wittliff | *The Perfect Storm* |
| **9** Joss Whedon | *X-Men, Titan A.E.* |
| **10** Susannah Grant | *Erin Brockovich, 28 Days, Center Stage* |

\* *Including writing teams*

# *Ranking based on total domestic gross of all films by these writers released in 2000*

## MILES AHEAD

*The Green Mile is by far the highest-earning film based on a Stephen King story. To date, some 40 film adaptations of his work have been released.*

## TOP 10 ★

# PRODUCERS, 2000

| PRODUCER* | HIGHEST-EARNING FILM# |
|---|---|
| **1** Steven Spielberg | *Gladiator* |
| **2** Bob Weinstein | *Scary Movie* |
| **3** Harvey Weinstein | *Scary Movie* |
| **4** Douglas Wick | *Gladiator* |
| **5** Jerry Bruckheimer, Chad Oman, Pat Sandston, Mike Stenson | *Remember the Titans* |
| **6** Brian Grazer | *How the Grinch Stole Christmas* |
| **7** Cary Granat | *Scary Movie* |
| **8** Mark Johnson | *What Lies Beneath* |
| **9** Terence Chang | *Mission: Impossible 2* |
| **10** Todd Hallowell, Aldric L'Auli Porter, Louisa Velis, David Womark | *How the Grinch Stole Christmas* |

\* *Including producer teams*

# *Ranking based on total domestic gross of all films released in 2000*

# The Studios

## TOP 10 NEW LINE FILMS

1. *Se7en*, 1995  2. *The Mask*, 1994  3. *Austin Powers: The Spy Who Shagged Me*, 1999
4. *Dumb and Dumber*, 1994  5. *Rush Hour*, 1998  6. *Teenage Mutant Ninja Turtles*, 1990
7. *Lost in Space*, 1998  8. *Blade*, 1998  9. *Mortal Kombat*, 1995
10. *The Wedding Singer*, 1998

## TOP 10 ★ PARAMOUNT FILMS

| | | |
|---|---|---|
| 1 | Titanic* | 1997 |
| 2 | Forrest Gump | 1994 |
| 3 | Mission: Impossible 2 | 2000 |
| 4 | Ghost | 1990 |
| 5 | Indiana Jones and the Last Crusade | 1989 |
| 6 | Mission: Impossible | 1996 |
| 7 | Grease | 1978 |
| 8 | Raiders of the Lost Ark | 1981 |
| 9 | Deep Impact | 1998 |
| 10 | Top Gun | 1986 |

\* Coproduction with Fox, which had overseas rights

## TOP 10 ★ MCA/UNIVERSAL FILMS

| | | |
|---|---|---|
| 1 | Jurassic Park | 1993 |
| 2 | E.T.: The Extra-Terrestrial | 1982 |
| 3 | The Lost World: Jurassic Park | 1997 |
| 4 | Jaws | 1975 |
| 5 | The Mummy | 1999 |
| 6 | The Flintstones | 1994 |
| 7 | Notting Hill | 1999 |
| 8 | Back to the Future | 1985 |
| 9 | How the Grinch Stole Christmas | 2000 |
| 10 | Apollo 13 | 1995 |

## TOP 10 ★ DREAMWORKS FILMS

| | | |
|---|---|---|
| 1 | Saving Private Ryan* | 1998 |
| 2 | Gladiator* | 2000 |
| 3 | Deep Impact* | 1998 |
| 4 | American Beauty | 1999 |
| 5 | What Lies Beneath* | 2000 |
| 6 | The Prince of Egypt | 1998 |
| 7 | The Haunting | 1990 |
| 8 | Chicken Run | 2000 |
| 9 | Antz | 1998 |
| 10 | Mouse Hunt | 1997 |

\* Coproduction with another studio

## TOP 10 ★ WARNER BROS. FILMS

| | | |
|---|---|---|
| 1 | Twister | 1996 |
| 2 | The Matrix | 1999 |
| 3 | Batman | 1989 |
| 4 | The Bodyguard | 1992 |
| 5 | Robin Hood: Prince of Thieves | 1991 |
| 6 | The Fugitive | 1993 |
| 7 | Batman Forever | 1995 |
| 8 | The Perfect Storm | 2000 |
| 9 | Lethal Weapon 3 | 1992 |
| 10 | The Exorcist | 1973 |

## TOP 10 MIRAMAX FILMS

1. *Shakespeare in Love*, 1998  2. *Scary Movie*, 2000  3. *The English Patient*, 1996
4. *Good Will Hunting*, 1997  5. *Life is Beautiful (La Vita è Bella)*, 1998
6. *Pulp Fiction*, 1994  7. *Scream*, 1996  8. *Scream 2*, 1997  9. *Scream 3*, 2000
10. *The Talented Mr. Ripley*, 1999

It was the coming of sound that launched the newly formed Warner Bros. into its important place in cinema history with *The Jazz Singer* (1927), its best-known early sound production. The Depression years were not easy for the company, but in the 1940s it produced a number of films that received acclaim from both critics and the public. Meanwhile, it came to be acknowledged as one of the major forces in the field of animation with its *Bugs Bunny* and other cartoons.

### STORMING AHEAD

*Each of the top four films produced by Warner Bros. has earned more than $400 million at the world box office, while earnings from Twister approach half a billion dollars.*

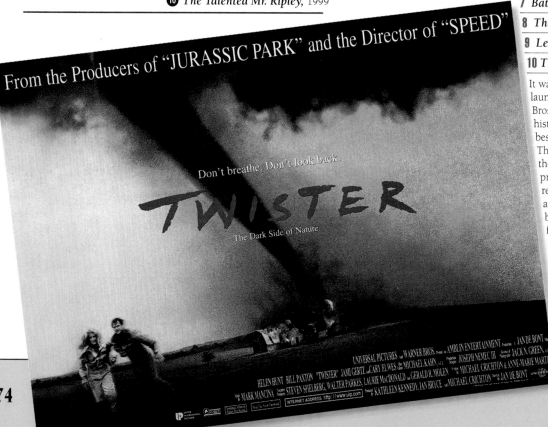

# TOP 10 TWENTIETH CENTURY-FOX FILMS

**1** *Titanic**, 1997 **2** *Star Wars: Episode I – The Phantom Menace*, 1999 **3** *Independence Day*, 1996 **4** *Star Wars*, 1977 **5** *The Empire Strikes Back*, 1980 **6** *Home Alone*, 1990 **7** *Return of the Jedi*, 1983 **8** *Mrs. Doubtfire*, 1993 **9** *True Lies*, 1994 **10** *Die Hard: With a Vengeance*, 1995

\* *Coproduced with Paramount; Twentieth Century-Fox controlled overseas rights*

## TOP 10 ★
## WALT DISNEY/ BUENA VISTA FILMS

| 1 | The Lion King | 1994 |
|---|---|---|
| 2 | The Sixth Sense | 1999 |
| 3 | Armageddon | 1998 |
| 4 | Toy Story 2 | 1999 |
| 5 | Aladdin | 1992 |
| 6 | Pretty Woman | 1990 |
| 7 | Tarzan | 1999 |
| 8 | A Bug's Life | 1998 |
| 9 | Toy Story | 1995 |
| 10 | Beauty and the Beast | 1991 |

## TOP 10 ★
## STUDIOS WITH THE MOST "BEST PICTURE" OSCARS

| | STUDIO | AWARDS |
|---|---|---|
| 1 | United Artists | 13 |
| 2 | Columbia | 12 |
| 3 | Paramount | 11 |
| 4 | MGM | 9 |
| 5 | Twentieth Century-Fox | 7 |
| 6 | Warner Bros. | 6 |
| 7 | Universal | 5 |
| 8 | Orion | 4 |
| 9 | =Deamworks | 2 |
| | =Miramax | 2 |
| | =RKO | 2 |

## TOP 10 ★
## SONY (COLUMBIA/ TRI-STAR) FILMS

| 1 | Men in Black | 1997 |
|---|---|---|
| 2 | Terminator 2: Judgment Day | 1991 |
| 3 | Godzilla | 1998 |
| 4 | Basic Instinct | 1992 |
| 5 | Close Encounters of the Third Kind | 1977/80 |
| 6 | As Good as It Gets | 1997 |
| 7 | Air Force One | 1997 |
| 8 | Hook | 1991 |
| 9 | Rambo: First Blood Part II | 1985 |
| 10 | Look Who's Talking | 1989 |

Founded in 1924 by Harry Cohn and his brother Jack, Columbia was built up into a studio to rival the established giants MGM and Paramount. In 1934, Frank Capra's *It Happened One Night*, starring Clark Gable and Claudette Colbert, swept the board, unprecedentedly winning "Best Picture," "Best Director," "Best Actor," and "Best Actress" Oscars. In subsequent years, films such as *Lost Horizon* (1937) and *The Jolson Story* (1946) consolidated Columbia's commercial success.

**SENSE OF ACHIEVEMENT**

*Disney's* The Lion King *remains its most successful film so far, but* The Sixth Sense *comes an honorable second, with world earnings of nearly $700 million.*

## TOP 10 ★
## STUDIOS, 2000

| | STUDIO | EARNINGS ($)* | MARKET SHARE (%) |
|---|---|---|---|
| 1 | Buena Vista | 1,174,000,000 | 15.78 |
| 2 | Universal | 1,053,600,000 | 14.16 |
| 3 | Warner Bros. | 903,400,000 | 12.14 |
| 4 | DreamWorks | 789,800,000 | 10.62 |
| 5 | Paramount | 781,000,000 | 10.50 |
| 6 | Sony | 688,200,000 | 9.25 |
| 7 | Twentieth Century-Fox | 659,300,000 | 8.86 |
| 8 | New Line | 372,500,000 | 5.01 |
| 9 | Dimension | 322,500,000 | 4.44 |
| 10 | Miramax | 128,400,000 | 1.73 |

\* *Domestic (US) box office gross in 2000*

Total US box office gross for 2000 was estimated as $7,439,400,655, of which the Top 10 studios earned $6,872,700,000, or 92 percent.

**Did You Know?** Although United Artists has won the most "Best Picture" Oscars, MGM has received the most wins in all categories, with a total of 190.

# Film Out-Takes

## TOP 10 ★

### MOST EXPENSIVE ITEMS OF FILM MEMORABILIA EVER SOLD AT AUCTION

| ITEM/SALE | PRICE ($) |
|---|---|
| 1 Judy Garland's ruby slippers from *The Wizard of Oz*, Christie's, New York, May 26, 2000 | 666,000 |
| 2 Clark Gable's Oscar for *It Happened One Night*, Christie's, Los Angeles, Dec 15, 1996 | 607,500 |
| 3 Vivien Leigh's Oscar for *Gone With the Wind*, Sotheby's, New York, Dec 15, 1993 | 562,500 |
| 4 Poster for *The Mummy*, 1932, Sotheby's, New York, Mar 1, 1997 | 453,500 |
| 5 James Bond's Aston Martin DB5 from *Goldfinger*, Sotheby's, New York, June 28, 1986 | 275,000 |
| 6 Clark Gable's personal script for *Gone With the Wind*, Christie's, Los Angeles, Dec 15, 1996 | 244,500 |
| 7 "Rosebud" sled from *Citizen Kane*, Christie's, Los Angeles, Dec 15, 1996 | 233,500 |
| 8 Herman J. Mankiewicz's scripts for *Citizen Kane* and *The American*, Christie's, New York, June 21, 1989 | 231,000 |
| 9 Mel Gibson's 5ft broadsword from *Braveheart*, Sotheby's, New York, Mar 6, 2001 | 170,000 |
| 10 Judy Garland's ruby slippers from *The Wizard of Oz*, Christie's, New York, June 21, 1988 | 165,000 |

## TOP 10 ★

### FILMS WITH THE MOST EXTRAS

| FILM/COUNTRY/YEAR | EXTRAS |
|---|---|
| 1 *Gandhi*, UK, 1982 | 300,000 |
| 2 *Kolberg*, Germany, 1945 | 187,000 |
| 3 *Monster Wang-magwi*, South Korea, 1967 | 157,000 |
| 4 *War and Peace*, USSR, 1967 | 120,000 |
| 5 *Ilya Muromets*, USSR, 1956 | 106,000 |
| 6 *Tonko*, Japan, 1988 | 100,000 |
| 7 *The War of Independence*, Romania, 1912 | 80,000 |
| 8 *Around the World in 80 Days*, US, 1956 | 68,894 |
| 9 =*Dny Zrady*, Czechoslovakia, 1972 | 60,000 |
| =*Intolerance*, US, 1916 | 60,000 |

## TOP 10 ★

### COUNTRIES WITH THE BIGGEST INCREASES IN MOVIE VISITS

| COUNTRY | TOTAL ATTENDANCE 1998 | 1999 | INCREASE |
|---|---|---|---|
| 1 Mexico | 104,000,000 | 120,000,000 | 16,000,000 |
| 2 Australia | 80,000,000 | 88,000,000 | 8,000,000 |
| 3 Poland | 19,900,000 | 26,620,000 | 6,720,000 |
| 4 UK | 136,500,000 | 140,260,000 | 3,760,000 |
| 5 Finland | 6,320,000 | 7,040,000 | 720,000 |
| 6 New Zealand | 16,270,000 | 16,760,000 | 490,000 |
| 7 Germany | 148,880,000 | 149,000,000 | 120,000 |
| 8 Sweden | 15,890,000 | 15,980,000 | 90,000 |
| 9 Iceland | 1,510,000 | 1,570,000 | 60,000 |
| 10 Spain | 112,140,000 | 131,350,000 | 19,210 |

Source: Screen Digest

### TOP 10 MOST PROLIFIC FILM-PRODUCING COUNTRIES

*(Country/films produced, 1999)*

❶ India, 764 ❷ US, 628 ❸ Japan, 270 ❹ Philippines, 220 ❺ France, 181 ❻ Hong Kong, 146 ❼ Italy, 108 ❽ Spain, 97 ❾ UK, 92 ❿ China, 85

Source: Screen Digest

**JUDY'S RUBY SLIPPERS**

*One of several pairs made for her most famous role, the ruby slippers worn by Judy Garland in* The Wizard of Oz *top the list of expensive film memorabilia.*

## TOP 10 ★
# COUNTRIES IN WHICH THE TOP FILM TAKES THE LARGEST SHARE OF THE BOX OFFICE

| COUNTRY | TOP FILM'S PERCENTAGE OF BOX OFFICE, 1998 |
|---|---|
| 1 Poland | 24.2 |
| 2 Japan | 18.3 |
| 3 Denmark | 16.9 |
| 4 Sweden | 16.5 |
| 5 Czech Republic | 15.5 |
| 6 Norway | 14.7 |
| 7 Argentina | 14.1 |
| 8 France | 12.2 |
| 9 = Germany | 12.1 |
| = UK | 12.1 |

Source: Screen Digest

## TOP 10 ★
# MOVIE-GOING COUNTRIES

| COUNTRY | TOTAL ATTENDANCE, 1999 |
|---|---|
| 1 India | 2,860,000,000 |
| 2 US | 1,465,200,000 |
| 3 Indonesia | 222,200,000 |
| 4 France | 155,500,000 |
| 5 Germany | 149,000,000 |
| 6 Japan | 144,760,000 |
| 7 UK | 140,260,000 |
| 8 Spain | 131,350,000 |
| 9 China | 121,000,000 |
| 10 Mexico | 120,000,000 |

Source: Screen Digest

Countries such as the former Soviet Union and China have long reported massive movie attendance figures – the latter once claiming a figure of over 20 billion. However, such inflated statistics include local screenings of propaganda films in mobile movie theaters as well as the commercial feature films on which this list is based. Ranked on a per capita basis, Iceland edges ahead of the US with 5.71 annual movie visits per person compared with the US's 5.45, while India drops out of the Top 10 with 2.99.

## TOP 10 ★
# COUNTRIES WITH THE MOST MOVIE THEATERS

| COUNTRY | MOVIE SCREENS |
|---|---|
| 1 China | 65,000 |
| 2 US | 37,185 |
| 3 India | 12,900 |
| 4 France | 5,000 |
| 5 Germany | 4,651 |
| 6 Spain | 3,343 |
| 7 UK | 2,825 |
| 8 Italy | 2,740 |
| 9 Canada | 2,685 |
| 10 Indonesia | 2,100 |

Source: Screen Digest

## TOP 10 ★
# COUNTRIES WITH THE MOST BOX OFFICE REVENUE

| COUNTRY | BOX OFFICE REVENUE, 1999 ($) |
|---|---|
| 1 US | 7,490,000,000 |
| 2 UK | 1,037,800,000 |
| 3 France | 891,100,000 |
| 4 Germany | 860,900,000 |
| 5 Italy | 566,700,000 |
| 6 Spain | 528,200,000 |
| 7 Canada | 399,000,000 |
| 8 Switzerland | 135,100,000 |
| 9 Belgium | 113,700,000 |
| 10 Netherlands | 111,400,000 |

Source: Screen Digest

## TOP 10 ★
# FILM-RELEASING COUNTRIES

| COUNTRY* | NEW RELEASES, 1999 |
|---|---|
| 1 Japan | 568 |
| 2 Spain | 505 |
| 3 Belgium | 500 |
| 4 France# | 448 |
| 5 US | 442 |
| 6 Taiwan# | 441 |
| 7 Hong Kong | 439 |
| 8 Italy | 423 |
| 9 UK | 387 |
| 10 South Korea | 370 |

\* No reliable figures available for India
\# 1998 figure

Source: Screen Digest

## TOP 10 ★
# COUNTRIES SPENDING THE MOST ON FILM PRODUCTION

| COUNTRY | INVESTMENT, 1999 ($) |
|---|---|
| 1 US | 8,699,000,000 |
| 2 Japan | 1,053,160,000 |
| 3 UK | 817,850,000 |
| 4 France | 732,580,000 |
| 5 Bulgaria | 544,020,000 |
| 6 Germany | 380,450,000 |
| 7 Canada | 225,950,000 |
| 8 Italy | 171,100,000 |
| 9 Spain | 168,460,000 |
| 10 Argentina | 133,330,000 |

Source: Screen Digest

# TOP 10 COUNTRIES WITH THE BIGGEST INCREASE IN FILM PRODUCTION
*(Country/percentage increase in production, 1989–98)*

**1** Ireland, 400.0  **2** Luxembourg, 200.0  **3** UK, 117.5  **4** Iceland, 100.0
**5** New Zealand, 75.0  **6** Australia, 72.7  **7** Norway, 55.6  **8** Venezuela, 42.9
**9** France, 33.6  **10** = Austria, 33.3;  = Brazil, 33.3

Source: Screen Digest

**Did You Know?** The longest nonstop film screening ran for 250 hours in Montreal, Canada, from midnight on Thursday, June 11 to dawn on Monday, June 22, 1992. Only one person sat through all of the 136 films that were shown.

# Film Music

## MUSICAL FILMS

| | FILM | YEAR |
|---|---|---|
| 1 | *Grease* | 1978 |
| 2 | *Saturday Night Fever* | 1977 |
| 3 | *The Sound of Music* | 1965 |
| 4 | *Evita* | 1996 |
| 5 | *The Rocky Horror Picture Show* | 1975 |
| 6 | *Staying Alive* | 1983 |
| 7 | *American Graffiti* | 1973 |
| 8 | *Mary Poppins* | 1964 |
| 9 | *Flashdance* | 1983 |
| 10 | *Fantasia 2000* | 2000 |

## POP MUSIC FILMS

| | FILM | YEAR |
|---|---|---|
| 1 | *Spice World* | 1997 |
| 2 | *Purple Rain* | 1984 |
| 3 | *The Blues Brothers* | 1980 |
| 4 | *La Bamba* | 1987 |
| 5 | *What's Love Got to Do With It?* | 1993 |
| 6 | *The Doors* | 1991 |
| 7 | *Blues Brothers 2000* | 1998 |
| 8 | *The Wall* | 1982 |
| 9 | *The Commitments* | 1991 |
| 10 | *Sgt. Pepper's Lonely Hearts Club Band* | 1978 |

## JAMES BOND FILM THEMES IN THE US

| | THEME/ARTIST OR GROUP | YEAR |
|---|---|---|
| 1 | *A View to a Kill*, Duran Duran | 1985 |
| 2 | *Nobody Does It Better* (from *The Spy Who Loved Me*), Carly Simon | 1977 |
| 3 | *Live and Let Die*, Paul McCartney and Wings | 1973 |
| 4 | *For Your Eyes Only*, Sheena Easton | 1981 |
| 5 | *Goldfinger*, Shirley Bassey | 1965 |
| 6 | *Thunderball*, Tom Jones | 1966 |
| 7 | *All Time High* (from *Octopussy*), Rita Coolidge | 1983 |
| 8 | *You Only Live Twice*, Nancy Sinatra | 1967 |
| 9 | *Diamonds Are Forever*, Shirley Bassey | 1972 |
| 10 | *Goldfinger*, John Barry | 1965 |

Not all the James Bond themes have been major US hits, especially those from the later movies, which failed to register at all. Only the first seven songs listed here made the Top 40.

## TOP 10 SOUNDTRACK ALBUMS IN THE US

*(Album/sales)*

❶ *The Bodyguard*, 17,000,000 ❷ *Purple Rain*, 13,000,000 ❸ *Forrest Gump*, 12,000,000 ❹ = *Dirty Dancing*, 11,000,000; = *Titanic*, 11,000,000 ❻ *The Lion King*, 10,000,000 ❼ *Top Gun*, 9,000,000 ❽ = *Footloose*, 8,000,000; = *Grease*, 8,000,000 ❿ *Saturday Night Fever*, 7,500,000    Source: *RIAA*

## "BEST SONG" OSCAR-WINNING SINGLES IN THE US

| | SINGLE/ARTIST OR GROUP | YEAR |
|---|---|---|
| 1 | *You Light up My Life*, Debby Boone | 1977 |
| 2 | *Up Where We Belong*, Joe Cocker and Jennifer Warnes | 1982 |
| 3 | *Love Theme* (from *A Star Is Born/Evergreen*), Barbra Streisand | 1976 |
| 4 | *My Heart Will Go On*, Celine Dion | 1997 |
| 5 | *I Just Called to Say I Love You*, Stevie Wonder | 1984 |
| 6 | *Arthur's Theme (Best That You Can Do)*, Christopher Cross | 1981 |
| 7 | *The Way We Were*, Barbra Streisand | 1973 |
| 8 | *A Whole New World*, Peabo Bryson and Regina Belle | 1992 |
| 9 | *Raindrops Keep Falling on My Head*, B. J. Thomas | 1969 |
| 10 | *(I've Had the) Time of My Life*, Bill Medley and Jennifer Warnes | 1987 |

Source: *The Popular Music Database*

### ON AND ON

*Featured in the world's most successful film,* Titanic, *Celine Dion's* My Heart Will Go On *became one of the best-selling Oscar-winning singles of all time.*

**BREAKFAST AT TIFFANY'S**

*Sung by Audrey Hepburn in the film Breakfast at Tiffany's, Oscar-winning song Moon River became a chart hit for Andy Williams in the US and for Danny Williams in the UK.*

# THE 10 ★
## LATEST "BEST SONG" OSCAR WINNERS

| YEAR | SONG/FILM |
| --- | --- |
| 2000 | *Things Have Changed*, Wonder Boys |
| 1999 | *You'll Be in My Heart*, Tarzan |
| 1998 | *When You Believe*, The Prince of Egypt |
| 1997 | *My Heart Will Go On*, Titanic |
| 1996 | *You Must Love Me*, Evita |
| 1995 | *Colors of the Wind*, Pocahontas |
| 1994 | *Can You Feel the Love Tonight*, The Lion King |
| 1993 | *Streets of Philadelphia*, Philadelphia |
| 1992 | *Whole New World*, Aladdin |
| 1991 | *Beauty and the Beast*, Beauty and the Beast |

# TOP 10 ★
## "BEST SONG" OSCAR WINNERS OF THE 1980s

| YEAR | SONG/FILM |
| --- | --- |
| 1980 | *Fame*, Fame |
| 1981 | *Up Where We Belong*, An Officer and a Gentleman |
| 1982 | *Arthur's Theme (Best That You Can Do)*, Arthur |
| 1983 | *Flashdance*, Flashdance |
| 1984 | *I Just Called to Say I Love You*, The Woman in Red |
| 1985 | *Say You, Say Me*, White Nights |
| 1986 | *Take My Breath Away*, Top Gun |
| 1987 | *(I've Had) The Time of My Life*, Dirty Dancing |
| 1988 | *Let the River Run*, Working Girl |
| 1989 | *Under the Sea*, The Little Mermaid |

# TOP 10 ★
## "BEST SONG" OSCAR WINNERS OF THE 1970s

| YEAR | SONG/FILM |
| --- | --- |
| 1970 | *For All We Know*, Lovers and Other Strangers |
| 1971 | *Theme from Shaft*, Shaft |
| 1972 | *The Morning After*, The Poseidon Adventure |
| 1973 | *The Way We Were*, The Way We Were |
| 1974 | *We May Never Love Like This Again*, The Towering Inferno |
| 1975 | *I'm Easy*, Nashville |
| 1976 | *Evergreen*, A Star Is Born |
| 1977 | *You Light up My Life*, You Light up My Life |
| 1978 | *Last Dance*, Thank God It's Friday |
| 1979 | *It Goes Like It Goes*, Norma Rae |

# TOP 10 ★
## "BEST SONG" OSCAR WINNERS OF THE 1960s

| YEAR | SONG/FILM |
| --- | --- |
| 1960 | *Never on Sunday*, Never on Sunday |
| 1961 | *Moon River*, Breakfast at Tiffany's |
| 1962 | *Days of Wine and Roses*, Days of Wine and Roses |
| 1963 | *Call Me Irresponsible*, Papa's Delicate Condition |
| 1964 | *Chim Chim Cheree*, Mary Poppins |
| 1965 | *The Shadow of Your Smile*, The Sandpiper |
| 1966 | *Born Free*, Born Free |
| 1967 | *Talk to the Animals*, Dr. Doolittle |
| 1968 | *The Windmills of Your Mind*, The Thomas Crown Affair |
| 1969 | *Raindrops Keep Falling on My Head*, Butch Cassidy and the Sundance Kid |

**Did You Know?** First-ever "Best Song" Oscar winner *The Continental*, from the 1934 film *The Gay Divorcee*, entered the charts 42 years later when it was released by Maureen McGovern.

# Animated Action

## ANIMATED FILMS

| | | |
|---|---|---|
| 1 | The Lion King | 1994 |
| 2 | Toy Story 2 | 1999 |
| 3 | Aladdin | 1992 |
| 4 | Tarzan | 1999 |
| 5 | A Bug's Life | 1998 |
| 6 | Toy Story | 1995 |
| 7 | Beauty and the Beast | 1991 |
| 8 | Who Framed Roger Rabbit* | 1988 |
| 9 | Pocahontas | 1995 |
| 10 | The Hunchback of Notre Dame | 1996 |

*\* Part animated, part live action*

The 1990s provided nine of the 10 most successful animated films of all time, which in turn ejected a number of their high-earning predecessors from this Top 10. Animated films stand out among the leading moneymakers of each decade: *Snow White* was the second highest earning film of the 1930s (after *Gone With the Wind*), while *Bambi*, *Fantasia*, *Cinderella*, and, through additional earnings from its rerelease, *Pinocchio* were the four most successful films of the 1940s.

## FIRST TOM AND JERRY CARTOONS

| | CARTOON | RELEASE DATE |
|---|---|---|
| 1 | Puss Gets The Boot* | Feb 20, 1940 |
| 2 | The Midnight Snack | July 19, 1941 |
| 3 | The Night Before Christmas* | Dec 6, 1941 |
| 4 | Fraidy Cat | Jan 17, 1942 |
| 5 | Dog Trouble | Apr 18, 1942 |
| 6 | Puss 'N' Toots | May 30, 1942 |
| 7 | The Bowling Alley-Cat | July 18, 1942 |
| 8 | Fine Feathered Friend | Oct 10, 1942 |
| 9 | Sufferin' Cats! | Jan 16, 1943 |
| 10 | The Lonesome Mouse | May 22, 1943 |

*\* Academy Award nomination; although in their debut Tom is called Jasper and the mouse is unnamed*

Created by William Hanna and Joseph Barbera, Tom and Jerry have been perennially popular during six decades. Hannah and Barbera directed 114 cartoons featuring them from 1940 to 1958, when MGM closed its animation department.

## FIRST FULL-LENGTH SIMPSONS EPISODES

| | EPISODE | FIRST SCREENED |
|---|---|---|
| 1 | Simpsons Roasting on an Open Fire | Dec 17, 1989 |
| 2 | Bart the Genius | Jan 14, 1990 |
| 3 | Homer's Odyssey | Jan 21, 1990 |
| 4 | There's No Disgrace Like Homer | Jan 28, 1990 |
| 5 | Bart the General | Feb 4, 1990 |
| 6 | Moaning Lisa | Feb 11, 1990 |
| 7 | The Call of the Simpsons | Feb 18, 1990 |
| 8 | The Telltale Head | Feb 25, 1990 |
| 9 | Life in the Fast Lane | Mar 18, 1990 |
| 10 | Homer's Night Out | Mar 25, 1990 |

Matt Groening's enormously successful animated series originally appeared in 1987 as short episodes screened on the Tracey Ullman Show.

## FIRST DISNEY ANIMATED FEATURES

| | | |
|---|---|---|
| 1 | Snow White and the Seven Dwarfs | 1937 |
| 2 | Pinocchio | 1940 |
| 3 | Fantasia | 1940 |
| 4 | Dumbo | 1941 |
| 5 | Bambi | 1942 |
| 6 | Victory Through Air Power | 1943 |
| 7 | The Three Caballeros | 1945 |
| 8 | Make Mine Music | 1946 |
| 9 | Fun and Fancy Free | 1947 |
| 10 | Melody Time | 1948 |

Excluding part-animated films such as *Song of the South* and *Mary Poppins*, and films made specially for television serialization, Disney had made a total of 42 full-length animated feature films by the end of 2000.

### SMALL SOLDIERS, BIG SUCCESS

*Part animation/part live-action films are comparatively rare, but* Small Soldiers *stands out as the highest earner of the last year of the 20th century.*

## PART ANIMATION/PART LIVE-ACTION FILMS

| | | | | | |
|---|---|---|---|---|---|
| 1 | Who Framed Roger Rabbit | 1988 | 6 | Small Soldiers | 1999 |
| 2 | Casper | 1995 | 7 | Song of the South | 1946 |
| 3 | Space Jam | 1996 | 8 | Fantasia 2000 | 2000 |
| 4 | 9 to 5 | 1980 | 9 | James and the Giant Peach | 1996 |
| 5 | Mary Poppins | 1964 | 10 | Pete's Dragon | 1977 |

**MONSTER MOVIE**

*Riding high on 1999's preeminent marketing phenomenon,* Pokémon The First Movie *earned over $150 million worldwide.*

## TOP 10 ★
### NON-DISNEY ANIMATED FEATURE FILMS

| | | |
|---|---|---|
| 1 | *The Prince of Egypt* | 1998 |
| 2 | *Chicken Run* | 2000 |
| 3 | *Antz* | 1998 |
| 4 | *Pokémon The First Movie: Mewtwo Strikes Back* | 1999 |
| 5 | *Pocket Monsters Revelation Lugia* | 1999 |
| 6 | *The Rugrats Movie* | 1998 |
| 7 | *South Park: Bigger, Longer and Uncut* | 1999 |
| 8 | *The Land Before Time* | 1988 |
| 9 | *Pokémon: The Movie 2000* | 2000 |
| 10 | *An American Tail* | 1986 |

Such was the success of *Pocket Monsters Revelation Lugia* in Japan that it earned a place in this list even before being released internationally.

## THE 10 ★
### FIRST BUGS BUNNY CARTOONS

| | TITLE | RELEASED |
|---|---|---|
| 1 | *Porky's Hare Hunt* | Apr 30, 1938 |
| 2 | *Hare-um Scare-um* | Aug 12, 1939 |
| 3 | *Elmer's Candid Camera* | Mar 2, 1940 |
| 4 | *A Wild Hare* | July 27, 1940 |
| 5 | *Elmer's Pet Rabbit* | Jan 4, 1941 |
| 6 | *Tortoise Beats Hare* | Mar 15, 1941 |
| 7 | *Hiawatha's Rabbit Hunt* | June 7, 1941 |
| 8 | *The Heckling Hare* | July 5, 1941 |
| 9 | *All This and Rabbit Stew* | Sep 13, 1941 |
| 10 | *Wabbit Twouble* | Dec 20, 1941 |

Bugs Bunny's debut was as a costar alongside Porky Pig in *Porky's Hare Hunt*, but he was not named until the release of *Elmer's Pet Rabbit*. *A Wild Hare* was the first in which he said the line that became his trademark: "Eh, what's up, Doc?"

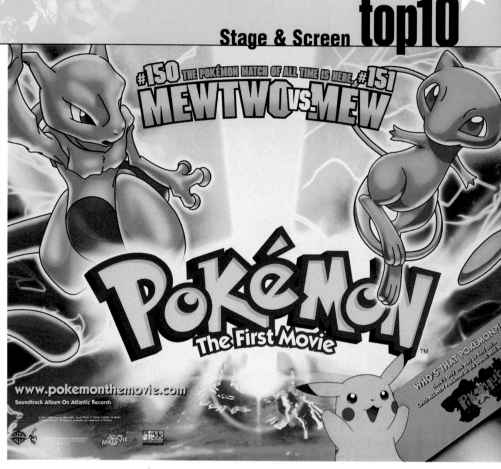

## THE 10 ★
### FIRST OSCAR-WINNING ANIMATED FILMS*

| | FILM | YEAR |
|---|---|---|
| 1 | *Flowers and Trees* | 1931/32 |
| 2 | *The Three Little Pigs* | 1932/33 |
| 3 | *The Tortoise and the Hare* | 1934 |
| 4 | *Three Orphan Kittens* | 1935 |
| 5 | *The Country Cousin* | 1936 |
| 6 | *The Old Mill* | 1937 |
| 7 | *Ferdinand the Bull* | 1938 |
| 8 | *The Ugly Duckling* | 1939 |
| 9 | *The Milky Way* | 1940 |
| 10 | *Lend a Paw* | 1941 |

\* In the category "Short Subjects (Cartoons)"

With the exception of *The Milky Way*, which was directed by Rudolf Ising, all were directed by Walt Disney. Oscars were awarded in the category "Short Subjects (Cartoons)" until 1971, when it was altered to "Short Subjects (Animated Films)"; in 1974 it changed again, to "Short Films (Animated)."

## THE 10 ★
### LATEST OSCAR-WINNING ANIMATED FILMS*

| YEAR | FILM/DIRECTOR/COUNTRY |
|---|---|
| 2000 | *Father and Daughter*, Michel Dudok de Wit, Netherlands |
| 1999 | *The Old Man and the Sea*, Aleksandr Petrov, US |
| 1998 | *Bunny*, Chris Wedge, US |
| 1997 | *Geri's Game*, Jan Pinkava, US |
| 1996 | *Quest*, Tyron Montgomery, UK |
| 1995 | *A Close Shave*, Nick Park, UK |
| 1994 | *Bob's Birthday*, David Fine and Alison Snowden, UK |
| 1993 | *The Wrong Trousers*, Nick Park, UK |
| 1992 | *Mona Lisa Descending a Staircase*, Joan C. Gratz, US |
| 1991 | *Manipulation*, Daniel Greaves, UK |

\* In the category "Short Films (Animated)"

**What is the name of the character played by Michael J. Fox in the *Back to the Future* films?**
*see p.161 for the answer*

A Minty Maclean
B Marty McFly
C Mickey McQueen

# On the Radio

TOP 10

## STATES WITH THE MOST NATIONAL PUBLIC RADIO MEMBER STATIONS

| | STATE | NPR STATIONS |
|---|---|---|
| 1 | New York | 42 |
| 2 | California | 35 |
| 3 | Michigan | 31 |
| 4 | Ohio | 25 |
| 5 | Wisconsin | 22 |
| 6 | Alaska | 21 |
| 7 | Texas | 19 |
| 8 | =Colorado | 17 |
| | =Florida | 17 |
| | =North Carolina | 17 |
| | =Wyoming | 17 |

Source: National Public Radio

## TOP 10

## RADIO FORMATS IN THE US BY NUMBER OF STATIONS

| | FORMAT | STATIONS |
|---|---|---|
| 1 | Country | 2,320 |
| 2 | News/Talk | 1,695 |
| 3 | Adult Contemporary | 784 |
| 4 | Oldies | 771 |
| 5 | Religion (teaching and variety) | 703 |
| 6 | Adult Standards | 602 |
| 7 | Spanish | 600 |
| 8 | Contemporary Christian | 529 |
| 9 | CHR (Top 40) | 439 |
| 10 | Variety | 436 |

Source: M Street

## TOP 10

## RADIO-OWNING COUNTRIES

| | COUNTRY | RADIO SETS PER 1,000 POPULATION* |
|---|---|---|
| 1 | US | 2,116 |
| 2 | Finland | 1,498 |
| 3 | UK | 1,443 |
| 4 | Gibraltar | 1,429 |
| 5 | Guam | 1,400 |
| 6 | Australia | 1,391 |
| 7 | Denmark | 1,145 |
| 8 | Canada | 1,067 |
| 9 | Monaco | 1,039 |
| 10 | New Zealand | 997 |

* In latest year for which data available

Source: UNESCO

## TOP 10

## FASTEST-GROWING RADIO MARKETS IN THE US

| | MARKET | PERCENTAGE INCREASE IN REVENUE (1996–2000) |
|---|---|---|
| 1 | San Francisco | 140.3 |
| 2 | Atlanta | 117.1 |
| 3 | Las Vegas | 110.5 |
| 4 | Austin | 110.1 |
| 5 | Raleigh | 105.9 |
| 6 | Boston | 101.9 |
| 7 | Wilmington, North Carolina | 100.0 |
| 8 | Phoenix | 94.9 |
| 9 | Seattle | 94.3 |
| 10 | Los Angeles | 94.0 |

Source: Duncan's Radio

During the year 1999–2000, San Jose showed the greatest growth in revenue for radio, at 26.1 percent.

## THE 10

## LATEST GEORGE FOSTER PEABODY AWARDS FOR BROADCASTING WON BY NATIONAL PUBLIC RADIO*

| YEAR | AWARD WINNER |
|---|---|
| 2000 | The NPR 100 |
| 1999 | =Lost & Found Sound |
| | =Morning Edition with Bob Edwards |
| 1998 | =Coverage of Africa |
| | =I Must Keep Fightin': The Art of Paul Robeson |
| | =Performance Today |
| 1997 | Jazz from Lincoln Center |
| 1996 | Remorse: The 14 Stories of Eric Morse |
| 1995 | Wynton Marsalis: Making the Music/Marsalis on Music |
| 1994 | Tobacco Stories and Wade in the Water: African American Sacred Music Traditions (NPR/Smithsonian Institution) |

* Includes only programs made or coproduced by NPR

Source: Peabody Awards

## THE 10

## LATEST NAB MARCONI ROCK STATIONS OF THE YEAR

| YEAR* | STATION/LOCATION |
|---|---|
| 2000 | WFBQ, Indianapolis, Indiana |
| 1999 | WEBN, Cincinnati, Ohio |
| 1998 | WFBQ-FM, Indianapolis, Indiana |
| 1997 | WDVE-FM, Pittsburgh, Pennsylvania |
| 1996 | WFBQ-FM, Indianapolis, Indiana |
| 1995 | KROQ-FM, Los Angeles, California |
| 1994 | KQRS-AM/FM, El Paso, Texas |
| 1993 | WXRT-FM, Chicago, Illinois |
| 1992 | KLOS-FM, Los Angeles, California |
| 1991 | KLOS-FM, Los Angeles, California |

* Prior to 1994, the award was for AOR/Classic rock.

## TOP 10 TIMES OF DAY FOR IN-CAR RADIO

(Time of day)

1 7.00–7.15 am 2 7.15–7.30 am 3 5.00–5.15 pm 4 5.15–5.30 pm 5 6.45–7.00 am
6 7.45–8.00 am 7 5.30–5.45 pm 8 6.45–7.00 am 9 4.15–4.30 pm 10 8.00–8.15 am

Source: Research Director, 1999 PD Profile®

## THE 10 ⭐
# LATEST NAB MARCONI NETWORK/SYNDICATED PERSONALITIES OF THE YEAR

| YEAR | WINNER/NETWORK OR SYNDICATION |
|------|-------------------------------|
| 2000 | Rush Limbaugh, Premiere Radio Networks |
| 1999 | Bob Kevoian and Tom Griswold, AMFM Radio Networks |
| 1998 | Paul Harvey, ABC Radio Networks |
| 1997 | Dr. Laura Schlessinger, Synergy Broadcasting |
| 1996 | Paul Harvey, ABC Radio Networks |
| 1995 | Rush Limbaugh, EFM Media Management |
| 1994 | Don Imus, Westwood One Radio Networks |
| 1993 | Charles Osgood, CBS Radio Networks |
| 1992 | Rush Limbaugh, EFM Media Management |
| 1991 | Paul Harvey, ABC Radio Networks |

The US National Association of Broadcasters presents annual awards in 22 different categories. They are known as the Marconi Awards in honor of radio pioneer, inventor, and 1909 Nobel Physics Prize winner Guglielmo Marconi.

## THE 10 ⭐
# LATEST NAB MARCONI NEWS/TALK/SPORT STATIONS OF THE YEAR

| YEAR* | STATION/LOCATION |
|-------|------------------|
| 2000 | WTMJ, Milwaukee, Wisconsin |
| 1999 | WBZ, Boston, Massachusetts |
| 1998 | WCCO-AM, Minneapolis, Minnesota |
| 1997 | KFGO-AM, Fargo, North Dakota |
| 1996 | WFAN-AM, New York, New York |
| 1995 | WLS-AM, Chicago, Illinois |
| 1994 | KRLD-AM, Dallas, Texas |
| 1993 | WGN-AM, Chicago, Illinois |
| 1992 | KGO-AM, San Francisco, California |
| 1991 | KABC-AM, Los Angeles, California |

* Prior to 1994 the award was for news/talk

## THE 10 ⭐
# LATEST NAB MARCONI OLDIES STATIONS OF THE YEAR

| YEAR* | STATION/LOCATION |
|-------|------------------|
| 2000 | WOMC, Detroit, Michigan |
| 1999 | WWSW, Pittsburgh, Pennsylvania |
| 1998 | WBIG-FM, Washington, DC |
| 1997 | WWSW-AM/FM, Pittsburgh, Pennsylvania |
| 1996 | WQSR-FM, Baltimore, Maryland |
| 1995 | WWSW-AM/FM, Pittsburgh, Pennsylvania |
| 1993 | WCBS-FM, New York, New York |
| 1992 | KOOL-FM, Phoenix, Arizona |
| 1991 | WCBS-FM, New York, New York |
| 1990 | WCBS-FM, New York, New York |

* No award in this category in 19940

## THE 10 ⭐
# LATEST NAB MARCONI LEGENDARY STATIONS OF THE YEAR

| YEAR | STATION/LOCATION |
|------|------------------|
| 2000 | WEBN, Cincinnati, Ohio |
| 1999 | KOA, Denver, Colorado |
| 1998 | WCBS-FM, New York, New York |
| 1997 | KVIL-FM, Dallas, Texas |
| 1996 | WJR-AM, Detroit, Michigan |
| 1995 | KGO-AM, San Francisco, California |
| 1994 | KDKA-AM, Pittsburgh, Pennsylvania |
| 1993 | WHO-AM, Des Moines, Iowa |
| 1992 | WCCO-AM, Minneapolis, Minnesota |
| 1991 | KMOX-AM, St. Louis, Missouri |

Unlike the National Association of Broadcasters' other awards (which are concerned with a station's or personality's achievements during the preceding year), the "Legendary Station" award can be presented only once to a station. It recognizes overall excellence in radio, and considers the station's history and heritage. A task force of broadcasters chooses five finalists, with the eventual winner being voted on by their peers.

## THE 10 ⭐
# LATEST NAB HALL OF FAME INDUCTEES

| YEAR | INDUCTEE |
|------|----------|
| 2001 | Bruce Morrow, radio personality |
| 2000 | Tom Joyner, radio personality |
| 1999 | Wolfman Jack, radio personality |
| 1998 | Rush Limbaugh, radio personality |
| 1997 | Wally Phillips, radio personality |
| 1996 | Don Imus, radio personality |
| 1995 | Gary Owens, radio personality |
| 1994 | Harry Caray, radio sportscaster |
| 1993 | Grand Ole Opry, radio program |
| 1992 | Larry King, radio personality |

Since 1977, the National Association of Broadcasters' Hall of Fame has been honoring radio personalities and programs that have earned a place in US broadcasting history. Among its earlier inductees were Orson Welles and Bing Crosby, while two US Presidents have also been included: Herbert Hoover in 1977 and former radio sportscaster Ronald Reagan in 1981.

## TOP 10 ⭐
# LONGEST-RUNNING PROGRAMS ON NATIONAL PUBLIC RADIO

| | PROGRAM | FIRST BROADCAST |
|---|---------|-----------------|
| 1 | All Things Considered | 1971 |
| 2 | Weekend All Things Considered | 1974 |
| 3 | Fresh Air with Terry Gross | 1977 |
| 4 | Marian McPartland's Piano Jazz | 1978 |
| 5 | Morning Edition | 1979 |
| 6 | Weekend Edition/ Saturday with Scott Simon | 1985 |
| 7 | Performance Today | 1987 |
| 8 | Weekend Edition/ Sunday with Liane Hansen | 1987 |
| 9 | Car Talk | 1987 |
| 10 | Talk of the Nation | 1991 |

All Things Considered, the longest-running NPR program, was first broadcast on May 3, 1971.

Source: National Public Radio

# Top TV

## TV REVENUE-EARNING COMPANIES

| COMPANY/COUNTRY | TV REVENUE IN 1999 ($) |
|---|---|
| 1 Time Warner, US | 18,802,000,000 |
| 2 Viacom, US | 7,663,600,000 |
| 3 Walt Disney, US | 7,512,000,000 |
| 4 GE/NBC, US | 5,790,000,000 |
| 5 NHK, Japan | 5,275,700,000 |
| 6 CBS, US | 4,915,000,000 |
| 7 AT&T, US | 4,871,000,000 |
| 8 News Corporation, Australia | 4,004,700,000 |
| 9 Cablevision, US | 3,943,000,000 |
| 10 DirecTV, US | 3,785,000,000 |

Source: Television Business International

## PRIMETIME PROGRAMS ON US TELEVISION, 1999–2000

| PROGRAM | DATE | VIEWERS |
|---|---|---|
| 1 The Academy Awards | Mar 26, 2000 | 29,437,000 |
| 2 Who Wants to Be a Millionaire? | May 1, 2000 | 22,715,000 |
| 3 Who Wants to Be a Millionaire? | Mar 1, 2000 | 20,862,000 |
| 4 Countdown to the Oscars 2000 | Mar 26, 2000 | 20,795,000 |
| 5 Who Wants to Be a Millionaire? | Jan 12, 2000 | 20,722,000 |
| 6 Who Wants to Be a Millionaire? | Feb 2, 2000 | 20,304,000 |
| 7 ER | Oct 7, 1999 | 19,993,000 |
| 8 Who Wants to Be a Millionaire? | Feb 28, 2000 | 18,962,000 |
| 9 Who Wants to Be a Millionaire? | Jan 27, 2000 | 18,864,000 |
| 10 Who Wants to Be a Millionaire? | Jan 18, 2000 | 18,726,000 |

Source: Nielsen Media Research

## TELEVISION-WATCHING COUNTRIES*

| COUNTRY | AVERAGE DAILY VIEWING TIME HRS | MINS |
|---|---|---|
| 1 US | 3 | 58 |
| 2 Greece | 3 | 39 |
| 3 = Italy | 3 | 36 |
| = UK | 3 | 36 |
| 5 Spain | 3 | 31 |
| 6 = Canada | 3 | 14 |
| = Ireland | 3 | 14 |
| 8 Germany | 3 | 8 |
| 9 France | 3 | 7 |
| 10 Belgium | 2 | 57 |

* In Western Europe and North America
Source: Screen Digest

A survey of TV-viewing habits in Western Europe and North America showed that the number of channels, including new digital channels, is proliferating at a much faster rate than the time spent actually watching them, thus creating, in the jargon of the industry, "audience fragmentation."

## MOST WATCHED DAYTIME DRAMAS ON US TELEVISION, 1999–2000

| PROGRAM | NETWORK | VIEWERS |
|---|---|---|
| 1 Young and the Restless | CBS | 6,130,000 |
| 2 Bold and the Beautiful | CBS | 4,543,000 |
| 3 Days of Our Lives | NBC | 4,297,000 |
| 4 General Hospital | ABC | 4,219,000 |
| 5 All My Children | ABC | 3,875,000 |
| 6 As the World Turns | CBS | 3,830,000 |
| 7 Guiding Light | CBS | 3,535,000 |
| 8 One Life to Live | ABC | 3,477,000 |
| 9 Port Charles | ABC | 2,080,000 |
| 10 Passions | NBC | 2,051,000 |

Source: Nielsen Media Research

## MOST WATCHED PROGRAMS ON PBS TELEVISION

| PROGRAM | BROADCAST | AVERAGE AUDIENCE |
|---|---|---|
| 1 The Civil War | Sep 1990 | 8,800,000 |
| 2 Life On Earth | Jan 1982 | 7,900,000 |
| 3 The Living Planet: A Portrait of the Earth | Feb 1985 | 7,800,000 |
| 4 The American Experience: The Kennedys | Sep 1992 | 7,000,000 |
| 5 Nature: Kingdom of the Ice Bear | Feb 1986 | 6,900,000 |
| 6 Cosmos | Sep 1980 | 6,500,000 |
| 7 = Planet Earth | Jan 1986 | 6,300,000 |
| = Lewis & Clark: The Journey of the Corps of Discovery | Nov 1997 | 6,300,000 |
| 9 The Scarlet Letter | Sep 1979 | 5,700,000 |
| 10 Baseball | Sep 1994 | 5,500,000 |

Source: PBS

## MOST WATCHED TALK SHOWS ON US TELEVISION, 1999–2000

| PROGRAM | VIEWERS |
|---|---|
| 1 Oprah Winfrey Show | 6,265,000 |
| 2 Jerry Springer | 4,180,000 |
| 3 Live! With Regis and Kelly | 3,657,000 |
| 4 Maury Povich Show | 3,520,000 |
| 5 Montel Williams Show | 3,303,000 |
| 6 Sally Jessy Raphael | 3,161,000 |
| 7 Ricki Lake | 2,701,000 |
| 8 The View | 2,583,000 |
| 9 Jenny Jones Show | 2,362,000 |
| 10 Change of Heart | 2,181,000 |

Source: Nielsen Media Research

## TOP 10 ★
### MOST WATCHED MOVIES ON US TELEVISION, 1999–2000

| | MOVIE | NETWORK | VIEWERS |
|---|---|---|---|
| 1 | ABC Original: *Tuesdays with Morrie* | ABC | 15,321,000 |
| 2 | ABC Premiere Event: *The Beach Boys, Part 1* | ABC | 11,368,000 |
| 3 | ABC Premiere Event: *Arabian Nights, Part 1* | ABC | 11,298,000 |
| 4 | CBS Sunday Movie: *Song from the Heart* | CBS | 10,756,000 |
| 5 | *Murder She Wrote* special: *A Story to Die For* | CBS | 9,589,000 |
| 6 | CBS Tuesday Movie Special: *Aftershock: Earthquake in New York, Part 2* | CBS | 9,371,000 |
| 7 | ABC Monday Night Movie: *Jack* | ABC | 9,066,000 |
| 8 | CBS Wednesday Movie: *Final Run* | CBS | 8,848,000 |
| 9 | Buena Vista 1 | Buena Vista Televison | 8,820,000 |
| 10 | Fox Movie Special: *Jerry Maguire* | Fox | 7,806,000 |

Source: *Nielsen Media Research*

## TOP 10 ★
### MOST-WATCHED CHILDREN'S PROGRAMS ON US TELEVISION, 1999–2000

| | PROGRAM | DATE | VIEWERS |
|---|---|---|---|
| 1 | *Pokémon** | Mar 18, 2000 | 3,625,000 |
| 2 | *Batman Beyond* | Feb 5, 2000 | 2,561,000 |
| 3 | *Disney's 1 Saturday Morning* | Sep 25, 2000 | 2,522,000 |
| 4 | *Caitlin's Way* (movie) | Mar 11, 2000 | 2,458,000 |
| 5 | *Rugrats on Vacation* | Dec 10, 2000 | 2,424,000 |
| 6 | *Hang Time* | Oct 2, 2000 | 2,407,000 |
| 7 | *Saved by the Bell* | Oct 2, 2000 | 2,309,000 |
| 8 | *City Guys* | Oct 2, 2000 | 2,289,000 |
| 9 | *Digimon: Digital Monsters* | Mar 25, 2000 | 2,270,000 |
| 10 | *Tiny Toons Adventure* | Jan 29, 2000 | 2,215,000 |

*\* Highest-rated telecast only listed*     Source: *Nielsen Media Research*

### TOP 10 CABLE TELEVISION COUNTRIES
*(Country/subscribers)*

❶ US, 67,011,180 ❷ Germany, 18,740,260 ❸ Netherlands, 6,227,472 ❹ Russia, 5,784,432 ❺ Belgium, 3,945,342 ❻ Poland, 3,830,788 ❼ Romania, 3,000,000 ❽ UK, 2,666,783 ❾ France, 2,478,630 ❿ Switzerland, 2,156,120

Source: *The Phillips Group*

## TOP 10 ★
### NIELSEN'S TV AUDIENCES OF ALL TIME IN THE US

| | PROGRAM | DATE | HOUSEHOLDS TOTAL | VIEWING (%) |
|---|---|---|---|---|
| 1 | *M\*A\*S\*H Special* | Feb 28, 1983 | 50,150,000 | 60.2 |
| 2 | *Dallas* | Nov 21, 1980 | 41,470,000 | 53.3 |
| 3 | *Roots* Part 8 | Jan 30, 1977 | 36,380,000 | 51.1 |
| 4 | Super Bowl XVI | Jan 24, 1982 | 40,020,000 | 49.1 |
| 5 | Super Bowl XVII | Jan 30, 1983 | 40,480,000 | 48.6 |
| 6 | XVII Winter Olympics | Feb 23, 1994 | 45,690,000 | 48.5 |
| 7 | Super Bowl XX | Jan 26, 1986 | 41,490,000 | 48.3 |
| 8 | *Gone With the Wind* Pt.1 | Nov 7, 1976 | 33,960,000 | 47.7 |
| 9 | *Gone With the Wind* Pt.2 | Nov 8, 1976 | 33,750,000 | 47.4 |
| 10 | Super Bowl XII | Jan 15, 1978 | 34,410,000 | 47.2 |

© Copyright 2000 Nielsen Media Research

Historically, as more households acquired television sets (there are currently 98 million "TV households" in the US), audiences generally increased. However, the rise in channel choice and the use of VCRs has somewhat checked this trend. Listing the Top 10 according to percentage of households viewing provides a clearer picture of who watches what.

## TOP 10 ★
### FASTEST-GROWING CABLE AND SATELLITE TV COMPANIES

| | COMPANY/COUNTRY | CABLE AND SATELLITE SUBSCRIBERS 1998 | 1999 | GROWTH % |
|---|---|---|---|---|
| 1 | **BSkyB**, UK | 244,000 | 2,600,000 | 965.6 |
| 2 | **Premiere World**, Germany | 145,000 | 1,300,000 | 796.6 |
| 3 | **Cyfra Plus**, Poland | 60,000 | 295,000 | 391.7 |
| 4 | **Foxtel**, Australia | 40,000 | 131,800 | 229.5 |
| 5 | **Wizja TV**, Poland | 94,000 | 300,000 | 219.1 |
| 6 | **Canal Digitaal** (Flemish), Belgium | 11,900 | 25,400 | 113.4 |
| 7 | **Bell ExpressVu**, Canada | 180,000 | 370,000 | 105.6 |
| 8 | **Tele+**, Italy | 502,300 | 962,000 | 91.5 |
| 9 | **Star Choice**, Canada | 175,000 | 320,000 | 82.9 |
| 10 | **Echostar** (DISH), US | 1,940,000 | 3,410,000 | 75.8 |

Source: *Screen Digest*

The arrival of digital broadcasting and attractive incentives offered by many service providers have attracted large numbers of first-time subscribers.

# TV Awards

## LATEST WINNERS OF THE DAYTIME EMMY AWARD FOR OUTSTANDING CHILDREN'S SPECIAL

SEASON
ENDING PROGRAM

| | |
|---|---|
| 2000 | Summer's End |
| 1999 | The Island on Bird Street |
| 1998 | In His Father's Shoes |
| 1997 | Elmo Saves Christmas |
| 1996 | Stand Up |
| 1995 | A Child Betrayed: The Calvin Mire Story |
| 1994 | Dead Drunk: The Kevin Tunnel Story |
| 1993 | ABC Afterschool Special: Shades of a Single Protein |
| 1992 | Vincent and Me |
| 1991 | Lost in the Barrens |

## LATEST WINNERS OF THE DAYTIME EMMY AWARD FOR OUTSTANDING CHILDREN'S SERIES

SEASON
ENDING PROGRAM

| | |
|---|---|
| 2000 | Bill Nye the Science Guy |
| 1999 | Preschool: Sesame Street School Age: Bill Nye the Science Guy |
| 1998 | Sesame Street |
| 1997 | Preschool: Sesame Street School age: Reading Rainbow |
| 1996 | Reading Rainbow |
| 1995 | Nick News |
| 1994 | Sesame Street |
| 1993 | Reading Rainbow |
| 1992 | Sesame Street |
| 1991 | Sesame Street |

## LATEST WINNERS OF THE DAYTIME EMMY AWARD FOR OUTSTANDING CHILDREN'S ANIMATED PROGRAM

SEASON
ENDING PROGRAM

| | |
|---|---|
| 2000 | Steven Spielberg Presents: Pinky, Elmyra, and the Brain |
| 1999 | Steven Spielberg Presents: Pinky and the Brain |
| 1998 | Arthur |
| 1997 | Animaniacs |
| 1996 | Animaniacs |
| 1995 | Where on Earth is Carmen Santiago |
| 1994 | Rugrats |
| 1993 | Tiny Toon Adventures |
| 1992 | Rugrats |
| 1991 | Tiny Toon Adventures |

## FEMALE PERFORMERS WHO HAVE WON THE MOST EMMYS

| | NAME | EMMYS |
|---|---|---|
| 1 = | Mary Tyler Moore | 8 |
| = | Dinah Shore | 8 |
| 3 = | Carol Burnett | 5 |
| = | Cloris Leachman | 5 |
| = | Lily Tomlin | 5 |
| = | Tracey Ullman | 5 |
| 7 = | Candice Bergen | 4 |
| = | Tyne Daly | 4 |
| = | Valerie Harper | 4 |
| = | Helen Hunt | 4 |
| = | Michael Learned | 4 |
| = | Rhea Perlman | 4 |

The first woman to receive an Emmy was not an actress but a puppeteer called Shirley Dinsdale.

## PROGRAMS WITH THE MOST DAYTIME TV EMMY AWARDS*

| | PROGRAM | NOMINATIONS | WINS |
|---|---|---|---|
| 1 | The Young and the Restless | 244 | 77 |
| 2 | Sesame Street | 205 | 76 |
| 3 | Sixty Minutes | 144 | 58 |
| 4 | Guiding Light | 176 | 54 |
| 5 | All My Children | 268 | 50 |
| 6 | General Hospital | 181 | 43 |
| 7 | The Oprah Winfrey Show | 75 | 34 |
| 8 | The Price is Right | 92 | 29 |
| 9 | One Life to Live | 110 | 27 |
| 10 | The Bold and the Beautiful | 74 | 26 |

* Up to and including 1999/2000 awards

## MALE PERFORMERS WHO HAVE WON THE MOST EMMYS

| | NAME | EMMYS |
|---|---|---|
| 1 | Ed Asner | 7 |
| 2 | Art Carney | 6 |
| 3 = | Alan Alda | 5 |
| = | Dick Van Dyke | 5 |
| = | Peter Falk | 5 |
| = | Hal Holbrook | 5 |
| = | Don Knotts | 5 |
| = | Carroll O'Connor | 5 |
| = | Laurence Olivier | 5 |
| 10 = | Dennis Franz | 4 |
| = | Harvey Korman | 4 |
| = | John Larroquette | 4 |

The actual Emmy (adapted from "immy," the nickname for the image orthicon television camera) is a statuette of a winged figure holding an atom.

# THE 10 LATEST WINNERS OF THE EMMY AWARD FOR OUTSTANDING COMEDY SERIES

*(Season ending/program)*

❶ 2000 *Will and Grace* ❷ 1999 *Ally McBeal* ❸ 1998 *Frasier* ❹ 1997 *Frasier* ❺ 1996 *Frasier* ❻ 1995 *Frasier* ❼ 1994 *Frasier* ❽ 1993 *Seinfeld* ❾ 1992 *Murphy Brown* ❿ 1991 *Cheers*

## THE 10 ⭐
## LATEST WINNERS OF THE EMMY AWARD FOR OUTSTANDING LEAD ACTOR IN A DRAMA SERIES

SEASON
ENDING ACTOR/SERIES

| 2000 | James Gandolfini, *The Sopranos* |
| 1999 | Dennis Franz, *NYPD Blue* |
| 1998 | Andre Braugher, *Homicide: Life on the Street* |
| 1997 | Dennis Franz, *NYPD Blue* |
| 1996 | Dennis Franz, *NYPD Blue* |
| 1995 | Mandy Patinkin, *Chicago Hope* |
| 1994 | Dennis Franz, *NYPD Blue* |
| 1993 | Tom Skerritt, *Picket Fences* |
| 1992 | Christopher Lloyd, *Avonlea* |
| 1991 | James Earl Jones, *Gabriel's Fire* |

## TOP 10 ⭐
## EMMY AWARD-WINNING TV NETWORKS*

| | NETWORK | NOMINATIONS | WINS |
|---|---|---|---|
| 1 | CBS | 3,778 | 1,091 |
| 2 | ABC | 3,083 | 835 |
| 3 | NBC | 3,038 | 737 |
| 4 | PBS | 1,438 | 457 |
| 5 | Syndicated | 835 | 241 |
| 6 | HBO | 170 | 60 |
| 7 | ESPN | 158 | 53 |
| 8 | SYN | 183 | 47 |
| 9 | TBS | 108 | 42 |
| 10 | Fox | 147 | 33 |

* Up to and including 1999/2000 awards

## THE 10 ⭐
## LATEST WINNERS OF THE EMMY AWARD FOR OUTSTANDING LEAD ACTRESS IN A DRAMA SERIES

SEASON
ENDING* ACTRESS/SERIES

| 2000 | Sela Ward, *Once and Again* |
| 1999 | Edie Falco, *The Sopranos* |
| 1998 | Christine Lahti, *Chicago Hope* |
| 1997 | Gillian Anderson, *The X-Files* |
| 1995 | Kathy Baker, *Picket Fences* |
| 1994 | Sela Ward, *Sisters* |
| 1993 | Kathy Baker, *Picket Fences* |
| 1992 | Dana Delaney, *China Beach* |
| 1991 | Patricia Wettig, *thirtysomething* |
| 1990 | Patricia Wettig, *thirtysomething* |

* No award in 1996

## THE 10 ⭐
## LATEST WINNERS OF THE EMMY AWARD FOR OUTSTANDING DRAMA

SEASON
ENDING PROGRAM

| 2000 | *The West Wing* |
| 1999 | *The Practice* |
| 1998 | *The Practice* |
| 1997 | *Law & Order* |
| 1996 | *ER* |
| 1995 | *NYPD Blue* |
| 1994 | *Picket Fences* |
| 1993 | *Picket Fences* |
| 1992 | *Northern Exposure* |
| 1991 | *L.A. Law* |

## THE 10 ⭐
## LATEST WINNERS OF THE EMMY AWARD FOR OUTSTANDING LEAD ACTOR IN A COMEDY SERIES

SEASON
ENDING ACTOR/PROGRAM

| 2000 | Micheal J. Fox, *Spin City* |
| 1999 | John Lithgow, *3rd Rock from the Sun* |
| 1998 | Kelsey Grammer, *Frasier* |
| 1997 | John Lithgow, *3rd Rock from the Sun* |
| 1996 | John Lithgow, *3rd Rock from the Sun* |
| 1995 | Kelsey Grammer, *Frasier* |
| 1994 | Kelsey Grammer, *Frasier* |
| 1993 | Ted Danson, *Cheers* |
| 1992 | Craig T. Nelson, *Coach* |
| 1991 | Burt Reynolds, *Evening Shade* |

## THE 10 ⭐
## LATEST WINNERS OF THE EMMY AWARD FOR OUTSTANDING LEAD ACTRESS IN A COMEDY SERIES

SEASON
ENDING ACTRESS/PROGRAM

| 2000 | Patricia Heaton, *Everybody Loves Raymond* |
| 1999 | Helen Hunt, *Mad About You* |
| 1998 | Helen Hunt, *Mad About You* |
| 1997 | Helen Hunt, *Mad About You* |
| 1996 | Helen Hunt, *Mad About You* |
| 1995 | Candice Bergen, *Murphy Brown* |
| 1994 | Candice Bergen, *Murphy Brown* |
| 1993 | Roseanne, *Roseanne* |
| 1992 | Candice Bergen, *Murphy Brown* |
| 1991 | Kirstie Alley, *Cheers* |

Helen Hunt's record four-year run of wins followed a three-year interval from 1993–5 when she was nominated for the Emmy in this category but failed to win it.

# Top Videos

188

## TOP 10 ★
### COUNTRIES WITH THE MOST VCRS

| | COUNTRY | VIDEO-OWNING HOUSEHOLDS |
|---|---|---|
| 1 | US | 91,602,000 |
| 2 | Japan | 38,982,000 |
| 3 | Germany | 31,425,000 |
| 4 | China | 23,956,000 |
| 5 | Brazil | 21,330,000 |
| 6 | UK | 21,306,000 |
| 7 | France | 18,903,000 |
| 8 | Russia | 14,555,000 |
| 9 | Italy | 12,706,000 |
| 10 | South Korea | 11,616,000 |

Source: Screen Digest

## TOP 10 ★
### BEST-SELLING VIDEOS IN THE US*

| | TITLE/LABEL/RELEASE DATE | SALES ($) |
|---|---|---|
| 1 | *Titanic*, Paramount, Sep 9, 1998 | 30,000,000 |
| 2 | *The Lion King*, Buena Vista/Disney, Mar 3, 1995 | 27,500,000 |
| 3 | *Snow White*, Buena Vista/Disney, Oct 28, 1994 | 27,000,000 |
| 4 | *Aladdin*, Buena Vista/Disney, Oct 1, 1993 | 25,000,000 |
| 5 | *Independence Day*, Fox Video, Nov 19, 1996 | 21,955,000 |
| 6 | *Jurassic Park*, MCA/Universal, Oct 4, 1994 | 21,500,000 |
| 7 | *Toy Story*, Buena Vista/Disney, Oct 29, 1996 | 21,000,000 |
| 8 | *Beauty and the Beast*, Buena Vista/Disney, Oct 30, 1992 | 20,000,000 |
| 9 = | *Pocahontas*, Buena Vista/Disney, Feb 26, 1996 | 18,000,000 |
| = | *Men in Black*, Columbia TriStar, Nov 25, 1997 | 18,000,000 |

*\* Since 1992*

Source: Video Store

## TOP 10 ★
### BEST-SELLING MUSIC VIDEOS OF 2000 IN THE US

VIDEO/ARTIST

1 *Time Out With Britney Spears*, Britney Spears

2 *S&M*, Metallica

3 *Listener Supported*, Dave Matthews Band

4 *A Farewell Celebration*, Cathedrals

5 *Hell Freezes Over*, Eagles

6 *Come On Over: Video Collection*, Shania Twain

7 *Welcome to Our Neighborhood*, Slipknot

8 *Death Row Uncut*, 2 Pac/Snoop Doggy Dogg

9 *'N the Mix With 'N Sync*, 'N Sync

10 *Baller Blockin'*, Cash Money Millionaires

Source: VideoScan

## TOP 10 ★
### BEST-SELLING CHILDREN'S VIDEOS OF 2000 IN THE US

VIDEO/LABEL

1 *Mary-Kate & Ashley: Passport to Paris*, DualStar/Warner

2 *Tarzan*, Walt Disney/Buena Vista

3 *Mary-Kate & Ashley: Switching Goals*, DualStar/Warner

4 *The Adventures of Elmo in Grouchland*, Columbia Tristar

5 *Pinocchio*, Walt Disney/Buena Vista

6 *Pokémon: The First Movie*, Warner

7 *Mulan*, Walt Disney/Buena Vista

8 *The Prince of Egypt*, DreamWorks

9 *Barney: More Barney Songs*, Barney/The Lyons Group

10 = *An Extremely Goofy Movie*, Walt Disney/Buena Vista

= *The Iron Giant*, Warner

Source: VideoScan

## TOP 10 ★
### BEST-SELLING SPORT VIDEOS OF 2000 IN THE US

VIDEO/SPORT

1 *WWF: The Rock – The People's Champ*, Wrestling

2 *WWF: The Rock – Know Your Role*, Wrestling

3 *WWF: Austin Vs. McMahon*, Wrestling

4 *MLB: 1999 Official World Series*, Baseball

5 *WWF: Hell Yeah – Stone Cold's Saga Continues*, Wrestling

6 *WWF: Best of Raw Vol. 1*, Wrestling

7 *WWF: Eve of Destruction*, Wrestling

8 *WWF: It's Our Time – Triple H and Chyna*, Wrestling

9 *WWF: Tables Ladders Chairs*, Wrestling

10 *NBA: 2000 NBA Finals Championship*, Basketball

Source: VideoScan

## TOP 10 ★
### BEST-SELLING VIDEOS OF THE LAST DECADE IN THE US*

| YEAR | FILM/LABEL |
|---|---|
| 2000 | *The Matrix,* Warner |
| 1999 | *Austin Powers: International Man of Mystery*, New Line/Warner |
| 1998 | *Titanic*, Paramount/20th Century-Fox |
| 1997 | *Men in Black*, Columbia |
| 1996 | *Babe*, Universal |
| 1995 | *The Lion King*, Buena Vista |
| 1994 | *Aladdin*, Walt Disney |
| 1993 | *Beauty and the Beast*, Walt Disney |
| 1992 | *Fantasia*, Walt Disney |
| 1991 | *Pretty Woman*, Touchstone |

*\* By year*

**Did You Know?** By 2002 it is estimated that 58 percent of homes in the US and 34 percent in Europe will own a DVD player, and that in 2003 DVD sales will overtake those of VHS tapes.

**THE NUMBER ONE...**

*The Matrix, a special effects extravaganza starring Keanu Reeves, is the fastest-selling DVD of all time in the US, as well as the bestselling.*

### TOP 10 ⭐

## DVD SALES
## IN THE US, 2000

TITLE/LABEL

1  *The Matrix*, Warner

2  *The Sixth Sense*,
   Hollywood Pictures/Buena Vista

3  *The Green Mile*, Warner

4  *American Pie*, Universal Studios

5  *Austin Powers: The Spy Who Shagged
   Me*, New Line/Warner

6  *Toy Story/Toy Story 2: 2-Pack*,
   Walt Disney/Buena Vista

7  *Braveheart*, Paramount

8  *The Patriot*, Columbia TriStar

9  *Independence Day*, FoxVideo

10 *Saving Private Ryan*, DreamWorks

Source: *VideoScan*

DVD was launched in the US in March 1997. In that year, total sales of DVD players was 315,136. This increased in 1998 to 1,089,261, and in 1999 to 4,019,389, as traditional videotape recordings became progressively eclipsed by DVD.

### TOP 10 ⭐

## MOVIE RENTALS
## ON VIDEO, 2000

FILM/LABEL

1  *American Pie*, Universal Studios

2  *The Matrix*, Warner

3  *American Beauty*, DreamWorks

4 =*Fight Club*, FoxVideo

  =*Magnolia*, New Line/Warner

6  *Girl, Interrupted*, Columbia TriStar

7  *Notting Hill*, Universal Studios

8  *Erin Brockovich*, Universal Studios

9  *Austin Powers: The Spy Who Shagged
   Me*, New Line/Warner

10 *Double Jeopardy*, Paramount

Source: *VideoScan*

# COMMERCE & INDUSTRY

# Wealth of Nations

## POOREST COUNTRIES

| COUNTRY | 1998 GDP PER CAPITA ($) |
|---|---|
| 1 Ethiopia | 100 |
| 2 Dem. Rep. of Congo | 110 |
| 3 =Burundi | 140 |
| =Sierra Leone | 140 |
| 5 Guinea-Bissau | 160 |
| 6 Niger | 190 |
| 7 =Eritrea | 200 |
| =Malawi | 200 |
| 9 =Mozambique | 210 |
| =Nepal | 210 |
| =Tanzania | 210 |

Source: *World Bank*, World Development Indicators

---

## TOP 10 ★

## COUNTRIES WITH THE HIGHEST ANNUAL PER CAPITA EXPENDITURE

| COUNTRY | EXPENDITURE PER CAPITA ($) |
|---|---|
| 1 Switzerland | 26,060 |
| 2 Japan | 24,670 |
| 3 US | 18,840 |
| 4 Denmark | 17,730 |
| 5 Germany | 16,850 |
| 6 Norway | 16,570 |
| 7 Belgium | 16,550 |
| 8 Austria | 16,020 |
| 9 Iceland | 15,850 |
| 10 France | 15,810 |

Average per capita expenditure varies enormously from country to country, from the levels encountered in the Top 10 to those in the low hundreds of dollars, or less. In Western industrial economies, the proportion of expenditure that is devoted to food is often about 20 percent, but this rises to 50 and even as much as 70 percent in less developed countries. Depending on levels of taxation, the more disposable expenditure that is not allocated to such essential items, the more may be spent on consumer goods, on education, and on leisure activities.

---

## TOP 10 ★

## RICHEST COUNTRIES

| COUNTRY | 1998 GDP PER CAPITA ($) |
|---|---|
| 1 Liechtenstein | 50,000* |
| 2 Luxembourg | 43,570 |
| 3 Switzerland | 40,080 |
| 4 Norway | 34,330 |
| 5 Denmark | 33,260 |
| 6 Japan | 32,380 |
| 7 Singapore | 30,060 |
| 8 US | 29,340 |
| 9 Iceland | 28,010 |
| 10 Austria | 26,850 |
| *World* | 4,890 |

\* World Bank estimate for the purpose of ranking

Source: *World Bank*, World Development Indicators

GDP (Gross Domestic Product) is the total value of all the goods and services provided annually within a country. Gross National Product, or GNP, also includes income from overseas. Dividing GDP by the country's population produces the GDP per capita, often used as a measure of how "rich" a country is.

---

## THE 10 ★

## COUNTRIES WITH THE FASTEST-SHRINKING INCOME PER CAPITA

| COUNTRY | AVERAGE ANNUAL GROWTH IN GNP PER CAPITA, 1997–98 (%) |
|---|---|
| 1 Guinea-Bissau | -30.4 |
| 2 Indonesia | -18.0 |
| 3 United Arab Emirates | -10.6 |
| 4 Moldova | -9.2 |
| 5 Thailand | -8.6 |
| 6 Romania | -8.1 |
| 7 Malaysia | -8.0 |
| 8 South Korea | -7.5 |
| 9 Eritrea | -6.7 |
| 10 Russia | -6.4 |

Source: *World Bank*, World Development Indicators 2000

---

## TOP 10 ★

## FASTEST-GROWING ECONOMIES

| COUNTRY | AVERAGE ANNUAL GROWTH IN GNP PER CAPITA, 1997–98 (%) |
|---|---|
| 1 Angola | 16.3 |
| 2 Tajikistan | 13.3 |
| 3 Belarus | 10.8 |
| 4 Mozambique | 9.7 |
| 5 Azerbaijan | 8.9 |
| 6 Republic of Congo | 8.4 |
| 7 Ireland | 7.4 |
| 8 Chile | 7.2 |
| 9 Rwanda | 7.1 |
| 10 Albania | 6.8 |
| *US* | 1.5 |

Source: *World Bank*, World Development Indicators 2000

---

## THE 10 ★

## COUNTRIES WITH THE LOWEST ANNUAL PER CAPITA EXPENDITURE

| COUNTRY | ANNUAL EXPENDITURE PER CAPITA ($) |
|---|---|
| 1 Somalia | 17 |
| 2 Mozambique | 57 |
| 3 Ethiopia | 87 |
| 4 Malawi | 109 |
| 5 Laos | 140 |
| 6 Tanzania | 150 |
| 7 =Bangladesh | 170 |
| =Bhutan | 170 |
| =Chad | 170 |
| =Eritrea | 170 |
| =Nepal | 170 |

It is hard for those brought up in Western consumer cultures to comprehend the poverty of the countries appearing in this Top – or Bottom – 10, where the total average annual expenditure of an individual would barely cover the cost of a few meals in the West. Such economies inevitably rely on a greater degee of self-sufficiency in food production.

# THE 10 ⭐
## COUNTRIES MOST IN DEBT

| COUNTRY | TOTAL EXTERNAL DEBT ($) |
|---|---|
| 1 Brazil | 232,004,000,000 |
| 2 Russia | 183,601,000,000 |
| 3 Mexico | 159,959,000,000 |
| 4 China | 154,599,000,000 |
| 5 Indonesia | 150,875,000,000 |
| 6 Argentina | 144,050,000,000 |
| 7 South Korea | 139,097,000,000 |
| 8 Turkey | 102,074,000,000 |
| 9 India | 98,232,000,000 |
| 10 Thailand | 86,172,000,000 |

Source: *World Bank*, World Development Indicators 2000

# TOP 10 ⭐
## COINS AND NOTES IN CIRCULATION IN THE US

| DENOMINATION | UNITS IN CIRCULATION * |
|---|---|
| 1 Penny | 106,000,000,000 |
| 2 Dime | 18,400,000,000 |
| 3 Quarter | 16,300,000,000 |
| 4 Nickel | 12,100,000,000 |
| 5 $1 bill | 7,218,985,378 |
| 6 $20 bill | 4,552,499,462 |
| 7 $100 bill | 3,653,250,477 |
| 8 $5 bill | 1,644,304,095 |
| 9 $10 bill | 1,360,224,091 |
| 10 $50 bill | 1,047,150,200 |

\* As of November 2000

Source: *United States Mint*

At number 11 is the $2 bill with a total of 611,632,251 in circulation. The number of coins being minted annually is declining for each denomination. Congress began discussing the withdrawal of the penny in 1994. Some of the paper money taken out of circulation is now recycled by Crane & Co., Inc. (which makes paper for US currency) in its distinctive stationery paper, "Old Money."

# TOP 10 ⭐
## COUNTRIES WITH THE MOST CURRENCY IN CIRCULATION 100 YEARS AGO

| COUNTRY | TOTAL CURRENCY IN CIRCULATION ($) |
|---|---|
| 1 France | 2,126,400,000 |
| 2 US | 2,092,800,000 |
| 3 Germany | 1,142,400,000 |
| 4 India | 921,600,000 |
| 5 Russia | 844,800,000 |
| 6 UK | 782,400,000 |
| 7 China | 720,000,000 |
| 8 Austria | 494,400,000 |
| 9 Italy | 432,000,000 |
| 10 Spain | 350,400,000 |

# TOP 10 ⭐
## AID DONORS

| COUNTRY | ANNUAL CONTRIBUTION ($) |
|---|---|
| 1 Japan | 9,358,000,000 |
| 2 US | 6,878,000,000 |
| 3 France | 6,307,000,000 |
| 4 Germany | 5,857,000,000 |
| 5 UK | 3,433,000,000 |
| 6 Netherlands | 2,947,000,000 |
| 7 Canada | 2,045,000,000 |
| 8 Sweden | 1,731,000,000 |
| 9 Denmark | 1,637,000,000 |
| 10 Norway | 1,306,000,000 |

## TOP 10 AID RECIPIENTS
*(Country/annual amount received in $)*

❶ **China**, 2,040,000,000 ❷ **Egypt**, 1,947,000,000 ❸ **India**, 1,678,000,000 ❹ **Israel**, 1,191,000,000 ❺ **Bangladesh**, 1,009,000,000 ❻ **Vietnam**, 997,000,000 ❼ = **Mozambique**, 963,000,000; = **Tanzania**, 963,000,000 ❾ **Bosnia**, 863,000,000 ❿ **Uganda**, 840,000,000

# TOP 10 ⭐
## RECIPIENTS OF FOREIGN AID FROM THE US

| COUNTRY | TOTAL INCOME ($) |
|---|---|
| 1 Israel | 1,200,000,000 |
| 2 Egypt | 828,440,000 |
| 3 Bosnia Herzegovina | 277,913,000 |
| 4 Ukraine | 156,591,000 |
| 5 Russia | 132,090,000 |
| 6 India | 126,668,000 |
| 7 Ethiopia | 112,260,000 |
| 8 Peru | 108,264,000 |
| 9 Haiti | 100,860,000 |
| 10 Indonesia | 98,666,000 |

Source: *US Agency for International Development*

Israel leads both this Top 10 and the per capita league table, with a total of $200,969 in US aid for every Israeli inhabitant. The only other country receiving aid in six figures is Bosnia Herzegovina ($112,973 per capita).

# TOP 10 ⭐
## MOST EXPENSIVE COUNTRIES IN WHICH TO BUY A BIG MAC

| COUNTRY | COST OF A BIG MAC ($) |
|---|---|
| 1 Switzerland | 3.65 |
| 2 Denmark | 2.93 |
| 3 UK | 2.85 |
| 4 US | 2.54 |
| 5 Argentina | 2.50 |
| 6 France | 2.49 |
| 7 Japan | 2.38 |
| 8 Mexico | 2.36 |
| 9 Sweden | 2.33 |
| 10 Germany | 2.30 |

Source: *The Economist*/McDonald's price data

*The Economist*'s Big Mac index assesses the value of countries' currencies against the standard US price of a Big Mac, by assuming that an identical amount of goods and services should cost the same in all countries.

**Did You Know?** Inflation in Hungary in June 1946 reached such a record level that the prewar gold pengō coin was valued at 130 million trillion paper pengōs, and notes with a face value of 1,000 trillion pengōs were printed.

# Workers of the World

## COUNTRIES WITH THE MOST WORKERS

| | COUNTRY | WORKERS* |
|---|---|---|
| 1 | China | 743,000,000 |
| 2 | India | 431,000,000 |
| 3 | US | 138,000,000 |
| 4 | Indonesia | 98,000,000 |
| 5 | Russia | 78,000,000 |
| 6 | Brazil | 76,000,000 |
| 7 | Japan | 68,000,000 |
| 8 | Bangladesh | 64,000,000 |
| 9 | Pakistan | 49,000,000 |
| 10 | Nigeria | 48,000,000 |

\* Based on people aged 15–64 who are currently employed; unpaid groups are not included

Source: *World Bank*, World Development Indicators 2000

## COUNTRIES WITH THE HIGHEST PROPORTION OF CHILD WORKERS

| | COUNTRY | PERCENTAGE OF CHILDREN WORKING* |
|---|---|---|
| 1 | Mali | 52 |
| 2 | Burundi | 49 |
| 3 | Burkina Faso | 47 |
| 4 = | Niger | 44 |
| = | Uganda | 44 |
| 6 | Nepal | 43 |
| 7 | Ethiopia | 42 |
| 8 | Rwanda | 41 |
| 9 | Kenya | 40 |
| 10 | Tanzania | 38 |

\* Aged 10–14 years

Source: *World Bank*, World Development Indicators 2000

## COUNTRIES WITH THE HIGHEST PROPORTION OF WORKERS IN SERVICE INDUSTRIES*

| | COUNTRY | LABOR FORCE PERCENTAGE |
|---|---|---|
| 1 | Puerto Rico | 77.0 |
| 2 = | Argentina | 76.5 |
| = | Jordan | 76.5 |
| 4 | Canada | 74.5 |
| 5 = | Australia | 74.0 |
| = | US | 74.0 |
| 7 = | Ecuador | 73.5 |
| = | Netherlands | 73.5 |
| 9 = | Peru | 73.0 |
| = | Norway | 73.0 |

\* Service industries include wholesale and retail trade, restaurants, and hotels; transportation, storage, and communications; financing, insurance, real estate, and business services; and community, social, and personal services

Source: *World Bank*, World Development Indicators 2000

## TOP 10 LEAST STRESSFUL JOBS IN THE US

1. Musical instrument repairer
2. Industrial machine repairer
3. Medical records technician
4. Pharmacist  5. Software engineer
6. Typist/word processor  7. Librarian
8. Janitor  9. Bookkeeper
10. Forklift operator

**HARD LABOR**

*India's huge workforce relies on traditional manual labor, but the country is increasingly becoming a major center for computer technology.*

# TOP 10 EMPLOYERS IN THE US
*(Company/employees, 2000)*

**1** **Wal-Mart Stores**, 1,244,000  **2** **U.S. Postal Service**, 859,484
**3** **General Motors**, 386,000  **4** **McDonalds**, 364,000
**5** **United Parcel Service**, 359,000  **6** **Ford Motor Co.**, 345,991
**7** **General Electric**, 341,000  **8** **Sears Roebuck**, 323,000
**9** **IBM**, 316,303  **10** **Kroger**, 312,000

Source: *Fortune 500/Universal Postal Union*

## OCCUPATIONS IN THE US

| | JOB SECTOR* | EMPLOYEES (2000) |
|---|---|---|
| 1 | Machine operators, assemblers, and inspectors | 7,319,000 |
| 2 | Sales workers (retail and personal services) | 6,782,000 |
| 3 | Food service | 6,327,000 |
| 4 | Construction trades | 6,120,000 |
| 5 | Handlers, equipment cleaners, helpers, and laborers | 5,443,000 |
| 6 | Teachers (except college and university) | 5,353,000 |
| 7 | Sales supervisors and proprietors | 4,937,000 |
| 8 | Management-related | 4,932,000 |
| 9 | Mechanics and repairers | 4,875,000 |
| 10 | Motor vehicle operators | 4,222,000 |
| | US total (including occupations not in Top 10) | 135,208,000 |

*\* Excluding general and miscellaneous group categories*

Source: *US Bureau of Labor Statistics*

## LABOR UNIONS IN THE US

| | UNION | MEMBERS |
|---|---|---|
| 1 | National Education Association | 2,500,000 |
| 2 | International Brotherhood of Teamsters | 1,500,000 |
| 3 | United Food and Commercial Workers' International Union | 1,400,000 |
| 4= | American Federation of State, County, and Municipal Employees | 1,300,000 |
| = | Service Employees International Union | 1,300,000 |
| 6 | American Federation of Teachers | 1,000,000 |
| 7 | United International Union of Automobile, Aerospace, and Agricultural Implement Workers of America | 800,000 |
| 8 | International Brotherhood of Electrical Workers | 760,000 |
| 9 | Laborers' International Union of North America | 741,000 |
| 10 | United Steelworkers of America | 700,000 |

**FACTORY MADE**
*Despite the growth of the service sector, manufacturing remains a vital component of most developed economies, providing employment for countless workers in factories across the world.*

## BEST PAID JOBS IN THE US

| | JOB | AVERAGE ANNUAL SALARY, 2000 ($) |
|---|---|---|
| 1 | Physician | 69,680 |
| 2 | Lawyer | 67,808 |
| 3 | Airplane pilot/navigator | 66,716 |
| 4 | Aerospace engineer | 66,248 |
| 5 | Pharmacist | 64,636 |
| 6 | Chemical engineer | 62,868 |
| 7 | Electrical/electronic engineer | 59,488 |
| 8 | Mechanical engineer | 58,552 |
| 9 | Management analyst/manager, marketing, advertising, PR | 55,848 |
| 10 | Architect | 54,704 |

Source: *US Bureau of Labor Statistics*

These are the average annual salaries for male employees in the highest-paid professions. Women earn average salaries that are much lower than these (women physicians, for example, averaging $46,748), and only female lawyers (with an average of $54,756) earn salaries that qualify for the Top 10.

# TOP 10 COUNTRIES WITH THE HIGHEST PROPORTION OF FARMERS
*(Country/percentage in agriculture, 1999)*

**1** **Bhutan**, 93.8  **2** **Nepal**, 93.1  **3** **Burkina Faso**, 92.2
**4** **Rwanda**, 90.5  **5** **Burundi**, 90.4  **6** **Niger**, 88.1  **7** **Guinea Bissau**, 83.1  **8** **Ethiopia**, 82.8  **9** **Mali**, 81.5  **10** **Uganda**, 79.5

Source: *Food and Agriculture Organization of the United Nations*
This is based on a study of the number of people who depend on agriculture for their livelihood as a proportion of the total population of the country.

Which is the only South American country to appear among the world's Top 10 gold producers?
*see p.204 for the answer*

A  Brazil
B  Bolivia
C  Peru

# Company Matters

## BANKS (BY ASSETS)

| BANK/COUNTRY | ASSETS ($) |
|---|---|
| 1 Deutsche Bank, Germany | 841,796,920,000 |
| 2 Bank of Tokyo-Mitsubishi, Japan | 729,249,600,000 |
| 3 BNP Paribas, France | 700,232,030,000 |
| 4 Bank of America Corp., US | 632,574,000,000 |
| 5 UBS, Switzerland | 613,198,370,000 |
| 6 Fuji Bank, Japan | 567,899,800,000 |
| 7 HSBC Holdings, UK | 567,793,290,000 |
| 8 Sumitomo Bank, Japan | 524,227,780,000 |
| 9 Dai-Ichi Kangyo Bank, Japan | 506,980,440,000 |
| 10 HypoVereinsbank, Germany | 504,412,630,000 |

Source: Fortune Global 500

## LARGEST BANKS (BY REVENUE)

| BANK/COUNTRY | REVENUE ($) |
|---|---|
| 1 J. P. Morgan Chase, US | 60,065,000,000 |
| 2 Deutsche Bank, Germany | 58,585,150,000 |
| 3 Bank of America Corp., US | 57,757,000,000 |
| 4 Credit Suisse, Switzerland | 49,361,980,000 |
| 5 Fortis, Belgium | 43,660,190,000 |
| 6 BNP Paribas, France | 40,098,550,000 |
| 7 HSBC Holdings, UK | 39,348,150,000 |
| 8 ABN AMRO Holdings, Netherlands | 38,820,670,000 |
| 9 Crédit Agricole, France | 32,923,500,000 |
| 10 Bank of Tokyo-Mitsubishi, Japan | 32,624,000,000 |

Source: Fortune 5000/Fortune Global 500

## INTERNATIONAL INDUSTRIAL COMPANIES

| COMPANY/SECTOR/LOCATION | ANNUAL SALES ($) |
|---|---|
| 1 Exxon Mobil, Oil, gas, fuel, US | 210,392,000,000 |
| 2 Wal-Mart Stores, Inc, Retailing, US | 193,295,000,000 |
| 3 General Motors Corp., Transport, US | 184,632,000,000 |
| 4 Ford Motor Co., Transport, US | 180,598,000,000 |
| 5 DaimlerChrysler, Transport, Germany | 159,986,000,000 |
| 6 General Electric, Electronics, electrical equipment, US | 129,853,000,000 |
| 7 Mitsui and Co. Ltd., Trading, Japan | 118,555,000,000 |
| 8 Mitsubishi Corp., Trading, Japan | 117,766,000,000 |
| 9 Toyota Motor, Transport, Japan | 115,671,000,000 |
| 10 Itochu Corp., Trading, Japan | 109,069,000,000 |

Source: Fortune Global 500

*Fortune* magazine's authoritative Global 500 list contains 500 companies each with annual sales in excess of $9.7 billion. All those in the Top 100 achieve sales of more than $32.7 billion, but only those in the Top 10 (plus one other – the Royal Dutch/Shell Group) make the stratospheric $100-billion-plus league.

### AS LONG AS IT'S BLACK...

*Long the world's best-selling car, the Model T Ford established the company's place among the foremost global manufacturers.*

## TOP 10 ★
## BANKS IN THE US

| BANK | REVENUE ($) |
|------|-------------|
| 1 J. P. Morgan Chase | 65,065,000,000 |
| 2 Bank of America | 57,757,000,000 |
| 3 Wells Fargo | 27,568,000,000 |
| 4 Bank One Corp. | 25,168,000,000 |
| 5 First Union Corp. | 24,246,000,000 |
| 6 FleetBoston | 22,608,000,000 |
| 7 U.S. Bancorp | 9,966,000,000 |
| 8 National City Corp. | 9,051,000,000 |
| 9 SunTrust Banks | 8,619,000,000 |
| 10 KeyCorp | 8,471,000,000 |

Source: Fortune Global 500

## TOP 10 ★
## CORPORATIONS IN THE US

| CORPORATION | REVENUE* ($) |
|-------------|--------------|
| 1 Exxon Mobil | 210,392,000,000 |
| 2 Wal-Mart Stores | 193,295,000,000 |
| 3 General Motors | 184,632,000,000 |
| 4 Ford Motor Company | 180,598,000,000 |
| 5 General Electric | 129,853,000,000 |
| 6 Citigroup | 111,826,000,000 |
| 7 Enron | 100,789,000,000 |
| 8 IBM | 88,396,000,000 |
| 9 AT&T | 65,981,000,000 |
| 10 Verizon Communications | 64,707,000,000 |

* In latest year for which data available

Source: Fortune Global 500

Despite their involvement in new technologies, several of the corporations listed here have a history dating back to the late 19th century: AT&T – originally the American Telephone and Telegraph Company – dates from 1885, while General Electric was established in 1892, when the Edison General Electric Company and Thomson Houston Company were merged. Even portions of IBM have their roots back in the 1880s.

## TOP 10 ★
## US COMPANIES MAKING THE GREATEST PROFIT PER SECOND

| COMPANY | PROFIT PER SECOND ($) |
|---------|------------------------|
| 1 Exxon Mobil | 561 |
| 2 Citigroup | 428 |
| 3 General Electric | 403 |
| 4 Verizon Communications | 374 |
| 5 Intel Corp. | 334 |
| 6 Microsoft | 298 |
| 7 Philip Morris | 269 |
| 8 IBM | 256 |
| 9 SBC Communications | 252 |
| 10 Bank of America Corporation | 238 |

## TOP 10 ★
## MAJORITY EMPLOYEE-OWNED COMPANIES IN THE US

| COMPANY/LOCATION | 1999 REVENUE ($) |
|------------------|-------------------|
| 1 United Airlines, Chicago, IL | 17,967,000,000 |
| 2 Publix Super Markets, Lakeland, FL | 13,069,000,000 |
| 3 Arrow Electronics, Melville, NY | 9,300,000,000 |
| 4 Science Applications International, San Diego, CA | 5,529,000,000 |
| 5 Graybar Electric, St. Louis, MI | 4,300,000,000 |
| 6 Hy-Vee, West Des Moines, IA | 3,500,000,000 |
| 7 Parsons Corp., Pasadena, CA | 2,000,000,000 |
| 8 Edward Jones Investments, St. Louis, MI | 1,800,000,000 |
| 9 CH2M Hill, Inc., Greenwood Village, CO | 1,600,000,000 |
| 10 Amsted Industries, Chicago, IL | 1,370,000,000 |

Source: Business Ethics

## TOP 10 ★
## OLDEST ESTABLISHED BUSINESSES IN THE US

| COMPANY*/LOCATION | FOUNDED |
|-------------------|---------|
| 1 White Horse Tavern, Newport, RI | 1673 |
| 2 J. E. Rhoads & Sons, Branchburg, NJ | 1702 |
| 3 Wayside Inn, Sudbury, MA | 1716 |
| 4 Elkridge Furnace Inn, Elkridge, MD | 1744 |
| 5 Moravian Book Shop, Bethlehem, PA | 1745 |
| 6 Pennsylvania Hospital, Philadelphia, PA | 1751 |
| 7 Philadelphia Contributorship, Philadelphia, PA | 1752 |
| 8 *New Hampshire Gazette*, Portsmouth, NH | 1756 |
| 9 *Hartford Courant*, Hartford, CT | 1764 |
| 10 Bachman Funeral Home, Strasburg, PA | 1769 |

* Excluding mergers and transplanted companies

Source: Institute for Family Enterprise, Bryant College

## TOP 10 ★
## PRIVATE COMPANIES IN THE US

| COMPANY | ANNUAL REVENUE ($) |
|---------|---------------------|
| 1 Cargill | 48,000,000,000 |
| 2 Koch Industries | 36,000,000,000 |
| 3 Pricewaterhouse Coopers | 20,000,000,000 |
| 4 Mars | 15,300,000,000 |
| 5 Bechtel Group | 15,100,000,000 |
| 6 KPMG International | 14,200,000,000 |
| 7 Publix Super Markets | 13,069,000,000 |
| 8 Deloitte Touche Tohmatsu | 12,300,000,000 |
| 9 ContiGroup Cos. | 10,000,000,000 |
| 10 Ernst & Young | 9,550,000,000 |

Source: Forbes

A private company is one that does not have commonly traded stock – in other words, outsiders cannot buy shares in it.

**Did You Know?** General Motors, the world's biggest carmaker, became the first company in the world to assemble 100 million vehicles when, on March 16, 1966, an Oldsmobile Toronado rolled off the production line.

# Advertising & Brands

## TOP 10 ★
## GLOBAL MARKETERS

| COMPANY/BASE | MEDIA SPENDING, 1998 ($) |
|---|---|
| **1 Procter & Gamble Company**, US | 4,747,600,000 |
| **2 Unilever**, Netherlands/UK | 3,428,500,000 |
| **3 General Motors Corporation**, US | 3,193,500,000 |
| **4 Ford Motor Company**, US | 2,229,500,000 |
| **5 Philip Morris Companies**, US | 1,980,300,000 |
| **6 DaimlerChrysler**, Germany/US | 1,922,200,000 |
| **7 Nestlé**, Switzerland | 1,833,000,000 |
| **8 Toyota Motor Corporation**, Japan | 1,692,400,000 |
| **9 Sony Corporation**, Japan | 1,337,700,000 |
| **10 Coca-Cola Company**, US | 1,327,300,000 |

Source: *Competitive Media Reporting/ACNielsen MMS/Advertising Age*

## TOP 10 ★
## ADVERTISERS BY CATEGORY IN THE US

| CATEGORY | TOTAL AD SPENDING IN 1999 ($) |
|---|---|
| **1 Automotive, access and equipment** | 10,454,795,800 |
| **2 Retail** | 8,501,141,700 |
| **3 Media and advertising** | 4,978,059,100 |
| **4 Financial** | 3,965,350,100 |
| **5 Drugs and proprietary remedies** | 3,903,115,600 |
| **6 Telecommunications** | 3,344,281,600 |
| **7 Automotive dealers and services** | 3,311,770,500 |
| **8 Restaurants** | 3,111,872,400 |
| **9 Public transportation, hotels, and resorts** | 2,800,402,900 |
| **10 Department stores** | 2,641,114,800 |

Source: *Competitive Media Reporting/ Publishers Information Bureau*

## TOP 10 ★
## ADVERTISERS ON THE WEB

| WEBSITE | IMPRESSIONS* |
|---|---|
| **1 TRUSTe** | 504,182,490 |
| **2 Microsoft** | 370,575,192 |
| **3 Yahoo!** | 228,032,781 |
| **4 America Online** | 128,433,841 |
| **5 AllAdvantage** | 120,408,883 |
| **6 Amazon** | 110,318,224 |
| **7 eBay** | 95,391,668 |
| **8 Casino On Net** | 90,831,841 |
| **9 Next Card** | 71,844,247 |
| **10 Barnes and Noble** | 67,581,608 |

\* *Number of times the advertising banner has been loaded within a browser, week ending July 23, 2000*

## TOP 10 ★
## CORPORATE ADVERTISERS IN THE US

| ADVERTISER | TOTAL ADVERTISING COSTS IN 1999 ($) |
|---|---|
| **1 General Motors Corp.** | 2,921,275,200 |
| **2 Proctor & Gamble Co.** | 1,738,686,100 |
| **3 DaimlerChrysler** | 1,511,578,900 |
| **4 Philip Morris Cos.** | 1,371,333,800 |
| **5 Ford Motor Co.** | 1,191,082,200 |
| **6 Time Warner Inc.** | 1,075,013,200 |
| **7 Walt Disney Co.** | 889,797,200 |
| **8 Johnson & Johnson** | 852,038,900 |
| **9 AT&T Corp.** | 828,708,400 |
| **10 MCI Worldcom Inc.** | 759,898,300 |

Source: *Competitive Media Reporting/ Publishers Information Bureau*

Despite the huge advertising budgets of these major corporations, the amounts represent only a relatively small proportion of total revenue: for General Motors, for example, less than 2 percent.

**BIG MAC**

*Global fast food company McDonald's is ranked second only to Coca-Cola as the world's most valuable food and beverage brand.*

**THE REAL THING**

*Best-selling, most advertised, and most valuable are only three of the many superlatives applied to Coca-Cola's top international status.*

### TOP 10 ★
## MOST VALUABLE GLOBAL BRANDS

| | BRAND* | INDUSTRY | BRAND VALUE ($) |
|---|---|---|---|
| 1 | Coca-Cola | Beverages | 72,537,000,000 |
| 2 | Microsoft-Windows | Technology | 70,197,000,000 |
| 3 | IBM | Technology | 53,184,000,000 |
| 4 | Intel | Technology | 39,049,000,000 |
| 5 | Nokia, Finland | Technology | 38,528,000,000 |
| 6 | General Electric | Diversified | 38,128,000,000 |
| 7 | Ford | Automobiles | 36,368,000,000 |
| 8 | Disney | Leisure | 33,553,000,000 |
| 9 | McDonald's | Food retail | 27,859,000,000 |
| 10 | AT&T | Telecommunications | 25,548,000,000 |

*\* All US-owned unless otherwise stated*

Source: *Interbrand*

Brand consultant Interbrand uses a method of estimating value that takes account of the profitability of individual brands within a business (rather than the companies that own them), as well as such factors as their potential for growth. Well over half of the 75 most valuable global brands surveyed by Interbrand are US-owned, with Europe accounting for another 30 percent.

Crowd cheers! Coke nears!
Game goes better refreshed.
Coca-Cola, never too sweet,
gives that special zing...refreshes best.

### TOP 10 ★
## BEST-SELLING GLOBAL BRANDS*

| | BRAND/COUNTRY | INDUSTRY | SALES, 1999 ($) |
|---|---|---|---|
| 1 | Ford, US | Automobiles | 121,603,000,000 |
| 2 | General Electric, US | Diversified | 105,840,000,000 |
| 3 | Shell, UK | Oil | 105,366,000,000 |
| 4 | Toyota, Japan | Automobiles | 100,704,000,000 |
| 5 | IBM, US | Technology | 87,548,000,000 |
| 6 | Mercedes, Germany | Automobiles | 65,249,000,000 |
| 7 | AT&T, US | Telecommunications | 62,391,000,000 |
| 8 | Honda, Japan | Automobiles | 60,902,000,000 |
| 9 | Panasonic, Japan | Electronics | 60,314,000,000 |
| 10 | BP, UK | Oil | 56,464,000,000 |

*\* By value of sales*

Source: *Interbrand*

Most of the companies appearing in this list have in common not only their impressive size and status but also a long history. Ford, Mercedes, and Shell, for example, date back over 100 years.

### TOP 10 ★
## MOST VALUABLE FOOD AND BEVERAGE BRANDS

| | BRAND* | INDUSTRY | BRAND VALUE ($) |
|---|---|---|---|
| 1 | Coca-Cola | Food/beverages | 72,537,000,000 |
| 2 | McDonald's | Food retail | 27,859,000,000 |
| 3 | Marlboro | Tobacco | 22,111,000,000 |
| 4 | Nescafé, Switzerland | Beverages | 13,681,000,000 |
| 5 | Heinz | Food/beverages | 11,742,000,000 |
| 6 | Budweiser | Alcohol | 10,685,000,000 |
| 7 | Kelloggs | Food/beverages | 7,357,000,000 |
| 8 | Pepsi-Cola | Beverages | 6,637,000,000 |
| 9 | Wrigley's | Food | 4,324,000,000 |
| 10 | Bacardi | Alcohol | 3,187,000,000 |

*\* All US-owned unless otherwise stated*

Source: *Interbrand*

Nearly half of these companies (McDonald's, Heinz, Kelloggs, Wrigley's, and Bacardi) are eponymous, deriving their names from those of their founders.

---

**Which European country has the most dollar billionaires?**
*see p.202 for the answer*

A Germany
B France
C Luxembourg

# Retail Therapy

## LARGEST SHOPPING MALLS IN THE US

| MALL/LOCATION | GROSS LEASABLE AREA (SQ FT) |
|---|---|
| 1 Del Amo Fashion Center, Torrance, CA | 3,000,000 |
| 2 Mall of America, Bloomington, MN | 2,796,516 |
| 3 = South Coast Plaza/Crystal Court, Costa Mesa, CA | 2,700,000 |
| = Woodfield Mall, Schamuberg, IL | 2,700,000 |
| 5 Northland Center, Southfield, MI | 2,200,000 |
| 6 Roosevelt Field Mall, Garden City, NY | 2,146,029 |
| 7 Sawgrass Mills, Sunrise, FL | 2,120,500 |
| 8 = Meadowlands Mills, Carlstadt, NJ | 2,100,000 |
| = North Park Center, Dallas, TX | 2,100,000 |
| = Plaza Las Amaricas, San Juan, PR | 2,100,000 |

Source: *International Council of Shopping Centers*

Gross leasable area is defined as "the total floor area designated for tenant occupancy," and includes square footage occupied by anchor stores.

## SUPERMARKETS IN THE US

| COMPANY | MARKET SHARE PERCENTAGE | SALES, 2000 ($) |
|---|---|---|
| 1 Wal-Mart Supercenters | 11.1 | 57,200,000,000* |
| 2 The Kroger Co. | 9.5 | 49,000,000,000 |
| 3 Albertson's | 7.1 | 36,400,000,000* |
| 4 Safeway | 6.2 | 32,000,000,000 |
| 5 Ahold USA | 5.4 | 27,800,000,000 |
| 6 Supervalu | 4.5 | 23,300,000,000* |
| 7 Publix Super Markets | 2.8 | 14,600,000,000 |
| 8 Fleming | 2.8 | 14,400,000,000 |
| 9 = Loblaw Cos. | 0.0# | 13,800,000,000 |
| = Winn-Dixie Stores | 2.7 | 13,800,000,000* |

\* *Estimated*

# *Canadian company, not assigned a share since the calculation is based on the US market*

Source: Supermarket News

## COMPLAINTS TO CONSUMER AGENCIES IN THE US

| CATEGORY | % OF AGENCIES REPORTING MAJOR COMPLAINTS IN 1999 |
|---|---|
| 1 Home improvement | 82 |
| 2 Auto sales | 75 |
| 3 Household goods | 66 |
| 4 Auto repair | 64 |
| 5 Credit/lending | 57 |
| 6 Utilities | 34 |
| 7 Mail order | 27 |
| 8 = Collections | 16 |
| = Landlord/tenant | 16 |
| 10 Leisure/travel | 14 |

Source: *The National Association of Consumer Agency Administrators*

### SHOPPING SPREE

*Despite the growth of online retailing, traditional shopping continues to be an activity enjoyed by many, and is both a yardstick and a mainstay of Western economies.*

## TOP 10 ⭐
## WORLD RETAIL SECTORS

| | SECTOR | COMPANIES* |
|---|---|---|
| 1 | Supermarket | 108 |
| 2 | Specialty | 94 |
| 3 | Department | 62 |
| 4 | Hypermarket | 53 |
| 5 | =Convenience | 40 |
| | =Discount | 40 |
| 7 | Mail order | 22 |
| 8 | Restaurant | 21 |
| 9 | Drug | 16 |
| 10 | DIY | 15 |

*Of those listed in Stores' Top 200 Global Retailers; stores can operate in more than one area*

Source: Stores

A survey of the global retail industry in 1999 revealed that the overall sales of the 200 largest retailers reached $2 trillion. Of the 200, 39 percent are in the US, followed by Japan with 14 percent, and the UK with 9 percent. The 77 US companies in the full list are even more dominant in terms of total sales, achieving some $922 billion, or 47 percent of the combined revenue of the global 200.

## TOP 10 ⭐
## RETAILERS IN THE US

| | COMPANY | STORES | RETAIL SALES, 2000 ($) |
|---|---|---|---|
| 1 | Wal-Mart Inc. | 3,989 | 193,215,000,000 |
| 2 | The Kroger Co. | 3,473 | 49,000,400,000 |
| 3 | The Home Depot | 930 | 45,738,000,000 |
| 4 | Sears, Roebuck and Co. | 3,011 | 40,937,000,000 |
| 5 | Kmart Corp. | 2,171 | 37,028,000,000 |
| 6 | Target Corp. | 1,243 | 36,903,000,000 |
| 7 | Albertson's | 2,492 | 36,762,000,000 |
| 8 | J.C. Penney | 4,076 | 32,965,000,000 |
| 9 | Costco | 302 | 32,164,300,000 |
| 10 | Safeway | 1,659 | 31,976,900,000 |

Source: Chain Store Age/Fortune 500

## TOP 10 ⭐
## SPORTING GOODS RETAILERS IN THE US

| | STORE | ANNUAL SALES ($) |
|---|---|---|
| 1 | Foot Locker | 2,268,000,000 |
| 2 | The Sports Authority Inc. | 1,500,000,000 |
| 3 | L.L. Bean | 1,000,000,000 |
| 4 | Bass Pro Shops | 960,000,000 |
| 5 | Just For Feet | 774,000,000 |
| 6 | Champs | 727,000,000 |
| 7 | Gart Sports/ Sportmart | 681,000,000 |
| 8 | Cabela's | 666,000,000 |
| 9 | Footaction | 643,000,000 |
| 10 | REI | 620,000,000 |

Source: Sports Business Research Network

## TOP 10 ⭐
## TYPES OF RETAILERS IN THE US, BY SALES

| | INDUSTRY | RETAIL SALES, 1999 ($) |
|---|---|---|
| 1 | Motor vehicle dealers | 668,216,000,000 |
| 2 | Grocery stores | 434,695,000,000 |
| 3 | Discount department stores | 203,257,000,000 |
| 4 | Gasoline service stations | 180,973,000,000 |
| 5 | Restaurants and eating places | 143,568,000,000 |
| 6 | Building materials, supply stores | 138,379,000,000 |
| 7 | Refreshment places | 122,818,000,000 |
| 8 | Drug and proprietary stores | 120,733,000,000 |
| 9 | Mail order | 89,633,000,000 |
| 10 | Conventional department stores | 56,621,000,000 |

Source: US Census Bureau Department of Commerce

In addition to those listed here, "Miscellaneous shopping goods stores" accounted for sales of $106,253,000,000, and "Miscellaneous general merchandise" $67,972,000,000.

## TOP 10 ⭐
## FASTEST-GROWING RETAIL SECTORS IN THE US

| | RETAIL SECTOR* | PERCENTAGE SALES INCREASE# |
|---|---|---|
| 1 | Gasoline | 20.1 |
| 2 | Meat, fish, and seafood | 13.4 |
| 3 | Radio, television, and electronics | 13.2 |
| 4 | Sporting goods and bicycles | 12.3 |
| 5 | Books | 9.7 |
| 6 | Drug and proprietary stores | 9.2 |
| 7 | =Liquor stores | 8.0 |
| | =Restaurants, lunchrooms, and cafeterias | 8.0 |
| 9 | Retail bakery products | 7.9 |
| 10 | Floor coverings | 7.5 |
| | Total retail sales | 7.0 |

*Excluding general categories*

\# 2000 compared with 1999

Source: US Census Bureau

## TOP 10 ⭐
## SPECIALTY RETAILERS IN THE US

| | COMPANY/SPECIALTY | RETAIL SALES, 2000 ($) |
|---|---|---|
| 1 | Home Depot, home improvements, DIY, building materials | 45,738,000,000 |
| 2 | Lowe's, home improvements, DIY, building materials | 18,779,000,000 |
| 3 | Gap, apparel | 13,674,000,000 |
| 4 | Circuit City, consumer electronics | 12,614,000,000 |
| 5 | Best Buy, consumer electronics | 12,494,000,000 |
| 6 | Office Depot, office supplies | 11,570,000,000 |
| 7 | Toys R Us, toys and games | 11,332,000,000 |
| 8 | Staples, office supplies | 10,674,000,000 |
| 9 | Limited, women's apparel | 10,105,000,000 |
| 10 | TJX, apparel | 9,579,000,000 |

Source: Fortune

How many patents did Thomas A. Edison register?
*see p.208 for the answer*
A 87
B 302
C 1,093

# That's Rich

## RICHEST RULERS

| RULER/COUNTRY | ASSETS ($) |
|---|---|
| 1 King Fahd Bin Abdulaziz Alsaud, Saudi Arabia | 30,000,000,000 |
| 2 Sheikh Zayed Bin Sultan al Nahyan, UAE (Abu Dhabi) | 23,000,000,000 |
| 3 Amir Jaber Al-Ahmed Al Jaber Al-Sabah, Kuwait | 18,000,000,000 |
| 4 Sultan Hassanal Bolkiah, Brunei | 16,000,000,000 |
| 5 Sheikh Maktoum Bin Rashid Al Maktoum, UAE (Dubai) | 12,000,000,000 |
| 6 President Saddam Hussein, Iraq | 7,000,000,000 |
| 7 Amir Hamad Bin Khalifa Al Thani, Qatar, 1995 | 5,000,000,000 |
| 8 Queen Beatrix, Netherlands | 3,500,000,000 |
| 9 Bashar Al-Assad*, Syria | 2,300,000,000 |
| 10 Queen Elizabeth II, UK | 450,000,000 |

*Est. wealth of his father President Hafez Al-Assad*

Based on data published in Forbes magazine

## TOP 10 ★

## HIGHEST-EARNING ENTERTAINERS*

| ENTERTAINER(S)/PROFESSION | 2000 INCOME ($) |
|---|---|
| 1 George Lucas, Film producer/director | 250,000,000 |
| 2 Oprah Winfrey, TV host/producer | 150,000,000 |
| 3 The Beatles, Rock band | 70,000,000 |
| 4 David Copperfield, Illusionist | 60,000,000 |
| 5 Steven Spielberg, Film producer/director | 51,000,000 |
| 6 Siegfried & Roy, Illusionists | 50,000,000 |
| 7 Brian Grazer/Ron Howard, Film producers | 45,000,000 |
| 8 Stephen King, Writer | 44,000,000 |
| 9 'N Sync, Male vocal group | 42,000,000 |
| 10 Britney Spears, Pop singer | 38,500,000 |

*Excluding actors, actresses, and sports stars*

Used by permission of Forbes magazine

## TOP 10 ★

## RICHEST PEOPLE

| NAME/COUNTRY | NET WORTH ($) |
|---|---|
| 1 William H. Gates III, US | 63,000,000,000 |
| 2 Lawrence Joseph Ellison, US | 58,000,000,000 |
| 3 Paul Gardner Allen, US | 36,000,000,000 |
| 4 Warren Edward Buffett, US | 28,000,000,000 |
| 5 Gordon Earle Moore, US | 26,000,000,000 |
| 6 = Prince Alwaleed Bin Talal Alsaud, Saudi Arabia | 20,000,000,000 |
| = Theo & Karl Albrecht and family, Germany | 20,000,000,000 |
| 8 Masayoshi Son, Japan | 19,400,000,000 |
| 9 Philip F. Anschutz, US | 18,000,000,000 |
| 10 = Steven Anthony Ballmer, US | 17,000,000,000 |
| = S. Robson Walton*, US | 17,000,000,000 |

*Other members of the Walton family have equal wealth*

Based on data published in Forbes magazine

## TOP 10 ★

## HIGHEST-EARNING ACTORS AND ACTRESSES

| ACTOR OR ACTRESS | 2000 INCOME ($) |
|---|---|
| 1 Bruce Willis | 70,000,000 |
| 2 Tom Cruise | 43,200,000 |
| 3 Eddie Murphy | 39,500,000 |
| 4 Mel Gibson | 31,800,000 |
| 5 Nicolas Cage | 28,400,000 |
| 6 Keanu Reeves | 25,500,000 |
| 7 Brad Pitt | 23,800,000 |
| 8 Julia Roberts | 18,900,000 |
| 9 Ben Affleck | 18,300,000 |
| 10 Robin Williams | 17,100,000 |

*Used by permission of Forbes magazine*

Actors such as Bruce Willis and Tom Cruise can routinely command $20 million or more per film.

**CLOSING ON GATES**

*The fortune of Oracle software magnate Larry Ellison has risen sharply, placing him a close second to the world's richest person, Bill Gates.*

## TOP 10 ★

## COUNTRIES WITH THE MOST DOLLAR BILLIONAIRES

| COUNTRY | $ BILLIONAIRES* |
|---|---|
| 1 US | 55 |
| 2 Japan | 43 |
| 3 Germany | 42 |
| 4 = Canada | 15 |
| = UK | 15 |
| 6 = France | 14 |
| = Switzerland | 14 |
| 8 = China (Hong Kong) | 13 |
| = Mexico | 13 |
| 10 = Brazil | 9 |
| = India | 9 |

*Individuals/families with a net worth of $1 billion or more*   Source: Forbes magazine

# TOP 10 ★
## MOST EXPENSIVE SINGLE PRECIOUS STONES EVER SOLD AT AUCTION*

| | STONE/SALE | PRICE ($) |
|---|---|---|
| 1 | *The Patino*, cushion-cut Burmese ruby of 32.08 carats, Chaumet (from the Patiño collection), Sotheby's, New York, Oct 26, 1989 | 4,620,000 |
| 2 | Cushion-cut Burmese ruby of 27.37 carats, Sotheby's, Geneva, May 17, 1995 | 4,036,250 (SF4,843,500) |
| 3 | Cushion-cut Burmese ruby of 15.97 carats, Sotheby's, New York, Oct 18, 1988 | 3,630,000 |
| 4 | Oval-cut Burmese ruby of 16.51 carats, Sotheby's, Geneva, May 26, 1993 | 3,036,896 (SF4,403,500) |
| 5 | *The Rockefeller Sapphire*, step-cut Burmese sapphire of 62.02 carats, Sotheby's, St. Moritz, Feb 20, 1988 | 2,828,571 (SF3,960,000) |
| 6 | Cushion-cut Burmese ruby of 16.20 carats, Christie's, New York, Oct 23, 1990 | 2,750,000 |
| 7 | Jadeite cabochon ring, 1.3 x 0.74 x 0.58 in (33.08 x 18.78 x 14.83 mm), Christie's, Hong Kong, Nov 1, 1999 | 2,405,000 (HK$18,500,000) |
| 8 | Cushion-cut sapphire of 337.66 carats in a diamond pendant, Christie's, Geneva, May 16, 1991 | 2,340,000 (SF3,300,000) |
| 9 | Rectangular step-cut emerald of 19.77 carats, Cartier (from the Duchess of Windsor collection), Sotheby's, Geneva, Apr 2, 1987 | 2,126,667 (SF3,190,000) |
| 10 | Cushion-cut Burmese ruby of 12.10 carats, Christie's, Geneva, Nov 19, 1992 | 2,000,000 (SF2,860,000) |

* Excluding diamonds

# TOP 10 ★
## COUNTRIES MAKING GOLD JEWELRY

| | COUNTRY | GOLD USED IN 1999 (TONNES) |
|---|---|---|
| 1 | India | 644.0 |
| 2 | Italy | 511.0 |
| 3 | US | 178.2 |
| 4 | China | 166.0 |
| 5 | Saudi Arabia and Yemen | 149.2 |
| 6 | Indonesia | 126.0 |
| 7 | Turkey | 115.0 |
| 8 | Egypt | 114.3 |
| 9 | Malaysia | 68.0 |
| 10 | Taiwan | 63.0 |
| | World | 3,128.0 |

Source: *Gold Fields Mineral Services Ltd.*, Gold Survey 2000

# TOP 10 ★
## GOLD MANUFACTURERS

| | COUNTRY | GOLD USED IN FABRICATION, 1999 (TONNES) |
|---|---|---|
| 1 | India | 685.2 |
| 2 | Italy | 522.8 |
| 3 | US | 323.1 |
| 4 | China | 181.5 |
| 5 | Japan | 158.7 |
| 6 | Saudi Arabia and Yemen | 149.2 |
| 7 | Turkey | 139.3 |
| 8 | Indonesia | 126.0 |
| 9 | Egypt | 114.3 |
| 10 | South Korea | 93.5 |
| | World | 3,722.3 |

Source: *Gold Fields Mineral Services Ltd.*, Gold Survey 2000

# TOP 10 ★
## PIECES OF JEWELRY AUCTIONED BY CHRISTIE'S

| | JEWELLERY/SALE | PRICE ($) |
|---|---|---|
| 1 | Single strand jadeite necklace of 27 beads, 0.59 to 0.62 in (15.09 to 15.84 mm), Christie's, Hong Kong, Nov 6, 1997 (HK$72,620,000) | 9,394,566 |
| 2 | *The Begum Blue* (from the collection of Princess Salimah Aga Khan), Christie's, Geneva, Nov 13, 1995 (SF8,803,500). *Fancy, deep blue, heart-shaped diamond of 13.78 carats and a heart-shaped diamond of 16.03 carats, D color, internally flawless.* | 7,790,000 |
| 3 | *The Mouna Diamond*, Christie's, Geneva, May 15, 1996 (SF3,743,500). *Fancy, intense yellow diamond brooch of 102.07 carats by Cartier, 1953.* | 3,237,868 |
| 4 | *The Allnat*, Christie's, Geneva, Nov 16, 1998 (SF4,403,500). *Fancy, intense yellow cushion-shaped diamond pendant of 112.53 carats (VS1), mounted by Bulgari.* | 3,043,496 |
| 5 | *The Harcourt Emeralds*, Christie's, London, June 21, 1989 (£1,870,000). *Necklace set with diamonds and 13 emeralds weighing 16.219 carats.* | 2,879,800 |
| 6 | Single strand jadeite and diamond lavalière of 29 jadeite beads, 0.19 to 0.64 in (4.78 to 16.22 mm), Christie's, Hong Kong, Nov 1, 1999 (HK$22,020,000) | 2,862,600 |
| 7 | *The Indore Pears*, Christie's, Geneva, Nov 12, 1987 (SF3,630,000) | 2,686,200 |
| 8 | A diamond necklace suspending a 17.57-carat heart-shaped diamond, with matching diamond ear pendants, Christie's, Geneva, Nov 15, 1995 (SF2,643,500) | 2,643,500 |
| 9 | Jadeite bangle, Christie's, Hong Kong, Nov 1, 1999 (HK$19,820,000) | 2,576,600 |
| 10 | Jadeite ring, 1.30 x 0.74 x 0.58 in (33.08 x 18.78 x 14.83 mm), Christie's, Hong Kong, Nov 1, 1999 (HK$18,500,000) | 2,405,000 |

## WORTH ITS WEIGHT IN GOLD

*International trade in gold is customarily carried out with either 32.15-troy ounce (1-kg) or 400-troy ounce (12.5-kg) gold bars.*

# Natural Resources

## TOP 10 ★ MOST PRODUCED NON-FUEL MINERALS

| | MINERAL | 1998 PRODUCTION (TONS) |
|---|---|---|
| 1 | Iron ore* | 1,003,890,630 |
| 2 | Bauxite | 120,073,193 |
| 3 | Clay, kaolin | 113,183,644 |
| 4 | Aluminium | 21,750,963 |
| 5 | Manganese ore | 18,404,661 |
| 6 | Chromite | 12,499,422 |
| 7 | Copper | 12,007,319 |
| 8 | Clay, bentonite | 9,182,647 |
| 9 | Feldspar | 7,952,389 |
| 10 | Zinc | 7,420,917 |

* From which iron and steel are produced

Source: U.S. Geological Survey, Minerals Yearbook

## TOP 10 ★ SALT PRODUCERS

| | COUNTRY | 1998 PRODUCTION (TONS)* |
|---|---|---|
| 1 | US | 40,647,728 |
| 2 | China | 30,313,560 |
| 3 | Germany | 15,452,042 |
| 4 | Canada | 13,089,946 |
| 5 | India | 9,349,962 |
| 6 | Australia | 8,759,439 |
| 7 | Mexico | 8,267,337 |
| 8 | France | 6,889,445 |
| 9 | UK | 6,495,763 |
| 10 | Brazil | 6,397,342 |
| | World | 183,062,409 |

* Includes salt in brine

Source: The Salt Institute

## TOP 10 ★ DIAMOND PRODUCERS, BY VALUE

| | COUNTRY | 1999 VALUE ($) |
|---|---|---|
| 1 | Botswana | 1,600,000,000 |
| 2 | Russia | 1,500,000,000 |
| 3 | South Africa | 900,000,000 |
| 4 | Dem. Rep. of Congo | 700,000,000 |
| 5 | Angola | 500,000,000 |
| 6 = | Australia | 400,000,000 |
| = | Canada | 400,000,000 |
| = | Namibia | 400,000,000 |
| 9 = | Guinea | 100,000,000 |
| = | Sierra Leone | 100,000,000 |

Source: De Beers

## TOP 10 ★ GOLD PRODUCERS

| | COUNTRY | 1999 PRODUCTION (TONS) |
|---|---|---|
| 1 | South Africa | 442.4 |
| 2 | US | 336.5 |
| 3 | Australia | 289.0 |
| 4 | Canada | 155.4 |
| 5 | China | 153.8 |
| 6 | Indonesia | 152.1 |
| 7 | Russia | 136.0 |
| 8 | Peru | 125.4 |
| 9 | Uzbekistan | 84.3 |
| 10 | Ghana | 76.9 |

Source: Gold Fields Mineral Services Ltd

World-dominating gold producer South Africa saw its output fall yet again for the seventh consecutive year. Australia's output also fell in 1999, after having increased dramatically over recent years: the country's record annual production had stood at 117 tons since 1903, but in 1988 it rocketed to 150 tons, a total it doubled in 1998. During the 1990s, several other countries increased their mine output dramatically, most notably Indonesia and Peru, each of which escalated production by a factor of almost nine, while Papua-New Guinea's production falls only just outside the Top 10.

## TOP 10 ★ SILVER PRODUCERS

| | COUNTRY | 1998 PRODUCTION (TONS) |
|---|---|---|
| 1 | Mexico | 2,643 |
| 2 | US | 2,027 |
| 3 | Peru | 1,903 |
| 4 | Australia | 1,446 |
| 5 | China | 1,378 |
| 6 | Chile | 1,377 |
| 7 | Canada | 1,160 |
| 8 | Poland | 984 |
| 9 | Kazakhstan | 462 |
| 10 | Bolivia | 373 |
| | World | 16,141 |

Source: U.S. Geological Survey, Minerals Yearbook

## TOP 10 ★ IRON PRODUCERS

| | COUNTRY | 1999 PRODUCTION (TONS)* |
|---|---|---|
| 1 | China | 123,409,653 |
| 2 | Japan | 73,343,068 |
| 3 | US | 45,568,761 |
| 4 | Russia | 39,400,739 |
| 5 | Germany | 27,489,872 |
| 6 | Brazil | 24,664,215 |
| 7 | South Korea | 22,960,553 |
| 8 | Ukraine | 21,590,538 |
| 9 | India | 19,820,935 |
| 10 | France | 13,635,197 |
| | World | 532,455,717 |

* Pig iron

Source: U.S. Geological Survey, Minerals Yearbook

## TOP 10 ALUMINUM PRODUCERS

(Country/1999 production in tons)

❶ US, 3,719,316 ❷ Russia, 3,096,314 ❸ China, 2,411,306 ❹ Canada, 2,352,254 ❺ Australia, 1,690,867 ❻ Brazil, 1,230,258 ❼ Norway, 1,017,669 ❽ South Africa, 676,149 ❾ Germany, 590,524 ❿ Venezuela, 560,998

World 22,735,170

Source: U.S. Geological Survey, Minerals Yearbook

**Did You Know?** Estimates indicate that if current production levels are maintained, US oil reserves will be exhausted in 2009, while those of the Middle East will last until 2086.

# COAL PRODUCERS

| | COUNTRY | 1999 PRODUCTION (TONS OIL EQUIVALENT*) |
|---|---|---|
| 1 | US | 571,331,873 |
| 2 | China | 504,012,149 |
| 3 | Australia | 147,434,134 |
| 4 | India | 141,824,157 |
| 5 | South Africa | 114,856,898 |
| 6 | Russia | 110,821,652 |
| 7 | Poland | 71,945,495 |
| 8 | Germany | 58,658,707 |
| 9 | Ukraine | 41,631,935 |
| 10 | Indonesia | 39,466,681 |

\* Commercial solid fuels only, i.e. bituminous coal and anthracite (hard coal), lignite, and brown (subbituminous) coal

Source: BP Amoco Statistical Review of World Energy 2000

# NATURAL GAS PRODUCERS

| | COUNTRY | 1999 PRODUCTION (TONS OIL EQUIVALENT*) |
|---|---|---|
| 1 | Russia | 488,068,003 |
| 2 | US | 478,718,042 |
| 3 | Canada | 143,792,569 |
| 4 | UK | 88,283,323 |
| 5 | Algeria | 72,831,281 |
| 6 | Indonesia | 58,855,549 |
| 7 | Netherlands | 53,245,572 |
| 8 | Uzbekistan | 45,962,443 |
| 9 | Norway | 45,175,078 |
| 10 | Saudi Arabia | 40,942,990 |

\* The amount of oil that would be required to produce the same energy output

Source: BP Amoco Statistical Review of World Energy 2000

# OIL PRODUCERS

| | COUNTRY | 1999 PRODUCTION (TONS) |
|---|---|---|
| 1 | Saudi Arabia | 405,296,236 |
| 2 | US | 349,098,046 |
| 3 | Russia | 299,986,141 |
| 4 | Iran | 172,432,979 |
| 5 | Mexico | 163,476,699 |
| 6 | Venezuela | 157,965,143 |
| 7 | China | 156,784,095 |
| 8 | Norway | 146,745,189 |
| 9 | UK | 134,934,711 |
| 10 | Iraq | 123,517,916 |
| | World | 3,397,480,838 |

Source: BP Amoco Statistical Review of World Energy 2000

While most leading countries have increased their oil production, Russia has fallen from the No. 1 slot in the global ranking it occupied 10 years ago.

# COUNTRIES WITH THE GREATEST COAL RESERVES

| | COUNTRY | RESERVES AT END OF 1999 (TONS) |
|---|---|---|
| 1 | US | 242,747,643,780 |
| 2 | Russia | 154,530,262,565 |
| 3 | China | 112,691,644,250 |
| 4 | Australia | 88,972,267,600 |
| 5 | India | 73,552,704,364 |
| 6 | Germany | 65,941,835,500 |
| 7 | South Africa | 54,459,098,264 |
| 8 | Ukraine | 33,813,398,514 |
| 9 | Kazakhstan | 33,463,021,000 |
| 10 | Poland | 14,083,010,808 |

Source: BP Amoco Statistical Review of World Energy 2000

Coal reserves are quantities of coal that can be recovered from known deposits, based on existing engineering and economic conditions, which, of course, may change over time.

# COUNTRIES WITH THE GREATEST NATURAL GAS RESERVES

| | COUNTRY | RESERVES 1999 TRILLION FT³ | TRILLION M³ |
|---|---|---|---|
| 1 | Russia | 1,700.0 | 48.14 |
| 2 | Iran | 812.3 | 23.00 |
| 3 | Qatar | 300.0 | 8.49 |
| 4 | United Arab Emirates | 212.0 | 6.00 |
| 5 | Saudi Arabia | 204.5 | 5.79 |
| 6 | USA | 164.0 | 4.65 |
| 7 | Algeria | 159.7 | 4.52 |
| 8 | Venezuela | 142.5 | 4.04 |
| 9 | Nigeria | 124.0 | 3.51 |
| 10 | Iraq | 109.8 | 3.11 |

Source: BP Amoco Statistical Review of World Energy 2000

Total world reserves in 1999 were put at 5,171.8 trillion cubic feet (146.43 trillion cubic meters), more than double the 1979 estimate.

# COUNTRIES WITH THE GREATEST CRUDE OIL RESERVES

| | COUNTRY | RESERVES AT END OF 1999 (TONS) |
|---|---|---|
| 1 | Saudi Arabia | 35,431,434,000 |
| 2 | Iraq | 14,861,518,150 |
| 3 | Kuwait | 13,089,946,450 |
| 4 | United Arab Emirates | 12,401,001,900 |
| 5 | Iran | 12,105,739,950 |
| 6 | Venezuela | 10,334,168,250 |
| 7 | Russia | 6,594,183,550 |
| 8 | Mexico | 4,035,246,650 |
| 9 | Libya | 3,838,405,350 |
| 10 | US | 3,444,722,750 |

Source: BP Amoco Statistical Review of World Energy 2000

The discovery of new oil means that total world reserves at the end of 1999 stood at 148 billion tons, 63 percent more than the 1979 estimate.

Background image: COPPER, NICKEL, AND IRON ORES

# Energy & Environment

## NUCLEAR ELECTRICITY-PRODUCING COUNTRIES

| | COUNTRY | 1999 PRODUCTION (KW/HR) |
|---|---|---|
| 1 | US | 728,200,000,000 |
| 2 | France | 375,100,000,000 |
| 3 | Japan | 308,700,000,000 |
| 4 | Germany | 161,000,000,000 |
| 5 | Russia | 110,900,000,000 |
| 6 | South Korea | 97,900,000,000 |
| 7 | UK | 91,500,000,000 |
| 8 | Canada | 69,800,000,000 |
| 9 | Ukraine | 67,300,000,000 |
| 10 | Sweden | 66,600,000,000 |
| | *World* | *2,395,900,000,000* |

Source: *Energy Information Administration*

## PAPER-RECYCLING COUNTRIES

| | COUNTRY | 1999 RECYCLING (TONNES) |
|---|---|---|
| 1 | US | 41,167,828 |
| 2 | Japan | 14,841,000 |
| 3 | China | 12,014,000 |
| 4 | Germany | 10,292,000 |
| 5 | France | 5,000,000 |
| 6 | South Korea | 3,869,000 |
| 7 | UK | 3,675,000 |
| 8 | Italy | 3,628,800 |
| 9 | Netherlands | 2,417,000 |
| 10 | Canada | 1,478,000 |
| | *World* | *115,331,303* |

Source: *Food and Agriculture Organization of the United Nations*

## WATT

James Watt (1736–1819) is remembered as the inventor of the modern steam engine, and the man after whom the unit of power is named. He introduced great improvements to the steam engine invented by Thomas Newcomen, patented many other inventions, and undertook experiments relating to power, introducing the concept of "horsepower." The use of the term "watt" was proposed in 1882, and is equivalent to an amp multiplied by a volt (each named after other electrical pioneers, André Marie Ampère and Allessandro Volta), or one joule per second. It is most commonly used as a measure of the intensity of light-bulbs, and in terms of electrical consumption in kilowatt/hours.

WHO WAS • WHO WAS • WHO WAS • WHO WAS •
?

## TOP 10 COUNTRIES WITH THE MOST RELIANCE ON NUCLEAR POWER

*(Country/nuclear electricity as percentage of total electricity)*

**1** France, 75.00 **2** Lithuania, 73.11 **3** Belgium, 57.74 **4** Bulgaria, 47.12
**5** Slovak Republic, 47.02 **6** Sweden, 46.80 **7** Ukraine, 43.77 **8** South Korea, 42.84
**9** Hungary, 38.30 **10** Slovenia, 37.18   *UK, 28.87*

Source: *International Atomic Energy Agency*

## ALTERNATIVE POWER-CONSUMING COUNTRIES*

| | COUNTRY | 1999 CONSUMPTION (KW/HR) |
|---|---|---|
| 1 | US | 83,000,000,000 |
| 2 | Japan | 24,700,000,000 |
| 3 | Germany | 15,000,000,000 |
| 4 | Brazil | 9,900,000,000 |
| 5 | Finland | 9,500,000,000 |
| 6 | Philippines | 8,300,000,000 |
| 7 | UK | 8,200,000,000 |
| 8 | Canada | 7,500,000,000 |
| 9 | Italy | 7,000,000,000 |
| 10 | Mexico | 5,300,000,000 |
| | *World* | *227,400,000,000* |

\* *Includes geothermal, solar, wind, wood, and waste electric power*

Source: *Energy Information Administration*

## NUCLEAR REACTOR

*Opened in 1985–86, Pacific Gas and Electric's Diablo Canyon Nuclear Power Station in California is one of the US's 104 nuclear reactors.*

206

TOP 10 ★

# CARBON DIOXIDE-EMITTING COUNTRIES

| | COUNTRY | CO₂ EMISSIONS PER HEAD, 1997 (TONS OF CARBON) |
|---|---|---|
| 1 | Qatar | 20.05 |
| 2 | United Arab Emirates | 10.36 |
| 3 | Kuwait | 8.69 |
| 4 | Guam | 7.76 |
| 5 | Bahrain | 7.66 |
| 6 | Singapore | 7.04 |
| 7 | US | 6.04 |
| 8 | Luxembourg | 5.69 |
| 9 | Brunei | 5.28 |
| 10 | Australia | 5.19 |

Source: *Gregg Marland and Tom Boden (Oak Ridge National Laboratory) and Bob Andres (University of North Dakota)*

$CO_2$ emissions derive from three principal sources: fossil fuel burning, cement manufacturing, and gas flaring. Since World War II, increasing industrialization in many countries has resulted in huge increases in carbon output, a trend that most countries are now actively attempting to reverse. There has been some degree of success among the former leaders in this Top 10, although the US remains the worst offender in total, with 1.7 billion tons released in 1997.

## TOP 10 ★

# DEFORESTING COUNTRIES

| | COUNTRY | AVERAGE ANNUAL FOREST LOSS, 1990-95 SQ MILES | SQ KM |
|---|---|---|---|
| 1 | Brazil | 9,863 | 25,544 |
| 2 | Indonesia | 4,187 | 10,844 |
| 3 | Dem. Rep. of Congo | 2,857 | 7,400 |
| 4 | Bolivia | 2,245 | 5,814 |
| 5 | Mexico | 1,961 | 5,080 |
| 6 | Venezuela | 1,944 | 5,034 |
| 7 | Malaysia | 1,545 | 4,002 |
| 8 | Myanmar (Burma) | 1,496 | 3,874 |
| 9 | Sudan | 1,361 | 3,526 |
| 10 | Thailand | 1,271 | 3,294 |

Source: *Food and Agriculture Organization of the United Nations*

Some 18,433 sq miles (47,740 sq km) of tropical forest was lost in South America each year between 1990 and 1995, plus a further 14,471 sq miles (37,480 sq km) in Africa, and 12,849 sq miles (33,280 sq km) in Asia. The total global loss during that five-year period was 217,553 sq miles (563,460 sq km), an area equivalent to twice the size of the UK. However, while Brazil tops the list of countries with the highest amount of forest loss, the rate of deforestation is only 0.5 percent.

**POWER TO THE PEOPLE**

*In the 20th century the creation of national grids for the transmission of electricity brought power to even the most remote communities.*

## TOP 10 ★

# ENERGY-CONSUMING COUNTRIES

| | COUNTRY | 1999 ENERGY CONSUMPTION* | | | | | |
|---|---|---|---|---|---|---|---|
| | | OIL | GAS | COAL | NUCLEAR | HEP[#] | TOTAL |
| 1 | US | 882.8 | 555.3 | 543.3 | 197.7 | 25.8 | 2,204.9 |
| 2 | China | 200.0 | 19.3 | 511.0 | 4.1 | 18.2 | 752.6 |
| 3 | Russia | 126.2 | 327.3 | 109.3 | 31.2 | 13.8 | 607.8 |
| 4 | Japan | 258.8 | 67.1 | 91.5 | 82.0 | 8.0 | 507.4 |
| 5 | Germany | 132.4 | 72.1 | 80.6 | 43.8 | 2.0 | 330.9 |
| 6 | India | 94.8 | 21.4 | 150.0 | 3.3 | 6.9 | 276.4 |
| 7 | France | 96.4 | 33.9 | 14.1 | 101.5 | 6.6 | 252.4 |
| 8 | Canada | 83.0 | 64.3 | 31.9 | 19.0 | 29.6 | 227.8 |
| 9 | UK | 78.7 | 82.5 | 35.8 | 24.8 | 0.6 | 222.4 |
| 10 | South Korea | 99.9 | 16.9 | 38.1 | 26.6 | 0.5 | 182.0 |
| | World | 3,462.4 | 2,063.9 | 2,129.5 | 650.8 | 226.8 | 8,533.6 |

*\* Millions of tonnes of oil equivalent    # Hydroelectric power*

Source: BP Amoco Statistical Review of World Energy 2000

## TOP 10 ★

# ELECTRICITY-CONSUMING COUNTRIES

| | COUNTRY | 1999 CONSUMPTION (KW/HR) |
|---|---|---|
| 1 | US | 3,254,900,000,000 |
| 2 | China | 1,084,100,000,000 |
| 3 | Japan | 947,000,000,000 |
| 4 | Russia | 728,200,000,000 |
| 5 | Canada | 497,500,000,000 |
| 6 | Germany | 495,200,000,000 |
| 7 | India | 424,000,000,000 |
| 8 | France | 398,800,000,000 |
| 9 | Brazil | 353,700,000,000 |
| 10 | UK | 333,000,000,000 |
| | World | 12,832,700,000,000 |

Source: *Energy Information Administration*

**Did You Know?** While other countries have steadily increased their energy consumption, in the 15 years from 1984 to 1999 India more than doubled its requirements.

# Science & Invention

## FIRST TRADEMARKS ISSUED IN THE US

| | ISSUED TO | PRODUCT |
|---|---|---|
| 1 | Averill Chemical-Paint Company | Liquid paint |
| 2 | J. B. Baldy & Co. | Mustard |
| 3 | Ellis Branson | Retail coal |
| 4 | Tracy Coit | Fish |
| 5 | William Lanfair Ellis & Co. | Oyster packing |
| 6 | Evans, Clow, Dalzell & Co. | Wrought-iron pipe |
| 7 | W. E. Garrett & Sons | Snuff |
| 8 | William G. Hamilton | Cartwheel |
| 9 | John K. Hogg | Soap |
| 10 | Abraham P. Olzendam | Woolen hose |

All of these trademarks were registered on the same day, October 25, 1870 and are distinguished in the ranking only by the trademark numbers assigned to them.

## FIRST PATENTEES IN THE US

| | PATENTEE/PATENT | DATE |
|---|---|---|
| 1 | Samuel Hopkins, Making pot and pearl ash | July 31, 1790 |
| 2 | Joseph S. Sampson, Candle making | Aug 6, 1790 |
| 3 | Oliver Evans, Flour and meal making | Dec 18, 1790 |
| 4 = | Francis Bailey, Punches for type | Jan 29, 1791 |
| = | Aaron Putnam, Improvement in distilling | Jan 29, 1791 |
| 6 | John Stone, Driving piles | Mar 10, 1791 |
| 7 = | Samuel Mullikin, Threshing machine | Mar 11, 1791 |
| = | Samuel Mullikin, Breaking hemp | Mar 11, 1791 |
| = | Samuel Mullikin, Polishing marble | Mar 11, 1791 |
| = | Samuel Mullikin, Raising nap on cloth | Mar 11, 1791 |

## PATENT COMPANIES IN THE US

| | COMPANY | PATENTS (1999) |
|---|---|---|
| 1 | International Business Machines Corp. | 2,756 |
| 2 | NEC Corporation | 1,842 |
| 3 | Canon Kabushiki Kaisha | 1,795 |
| 4 | Samsung Electronics Co. Ltd. | 1,545 |
| 5 | Sony Corporation | 1,409 |
| 6 | Toshiba Corporation | 1,200 |
| 7 | Fujitsu Limited | 1,193 |
| 8 | Motorola Inc. | 1,192 |
| 9 | Lucent Technologies Inc. | 1,153 |
| 10 | Mitsubishi Denki Kabushiki Kaisha | 1,054 |

For the seventh consecutive year, the International Business Machines Corporation (IBM) received more patents than any other organization.

## MOST PROLIFIC PATENTEES IN THE US

| | PATENTEE | PATENTS* |
|---|---|---|
| 1 | Thomas A. Edison | 1,093 |
| 2 | Donald E. Weder | 934 |
| 3 | Shunpei Yamazaki | 679 |
| 4 | Francis H. Richards | 619 |
| 5 | Edwin Herbert Land | 533 |
| 6 = | Marvin Camras | 500 |
| = | Jerome H. Lemelson | 500 |
| 8 | Elihu Thomson | 444 |
| 9 | George Westinghouse | 400 |
| 10 | Charles E. Scribner | 374 |

*Minimum number credited to each inventor*

Such is the complexity of the whole subject of patent registration (patents may be registered to individuals or to the companies that employ them) that this list can only be a tentative attempt to rank the 10 leading US inventors. Electricity, radio, and television feature prominently among the many patents credited to these individuals, but their inventions also encompass Land's Polaroid camera and Lemelson's tape drive, used in the Sony Walkman, and his Velcro dart-board.

## COUNTRIES TO REGISTER THE MOST PATENTS

| | COUNTRY | PATENTS REGISTERED (1998) |
|---|---|---|
| 1 | US | 147,520 |
| 2 | Japan | 141,448 |
| 3 | Germany | 51,685 |
| 4 | France | 46,213 |
| 5 | UK | 43,181 |
| 6 | Italy | 38,988 |
| 7 | Russia | 23,368 |
| 8 | Netherlands | 22,411 |
| 9 | Spain | 20,128 |
| 10 | Sweden | 18,482 |

Source: *World Intellectual Property Organization*

A patent is an exclusive license to manufacture and exploit a unique product or process for a fixed period. The figures refer to the number of patents actually granted during 1998 – which, in most instances, represents only a fraction of the patents applied for. For example, a total of 262,787 applications were registered in the US, but the process of obtaining a patent can be tortuous, and many are refused after investigations show that the product is too similar to one already patented.

## US STATES FOR PATENTS

| | STATE* | PATENTS GRANTED (1999) |
|---|---|---|
| 1 | California | 16,778 |
| 2 | New York | 6,107 |
| 3 | Texas | 6,049 |
| 4 | New Jersey | 3,988 |
| 5 | Pennsylvania | 3,752 |
| 6 | Illinois | 3,736 |
| 7 | Michigan | 3,690 |
| 8 | Massachusetts | 3,523 |
| 9 | Ohio | 3,362 |
| 10 | Minnesota | 2,651 |

*Residence of patentee*

The overall total of patents for 1999 was 83,911. Wyoming residents registered the fewest: just 52.

## TOP 10 ★
## COUNTRIES TO REGISTER THE MOST TRADEMARKS

| | COUNTRY | TRADEMARKS REGISTERED (1998) |
|---|---|---|
| 1 | Japan | 132,066 |
| 2 | US | 129,871 |
| 3 | China | 98,961 |
| 4 | Argentina | 61,671 |
| 5 | Spain | 59,810 |
| 6 | Germany | 57,919 |
| 7 | UK | 48,600 |
| 8 | Italy | 46,707 |
| 9 | Benelux | 32,093 |
| 10 | Mexico | 28,362 |

Source: *World Intellectual Property Organization*

## TOP 10 ★
## US ACADEMIC INSTITUTIONS FOR RESEARCH AND DEVELOPMENT FUNDING

| | INSTITUTION | TOTAL R&D FUNDING (1997) |
|---|---|---|
| 1 | University of Michigan | 483,000,000 |
| 2 | Johns Hopkins University | 421,000,000 |
| 3 | University of Wisconsin-Madison | 420,000,000 |
| 4 | Massachusetts Institute of Technology | 411,000,000 |
| 5 | University of Washington-Seattle | 410,000,000 |
| 6 | Johns Hopkins University Applied Physics Laboratory | 408,000,000 |
| 7 | Stanford University | 395,000,000 |
| 8 | University of California-San Diego | 378,000,000 |
| 9 | University of California-Los Angeles | 375,000,000 |
| 10 | Texas A&M University | 367,000,000 |
| | Total (all institutions) | 24,348,000,000 |

Source: *US National Science Foundation*

## TOP 10 ★
## COUNTRIES FOR RESEARCH AND DEVELOPMENT EXPENDITURE

| | COUNTRY | R&D EXPENDITURE AS PERCENTAGE OF GNP* |
|---|---|---|
| 1 | Sweden | 3.76 |
| 2 | South Korea | 2.82 |
| 3 | Japan | 2.80 |
| 4 | Finland | 2.78 |
| 5 | US | 2.63 |
| 6 | Switzerland | 2.60 |
| 7 | Germany | 2.41 |
| 8 | Israel | 2.35 |
| 9 | France | 2.25 |
| 10 | Italy | 2.21 |

* In latest year for which statistics available

Source: *World Bank*, World Development Indicators 2000

## TOP 10 ★
## COUNTRIES FOR SCIENTIFIC AND TECHNICAL JOURNAL ARTICLES

| | COUNTRY | AVERAGE NUMBER PUBLISHED PER ANNUM (1995–97) |
|---|---|---|
| 1 | US | 173,233 |
| 2 | Japan | 43,655 |
| 3 | UK | 39,670 |
| 4 | Germany | 35,294 |
| 5 | France | 26,455 |
| 6 | Canada | 20,989 |
| 7 | Russia | 17,589 |
| 8 | Italy | 16,256 |
| 9 | Australia | 11,830 |
| 10 | Netherlands | 10,914 |
| | World total | 515,708 |

Source: *US National Science Foundation*

## TOP 10 ★
## COUNTRIES FOR RESEARCH AND DEVELOPMENT SCIENTISTS AND ENGINEERS

| | COUNTRY | R&D SCIENTISTS AND ENGINEERS PER MILLION* |
|---|---|---|
| 1 | Japan | 4,909 |
| 2 | Sweden | 3,826 |
| 3 | US | 3,676 |
| 4 | Norway | 3,664 |
| 5 | Russia | 3,587 |
| 6 | Australia | 3,357 |
| 7 | Denmark | 3,259 |
| 8 | Switzerland | 3,006 |
| 9 | Germany | 2,831 |
| 10 | Finland | 2,799 |

* In latest year for which statistics available

Source: *World Bank*, World Development Indicators 2000

## TOP 10 ★
## COUNTRIES FOR HIGH-TECHNOLOGY EXPORTS

| | COUNTRY | HIGH-TECHNOLOGY EXPORTS ($)* |
|---|---|---|
| 1 | US | 170,681,000,000 |
| 2 | Japan | 94,777,000,000 |
| 3 | UK | 64,461,000,000 |
| 4 | Germany | 63,698,000,000 |
| 5 | Singapore | 54,783,000,000 |
| 6 | France | 54,183,000,000 |
| 7 | Netherlands | 35,377,000,000 |
| 8 | Malaysia | 31,419,000,000 |
| 9 | South Korea | 30,582,000,000 |
| 10 | Ireland | 23,944,000,000 |

* In latest year for which statistics available

Source: *World Bank*, World Development Indicators 2000

**Did You Know?** In 1870, William Underwood & Co. of Boston registered the first US trademark for a food product. It was the image of a devil for the canned deviled ham that the company had launched three years earlier.

# Communication Matters

## TOP 10 ★
## COUNTRIES WITH THE MOST TELEPHONES

| | COUNTRY | TOTAL TELEPHONE LINES | TELEPHONE LINES PER 100 INHABITANTS | | COUNTRY | TOTAL TELEPHONE LINES | TELEPHONE LINES PER 100 INHABITANTS |
|---|---|---|---|---|---|---|---|
| 1 | Luxembourg | 308,000 | 73.33 | 7 | Iceland | 183,000 | 65.36 |
| 2 | Norway | 3,155,000 | 71.19 | 8 | Canada | 19,630,000 | 63.67 |
| 3 | US | 193,862,000 | 70.98 | 9 | Netherlands | 9,878,000 | 62.60 |
| 4 | Switzerland | 5,023,000 | 70.11 | 10 | Australia | 11,609,000 | 61.04 |
| 5 | Sweden | 6,160,000 | 69.45 | | | | |
| 6 | Denmark | 3,555,000 | 67.08 | | | | |

Source: *Siemens AG,* International Telecom Statistics 2000

## TOP 10 ★
## COUNTRIES WITH THE HIGHEST RATIO OF CELLULAR MOBILE PHONE USERS

| | COUNTRY | SUBSCRIBERS | MOBILES PER 100 INHABITANTS |
|---|---|---|---|
| 1 | Finland | 3,499,000 | 67.8 |
| 2 | Norway | 2,779,000 | 62.7 |
| 3 | Sweden | 5,234,000 | 59.0 |
| 4 | Italy | 30,068,000 | 52.2 |
| 5 | Austria | 4,147,000 | 51.3 |
| 6 | Denmark | 2,682,000 | 50.6 |
| 7 | South Korea | 23,493,000 | 49.9 |
| 8 | Taiwan | 10,835,000 | 49.4 |
| 9 | Portugal | 4,720,000 | 47.4 |
| 10 | Switzerland | 3,164,000 | 44.2 |
| | US | 86,000,000 | 31.5 |

Source: *Siemens AG,* International Telecom Statistics 2000

## TOP 10 ★
## COUNTRIES MAKING THE MOST INTERNATIONAL PHONE CALLS

| | COUNTRY | MINUTES PER HEAD, 1999 | TOTAL MINUTES OUTGOING CALLS, 1999 |
|---|---|---|---|
| 1 | US | 102.7 | 28,363,000,000 |
| 2 | Germany | 89.9 | 7,385,000,000 |
| 3 | UK | 101.9 | 6,066,000,000 |
| 4 | Canada | 174.1 | 5,310,000,000 |
| 5 | France | 74.9 | 4,386,000,000 |
| 6 | Italy | 54.0 | 3,100,000,000 |
| 7 | Switzerland | 335.9 | 2,400,000,000 |
| 8 | Netherlands | 135.7 | 2,150,000,000 |
| 9 | Japan | 15.5 | 1,957,000,000 |
| 10 | China | 1.5 | 1,950,000,000 |

Source: *International Telecommunication Union*

### THE FIRST TRANSPACIFIC TELEGRAPH CABLE

In 1858, the first transatlantic cable was laid, and, following this, the idea of a transpacific cable between Canada and Australia was proposed in 1887. It was not until 1902, however, that the dream became a reality. In that year, a specially built ship, the *Colonia*, laid an undersea cable from Bamfield, Vancouver Island, in Canada, to the Fanning, Fiji, and Norfolk islands. From here it branched to Brisbane, Australia, and Doubtless Bay on the north island of New Zealand. Despite the technical difficulties of laying some 8,000 miles (12,875 km) of cable, often at great depths, the project was completed on schedule. On October 31, Canadian engineer Sir Sandford Fleming sent the first telegram from Canada to Australia, and the whole system was opened on December 8, remaining in service until 1964.

• YEARS AGO • YEARS AGO • YEARS AGO • **100**

**END OF THE LINE**

*In many countries, the recent expansion of cellular phone networks has resulted in a decline in the popularity of public telephones.*

## TOP 10 ★
### LETTER-POSTING COUNTRIES

| | COUNTRY | AVERAGE NO. OF LETTER POST ITEMS POSTED PER INHABITANT* |
|---|---|---|
| 1 | Vatican City | 5,740.0 |
| 2 | US | 734.4 |
| 3 | Sweden | 502.8 |
| 4 | France | 442.8 |
| 5 | Finland | 396.5 |
| 6 | Austria | 371.6 |
| 7 | Belgium | 344.1 |
| 8 | Norway | 338.0 |
| 9 | Luxembourg | 336.1 |
| 10 | Denmark | 334.7 |

\* In 1999 or latest year for which data available
Source: *Universal Postal Union*

The Vatican's population (which is variable, but seldom exceeds 750) is small. This statistical anomaly results in part from the large numbers of official missives dispatched via the Holy See's post office and its 32 postboxes, but mainly because Rome's inhabitants have discovered that mail posted in the Vatican City and bearing Vatican stamps is treated as priority.

## TOP 10 ★
### COUNTRIES WITH THE MOST POST OFFICES

| | COUNTRY | POST OFFICES* |
|---|---|---|
| 1 | India | 154,149 |
| 2 | China | 117,052 |
| 3 | Russia | 41,556 |
| 4 | US | 38,169 |
| 5 | Japan | 24,755 |
| 6 | Indonesia | 20,139 |
| 7 | UK | 18,341 |
| 8 | France | 16,930 |
| 9 | Italy | 15,079 |
| 10 | Ukraine | 14,931 |

\* 1999 or latest year for which data available
Source: *Universal Postal Union*

There are some 770,000 post offices around the world. These range from major city post offices offering a wide range of services, to small establishments providing only basic facilities, such as the sale of postage stamps. The average number of inhabitants served by each post office also varies considerably, from fewer than 2,000 people in countries such as Cyprus and Belize to as many as 230,000 people in Burundi.

## THE 10 COUNTRIES RECEIVING THE MOST LETTERS FROM ABROAD

*(Country/items of mail handled, 1999\*)*

❶ Germany, 702,000,000 ❷ India, 561,640,000
❸ UK, 535,812,069 ❹ France, 476,000,000
❺ US, 474,347,500 ❻ Saudi Arabia, 340,105,000
❼ Netherlands, 299,000,000 ❽ Japan, 289,593,000
❾ Algeria, 217,600,000 ❿ Italy, 217,446,283

\* Or latest year for which data available
Source: *Universal Postal Union*

## THE 10 COUNTRIES SENDING THE MOST LETTERS ABROAD

*(Country/items of mail handled, 1999\*)*

❶ UK, 986,786,244 ❷ US, 904,600,000 ❸ France, 576,200,000
❹ Germany, 402,600,000 ❺ Saudi Arabia, 347,696,000
❻ Finland, 306,300,000 ❼ Russia, 221,800,000 ❽ Algeria, 201,000,000 ❾ Belgium, 193,793,831 ❿ India, 177,300,000

\* Or latest year for which data available
Source: *Universal Postal Union*

भारत INDIA · SAUSSUREA SIMPSONIANA · 5.00
भारत INDIA · CAPRA FALCONERI · 5.00
भारत INDIA · ITHAGINIS CRUENTUS · 5.00
भारत INDIA · MECONOPSIS HORRIDULA · 5.00

**INDIAN STAMPS**

*India has more post offices and more postal workers than any other country in the world. Its system handles over 16 billion letters and 285 million packages a year.*

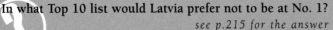

In what Top 10 list would Latvia prefer not to be at No. 1?
*see p.215 for the answer*

A  Most accident-prone country
B  Country with the most bank robberies
C  Country with the highest suicide rate

# The World Wide Web

## ONLINE LANGUAGES

| LANGUAGE | INTERNET ACCESS* |
|---|---|
| 1 English | 230,000,000 |
| 2 Chinese | 160,000,000 |
| 3 Spanish | 60,000,000 |
| 4 Japanese | 58,000,000 |
| 5 German | 46,000,000 |
| 6 Korean | 35,000,000 |
| 7 Portuguese | 32,000,000 |
| 8 French | 30,000,000 |
| 9 Italian | 23,000,000 |
| 10 Russian | 15,000,000 |
| *World total* | 774,000,000 |

\* *Online population estimate for 2003*

Source: *Global Reach*

## BUSIEST INTERNET SITES

| SITE | HITS* |
|---|---|
| 1 yahoo.com | 65,910,000 |
| 2 aol.com | 53,373,000 |
| 3 msn.com | 47,330,000 |
| 4 microsoft.com | 39,905,000 |
| 5 passport.com | 37,807,000 |
| 6 geocities.com | 36,294,000 |
| 7 AOLProprietary.aol | 32,879,000 |
| 8 amazon.com | 28,534,000 |
| 9 lycos.com | 25,898,000 |
| 10 ebay.com | 25,031,000 |

\* *Number of accesses during December 2000*

Source: *PC Data Online*

## INTERNET DOMAINS

| DOMAIN | COUNTRY | REGISTRATIONS |
|---|---|---|
| 1 .com | US/International | 21,151,560 |
| 2 .net | International | 3,986,781 |
| 3 .org | International | 2,503,682 |
| 4 .co.uk | UK | 2,317,009 |
| 5 .de | Germany | 1,032,618 |
| 6 .nl | Netherlands | 544,594 |
| 7 .it | Italy | 404,893 |
| 8 .co.kr | South Korea | 332,801 |
| 9 .com.ar | Argentina | 301,394 |
| 10 .org.uk | UK | 154,838 |
| | *World total* | 34,995,298 |

## ITEMS MOST PURCHASED ONLINE IN THE US

| ITEM | PERCENTAGE* |
|---|---|
| 1 Computers and computer products | 66 |
| 2 Books | 62 |
| 3 CDs, recorded music | 60 |
| 4 = Electronic products | 35 |
| = Toys | 35 |
| 6 Videos, filmed entertainment | 33 |
| 7 Cosmetics, fragrances, health and beauty aids | 32 |
| 8 Clothing and accessories (women's) | 30 |
| 9 = Air travel reservations | 28 |
| = Magazines | 28 |

\* *Percentage of purchasers who have bought item online*

Source: Stores/*Ernst & Young*, Global Online Retailing, 2000

iBook

DORLING KINDERSLEY

**E-SHOPPING**

*The ability to locate and purchase both new and used books online has been heralded as among the most popular of the internet's many benefits.*

## TOP 10 ★
# COUNTRIES WITH THE HIGHEST DENSITY OF INTERNET HOSTS

| | COUNTRY | INTERNET HOSTS PER 1,000 PEOPLE |
|---|---|---|
| 1 | Finland | 108.00 |
| 2 | US | 88.90 |
| 3 | Iceland | 78.70 |
| 4 | Norway | 71.80 |
| 5 | Canada | 53.50 |
| 6 | New Zealand | 49.70 |
| 7 | Australia | 42.70 |
| 8 | Sweden | 35.10 |
| 9 | Netherlands | 34.60 |
| 10 | Switzerland | 27.90 |

Source: *United Nations,* Human Development Report, 1999

An internet host is a computer system connected to the internet – either a single terminal directly connected, or a computer that allows multiple users to access network services through it. The ratio of hosts to population is a crude measure of how "wired" a country is.

## TOP 10 ★
# COMPUTER COMPANIES

| | COMPANY/COUNTRY | ANNUAL SALES ($)* |
|---|---|---|
| 1 | IBM, US | 88,396,000,000 |
| 2 | Hewlett-Packard, US | 48,782,000,000 |
| 3 | Fujitsu, Japan | 47,196,000,000 |
| 4 | Compaq Computer, US | 42,383,000,000 |
| 5 | Dell Computer, US | 31,888,000,000 |
| 6 | Canon, Japan | 23,062,000,000 |
| 7 | Xerox, US | 18,632,000,000 |
| 8 | Sun Microsystems, US | 15,721,000,000 |
| 9 | Ricoh, Japan | 12,997,000,000 |
| 10 | Gateway, US | 9,601,000,000 |

* In latest year for which figures are available

Source: Fortune *Global 500*

## TOP 10 ★
# COUNTRIES WITH THE MOST INTERNET USERS

| | COUNTRY | PERCENTAGE OF POPULATION | INTERNET USERS* | | COUNTRY | PERCENTAGE OF POPULATION | INTERNET USERS* |
|---|---|---|---|---|---|---|---|
| 1 | US | 54.7 | 153,840,000 | 7 | Italy | 23.4 | 13,420,000 |
| 2 | Japan | 30.5 | 38,640,000 | 8 | Canada | 42.6 | 13,280,000 |
| 3 | Germany | 24.4 | 20,100,000 | 9 | Brazil | 5.8 | 9,840,000 |
| 4 | UK | 33.9 | 19,940,000 | 10 | Russia | 6.3 | 9,200,000 |
| 5 | China | 1.3 | 16,900,000 | | World total | 6.7 | 407,100,000 |
| 6 | South Korea | 35.0 | 16,400,000 | | | | |

* Estimates for weekly usage as of end of 2000

Source: *Computer Industry Almanac, Inc.*

## TOP 10 ★
# COUNTRIES WITH THE MOST COMPUTERS

| | COUNTRY | PERCENTAGE OF WORLD TOTAL | COMPUTERS |
|---|---|---|---|
| 1 | US | 28.32 | 164,100,000 |
| 2 | Japan | 8.62 | 49,900,000 |
| 3 | Germany | 5.28 | 30,600,000 |
| 4 | UK | 4.49 | 26,000,000 |
| 5 | France | 3.77 | 21,800,000 |
| 6 | Italy | 3.02 | 17,500,000 |
| 7 | Canada | 2.76 | 16,000,000 |
| 8 | China | 2.75 | 15,900,000 |
| 9 = | Australia | 1.82 | 10,600,000 |
| = | South Korea | 1.82 | 10,600,000 |

Source: *Computer Industry Almanac, Inc.*

Computer industry estimates put the number of computers in the world at 98 million in 1990, 222 million in 1995, and 579 million in 2000 – a sixfold increase over the decade – with the Top 10 countries owning over 62 percent of the total.

## TOP 10 ★
# USES OF THE INTERNET

| | ACTVITY | PERCENTAGE OF INTERNET USERS* |
|---|---|---|
| 1 | Email | 90 |
| 2 | General information | 77 |
| 3 | Surfing | 69 |
| 4 | Reading | 67 |
| 5 | Hobbies | 63 |
| 6 | Product information | 62 |
| 7 | Travel information | 54 |
| 8 | Work/business | 46 |
| 9 = | Entertainment/games | 36 |
| = | Buying | 36 |

* Based on US sample survey, 2000

Source: *Stanford Institute for the Quantitative Study of Society*

In addition, those polled also identified stock quotations (27%), job search (26%), chat rooms (24%), homework (21%), auctions (13%), banking (12%), and trading stocks (7%).

## COMPUTER POWER FIRST DEMONSTRATED

Automatic programming of computers is credited to Grace Hopper, an employee of US manufacturers Remington-Rand. In 1951, her company had created the Univac I (UNIVersal Automatic Computer), an expensive and gigantic machine weighing some 35 tons (32 tonnes). It was slow (its clock speed was 2.25 MHz, while 500 MHz or more is now commonplace), and it required the operator to write programs on punch cards and then transfer them on to magnetic tape. Despite these drawbacks, the Univac I proved its accuracy when it was used by the CBS television network to correctly predict a landslide victory for Eisenhower at the 1952 US election. In 1954, General Electric purchased a Univac, thus becoming the first commercial organization to use a computer.

*50 YEARS AGO · YEARS AGO · YEARS AGO*

**Did You Know?** In 1943 Thomas Watson, chairman of IBM, stated "I think there is a world market for maybe five computers." Six years later, *Popular Mechanics* magazine predicted that "Computers in the future may weigh no more than 1.5 tons."

213

# Hazards at Home & Work

## MOST DANGEROUS OCCUPATIONS IN THE US

| OCCUPATION | FATAL INJURIES, 1999 |
|---|---|
| 1 Truck drivers | 898 |
| 2 Management/administrative executive | 371 |
| 3 Farming operators and managers | 362 |
| 4 Mechanics and repairers | 353 |
| 5 Construction laborers | 341 |
| 6 Farmers (except horticultural) | 233 |
| 7 Professional specialty | 226 |
| 8 Machine operators, assemblers, and inspectors | 216 |
| 9 Other farm workers, including supervisors | 206 |
| 10 Material moving equipment operators | 205 |

Source: *US Bureau of Labor Statistics*, National Census of Fatal Occupational Injuries, 1999

Of the total of 6,023 occupational fatalities reported, those involving truck drivers comprise some 15 percent.

**DANGER ON DECK**

*Exposure to extreme weather conditions and other hazards places fishing among the world's most dangerous industries.*

## THE 10 MOST COMMON CAUSES OF ACCIDENTAL DEATH IN THE US

*(Type of accident/total deaths, 1997)*

❶ **Motor vehicle**, 42,340 ❷ **Fall**, 11,858 ❸ **Poisoning**, 10,163 ❹ **Suffocation**, 4,420 ❺ **Drowning and submersion**, 4,051 ❻ **Adverse event-related** (medical care and drugs), 3,291 ❼ **Residential fire and flames**, 3,146 ❽ **Firearm**, 981 ❾ **Striking by/against**, 974 ❿ **Cutting and piercing**, 104

*Total unintentional and adverse event-related deaths 95,644*

Source: *National Center for Injury Prevention and Control*

## MOST COMMON WORK INJURIES IN THE US

| INJURY/ILLNESS* | NONFATAL INJURIES, 1998 |
|---|---|
| 1 Sprains/strains | 760,000 |
| 2 Bruises/contusions | 153,100 |
| 3 Cuts/lacerations | 137,600 |
| 4 Fractures | 115,400 |
| 5 Multiple traumatic injuries | 57,600 |
| 6 Heat burns | 28,400 |
| 7 Carpal tunnel syndrome | 26,300 |
| 8 Tendonitis | 16,900 |
| 9 Chemical burns | 11,700 |
| 10 Amputations | 10,200 |
| Total cases | 1,730,500 |

\* *Requiring days away from work*
Source: *US Bureau of Labor Statistics*

## MOST COMMON PRODUCTS INVOLVED IN ACCIDENTS IN US HOMES

| PRODUCT GROUP | ACCIDENTS, 1999 |
|---|---|
| 1 Stairs, ramps, landings, and floors | 2,052,256 |
| 2 Beds, mattresses, and pillows | 472,012 |
| 3 Chairs, sofas, and sofa beds | 417,366 |
| 4 Tables | 304,758 |
| 5 Bathroom structures and fixtures | 273,551 |
| 6 Cans and other containers | 239,780 |
| 7 Desks, cabinets, shelves, and racks | 239,535 |
| 8 Exercise equipment | 224,551 |
| 9 Ladders and stools | 178,199 |
| 10 Glass doors, windows, and panels | 169,329 |

Source: *US Consumer Product Safety Commission/ NEISS (National Electronic Injury Surveillance System)*

These figures are based on the results of a survey of injuries caused by some 15,000 types of product, based on a sample of 100 US hospitals during 1999. Excluded from the list are many of the sports and transportation products with which most injuries occur outside the home. If they had been included, bicycles and accessories, for instance, would have taken second place with 614,594 injuries. The highest rate of injury recorded is for people aged 65 and over, who hurt themselves on stairs, ramps, landings, and floors at a rate of 1,698.5 per 100,000. Ten percent of the injuries in the stairs category were serious, and over 63 percent of victims were women.

## THE 10 ★
## MOST COMMON CAUSES OF DEATH AT WORK IN THE US

| | INJURY EVENT/EXPOSURE | FATALITIES, 1999 |
|---|---|---|
| 1 | Highway: collision between moving vehicles | 711 |
| 2 | Homicide | 645 |
| 3 | Fall to lower level | 634 |
| 4 | Struck by object | 585 |
| 5 | Highway: noncollision | 388 |
| 6 | Worker struck by a vehicle | 377 |
| 7 | Nonhighway (farm/industrial premises) | 353 |
| 8 | Highway: vehicle struck stationary object or equipment | 334 |
| 9 | Caught in or compressed by equipment or machinery | 302 |
| 10 | Contact with electric current | 278 |

Source: *US Bureau of Labor Statistics*, National Census of Fatal Occupational Injuries, 1999

## THE 10 ★
## MOST COMMON CAUSES OF DOMESTIC FIRES IN THE US*

| | MAJOR CAUSE | FIRES |
|---|---|---|
| 1 | Cooking equipment | 95,300 |
| 2 | Heating equipment | 65,900 |
| 3 | Incendiary or suspicious causes | 50,700 |
| 4 | Other equipment | 43,900 |
| 5 | Electrical distribution system | 39,200 |
| 6 | Appliance, tool, or air conditioning | 30,100 |
| 7 | Smoking materials | 22,000 |
| 8 | Open flame, torch | 20,500 |
| 9 | Child playing | 19,800 |
| 10 | Exposure (to other hostile fire) | 15,700 |

* Based on a survey conducted by the NFIRS and NFPA covering the period 1993–97

Source: *National Fire Protection Association*

**DOMESTIC INFERNO**
*A combination of deliberate and accidental fires, many of which result from avoidable causes, contributes to losses of life and property.*

## THE 10 ★
## MOST ACCIDENT-PRONE COUNTRIES

| | COUNTRIES | ACCIDENT DEATH RATE PER 100,000* |
|---|---|---|
| 1 | Latvia | 104.2 |
| 2 | Estonia | 103.0 |
| 3 | Belarus | 99.6 |
| 4 | Russia | 98.8 |
| 5 | Lithuania | 88.0 |
| 6 | Ukraine | 76.4 |
| 7 | Moldova | 63.2 |
| 8 | Kazakhstan | 59.6 |
| 9 | Romania | 56.0 |
| 10 | South Korea | 53.9 |

* In those countries/latest year for which data available

Source: UN Demographic Yearbook

**What gaseous phenomenon did safety lamp inventor Sir Humphrey Davy also discover?**
*see p.216 for the answer*

A  Hydrogen can be used in balloons
B  The effects of laughing gas
C  Inhaling helium makes human voices squeaky

# Industrial & Other Disasters

## THE 10 ★ WORST FIRES*

| LOCATION/DATE/TYPE | ESTIMATED NO. KILLED |
|---|---|
| 1 **Moscow**, Russia, 1570#, City | 200,000 |
| 2 **Constantinople**, Turkey, 1729#, City | 7,000 |
| 3 **London**, UK, July 11, 1212, London Bridge | 3,000+ |
| 4 **Peshtigo**, Wisconsin, US, Oct 8, 1871, Forest | 2,682 |
| 5 **Santiago**, Chile, Dec 8, 1863, Church of La Compañia | 2,500 |
| 6 **Chungking**, China, Sep 2, 1949, Docks | 1,700 |
| 7 **Hakodate**, Japan, Mar 22, 1934, City | 1,500 |
| 8 **Constantinople**, Turkey, June 5, 1870, City | 900 |
| 9 **Cloquet**, Minnesota, US, Oct 12, 1918, Forest | 559 |
| 10 =**Lagunillas**, Venezuela, Nov 14, 1939, Oil refinery and city | over 500 |
| =**Mandi Dabwali**, India, Dec 23, 1995, School tent | over 500 |

\* Excluding sports and entertainment venues, mining disasters, the results of military action, and fires associated with earthquakes

\# Precise date unknown

\+ Burned, crushed, and drowned in ensuing panic; some chroniclers give the year as 1213

## THE 10 ★ WORST DISASTERS AT SPORTS VENUES

| LOCATION/DATE/TYPE | NO. KILLED |
|---|---|
| 1 **Hong Kong Jockey Club**, Hong Kong, Feb 26, 1918, Stand collapse and fire | 604 |
| 2 **Lenin Stadium**, Moscow, USSR, Oct 20, 1982, Crush in soccer stadium | 340 |
| 3 **Lima**, Peru, May 24, 1964, Riot in soccer stadium | 320 |
| 4 **Sinceljo**, Colombia, Jan 20, 1980, Bullring stand collapse | 222 |
| 5 **Hillsborough**, Sheffield, UK, Apr 15, 1989, Crush in soccer stadium | 96 |
| 6 **Guatemala City**, Guatemala, Oct 16, 1996, Stampede in Mateo Flores National Stadium during World Cup soccer qualifying match, Guatemala v Costa Rica, with 127 injured | 83 |
| 7 **Le Mans**, France, June 11, 1955, Racing car crash | 82 |
| 8 **Katmandu**, Nepal, Mar 12, 1988 Stampede in soccer stadium | 80 |
| 9 **Buenos Aires**, Argentina, May 23, 1968, Riot in soccer stadium | 74 |
| 10 **Ibrox Park**, Glasgow, Scotland, Jan 2, 1971, Barrier collapse in soccer stadium | 66 |

## THE 10 ★ WORST MINING DISASTERS

| LOCATION/DATE | NO. KILLED |
|---|---|
| 1 **Honkeiko**, China, Apr 26, 1942 | 1,549 |
| 2 **Courrières**, France, Mar 10, 1906 | 1,060 |
| 3 **Omuta**, Japan, Nov 9, 1963 | 447 |
| 4 **Senghenydd**, UK, Oct 14, 1913 | 439 |
| 5 =**Hokkaido**, Japan, Dec 1, 1914 | 437 |
| =**Coalbrook**, South Africa, Jan 21, 1960 | 437 |
| 7 **Wankie**, Rhodesia, June 6, 1972 | 427 |
| 8 **Tsinan**, China, May 13, 1935 | 400 |
| 9 **Dhanbad**, India, May 28, 1965 | 375 |
| 10 **Chasnala**, India, Dec 27, 1975 | 372 |

A mine disaster at the Fushun mines, Manchuria, on February 12, 1931, may have resulted in up to 3,000 deaths, but information was suppressed by the Chinese government. Soviet security was also responsible for obscuring details of an explosion at the East German Johanngeorgendstadt uranium mine on November 29, 1949, when as many as 3,700 may have died. The two worst disasters in the Top 10 both resulted from underground explosions, and the large numbers of deaths among mine workers resulted from that cause and from asphyxiation by poisonous gases. Among the most tragic disasters of the last century was the collapse of a slag heap at Aberfan, Wales, which killed 144, most of them children.

## THE 10 ★ WORST FIRES AT THEATER AND ENTERTAINMENT VENUES*

| LOCATION/DATE/TYPE | NO. KILLED |
|---|---|
| 1 **Canton**, China, May 25, 1845, Theater | 1,670 |
| 2 **Shanghai**, China, June 1871, Theater | 900 |
| 3 **Vienna**, Austria, Dec 8, 1881, Ring Theater | 640–850 |
| 4 **St. Petersburg**, Russia, Feb 14, 1836, Lehmann Circus | 800 |
| 5 **Antoung**, China, Feb 13, 1937, Cinema | 658 |
| 6 **Chicago**, IL, US, Dec 30, 1903, Iroquois Theater | 602 |
| 7 **Boston**, MA, US, Nov 28, 1942, Cocoanut Grove Night Club | 491 |
| 8 **Berditschoft**, Poland, Jan 13, 1883, Circus Ferroni | 430 |
| 9 **Abadan**, Iran, Aug 20, 1978, Theater | 422 |
| 10 **Niterói**, Brazil, Dec 17, 1961, Circus | 323 |

\* 19th and 20th centuries, excluding sports stadiums and race tracks

**TROUBLE IN STORE**

*Some 1,500 people were inside the Sampoong Department Store, Seoul, when it collapsed, leaving over a third of them dead and as many as 900 injured.*

## THE 10 ★
## WORST EXPLOSIONS*

| | LOCATION/DATE | TYPE | ESTIMATED NO. KILLED |
|---|---|---|---|
| 1 | **Rhodes**, Greece, 1856# | Lightning strike of gunpowder store | 4,000 |
| 2 | **St. Nazaiere**, Breschia, Italy, 1769# | Arsenal | over 3,000 |
| 3 | **Salang Tunnel**, Afghanistan, Nov 3, 1982 | Petrol tanker colision | over 2,000 |
| 4 | **Lanchow**, China, Oct 26, 1935 | Arsenal | 2,000 |
| 5 | **Halifax**, Canada, Dec 6, 1917 | Ammunition ship *Mont Blanc* | 1,963 |
| 6 | **Hamont Station**, Belgium, Aug 3, 1918 | Ammunition trains | 1,750 |
| 7 | **Memphis**, TN, US, Apr 27, 1865 | *Sultana* boiler explosion | 1,547 |
| 8= | **Archangel**, Russia, Feb 20, 1917 | Munitions ship | 1,500 |
| = | **Ft. Smederovo**, Yugoslavia, June 9, 1941 | Ammunition dump | 1,500 |
| 10 | **Bombay**, India, Apr 14, 1944 | Ammunition ship *Fort Stikine* | 1,376 |

*\* Excluding mining disasters, terrorist and military bombs, and natural explosions, such as volcanoes    # Precise date unknown*

## THE 10 ★
## WORST COMMERCIAL AND INDUSTRIAL DISASTERS*

| | LOCATION/DATE | TYPE | NO. KILLED |
|---|---|---|---|
| 1 | **Bhopal**, India, Dec 3, 1984 | Methylisocyante gas escape at Union Carbide plant | up to 3,000 |
| 2 | **Seoul**, S. Korea, June 29, 1995 | Collapse of Sampoong Department Store | 640 |
| 3 | **Oppau**, Germany, Sep 21, 1921 | Chemical plant explosion | 561 |
| 4 | **Mexico City**, Mexico, Nov 20, 1984 | Explosion at a PEMEX liquified petroleum gas plant | 540 |
| 5 | **Brussels**, Belgium, May 22, 1967 | Fire in l'Innovation department store | 322 |
| 6 | **Novosibirsk**, USSR, Apr 1979 (precise date unknown) | Anthrax infection following accident at biological and chemical warfare plant | up to 300 |
| 7 | **Guadalajara**, Mexico, Apr 22, 1992 | Explosions caused by gas leak into sewers | 230 |
| 8 | **São Paulo**, Brazil, Feb 1, 1974 | Fire in Joelma bank and office building | 227 |
| 9 | **Oakdale**, Pennsylvania, US, May 18, 1918 | Chemical plant explosion | 193 |
| 10 | **Bangkok**, Thailand, May 10, 1993 | Fire at a 4-story doll factory | 187 |

*\* Including industrial sites, factories, offices, and stores; excluding military, mining, marine, and other transport disasters, and mass poisonings*

**In the per capita consumption of what foods does the UK lead the world?**
*see p.218 for the answer*

A Avocados and tomatoes
B Baked beans and potato chips
C Hamburgers and bread

# Food for Thought

TOP 10 ★

## FROZEN FOOD CONSUMERS

| COUNTRY | ANNUAL CONSUMPTION PER CAPITA | | |
|---|---|---|---|
| | LB | OZ | KG |
| 1 Norway | 78 | 8 | 35.6 |
| 2 Denmark | 71 | 10 | 32.5 |
| 3 UK | 68 | 2 | 30.9 |
| 4 Israel | 63 | 8 | 28.8 |
| 5 Czech Republic | 46 | 15 | 21.3 |
| 6 Sweden | 44 | 12 | 20.3 |
| 7 Ireland | 41 | 11 | 18.9 |
| 8 Belgium | 39 | 4 | 17.8 |
| 9 Finland | 36 | 10 | 16.6 |
| 10 US | 35 | 15 | 16.3 |

Source: *Euromonitor*

## TOP 10 ★ POTATO CHIP CONSUMERS

| COUNTRY | ANNUAL CONSUMPTION PER CAPITA | | |
|---|---|---|---|
| | LB | OZ | KG |
| 1 =UK | 6 | 13 | 3.1 |
| =US | 6 | 13 | 3.1 |
| 3 =Ireland | 5 | 15 | 2.7 |
| =New Zealand | 5 | 15 | 2.7 |
| 5 Norway | 5 | 12 | 2.6 |
| 6 Portugal | 5 | 5 | 2.4 |
| 7 Netherlands | 5 | 1 | 2.3 |
| 8 Australia | 4 | 7 | 2.0 |
| 9 =Israel | 3 | 8 | 1.6 |
| =Sweden | 3 | 8 | 1.6 |

Source: *Euromonitor*

## BIRDSEYE

In 1915, while conducting a survey for the US Government in Labrador, Brooklyn-born Clarence "Bob" Birdseye (1886–1956) experimented with the Eskimo method of preserving food in the winter by freezing it in barrels. After returning to the US in 1917, he became interested in the possibility of preserving food commercially by the same method. In Gloucester, Mass., he opened General Seafoods and began preserving fish by rapid freezing. In 1929 he sold the company for $22 million. Birdseye himself became a millionaire, devoting his life to inventing.

WHO WAS • WHO WAS • WHO WAS • WHO WAS •

## TOP 10 ★ BAKED BEAN CONSUMERS

| COUNTRY | ANNUAL CONSUMPTION PER CAPITA | | |
|---|---|---|---|
| | LB | OZ | KG |
| 1 UK | 11 | 11 | 5.3 |
| 2 Ireland | 11 | 4 | 5.1 |
| 3 Mexico | 9 | 4 | 4.2 |
| 4 New Zealand | 4 | 14 | 2.2 |
| 5 =Australia | 4 | 0 | 1.8 |
| =France | 4 | 0 | 1.8 |
| 7 Switzerland | 3 | 5 | 1.5 |
| 8 Saudi Arabia | 3 | 1 | 1.4 |
| 9 =Canada | 2 | 14 | 1.3 |
| =US | 2 | 14 | 1.3 |

Source: *Euromonitor*

## TOP 10 ★ BREAD CONSUMERS

| COUNTRY | ANNUAL CONSUMPTION PER CAPITA | | |
|---|---|---|---|
| | LB | OZ | KG |
| 1 Slovak Republic | 286 | 6 | 129.9 |
| 2 Turkey | 285 | 15 | 129.7 |
| 3 Bulgaria | 285 | 12 | 129.6 |
| 4 Saudi Arabia | 247 | 2 | 112.1 |
| 5 Egypt | 234 | 2 | 106.2 |
| 6 Romania | 211 | 14 | 96.1 |
| 7 Chile | 176 | 13 | 80.2 |
| 8 Poland | 175 | 1 | 79.4 |
| 9 =Denmark | 164 | 11 | 74.7 |
| =Hungary | 164 | 11 | 74.7 |
| *US* | 46 | 15 | 21.3 |

Source: *Euromonitor*

## TOP 10 ★ MEAT CONSUMERS

| COUNTRY | ANNUAL CONSUMPTION PER CAPITA | | |
|---|---|---|---|
| | LB | OZ | KG |
| 1 US | 270 | 1 | 122.5 |
| 2 Cyprus | 250 | 7 | 113.6 |
| 3 New Zealand | 242 | 11 | 110.1 |
| 4 Australia | 238 | 8 | 108.2 |
| 5 Spain | 236 | 9 | 107.3 |
| 6 Austria | 231 | 0 | 104.8 |
| 7 Denmark | 227 | 8 | 103.2 |
| 8 Netherlands | 223 | 9 | 101.4 |
| 9 Bahamas | 222 | 7 | 100.9 |
| 10 France | 219 | 9 | 99.6 |

Figures from the Meat and Livestock Commission show a huge range of meat consumption in countries around the world, ranging from the No. 1 meat consumer, the US, at 270 lb 1 oz (122.5 kg) per person per year, to very poor countries such as India, where meat consumption may be as little as 10 lb 2 oz (4.6 kg) per person per year. In general, meat is an expensive food and in poor countries is saved for special occasions, so the richer the country, the more likely it is to have a high meat consumption. In recent years, however, health scares relating to meat, and the rise in the number of vegetarians, have contributed to deliberate declines in consumption.

## TOP 10 HOTTEST CHILLIES

*(Chilli\*/Scoville units#)*

1 Datil, Habanero, Scotch Bonnet, 100,000–350,000  2 Chiltepin, Santaka, Thai, 50,000–100,000  3 Aji, Cayenne, Piquin, Tabasco, 30,000–50,000  4 de Arbol, 15,000–30,000  5 Serrano, Yellow Wax, 5,000–15,000  6 Chipotle, Jalapeno, Mirasol, 2,500–5,000  7 Cascabel, Sandia, Rocotillo, 1,500–2,500  8 Ancho, Espanola, Pasilla, Poblano, 1,000–1,500  9 Anaheim, New Mexico, 500–1,000  10 Cherry, Peperoncini, 100–500

*\* Examples – there are others in most categories*
*# One part of capsaicin (the principal substance that determines how "hot" a chilli is) per million equals 15,000 Scoville units; the test was pioneered by pharmacist Wilbur Scoville*

## TOP 10 ★
# SPICE CONSUMERS

| COUNTRY | LB | OZ | KG |
|---|---|---|---|
| **1** United Arab Emirates | 13 | 1 | 6.3 |
| **2** Hungary | 13 | 0 | 5.9 |
| **3** Jamaica | 9 | 14 | 4.5 |
| **4** Brunei | 9 | 0 | 4.1 |
| **5** =Slovenia | 8 | 3 | 3.7 |
| =Sri Lanka | 8 | 3 | 3.7 |
| **7** Seychelles | 7 | 4 | 3.3 |
| **8** Cape Verdi | 6 | 13 | 3.1 |
| **9** Kuwait | 6 | 10 | 3.0 |
| **10** Bermuda | 6 | 3 | 2.8 |
| *US* | 1 | 12 | 0.8 |
| *World* | 1 | 12 | 0.8 |

ANNUAL CONSUMPTION PER CAPITA

Source: *Food and Agriculture Organization of the United Nations*

This list inevitably features those countries where spices play an important part in national cuisine. India just fails to find a place in the list, its per capita consumption being estimated at 4 lb 6 oz (2 kg).

## TOP 10 ★
# VEGETABLE CONSUMERS

| COUNTRY | LB | OZ | KG |
|---|---|---|---|
| **1** Lebanon | 766 | 1 | 347.9 |
| **2** United Arab Emirates | 599 | 0 | 271.9 |
| **3** Greece | 579 | 0 | 262.8 |
| **4** Israel | 495 | 0 | 224.7 |
| **5** Libya | 491 | 0 | 222.8 |
| **6** Turkey | 471 | 1 | 213.9 |
| **7** South Korea | 457 | 0 | 207.5 |
| **8** Kuwait | 432 | 5 | 196.1 |
| **9** Iran | 416 | 4 | 188.8 |
| **10** Portugal | 410 | 0 | 186.2 |
| *US* | 266 | 15 | 121.1 |
| *World* | 208 | 0 | 94.6 |

ANNUAL CONSUMPTION PER CAPITA

Source: *Food and Agriculture Organization of the United Nations*

## TOP 10 ★
# FOOD ITEMS CONSUMED IN THE US BY WEIGHT

| ITEM | LB | OZ | KG |
|---|---|---|---|
| **1** Dairy products | 582 | 5 | 264.1 |
| **2** Processed vegetables | 231 | 10 | 105.1 |
| **3** Flour and cereal products | 196 | 13 | 89.3 |
| **4** Fresh vegetables | 186 | 8 | 84.6 |
| **5** Caloric sweeteners | 155 | 2 | 70.4 |
| **6** Processed fruit | 149 | 11 | 67.9 |
| **7** Fresh fruit | 131 | 13 | 59.8 |
| **8** Red meat | 115 | 10 | 52.4 |
| **9** Fats and oils | 65 | 5 | 29.6 |
| **10** Poultry | 65 | 0 | 29.5 |

ANNUAL CONSUMPTION PER CAPITA

Source: *US Department of Agriculture/Economic Research Service*

While healthy-eating concerns have led to a reduction of red meat and whole milk consumption, and an increase in fruit and vegetable intake, overall consumption of dairy products and fats and oils has actually increased.

## TOP 10 ★
# POTATO CONSUMERS

| COUNTRY | LB | OZ | KG |
|---|---|---|---|
| **1** Belarus | 411 | 0 | 168.5 |
| **2** Ukraine | 303 | 9 | 137.7 |
| **3** Latvia | 301 | 9 | 136.8 |
| **4** Poland | 296 | 1 | 134.3 |
| **5** Lithuania | 289 | 14 | 131.5 |
| **6** Ireland | 286 | 3 | 129.8 |
| **7** Portugal | 280 | 1 | 127.4 |
| **8** Russia | 272 | 2 | 123.4 |
| **9** Croatia | 251 | 2 | 113.9 |
| **10** Malawi | 250 | 0 | 113.4 |
| *US* | 141 | 0 | 64.0 |
| *World* | 66 | 0 | 30.0 |

ANNUAL CONSUMPTION PER CAPITA

Source: *Food and Agriculture Organization of the United Nations*

The potato has long been a staple part of the national diet for the countries at the top of the list.

## TOP 10 ★
# BUTTER CONSUMERS

| COUNTRY | LB | OZ | KG |
|---|---|---|---|
| **1** New Zealand | 20 | 15 | 9.5 |
| **2** France | 19 | 13 | 9.0 |
| **3** Estonia | 17 | 5 | 8.0 |
| **4** Germany | 15 | 6 | 7.0 |
| **5** Switzerland | 13 | 10 | 6.2 |
| **6** =Belgium–Luxembourg | 12 | 12 | 5.8 |
| =Fiji Islands | 12 | 12 | 5.8 |
| **8** Iceland | 12 | 9 | 5.7 |
| **9** Belarus | 12 | 2 | 5.5 |
| **10** Macedonia | 11 | 0 | 5.0 |
| *US* | 3 | 15 | 1.8 |
| *World* | 2 | 6 | 1.1 |

ANNUAL CONSUMPTION PER CAPITA

Source: *Food and Agriculture Organization of the United Nations*

## TOP 10 ★
# FISH CONSUMERS

| COUNTRY | LB | OZ | KG |
|---|---|---|---|
| **1** Maldives | 353 | 2 | 160.2 |
| **2** Iceland | 202 | 2 | 91.7 |
| **3** Kiribati | 170 | 3 | 77.2 |
| **4** Japan | 159 | 2 | 72.2 |
| **5** Seychelles | 142 | 13 | 64.8 |
| **6** Portugal | 129 | 7 | 58.7 |
| **7** Norway | 120 | 6 | 54.6 |
| **8** Malaysia | 119 | 4 | 54.1 |
| **9** French Polynesia | 114 | 3 | 51.8 |
| **10** South Korea | 113 | 12 | 51.6 |
| *US* | 50 | 7 | 22.9 |
| *World* | 44 | 14 | 20.4 |

ANNUAL CONSUMPTION PER CAPITA*

* Combines sea and freshwater fish totals

Source: *Food and Agriculture Organization of the United Nations*

The majority of the fish consumed in the world comes from the sea, the average annual consumption of freshwater fish being 9 lb 11 oz (4.4 kg). The largest consumers are Norwegians, who each consume 26 lb (11.8 kg) per annum.

**Did You Know?** The cultivation of potatoes was banned in Scotland in 1728 because they were considered an "unholy nightshade" and were not mentioned in the Bible.

# Sweet Dreams

## TOP 10 ★
### SUGAR PRODUCERS

| | COUNTRY | 2000 SUGAR PRODUCTION (TONS)* |
|---|---|---|
| 1 | India | 20,872,300 |
| 2 | Brazil | 15,983,500 |
| 3 | China | 9,236,100 |
| 4 | US | 8,749,100 |
| 5 | Australia | 6,369,200 |
| 6 | Thailand | 6,206,000 |
| 7 | Mexico | 5,493,900 |
| 8 | France | 4,828,100 |
| 9 | Cuba | 4,557,000 |
| 10 | Germany | 4,519,500 |
| | World | 141,989,100 |

* Raw centrifugal sugar

Source: Food and Agriculture Organization of the United Nations

## TOP 10 ★
### CHEWING GUM CONSUMERS

| | COUNTRY | ANNUAL CONSUMPTION PER CAPITA | | |
|---|---|---|---|---|
| | | LB | OZ | KG |
| 1 | Denmark | 2 | 10 | 1.2 |
| 2 | Norway | 2 | 3 | 1.0 |
| 3 = | Switzerland | 1 | 9 | 0.7 |
| = | US | 1 | 9 | 0.7 |
| 5 = | Israel | 1 | 5 | 0.6 |
| = | Spain | 1 | 5 | 0.6 |
| 7 = | Argentina | 1 | 2 | 0.5 |
| = | France | 1 | 2 | 0.5 |
| = | Germany | 1 | 2 | 0.5 |
| 10 = | Canada | 0 | 14 | 0.4 |
| = | Ireland | 0 | 14 | 0.4 |
| = | Japan | 0 | 14 | 0.4 |
| = | Mexico | 0 | 14 | 0.4 |
| = | Morocco | 0 | 14 | 0.4 |
| = | UK | 0 | 14 | 0.4 |

Source: Euromonitor

Worldwide chewing gum consumption in 1999 was estimated as 838,945.2tonnes.

## TOP 10 ★
### SUGAR CONSUMERS

| | COUNTRY | ANNUAL CONSUMPTION PER CAPITA* | | |
|---|---|---|---|---|
| | | LB | OZ | KG |
| 1 | Belize | 136 | 10 | 62.0 |
| 2 | Cape Verde | 130 | 8 | 59.2 |
| 3 | Cuba | 130 | 1 | 59.0 |
| 4 | Ecuador | 121 | 4 | 55.0 |
| 5 | Barbados | 115 | 11 | 52.2 |
| 6 = | Brazil | 113 | 8 | 51.5 |
| = | Trinidad and Tobago | 113 | 8 | 51.5 |
| 8 | Iceland | 111 | 8 | 50.6 |
| 9 | Macedonia | 111 | 1 | 50.4 |
| 10 | Swaziland | 108 | 14 | 49.4 |
| | US | 66 | 12 | 30.3 |
| | World | 41 | 14 | 19.0 |

* Refined equivalent

Source: Food and Agriculture Organization of the United Nations

Each citizen of Belize, the current world leader in the sweet-tooth stakes, would appear to consume more than 2.2 lb (1 kg) of sugar every week.

## TOP 10 ★
### SWEETENER CONSUMERS*

| | COUNTRY | ANNUAL CONSUMPTION PER CAPITA | | |
|---|---|---|---|---|
| | | LB | OZ | KG |
| 1 | US | 88 | 6 | 40.1 |
| 2 | South Korea | 30 | 13 | 14.0 |
| 3 | Brunei | 26 | 14 | 12.2 |
| 4 | Bermuda | 25 | 9 | 11.6 |
| 5 = | Hungary | 25 | 2 | 11.4 |
| = | Iceland | 25 | 2 | 11.4 |
| 7 | Japan | 23 | 5 | 10.6 |
| 8 | Bahamas | 18 | 11 | 8.5 |
| 9 | Canada | 18 | 4 | 8.3 |
| 10 | Estonia | 14 | 15 | 6.8 |
| | World | 6 | 2 | 2.8 |

* Excluding sugar

Source: Food and Agriculture Organization of the United Nations

## TOP 10 ★
### FRUIT CONSUMERS

| | COUNTRY | ANNUAL CONSUMPTION PER CAPITA | | |
|---|---|---|---|---|
| | | LB | OZ | KG |
| 1 | Dominica | 885 | 9 | 401.7 |
| 2 | Belize | 709 | 0 | 321.8 |
| 3 | Lebanon | 532 | 14 | 241.7 |
| 4 | Uganda | 522 | 11 | 237.1 |
| 5 | Saint Lucia | 486 | 12 12 | 220.8 |
| 6 | São Tomé and Principe | 478 | 6 | 217.0 |
| 7 | Rwanda | 477 | 8 | 216.6 |
| 8 | Bermuda | 456 | 13 | 207.2 |
| 9 | Papua New Guinea | 451 | 1 | 204.6 |
| 10 | Bahamas | 425 | 8 | 193.0 |
| | US | 261 | 0 | 118.4 |
| | World | 125 | 10 | 57.0 |

Source: Food and Agriculture Organization of the United Nations

World fruit consumption varies from those in the list – where some people devour more than five times their own body weight every year – to Eritrea, with just 3 lb (1.4 kg) per capita.

## TOP 10 ★
### HONEY CONSUMERS

| | COUNTRY | ANNUAL CONSUMPTION PER CAPITA | | |
|---|---|---|---|---|
| | | LB | OZ | KG |
| 1 | Central African Republic | 6 | 10 | 3.0 |
| 2 | Turkmenistan | 5 | 1 | 2.3 |
| 3 | Angola | 3 | 15 | 1.8 |
| 4 = | Greece | 3 | 8 | 1.6 |
| = | New Zealand | 3 | 8 | 1.6 |
| 6 | Switzerland | 3 | 1 | 1.4 |
| 7 = | Germany | 2 | 10 | 1.2 |
| = | Ukraine | 2 | 10 | 1.2 |
| 9 = | Austria | 2 | 0 | 1.1 |
| = | Canada | 2 | 0 | 1.1 |
| = | Slovenia | 2 | 0 | 1.1 |
| | US | 1 | 5 | 0.6 |
| | World | 0 | 7 | 0.2 |

Source: Food and Agriculture Organization of the United Nations

# TOP 10 CANDY MANUFACTURERS IN THE US*

❶ Hershey Chocolate ❷ Mars ❸ Nestlé USA ❹ Nabisco
❺ William Wrigley Jr. Co. ❻ Warner-Lambert ❼ Favorite Brands International
❽ = Brach & Brock Confections; = Russell Stover Candies ❿ Tootsie Roll Industries

*\* Based on $ sales volume*
Source: *Euromonitor*

## TOP 10 ★
## NON-CHOCOLATE BRANDS IN THE US

| BRAND | 1998 MARKET SHARE (%) |
|---|---|
| 1 Y&S Twizzler | 6.0 |
| 2 Starburst | 4.2 |
| 3 Farley's | 4.0 |
| 4 Life Savers | 3.9 |
| 5 Jolly Rancher | 2.6 |
| 6 =Brach's | 2.5 |
| =Skittles | 2.5 |
| 8 Werther's | 2.3 |
| 9 Sathers | 2.1 |
| 10 =Brock | 2.0 |
| =Halls | 2.0 |

Source: *Euromonitor*

## TOP 10 ★
## CHOCOLATE CONSUMERS

| COUNTRY | ANNUAL CONSUMPTION PER CAPITA LB | OZ | KG |
|---|---|---|---|
| 1 Switzerland | 26 | 0 | 11.8 |
| 2 UK | 21 | 10 | 9.8 |
| 3 Belgium | 18 | 12 | 8.5 |
| 4 Ireland | 17 | 3 | 7.8 |
| 5 Norway | 17 | 0 | 7.7 |
| 6 Germany | 16 | 1 | 7.3 |
| 7 Austria | 13 | 14 | 6.3 |
| 8 Australia | 12 | 13 | 5.8 |
| 9 US | 12 | 9 | 5.7 |
| 10 Sweden | 10 | 9 | 4.8 |

Source: *Euromonitor*

## TOP 10 ★
## CHOCOLATE BRANDS IN THE US

| BRAND | 1999 MARKET SHARE (%) |
|---|---|
| 1 Snickers | 21.1 |
| 2 Reese's Peanut Butter Cup | 17.0 |
| 3 Kit Kat | 9.2 |
| 4 Milky Way | 7.7 |
| 5 Twix | 5.9 |
| 6 York | 5.8 |
| 7 Three Musketeers | 5.1 |
| 8 Butterfinger | 4.3 |
| 9 Hershey's Sweet Escapes | 2.1 |
| 10 Almond Joy | 1.5 |

Source: *Euromonitor*

## TOP 10 ★
## ICE CREAM CONSUMERS

| COUNTRY | ANNUAL CONSUMPTION PER CAPITA PINTS | LITERS |
|---|---|---|
| 1 Australia | 29.2 | 16.6 |
| 2 Italy | 25.0 | 14.2 |
| 3 US | 24.5 | 13.9 |
| 4 New Zealand | 23.2 | 13.2 |
| 5 Sweden | 21.5 | 12.2 |
| 6 Ireland | 18.1 | 10.3 |
| 7 Norway | 16.2 | 9.2 |
| 8 Canada | 16.0 | 9.1 |
| 9 Israel | 15.8 | 9.0 |
| 10 Finland | 15.5 | 8.8 |

Source: *Euromonitor*

## TOP 10 ★
## DATE CONSUMERS

| COUNTRY | ANNUAL CONSUMPTION PER CAPITA LB | OZ | KG |
|---|---|---|---|
| 1 United Arab Emirates | 77 | 10 | 35.2 |
| 2 Saudi Arabia | 67 | 11 | 30.7 |
| 3 Iraq | 36 | 13 | 16.7 |
| 4 Libya | 31 | 5 | 14.2 |
| 5 Algeria | 26 | 12 | 12.1 |
| 6 Iran | 25 | 12 | 11.7 |
| 7 Egypt | 25 | 2 | 11.4 |
| 8 =Sudan | 12 | 2 | 5.5 |
| =Tunisia | 12 | 2 | 5.5 |
| 10 Kuwait | 10 | 6 | 4.7 |
| US | 0 | 3 | 0.1 |
| World | 1 | 12 | 0.8 |

Source: *Food and Agriculture Organization of the United Nations*

## TOP 10 ★
## COCOA CONSUMERS

| COUNTRY | TOTAL COCOA CONSUMPTION (TONS) |
|---|---|
| 1 US | 723,300 |
| 2 Germany | 313,600 |
| 3 UK | 233,900 |
| 4 France | 205,000 |
| 5 Japan | 145,400 |
| 6 Brazil | 137,300 |
| 7 Italy | 107,100 |
| 8 Russia | 105,400 |
| 9 Spain | 74,500 |
| 10 Canada | 70,000 |
| World | 3,050,400 |

Cocoa is the principal ingredient of chocolate, and its consumption is therefore closely linked to the production of chocolate in each consuming country. Like coffee, the consumption of chocolate tends to occur mainly in the Western world and in more affluent countries. Europe has the highest intake of the world's regions, with a total cocoa consumption of 1,523,000 tons; the Americas are next with 1,125,800 (over half of which is accounted for by the US); Asia and Oceania consume 334,400; and lastly, Africa, where 67,000 tons are consumed.

**Did You Know?** Chocolate was consumed mostly as a drink until 1879, when Swiss manufacturer Rudolphe Lindt added cocoa butter, and Daniel Peter pioneered the first milk chocolate bar.

# Alcoholic & Soft Drinks

## ALCOHOL-CONSUMING COUNTRIES

| COUNTRY | CONSUMPTION PER CAPITA, 1999 (100 PERCENT ALCOHOL) PINTS | LITERS |
|---|---|---|
| 1 Luxembourg | 21.5 | 12.2 |
| 2 Ireland | 20.4 | 11.6 |
| 3 Portugal | 19.4 | 11.0 |
| 4 France | 18.8 | 10.7 |
| 5 Germany | 18.7 | 10.6 |
| 6 Czech Republic | 18.5 | 10.5 |
| 7 Romania | 18.1 | 10.3 |
| 8 Spain | 17.4 | 9.9 |
| 9 Hungary | 17.1 | 9.7 |
| 10 Denmark | 16.7 | 9.5 |
| US | 11.8 | 6.7 |

Source: *Productschap voor Gedistilleerde Dranken*

After heading this list for many years – and with an annual consumption that peaked at 31.2 pints (17.7 liters) per head in 1961 – France was overtaken by Luxembourg, which is acknowledged as the world's leading alcohol consumer. While Western European countries have the highest average consumption of alcohol in the world – 14.1 pints (8.0 liters) per person per annum, compared to a world average of 6.7 pints (3.8 liters) – the trend is toward lower drinking levels. Average consumption in Western Europe fell by 5.9 percent between 1990 and 1999.

### SCHWEPPES

German-born Jean Jacob Schweppe (1740–1821), an amateur scientist, moved to Geneva, Switzerland, where he became interested in the manufacture of artificial mineral waters. He moved to London in 1792 and began producing his own brand of soda water, forming Schweppe & Co. (later Schweppes Ltd.). By the 1870s, the company was also making ginger ale and "Indian Tonic Water," adding quinine to sweetened soda water after the style of the British in India, who drank it as an antidote to malaria, and thus beginning the fashion for gin and tonic.

WHO WAS · WHO WAS · WHO WAS · WHO WAS

## TOP 10 COUNTRIES WITH THE BIGGEST INCREASE IN BEER PRODUCTION

*(Country/percentage increase, 1980–98)*

1 China, 2,783  2 Argentina, 435  3 South Africa, 208  4 Brazil, 207  5 Turkey, 116  6 Mexico, 105  7 Chile, 94  8 Portugal, 91  9 Poland, 81  10 Finland, 66

US, 5

Source: *Productschap voor Gedistilleerde Dranken*

## BEER-DRINKING COUNTRIES

| COUNTRY | CONSUMPTION PER CAPITA, 1999 PINTS | LITERS |
|---|---|---|
| 1 Czech Republic | 280.5 | 159.4 |
| 2 Ireland | 272.2 | 154.7 |
| 3 Germany | 224.3 | 127.5 |
| 4 Luxembourg | 191.8 | 109.0 |
| 5 Austria | 191.6 | 108.9 |
| 6 Denmark | 179.3 | 101.9 |
| 7 UK | 174.2 | 99.0 |
| 8 Belgium | 171.5 | 97.5 |
| 9 Australia | 160.4 | 91.2 |
| 10 Slovak Republic | 155.0 | 88.1 |

Source: *Productschap voor Gedistilleerde Dranken*

## WINE-PRODUCING COUNTRIES

| COUNTRY | PRODUCTION, 1998 PINTS | LITERS |
|---|---|---|
| 1 Italy | 9,535,749,556 | 5,418,800,000 |
| 2 France | 9,268,795,026 | 5,267,100,000 |
| 3 Spain | 5,335,571,096 | 3,032,000,000 |
| 4 US | 3,291,266,036 | 1,870,300,000 |
| 5 Argentina | 2,230,134,977 | 1,267,300,000 |
| 6 Germany | 1,900,533,240 | 1,080,000,000 |
| 7 South Africa | 1,435,078,572 | 815,500,000 |
| 8 Australia | 1,304,856,850 | 741,500,000 |
| 9 Chile | 963,464,767 | 547,500,000 |
| 10 Romania | 880,228,451 | 500,200,000 |

Source: *Productschap voor Gedistilleerde Dranken*

## BEER-PRODUCING COUNTRIES

| COUNTRY | PRODUCTION, 1998 PINTS | LITERS |
|---|---|---|
| 1 US | 41,829,328,810 | 23,770,000,000 |
| 2 China | 30,443,726,900 | 17,300,000,000 |
| 3 Germany | 19,656,441,010 | 11,170,000,000 |
| 4 Brazil | 14,352,545,470 | 8,156,000,000 |
| 5 Japan | 12,633,090,810 | 7,178,900,000 |
| 6 UK | 9,969,352,696 | 5,665,200,000 |
| 7 Mexico | 9,618,281,972 | 5,465,700,000 |
| 8 Russia | 5,724,476,509 | 3,253,000,000 |
| 9 South Africa | 4,511,830,717 | 2,563,900,000 |
| 10 Spain | 4,397,798,722 | 2,499,100,000 |

Source: *Productschap voor Gedistilleerde Dranken*

## WINE-DRINKING COUNTRIES

| COUNTRY | CONSUMPTION PER CAPITA, 1999 PINTS | LITERS |
|---|---|---|
| 1 Luxembourg | 107.3 | 61.0 |
| 2 France | 100.7 | 57.2 |
| 3 Portugal | 91.0 | 51.7 |
| 4 Italy | 90.6 | 51.5 |
| 5 Switzerland | 76.7 | 43.6 |
| 6 Argentina | 62.6 | 35.6 |
| 7 Greece | 61.9 | 35.2 |
| 8 Spain | 59.3 | 33.7 |
| 9 Uruguay | 56.3 | 32.0 |
| 10 Austria | 54.4 | 30.9 |
| US | 13.4 | 7.6 |

Source: *Productschap voor Gedistilleerde Dranken*

## TOP 10 ★
### COLA-DRINKING COUNTRIES

| | COUNTRY | CONSUMPTION PER CAPITA, 1998 | |
| | | PINTS | LITERS |
|---|---|---|---|
| 1 | Mexico | 172.3 | 97.9 |
| 2 | United Arab Emirates | 167.4 | 95.1 |
| 3 | Bermuda | 157.7 | 89.6 |
| 4 | US | 150.1 | 85.3 |
| 5 | St. Lucia | 136.0 | 77.3 |
| 6 | Bahrain | 135.0 | 76.7 |
| 7 | Dominica | 134.8 | 76.6 |
| 8 | Belize | 129.7 | 73.7 |
| 9 | Luxembourg | 118.1 | 67.1 |
| 10 | Grenada | 117.7 | 66.9 |

Source: *Euromonitor*

## TOP 10 ★
### SPARKLING WINE-DRINKING COUNTRIES

| | COUNTRY | CONSUMPTION PER CAPITA, 1999 | |
| | | PINTS | LITERS |
|---|---|---|---|
| 1 | France | 7.6 | 4.3 |
| 2 | Germany | 6.9 | 3.9 |
| 3 = | Hungary | 3.7 | 2.1 |
| = | New Zealand | 3.7 | 2.1 |
| 5 | Australia | 2.8 | 1.6 |
| 6 | Czech Republic | 2.5 | 1.4 |
| 7 | Belgium | 2.3 | 1.3 |
| 8 = | Italy | 2.1 | 1.2 |
| = | Poland | 2.1 | 1.2 |
| 10 = | Portugal | 1.8 | 1.0 |
| = | Romania | 1.8 | 1.0 |

Source: *Euromonitor*

## TOP 10 ★
### COFFEE-DRINKING COUNTRIES

| | COUNTRY | ANNUAL CONSUMPTION PER HEAD | | | |
| | | LB | OZ | KG | CUPS* |
|---|---|---|---|---|---|
| 1 | Finland | 25 | 1 | 11.37 | 1,706 |
| 2 | Norway | 23 | 4 | 10.56 | 1,584 |
| 3 | Denmark | 22 | 4 | 10.09 | 1,514 |
| 4 | Sweden | 19 | 3 | 8.70 | 1,305 |
| 5 | Austria | 18 | 1 | 8.19 | 1,229 |
| 6 | Germany | 16 | 11 | 7.58 | 1,137 |
| 7 | Switzerland | 16 | 0 | 7.26 | 1,089 |
| 8 | Netherlands | 13 | 10 | 6.19 | 929 |
| 9 | France | 12 | 3 | 5.52 | 828 |
| 10 | Belgium and Luxembourg | 11 | 12 | 5.33 | 800 |

* *Based on 150 cups per 2 lb 3 oz (1 kg)*

Source: *International Coffee Organization*

## TOP 10 ★
### CHAMPAGNE-IMPORTING COUNTRIES

| | COUNTRY | BOTTLES IMPORTED, 2000 |
|---|---|---|
| 1 | UK | 20,433,640 |
| 2 | US | 19,268,837 |
| 3 | Germany | 14,235,737 |
| 4 | Italy | 8,239,536 |
| 5 | Belgium | 7,320,681 |
| 6 | Switzerland | 6,518,658 |
| 7 | Japan | 3,174,914 |
| 8 | Netherlands | 2,122,547 |
| 9 | Spain | 2,035,983 |
| 10 | Australia | 1,434,895 |

Source: *Comité Interprofessionnel du Vin de Champagne (CIVC)*

## TOP 10 ★
### SOFT DRINK-DRINKING COUNTRIES

| | COUNTRY | ANNUAL CONSUMPTION PER CAPITA* | |
| | | PINTS | LITERS |
|---|---|---|---|
| 1 | US | 385 | 219 |
| 2 | Mexico | 265 | 151 |
| 3 | Iceland | 246 | 140 |
| 4 | Malta | 236 | 134 |
| 5 | Norway | 222 | 126 |
| 6 | Canada | 215 | 122 |
| 7 | Australia | 211 | 120 |
| 8 | Israel | 195 | 111 |
| 9 | Chile | 194 | 110 |
| 10 | Ireland | 192 | 109 |

* *Carbonated only*

Source: *Zenith International*

As one might expect, affluent Western countries feature prominently in this list and, despite the spread of so-called "Coca-Cola culture," former Eastern Bloc and Third World countries rank very low – some African nations recording consumption figures of less than 1.76 pints (1 liter) per annum.

## TOP 10 ★
### SOFT DRINK BRANDS IN THE US

| | BRAND | SALES IN 2000 (GALLONS)* |
|---|---|---|
| 1 | Coca-Cola Classic | 3,106,400,000 |
| 2 | Pepsi | 2,133,700,000 |
| 3 | Diet Coke | 1,322,700,000 |
| 4 | Mountain Dew | 1,095,000,000 |
| 5 | Sprite | 1,002,100,000 |
| 6 | Dr. Pepper | 947,900,000 |
| 7 | Diet Pepsi | 750,500,000 |
| 8 | 7-Up | 305,100,000 |
| 9 | Caffeine Free Diet Coke | 263,300,000 |
| 10 | Minute Maid Regular & Diet | 226,100,000 |

* *Wholesale sales*

Source: *Beverage Marketing Corporation*

A total of 15,328,000,000 gallons of soft drinks was sold in the US in 1998.

## TOP 10 COUNTRIES WITH THE BIGGEST INCREASE IN ALCOHOL CONSUMPTION

*(Country/percentage increase, 1970–99)*

**1** Brazil, 466.8 **2** Paraguay, 275.0 **3** Turkey, 177.8 **4** Colombia, 166.6 **5** Cyprus, 114.8 **6** Ireland, 97.0 **7** Venezuela, 96.8 **8** Finland, 70.7 **9** Greece, 69.6 **10** Cuba, 69.3 *UK, 52.1*

Source: *Productschap voor Gedistilleerde Dranken*

**Did You Know?** Champagne was invented by blind Benedictine monk Dom Pierre Pérignon (1639–1715), cellar master of the Abbey of Hautvilliers, France.

# ON THE MOVE

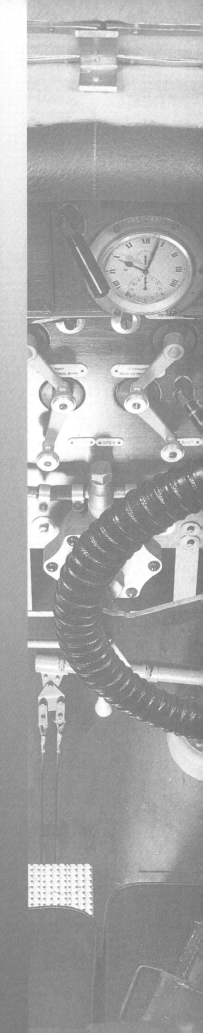

# Speed Records

## THE 10 ★
## FIRST AMERICAN HOLDERS OF THE LAND SPEED RECORD

| | DRIVER*/CAR/LOCATION | DATE | MPH | KM/H |
|---|---|---|---|---|
| 1 | **William Vanderbilt**, *Mors*, Albis, France | Aug 5, 1902 | 76.08 | 122.44 |
| 2 | **Henry Ford#**, Ford *Arrow*, Lake St. Clair, US | Jan 12, 1904 | 91.37 | 147.05 |
| 3 | **Fred Marriott#**, Stanley *Rocket*, Daytona Beach, US | Jan 23, 1906 | 121.57 | 195.65 |
| 4 | **Barney Oldfield#**, Benz, Daytona Beach, US | Mar 16, 1910 | 131.27 | 211.26 |
| 5 | **Bob Burman#**, Benz, Daytona Beach, US | Apr 23, 1911 | 141.37 | 227.51 |
| 6 | **Ralph de Palma#**, Packard, Daytona Beach, US | Feb 17, 1919 | 149.87 | 241.19 |
| 7 | **Tommy Milton#**, Duesenberg, Daytona Beach, US | Apr 27, 1920 | 156.03 | 251.11 |
| 8 | **Ray Keech**, White *Triplex*, Daytona Beach, US | Apr 22, 1928 | 207.55 | 334.02 |
| 9 | **Craig Breedlove#**, *Spirit of America*, Bonneville Salt Flats, Utah, US | Aug 5, 1963 | 407.45 | 655.73 |
| 10 | **Tom Green**, *Wingfoot Express*, Bonneville Salt Flats, Utah, US | Oct 2, 1964 | 413.20 | 664.98 |

\* *Excluding those who subsequently broke their own records*

\# *Record not recognized in Europe*

**COOL RUNNER**

*In 1904 Henry Ford set the land speed record – although it was actually achieved on ice – on the frozen Lake St. Clair, near Detroit. A former employee of Thomas Edison, Ford (standing) had established the Ford Motor Company the previous year.*

## THE 10 ★
## LATEST HOLDERS OF THE MOTORCYCLE SPEED RECORD

| | RIDER/MOTORCYCLE | YEAR | MPH | KM/H |
|---|---|---|---|---|
| 1 | **Dave Campos**, Twin 1,491cc Ruxton Harley-Davidson *Easyriders* | 1990 | 322.15 | 518.45 |
| 2 | **Donald A. Vesco**, Twin 1,016cc Kawasaki *Lightning Bolt* | 1978 | 318.60 | 512.73 |
| 3 | **Donald A. Vesco**, 1,496cc Yamaha *Silver Bird* | 1975 | 302.93 | 487.50 |
| 4 | **Calvin Rayborn**, 1,480cc Harley-Davidson | 1970 | 264.96 | 426.40 |
| 5 | **Calvin Rayborn**, 1,480cc Harley-Davidson | 1970 | 254.99 | 410.37 |
| 6 | **Donald A. Vesco**, 700cc Yamaha | 1970 | 251.82 | 405.25 |
| 7 | **Robert Leppan**, 1,298cc Triumph | 1966 | 245.62 | 395.27 |
| 8 | **William A. Johnson**, 667cc Triumph | 1962 | 224.57 | 361.40 |
| 9 | **Wilhelm Herz**, 499cc NSU | 1956 | 210.08 | 338.08 |
| 10 | **Russell Wright**, 998cc Vincent HRD | 1955 | 184.95 | 297.64 |

All the records listed here were achieved at the Bonneville Salt Flats, Utah, US, with the exception of No. 10 (Christchurch, New Zealand). Nos. 1 and 2 had two engines and were stretched to 21 ft (6.4 m) and 23 ft (7 m) respectively.

## TOP 10 ★
## LATEST HOLDERS OF THE LAND SPEED RECORD

| | DRIVER/CAR | DATE | MPH | KM/H |
|---|---|---|---|---|
| 1 | **Andy Green**, *Thrust SSC*\* | Oct 15, 1997 | 763.04 | 1,227.99 |
| 2 | **Richard Noble**, *Thrust 2*\* | Oct 4, 1983 | 633.47 | 1,013.47 |
| 3 | **Gary Gabelich**, *The Blue Flame* | Oct 23, 1970 | 622.41 | 995.85 |
| 4 | **Craig Breedlove**, *Spirit of America – Sonic 1* | Nov 15, 1965 | 600.60 | 960.96 |
| 5 | **Art Arfons**, *Green Monster* | Nov 7, 1965 | 576.55 | 922.48 |
| 6 | **Craig Breedlove**, *Spirit of America – Sonic 1* | Nov 2, 1965 | 555.48 | 888.76 |
| 7 | **Art Arfons**, *Green Monster* | Oct 27, 1964 | 536.71 | 858.73 |
| 8 | **Craig Breedlove**, *Spirit of America* | Oct 15, 1964 | 526.28 | 842.04 |
| 9 | **Craig Breedlove**, *Spirit of America* | Oct 13, 1964 | 468.72 | 749.95 |
| 10 | **Art Arfons**, *Green Monster* | Oct 5, 1964 | 434.02 | 694.43 |

\* *Achieved at Black Rock Desert, Nevada, US; all other speeds were achieved at Bonneville Salt Flats, Utah, US*

## FERRARI

Enzo Ferrari (1898–1988) attended his first motor race at the age of 10, vowing to become a race car driver. He achieved his ambition while working for a carmaker, later becoming part of the Alfa Romeo team and starting his own firm in 1929. Ferrari retired from driving and began producing his first race cars in 1940, and his first Grand Prix cars in the late 1940s. For over half a century, Ferraris have been among the most desirable – as well as the most expensive – of all cars, while the company's Formula One cars lead the constructors' table for the most wins.

WHO WAS • WHO WAS • WHO WAS • WHO WAS • WHO WAS

# TOP 10 ★
## FASTEST PRODUCTION MOTORCYCLES

| | MAKE/MODEL | MPH | KM/H |
|---|---|---|---|
| 1 | Suzuki GSX1300R Hayabusa | 192 | 309 |
| 2= | Honda CBR1100XX Blackbird | 181 | 291 |
| = | Honda RC45(m) | 181 | 291 |
| 4= | Harris Yamaha YZR500 | 180 | 289 |
| = | Kawasaki ZZR1100 D7 | 180 | 289 |
| 6 | Bimota YB10 Biposto | 176 | 283 |
| 7 | Suzuki GSX-R1100WP (d) | 174 | 280 |
| 8 | Suzuki GSX-R750-WV | 173 | 279 |
| 9= | Bimota Furano | 173 | 278 |
| = | Kawasaki ZZR1100 C1 | 173 | 278 |

# TOP 10 ★
## FASTEST PRODUCTION CARS

| | MODEL*/ COUNTRY OF MANUFACTURE | MPH | KM/H# |
|---|---|---|---|
| 1 | McLaren F1, UK | 240 | 386 |
| 2 | Lamborghini Diablo 6.0, Italy | 208 | 335 |
| 3 | Lister Storm, UK | 201 | 323 |
| 4 | Marcos Mantara LM 600 Coupe/Cabriolet, UK | 200 | 322 |
| 5 | Ferrari 550 Maranello, Italy | 199 | 320 |
| 6 | Renault Espace Privilege/Initiale 3.0 Auto, France | 194 | 312 |
| 7= | Ascari Escosse, Italy | >190 | >305 |
| = | Pagani Zonda, Italy | >190 | >305 |
| 9= | Callaway C12, US | 190 | 305 |
| = | Porsche 911 Turbo, Germany | 190 | 305 |

\* *Fastest of each manufacturer*

\# *May vary according to specification modifications to meet national legal requirements*

Source: Auto Express/Top Gear Magazine

It is believed that it would be virtually impossible to build a road car capable of more than 250 mph (402 km/h), but these supercars come closest to that limit. The list includes the fastest example of each marque, but excludes "limited edition" cars.

# TOP 10 ★
## PRODUCTION CARS WITH THE FASTEST 0–60MPH TIMES

| | MODEL*/ COUNTRY OF MANUFACTURE | SECONDS TAKEN# |
|---|---|---|
| 1 | Renault Espace F1, France | 2.8 |
| 2 | McLaren F1, UK | 3.2 |
| 3 | Caterham Seven Superlight R500, UK | 3.4 |
| 4= | Marcos Mantara LM600 Coupe/Cabriolet, UK | 3.6 |
| = | Westfield FW400, UK | 3.6 |
| 6 | Lamborghini Diablo 6.0, Italy | 3.9 |
| 7 | Ascari Escosse, Italy | 4.1 |
| 8= | AC Cobra Superblower, UK | 4.2 |
| = | Callaway C12, US | 4.2 |
| = | TVR Tuscan Speed Six 4.0, UK | 4.2 |

\* *Fastest of each manufacturer*

\# *May vary according to specification modifications to meet national legal requirements*

Source: Auto Express/Top Gear Magazine

### SUPERCAR

*Racing technology applied to a road car in the McLaren F1 set new records for speed and acceleration. It was also at one time the highest-priced production car ever built.*

# Cars & Road Transport

## US STATES WITH THE LONGEST ROAD NETWORKS

|  | STATE | TOTAL LENGTH MILES | KM |
|---|---|---|---|
| 1 | Texas | 300,507 | 483,619 |
| 2 | California | 166,973 | 268,717 |
| 3 | Illinois | 138,246 | 222,485 |
| 4 | Kansas | 133,963 | 215,593 |
| 5 | Minnesota | 131,996 | 212,427 |
| 6 | Missouri | 122,831 | 197,677 |
| 7 | Michigan | 121,722 | 195,893 |
| 8 | Pennsylvania | 119,384 | 192,130 |
| 9 | Ohio | 116,371 | 187,281 |
| 10 | Florida | 115,956 | 186,613 |
|  | *US total* | 3,917,240 | 6,304,187 |

Source: *Federal Highway Administration*

Texas's total includes its 141,977 miles (228,490 km) of county roads, 79,185 miles (127,436 km) of state-maintained highways and other roads, and 78,488 miles (119,877 km) of city streets.

## COUNTRIES WITH THE LONGEST ROAD NETWORKS

|  | COUNTRY | LENGTH* MILES | KM |
|---|---|---|---|
| 1 | US | 3,944,605 | 6,348,227 |
| 2 | India | 2,062,731 | 3,319,644 |
| 3 | Brazil | 1,230,315 | 1,980,000 |
| 4 | China | 751,859 | 1,210,000 |
| 5 | Japan | 715,948 | 1,152,207 |
| 6 | Russia | 589,060 | 948,000 |
| 7 | Australia | 567,312 | 913,000 |
| 8 | Canada | 560,416 | 901,902 |
| 9 | France | 555,071 | 893,300 |
| 10 | Germany | 407,706 | 656,140 |

* *Both paved and unpaved roads*

The proportion of paved roads varies considerably: India's overall total, for example, comprises 942,668 miles (1,517,077 km) paved and 1,120,063 miles (1,802,567 km) unpaved, while only 114,419 miles (184,140 km) of Brazil's and 168,578 miles (271,300 km) of China's total are paved.

## FIRST COUNTRIES TO MAKE SEAT BELTS COMPULSORY

|  | COUNTRY | INTRODUCED |
|---|---|---|
| 1 | Czechoslovakia | Jan 1969 |
| 2 | Ivory Coast | Jan 1970 |
| 3 | Japan | Dec 1971 |
| 4 | Australia | Jan 1972 |
| 5 = | Brazil | June 1972 |
| = | New Zealand | June 1972 |
| 7 | Puerto Rico | Jan 1974 |
| 8 | Spain | Oct 1974 |
| 9 | Sweden | Jan 1975 |
| 10 = | Belgium | June 1975 |
| = | Luxembourg | June 1975 |
| = | Netherlands | June 1975 |

Seat belts were not designed for use in private cars until the 1950s. Ford was the first manufacturer in Europe to fit anchorage-points; belts were first equipped as standard in Swedish Volvos in 1959.

## COUNTRIES WITH THE MOST SALES OF MOTOR VEHICLES

|  | COUNTRY | CARS | COMMERCIAL VEHICLES | TOTAL SALES, 1999 |
|---|---|---|---|---|
| 1 | US | 8,698,284 | 8,716,444 | 17,414,728 |
| 2 | Japan | 4,154,084 | 1,707,132 | 5,861,216 |
| 3 | Germany | 3,802,176 | 318,901 | 4,127,077 |
| 4 | Italy | 2,349,200 | 196,298 | 2,545,498 |
| 5 | France | 2,148,423 | 386,983 | 2,535,416 |
| 6 | UK | 2,197,615 | 288,100 | 2,485,715 |
| 7 | China | 610,814 | 1,314,282 | 1,925,096 |
| 8 | Spain | 1,406,907 | 227,516 | 1,634,423 |
| 9 | Canada | 806,440 | 733,939 | 1,540,379 |
| 10 | South Korea | 910,725 | 362,304 | 1,273,029 |

Source: Ward's Motor Vehicle Data Book, *2000 edition*

**FRENCH JAM**

*France has one of the world's highest ratios of cars to people and can claim a record traffic jam of 190 miles (176 km), which occurred between Paris and Lyons on Feb 16, 1980.*

## TOP 10 ★
# COUNTRIES PRODUCING THE MOST MOTOR VEHICLES

| | COUNTRY | CARS | COMMERCIAL VEHICLES | TOTAL (1999) |
|---|---|---|---|---|
| 1 | US | 5,554,390 | 6,451,689 | 12,006,079 |
| 2 | Japan | 8,055,736 | 1,994,029 | 10,049,792 |
| 3 | Germany | 5,348,115 | 378,673 | 5,726,788 |
| 4 | France | 2,603,021 | 351,139 | 2,954,160 |
| 5 | Spain | 2,216,571 | 609,492 | 2,826,063 |
| 6 | Canada | 1,122,287 | 1,050,375 | 2,172,662 |
| 7 | UK | 1,748,277 | 232,793 | 1,981,070 |
| 8 | South Korea | 1,625,125 | 329,369 | 1,954,494 |
| 9 | Italy | 1,402,382 | 290,355 | 1,692,737 |
| 10 | China | 507,103 | 1,120,726 | 1,627,829 |

Source: Ward's Motor Vehicle Facts and Figures

### A CAR IS BORN
*Japan's car production, which places increasing reliance on advanced robotic technology, closely rivals that of world leader the US.*

## TOP 10 ★
# BEST-SELLING CARS OF ALL TIME

| | MANUFACTURER/MODEL | YEARS IN PRODUCTION | ESTIMATED NO. MADE* |
|---|---|---|---|
| 1 | Toyota Corolla | 1966– | 23,000,000 |
| 2 | Volkswagen Beetle | 1937–# | 21,500,000 |
| 3 | Volkswagen Golf | 1974– | over 20,000,000 |
| 4 | Lada Riva | 1972–97 | 19,000,000 |
| 5 | Ford Model T | 1908–27 | 16,536,075 |
| 6 | Honda Civic | 1972– | 14,000,000 |
| 7 | Nissan Sunny/Pulsar | 1966–94 | 13,571,100 |
| 8 | Ford Escort/Orion | 1967–84 | 12,000,000 |
| 9 | Honda Accord | 1976– | 11,500,000 |
| 10 | Volkswagen Passat | 1973– | 10,435,700 |

\* Up to January 1, 2001

\# Still produced in Mexico

Estimates of manufacturers' output of their best-selling models vary from the vague to the unusually precise 16,536,075 of the Model T Ford, with 15,007,033 produced in the US and the rest in Canada and the UK between 1908 and 1927.

### THE CAR IN FRONT ...
*The Toyota Motor Company was started in 1937, in Koromo, Japan, by Kiichiro Toyoda. Its Corolla model became the world's best-selling car.*

## TOP 10 ★
# BEST-SELLING CARS IN THE US, 2000

| | MODEL | SALES (2000) |
|---|---|---|
| 1 | Toyota Camry | 422,961 |
| 2 | Honda Accord | 404,515 |
| 3 | Ford Taurus | 382,035 |
| 4 | Honda Civic | 324,528 |
| 5 | Ford Focus | 286,166 |
| 6 | Chevrolet Cavalier | 236,803 |
| 7 | Toyota Corolla | 230,156 |
| 8 | Pontiac Grand Am | 214,923 |
| 9 | Chevrolet Malibu | 207,376 |
| 10 | Saturn S-series | 177,355 |

Source: *Ward's AutoInfoBank*

COR 163

# Road Accidents

## AGE GROUPS MOST VULNERABLE FOR ROAD FATALITIES IN THE US

| | AGE GROUP | DEATHS | DEATH RATE PER 100,000 (1999) |
|---|---|---|---|
| 1 | 16–20 | 5,917 | 28.08 |
| 2 | 21–24 | 3,884 | 25.52 |
| 3 | 74+ | 4,025 | 20.57 |
| 4 | 25–34 | 6,821 | 16.10 |
| 5 | 65–74 | 3,063 | 14.06 |
| 6 | 35–44 | 6,719 | 12.60 |
| 7 | 55–64 | 3,235 | 11.50 |
| 8 | 45–54 | 4,908 | 11.47 |
| 9 | 10–15 | 1,403 | 4.46 |
| 10 | 0–5 | 733 | 2.93 |

Source: *National Highway Traffic Safety Administration*

## THE 10 WORST YEARS FOR ROAD FATALITIES IN THE US

*(Year/no. killed*)*

**1** 1972, 54,589 **2** 1973, 54,052 **3** 1969, 53,543 **4** 1968, 52,725 **5** 1970, 52,627 **6** 1971, 52,542 **7** 1979, 51,093 **8** 1980, 51,091 **9** 1966, 50,894 **10** 1967, 50,724

* *Traffic fatalities occurring within 30 days of accident*
Source: *National Highway Traffic Safety Administration*

## MOST COMMON CAUSES OF FATAL CRASHES IN THE US

| | CAUSE | FATALITIES (1999) |
|---|---|---|
| 1 | Failure to keep in correct lane, or running off road | 16,904 |
| 2 | Driving too fast for conditions, or in excess of posted speed limit | 11,100 |
| 3 | Failure to yield right of way | 5,076 |
| 4 | Inattention (talking, eating, etc.) | 3,908 |
| 5 | Operating vehicle in erratic, reckless, careless, or negligent manner | 2,985 |
| 6 | Failure to obey traffic signs, signals, or officer | 2,817 |
| 7 | Swerving due to wind or slippery surface, or avoiding vehicle, object, nondriver in road, etc. | 1,986 |
| 8 | Drowsiness, sleep, fatigue, illness, or blackout | 1,808 |
| 9 | Overcorrecting/ oversteering | 1,793 |
| 10 | Making improper turn | 1,323 |

Source: *National Highway Traffic Safety Administration*

In this list – which remains astonishingly consistent from year to year – other causes include obscured vision (1,310 fatalities) and driving on the wrong side of the road (1,256), with a further 20,552 fatalities being reported with no cause listed and 601 as "unknown." The total number of drivers involved is 56,352, with the sum of the numbers and percentages being greater because in some cases more than one factor resulted in the fatal accident.

**SPEED LIMIT**
*Excess speed is a major cause of accidents the world over. Speed limits, increasing surveillance by speed cameras, and rigorous enforcement attempt to reduce the toll that speeding drivers take on lives.*

## MOST ACCIDENT-PRONE CAR COLORS

| | COLOR | ACCIDENTS PER 10,000 CARS OF EACH COLOR |
|---|---|---|
| 1 | Black | 179 |
| 2 | White | 160 |
| 3 | Red | 157 |
| 4 | Blue | 149 |
| 5 | Gray | 147 |
| 6 | Gold | 145 |
| 7 | Silver | 142 |
| 8 | Beige | 137 |
| 9 | Green | 134 |
| 10= | Brown | 133 |
| = | Yellow | 133 |

Research figures appear to refute the notion that white cars are safest because they are the easiest to see, especially at night. These statistics were immediately disputed by some car manufacturers, insurance companies, and psychologists, who pointed out that the type of vehicle and age and experience of drivers were equally salient factors. In the light of these comments, until further surveys are conducted it would be misleading to consider any color "safer" than another.

## STATES WITH THE MOST MOTOR VEHICLE FATALITIES

| | STATE | TOTAL FATALITIES (1999) |
|---|---|---|
| 1 | California | 3,559 |
| 2 | Texas | 3,518 |
| 3 | Florida | 2,918 |
| 4 | Pennsylvania | 1,549 |
| 5 | New York | 1,548 |
| 6 | Georgia | 1,508 |
| 7 | North Carolina | 1,505 |
| 8 | Illinois | 1,456 |
| 9 | Ohio | 1,430 |
| 10 | Michigan | 1,382 |

Source: *National Highway Traffic Safety Administration*

## THE 10 ★
# COUNTRIES WITH THE MOST DEATHS BY CAR ACCIDENTS

| | COUNTRY | DEATH RATE PER 100,000 POPULATION* |
|---|---|---|
| 1 | South Korea | 32.3 |
| 2 | Latvia | 27.1 |
| 3 | El Salvador | 24.4 |
| 4 | Lithuania | 23.8 |
| 5 | Venezuela | 22.3 |
| 6 | Greece | 22.1 |
| 7 | Estonia | 20.7 |
| 8 | Portugal | 19.2 |
| 9 | Russia | 18.5 |
| 10 | Belarus | 18.3 |
| | US | 15.8 |

\* In those countries/latest year for which data available

Source: *United Nations*

This Top 10 represents countries in which visitors clearly need to take special care on the road.

## THE 10 ★
# MOST COMMON COLLISIONS IN THE US

| | OBJECT/EVENT | COLLISIONS (1999) |
|---|---|---|
| 1 | Another vehicle, at an angle | 1,948,000 |
| 2 | Another vehicle, rear end | 1,859,000 |
| 3 | Another vehicle, sideswipe | 514,000 |
| 4 | Parked motor vehicle | 329,000 |
| 5 | Animal | 267,000 |
| 6 | Culvert, curb, or ditch | 197,000 |
| 7 | Pole or post | 180,000 |
| 8 | Shrubbery or tree | 126,000 |
| 9 | Rollover | 124,000 |
| 10 | Another vehicle, head on | 109,000 |

Source: *National Highway Traffic Safety Administration*

Out of a total of 6,279,000 crashes recorded in 1999 (omitting those described as "other" or "unknown"), the next most common event is a collision with a guard rail, with 91,000 cases.

## THE 10 ★
# WORST MOTOR VEHICLE AND ROAD DISASTERS

| | LOCATION/DATE/INCIDENT | NO. KILLED |
|---|---|---|

**1  Afghanistan**, Nov 3, 1982 — over 2,000
*Following a collision with a Soviet army truck, a gasoline tanker exploded in the 1.7-mile (2.7-km) Salang Tunnel. Some authorities have put the death toll from the explosion, fire, and fumes as high as 3,000.*

**2  Colombia**, Aug 7, 1956 — 1,200
*Seven army ammunition trucks exploded at night in the center of Cali, destroying eight city blocks, including a barracks where 500 soldiers were sleeping.*

**3  Thailand**, Feb 15, 1990 — over 150
*A dynamite truck exploded.*

**4  Nigeria**, Nov 4, 2000 — 150
*A gasoline tanker collided with a line of parked cars on the Ile-Ife-Ibadan Expressway, exploding and burning many to death. Some 96 bodies were recovered, but some estimates put the final toll as high as 200.*

**5  Nepal**, Nov 23, 1974 — 148
*Hindu pilgrims were killed when a suspension bridge over the River Mahahali collapsed.*

**6  Egypt**, Aug 9, 1973 — 127
*A bus drove into an irrigation canal.*

**7  Togo**, Dec 6, 1965 — over 125
*Two trucks collided with dancers during a festival at Sotouboua.*

**8  Spain**, July 11, 1978 — over 120
*A liquid gas tanker exploded in a camping site at San Carlos de la Rapita.*

**9  South Korea**, Apr 28, 1995 — 110
*An undergound explosion destroyed vehicles and caused about 100 cars and buses to plunge into the pit it created.*

**10=The Gambia**, Nov 12, 1992 — c.100
*After brake failure, a bus ferrying passengers to a dock plunged into a river.*

**=Kenya**, early Dec, 1992 — c.100
*A bus carrying 112 skidded, hit a bridge, and plunged into a river.*

The worst-ever car racing accident occurred on June 13, 1955, at Le Mans, France, when, in attempting to avoid other cars, French driver Pierre Levegh's Mercedes-Benz 300 SLR went out of control, hit a wall, and exploded in midair, showering wreckage into the crowd and thereby killing a total of 82.

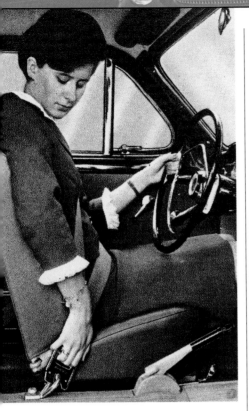

**BELTING UP**
*Seat belts were first included as standard equipment in Swedish Volvos in 1959, and became compulsory in most countries from the 1970s onward.*

## THE 10 ★
# COUNTRIES WITH THE HIGHEST NUMBER OF ROAD DEATHS

| | COUNTRY | TOTAL DEATHS* |
|---|---|---|
| 1 | US | 41,471 |
| 2 | Thailand | 15,176 |
| 3 | Japan | 10,805 |
| 4 | South Korea | 10,416 |
| 5 | France | 8,918 |
| 6 | Germany | 7,792 |
| 7 | Poland | 7,080 |
| 8 | Brazil | 6,759 |
| 9 | Turkey | 6,416 |
| 10 | Italy | 6,326 |

\* In latest year for which figures available

Which country does not appear among those with the Top 10 longest rail networks?
*see p.233 for the answer*

A  Japan
B  Mexico
C  Argentina

# Rail Transport

## WORST RAIL DISASTERS

LOCATION/DATE/INCIDENT     NO. KILLED

**1 Bagmati River**, India, June 6, 1981   c.800
*The carriages of a train traveling from Samastipur to Banmukhi in Bihar plunged off a bridge over the River Bagmati near Mansi when the driver braked, apparently to avoid hitting a sacred cow. Although the official death toll was said to have been 268, many authorities have claimed that the train was so massively overcrowded that the actual figure was in excess of 800.*

**2 Chelyabinsk**, Russia, June 3, 1989   up to 800
*Two passenger trains, laden with vacationers heading to and from Black Sea resorts, were destroyed when liquid gas from a nearby pipeline exploded.*

**3 Guadalajara**, Mexico, Jan 18, 1915   over 600
*A train derailed on a steep incline, but political strife in the country meant that full details of the disaster were suppressed.*

**4 Modane**, France, Dec 12, 1917   573
*A troop-carrying train ran out of control and was derailed. It has been claimed that the train was overloaded and that as many as 1,000 may have died.*

**5 Balvano**, Italy, Mar 2, 1944   521
*A heavily laden train stalled in the Armi Tunnel, and many passengers were asphyxiated. Like the disaster at Torre (No. 6), wartime secrecy prevented full details from being published.*

**6 Torre**, Spain, Jan 3, 1944   over 500
*A double collision and fire in a tunnel resulted in many deaths – some have put the total as high as 800.*

**7 Awash**, Ethiopia, Jan 13, 1985   428
*A derailment hurled a train laden with some 1,000 passengers into a ravine.*

**8 Cireau**, Romania, Jan 7, 1917   374
*An overcrowded passenger train crashed into a military train and was derailed.*

**9 Quipungo**, Angola, May 31, 1993   355
*A train was derailed by UNITA guerrilla action.*

**10 Sangi**, Pakistan, Jan 4, 1990   306
*A train was diverted on to the wrong line, resulting in a fatal collision.*

Figures for rail accidents are often extremely imprecise, especially during wartime, and half of these disasters occurred during the two world wars.

## FIRST COUNTRIES WITH RAILWAYS

| | COUNTRY | FIRST RAILWAY ESTABLISHED |
|---|---|---|
| 1 | UK | Sep 27, 1825 |
| 2 | France | Nov 7, 1829 |
| 3 | US | May 24, 1830 |
| 4 | Ireland | Dec 17, 1834 |
| 5 | Belgium | May 5, 1835 |
| 6 | Germany | Dec 7, 1835 |
| 7 | Canada | July 21, 1836 |
| 8 | Russia | Oct 30, 1837 |
| 9 | Austria | Jan 6, 1838 |
| 10 | Netherlands | Sep 24, 1839 |

Although there were earlier horse-drawn railways, the Stockton & Darlington Railway inaugurated the world's first steam service. In their early years some of those listed here offered only limited services over short distances, but their opening dates mark the generally accepted beginning of each country's steam railway system. By 1850, railways had also begun operating in Italy, Hungary, Denmark, and Spain.

## LONGEST UNDERGROUND RAILWAY NETWORKS

| | CITY/COUNTRY | OPENED | STATIONS | TOTAL TRACK LENGTH MILES | KM |
|---|---|---|---|---|---|
| 1 | **London**, UK | 1863 | 267 | 244 | 392 |
| 2 | **New York**, US | 1904 | 468 | 231 | 371 |
| 3 | **Moscow**, Russia | 1935 | 150 | 163 | 262 |
| 4 | **Paris**, France* | 1900 | 297 | 125 | 201 |
| 5 | **Copenhagen**, Denmark# | 1934 | 79 | 119 | 192 |
| 6 | **Seoul**, South Korea | 1974 | 114 | 113 | 183 |
| 7 | **Mexico City**, Mexico | 1969 | 154 | 112 | 178 |
| 8 | **Chicago**, US | 1943 | 145 | 108 | 173 |
| 9 | **Tokyo**, Japan+ | 1927 | 150 | 107 | 172 |
| 10 | **Berlin**, Germany | 1902 | 135 | 89 | 143 |

*\* Metro + RER   # Only partly underground   + Through-running extensions raise total to 391 miles (683 km), with 502 stations*

Source: Tony Pattison, Centre for Environmental Initiatives Researcher

### GOING UNDERGROUND

*Now over 100 years old, the Paris Metro – with its distinctive Art Deco entrances – is among the world's longest and most used underground railway systems.*

**RAILROAD**
*Although the US still has the longest rail network in the world, US rail mileage has declined considerably since its 1916 peak of 254,000 miles (408,773 km).*

## TOP 10 ★
## LONGEST RAIL NETWORKS

| LOCATION | TOTAL RAIL LENGTH MILES | KM |
|---|---|---|
| 1 US | 149,129 | 240,000 |
| 2 Russia | 93,205 | 150,000 |
| 3 China | 40,793 | 65,650 |
| 4 India | 39,093 | 62,915 |
| 5 Germany | 25,368 | 40,826 |
| 6 Argentina | 23,815 | 38,326 |
| 7 Canada | 22,440 | 36,114 |
| 8 Australia | 21,014 | 33,819 |
| 9 France | 19,846 | 31,939 |
| 10 Mexico | 19,292 | 31,048 |

The total of all world networks is today considered to be 746,476 miles (1,201,337 km). Of this, 148,775 miles (239,430 km) are narrow gauge and some 118,061 to 121,167 miles (190,000 to 195,000 km) are electrified.

## TOP 10 ★
## FASTEST RAIL JOURNEYS*

| JOURNEY | COUNTRY | TRAIN | DISTANCE MILES | KM | SPEED MPH | KM/H |
|---|---|---|---|---|---|---|
| 1 Hiroshima–Kokura | Japan | Nozomi 500 | 119.3 | 192.0 | 162.7 | 261.8 |
| 2 Massy–St. Pierre des Corps | France | 7 TGV | 128.5 | 206.9 | 157.4 | 253.3 |
| 3 Brussels–Paris | International | Thalys 9342 | 194.7 | 313.4 | 140.7 | 226.5 |
| 4 Madrid–Seville | Spain | 5 AVE | 292.4 | 470.5 | 129.9 | 209.1 |
| 5 Karlsruhe–Mannheim | Germany | 2 trains | 44.1 | 71.0 | 120.4 | 193.8 |
| 6 London–York | UK | 1 IC225 | 188.5 | 303.4 | 112.0 | 180.2 |
| 7 Skövde–Södertälje | Sweden | 3 X2000 | 172.1 | 277.0 | 106.4 | 171.3 |
| 8 Piacenza–Parma | Italy | ES 9325 | 35.4 | 57.0 | 106.2 | 171.0 |
| 9 North Philadelphia–Newark Penn | US | 1 NE Direct | 76.0 | 122.4 | 95.0 | 153.0 |
| 10 Salo–Karjaa | Finland | S220 132 | 33.0 | 53.1 | 94.3 | 151.7 |

*\* Fastest journey for each country; all those in the Top 10 have other similarly or equally fast services*
Source: Railway Gazette International

Japan is the leader not only for scheduled train journeys: its MLX01 Maglev train holds the world speed record for an experimental vehicle, traveling at over 341.7 mph (550 km/h). At the other end of the scale, Albania has achieved a 47 percent increase from 21.3 mph (34.2 km/h) to 31.3 mph (50.5 km/h).

# Water Transport

## LONGEST CRUISE SHIPS

| SHIP/COUNTRY/YEAR BUILT | LENGTH | | |
|---|---|---|---|
| | FT | IN | M |
| 1 *Norway* (former *France*), France, 1961 | 1,035 | 2 | 315.53 |
| 2 = *Voyager of the Seas*, Finland, 1999 | 1,020 | 9 | 311.12 |
| = *Explorer of the Seas*, Finland, 2000 | 1,020 | 9 | 311.12 |
| 4 *Disney Magic*, Italy, 1998 | 964 | 8 | 294.06 |
| 5 = *Disney Wonder*, Italy, 1999 | 964 | 7 | 294.00 |
| = *Millennium*, France, 2000 | 964 | 7 | 294.00 |
| 7 *Queen Elizabeth 2*, UK, 1969 | 963 | 0 | 293.53 |
| 8 *Costa Atlantica*, Finland, 2000 | 957 | 0 | 291.70 |
| 9 *Grand Princess*, Italy, 1998 | 949 | 10 | 289.51 |
| 10 *Enchantment of the Seas*, Finland, 1997 | 917 | 4 | 279.60 |

Source: *Lloyd's Register, MIPG/PPMS*

For comparison, the *Great Eastern* (launched in 1858) measured 692 ft (211 m) long. The *Titanic*, which sank dramatically on its maiden voyage in 1912, was 882 ft (269 m) long and, until the influx of new vessels in 1998, would have ranked 8th in this Top 10. Former entrant in this list the *Queen Mary* (1,019 ft/311 m) is now a floating museum in Long Beach, California.

**PORT OF CALL**
*Its substantial and well-protected harbor has contributed to Singapore's becoming the most important commercial center in Southeast Asia.*

## TOP 10 BUSIEST PORTS*

*(Port/location)*

**①** Singapore **②** Hong Kong, China
**③** Kaohsiung, Taiwan **④** Rotterdam, Netherlands **⑤** Pusan, South Korea
**⑥** Long Beach, US **⑦** Hamburg, Germany
**⑧** Antwerp, Belgium
**⑨** Los Angeles, US **⑩** Shanghai, China

\* *Ports handling the most TEUs (Twenty-foot Equivalent Units)*
Source: *International Association of Ports & Harbors*

## COUNTRIES WITH THE LONGEST INLAND WATERWAY NETWORKS*

| COUNTRY | LENGTH | |
|---|---|---|
| | MILES | KM |
| 1 China | 68,351 | 110,000 |
| 2 Russia | 62,758 | 101,000 |
| 3 Brazil | 31,069 | 50,000 |
| 4 US# | 25,482 | 41,009 |
| 5 Indonesia | 13,409 | 21,579 |
| 6 Colombia | 11,272 | 18,140 |
| 7 Vietnam | 11,000 | 17,702 |
| 8 India | 10,054 | 16,180 |
| 9 Dem. Rep. of Congo | 9,321 | 15,000 |
| 10 France | 9,278 | 14,932 |

\* *Canals and navigable rivers*
# *Excluding Great Lakes*
Source: *Central Intelligence Agency*

The navigability of the world's waterways varies greatly: only 2,256 miles (3,631 km) of those of India, for example, are navigable by large vessels.

### THE *UNITED STATES* GAINS THE BLUE RIBAND

From the 19th century onward, ocean liners vied for the prize for the fastest transatlantic crossing by a passenger ship. The record, popularly known as the "Blue Riband," and the Hales Trophy, awarded since 1935, go to the vessel with the fastest crossing, which is based on average speed rather than shortest time because the route lengths vary. In 1838 the record stood at 7.3 knots over an 18-day voyage. This was steadily improved upon until, in 1938, the *Queen Mary* established the westbound record crossing at a speed of 30.99 knots. It took until July 15, 1952, for the *United States* to establish a new record of 3 days 10 hours 40 minutes at an average speed of 34.51 knots. A new eastbound record of 2 days 20 hours 9 minutes (41.28 knots) was set in 1998, but the *United States'* westbound record has remained unbeaten for half a century.

**50 YEARS AGO · YEARS AGO · YEARS AGO · YEARS**

## THE 10 ★
# WORST MARINE DISASTERS

| LOCATION/DATE/INCIDENT | APPROX. NO. KILLED |
|---|---|
| **1 Off Gdansk**, Poland, January 30, 1945 | up to 7,800 |

*The German liner* Wilhelm Gustloff, *laden with refugees, was torpedoed by a Soviet submarine, S-13. The precise death toll remains uncertain, but is in the range of 5,348 to 7,800.*

| | |
|---|---|
| **2 Off Cape Rixhöft** (Rozeewie), Poland, April 16, 1945 | 6,800 |

*A German ship,* Goya, *carrying evacuees from Gdansk, was torpedoed in the Baltic.*

| | |
|---|---|
| **3 Off Yingkow**, China, December 3, 1948 | over 6,000 |

*The boilers of an unidentified Chinese troop ship carrying Nationalist soldiers from Manchuria exploded, detonating ammunition.*

| | |
|---|---|
| **4 Lübeck**, Germany, May 3, 1945 | 5,000 |

*The German ship* Cap Arcona, *carrying concentration camp survivors, was bombed and sunk by British aircraft.*

| | |
|---|---|
| **5 Off St. Nazaire**, France, June 17, 1940 | 3,050 |

*The British troop ship* Lancastria *sank.*

| | |
|---|---|
| **6 Off Stolpmünde** (Ustka), Poland, February 9, 1945 | 3,000 |

*German war-wounded and refugees were lost when the* Steuben *was torpedoed by the same Russian submarine that had sunk the* Wilhelm Gustloff.

| LOCATION/DATE/INCIDENT | APPROX. NO. KILLED |
|---|---|
| **7 Tabias Strait**, Philippines, December 20, 1987 | up to 3,000 |

*The ferry* Dona Paz *was struck by oil tanker MV Victor.*

| | |
|---|---|
| **8 Woosung**, China, December 3, 1948 | over 2,750 |

*The overloaded steamship* Kiangya, *carrying refugees, struck a Japanese mine.*

| | |
|---|---|
| **9 Lübeck**, Germany, May 3, 1945 | 2,750 |

*The refugee ship* Thielbeck *sank during the British bombardment of Lübeck harbor in the closing weeks of World War II.*

| | |
|---|---|
| **10 South Atlantic**, September 12, 1942 | 2,279 |

*The British passenger vessel* Laconia, *carrying Italian prisoners-of-war, was sunk by German U-boat U-156.*

Recent reassessments of the death tolls in some of the World War II marine disasters mean that the most famous marine disaster of all, the sinking of the *Titanic*, the British liner that struck an iceberg in the North Atlantic and sank on April 15, 1912, with the loss of 1,517 lives, no longer ranks in this list. However, the *Titanic* tragedy remains one of the worst-ever peacetime disasters, along with such notable incidents as that involving the *General Slocum*, an excursion liner that caught fire in the port of New York on June 15, 1904, with the loss of 1,021 lives.

## THE 10 ★
# WORST OIL TANKER SPILLS

| TANKER/LOCATION/DATE | APPROX. SPILLAGE (TONS) |
|---|---|
| **1** *Atlantic Empress* and *Aegean Captain*, Trinidad, July 19, 1979 | 269,549 |
| **2** *Castillio de Bellver*, Cape Town, South Africa, Aug 6, 1983 | 251,097 |
| **3** *Olympic Bravery*, Ushant, France, Jan 24, 1976 | 246,051 |
| **4** *Amoco Cadiz*, Finistère, France, Mar 16, 1978 | 219,748 |
| **5** *Odyssey*, Atlantic, off Canada, Nov 10, 1988 | 137,862 |
| **6** *Haven*, off Genoa, Italy, Apr 11, 1991 | 134,344 |
| **7** *Torrey Canyon*, Scilly Isles, UK, Mar 18, 1967 | 122,189 |
| **8** *Sea Star*, Gulf of Oman, Dec 19, 1972 | 121,229 |
| **9** *Irenes Serenade*, Pilos, Greece, Feb 23, 1980 | 117,071 |
| **10** *Texaco Denmark*, North Sea, off Belgium, Dec 7, 1971 | 100,758 |

Source: *Environmental Technology Center,* Oil Spill Intelligence Report

**ENVIRONMENTAL DISASTER**
*The 1979 collision of the* Atlantic Empress *and the* Aegean Captain *off Trinidad resulted in the worst oil spill of all time.*

**What is Charles W. Furnas's claim to aviation fame?**
*see p.236 for the answer*

A The first airplane passenger in the US
B The first to use a parachute
C The first to land an aircraft on water

# Air Records

## FIRST TRANSATLANTIC FLIGHTS

| AIRCRAFT/CREW/COUNTRY | CROSSING | DATE* |
|---|---|---|
| 1 **US Navy/Curtiss flying boat** *NC-4*, Lt.-Cdr. Albert Cushing Read and crew of five, US | Trepassy Harbor, Newfoundland, to Lisbon, Portugal | May 16–27, 1919 |
| 2 **Twin Rolls-Royce-engined converted Vickers Vimy bomber**#, Capt. John Alcock and Lt. Arthur Whitten Brown, UK | St. John's, Newfoundland, to Galway, Ireland | June 14–15, 1919 |
| 3 **British airship** *R-34*+, Maj. George Herbert Scott and crew of 30, UK | East Fortune, Scotland, to Roosevelt Field, New York | July 2–6, 1919 |
| 4 **Fairey IIID seaplane** *Santa Cruz*, Adm. Gago Coutinho and Cdr. Sacadura Cabral, Portugal | Lisbon, Portugal, to Recife, Brazil | Mar 30–June 5, 1922 |
| 5 **Two Douglas seaplanes,** *Chicago* **and** *New Orleans*, Lt. Lowell H. Smith and Leslie P. Arnold/Erik Nelson and John Harding, US | Orkneys, Scotland, to Labrador, Canada | Aug 2–31, 1924 |
| 6 **Renamed German-built** *ZR 3* **airship** *Los Angeles*, Dr. Hugo Eckener with 31 passengers and crew, Germany | Friedrichshafen, Germany, to Lakehurst, New Jersey | Oct 12–15, 1924 |
| 7 **Dornier Wal twin-engined flying boat** *Plus Ultra*, Capt. Julio Ruiz de Alda and crew, Spain | Huelva, Spain, to Recife, Brazil | Jan 22–Feb 10, 1926 |
| 8 **Savoia-Marchetti S.55 flying boat** *Santa Maria*, Francesco Marquis de Pinedo, Capt. Carlo del Prete, and Lt. Vitale Zacchetti, Italy | Cagliari, Sardinia, to Recife, Brazil | Feb 8–24, 1927 |
| 9 **Dornier Wal flying boat**, Sarmento de Beires and Jorge de Castilho, Portugal | Lisbon, Portugal, to Natal, Brazil | Mar 16–17, 1927 |
| 10 **Savoia-Marchetti flying boat**, João De Barros and crew, Brazil | Genoa, Italy, to Natal, Brazil | Apr 28–May 14, 1927 |

\* All dates refer to the actual Atlantic legs of the journeys; some started earlier and ended beyond their first transatlantic landfalls

\# First nonstop flight

\+ First east–west flight

**ATLANTIC FLIER**

*Alcock and Brown made the first nonstop Atlantic crossing in 16 hours 28 minutes in a converted Vickers Vimy bomber.*

## FIRST PEOPLE TO FLY IN HEAVIER-THAN-AIR AIRCRAFT

| PILOT/NATIONALITY/AIRCRAFT | DATE |
|---|---|
| 1 **Orville Wright**, US, *Wright Flyer I* | Dec 17, 1903 |
| 2 **Wilbur Wright**, US, *Wright Flyer I* | Dec 17, 1903 |
| 3 **Alberto Santos-Dumont**, Brazil, *No. 14-bis* | Oct 23, 1906 |
| 4 **Charles Voisin**, France, *Voisin-Delagrange I* | Mar 30, 1907 |
| 5 **Henri Farman**, UK, later France, *Voisin-Farman I-bis* | Oct 7, 1907 |
| 6 **Léon Delagrange**, France, *Voisin-Delagrange I* | Nov 5, 1907 |
| 7 **Robert Esnault-Pelterie**, France, *REP No. 1* | Nov 16, 1907 |
| 8 **Charles W. Furnas**\*, US, *Wright Flyer III* | May 14, 1908 |
| 9 **Louis Blériot**, France, *Blériot VIII* | June 29, 1908 |
| 10 **Glenn Hammond Curtiss**, US, *AEA June Bug* | July 4, 1908 |

\* As a passenger in a plane piloted by Wilbur Wright, Furnas was the first airplane passenger in the US

## FIRST ROCKET AND JET AIRCRAFT

| AIRCRAFT/COUNTRY | FIRST FLIGHT |
|---|---|
| 1 **Heinkel He 176**\*, Germany | June 20, 1939 |
| 2 **Heinkel He 178**, Germany | Aug 27, 1939 |
| 3 **DFS 194**\*, Germany | Aug, 1940# |
| 4 **Caproni-Campini N-1**, Italy | Aug 28, 1940 |
| 5 **Heinkel He 280V-1**, Germany | Apr 2, 1941 |
| 6 **Gloster E.28/39**, UK | May 15, 1941 |
| 7 **Messerschmitt Me 163 Komet**\*, Germany | Aug 13, 1941 |
| 8 **Messerschmitt Me 262V-3**, Germany | July 18, 1942 |
| 9 **Bell XP-59A Airacomet**, US | Oct 1, 1942 |
| 10 **Gloster Meteor F Mk 1**, UK | Mar 5, 1943 |

\* Rocket-powered    # Precise date unknown

# FIRST FLIGHTS OF MORE THAN ONE HOUR

| | PILOT | HR:MIN:SEC | DATE |
|---|---|---|---|
| 1 | Orville Wright | 1:02:15 | Sep 9, 1908 |
| 2 | Orville Wright | 1:05:52 | Sep 10, 1908 |
| 3 | Orville Wright | 1:10:00 | Sep 11, 1908 |
| 4 | Orville Wright | 1:15:20 | Sep 12, 1908 |
| 5 | Wilbur Wright | 1:31:25 | Sep 21, 1908 |
| 6 | Wilbur Wright | 1:07:24 | Sep 28, 1908 |
| 7 | Wilbur Wright* | 1:04:26 | Oct 6, 1908 |
| 8 | Wilbur Wright | 1:09:45 | Oct 10, 1908 |
| 9 | Wilbur Wright | 1:54:53 | Dec 18, 1908 |
| 10 | Wilbur Wright | 2:20:23 | Dec 31, 1908 |

\* First-ever flight of more than one hour with a passenger (M. A. Fordyce)

**ROCKET PILOT**
*X-15 pilot Joseph A. Walker held the world record seven times in 1960–62, before finally losing the mantle to William J. Knight.*

# FASTEST X-15 FLIGHTS

| | PILOT/DATE | MACH* | FLIGHT MPH | KM/H |
|---|---|---|---|---|
| 1 | William J. Knight, Oct 3, 1967 | 6.70 | 4,520 | 7,274 |
| 2 | William J. Knight, Nov 18, 1966 | 6.33 | 4,261 | 6,857 |
| 3 | Joseph A. Walker, June 27, 1962 | 5.92 | 4,105 | 6,606 |
| 4 | Robert M. White, Nov 9, 1961 | 6.04 | 4,094 | 6,589 |
| 5 | Robert A. Rushworth, Dec 5, 1963 | 6.06 | 4,018 | 6,466 |
| 6 | Neil A. Armstrong, July 26, 1962 | 5.74 | 3,989 | 6,420 |
| 7 | John B. McKay, June 22, 1965 | 5.64 | 3,938 | 6,388 |
| 8 | Robert A. Rushworth, July 18, 1963 | 5.63 | 3,925 | 6,317 |
| 9 | Joseph A. Walker, June 25, 1963 | 5.51 | 3,911 | 6,294 |
| 10 | William H. Dan, Oct 4, 1967 | 5.53 | 3,910 | 6,293 |

\* *Mach no. varies with altitude – the list is ranked on actual speed*

Although achieved more than 33 years ago, the speeds attained by the rocket-powered X-15 and X-15A-2 aircraft are the greatest ever attained by piloted vehicles in the Earth's atmosphere.

# BIGGEST AIRSHIPS EVER BUILT

| | AIRSHIP | COUNTRY | YEAR | VOLUME CU FT | CU M | LENGTH FT | M |
|---|---|---|---|---|---|---|---|
| 1 = | *Hindenburg* | Germany | 1936 | 7,062,934 | 200,000 | 804 | 245 |
| = | *Graf Zeppelin II* | Germany | 1938 | 7,062,934 | 200,000 | 804 | 245 |
| 3 = | *Akron* | US | 1931 | 6,500,000 | 184,060 | 785 | 239 |
| = | *Macon* | US | 1933 | 6,500,000 | 184,060 | 785 | 239 |
| 5 | *R101* | UK | 1930 | 5,500,000 | 155,744 | 777 | 237 |
| 6 | *Graf Zeppelin* | Germany | 1928 | 3,708,040 | 105,000 | 776 | 237 |
| 7 | *L72* | Germany | 1920 | 2,419,055 | 68,500 | 743 | 226 |
| 8 | *R100* | UK | 1929 | 5,500,000 | 155,744 | 709 | 216 |
| 9 | *R38* | UK* | 1921 | 2,724,000 | 77,136 | 699 | 213 |
| 10 = | *L70* | Germany | 1918 | 2,418,700 | 62,200 | 694 | 212 |
| = | *L71* | Germany | 1918 | 2,418,700 | 62,200 | 694 | 212 |

\* *UK-built, but sold to US Navy*

## THE FIRST JET AIRLINER

The jet airliner began life only 50 years ago, with the launch on May 3, 1952, of the scheduled BOAC de Havilland Comet service between London and Johannesburg, a distance of 6,724 miles (10,821 km) flown in stages with a journey time of 23 hours 34 minutes. The 36-seat aircraft *Yoke Peter* inaugurated the route, following exhaustive tests on freight-only flights to destinations such as Beirut, New Delhi, Jakarta, and Singapore. By August 1952, a weekly Comet service to Colombo, Ceylon (Sri Lanka), had also been established. Soon after, several crashes involving Comets cast doubts over the safety of passenger jets, but these were overcome as the world's airline routes became established.

**50 YEARS AGO · YEARS AGO · YEARS AGO · YEARS**

**Did You Know?** Following a feud with the Smithsonian Institution in Washington, DC, the Wright Brothers' *Flyer*, the first aircraft to fly, was kept in the Science Museum, London, from 1928 until 1948.

# Air Transport

## WORST AIRSHIP DISASTERS

| LOCATION/DATE/INCIDENT | NO. KILLED |
| --- | --- |
| **1  Off the New Jersey coast**, US, Apr 4, 1933 | 73 |
| *US Navy airship Akron crashed into the sea in a storm, leaving only three survivors.* | |
| **2  Over the Mediterranean**, Dec 21, 1923 | 52 |
| *French airship Dixmude is assumed to have been struck by lightning, and broke up and crashed into the sea.* | |
| **3  Near Beauvais**, France, Oct 5, 1930 | 50 |
| *British airship R101 crashed into a hillside leaving 48 dead, with two dying later, and six survivors.* | |
| **4  Off the coast near Hull**, UK, Aug 24, 1921 | 44 |
| *Airship R38 broke in two on a training and test flight.* | |
| **5  Lakehurst**, New Jersey, US, May 6, 1937 | 36 |
| *German Zeppelin Hindenburg caught fire when mooring.* | |
| **6  Hampton Roads**, Virginia, US, Feb 21, 1922 | 34 |
| *Roma, an Italian airship bought by the US Army, crashed, killing all but 11 men on board.* | |
| **7  Berlin**, Germany, Oct 17, 1913 | 28 |
| *German airship LZ18 crashed after engine failure during a test flight at Berlin-Johannisthal.* | |
| **8  Baltic Sea**, Mar 30, 1917 | 23 |
| *German airship SL9 was struck by lightning on a flight from Seerappen to Seddin, and crashed into the sea.* | |
| **9  Mouth of the River Elbe**, Germany, Sep 3, 1915 | 19 |
| *German airship L10 was struck by lightning and plunged into the sea.* | |
| **10=Off Heligoland**, Sep 9, 1913 | 14 |
| *German Navy airship L1 crashed into the sea, leaving six survivors.* | |
| **=Caldwell**, Ohio, US, Sep 3, 1925 | 14 |
| *US dirigible Shenandoah broke up in a storm, scattering sections over many miles of the Ohio countryside.* | |

Fatalities occurred from the earliest days of airships: the *Pax* crashed in Paris on May 12, 1902, killing its Brazilian inventor and pilot Augusto Severo and his assistant, and on October 13 of the same year Ottokar de Bradsky and his mechanic were killed in an airship crash, also in Paris.

## TOP 10 AIRLINERS IN SERVICE

*(Aircraft/no. in service)*

**1** Boeing B-737-300, 1,076  **2** Boeing B-757-200, 913  **3** Airbus A-320, 839  **4** Boeing B-727-200, 771  **5** Boeing B-737-200, 752  **6** Boeing B-767-300, 560  **7** Boeing B-747-400, 524  **8** Boeing B-737-400, 460  **9** Raytheon Beech 1900, 408  **10** Saab 340, 407

Source: *Air Transport Intelligence at www.rati.com*

## WORST AIR DISASTERS

| LOCATION/DATE/INCIDENT | NO. KILLED |
| --- | --- |
| **1  Tenerife**, Canary Islands, Mar 27, 1977 | 583 |
| *Two Boeing 747s (Pan Am and KLM, carrying 364 passengers and 16 crew and 230 passengers and 11 crew respectively) collided and caught fire on the runway of Los Rodeos airport after the pilots received incorrect control-tower instructions.* | |
| **2  Mt. Ogura**, Japan, Aug 12, 1985 | 520 |
| *A JAL Boeing 747 on an internal flight from Tokyo to Osaka crashed, killing all but four on board in the worst-ever disaster involving a single aircraft.* | |
| **3  Charkhi Dadri**, India, Nov 12, 1996 | 349 |
| *Soon after taking off from New Delhi's Indira Gandhi International Airport, a Saudi Airways Boeing 747 collided with a Kazakh Airlines Ilyushin IL-76 cargo aircraft on its descent and exploded, killing all 312 on the Boeing and 37 on the Ilyushin, in the world's worst midair crash.* | |
| **4  Paris**, France, Mar 3, 1974 | 346 |
| *A Turkish Airlines DC-10 crashed at Ermenonville, north of Paris, just after takeoff for London, with many English rugby fans among the dead.* | |
| **5  Off the Irish coast**, June 23, 1985 | 329 |
| *An Air India Boeing 747 on a flight from Vancouver to Delhi exploded in midair, perhaps as a result of a terrorist bomb.* | |
| **6  Riyadh**, Saudi Arabia, Aug 19, 1980 | 301 |
| *A Saudia (Saudi Arabian) Airlines Lockheed Tristar caught fire during an emergency landing.* | |
| **7  Kinshasa**, Zaïre, Jan 8, 1996 | 298 |
| *A Zaïrean Antonov-32 cargo plane crashed shortly after takeoff, killing shoppers in a city center market.* | |
| **8  Off the Iranian coast**, July 3, 1988 | 290 |
| *An Iran Air A300 airbus was shot down in error by a missile fired by the USS Vincennes.* | |
| **9  Chicago**, US, May 25, 1979 | 273 |
| *The worst air disaster in the US occurred when an engine fell off an American Airlines DC-10 as it took off from Chicago O'Hare airport and the plane plunged out of control, killing all 271 on board and two on the ground.* | |
| **10  Lockerbie**, Scotland, Dec 21, 1988 | 270 |
| *Pan Am Flight 103 from London Heathrow to New York exploded in midair as a result of a terrorist bomb, killing 243 passengers, 16 crew, and 11 on the ground, in the UK's worst-ever air disaster.* | |

### FIERY FINALE

*Astonishingly, 61 of the 97 people on board the Hindenburg survived its explosion, but the awesome images of the catastrophe heralded the end of the airship era.*

**FLYING HIGH**

*First flown in 1982, and now costing upward of $70 million each, the Boeing B-757-200 has a maximum range of 4,520 miles (7,240 km) and is extensively used on both short- and long-haul routes.*

## TOP 10 ★
### BUSIEST INTERNATIONAL AIRPORTS

| AIRPORT/LOCATION | INTERNATIONAL PASSENGERS PER ANNUM |
|---|---|
| 1 **London Heathrow**, London, UK | 50,612,000 |
| 2 **Frankfurt**, Frankfurt, Germany | 32,333,000 |
| 3 **Charles de Gaulle**, Paris, France | 31,549,000 |
| 4 **Schiphol**, Amsterdam, Netherlands | 30,832,000 |
| 5 **Hong Kong**, Hong Kong, China | 28,316,000 |
| 6 **London Gatwick**, Gatwick, UK | 24,385,000 |
| 7 **Singapore International**, Singapore | 23,799,000 |
| 8 **New Tokyo International (Narita)**, Tokyo, Japan | 22,941,000 |
| 9 **J.F. Kennedy International**, New York, US | 17,378,000 |
| 10 **Zurich**, Zurich, Switzerland | 16,747,000 |

Source: *International Civil Aviation Organization*

## TOP 10 AIRLINES WITH THE MOST AIRCRAFT
*(Airline/country*/fleet size)*

❶ **American Airlines**, 714  ❷ **United Airlines**, 603  ❸ **Delta Airlines**, 600
❹ **Northwest Airlines**, 424  ❺ **US Airways**, 384  ❻ **Continental Airlines**, 364
❼ **Southwest Airlines**, 327  ❽ **British Airways**, UK, 268
❾ **American Eagle Airlines**, 245  ❿ **Lufthansa German Airlines**, Germany, 233

*\* All from the US unless otherwise stated*
Source: Airline Business/Air Transport Intelligence at www.rati.com

## TOP 10 ★
### AIRLINES CARRYING THE MOST PASSENGERS

| AIRLINE/COUNTRY | PASSENGERS, 1999 |
|---|---|
| 1 **Delta Airlines**, US | 105,500,000 |
| 2 **United Airlines**, US | 87,100,000 |
| 3 **American Airlines**, US | 84,700,000 |
| 4 **US Airways**, US | 58,800,000 |
| 5 **Southwest Airlines**, US | 57,700,000 |
| 6 **Northwest Airlines**, US | 56,100,000 |
| 7 **Continental Airlines**, US | 45,500,000 |
| 8 **All Nippon Airways**, Japan | 42,700,000 |
| 9 **Air France**, France | 39,800,000 |
| 10 **Lufthansa**, Germany | 38,900,000 |

Source: Airline Business/*Air Transport Intelligence* at www.rati.com

**BOEING**

The name of William Edward Boeing (1881–1956) is known the world over from the aircraft made by his company – the world's largest. Detroit-born Boeing made a fortune in the timber industry and, having become passionate about aviation, set up an aircraft manufacturing company in 1916. The firm prospered, and in 1927 set up an airline, Boeing Air Transport. Boeing retired from the business in 1934, when US government antitrust legislation made it illegal for a company to build aircraft and operate an airline. The airline was sold off and became United – one of the world's largest – while the Boeing Company continued to supply the world's airlines with its aircraft.

**On what unusual surface did Henry Ford set the land speed record in 1904?**
*see p.226 for the answer*

A  Ice
B  Salt
C  Volcanic lava

# World Tourism

TOP 10 ★

## TOURIST DESTINATIONS IN ASIA AND THE PACIFIC

| | COUNTRY | TOTAL VISITORS (2000) |
|---|---|---|
| 1 | China | 31,236,000 |
| 2 | Hong Kong | 13,059,000 |
| 3 | Malaysia | 10,000,000 |
| 4 | Thailand | 9,574,000 |
| 5 | Singapore | 7,003,000 |
| 6 | Macau | 6,682,000 |
| 7 | South Korea | 5,336,000 |
| 8 | Indonesia | 5,012,000 |
| 9 | Australia | 4,882,000 |
| 10 | Japan | 4,758,000 |

Source: *World Tourism Organization*

TOP 10 ★

## TOURIST DESTINATIONS IN THE AMERICAS

| | COUNTRY | TOTAL VISITORS (2000) |
|---|---|---|
| 1 | US | 52,690,000 |
| 2 | Canada | 20,423,000 |
| 3 | Mexico | 20,000,000 |
| 4 | Brazil | 5,190,000 |
| 5 | Puerto Rico | 3,094,000 |
| 6 | Argentina | 2,988,000 |
| 7 | Dominican Republic | 2,977,000 |
| 8 | Uruguay | 1,968,000 |
| 9 | Chile | 1,719,000 |
| 10 | Cuba | 1,700,000 |

Source: *World Tourism Organization*

TOP 10 ★

## DESTINATIONS FOR US TOURISTS

| | DESTINATION COUNTRY | US VISITORS (1999) |
|---|---|---|
| 1 | Mexico | 17,743,000 |
| 2 | Canada | 16,036,000 |
| 3 | UK | 4,129,000 |
| 4 | France | 2,728,000 |
| 5 | Germany | 1,966,000 |
| 6 | Italy | 1,893,000 |
| 7 | Jamaica | 1,499,000 |
| 8 = | Bahamas | 1,254,000 |
| = | Japan | 1,254,000 |
| 10 | Netherlands | 1,032,000 |

Source: *Tourism Industries/International Trade Administration, Department of Commerce*

TOP 10 ★

## TOURIST DESTINATIONS IN EUROPE

| | COUNTRY | TOTAL VISITORS (2000) | | COUNTRY | TOTAL VISITORS (2000) |
|---|---|---|---|---|---|
| 1 | France | 74,500,000 | 6 | Germany | 18,916,000 |
| 2 | Spain | 48,500,000 | 7 | Poland | 18,183,000 |
| 3 | Italy | 41,182,000 | 8 | Austria | 17,818,000 |
| 4 | UK | 24,900,000 | 9 | Hungary | 15,571,000 |
| 5 | Russia | 22,783,000 | 10 | Greece | 12,500,000 |

Source: *World Tourism Organization*

TOP 10 ★

## OLDEST AMUSEMENT PARKS

| | PARK/LOCATION | YEAR FOUNDED |
|---|---|---|
| 1 | **Bakken**, Klampenborg, Denmark | 1583 |
| 2 | **The Prater**, Vienna, Austria | 1766 |
| 3 | **Blackgang Chine Cliff Top Theme Park**, Ventnor, Isle of Wight, UK | 1842 |
| 4 | **Tivoli Gardens**, Copenhagen, Denmark | 1843 |
| 5 | **Lake Compounce Amusement Park**, Bristol, Connecticut | 1846 |
| 6 | **Hanayashiki**, Tokyo, Japan | 1853 |
| 7 | **Grand Pier**, Teignmouth, UK | 1865 |
| 8 | **Blackpool Central Pier**, Blackpool, UK | 1868 |
| 9 | **Cedar Point**, Sandusky, Ohio | 1870 |
| 10 | **Clacton Pier**, Clacton, UK | 1871 |

**IT JUST KEEPS ROLLING ALONG**

*In operation since 1914, the Rutschbanen in Copenhagen's Tivoli Gardens is Europe's oldest working roller coaster. The oldest one in the US predates this by 12 years.*

## TOP 10 ★
# WORLDWIDE AMUSEMENT AND THEME PARKS, 2000

| PARK/LOCATION | ATTENDANCE |
|---|---|
| 1 Tokyo Disneyland, Tokyo, Japan | 16,507,000 |
| 2 The Magic Kingdom at Walt Disney World, Lake Buena Vista, Florida, | 15,400,000 |
| 3 Disneyland, Anaheim, California | 13,900,000 |
| 4 Disneyland Paris, Marne-La-Vallée, France | 12,000,000 |
| 5 Epcot at Walt Disney World | 10,600,000 |
| 6 Everland, Kyonggi-Do, South Korea | 9,153,000 |
| 7 Disney–MGM Studios at Walt Disney World | 8,900,000 |
| 8 Disney's Animal Kingdom at Walt Disney World | 8,300,000 |
| 9 Universal Studios Florida, Orlando, Florida | 8,100,000 |
| 10 Lotte World, Seoul, South Korea | 7,200,000 |

Source: *Amusement Business*

## TOP 10 ★
# MOST VISITED CITIES IN THE US

| CITY/STATE | % MARKET SHARE | VISITORS 1999 |
|---|---|---|
| 1 New York City, New York | 22.5 | 5,505,000 |
| 2 Los Angeles, California | 14.6 | 3,572,000 |
| 3 = Miami, Florida | 11.7 | 2,863,000 |
| = Orlando, Florida | 11.7 | 2,863,000 |
| 5 San Francisco, California | 11.4 | 2,789,000 |
| 6 Las Vegas, Nevada | 9.2 | 2,251,000 |
| 7 Oahu/Honolulu, Hawaii | 9.0 | 2,202,000 |
| 8 Washington, DC | 5.3 | 1,297,000 |
| 9 Chicago, Illinois | 5.2 | 1,272,000 |
| 10 Boston, Massachusetts | 4.9 | 1,199,000 |

Source: *Tourism Industries/International Trade Administration, Department of Commerce*

## TOP 10 ★
# OLDEST ROLLER COASTERS*

| ROLLER COASTER/LOCATION | YEAR FOUNDED |
|---|---|
| 1 Leap-the-Dips, Lakemont Park, Altoona, Pennsylvania | 1902 |
| 2 Scenic Railway, Luna Park, Melbourne, Australia | 1912 |
| 3 Rutschbanen, Tivoli Gardens, Copenhagen, Denmark | 1914 |
| 4 Jack Rabbit, Clementon Amusement Park, Clementon, New Jersey | 1919 |
| 5 = Jack Rabbit, Sea Breeze Park, Rochester, New York | 1920 |
| = Scenic Railway, Dreamland, Margate, UK | 1920 |
| 7 = Jack Rabbit, Kennywood, West Mifflin, Pennsylvania | 1921 |
| = Roller Coaster, Lagoon, Farmington, Utah | 1921 |
| 9 = Big Dipper, Blackpool Pleasure Beach, Blackpool, UK | 1923 |
| = Thunderhawk, Dorney Park, Allentown, Pennsylvania | 1923 |
| = Zippin Pippin, Libertyland, Memphis, Tennessee | 1923 |

\* *In operation at same location since founded*

Leap-the-Dips at Lakemont Park, Altoona, Pennsylvania, the world's oldest roller coaster, was out of operation from 1985, but was restored and reopened in 1999.

## TOP 10 ★
# FASTEST ROLLER COASTERS

| ROLLER COASTER/ LOCATION/YEAR OPENED | SPEED MPH | KM/H |
|---|---|---|
| 1 = Superman The Escape, Six Flags Magic Mountain, Valencia, California, 1997 | 100 | 161 |
| = Tower of Terror, Dreamworld, Gold Coast, Australia, 1997 | 100 | 161 |
| 3 Millennium Force, Cedar Point, Sandusky, Ohio, 2000 | 92 | 148 |
| 4 = Goliath, Six Flags Magic Mountain, Valencia, California, 2000 | 85 | 137 |
| = Titan, Six Flags Over Texas, Arlington, Texas, 2001* | 85 | 137 |
| 6 = Desperado, Buffalo Bill's Resort and Casino, Primm, Nevada, 1994 | 80 | 129 |
| = HyperSonic XLC, Paramount's Kings Dominion, Doswell, Virginia, 2001* | 80 | 129 |
| = Nitro, Six Flags Great Adventure, Jackson, New Jersey, 2001* | 80 | 129 |
| = Phantom's Revenge, Kennywood Park, West Mifflin, Pennsylvania, 2001# | 80 | 129 |
| = Superman The Ride of Steel, Six Flags, Darien Lake, New York, 2000 | 80 | 129 |

\* *Under construction at time of going to press*

### THE OLDEST ROLLER COASTER

The first simple roller coasters were built in 1884 at Coney Island, New York, by Lemarcus Adna Thompson, but the world's oldest surviving example is Leap-the-Dips at Lakemont Park, Altoona, Pennsylvania. Invented and built in 1902 by the Edward Joy Morris Company to a design Morris had patented in 1894, it is small and slow by modern standards, measuring only 1,452 ft (443 m) long and standing 41 ft (12 m) at its highest point, with a maximum speed of 10 mph (16 km/h). A figure-of-eight design, it operates on a principle known as side friction. As one of remaining examples of the type, it was placed in the National Register of Historical Places in 1991 and attained National Landmark status in 1996. Leap-the-Dips was recently restored and reopened in advance of its 100th anniversary.

**100 YEARS AGO · YEARS AGO · YEARS AGO · YEARS AGO ·**

**Did You Know?** The world's oldest surviving Ferris wheel, dating from 1895, is in Asbury Park, New Jersey. Europe's oldest has stood in the Prater, Vienna, Austria, since 1897.

# THE SPORTS WORLD

# Summer Olympics

## MOST SUCCESSFUL COUNTRIES AT ONE SUMMER OLYMPICS

| | COUNTRY | VENUE | YEAR | GOLD | MEDALS SILVER | BRONZE | TOTAL |
|---|---|---|---|---|---|---|---|
| 1 | US | St. Louis | 1904 | 80 | 86 | 72 | 238 |
| 2 | USSR | Moscow | 1980 | 80 | 69 | 46 | 195 |
| 3 | US | Los Angeles | 1984 | 83 | 61 | 30 | 174 |
| 4 | Great Britain | London | 1908 | 56 | 50 | 39 | 145 |
| 5 | USSR | Seoul | 1988 | 55 | 31 | 46 | 132 |
| 6 | East Germany | Moscow | 1980 | 47 | 37 | 42 | 126 |
| 7 | USSR | Montreal | 1976 | 49 | 41 | 35 | 125 |
| 8 | EUN* | Barcelona | 1992 | 45 | 38 | 29 | 112 |
| 9 | US | Barcelona | 1992 | 37 | 34 | 37 | 108 |
| 10 | US | Mexico City | 1968 | 45 | 28 | 34 | 107 |

* Unified Team representing the Commonwealth of Independent States (former Soviet republics), formed in 1991

## OLYMPIC MEDAL-WINNING COUNTRIES THAT HAVE NEVER WON A GOLD MEDAL

| | COUNTRY | SILVER | MEDALS BRONZE | TOTAL |
|---|---|---|---|---|
| 1 | Mongolia | 5 | 9 | 14 |
| 2 | Taipai | 4 | 6 | 10 |
| 3 = | Chile | 6 | 3 | 9 |
| = | Philippines | 2 | 7 | 9 |
| 5 | Georgia | 0 | 8 | 8 |
| 6 = | Latvia | 5 | 2 | 7 |
| = | Slovenia | 2 | 5 | 7 |
| 8 | Puerto Rico | 1 | 5 | 6 |
| 9 = | Ghana | 1 | 3 | 4 |
| = | Israel | 1 | 3 | 4 |
| = | Lebanon | 2 | 2 | 4 |
| = | Moldovia | 2 | 2 | 4 |
| = | Namibia | 4 | 0 | 4 |
| = | Nigeria | 1 | 3 | 4 |

## SUMMER OLYMPICS ATTENDED BY THE MOST COMPETITORS, 1896–2000

| | LOCATION | YEAR | COUNTRIES REPRESENTED | COMPETITORS |
|---|---|---|---|---|
| 1 | Atlanta | 1996 | 197 | 10,310 |
| 2 | Sydney | 2000 | 199 | 10,000* |
| 3 | Barcelona | 1992 | 169 | 9,364 |
| 4 | Seoul | 1988 | 159 | 8,465 |
| 5 | Munich | 1972 | 121 | 7,123 |
| 6 | Los Angeles | 1984 | 140 | 6,797 |
| 7 | Montreal | 1976 | 92 | 6,028 |
| 8 | Mexico City | 1968 | 112 | 5,530 |
| 9 | Rome | 1960 | 83 | 5,346 |
| 10 | Moscow | 1980 | 80 | 5,217 |

* Estimated

**OLYMPIAN OPENING**

Widely regarded as one of the most successful Olympics of modern times, the 2000 Sydney Games were launched by the arrival of the Olympic flame borne by 400-m champion Cathy Freeman.

**OAR INSPIRING**

*British rower Steve Redgrave, here with team members Matthew Pinsent, Tim Foster, and James Cracknell, won his fifth consecutive gold at the 2000 Olympics.*

## TOP 10 ★
# SPORTS WITH THE MOST OLYMPICS MEDALS FOR THE US

| SPORT | GOLD | SILVER | BRONZE | TOTAL |
|---|---|---|---|---|
| 1 Athletics | 309 | 220 | 183 | 712 |
| 2 Swimming* | 192 | 138 | 104 | 434 |
| 3 Diving | 47 | 40 | 41 | 128 |
| 4 Wrestling | 47 | 44 | 25 | 119 |
| 5 Boxing | 47 | 23 | 37 | 107 |
| 6 Shooting | 46 | 26 | 23 | 95 |
| 7 Rowing | 29 | 29 | 21 | 79 |
| 8 Gymnastics | 26 | 23 | 28 | 77 |
| 9 Yachting | 17 | 21 | 17 | 55 |
| 10 Speed skating | 22 | 16 | 10 | 48 |

\* *Not including diving, water polo, or synchronized swimming*

## TOP 10 ★
# COUNTRIES WITH THE MOST SUMMER OLYMPICS MEDALS, 1896–2000

| COUNTRY | GOLD | SILVER | BRONZE | TOTAL |
|---|---|---|---|---|
| 1 US | 872 | 659 | 581 | 2,112 |
| 2 USSR* | 485 | 395 | 354 | 1,234 |
| 3 Great Britain | 188 | 245 | 232 | 665 |
| 4 France | 189 | 195 | 217 | 601 |
| 5 Germany# | 165 | 198 | 210 | 573 |
| 6 Italy | 179 | 144 | 155 | 478 |
| 7 Sweden | 138 | 157 | 176 | 471 |
| 8 Hungary | 150 | 134 | 158 | 442 |
| 9 East Germany | 153 | 130 | 127 | 410 |
| 10 Australia | 103 | 110 | 139 | 352 |

\* *Includes Unified Team of 1992; excludes Russia since then*

# *Not including West/East Germany 1968–88*

## TOP 10 ★
# MEDAL WINNERS IN A SUMMER OLYMPICS CAREER

| WINNER | COUNTRY | SPORT | YEARS | GOLD | SILVER | BRONZE | TOTAL |
|---|---|---|---|---|---|---|---|
| 1 Larissa Latynina | USSR | Gymnastics | 1956–64 | 9 | 5 | 4 | 18 |
| 2 Nikolay Andrianov | USSR | Gymnastics | 1972–80 | 7 | 5 | 3 | 15 |
| 3 =Edoardo Mangiarotti | Italy | Fencing | 1936–60 | 6 | 5 | 2 | 13 |
| =Takashi Ono | Japan | Gymnastics | 1952–64 | 5 | 4 | 4 | 13 |
| =Boris Shakhlin | USSR | Gymnastics | 1956–64 | 7 | 4 | 2 | 13 |
| 6 =Sawao Kato | Japan | Gymnastics | 1968–76 | 8 | 3 | 1 | 12 |
| =Paavo Nurmi | Finland | Athletics | 1920–28 | 9 | 3 | 0 | 12 |
| 8 =Matt Biondi | US | Swimming | 1984–92 | 8 | 2 | 1 | 11 |
| =Vera Cáslavská | Czechoslovakia | Gymnastics | 1964–68 | 7 | 4 | 0 | 11 |
| =Viktor Chukarin | USSR | Gymnastics | 1952–56 | 7 | 3 | 1 | 11 |
| =Carl Osburn | US | Shooting | 1912–24 | 5 | 4 | 2 | 11 |
| =Mark Spitz | US | Swimming | 1968–72 | 9 | 1 | 1 | 11 |

Larissa Latynina won six medals at each of three Games between 1956 and 1964. The only discipline at which she did not win a medal was on the beam in 1956, when she came fourth. The only Winter Games competitor who would be eligible for this list is Björn Dählie of Norway, who won a total of 12 medals (eight gold and four silver) for Nordic Skiing in the Olympics of 1992–98.

# TOP 10 COUNTRIES AT THE SYDNEY OLYMPICS WITH THE HIGHEST RATIO OF MEDALS

*(Country/medals per million population)*

**1** Bahamas, 6.80  **2** Barbados, 3.76  **3** Iceland, 3.65  **4** Australia, 3.09
**5** Jamaica, 2.72  **6** Cuba, 2.61  **7** Norway, 2.26  **8** Estonia, 2.07
**9** Hungary, 1.68  **10** Belarus, 1.66

*US, 0.36   Source: eCountries*

The Bahamas, with a population of 294,000, tops this list of Olympic medal winners with one silver and one gold won by their female sprinters. Barbados came 2nd, having won just one bronze in the men's 100 m.

**What sport was introduced in the 1998 Winter Olympics?**
*see p.247 for the answer*

A   Snowmobile racing
B   Women's ski jumping
C   Snowboarding

## TOP 10 ★
## COMPETITOR-ATTENDED WINTER OLYMPICS

| | HOST CITY | COUNTRY | YEAR | COMPETITORS |
|---|---|---|---|---|
| 1 | Nagano | Japan | 1998 | 2,177 |
| 2 | Albertville | France | 1992 | 1,801 |
| 3 | Lillehammer | Norway | 1994 | 1,736 |
| 4 | Calgary | Canada | 1988 | 1,425 |
| 5 | Sarajevo | Yugoslavia | 1984 | 1,274 |
| 6 | Grenoble | France | 1968 | 1,158 |
| 7 | Innsbruck | Austria | 1976 | 1,123 |
| 8 | Innsbruck | Austria | 1964 | 1,091 |
| 9 | Lake Placid | US | 1980 | 1,072 |
| 10 | Sapporo | Japan | 1972 | 1,006 |

The first Winter Games at Chamonix, France, in 1924 were attended by 258 competitors representing 16 countries. Subsequent Games have seen the numbers of both competitors and countries generally increase: a total of 72 countries took part at the XVIII Games at Nagano.

## TOP 10 ★
## WINTER OLYMPIC MEDAL-WINNING COUNTRIES, 1908–98

| | COUNTRY | GOLD | SILVER | BRONZE | TOTAL |
|---|---|---|---|---|---|
| 1 | Norway | 83 | 87 | 69 | 239 |
| 2 | Soviet Union* | 87 | 63 | 67 | 217 |
| 3 | US | 59 | 59 | 41 | 159 |
| 4 | Austria | 39 | 52 | 53 | 144 |
| 5 | Finland | 38 | 49 | 48 | 135 |
| 6 | Germany# | 46 | 38 | 32 | 116 |
| 7 | East Germany | 39 | 36 | 35 | 110 |
| 8 | Sweden | 39 | 28 | 35 | 102 |
| 9 | Switzerland | 29 | 32 | 32 | 93 |
| 10 | Canada | 25 | 25 | 29 | 79 |

*Includes Unified Team of 1992; excludes Russia since then*

*# Not including East/West Germany 1968–88*

Figure skating was first featured at the 1908 Summer Olympics held in London, and ice hockey as part of the 1920 Summer Olympics in Antwerp.

### FINNISH FIRST

*At the 1998 Nagano Games, Finland added two gold, four silver, and six bronze medals to its tally, with Jani Soininen winning gold in the ski jumping event.*

What is the nationality of mile record holder Hicham El Guerrouj?
*see p.250 for the answer*

A  Moroccan
B  Dutch
C  Egyptian

## TOP 10 ★
# INDIVIDUAL GOLD MEDALLISTS AT THE WINTER OLYMPICS

| MEDALLIST/COUNTRY/SPORT | GOLD MEDALS |
|---|---|
| **1** Bjørn Dählie, Nor, Nordic skiing | 8 |
| **2 =**Lydia Skoblikova, USSR, Speed skating | 6 |
| **=**Lyubov Yegorova, EUN*/Rus, Nordic skiing | 6 |
| **4 =**Bonnie Blair, US, Speed skating | 5 |
| **=**Eric Heiden, US, Speed skating | 5 |
| **=**Larissa Lazurtina, EUN*/Rus, Nordic skiing | 5 |
| **=**Clas Thunberg, Nor, Speed skating | 5 |
| **8 =**Ivar Ballangrud, Nor, Speed skating | 4 |
| **=**Yevgeni Grishin, USSR, Speed skating | 4 |
| **=**Sixten Jernberg, Swe, Nordic skiing | 4 |
| **=**Johan-Olav Koss, Nor, Speed skating | 4 |
| **=**Galina Kulakova, USSR, Nordic skiing | 4 |
| **=**Chun Lee-kyung, Kor, Short track speed skating | 4 |
| **=**Matti Nykänen, Fin, Ski jumping | 4 |
| **=**Nikolai Simyatov, USSR, Nordic skiing | 4 |
| **=**Raisa Smetanina, USSR, Nordic skiing | 4 |
| **=**Alexander Tikhonov, USSR, Biathlon | 4 |

* EUN = Unified Team (Commonwealth of Independent States 1992)

## TOP 10 ★
# WINTER OLYMPIC MEDAL-WINNING COUNTRIES, 1908–98 (MEN'S EVENTS)*

| | COUNTRY | GOLD | SILVER | BRONZE | TOTAL |
|---|---|---|---|---|---|
| **1** | Norway | 76 | 79 | 56 | 211 |
| **2** | Soviet Union# | 52 | 35 | 35 | 122 |
| **3** | Finland | 29 | 38 | 35 | 102 |
| **4** | Austria | 26 | 33 | 37 | 96 |
| **5** | Sweden | 32 | 23 | 31 | 86 |
| **6** | US | 33 | 32 | 20 | 85 |
| **7** | Switzerland | 19 | 24 | 25 | 68 |
| **8** | East Germany | 24 | 19 | 23 | 66 |
| **9** | Germany+ | 27 | 14 | 15 | 56 |
| **10** | Italy | 17 | 22 | 15 | 54 |

* In figure skating, men's singles and pairs have been counted together

# Includes Unified Team of 1992; excludes Russia since then

+ Not including East/West Germany 1968–88

The only person to win gold medals at both the Summer and Winter Games is Eddie Eagan of the US. After winning the 1920 light-heavyweight boxing title, he then went on to win a gold medal as a member of the American four-man bobsled team in 1932.

**SNOW FALL**

*Seen here in an uncharacteristic pose, Nordic skier Bjørn Dählie has won a record eight gold medals at three Winter Olympics, 1992–98.*

**ON BOARD**

*Introduced at the 1998 Games, the snowboarding halfpipe event was won by Nicola Thost, adding to the tally of German medal winners.*

## TOP 10 ★
# WINTER OLYMPIC MEDAL-WINNING COUNTRIES, 1908–98 (WOMEN'S EVENTS)*

| | COUNTRY | GOLD | SILVER | BRONZE | TOTAL |
|---|---|---|---|---|---|
| **1** | Soviet Union# | 35 | 28 | 32 | 95 |
| **2** | US | 26 | 27 | 21 | 74 |
| **3** | Germany+ | 19 | 24 | 17 | 60 |
| **4** | Austria | 13 | 19 | 16 | 48 |
| **5** | East Germany | 15 | 17 | 12 | 44 |
| **6** | Finland | 9 | 11 | 13 | 33 |
| **7 =** | Canada | 11 | 9 | 8 | 28 |
| **=** | Norway | 7 | 8 | 13 | 28 |
| **9** | Switzerland | 10 | 8 | 7 | 25 |
| **10** | Italy | 7 | 8 | 9 | 24 |

* In figure skating, women's singles and ice dance have been counted together

# Includes Unified Team of 1992; excludes Russia since then

+ Not including East/West Germany 1968–88

# Football Facts

## TOP 10 ★
### PLAYERS WITH THE MOST CAREER POINTS

| | PLAYER | POINTS |
|---|---|---|
| 1 | Gary Anderson* | 2,059 |
| 2 | George Blanda | 2,002 |
| 3 | Morten Andersen* | 1,934 |
| 4 | Norm Johnson | 1,736 |
| 5 | Nick Lowery | 1,711 |
| 6 | Jan Stenerud | 1,699 |
| 7 | Eddie Murray* | 1,591 |
| 8 | Al Del Greco* | 1,568 |
| 9 | Pat Leahy | 1,470 |
| 10 | Jim Turner | 1,439 |

* Still active 2000 season

Source: National Football League

## TOP 10 ★
### BIGGEST WINNING MARGINS IN THE SUPER BOWL

| | GAME* | YEAR | MARGIN |
|---|---|---|---|
| 1 | San Francisco 49ers v Denver Broncos | 1990 | 45 |
| 2 | Chicago Bears v New England | 1986 | 36 |
| 3 | Dallas Cowboys v Buffalo Bills | 1993 | 35 |
| 4 | Washington Redskins v Denver Broncos | 1988 | 32 |
| 5 | Los Angeles Raiders v Washington Redskins | 1984 | 29 |
| 6 | Baltimore Ravens v New York Giants | 2001 | 27 |
| 7 | Green Bay Packers v Kansas City Chiefs | 1967 | 25 |
| 8 | San Francisco 49ers v San Diego Chargers | 1995 | 23 |
| 9 | San Francisco 49ers v Miami Dolphins | 1985 | 22 |
| 10 | Dallas Cowboys v Miami Dolphins | 1972 | 21 |

* Winners listed first

Source: National Football League

## TOP 10 ★
### RUSHERS IN AN NFL CAREER

| | PLAYER | TOTAL YARDS GAINED RUSHING |
|---|---|---|
| 1 | Walter Payton | 16,726 |
| 2 | Barry Sanders | 15,269 |
| 3 | Emmitt Smith* | 15,146 |
| 4 | Eric Dickerson | 13,259 |
| 5 | Tony Dorsett | 12,739 |
| 6 | Jim Brown | 12,312 |
| 7 | Marcus Allen | 12,243 |
| 8 | Franco Harris | 12,120 |
| 9 | Thurman Thomas* | 12,072 |
| 10 | John Riggins | 11,352 |

* Still active 2000 season

Source: National Football League

## TOP 10 ★
### POINT SCORERS IN AN NFL SEASON

| | PLAYER/TEAM | YEAR | POINTS |
|---|---|---|---|
| 1 | Paul Hornung, Green Bay Packers | 1960 | 176 |
| 2 | Gary Anderson, Minnesota Vikings | 1998 | 164 |
| 3 | Mark Moseley, Washington Redskins | 1983 | 161 |
| 4 | Marshall Faulk, St. Louis Rams | 2000 | 160 |
| 5 | Gino Cappelletti, Boston Patriots | 1964 | 155* |
| 6 | Emmitt Smith, Dallas Cowboys | 1995 | 150 |
| 7 | Chip Lohmiller, Washington Redskins | 1991 | 149 |
| 8 | Gino Cappelletti, Boston Patriots | 1961 | 147 |
| 9 | Paul Hornung, Green Bay Packers | 1961 | 146 |
| 10= | Jim Turner, New York Jets | 1968 | 145 |
| = | John Kasay, Carolina Panthers | 1996 | 145 |
| = | Mike Vanderjagt, Indianapolis Colts | 1999 | 145 |

* Including a two-point conversion

Source: National Football League

## TOP 10 ★
### LONGEST CAREERS OF CURRENT NFL PLAYERS

| | PLAYER/TEAM | YEARS |
|---|---|---|
| 1= | Gary Anderson, Minnesota Vikings | 19 |
| = | Morten Andersen, Atlanta Falcons | 19 |
| = | Eddie Murray, Washington Redskins | 19 |
| 4 | Darrell Green, Washington Redskins | 18 |
| = | Trey Junkin, Arizona Cardinals | 18 |
| = | Bruce Matthews, Tennessee Titans | 18 |
| 7 | Irving Fryar, Washington Redskins | 17 |
| = | Al Del Greco, Tennessee Titans | 17 |
| = | Mike Horan, St. Louis Rams | 17 |
| = | Warren Moon, Kansas City Chiefs | 17 |

Source: National Football League

## TOP 10 ★
### PLAYERS WITH THE MOST PASSING YARDS IN AN NFL CAREER

| | PLAYER | PASSING YARDS |
|---|---|---|
| 1 | Dan Marino | 61,361 |
| 2 | John Elway | 51,475 |
| 3 | Warren Moon | 49,247 |
| 4 | Fran Tarkenton | 47,003 |
| 5 | Dan Fouts | 43,040 |
| 6 | Joe Montana | 40,551 |
| 7 | Johnny Unitas | 40,239 |
| 8 | Dave Krieg | 38,151 |
| 9 | Boomer Esiason | 37,920 |
| 10 | Vinny Testaverde | 36,296 |

Source: National Football League

**Did You Know?** Until improvements in the rules and equipment were introduced, college football was one of the most dangerous of all team sports, the 1905 season resulting in 18 deaths and 159 serious injuries.

## TOP 10 ★
# HEAVIEST PLAYERS IN THE NFL

| PLAYER/TEAM | WEIGHT LB | KG |
|---|---|---|
| 1 **Aaron Gibson**, Detroit Lions | 380 | 172 |
| 2 **Willie Jones**, Kansas City Chiefs | 372 | 169 |
| 3 **L. J. Shelton**, Arizona Cardinals | 360 | 163 |
| 4 **David Dixon**, Minnesota Vikings | 358 | 162 |
| 5 **Anthony Clement**, Arizona Cardinals | 351 | 159 |
| 6 =**Derrick Fletcher**, Washington Redskins | 350 | 159 |
| =**Stockar McDougle**, Detroit Lions | 350 | 159 |
| 8 **Tra Thomas**, Philadelphia Eagles | 349 | 158 |
| 9 **Yusuf Scott**, Arizona Cardinals | 348 | 158 |
| 10 =**Jon Clark**, Arizona Cardinals | 346 | 157 |
| =**Korey Stringer**, Minnesota Vikings | 346 | 157 |

Source: *National Football League*

## TOP 10 ★
# MOST SUCCESSFUL TEAMS

| TEAM | SUPER BOWL GAMES WINS | LOSSES | PTS* |
|---|---|---|---|
| 1 **Dallas Cowboys** | 5 | 3 | 13 |
| 2 **San Francisco 49ers** | 5 | 0 | 10 |
| 3 **Pittsburgh Steelers** | 4 | 1 | 9 |
| 4 **Washington Redskins** | 3 | 2 | 8 |
| 5 **Denver Broncos** | 2 | 4 | 8 |
| 6 =**Green Bay Packers** | 3 | 1 | 7 |
| =**Oakland/ Los Angeles Raiders** | 3 | 1 | 7 |
| 8 **Miami Dolphins** | 2 | 3 | 7 |
| 9 **New York Giants** | 2 | 1 | 5 |
| 10 =**Buffalo Bills** | 0 | 4 | 4 |
| =**Minnesota Vikings** | 0 | 4 | 4 |

*\* Based on two points for a Super Bowl win, and one for runner-up; wins take precedence over runners-up in determining ranking*

Source: *National Football League*

## TOP 10 ★
# LARGEST NFL STADIUMS

| STADIUM/HOME TEAM | CAPACITY |
|---|---|
| 1 **Pontiac Silverdome**, Detroit Lions | 80,311 |
| 2 **FedEx Field**, Washington Redskins | 80,116 |
| 3 **Giants Stadium**, New York Giants/Jets | 79,469 |
| 4 **Arrowhead Stadium**, Kansas City Chiefs | 79,409 |
| 5 **Ralph Wilson Stadium**, Buffalo Bills | 75,339 |
| 6 **Pro Player Stadium**, Miami Dolphins | 75,192 |
| 7 **Sun Devil Stadium**, Arizona Cardinals | 73,273 |
| 8 **Ericsson Stadium**, Carolina Panthers | 73,250 |
| 9 **Cleveland Browns Stadium**, Cleveland Browns | 73,200 |
| 10 **Alltel Stadium**, Jacksonville Jaguars | 73,000 |

Source: *National Football League*

## TOP 10 ★
# COLLEGES WITH THE MOST BOWL WINS

| COLLEGE | WINS |
|---|---|
| 1 **Alabama** | 28 |
| 2 **University of Southern California (USC)** | 25 |
| 3 **Penn State** | 23 |
| 4 **Tennessee** | 22 |
| 5 **Oklahoma** | 21 |
| 6 **Nebraska** | 20 |
| 7 **Georgia Tech** | 19 |
| 8 =**Georgia** | 18 |
| =**Texas** | 18 |
| 10 =**Florida State** | 17 |
| =**Michigan** | 17 |
| =**Mississippi** | 17 |

Bowl games are end-of-season college championship games, played at the end of December or beginning of January each year. The "Big Four" Bowl games, and members of the Bowl Championship Series, are the Rose Bowl (Pasadena), Orange Bowl (Miami), Sugar Bowl (New Orleans), and Cotton Bowl (Dallas).

# TOP 10 MOST SUCCESSFUL COACHES IN AN NFL CAREER
*(Coach/games won)*

❶ **Don Shula**, 347  ❷ **George Halas**, 324  ❸ **Tom Landry**, 270  ❹ **Curly Lambeau**, 229  ❺ **Chuck Noll**, 209  ❻ **Chuck Knox**, 193  ❼ **Dan Reeves\***, 179  ❽ **Paul Brown**, 170  ❾ **Bud Grant**, 168  ❿ **Marv Levy**, 154

*\* Still active 2000 season*  Source: *National Football League*

## THE FIRST ROSE BOWL

The Valley Hunt Club in Pasadena, California, first staged its Tournament of Roses in 1890. A celebration of California's mild winter weather, it grew in popularity and, following the event's famed parade, it was decided to stage a college football game. At the first-ever Rose Tournament game, held on New Year's Day 1902 at Tournament Park, the University of Michigan beat Stanford University with a score of 49–0 before a crowd of 8,000. So great was the defeat that the organizers decided not to stage the event again, the following year replacing it with a Roman-style chariot race. It was not until 1916 that football returned to the festivities, but as the crowd outgrew the seating capacity at Tournament Park, a new 57,000-seat stadium was constructed; the first game was held there on January 1, 1923. The stadium, and the annual game played there, were named the "Rose Bowl" by Harlan "Dusty" Hall, the Rose Tournament's press agent.

**100** YEARS AGO · YEARS AGO · YEARS AGO · YEARS AGO ·

# Athletic Achievements

## LONGEST LONG JUMPS*

| | ATHLETE/COUNTRY | YEAR | DISTANCE METERS |
|---|---|---|---|
| 1 | Mike Powell, US | 1991 | 8.95 |
| 2 | Bob Beamon, US | 1968 | 8.90 |
| 3 | Carl Lewis, US | 1991 | 8.87 |
| 4 | Robert Emmiyan, USSR | 1987 | 8.86 |
| 5 = | Larry Myricks, US | 1988 | 8.74 |
| = | Erick Walder, US | 1994 | 8.74 |
| 7 | Ivan Pedroso, Cuba | 1995 | 8.71 |
| 8 | Kareem Streete-Thompson, US | 1994 | 8.63 |
| 9 | James Beckford, Jamaica | 1997 | 8.62 |
| 10 | Yago Lamela, Spain# | 1999 | 8.56 |

* Longest by each athlete only    # Indoor

## HIGHEST POLE VAULTS*

| | ATHLETE/COUNTRY | YEAR | HEIGHT METERS |
|---|---|---|---|
| 1 | Sergei Bubka, Ukraine# | 1993 | 6.15 |
| 2 | Maxim Tarasov, Russia | 1999 | 6.05 |
| 3 = | Okkert Brits, South Africa | 1995 | 6.03 |
| = | Jeff Hartwig, US | 2000 | 6.03 |
| 5 | Rodion Gataullin, USSR# | 1989 | 6.02 |
| 6 | Igor Trandenkov, Russia | 1996 | 6.01 |
| 7 = | Jeane Galfione, France | 1999 | 6.00 |
| = | Tim Lobinger, Germany | 1997 | 6.00 |
| = | Dmitri Markov, Belarus | 1998 | 6.00 |
| 10 | Lawrence Johnson, US | 1996 | 5.98 |

* Highest by each athlete only    # Indoor

## FASTEST MILES EVER RUN

| | ATHLETE/COUNTRY | YEAR | TIME |
|---|---|---|---|
| 1 | Hicham El Guerrouj, Morocco | 1999 | 3:43.13 |
| 2 | Noah Ngeny, Kenya | 1999 | 3:43.40 |
| 3 | Novreddine Morceli, Algeria | 1993 | 3:44.39 |
| 4 | Hicham El Guerrouj | 1998 | 3:44.60 |
| 5 | Hicham El Guerrouj | 1997 | 3:44.90 |
| 6 | Novreddine Morceli | 1995 | 3:45.19 |
| 7 | Hicham El Guerrouj | 1997 | 3:45.64 |
| 8 | Hicham El Guerrouj | 2000 | 3:45.96 |
| 9 | Hicham El Guerrouj | 2000 | 3:46.24 |
| 10 | Steve Cram, UK | 1985 | 3:46.32 |

The current world record is almost 13 percent faster than Roger Bannister's breakthrough first sub-four-minute mile of 1954, and over 20 percent faster than the unofficial record set by British runner Walter Chinnery in 1868.

## THE 10 LATEST WINNERS OF THE JESSE OWENS INTERNATIONAL TROPHY

*(Year/athlete/sport)*

**1** 2001 Marion Jones, athletics **2** 2000 Lance Armstrong, cycling **3** 1999 Marion Jones, athletics **4** 1998 Haile Gebrselassie, athletics **5** 1997 Michael Johnson, athletics **6** 1996 Michael Johnson, athletics **7** 1995 Johann Olav Koss, speed skating **8** 1994 Wang Junxia, athletics **9** 1993 Vitaly Scherbo, gymnastics **10** 1992 Mike Powell, athletics

The Jesse Owens International Trophy has been presented by the International Amateur Athletic Association since 1981. It is named in honor of American athlete Jesse Owens (1913–80).

## HIGHEST HIGH JUMPS*

| | ATHLETE/COUNTRY | YEAR | HEIGHT METERS |
|---|---|---|---|
| 1 | Javier Sotomayor, Cuba | 1993 | 2.45 |
| 2 = | Patrik Sjöberg, Sweden | 1987 | 2.42 |
| = | Carlo Thränhardt, West Germany# | 1988 | 2.42 |
| 4 | Igor Paklin, USSR | 1985 | 2.41 |
| 5 = | Charles Austin, US | 1991 | 2.40 |
| = | Hollis Conway, US# | 1991 | 2.40 |
| = | Sorin Matei, Romania | 1990 | 2.40 |
| = | Rudolf Povarnitsyn, USSR | 1985 | 2.40 |
| = | Vyochaslav Voronin, Russia | 2000 | 2.40 |
| 10 = | Hollis Conway, US | 1989 | 2.39 |
| = | Zhu Jianhua, China | 1984 | 2.39 |
| = | Dietmar Mögenburg, West Germany# | 1985 | 2.39 |
| = | Ralph Sonn, Germany# | 1991 | 2.39 |

* Highest by each athlete only
# Indoor

## FASTEST TIMES IN THE BOSTON MARATHON

### MEN

| | RUNNER/COUNTRY | YEAR | HR:MIN:SEC |
|---|---|---|---|
| 1 | Cosmas Ndeti, Kenya | 1994 | 2:07:15 |
| 2 | Andres Espinosa, Mexico | 1994 | 2:07:19 |
| 3 | Moses Tanui, Kenya | 1998 | 2:07:34 |
| 4 | Joseph Chebet, Kenya | 1998 | 2:07:37 |
| 5 | Rob de Castella, Austria | 1986 | 2:07:51 |
| 6 | Gert Thys, S. Africa | 1998 | 2:07:52 |
| 7 | Jackson Kipngok, Kenya | 1994 | 2:08:08 |
| 8 | Hwant Young-Cho, Korea | 1984 | 2:08:09 |
| 9 | Ibrahim Hussein, Kenya | 1992 | 2:08:14 |
| 10 | Gelindo Bordin, Italy | 1980 | 2:08:19 |

Source: *Boston Athletic Association*

### WOMEN

| | RUNNER/COUNTRY | YEAR | HR:MIN:SEC |
|---|---|---|---|
| 1 | Uta Pippig, Germany | 1994 | 2:21:45 |
| 2 | Joan Benoit, US | 1983 | 2:22:43 |
| 3 | Fatuma Roba, Ethiopia | 1998 | 2:23:21 |
| 4 | Fatuma Roba | 1999 | 2:23:25 |
| 5 | Valentina Yegorova, Russia | 1994 | 2:23:33 |
| 6 | Olga Markova, CIS | 1992 | 2:23:43 |
| 7 | Wanda Panfil, Poland | 1991 | 2:24:18 |
| 8 | Rosa Mota, Portugal | 1988 | 2:24:30 |
| 9 | Ingrid Kristiansen, Norway | 1989 | 2:24:33 |
| 10 | Ingrid Kristiansen | 1986 | 2:24:55 |

## TOP 10 ★
# FASTEST WOMEN EVER*

| ATHLETE/COUNTRY | YEAR | SECONDS |
|---|---|---|
| 1 Florence Griffith Joyner, US | 1988 | 10.49 |
| 2 Marion Jones, US | 1998 | 10.65 |
| 3 Christine Arron, France | 1998 | 10.73 |
| 4 Merlene Ottey, Jamaica | 1996 | 10.74 |
| 5 Evelyn Ashford, US | 1984 | 10.76 |
| 6 Irina Privalova, Russia | 1994 | 10.77 |
| 7 Dawn Sowell, US | 1989 | 10.78 |
| 8 Inger Miller, US | 1999 | 10.79 |
| 9 Marlies Göhr, East Germany | 1983 | 10.81 |
| 10=Gail Devers, US | 1992 | 10.82 |
| =Gwen Torrence, US | 1994 | 10.82 |

* Based on fastest time for the 100 meters

## TOP 10 ★
# FASTEST MEN EVER*

| ATHLETE/COUNTRY | YEAR | SECONDS |
|---|---|---|
| 1 Maurice Greene, US | 1999 | 9.79 |
| 2=Donovan Bailey, Canada | 1996 | 9.84 |
| =Bruny Surin, Canada | 1999 | 9.84 |
| 4 Leroy Burrell, US | 1994 | 9.85 |
| 5=Ato Boldon, Trinidad | 1998 | 9.86 |
| =Frank Fredericks, Namibia | 1996 | 9.86 |
| =Carl Lewis, US | 1991 | 9.86 |
| 8=Linford Christie, UK | 1993 | 9.87 |
| =Obadele Thompson, Barbados | 1998 | 9.87 |
| 10 Dennis Mitchell, US | 1991 | 9.91 |

* Based on fastest time for the 100 metres

Many would argue that Michael Johnson (US) should be in this category with his remarkable 200-meter record of 19.32 seconds (equivalent to a 100-meter time of 9.66 seconds), but his best 100-meter time is only 10.09 seconds.

### KEEPING UP WITH THE JONES

*Marion Jones' personal best of 10.65 seconds for the 100 meters makes her the fastest living female athlete. The record-holder at 10.49 was Florence Griffith Joyner, who died in 1998.*

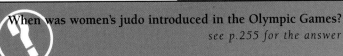
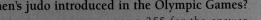

When was women's judo introduced in the Olympic Games?    A 1896
*see p.255 for the answer*    B 1936
                                                           C 1992

# Basketball Bests

## DIVISION 1 NCAA TEAMS

| COLLEGE | DIVISION 1 WINS |
| --- | --- |
| 1 Kentucky | 1,787 |
| 2 North Carolina | 1,778 |
| 3 Kansas | 1,732 |
| 4 Duke | 1,635 |
| 5 St. John's | 1,610 |
| 6 Temple | 1,563 |
| 7 Syracuse | 1,546 |
| 8 Pennsylvania | 1,505 |
| 9 Indiana | 1,493 |
| 10 Oregon State | 1,485 |

Source: *NCAA*

NCAA basketball was launched on March 17, 1939. Ironically, James Naismith, basketball's inventor, died on November 28 of the same year.

## TOP 10 ★ POINT SCORERS IN AN NBA CAREER

| PLAYER | TOTAL POINTS* |
| --- | --- |
| 1 Kareem Abdul-Jabbar | 38,387 |
| 2 Karl Malone# | 32,919 |
| 3 Wilt Chamberlain | 31,419 |
| 4 Michael Jordan | 29,277 |
| 5 Moses Malone | 27,409 |
| 6 Elvin Hayes | 27,313 |
| 7 Oscar Robertson | 26,710 |
| 8 Dominique Wilkins | 26,668 |
| 9 Hakeem Olajuwon# | 26,511 |
| 10 John Havlicek | 25,395 |

* *Regular season games only*

# *Still active at end of 2000–2001 season*

Source: *NBA*

## TOP 10 ★ COACHES IN THE NBA

| COACH | GAMES WON* |
| --- | --- |
| 1 Lenny Wilkens# | 1,226 |
| 2 Pat Riley# | 1,049 |
| 3 Don Nelson# | 979 |
| 4 Bill Fitch | 944 |
| 5 Red Auerbach | 938 |
| 6 Dick Motta | 935 |
| 7 Jack Ramsay | 864 |
| 8 Cotton Fitzsimmons | 832 |
| 9 =Gene Shue | 784 |
| =Jerry Sloan# | 784 |

* *Regular season games only*

# *Still active 2000–2001 season*

Source: *NBA*

Lenny Wilkens reached his 1,000th win on March 1, 1996 when the Atlanta Hawks beat the Cleveland Cavaliers 74–68 at The Omni. Pat Riley, as coach of the LA Lakers, the New York Knicks, and the Miami Heat, acquired the best percentage record, with 1,049 wins from 1,515 games, representing a 0.692 percent success rate.

## TOP 10 COACHES IN THE NCAA

*(Coach/wins)*

**1** Dean Smith, 879 **2** Adolph Rupp, 876 **3** Jim Phelan*, 816 **4** Henry Iba, 767 **5** Bob Knight*, 764 **6** Lefty Driesell*, 762 **7** = Jerry Tarkanian*, 759; = Ed Diddle, 759 **9** Phog Allen, 746 **10** Lou Henson*, 740

* *Still active 2000–2001 season*   Source: *NCAA*

## TOP 10 ★ BIGGEST ARENAS IN THE NBA

| ARENA/LOCATION | HOME TEAM | CAPACITY |
| --- | --- | --- |
| 1 **The Palace of Auburn Hills**, Auburn Hills, Michigan | Detroit Pistons | 22,076 |
| 2 **United Center**, Chicago, Illinois | Chicago Bulls | 21,711 |
| 3 **MCI Center**, Washington, DC | Washington Wizards | 20,674 |
| 4 **Gund Arena**, Cleveland, Ohio | Cleveland Cavaliers | 20,562 |
| 5 **Alamodome**, San Antonio, Texas | San Antonio Spurs | 20,557 |
| 6 **First Union Center**, Philadelphia, Pennsylvania | Philadelphia 76ers | 20,444 |
| 7 **Charlotte Coliseum**, Charlotte, North Carolina | Charlotte Hornets | 20,085 |
| 8 **Continental Airlines Arena**, East Rutherford, New Jersey | New Jersey Nets | 20,049 |
| 9 **The Rose Garden**, Portland, Oregon | Portland Trailblazers | 19,980 |
| 10 **Delta Center**, Salt Lake City, Utah | Utah Jazz | 19,911 |

The smallest arena is the 15,200-capacity Miami Arena, home of the Miami Heat. The largest-ever NBA stadium was the Louisiana Superdome, completed in May 1995 at a cost of $173 million, and used by Utah Jazz from then until 1979; the stadium was capable of holding crowds of up to 47,284.

Source: *NBA*

## TOP 10 ★ PLAYERS WITH THE HIGHEST POINTS AVERAGES

| PLAYER | POINTS SCORED | POINTS AVERAGE |
| --- | --- | --- |
| 1 Michael Jordan | 29,277 | 31.5 |
| 2 Wilt Chamberlain | 31,419 | 30.1 |
| 3 Shaquille O'Neal* | 16,812 | 27.7 |
| 4 Elgin Baylor | 23,149 | 27.4 |
| 5 Jerry West | 25,192 | 27.0 |
| 6 Bob Pettit | 20,880 | 26.4 |
| 7 George Gervin | 20,708 | 26.2 |
| 8 Karl Malone* | 32,919 | 25.9 |
| 9 Oscar Robertson, | 26,710 | 25.7 |
| 10 Dominique Wilkins | 26,668 | 24.8 |

* *Still active 2000–2001 season*

Source: *NBA*

In how many Olympic Games did Hungarian fencer Aladár Gerevich win seven golds?  **A** Three
*see p.255 for the answer*  **B** Five
**C** Six

## TOP 10 TEAMS WITH THE MOST NCAA CHAMPIONSHIP WINS

*(College/wins)*

**1** UCLA, 11 **2** Kentucky, 7 **3** Indiana, 5 **4** = North Carolina, 3; = Duke, 3 **6** = Cincinnati, 2; = Kansas, 2; = Louisville, 2; = Michigan State, 2; = North Carolina State, 2; = Oklahoma A & M*, 2; = San Francisco, 2

*\* Now known as Oklahoma State*

## TOP 10 ★
## POINTS SCORED IN THE WNBA

| PLAYER/GAME | DATE | PTS |
|---|---|---|
| **1** Cynthia Cooper, Houston v Sacramento | July 25, 1997 | 44 |
| **2** Cynthia Cooper, Houston v Utah | Aug 16, 1999 | 42 |
| **3** Cynthia Cooper, Houston v Charlotte | Aug 11, 1997 | 39 |
| **4** Jennifer Gillom, Phoenix v Cleveland | Aug 10, 1998 | 36 |
| **5** =Cynthia Cooper, Houston v Los Angeles | Aug 1, 1997 | 34 |
| =Cynthia Cooper, Houston v Phoenix | Aug 7, 1997 | 34 |
| =Ruthie Bolton-Holifield, Sacramento v Utah | Aug 8, 1997 | 34 |
| =Ruthie Bolton-Holifield, Sacramento v Cleveland | Aug 12, 1997 | 34 |
| =Cynthia Cooper, Houston v Sacramento | July 3, 1998 | 34 |
| =Cynthia Cooper, Houston v Detroit | Aug 7, 1998 | 34 |

Source: *WNBA*

## TOP 10 ★
## FREE THROW PERCENTAGES

| PLAYER | ATTEMPTS | MADE | PERCENTAGE |
|---|---|---|---|
| **1** Mark Price | 2,362 | 2,135 | 90.4 |
| **2** Rick Barry | 4,243 | 3,818 | 90.0 |
| **3** Calvin Murphy | 3,864 | 3,445 | 89.2 |
| **4** Scott Skiles | 1,741 | 1,548 | 88.9 |
| **5** Larry Bird | 4,471 | 3,960 | 88.6 |
| **6** Reggie Miller* | 6,038 | 5,338 | 88.4 |
| **7** Bill Sharman | 3,559 | 3,143 | 88.3 |
| **8** Ricky Pierce | 3,871 | 3,389 | 87.5 |
| **9** Kiki Vandeweghe | 3,997 | 3,484 | 87.2 |
| **10** Jeff Malone | 3,383 | 2,947 | 87.1 |

*\* Still active 2000–2001 season*
Source: *NBA*

## TOP 10 PLAYERS WITH THE MOST CAREER ASSISTS

*(Player/assists)*

**1** John Stockton*, 14,501 **2** Magic Johnson, 10,141 **3** Oscar Robertson, 9,887 **4** Mark Jackson*, 9,235 **5** Isiah Thomas, 9,061 **6** Maurice Cheeks, 7,392 **7** Lenny Wilkens, 7,211 **8** Rod Strickland*, 7,026 **9** Bob Cousy, 6,995 **10** Guy Rodgers, 6,917

*\* Still active at end of 2000–2001 season*
Source: *NBA*

**MAGIC TOUCH**
*Magic (Earvin) Johnson turned professional in 1979, becoming one of the NBA's most legendary players.*

## TOP 10 ★
## PLAYERS TO HAVE PLAYED MOST GAMES IN THE NBA AND ABA

| PLAYER | GAMES PLAYED* |
|---|---|
| **1** Robert Parish | 1,611 |
| **2** Kareem Abdul-Jabbar | 1,560 |
| **3** Moses Malone | 1,455 |
| **4** Buck Williams | 1,348 |
| **5** John Stockton# | 1,339 |
| **6** Artis Gilmore | 1,329 |
| **7** Elvin Hayes | 1,303 |
| **8** Caldwell Jones | 1,299 |
| **9** Sam Perkins# | 1,286 |
| **10** Karl Malone# | 1,273 |

*\* Regular season only*
*# Still active at end of 2000–2001 season*
Source: *NBA*

# Combat Sports

## TOP 10 ★
### BOXING CHAMPIONS WITH THE MOST CONSECUTIVE SUCCESSFUL DEFENSES*

| FIGHTER/DIVISION/REIGN YEARS | DEFENSES |
|---|---|
| 1 Joe Louis#, Heavyweight, 1937–49 | 25 |
| 2 Ricardo Lopez, Strawweight (WBC), 1990– | 22 |
| 3 =Henry Armstrong#, Welterweight, 1938–40 | 19 |
| =Khaosai Galaxy, Junior bantamweight (WBA), 1984–91 | 19 |
| =Eusebio Pedroza, Featherweight (WBA), 1978–85 | 19 |
| 6 =Wilfredo Gomez, Junior featherweight (WBC), 1977–83 | 17 |
| =Myung Woo Yuh, Junior flyweight (WBA), 1985–91 | 17 |
| 8 Orlando Canizales, Bantamweight (IBF), 1988–94 | 16 |
| 9 =Miguel Canto, Flyweight (WBC), 1975–79 | 14 |
| =Bob Foster#, Light heavyweight, 1968–74 | 14 |
| =Carlos Monzon#, Middleweight, 1970–77 | 14 |

\* One champion per division listed
\# Undisputed champion

## TOP 10 ★
### BOXERS WITH THE MOST KNOCKOUTS IN A CAREER

| | BOXER/COUNTRY* | CAREER | KNOCKOUTS |
|---|---|---|---|
| 1 | Archie Moore | 1936–63 | 129 |
| 2 | Young Stribling | 1921–63 | 126 |
| 3 | Billy Bird | 1920–48 | 125 |
| 4 | Sam Langford, Canada | 1902–26 | 116 |
| 5 | George Odwell | 1930–45 | 114 |
| 6 | Sugar Ray Robinson | 1940–65 | 110 |
| 7 | Sandy Saddler | 1944–65 | 103 |
| 8 | Henry Armstrong | 1931–45 | 100 |
| 9 | Jimmy Wilde, UK | 1911–23 | 99 |
| 10 | Len Wickwar | 1928–47 | 93 |

\* All from the US unless otherwise stated

Although this is the most generally accepted Top 10, boxing historians disagree considerably on this subject. Some, for example, include exhibition matches as well as the professional bouts on which this list is based. As the dates suggest, careers of this length, and the numbers of contests implied by knockout figures in the hundreds, are things of the past.

**HEAVYWEIGHT CHAMP**

*Evander Holyfield enjoyed a brief reign as undisputed World Heavyweight Champion, defeating Buster Douglas for the WBC, WBA, and IBF titles in October 1990, before losing two years later to Riddick Bowe.*

## TOP 10 ★
### BOXERS WHO HAVE FOUGHT THE MOST BOUTS*

| | BOXER/COUNTRY# | YEARS | BOUTS |
|---|---|---|---|
| 1 | Len Wickwar | 1928–47 | 466 |
| 2 | Wildcat Monte | 1923–37 | 406 |
| 3 | Jack Britton | 1904–30 | 357 |
| 4 | Johnny Dundee, Italy | 1910–32 | 340 |
| 5 | Billy Bird | 1920–48 | 318 |
| 6 | George Marsden | 1928–46 | 311 |
| 7 | Duke Tramel | 1922–36 | 305 |
| 8 | Maxie Rosenbloom | 1923–39 | 300 |
| 9 | Harry Greb | 1913–26 | 299 |
| 10 | Sam Langford, Canada | 1902–26 | 298 |

\* Excluding exhibition bouts
\# All from the US unless otherwise stated

## THE 10 ★
### LATEST UNDISPUTED WORLD HEAVYWEIGHT CHAMPIONS

| YEAR | FIGHTER/COUNTRY* |
|---|---|
| 2001 | Hasim Rahman |
| 1999 | Lennox Lewis, UK |
| 1992 | Riddick Bowe |
| 1990 | Evander Holyfield |
| 1990 | James Buster Douglas |
| 1987 | Mike Tyson |
| 1978 | Leon Spinks |
| 1974 | Muhammed Ali |
| 1973 | George Foreman |
| 1970 | Joe Frazier |

\* All from the US unless otherwise stated

"Undisputed" champions are those who are recognized by the four main governing bodies: the World Boxing Council (WBC), World Boxing Association (WBA), International Boxing Federation (IBF), and World Boxing Organization (WBO).

**JUDO CHAMPIONS**

*Brazil gained two silver medals for judo at the 2000 Olympics, one of them won by Tiago Camilo, seen here defeating Gil Offer of Israel in the Lightweight class.*

## TOP 10 OLYMPIC JUDO COUNTRIES

| | COUNTRY | MEDALS GOLD | SILVER | BRONZE | TOTAL |
|---|---|---|---|---|---|
| 1 | Japan | 23 | 12 | 13 | 48 |
| 2 | France | 10 | 5 | 17 | 32 |
| 3 | Korea | 7 | 10 | 13 | 30 |
| 4 | USSR* | 7 | 5 | 15 | 27 |
| 5 | Cuba | 5 | 7 | 8 | 20 |
| 6 | Great Britain | – | 7 | 9 | 16 |
| 7 | Netherlands | 4 | – | 7 | 11 |
| 8 | =Brazil | 2 | 3 | 5 | 10 |
| | =China | 4 | 1 | 5 | 10 |
| | =Germany# | 1 | 1 | 8 | 10 |
| | =Italy | 2 | 3 | 5 | 10 |

* *Includes Unified Team of 1992; excludes Russia since then*

# *Not including West/East Germany 1968–88*

Judo made its debut at the 1964 Tokyo Olympics, but for men only. Women's judo was not introduced until the 1992 Barcelona Games. Judo was not included in the 1968 Mexico City Games.

## TOP 10 OLYMPIC FENCING COUNTRIES

| | COUNTRY | MEDALS GOLD | SILVER | BRONZE | TOTAL |
|---|---|---|---|---|---|
| 1 | France | 39 | 38 | 33 | 110 |
| 2 | Italy | 40 | 36 | 26 | 102 |
| 3 | Hungary | 33 | 20 | 26 | 79 |
| 4 | USSR* | 19 | 17 | 18 | 54 |
| 5 | Germany# | 6 | 8 | 9 | 23 |
| 6 | Poland | 4 | 8 | 8 | 20 |
| 7 | US | 2 | 6 | 11 | 19 |
| 8 | West Germany | 7 | 8 | 1 | 16 |
| 9 | Belgium | 5 | 3 | 5 | 13 |
| 10 | Romania | 3 | 3 | 6 | 12 |

* *Includes Unified Team of 1992; excludes Russia since then*

# *Not including West/East Germany 1968–88*

Fencing was introduced at the first modern Olympics in 1896. Hungarian competitor Aladár Gerevich (1910–91) achieved the unique feat of winning seven gold medals at six consecutive Games, spanning the 28 years from 1932 to 1960.

## TOP 10 OLYMPIC FREESTYLE WRESTLING COUNTRIES

| | COUNTRY | MEDALS GOLD | SILVER | BRONZE | TOTAL |
|---|---|---|---|---|---|
| 1 | US | 44 | 35 | 24 | 103 |
| 2 | USSR* | 31 | 17 | 15 | 63 |
| 3 | =Bulgaria | 7 | 17 | 9 | 33 |
| | =Japan | 16 | 9 | 8 | 33 |
| | =Turkey | 16 | 11 | 6 | 33 |
| 6 | =Iran | 5 | 9 | 12 | 26 |
| | =Sweden | 8 | 10 | 8 | 26 |
| 8 | Finland | 8 | 7 | 10 | 25 |
| 9 | Korea | 4 | 7 | 8 | 19 |
| 10 | Great Britain | 3 | 4 | 10 | 17 |

* *Includes Unified Team of 1992; excludes Russia since then*

Freestyle wrestling was introduced in the 1904 Olympic Games.

## TOP 10 OLYMPIC GRECO-ROMAN WRESTLING COUNTRIES

| | COUNTRY | MEDALS GOLD | SILVER | BRONZE | TOTAL |
|---|---|---|---|---|---|
| 1 | USSR* | 37 | 19 | 13 | 69 |
| 2 | Finland | 19 | 21 | 19 | 59 |
| 3 | Sweden | 20 | 16 | 19 | 55 |
| 4 | Hungary | 15 | 10 | 11 | 36 |
| 5 | Bulgaria | 9 | 14 | 7 | 30 |
| 6 | Romania | 6 | 8 | 13 | 27 |
| 7 | Germany# | 4 | 13 | 8 | 25 |
| 8 | Poland | 5 | 8 | 6 | 19 |
| 9 | =Italy | 5 | 4 | 9 | 18 |
| | =Turkey | 11 | 4 | 3 | 18 |

* *Includes Unified Team of 1992; excludes Russia since then*

# *Not including West/East Germany 1968–88*

The principal difference between freestyle and Greco-Roman wrestling is that in the latter competitors may not seize their opponents below the hips or grip using their legs.

## THE 10 WRESTLING WEIGHT DIVISIONS

*(Weight/limit in lb/kg)*

❶ **Heavyweight plus**, over 220/over 100 ❷ **Heavyweight**, 220/100 ❸ **Light-heavyweight**, 198/90 ❹ **Middleweight**, 181/82 ❺ **Welterweight**, 163/74 ❻ **Lightweight**, 150/68 ❼ **Featherweight**, 137/62 ❽ **Bantamweight**, 126/57 ❾ **Flyweight**, 115/52 ❿ **Light-flyweight**, 106/48

**Did You Know?** Italian-born Angelo Parsi won four Olympic medals in judo for two different countries, competing for Great Britain in 1972, when he won a bronze, and for France in 1980 and 1984, winning a gold and two silvers.

# Baseball Teams

## TOP 10 ★
### NEWEST MAJOR LEAGUE TEAMS

| TEAM | AL/NL* | 1ST SEASON |
|---|---|---|
| 1 =Arizona Diamondbacks | NL | 1998 |
| =Tampa Bay Devil Rays | AL | 1998 |
| 3 =Colorado Rockies | NL | 1993 |
| =Florida Marlins | NL | 1993 |
| 5 =Seattle Mariners | AL | 1977 |
| =Toronto Blue Jays | AL | 1977 |
| 7 =Kansas City Royals | AL | 1969 |
| =Montreal Expos | NL | 1969 |
| =Seattle Pilots/ Milwaukee Brewers | AL | 1969 |
| 10 =Houston Astros | NL | 1962 |
| =New York Mets | NL | 1962 |

*AL = American League; NL = National League

Source: *Major League Baseball*

## TOP 10 ★
### AVERAGE ATTENDANCES

| TEAM | AVERAGE ATTENDANCE (2000) |
|---|---|
| 1 Cleveland Indians | 42,671 |
| 2 St. Louis Cardinals | 41,036 |
| 3 San Francisco Giants | 40,973 |
| 4 Colorado Rockies | 40,898 |
| 5 Baltimore Orioles | 40,428 |
| 6 New York Yankees | 40,346 |
| 7 Atlanta Braves | 39,930 |
| 8 Seattle Mariners | 38,868 |
| 9 Houston Astros | 37,757 |
| 10 Los Angeles Dodgers | 37,088 |

Source: *Major League Baseball*

## TOP 10 ★
### BIGGEST SINGLE GAME WINS IN THE WORLD SERIES

| TEAMS*/GAME | DATE | SCORE |
|---|---|---|
| 1 New York Yankees v New York Giants (Game 2) | Oct 2, 1936 | 18–4 |
| 2 New York Yankees v Pittsburgh Pirates (Game 2) | Oct 6, 1960 | 16–3 |
| 3 =New York Yankees v New York Giants (Game 5) | Oct 9, 1951 | 13–1 |
| =New York Yankees v Pittsburgh Pirates (Game 6) | Oct 12, 1960 | 12–0 |
| =Detroit Tigers v St. Louis Cardinals (Game 6) | Oct 9, 1968 | 13–1 |
| =New York Yankees v Milwaukee Brewers (Game 6) | Oct 19, 1982 | 13–1 |
| 7 =New York Yankees v Philadelphia Athletics (Game 6) | Oct 26, 1911 | 13–2 |
| =St. Louis Cardinals v Detroit Tigers (Game 7) | Oct 9, 1934 | 11–0 |
| =Chicago White Sox v Los Angeles Dodgers (Game 1) | Oct 1, 1959 | 11–0 |
| =Kansas City Royals v St. Louis Cardinals (Game 7) | Oct 27, 1985 | 11–0 |
| =Atlanta Braves v New York Yankees (Game 1) | Oct 20, 1996 | 12–1 |

* Winners listed first

Source: *Major League Baseball*

## THE 10 ★
### TOTAL ATTENDANCES OF EACH YEAR IN THE PAST DECADE

| YEAR | ATTENDANCE |
|---|---|
| 2000 | 71,755,353 |
| 1999 | 70,139,380 |
| 1998 | 70,372,221 |
| 1997 | 63,196,222 |
| 1996 | 60,097,381 |
| 1995 | 50,469,236* |
| 1994 | 50,010,016* |
| 1993 | 70,256,459 |
| 1992 | 55,872,271 |
| 1991 | 56,813,760 |

* Strike/lockout year

Source: *Major League Baseball*

## THE 10 ★
### LATEST WINNERS OF THE WORLD SERIES

| YEAR* | WINNER/LEAGUE LOSER/LEAGUE# | SCORE |
|---|---|---|
| 2000 | New York (AL) New York (NL) | 4–1 |
| 1999 | New York (AL) Atlanta (NL) | 4–0 |
| 1998 | New York (AL) San Diego (NL) | 4–0 |
| 1997 | Florida (NL) Cleveland (AL) | 4–3 |
| 1996 | New York (AL) Atlanta (NL) | 4–2 |
| 1995 | Atlanta (NL) Cleveland (AL) | 4–2 |
| 1993 | Toronto (AL) Philadelphia (NL) | 4–2 |
| 1992 | Toronto (AL) Atlanta (NL) | 4–2 |
| 1991 | Minnesota (AL) Atlanta (NL) | 4–2 |
| 1990 | Cincinnati (NL) Oakland (AL) | 4–0 |

* The 1994 event was canceled due to a players' strike

# AL = American League  NL = National League

Source: *Major League Baseball*

## THE 10 MAJOR LEAGUE PLAYERS' SALARIES OF THE LAST DECADE
### (Year/average salary in $)

❶ 2000 1,995,025  ❷ 1999 1,720,050  ❸ 1998 1,441,406  ❹ 1997 1,383,578
❺ 1996 1,176,967  ❻ 1995 1,071,029  ❼ 1994 1,188,679  ❽ 1993 1,120,254
❾ 1992 1,084,408  ❿ 1991 891,188

Source: *Associated Press*

## TOP 10 ★
# TEAMS WITH THE MOST WORLD SERIES WINS

| | TEAM* | WINS |
|---|---|---|
| 1 | New York Yankees | 26 |
| 2= | Philadelphia/Kansas City/Oakland Athletics | 9 |
| = | St. Louis Cardinals | 9 |
| 4 | Brooklyn/Los Angeles Dodgers | 6 |
| 5= | Boston Red Sox | 5 |
| = | Cincinnati Reds | 5 |
| = | New York/San Francisco Giants | 5 |
| = | Pittsburgh Pirates | 5 |
| 9 | Detroit Tigers | 4 |
| 10= | Boston/Milwaukee/Atlanta Braves | 3 |
| = | St. Louis/Baltimore Orioles | 3 |
| = | Washington Senators/Minnesota Twins | 3 |

* Teams separated by / indicate changes of franchise and are regarded as the same team for Major League record purposes

Source: *Major League Baseball*

Major League baseball started in the US with the formation of the National League in 1876. The rival American League was started in 1901, and two years later Pittsburgh, champion of the National League, invited American League champion Boston to take part in a best-of-nine games series to establish the "real" champion. Boston won 5–3. The following year the National League champion, New York, refused to play Boston, and there was no World Series. However, it was resumed in 1905 and has been held every year since, except in 1994, when a players' strike curtailed the season. It has been a best-of-seven games series since 1905, with the exception of 1919–21 when it reverted to a nine-game series.

## TOP 10 ★
# BASEBALL TEAM PAYROLLS

| | TEAM | AVERAGE 2000 SALARY ($) | TOTAL 2000 PAYROLL ($) |
|---|---|---|---|
| 1 | New York Yankees | 3,190,974 | 92,538,260 |
| 2 | Los Angeles Dodgers | 3,263,862 | 88,124,286 |
| 3 | Atlanta Braves | 2,817,928 | 84,537,836 |
| 4 | Baltimore Orioles | 2,808,532 | 81,447,435 |
| 5 | Arizona Diamondbacks | 2,893,851 | 81,027,833 |
| 6 | New York Mets | 3,180,391 | 79,509,776 |
| 7 | Boston Red Sox | 2,598,011 | 77,940,333 |
| 8 | Cleveland Indians | 2,918,495 | 75,880,871 |
| 9 | Texas Rangers | 2,722,920 | 70,795,921 |
| 10 | Tampa Bay Devil Rays | 2,024,682 | 62,765,129 |

Source: *Associated Press*

## TOP 10 ★
# LARGEST MAJOR LEAGUE BALLPARKS*

| | STADIUM | HOME TEAM | CAPACITY |
|---|---|---|---|
| 1 | Qualcomm Stadium | San Diego Padres | 66,307 |
| 2 | Veterans Stadium | Philadelphia Phillies | 62,411 |
| 3 | Dodger Stadium | Los Angeles Dodgers | 56,000 |
| 4 | Shea Stadium | New York Mets | 55,775 |
| 5 | Yankee Stadium | New York Yankees | 55,070 |
| 6 | Cinergy Field | Cincinnati Reds | 52,953 |
| 7 | SkyDome | Toronto Blue Jays | 50,516 |
| 8 | Coors Field | Colorado Rockies | 50,249 |
| 9 | Turner Field | Atlanta Braves | 50,062 |
| 10 | Busch Stadium | St. Louis Cardinals | 49,738 |

* By capacity

Source: *Major League Baseball*

Stadium capacities vary constantly, some being adjusted according to the event: Veterans Stadium, for example, holds fewer for baseball games than for football games.

## TOP 10 ★
# OLDEST STADIUMS IN MAJOR LEAGUE BASEBALL

| | STADIUM | HOME CLUB | FIRST GAME |
|---|---|---|---|
| 1 | Fenway Park | Boston Red Sox | Apr 20, 1912 |
| 2 | Wrigley Field | Chicago Cubs | Apr 23, 1914 |
| 3 | Yankee Stadium | New York Yankees | Apr 18, 1923 |
| 4 | Dodger Stadium | Los Angeles Dodgers | Apr 10, 1962 |
| 5 | Shea Stadium | New York Mets | Apr 17, 1964 |
| 6 | Edison International Field of Anaheim* | Anaheim Angels | Apr 19, 1966 |
| 7 | Busch Stadium | St. Louis Cardinals | May 12, 1966 |
| 8 | Qualcomm Stadium# | San Diego Padres | Apr 5, 1968 |
| 9 | Network Associates Coliseum+ | Oakland Athletics | Apr 17, 1968 |
| 10 | Cinergy Field | Cincinnati Reds | June 30, 1970 |

* Formerly known as Anaheim Stadium

# Formerly known as Jack Murphy Stadium

+ Formerly known as Oakland-Alameda County Coliseum

Source: *Major League Baseball*

Having outgrown its former Huntington Avenue ballpark, the Boston Red Sox moved to Fenway Park. Their inaugural game, when they defeated the New York Highlanders before a crowd of 27,000, was sadly overshadowed by taking place in the same week as the sinking of the *Titanic*.

What was C. A. Parker's 1878 cycling first?
*see p.263 for the answer*

A First to ride a one-wheeled cycle
B First to win a cycling race in the US
C First to cycle round the world

# Baseball Stars

## THE 10 ★
### FIRST PITCHERS TO THROW PERFECT GAMES

| PLAYER/MATCH | DATE |
|---|---|
| **1 Lee Richmond,** Worcester v Cleveland | June 12, 1880 |
| **2 Monte Ward,** Providence v Buffalo | June 17, 1880 |
| **3 Cy Young,** Boston v Philadelphia | May 5, 1904 |
| **4 Addie Joss,** Cleveland v Chicago | Oct 2, 1908 |
| **5 Charlie Robertson,** Chicago v Detroit | Apr 30, 1922 |
| **6 Don Larsen*,** New York v Brooklyn | Oct 8, 1956 |
| **7 Jim Bunning,** Philadelphia v New York | June 21, 1964 |
| **8 Sandy Koufax,** Los Angeles v Chicago | Sep 9, 1965 |
| **9 Catfish Hunter,** Oakland v Minnesota | May 8, 1968 |
| **10 Len Barker,** Cleveland v Toronto | May 15, 1981 |

*Larsen's perfect game was, uniquely, in the World Series*

## TOP 10 ★
### PLAYERS MOST AT-BAT IN A CAREER

| PLAYER | AT-BAT |
|---|---|
| **1 Pete Rose** | 14,053 |
| **2 Hank Aaron** | 12,364 |
| **3 Carl Yastrzemski** | 11,988 |
| **4 Ty Cobb** | 11,429 |
| **5 Eddie Murray** | 11,336 |
| **6 Cal Ripken Jr.** | 11,074 |
| **7 Robin Yount** | 11,008 |
| **8 Dave Winfield** | 11,003 |
| **9 Stan Musial** | 10,972 |
| **10 Willie Mays** | 10,881 |

Source: *Major League Baseball*

## TOP 10 ★
### PLAYERS WHO PLAYED THE MOST GAMES IN A CAREER

| PLAYER | GAMES |
|---|---|
| **1 Pete Rose** | 3,562 |
| **2 Carl Yastrzemski** | 3,308 |
| **3 Hank Aaron** | 3,298 |
| **4 Ty Cobb** | 3,034 |
| **5 =Eddie Murray** | 3,026 |
| **=Stan Musial** | 3,026 |
| **7 Willie Mays** | 2,992 |
| **8 Dave Winfield** | 2,973 |
| **9 Rusty Staub** | 2,951 |
| **10 Brooks Robinson** | 2,896 |

Source: *Major League Baseball*

## TOP 10 ★
### PLAYERS WITH THE MOST CAREER STRIKEOUTS

| PLAYER | STRIKEOUTS |
|---|---|
| **1 Nolan Ryan** | 5,714 |
| **2 Steve Carlton** | 4,136 |
| **3 Bert Blyleven** | 3,701 |
| **4 Tom Seaver** | 3,640 |
| **5 Don Sutton** | 3,574 |
| **6 Gaylord Perry** | 3,534 |
| **7 Walter Johnson** | 3,508 |
| **8 Roger Clemens*** | 3,504 |
| **9 Phil Niekro** | 3,342 |
| **10 Ferguson Jenkins** | 3,192 |

* *Still active 2000 season*

Source: *Major League Baseball*

Nolan Ryan was known as the "Babe Ruth of strikeout pitchers," pitching faster (a record 101 mph/162.5 km/h) and longer (27 seasons – 1966 and 1968–93) than any previous player. As well as his 5,714 strikeouts, including 383 in one season, he walked 2,795 batters and allowed the fewest hits (6.55) per nine innings.

## TOP 10 ★
### PITCHERS WITH THE MOST CAREER WINS

| PLAYER | WINS |
|---|---|
| **1 Cy Young** | 511 |
| **2 Walter Johnson** | 417 |
| **3 =Grover Alexander** | 373 |
| **=Christy Mathewson** | 373 |
| **5 Warren Spahn** | 363 |
| **6 =Pud Galvin** | 361 |
| **=Kid Nichols** | 361 |
| **8 Tim Keefe** | 344 |
| **9 Steve Carlton** | 329 |
| **10 =John Clarkson** | 326 |
| **=Eddie Plank** | 326 |

Source: *Major League Baseball*

## TOP 10 ★
### PLAYERS WITH THE HIGHEST CAREER BATTING AVERAGES

| PLAYER | AT-BAT | HITS | AVERAGE* |
|---|---|---|---|
| **1 Ty Cobb** | 11,434 | 4,189 | .366 |
| **2 Rogers Hornsby** | 8,173 | 2,930 | .358 |
| **3 Joe Jackson** | 4,981 | 1,772 | .356 |
| **4 Ed Delahanty** | 7,505 | 2,597 | .346 |
| **5 Tris Speaker** | 10,195 | 3,514 | .345 |
| **6 =Billy Hamilton** | 6,268 | 2,158 | .344 |
| **=Ted Williams** | 7,706 | 2,654 | .344 |
| **8 =Dan Brouthers** | 6,711 | 2,296 | .342 |
| **=Harry Heilmann** | 7,787 | 2,660 | .342 |
| **=Babe Ruth** | 8,399 | 2,873 | .342 |

* *Calculated by dividing the number of hits by the number of times a batter was "at-bat"*

Source: *Major League Baseball*

Second only to the legendary Ty Cobb, Rogers Hornsby stands as the best second-hitting baseman of all time, with an average of over .400 in a five-year period. Baseball's greatest right-handed hitter, slugging 20-plus homers on seven occasions, he achieved a career average of .358.

## THE 10 ⭐
## FIRST PLAYERS TO HIT FOUR HOME RUNS IN ONE GAME

| | PLAYER | CLUB | DATE |
|---|---|---|---|
| 1 | Bobby Lowe | Boston | May 30, 1884 |
| 2 | Ed Delahanty | Philadelphia | July 13, 1896 |
| 3 | Lou Gehrig | New York | June 3, 1932 |
| 4 | Chuck Klein | Philadelphia | July 10, 1936 |
| 5 | Pat Seerey | Chicago | July 18, 1948 |
| 6 | Gil Hodges | Brooklyn | Aug 31, 1950 |
| 7 | Joe Adcock | Milwaukee | July 31, 1954 |
| 8 | Rocky Colavito | Cleveland | June 10, 1959 |
| 9 | Willie Mays | San Francisco | Apr 30, 1961 |
| 10 | Mike Schmidt | Philadelphia | Apr 17, 1976 |

The only other players to score four homers in one game are Bob Horner, who did so for Atlanta on July 6, 1986, and Mark Whitten, for St. Louis, on September 7, 1993.

## TOP 10 ⭐
## PLAYERS WITH THE MOST HOME RUNS IN A CAREER

| | PLAYER | HOME RUNS |
|---|---|---|
| 1 | Hank Aaron | 755 |
| 2 | Babe Ruth | 714 |
| 3 | Willie Mays | 660 |
| 4 | Frank Robinson | 586 |
| 5 | Harmon Killebrew | 573 |
| 6 | Reggie Jackson | 563 |
| 7 | Mark McGwire | 554 |
| 8 | Mike Schmidt | 548 |
| 9 | Mickey Mantle | 536 |
| 10 | Jimmie Foxx | 534 |

Source: *Major League Baseball*

George Herman "Babe" Ruth set a home run record in 1919 by hitting 29, breaking it the next season by hitting 54. His career total of 714 came from 8,399 "at-bats," which represents an average of 8.5 percent. The next man in the averages, Harmon Killebrew, averages at 7.0 percent.

## TOP 10 ⭐
## PLAYERS WITH MOST CONSECUTIVE GAMES PLAYED

| | PLAYER | GAMES |
|---|---|---|
| 1 | Cal Ripken Jr. | 2,600 |
| 2 | Lou Gehrig | 2,130 |
| 3 | Everett Scott | 1,307 |
| 4 | Steve Garvey | 1,207 |
| 5 | Billy Williams | 1,117 |
| 6 | Joe Sewell | 1,103 |
| 7 | Stan Musial | 895 |
| 8 | Eddie Yost | 829 |
| 9 | Gus Suhr | 822 |
| 10 | Nellie Fox | 798 |

Source: *Major League Baseball*

Cal Ripken took himself out of the starting line-up on September 21, 1998, in a game between the Orioles and the Yankees, having played in every game since May 30, 1982.

## TOP 10 ⭐
## PLAYERS WITH THE MOST RUNS IN A CAREER

| | PLAYER | RUNS* |
|---|---|---|
| 1 | Ty Cobb | 2,245 |
| 2 | Rickey Henderson# | 2,178 |
| 3 = | Hank Aaron | 2,174 |
| = | Babe Ruth | 2,174 |
| 5 | Pete Rose | 2,165 |
| 6 | Willie Mays | 2,062 |
| 7 | Stan Musial | 1,949 |
| 8 | Lou Gehrig | 1,888 |
| 9 | Tris Speaker | 1,881 |
| 10 | Mel Ott | 1,859 |

*\* Regular season only, excluding World Series*

*# Still active in 2000 season*

Source: *Major League Baseball*

The still unbroken record of Tyrus Raymond "Ty" Cobb (1886–1961) was achieved in a career with Detroit and Philadelphia during 1905–28.

## TOP 10 ⭐
## BASEBALL PLAYERS WITH THE BIGGEST CONTRACTS

| | PLAYER/CLUB | PERIOD OF CONTRACT | TOTAL ($) |
|---|---|---|---|
| 1 | Alex Rodriguex, Texas Rangers | 2001–10 | 252,000,000 |
| 2 | Manny Ramirez, Boston Red Sox | 2001–08 | 160,000,000 |
| 3 | Mike Hampton, Colorado Rockies | 2001–08 | 121,000,000 |
| 4 | Ken Griffey Jr., Cincinnati Reds | 2000–08 | 116,500,000 |
| 5 | Kevin Brown, Los Angeles Dodgers | 1999–2005 | 105,000,000 |
| 6 | Mike Piazza, New York Mets | 1999–2005 | 91,000,000 |
| 7 | Chipper Jones, Atlanta Braves | 2001–06 | 90,000,000 |
| 8 | Mike Mussina, New York Yankees | 2001–06 | 88,500,000 |
| 9 | Bernie Williams, New York Yankees | 1999–2005 | 87,500,000 |
| 10 | Shawn Green, Los Angeles Dodgers | 2000–05 | 84,000,000 |

Source: *Major League Baseball*

## TOP 10 ⭐
## LOWEST EARNED RUN AVERAGES IN A CAREER

| | PLAYER | ERA |
|---|---|---|
| 1 | Ed Walsh | 1.82 |
| 2 | Addie Joss | 1.89 |
| 3 | "Three Finger" Brown | 2.06 |
| 4 | John Ward | 2.10 |
| 5 | Christy Mathewson | 2.13 |
| 6 | Rube Waddell | 2.16 |
| 7 | Walter Johnson | 2.17 |
| 8 | Orval Overall | 2.23 |
| 9 | Tommy Bond | 2.25 |
| 10 | Ed Reulbach | 2.28 |

Source: *Major League Baseball*

**What innovation did motorcycle makers Harley Davidson introduce in 1909?**   A The twist-grip throttle
*see p.264 for the answer*   B The kick-starter
C The crash helmet

259

# International Soccer

## MOST WATCHED WORLD CUP FINALS

| | HOST NATION | YEAR | MATCHES | SPECTATORS | AVERAGE |
|---|---|---|---|---|---|
| 1 | US | 1994 | 52 | 3,587,538 | 68,991 |
| 2 | Brazil | 1950 | 22 | 1,337,000 | 60,773 |
| 3 | Mexico | 1970 | 32 | 1,673,975 | 52,312 |
| 4 | England | 1966 | 32 | 1,614,677 | 50,459 |
| 5 | Italy | 1990 | 52 | 2,515,168 | 48,369 |
| 6 | West Germany | 1974 | 38 | 1,774,022 | 46,685 |
| 7 | France | 1998 | 64 | 2,775,400 | 43,366 |
| 8 | Argentina | 1978 | 38 | 1,610,215 | 42,374 |
| 9 | Mexico | 1986 | 52 | 2,184,522 | 42,010 |
| 10 | Switzerland | 1954 | 26 | 943,000 | 36,269 |

Since the World Cup's launch in 1930, a total of 24,814,267 people have watched the 580 final stage matches, at an average of 42,783 per game. The worst attended finals were in Italy in 1934, when the 17 matches were watched by 395,000, at an average of 23,235 per game.

## COUNTRIES IN THE WORLD CUP

| | COUNTRY | WIN | R/U | 3RD | 4TH | TOTAL PTS* |
|---|---|---|---|---|---|---|
| 1 | Brazil | 4 | 2 | 2 | 1 | 27 |
| 2 | Germany/West Germany | 3 | 3 | 2 | 1 | 26 |
| 3 | Italy | 3 | 2 | 1 | 1 | 21 |
| 4 | Argentina | 2 | 2 | – | – | 14 |
| 5 | Uruguay | 2 | – | – | 2 | 10 |
| 6 | France | 1 | – | 2 | 1 | 9 |
| 7 | Sweden | – | 1 | 2 | 1 | 8 |
| 8 | Holland | – | 2 | – | 1 | 7 |
| 9 = | Czechoslovakia | – | 2 | – | – | 6 |
| = | Hungary | – | 2 | – | – | 6 |

*Based on 4 points for winning the tournament, 3 points for runner-up, 2 points for 3rd place, and 1 point for 4th; up to and including the 1998 World Cup*

## LEAST SUCCESSFUL WORLD CUP COUNTRIES

| | COUNTRY | TOURNAMENTS | MATCHES PLAYED | WON |
|---|---|---|---|---|
| 1 | South Korea | 5 | 14 | 0 |
| 2 = | El Salvador | 2 | 6 | 0 |
| = | Bolivia | 3 | 6 | 0 |
| 4 | Republic of Ireland | 1 | 5 | 0 |
| 5 | Egypt | 2 | 4 | 0 |
| 6 = | Canada | 1 | 3 | 0 |
| = | Greece | 1 | 3 | 0 |
| = | Haiti | 1 | 3 | 0 |
| = | Iraq | 1 | 3 | 0 |
| = | Japan | 1 | 3 | 0 |
| = | New Zealand | 1 | 3 | 0 |
| = | South Africa | 1 | 3 | 0 |
| = | United Arab Emirates | 1 | 3 | 0 |
| = | Zaïre | 1 | 3 | 0 |

**FRANCE WINS WORLD CUP**

*Host nation France celebrates its win against Brazil in the 1998 World Cup, one of only seven different victorious countries since the first Cup in 1930.*

## HIGHEST-SCORING WORLD CUP FINALS

| | YEAR | GAMES | GOALS | AVERAGE PER GAME |
|---|---|---|---|---|
| 1 | 1954 | 26 | 140 | 5.38 |
| 2 | 1938 | 18 | 84 | 4.66 |
| 3 | 1934 | 17 | 70 | 4.11 |
| 4 | 1950 | 22 | 88 | 4.00 |
| 5 | 1930 | 18 | 70 | 3.88 |
| 6 | 1958 | 35 | 126 | 3.60 |
| 7 | 1970 | 32 | 95 | 2.96 |
| 8 | 1982 | 52 | 146 | 2.81 |
| 9 = | 1962 | 32 | 89 | 2.78 |
| = | 1966 | 32 | 89 | 2.78 |

## TOP 10 ★
### GOAL SCORERS IN FULL INTERNATIONALS

| | PLAYER | COUNTRY | YEARS | GOALS |
|---|---|---|---|---|
| 1 | Ferenc Puskás | Hungary/Spain | 1945–56 | 83 |
| 2 | Pelé | Brazil | 1957–91 | 77 |
| 3 | Sándor Kocsis | Hungary | 1947–56 | 75 |
| 4 | Hossam Hassan* | Egypt | 1985–2000 | 73 |
| 5 | Gerd Müller | West Germany | 1966–74 | 68 |
| 6 | Imre Schlosser | Hungary | 1906–27 | 60 |
| 7 | Kazuyoshi Miura* | Japan | 1990–2000 | 55 |
| 8 =Gabriel Batistuta* | | Argentina | 1991–2000 | 54 |
| =Ali Daei* | | Iran | 1993–2000 | 54 |
| 10 | Joachim Streich | East Germany | 1969–84 | 53 |

* Active in 2001 season

## TOP 10 RICHEST SOCCER CLUBS
*(Club/country/income in $)*

❶ **Manchester United**, England, 178,500,000 ❷ **Bayern Munich**, Germany, 134,400,000 ❸ **Real Madrid**, Spain, 122,500,000 ❹ **Chelsea**, England, 95,200,000 ❺ **Juventus**, Italy, 94,200,000 ❻ **Barcelona**, Spain, 89,700,000 ❼ **Milan**, Italy, 87,100,000 ❽ **Lazio**, Italy, 80,500,000 ❾ **Internazionale**, Italy, 79,000,000 ❿ **Arsenal**, England, 78,200,000

## TOP 10 ★
### MOST EXPENSIVE TRANSFERS

| | PLAYER | FROM | TO | YEAR | FEE ($) |
|---|---|---|---|---|---|
| 1 | Luis Figo | Barcelona | Real Madrid | 2000 | 56,514,000 |
| 2 | Christian Vieri | Lazio | Inter Milan | 1999 | 54,737,000 |
| 3 | Herman Crespi | Parma | Lazio | 2000 | 52,133,000 |
| 4 | Denilson | São Paulo | Real Betis | 1998 | 40,157,000 |
| 5 | Nicolas Anelka | Arsenal | Real Madrid | 1999 | 39,443,000 |
| 6 | Marcio Amoruso | Udinese | Parma | 1999 | 36,545,000 |
| 7 | Marc Overmars | Arsenal | Barcelona | 2000 | 36,508,000 |
| 8 | Gabriel Batistuta | Fiorentina | Roma | 2000 | 32,857,000 |
| 9 | Nicolas Anelka | Real Madrid | Paris St. Germain | 2000 | 32,127,000 |
| 10 | Rivaldo | Deportivo | Barcelona | 1997 | 30,125,000 |

**RAVELLI'S REIGN**
*Swedish goalkeeper Thomas Ravelli's record number of appearances for his country was unchallenged until Germany's Lothar Matthäus played his 143rd game in February 2000.*

## TOP 10 ★
### MOST CAPPED INTERNATIONAL PLAYERS

| | PLAYER | COUNTRY | YEARS | CAPS |
|---|---|---|---|---|
| 1 | Lothar Matthäus* | West Germany/Germany | 1980–2000 | 150 |
| 2 =Claudio Suarez* | | Mexico | 1992–2000 | 147 |
| =Hossam Hassan* | | Egypt | 1985–2000 | 147 |
| 4 | Thomas Ravelli | Sweden | 1981–97 | 143 |
| 5 =Majed Abdullah | | Saudi Arabia | 1978–94 | 140 |
| =Mohamed Al-Deayea* | | Saudi Arabia | 1990–2000 | 140 |
| 7 | Cobi Jones* | US | 1992–2000 | 134 |
| 8 | Marcelo Balboa* | US | 1988–2000 | 128 |
| 9 =Mohammed Al-Khilaiwi* | | South Korea | 1992–2000 | 127 |
| =Peter Schmeichel* | | Denmark | 1987–2000 | 127 |

* Active in 2001 season

## TOP 10 EUROPEAN CLUB SIDES WITH THE MOST DOMESTIC LEAGUE TITLES
*(Club/country/titles)*

❶ **Glasgow Rangers**, Scotland, 49 ❷ **Linfield**, Northern Ireland, 43 ❸ **Glasgow Celtic**, Scotland, 36 ❹ **Rapid Vienna**, Austria, 31* ❺ **Benfica**, Portugal, 30 ❻ **Olympiakos**, Greece, 29 ❼ **CSKA Sofia**, Bulgaria, 28 ❽ = **Ajax**, Holland, 27; = **Real Madrid**, Spain, 27 ❿ = **Ferencvaros**, Hungary, 26; = **Jeunesse Esch**, Luxembourg, 26

* Rapid Vienna also won one German League title, in 1941

In what sport has Park Joo-bong won the most world titles?
*see p.273 for the answer*

A  Badminton
B  Trampolining
C  Judo

# Free Wheelers

## STREET SKATEBOARDERS

| SKATEBOARDER/COUNTRY* | POINTS# |
|---|---|
| 1 Carlos de Andrade, Brazil | 490 |
| 2 Kerry Getz | 470 |
| 3 =Kyle Berard | 445 |
| =Eric Koston | 445 |
| 5 Chris Senn | 440 |
| 6 Pat Channita | 406 |
| 7 Rick McCrank, Canada | 377 |
| 8 Ryan Johnson | 340 |
| 9 Chad Fernandez | 320 |
| 10 Andy Macdonald | 310 |

\* All from the US unless otherwise stated

# Based on skateboarder's best four US events and best two from Europe/Brazil in the World Cup Skateboarding Tour

These skateboarders are ranked by World Cup Skateboarding (WCS), the organization recognized worldwide as the sanctioning body for skateboarding. The World Cup Skateboarding Tour has been held since 1994 and already includes 18 events in nine countries. Despite its name, street skateboarders rarely skate on the actual street itself, but prefer curbs, benches, handrails, and other elements of urban landscapes.

## VERT. SKATEBOARDERS

| SKATEBOARDER/COUNTRY | POINTS* |
|---|---|
| 1 Bob Burnquist, Brazil | 600 |
| 2 Andy Macdonald, US | 570 |
| 3 Pierre-Luc Gagnon, Canada | 535 |
| 4 Rune Glifberg, Denmark | 480 |
| 5 Sandro Dias, Brazil | 425 |
| 6 Lincoln Ueda, Brazil | 410 |
| 7 Anthony Furlong, US | 370 |
| 8 Max Schaaf, US | 350 |
| 9 Buster Halterman, US | 325 |
| 10 Cristiano Mateus, Brazil | 320 |

\* Based on skateboarder's best four US events and best two from Europe/Brazil in the World Cup Skateboarding Tour

Vert. skateboarding is skateboarding on the vertical rather than the horizontal plane, which usually involves skateboarding on ramps and other vertical structures specifically designed for skateboarding. Skateboarding first became popular with surfers as a means of keeping in shape when there were no waves to surf, but over the past 40 years the sport has gained worldwide recognition in its own right, with a world ranking system since 1995.

## DOWNHILL RIDERS IN THE UCI MOUNTAIN BIKE WORLD CUP, 2000 (MEN)

| RIDER/COUNTRY | POINTS* |
|---|---|
| 1 Nicolas Vouilloz, France | 1,256 |
| 2 Steve Peat, Great Britain | 1,184 |
| 3 David Vazquez, Spain | 1,166 |
| 4 Mickael Pascal, France | 966 |
| 5 Cedric Gracia, France | 944 |
| 6 Gerwin Peters, Netherlands | 942 |
| 7 Bas De Bever, Netherlands | 919 |
| 8 Eric Carter, US | 895 |
| 9 Fabien Barel, France | 890 |
| 10 Oscar Saiz, Spain | 854 |

\* Total points scored over a series of eight competitions

## DOWNHILL RIDERS IN THE UCI MOUNTAIN BIKE WORLD CUP, 2000 (WOMEN)

| RIDER/COUNTRY | POINTS* |
|---|---|
| 1 Anne Caroline Chausson, France | 1,340 |
| 2 Missy Giove, US | 1,203 |
| 3 Katja Repo, Finland | 1,117 |
| 4 Sari Jorgensen, Switzerland | 952 |
| 5 Leigh Donovan, US | 935 |
| 6 Sabrina Jonnier, France | 934 |
| 7 Marla Streb, US | 905 |
| 8 Nolvenn Le Caer, France | 897 |
| 9 Tara Llanes, US | 895 |
| 10 Sarah Stieger, Switzerland | 891 |

\* Total points scored over a series of eight competitions

**FINNISH THIRD**

*Born in Helsinki, Finland, in 1973, Katja Repo has competed in professional cycling events since 1993 and finished third in the 2000 World Cup.*

## TOP 10 ★
# INTERNATIONAL ROLLER HOCKEY COUNTRIES, 2000

| | COUNTRY | POINTS* |
|---|---|---|
| 1 | Argentina | 2,615 |
| 2 | Spain | 2,585 |
| 3 | Portugal | 2,560 |
| 4 | Italy | 2,485 |
| 5 | Brazil | 2,235 |
| 6 | France | 2,210 |
| 7 | Switzerland | 2,160 |
| 8 | Angola | 2,025 |
| 9 | Chile | 1,980 |
| 10 | Germany | 1,955 |

*\* Ranked by the ELO system, which employs a statistical formula to calculate the probability of winning future games based on the results so far attained*

## TOP 10 ★
# LONGEST TOURS DE FRANCE

| | WINNER/ COUNTRY/YEAR | STAGES | DISTANCE MILES | KM |
|---|---|---|---|---|
| 1 | Lucien Buysse, Belgium, 1926 | 17 | 3,570 | 5,745 |
| 2 | Firmin Lambot, Belgium, 1919 | 15 | 3,455 | 5,560 |
| 3 | Gustave Garrigou, France, 1911 | 15 | 3,445 | 5,544 |
| 4 | Philippe Thys, Belgium, 1920 | 15 | 3,419 | 5,503 |
| 5 | Léon Scieur, Belgium, 1921 | 15 | 3,408 | 5,484 |
| 6 | Ottavio Bottecchia, Italy, 1925 | 18 | 3,374 | 5,430 |
| 7 | Ottavio Bottecchia, 1924 | 15 | 3,372 | 5,427 |
| 8 | Philippe Thys, 1914 | 15 | 3,364 | 5,414 |
| 9 | Philippe Thys, 1913 | 15 | 3,347 | 5,387 |
| 10 | Henri Pélissier, France, 1923 | 15 | 3,347 | 5,386 |

**US IN TOUR DE FRANCE**
*After triumphing over illness, Lance Armstrong won the 2000 Tour de France, thereby elevating the US to fifth place among nationalities competing in the world's most prestigious cycle race.*

## TOP 10 ★
# COUNTRIES WITH THE MOST TOUR DE FRANCE WINNERS

| | COUNTRY | WINNERS |
|---|---|---|
| 1 | France | 36 |
| 2 | Belgium | 18 |
| 3 | Italy | 9 |
| 4 | Spain | 8 |
| 5 | US | 5 |
| 6 | Luxembourg | 4 |
| 7= | Holland | 2 |
| = | Switzerland | 2 |
| 9= | Denmark | 1 |
| = | Germany | 1 |
| = | Ireland | 1 |

The Tour de France is the toughest, longest, and most popular cycling race in the world.

## TOP 10 ★
# OLYMPIC CYCLING COUNTRIES

| | COUNTRY | MEDALS GOLD | SILVER | BRONZE | TOTAL |
|---|---|---|---|---|---|
| 1 | France | 37 | 21 | 23 | 81 |
| 2 | Italy | 34 | 15 | 7 | 56 |
| 3 | Great Britain | 10 | 22 | 18 | 50 |
| 4 | US | 12 | 14 | 17 | 43 |
| 5 | Germany* | 11 | 13 | 12 | 36 |
| 6 | Netherlands | 13 | 15 | 7 | 35 |
| 7 | Australia | 7 | 13 | 11 | 31 |
| 8= | Belgium | 6 | 8 | 10 | 24 |
| = | Soviet Union# | 11 | 4 | 9 | 24 |
| 10 | Denmark | 6 | 7 | 8 | 21 |

*\* Not including West/East Germany 1968–88*

*# Includes Unified Team of 1992; excludes Russia since then*

# TOP 10 OLDEST CLASSIC CYCLING RACES
*(Race/first held)*

❶ Bordeaux–Paris, 1891 ❷ Liège Bastogne–Liège, 1892 ❸ Paris–Brussels, 1893 ❹ Paris–Roubaix, 1896 ❺ Tour de France, 1903 ❻ Tour of Lombardy, 1905 ❼ Giro d'Italia (Tour of Italy), 1906 ❽ Milan–San Remo, 1907 ❾ Tour of Flanders, 1913 ❿ Grand Prix des Nations, 1932

**Did You Know?** The first cycle race in the US was held over a 3-mile course in Beacon Park, Boston, Mass., on May 24, 1878. It was won by C. A. Parker in a time of 12 minutes 27 seconds.

# Auto Racing

## LATEST DRIVERS KILLED DURING THE INDIANAPOLIS 500

| | DRIVER | YEAR |
|---|---|---|
| 1 | Swede Savage | 1973 |
| 2= | Eddie Sachs | 1964 |
| = | Dave MacDonald | 1964 |
| 4 | Pat O'Connor | 1958 |
| 5 | Bill Vukovich Sr. | 1955 |
| 6 | Carl Scarborough | 1953 |
| 7 | Shorty Cantlon | 1947 |
| 8 | Floyd Roberts | 1939 |
| 9 | Clay Weatherly | 1935 |
| 10= | Mark Billman | 1933 |
| = | Lester Spangler | 1933 |

Since the death of Harry Martin during practice for the first-ever Indianapolis 500 in 1911, the race has claimed the lives of a total of 38 drivers, 14 of them during the race, and a further 24 in practice or while qualifying.

## MONEY WINNERS AT THE INDIANAPOLIS 500

| | DRIVER | FINISHING POSITION | TOTAL PRIZES, 2000 ($) |
|---|---|---|---|
| 1 | Juan Montoya | 1 | 1,235,690 |
| 2 | Buddy Lazier | 2 | 567,100 |
| 3 | Eliseo Salazar | 3 | 468,900 |
| 4 | Greg Ray | 33 | 388,700 |
| 5 | Eddie Cheever Jr. | 5 | 360,000 |
| 6 | Jeff Ward | 4 | 355,000 |
| 7 | Scott Goodyear | 9 | 347,800 |
| 8 | Scott Sharp | 10 | 312,000 |
| 9 | Stephan Gregoire | 8 | 305,900 |
| 10 | Mark Dismore | 11 | 293,500 |
| | *Total prize money for all drivers* | | 9,436,505 |

Source: *Indianapolis Motor Speedway*

Drivers are ranked here according to their winnings, which vary according to such designations as first using a particular brand of tire.

## FASTEST WINNING SPEEDS OF THE DAYTONA 500

| | DRIVER*/CAR/YEAR | SPEED MPH | KM/H |
|---|---|---|---|
| 1 | Buddy Baker, Oldsmobile, 1980 | 177.602 | 285.823 |
| 2 | Bill Elliott, Ford, 1987 | 176.263 | 283.668 |
| 3 | Dale Earnhardt#, Chevrolet, 1998 | 172.712 | 277.953 |
| 4 | Bill Elliott, Ford, 1985 | 172.265 | 277.234 |
| 5 | Dale Earnhardt, Chevrolet, 1998 | 172.071 | 276.921 |
| 6 | Richard Petty, Buick, 1981 | 169.651 | 273.027 |
| 7 | Derrike Cope, Chevrolet, 1990 | 165.761 | 266.766 |
| 8 | Michael Waltrip, Chevrolet, 2001 | 161.783 | 260.364 |
| 9 | Jeff Gordon, Chevrolet, 1999 | 161.551 | 259.991 |
| 10 | A. J. Foyt Jr., Mercury, 1972 | 161.550 | 259.990 |

\* All winners from the US

\# Killed on final turn of last lap of 2001 Daytona 500

Source: *NASCAR*

## FASTEST WINNING SPEEDS OF THE INDIANAPOLIS 500

| | DRIVER/COUNTRY* | CAR | YEAR | SPEED MPH | KM/H |
|---|---|---|---|---|---|
| 1 | Arie Luyendyk, Netherlands | Lola-Chevrolet | 1990 | 185.984 | 299.307 |
| 2 | Rick Mears | Chevrolet-Lumina | 1991 | 176.457 | 283.980 |
| 3 | Bobby Rahal | March-Cosworth | 1986 | 170.722 | 274.750 |
| 4 | Emerson Fittipaldi, Brazil | Penske-Chevrolet | 1989 | 167.581 | 269.695 |
| 5 | Rick Mears | March-Cosworth | 1984 | 163.612 | 263.308 |
| 6 | Mark Donohue | McLaren-Offenhauser | 1972 | 162.962 | 262.619 |
| 7 | Al Unser | March-Cosworth | 1987 | 162.175 | 260.995 |
| 8 | Tom Sneva | March-Cosworth | 1983 | 162.117 | 260.902 |
| 9 | Gordon Johncock | Wildcat-Cosworth | 1982 | 162.029 | 260.760 |
| 10 | Al Unser | Lola-Cosworth | 1978 | 161.363 | 259.689 |

\* All from the US unless otherwise stated

Source: *Indianapolis Motor Speedway*

The first Indianapolis 500, known affectionately as the "Indy," was held on Memorial Day, May 30, 1911, and was won by Ray Harroun driving a bright yellow 447-cubic inch six-cylinder Marmon Wasp at an average speed of 74.59 mph. The race takes place over 200 laps of the 2.5-mile Indianapolis Raceway, which from 1927 to 1945 was owned by World War I flying ace Eddie Rickenbacker.

### HARLEY AND DAVIDSON

In Milwaukee, Wisconsin, in 1901, childhood friends William Harley (1880–1943) and Arthur Davidson (1881–1950) began their first motorcycle-building experiments, based on a bicycle with an engine they built themselves. Davidson's two brothers joined the firm, which steadily increased production and introduced such innovations as the twist-grip throttle (1909). The Harley-Davidson soon became sufficiently established that 20,000 were supplied to the US army in World War I, and 90,000 in World War II. The firm remains the oldest-established and one of the largest motorcycle companies in the world.

## TOP 10 ★
# NASCAR MONEY WINNERS OF ALL TIME*

| | DRIVER | TOTAL PRIZES ($) |
|---|---|---|
| 1 | Dale Earnhardt | 38,262,514 |
| 2 | Jeff Gordon | 29,570,670 |
| 3 | Rusty Wallace | 23,269,214 |
| 4 | Mark Martin | 23,126,188 |
| 5 | Bill Elliott | 23,005,860 |
| 6 | Terry Labonte | 22,632,033 |
| 7 | Dale Jarrett | 22,116,791 |
| 8 | Darrell Waltrip | 19,256,474 |
| 9 | Ricky Rudd | 18,970,391 |
| 10 | Geoffrey Bodine | 14,689,188 |

\* To December 6, 2000
Source: NASCAR

## TOP 10 ★
# DRIVERS WITH THE MOST WINSTON CUP WINS

| | DRIVER | YEARS | VICTORIES |
|---|---|---|---|
| 1 | Richard Petty | 1958–92 | 200 |
| 2 | David Pearson | 1960–86 | 105 |
| 3 = | Bobby Allison | 1975–88 | 84 |
| = | Darrell Waltrip* | 1975–92 | 84 |
| 5 | Cale Yarborough | 1957–88 | 83 |
| 6 | Dale Earnhardt# | 1979–2000 | 76 |
| 7 | Lee Petty | 1949–64 | 54 |
| 8 | Rusty Wallace* | 1986-2000 | 53 |
| 9 | Jeff Gordon* | 1994-2000 | 52 |
| 10 = | Ned Jarrett | 1953–66 | 50 |
| = | Junior Johnson | 1953–66 | 50 |

\* Still driving at end of 2000 season
# Killed on final turn of last lap of 2001 Daytona 500
Source: NASCAR

The Winston Cup is a season-long series of races organized by the National Association of Stock Car Auto Racing, Inc. (NASCAR). Races, which take place over enclosed circuits such as Daytona speedway, are among the most popular motor races in the US. The series started in 1949 as the Grand National series, but changed its name to the Winston Cup in 1970.

## TOP 10 ★
# CART MONEY WINNERS OF ALL TIME

| | DRIVER | TOTAL PRIZES* ($) |
|---|---|---|
| 1 | Al Unser Jr. | 18,342,156 |
| 2 | Michael Andretti | 16,841,369 |
| 2 | Bobby Rahal | 16,344,008 |
| 4 | Emerson Fittipaldi | 14,293,625 |
| 5 | Mario Andretti | 11,552,154 |
| 6 | Rick Mears | 11,050,807 |
| 7 | Jimmy Vasser | 9,809,994 |
| 8 | Danny Sullivan | 8,884,126 |
| 9 | Paul Tracy | 8,011,570 |
| 10 | Arie Luyendyk | 7,732,188 |

\* As at December 2000
Source: Championship Auto Racing Teams

## TOP 10 ★
# CART DRIVERS WITH THE MOST RACE WINS

| | DRIVER | YEARS | WINS |
|---|---|---|---|
| 1 | A. J. Foyt Jr. | 1960–81 | 67 |
| 2 | Mario Andretti | 1965–93 | 52 |
| 3 | Michael Andretti | 1986–2000 | 40 |
| 4 | Al Unser | 1965–87 | 39 |
| 5 | Bobby Unser | 1966–81 | 35 |
| 6 | Al Unser Jr. | 1984–95 | 31 |
| 7 | Rick Mears | 1978–91 | 29 |
| 8 | Johnny Rutherford | 1965–86 | 27 |
| 9 | Rodger Ward | 1953–66 | 26 |
| 10 | Gordon Johncock | 1965–83 | 25 |

Source: Championship Auto Racing Teams

Two generations of the Unser family dominate the CART scene. Al and Bobby are brothers, while Al's son Al Jr. also makes a showing here and as all-time money winner. In 1998, Bobby's son Robby also entered Indy car racing. Michael Andretti, who started his CART career in 1983, is the only current driver in this list. Youngest-ever champion and 2000 Indianapolis 500 winner Juan Montoya also seemed destined for inclusion, but transfered to Formula One.

## TOP 10 ★
# MOTORCYCLE RIDERS WITH THE MOST WORLD SUPERBIKE CHAMPIONSHIP WINS

| | RIDER/COUNTRY | WINS |
|---|---|---|
| 1 | Carl Fogarty, UK | 56 |
| 2 | Doug Polen, US | 27 |
| 3 | Raymand Roche, France | 23 |
| 4 | Troy Corser, Australia | 19 |
| 5 = | Colin Edwards, US | 15 |
| = | John Kocinski, US | 15 |
| 7 = | Pier Francesco Chili, Italy | 14 |
| = | Scott Russell, US | 14 |
| 9 | Giancarlo Falappa, Italy | 12 |
| 10 | Aalon Slight, New Zealand | 11 |

## THE 10 ★
# LATEST WORLD CHAMPION ENDURANCE MOTORCYCLE RIDERS

| YEAR | RIDER(S)/COUNTRY | BIKE |
|---|---|---|
| 2000 | Peter Linden, Sweden/ Warwick Nowland, UK | Suzuki |
| 1999 | Terry Rymer, UK/ Jéhan d'Orgeix, France | Suzuki |
| 1998 | Doug Polen, US/ Christian Lavielle, France | Honda |
| 1997 | Peter Goddard, Australia/ Doug Polen, US | Suzuki |
| 1996 | Brian Morrison, UK | Kawasaki |
| 1995 | Stephene Mertens, Belgium/ Jean Michel Mattioli, France | Honda |
| 1994 | Adrien Morillas, France | Kawasaki |
| 1993 | Doug Toland, US | Kawasaki |
| 1992 | Terry Rymer, UK/ Carl Fogarty, UK | Kawasaki |
| 1991 | Alex Vieira, Portugal | Kawasaki |

The World Endurance Championship includes four 24-hour races, at Le Mans (France), Spa Francorchamps (Belgium), Oschersleben (Germany), and Bol d'Or (France), and two eight-hour races at Estoril (Portugal) and Suzuka (Japan).

---

**After whom or what are Derby races named?**
*see p.268 for the answer*
A Edward Stanley, 12th Earl of Derby
B The city of Derby
C From the French *d'arbre*

# Golfing Greats

## YOUNGEST WINNERS OF THE BRITISH OPEN

| | PLAYER/COUNTRY | YRS | AGE MTHS |
|---|---|---|---|
| 1 | Tom Morris Jr., UK | 17 | 5 |
| 2 | Willie Auchterlonie, UK | 21 | 1 |
| 3 | Severiano Ballesteros, Spain | 22 | 3 |
| 4 | John H. Taylor, UK | 23 | 3 |
| 5 | Gary Player, South Africa | 23 | 8 |
| 6 | Bobby Jones, US | 24 | 3 |
| 7 | Tiger Woods, US | 24 | 6 |
| 8 | Peter Thomson, Australia | 24 | 11 |
| 9 | =Arthur Havers, UK | 25 | 0 |
| | =Tony Jacklin, UK | 25 | 0 |

The dates of birth for Tom Kidd and Jack Simpson, the 1873 and 1884 winners, have never been established. Hugh Kirkaldy, the 1891 winner, was born in 1865 and could have been either 25 or 26 when he won the title, but, again, his exact date of birth has never been confirmed.

## AMERICAN PLAYERS WITH THE MOST WINS IN THE RYDER CUP

| | PLAYER | WINS |
|---|---|---|
| 1 | Arnold Palmer | 22 |
| 2 | =Billy Casper | 20 |
| | =Lanny Wadkins | 20 |
| 4 | =Jack Nicklaus | 17 |
| | =Lee Trevino | 17 |
| 6 | Tom Kite | 15 |
| 7 | Gene Littler | 14 |
| 8 | Hale Irwin | 13 |
| 9 | =Sam Snead | 10 |
| | =Tom Watson | 10 |

The Ryder Cup was launched in 1927 by British seed merchant and golf enthusiast Samuel Ryder (1858–1936). Held every two years (with a break between 1939 and 1945 due to World War II), the venues alternate between the US and Great Britain, the US originally competing against Great Britain and Ireland, but, since 1979, against Europe.

## LOWEST WINNING SCORES IN THE US MASTERS

| | PLAYER* | YEAR | SCORE |
|---|---|---|---|
| 1 | Tiger Woods | 1997 | 270 |
| 2 | =Jack Nicklaus | 1965 | 271 |
| | =Raymond Floyd | 1976 | 271 |
| 4 | =Ben Hogan | 1953 | 274 |
| | =Ben Crenshaw | 1995 | 274 |
| 6 | =Severiano Ballesteros, Spain | 1980 | 275 |
| | =Fred Couples | 1992 | 275 |
| 8 | =Arnold Palmer | 1964 | 276 |
| | =Jack Nicklaus | 1975 | 276 |
| | =Tom Watson | 1977 | 276 |
| | =Nick Faldo, UK | 1996 | 276 |

* All from the US unless otherwise stated

The US Masters, the brainchild of American amateur golfer Robert Tyre "Bobby" Jones, is the only major played on the same course each year, at Augusta, Georgia. The course was built on the site of an old nursery, and the abundance of flowers, shrubs, and plants is a reminder of its former days, with each of the 18 holes named after the plants growing adjacent to it.

## WINNERS OF WOMEN'S MAJORS

| | PLAYER* | TITLES |
|---|---|---|
| 1 | Patty Berg | 16 |
| 2 | =Louise Suggs | 13 |
| | =Mickey Wright | 13 |
| 4 | Babe Zaharias | 12 |
| 5 | =Julie Inkster | 8 |
| | =Betsy Rawls | 8 |
| 7 | JoAnne Carner | 7 |
| 8 | =Pat Bradley | 6 |
| | =Glenna Collett Vare | 6 |
| | =Betsy King | 6 |
| | =Patty Sheehan | 6 |
| | =Kathy Whitworth | 6 |

* All from the US

**BEST OF THE REST**
*Swedish golfer Annika Sorenstam (b. 1970) won more LPGA tournaments (18) than any other player in the 1990s and is the highest-earning non-American woman golfer of all time.*

## CAREER EARNINGS BY WOMEN GOLFERS

| | PLAYER*/YEARS | WINNINGS# ($) |
|---|---|---|
| 1 | Betsy King, 1977–2000 | 6,828,688 |
| 2 | Annika Sorenstam, Sweden, 1992–2000 | 6,200,596 |
| 3 | Karrie Webb, Australia, 1995–2000 | 6,162,895 |
| 4 | Julie Inkster, 1983–2000 | 6,057,400 |
| 5 | Beth Daniel, 1979–2000 | 6,022,461 |
| 6 | Dottie Pepper, 1987–2000 | 5,882,131 |
| 7 | Pat Bradley, 1974–2000 | 5,743,605 |
| 8 | Patty Sheehan, 1980–2000 | 5,500,983 |
| 9 | Meg Mallon, 1987–2000 | 5,466,338 |
| 10 | Nancy Lopez, 1977–2000 | 5,297,955 |

* All from the US unless otherwise stated
# As of November 20, 2000

## TOP 10 ★
### WINS IN A US SEASON

| | PLAYER | YEAR | WINS |
|---|---|---|---|
| 1 | Byron Nelson | 1945 | 18 |
| 2 | Ben Hogan | 1946 | 13 |
| 3 | Sam Snead | 1950 | 11 |
| 4 | Ben Hogan | 1948 | 10 |
| 5 | Paul Runyan | 1933 | 9 |
| = | Tiger Woods | 2000 | 9* |
| 7= | Horton Smith | 1929 | 8 |
| = | Gene Sarazen | 1930 | 8 |
| = | Harry Cooper | 1937 | 8 |
| = | Sam Snead | 1938 | 8 |
| = | Henry Picard | 1939 | 8 |
| = | Byron Nelson | 1944 | 8 |
| = | Arnold Palmer | 1960 | 8 |
| = | Johnny Miller | 1974 | 8 |
| = | Tiger Woods | 1999 | 8 |

*\* Woods' total in 2000 includes his British Open win which, since 1995, has been included as an Official US PGA Tour event*

Source: *PGA*

Having won eight Tour events in 1944, Byron Nelson went on to shatter the US record the following year with a stunning 18 wins.

---

## TOP 10 MONEY-WINNING GOLFERS, 2000
*(Player\*/winnings in 2000#, $)*

❶ **Tiger Woods**, 9,501,387 ❷ **Phil Mickelson**, 4,791,743
❸ **Ernie Els**, South Africa, 3,855,829 ❹ **Hal Sutton**, 3,061,444 ❺ **Lee Westwood**, UK, 2,966,066 ❻ **Vijay Singh**, Fiji, 2,702,858 ❼ **Darren Clarke**, UK, 2,671,040 ❽ **Mike Weir**, 2,547,829 ❾ **Jesper Parnevik**, Sweden, 2,499,079 ❿ **David Duval**, 2,471,244

*\* All from the US unless otherwise stated*
*# As of December 18, 2000*
This list is based on winnings on the world's five top Tours: US PGA Tour, European PGA Tour, PGA Tour of Japan, Australasian PGA Tour, and FNB Tour of South Africa.

---

## TOP 10 ★
### PLAYERS TO WIN THE MOST MAJORS IN A CAREER

| | PLAYER* | BRITISH OPEN | US OPEN | US MASTERS | PGA | TOTAL |
|---|---|---|---|---|---|---|
| 1 | Jack Nicklaus | 3 | 4 | 6 | 5 | 18 |
| 2 | Walter Hagen | 4 | 2 | 0 | 5 | 11 |
| 3= | Ben Hogan | 1 | 4 | 2 | 2 | 9 |
| = | Gary Player, South Africa | 3 | 1 | 3 | 2 | 9 |
| 5 | Tom Watson | 5 | 1 | 2 | 0 | 8 |
| 6= | Bobby Jones | 3 | 4 | 0 | 0 | 7 |
| = | Arnold Palmer | 2 | 1 | 4 | 0 | 7 |
| = | Gene Sarazen | 1 | 2 | 1 | 3 | 7 |
| = | Sam Snead | 1 | 0 | 3 | 3 | 7 |
| = | Harry Vardon, UK | 6 | 1 | 0 | 0 | 7 |

*\* All from the US unless otherwise stated*

**GOOD AS GOLD**

*In a career spanning over 30 years, Jack Nicklaus, nicknamed the Golden Bear, won more majors than any other player in golfing history.*

# Horse Racing

## STEEPLECHASE TRAINERS, 2000

| | TRAINER | WINNINGS ($) | WINS |
|---|---|---|---|
| 1 | Tom Voss | 365,712 | 24 |
| 2 | Sanna Neilson | 602,314 | 21 |
| 3 = | Ricky Hendriks | 238,426 | 16 |
| = | Bruce Miller | 604,804 | 16 |
| = | Jonathan Sheppard | 596,074 | 16 |
| 6 | Jack Fisher | 317,692 | 11 |
| 7 | Neil Morris | 104,625 | 9 |
| 8 | Kathy Neilson | 88,865 | 8 |
| 9 | Janet Elliot | 415,536 | 7 |
| 10 | Charlie Fenwick | 202,622 | 6 |

Source: Steeplechase Times/National Steeplechase Association

## TOP 10 ★
## MONEY-WINNING HORSES, 2000

| | HORSE | WINNINGS ($) |
|---|---|---|
| 1 | Dubai Millennium | 3,600,000 |
| 2 | Tiznow | 3,445,950 |
| 3 | Fantastic Light | 3,238,998 |
| 4 | T.M. Opera O | 2,278,332 |
| 5 | Fusaichi Pegasus | 1,987,800 |
| 6 | Spain | 1,979,500 |
| 7 | Captain Steve | 1,882,276 |
| 8 | Behrens | 1,764,500 |
| 9 | Lemon Drop Kid | 1,673,900 |
| 10 | Giant's Causeway | 1,600,593 |

Source: National Thoroughbred Racing Association

## TOP 10 ★
## MONEY-WINNING HORSES

| | HORSE | WINS | WINNINGS ($) |
|---|---|---|---|
| 1 | Cigar | 19 | 9,999,815 |
| 2 | Skip Away | 18 | 9,616,360 |
| 3 | Hokuto Vega | 16 | 8,337,603 |
| 4 | Silver Charm | 12 | 6,944,369 |
| 5 | Alysheba | 11 | 6,679,242 |
| 6 | John Henry | 39 | 6,597,947 |
| 7 | Singspiel | 9 | 5,950,217 |
| 8 | Sakura Laurel | 9 | 5,763,926 |
| 9 | Best Pal | 18 | 5,668,245 |
| 10 | Taiki Blizzard | 6 | 5,544,484 |

Source: National Thoroughbred Racing Association

## TOP 10 ★
## FASTEST WINNING TIMES OF THE KENTUCKY DERBY

| | HORSE | YEAR | TIME MIN:SEC |
|---|---|---|---|
| 1 | Secretariat | 1973 | 1:59.2 |
| 2 | Northern Dancer | 1964 | 2:00.0 |
| 3 | Spend a Buck | 1985 | 2:00.2 |
| 4 | Decidedly | 1962 | 2:00.4 |
| 5 | Proud Clarion | 1967 | 2:00.6 |
| 6 | Grindstone | 1996 | 2:01.0 |
| 7 = | Lucky Debonair | 1965 | 2:01.2 |
| = | Affirmed | 1978 | 2:01.2 |
| = | Thunder Gulch | 1995 | 2:01.2 |
| = | Fusaichi Pegasus | 2000 | 2:01.2 |

Source: The Jockey Club

The Kentucky Derby is held on the first Saturday in May at Churchill Downs, Louisville, Kentucky. The course was established in 1874 by Colonel Lewis Clark. The first leg of the Triple Crown, it was first raced in 1875 over a distance of 1 mile 4 furlongs, but after 1896 was reduced to 1 mile 2 furlongs. It is said that the hat, known in England as a "bowler," manufactured in the US by James H. Knapp of South Norwalk, Connecticut, became popular attire at the first Kentucky Derbys, thereby acquiring the name "derby."

### DERBY

The man who gave his name to horse races in the UK, US, and elsewhere was Edward Stanley, 12th Earl of Derby (1752–1834). He offered a prize for a race for 3-year-old fillies, which was named after The Oaks, the house he lived in near the Epsom racecourse in Surrey, UK, and in 1780 he introduced a race for 3-year-old fillies or colts, which was named the Derby. Further Derbies followed – the Hong Kong Derby was first run in 1873, and the Kentucky Derby followed shortly after in 1875 – while the name came to be used in a more general way to describe other sporting events.

WHO WAS · WHO WAS · WHO WAS · WHO WAS · WHO WAS

## TOP 10 ★
## US JOCKEYS WITH THE MOST WINS IN A CAREER

| | JOCKEYS | YEARS RIDING | WINS |
|---|---|---|---|
| 1 | Laffit Pincay Jr. | 37 | 9,052 |
| 2 | Bill Shoemaker | 42 | 8,833 |
| 3 | Pat Day | 28 | 7,892 |
| 4 | David Gall | 43 | 7,396 |
| 5 | Russell Baze | 27 | 7,234 |
| 6 | Chris McCarron | 26 | 7,173 |
| 7 | Angel Cordero Jr. | 35 | 7,057 |
| 8 | Jorge Velasquez | 33 | 6,795 |
| 9 | Sandy Hawley | 31 | 6,449 |
| 10 | Larry Snyder | 35 | 6,388 |

Source: NTRA Communications

## TOP 10 ★
## MONEY-WINNING NORTH AMERICAN JOCKEYS

| | JOCKEY | EARNINGS ($) |
|---|---|---|
| 1 | Chris McCarron | 247,335,327 |
| 2 | Pat Day | 241,500,532 |
| 3 | Laffit Pincay Jr. | 215,819,671 |
| 4 | Jerry Bailey | 199,325,433 |
| 5 | Gary Stevens | 190,344,329 |
| 5 | Eddie Delahoussaye | 182,028,673 |
| 7 | Angel Cordero Jr. | 164,561,227 |
| 8 | Jose Santos | 132,564,875 |
| 9 | Jorge Velasquez | 125,534,962 |
| 10 | Bill Shoemaker | 123,375,524 |

Source: NTRA Communications

## TOP 10 ★
# JOCKEYS IN THE BREEDERS' CUP

| | JOCKEY | YEARS | WINS |
|---|---|---|---|
| 1 | Pat Day | 1984–99 | 11 |
| 2 | Jerry Bailey | 1991–2000 | 9 |
| 3 = | Chris McCarron | 1985–2000 | 8 |
| = | Mike Smith | 1992–97 | 8 |
| = | Gary Stevens | 1990–2000 | 8 |
| 6 = | Eddie Delahoussaye | 1984–93 | 7 |
| = | Laffit Pincay Jr. | 1985–93 | 7 |
| 8 = | Jose Santos | 1986–97 | 6 |
| = | Pat Valenzuela | 1986–92 | 6 |
| 10 | Corey Nakatani | 1996–99 | 5 |

Source: *The Breeders Cup*

Held at a different venue each year, the Breeders' Cup is an end-of-season gathering with seven races run during the day, with the season's best thoroughbreds competing in each category. Staged in October or November, there is $10 million prize money on offer, with $3 million going to the winner of the day's senior race, the Classic. Churchill Downs is the most-used venue, with five Breeders' Cups since the first in 1984.

## THE 10 ★
# LATEST TRIPLE CROWN-WINNING HORSES*

| | HORSE* | YEAR |
|---|---|---|
| 1 | Affirmed | 1978 |
| 2 | Seattle Slew | 1977 |
| 3 | Secretariat | 1973 |
| 4 | Citation | 1948 |
| 5 | Assault | 1946 |
| 6 | Count Fleet | 1943 |
| 7 | Whirlaway | 1941 |
| 8 | War Admiral | 1937 |
| 9 | Omaha | 1935 |
| 10 | Gallant Fox | 1930 |

* Horses that have won the Kentucky Derby, the Preakness, and Belmont Stakes in the same season

Since 1875, only 11 horses have won all three races in one season.

## TOP 10 ★
# MONEY-WINNING HORSES IN A HARNESS-RACING CAREER

| TROTTERS | | | PACERS | |
|---|---|---|---|---|
| HORSE | WINNINGS ($) | | WINNINGS ($) | HORSE |
| Moni Maker | 5,589,256 | 1 | 3,225,653 | Nihilator |
| Peace Corps | 4,180,001 | 2 | 3,085,083 | Artsplace |
| Ourasi | 4,010,105 | 3 | 3,021,363 | Presidential Ball |
| Mack Lobell | 3,917,594 | 4 | 2,944,591 | Matt's Scooter |
| Reve d'Udon | 3,611,351 | 5 | 2,819,102 | On The Road Again |
| Zoogin | 3,513,324 | 6 | 2,763,527 | Riyadh |
| Sea Cove | 3,138,986 | 7 | 2,580,171 | Gallo Blue Chip |
| Ina Scot | 2,897,044 | 8 | 2,570,357 | Beach Towel |
| Defi d'Aunou | 2,762,409 | 9 | 2,541,647 | Western Hanover |
| Ideal du Gazeau | 2,744,777 | 10 | 2,514,465 | Red Bow Tie |

Harness-racing is one of the oldest sports in the US, its origins going back to the Colonial period, when many races were held along the turnpikes of New York and the New England colonies. After growing in popularity in the 19th century, the exotically titled governing body, the National Association for the Promotion of the Interests of the Trotting Turf (now the National Trotting Association), was founded in 1870. While widespread in the US, harness-racing is also popular in Australia and New Zealand, and, increasingly, elsewhere around the globe. It has enjoyed a following in Britain since the 1960s, with the opening of a trotting track at Prestatyn, North Wales. Harness-racing horses pull a jockey on a two-wheeled "sulky" (introduced in 1829) around an oval track. Unlike thoroughbred racehorses, standardbred harness-racing horses are trained to trot and pace, but do not gallop. A trotter is a horse whose diagonally opposite legs move forward together, while a pacer's legs are extended laterally and with a "swinging motion." Pacers usually travel faster than trotters.

## TOP 10 ★
# JOCKEYS IN THE US TRIPLE CROWN RACES

| | JOCKEY | KENTUCKY | PREAKNESS | BELMONT | TOTAL |
|---|---|---|---|---|---|
| 1 | Eddie Arcaro | 5 | 6 | 6 | 17 |
| 2 | Bill Shoemaker | 4 | 2 | 5 | 11 |
| 3 = | Pat Day | 1 | 5 | 3 | 9 |
| = | Bill Hartack | 5 | 3 | 1 | 9 |
| = | Earle Sande | 3 | 1 | 5 | 9 |
| 6 | Jimmy McLaughlin | 1 | 1 | 6 | 8 |
| 7 = | Angel Cordero Jr. | 3 | 2 | 1 | 6 |
| = | Chas Kurtsinger | 2 | 2 | 2 | 6 |
| = | Gary Stevens | 3 | 1 | 2 | 6 |
| = | Ron Turcotte | 2 | 2 | 2 | 6 |

The US Triple Crown consists of the Kentucky Derby, Preakness Stakes (held at Pimlico, Maryland, since 1873), and Belmont Stakes (held at Belmont, New York, since 1867). The only jockey to complete the Triple Crown twice is Eddie Arcaro, on Whirlaway in 1941 and on Citation in 1948.

**Did You Know?** The first horse race trotting course in the US was established at Jamaica, New York. A horse called Screwdriver won the inaugural race there on May 16, 1825.

# Hockey Highlights

## BEST-PAID PLAYERS IN THE NHL, 2000–2001

| PLAYER | TEAM | SALARY ($) |
|---|---|---|
| 1 =Paul Kariya | Anaheim Mighty Ducks | 10,000,000 |
| =Peter Forsberg | Colorado Avalanche | 10,000,000 |
| 3 Jaromir Jagr | Pittsburgh Penguins | 9,482,708 |
| 4 Pavel Bure | Florida Panthers | 9,000,000 |
| 5 Keith Tkachuk | Phoenix Coyotes | 8,300,000 |
| 6 =Steve Yzerman | Detroit Red Wings | 8,000,000 |
| =Teemu Selanne | Anaheim Mighty Ducks | 8,000,000 |
| 8 Joe Sakic | Colorado Avalanche | 7,900,000 |
| 9 Brian Leetch | New York Rangers | 7,680,000 |
| 10 =Patrick Roy | Colorado Avalanche | 7,500,000 |
| =Dominik Hasek | Buffalo Sabres | 7,500,000 |
| =Mats Sundin | Toronto Maple Leafs | 7,500,000 |

Source: *National Hockey League Players Association*

## GOALIES WITH THE BEST SAVES PERCENTAGES IN THE NHL, 2000–2001

| PLAYER/TEAM | GAMES PLAYED* | TOTAL SAVES | SAVES % |
|---|---|---|---|
| 1 Marty Turco, Dallas Stars | 26 | 492 | 92.5 |
| 2 Mike Dunham, Nashville Predators | 48 | 1,274 | 92.3 |
| 3 Sean Burke, Phoenix Coyotes | 62 | 1,628 | 92.2 |
| 4 =Roman Cechmanek, Philidelphia Flyers | 59 | 1,349 | 92.1 |
| =Dominik Hasek, Buffalo Sabres | 67 | 1,589 | 92.1 |
| 6 =Emmanuel Fernandez, Minnesota Wild | 42 | 1,055 | 92.0 |
| =Manny Legace, Detroit Red Wings | 39 | 836 | 92.0 |
| =Roberto Luongo, Florida Panthers | 47 | 1,226 | 92.0 |
| 9 Ron Tugnutt, Columbus Blue Jackets | 53 | 1,401 | 91.7 |
| 10 =Curtis Joseph, Toronto Maple Leafs | 68 | 1,744 | 91.5 |
| =Evgeni Nabokov, San Jose Sharks | 66 | 1,447 | 91.5 |

* Minimum qualification 20 games
Source: *National Hockey League Players Association*

## TOP 10 TEAM SALARIES IN THE NHL, 2000–2001

*(Team/salary, $)*

❶ New York Rangers, 60,732,037 ❷ Detroit Red Wings, 55,807,500 ❸ Dallas Stars, 55,342,200 ❹ Colorado Avalanche, 51,061,076 ❺ Philadelphia Flyers, 41,924,500 ❻ Anaheim Mighty Ducks, 41,847,500 ❼ Florida Panthers, 41,742,500 ❽ Toronto Maple Leafs, 41,096,273 ❾ Washington Capitals, 40,165,000 ❿ St. Louis Blues, 38,840,833

Source: *National Hockey League Players Association*

## GOAL SCORERS IN AN NHL SEASON

| PLAYER/TEAM | SEASON | GOALS |
|---|---|---|
| 1 Wayne Gretzky, Edmonton Oilers | 1981–82 | 92 |
| 2 Wayne Gretzky, Edmonton Oilers | 1983–84 | 87 |
| 3 Brett Hull, St. Louis Blues | 1990–91 | 86 |
| 4 Mario Lemieux, Pittsburgh Penguins | 1988–89 | 85 |
| 5 =Phil Esposito, Boston Bruins | 1970–71 | 76 |
| =Alexander Mogilny, Buffalo Sabres | 1992–93 | 76 |
| =Teemu Selanne, Winnipeg Jets | 1992–93 | 76 |
| 8 Wayne Gretzky, Edmonton Oilers | 1984–85 | 73 |
| 9 Brett Hull, St. Louis Blues | 1989–90 | 72 |
| 10 =Wayne Gretzky, Edmonton Oilers | 1982–83 | 71 |
| =Jari Kurri, Edmonton Oilers | 1984–85 | 71 |

## GOAL-SCORING ROOKIES IN THE NHL, 2000–2001

| PLAYER/TEAM | GAMES PLAYED | GOALS |
|---|---|---|
| 1 Brad Richards, Tampa Bay Lightning | 82 | 21 |
| 2 =Daniel Sedin, Vancouver Canucks | 75 | 20 |
| =Shane Willis, Carolina Hurricanes | 73 | 20 |
| 4 Martin Havlat, Ottawa Senators | 73 | 19 |
| 5 Marian Gaborik, Minnesota Wild | 71 | 18 |
| 6 Ruslan Fedotenko, Philadelphia Flyers | 74 | 16 |
| 7 Steven Reinprecht, Colorado Avalanche | 80 | 15 |
| 8 =Tomi Kallio, Atlanta Thrashers | 56 | 14 |
| =Ville Nieminen, Colorado Avalanche | 50 | 14 |
| 10 =Serge Aubin, Columbus Blue Jackets | 81 | 13 |
| =David Vyborny, Columbus Blue Jackets | 79 | 13 |

Source: *National Hockey League Players Association*

## TOP 10 ★
# GOALIES
# IN AN NHL CAREER*

| PLAYER | SEASONS | GAMES WON |
|---|---|---|
| 1 Patrick Roy# | 17 | 484 |
| 2 Terry Sawchuk | 21 | 447 |
| 3 Jacques Plante | 18 | 434 |
| 4 Tony Esposito | 16 | 423 |
| 5 Glenn Hall | 18 | 407 |
| 6 Grant Fuhr# | 19 | 403 |
| 7 Mike Vernon# | 18 | 383 |
| 8 Andy Moog | 18 | 372 |
| 9 Rogie Vachon | 16 | 355 |
| 10 Tom Barrasso# | 17 | 353 |

* Regular season only

# Still active at end of 2000–2001 season

## TOP 10 ★
# TEAMS
# WITH THE MOST
# STANLEY CUP WINS

| TEAM | WINS |
|---|---|
| 1 Montreal Canadiens | 23 |
| 2 Toronto Maple Leafs | 13 |
| 3 Detroit Red Wings | 9 |
| 4 =Boston Bruins | 5 |
| =Edmonton Oilers | 5 |
| 6 =New York Islanders | 4 |
| =New York Rangers | 4 |
| =Ottawa Senators | 4 |
| 9 Chicago Black Hawks | 3 |
| 10 =Philadelphia Flyers | 2 |
| =Pittsburgh Penguins | 2 |
| =Montreal Maroons | 2 |

During his time as Governor General of Canada from 1888 to 1893, Sir Frederick Arthur Stanley (Lord Stanley of Preston and 16th Earl of Derby) became interested in what is called hockey in the US, and ice hockey elsewhere, and in 1893 presented a trophy to be contested by the best amateur teams in Canada. The first trophy went to the Montreal Amateur Athletic Association, which won it without a challenge from any other team.

## TOP 10 ★
# WINNERS
# OF THE HART TROPHY

| PLAYER | YEARS | WINS |
|---|---|---|
| 1 Wayne Gretzky | 1980–89 | 9 |
| 2 Gordie Howe | 1952–63 | 6 |
| 3 Eddie Shore | 1933–38 | 4 |
| 4 =Bobby Clarke | 1973–76 | 3 |
| =Howie Morenz | 1928–32 | 3 |
| =Bobby Orr | 1970–72 | 3 |
| =Mario Lemieux | 1988–96 | 3 |
| 8 =Jean Beliveau | 1956–64 | 2 |
| =Bill Cowley | 1941–43 | 2 |
| =Phil Esposito | 1969–74 | 2 |
| =Dominic Hasek | 1997–98 | 2 |
| =Bobby Hull | 1965–66 | 2 |
| =Guy Lafleur | 1977–78 | 2 |
| =Mark Messier | 1990–92 | 2 |
| =Stan Mikita | 1967–68 | 2 |
| =Nels Stewart | 1926–30 | 2 |

Source: National Hockey League

## TOP 10 ★
# GOAL SCORERS
# IN 2000–2001

| PLAYER/TEAM | GOALS |
|---|---|
| 1 Pavel Bure, Florida Panthers | 59 |
| 2 Joe Sakic, Colorado Avalanche | 54 |
| 3 Jaromir Jagr, Pittsburgh Penguins | 52 |
| 4 Peter Bondra, Washington Capitals | 45 |
| 5 Alexei Kovalev, Pittsburgh Penguins | 44 |
| 6 Alexander Mogilny, New Jersey Devils | 43 |
| 7 =Milan Hejduk, Colorado Avalanche | 41 |
| =Markus Naslund, Vancouver Canucks | 41 |
| =Jeff O'Neill, Carolina Hurricanes | 41 |
| 10 =Bill Guerin, Boston Bruins | 40 |
| =Patrik Elias, New Jersey Devils | 40 |
| =Alexei Yashin, Ottawa Senators | 40 |
| =Scott Young, St. Louis Blues | 40 |

Source: National Hockey League

## TOP 10 ★
# GOAL SCORERS
# IN AN NHL CAREER*

| PLAYER | SEASONS | GOALS |
|---|---|---|
| 1 Wayne Gretzky | 20 | 894 |
| 2 Gordie Howe | 26 | 801 |
| 3 Marcel Dionne | 18 | 731 |
| 4 Phil Esposito | 18 | 717 |
| 5 Mike Gartner | 19 | 708 |
| 6 Mark Messier# | 22 | 651 |
| 7 Mario Lemieux# | 13 | 648 |
| 8 Bobby Hull | 16 | 610 |
| 9 Dino Ciccarelli | 19 | 608 |
| 10 Jari Kurri | 17 | 601 |

* Regular season only

# Still active at end of 2000–2001 season

## TOP 10 ★
# BIGGEST NHL ARENAS

| STADIUM/LOCATION HOME TEAM | CAPACITY |
|---|---|
| 1 Molson Centre, Montreal, Montreal Canadiens | 21,631 |
| 2 United Center, Chicago, Chicago Blackhawks | 21,500 |
| 3 =Dallas, Dallas, Dallas North Stars | 21,000 |
| =Air Canada Center, Toronto, Toronto Maple Leafs | 21,000 |
| 5 Canadian Airlines Saddledrome, Calgary, Calgary Flames | 20,035 |
| 6 =Raleigh Entertainment & Sports Arena, Raleigh, Carolina Hurricanes | 20,000 |
| =Staples Center, Los Angeles, Los Angeles Kings | 20,000 |
| =MCI Center, Washington, Washington Capitals | 20,000 |
| =Philips Arena, Atlanta, Atlanta Thrashers | 20,000 |
| =Nashville Arena, Nashville, Nashville Predators | 20,000 |

In what Olympic sport has the US won more than three times as many medals as the next country?

A Cycling
B Swimming
C Figure skating

see p.275 for the answer

# What a Racket

## WINNERS OF THE TABLE TENNIS WORLD CHAMPIONSHIP

| | COUNTRY | MEN'S | WOMEN'S | TOTAL |
|---|---|---|---|---|
| 1 | China | 13 | 13 | 26 |
| 2 | Japan | 7 | 8 | 15 |
| 3 | Hungary | 12 | – | 12 |
| 4 | Czechoslovakia | 6 | 3 | 9 |
| 5 | Romania | – | 5 | 5 |
| 6 | Sweden | 4 | – | 4 |
| 7= | England | 1 | 2 | 3 |
| = | US | 1 | 2 | 3 |
| 9 | Germany | – | 2 | 2 |
| 10= | Austria | 1 | – | 1 |
| = | North Korea | – | 1 | 1 |
| = | South Korea | – | 1 | 1 |
| = | USSR | – | 1 | 1 |

Originally a European event, table tennis was later extended to a world championship. This Top 10 takes account of men's wins since 1926 and women's since 1934. Winning men's teams receive the Swaythling Cup, and women the Marcel Corbillon Cup. The championship has been held biennially since 1959.

## WINNERS OF WOMEN'S GRAND SLAM SINGLES TITLES

| | PLAYER/COUNTRY | A | F | W | US | TOTAL |
|---|---|---|---|---|---|---|
| 1 | Margaret Court (née Smith), Aus | 11 | 5 | 3 | 5 | 24 |
| 2 | Steffi Graf, Ger | 4 | 5 | 7 | 5 | 21 |
| 3 | Helen Wills-Moody, US | 0 | 4 | 8 | 7 | 19 |
| 4= | Chris Evert-Lloyd, US | 2 | 7 | 3 | 6 | 18 |
| = | Martina Navratilova, Cze/US | 3 | 2 | 9 | 4 | 18 |
| 6= | Billie Jean King (née Moffitt), US | 1 | 1 | 6 | 4 | 12 |
| = | Suzanne Lenglen, Fra | 0 | 6 | 6 | 0 | 12 |
| 8= | Maureen Connolly, US | 1 | 2 | 3 | 3 | 9 |
| = | Monica Seles, Yug/US | 4 | 3 | 0 | 2 | 9 |
| 10 | Molla Mallory (née Bjurstedt), US | 0 | 0 | 0 | 8 | 8 |

*A – Australian Open; F – French Open; W – Wimbledon; US – US Open*

## WINNERS OF INDIVIDUAL OLYMPIC TENNIS MEDALS

| | PLAYER/COUNTRY/YEARS | GOLD | TOTAL |
|---|---|---|---|
| 1 | Max Decugis, France, 1900–20 | 4 | 6 |
| 2 | Kitty McKane, GB, 1920–24 | 1 | 5 |
| 3= | Reginald Doherty, GB, 1900–08 | 3 | 4 |
| = | Gunnar Setterwall, Sweden, 1908–12 | 0 | 4 |
| 5= | Charles Dixon, GB, 1908–12 | 0 | 3 |
| = | Mary Joe Fernandez, US, 1992–96 | 2 | 3 |
| = | Suzanne Lenglen, France, 1920 | 2 | 3 |
| = | Harold Mahony, Ireland, 1900 | 0 | 3 |
| = | Jana Novotna, Czech Republic, 1988–96 | 0 | 3 |
| = | Vince Richards, US, 1924 | 2 | 3 |
| = | Josiah Ritchie, GB, 1908 | 1 | 3 |
| = | Arantxa Sanchez-Vicario, Spain, 1992–96 | 0 | 3 |
| = | Charles Winslow, South Africa, 1912–20 | 2 | 3 |

## TOP 10 MALE TENNIS PLAYERS*

*(Player/country/weeks at No. 1)*

❶ Pete Sampras, US, 276 ❷ Ivan Lendl, Czechoslovakia, 270 ❸ Jimmy Connors, US, 268 ❹ John McEnroe, US, 170 ❺ Bjorn Borg, Sweden, 109 ❻ Stefan Edberg, Sweden, 72 ❼ Jim Courier, US, 58 ❽ Andre Agassi, US, 51 ❾ Ilie Nastase, Romania, 40 ❿ Mats Wilander, Sweden, 20

*\* Based on weeks at No. 1 in ATP rankings (1973–2000)*

### BRILLIANT CAREER

*In 1995, Andre Agassi was the 12th player to be ranked world No. 1. In 1999, he became only the fifth male player to complete a Grand Slam.*

## THE 10
# LATEST WINNERS OF THE SQUASH WORLD OPEN (FEMALE)

| YEAR* | PLAYER/COUNTRY |
|---|---|
| 1999 | Cassandra Campion, England |
| 1998 | Sarah Fitz-Gerald, Australia |
| 1997 | Sarah Fitz-Gerald |
| 1996 | Sarah Fitz-Gerald |
| 1995 | Michelle Martin, Australia |
| 1994 | Michelle Martin |
| 1993 | Michelle Martin |
| 1992 | Susan Devoy, New Zealand |
| 1991 | Susan Devoy |
| 1990 | Martine le Moignan, Guernsey |

* No championship in 2000

Source: Women's International Squash Players Assoc.

## TOP 10
# DAVIS CUP-WINNING TEAMS

| | COUNTRY | WINS |
|---|---|---|
| 1 | US | 31 |
| 2 | Australia | 21 |
| 3 | France | 8 |
| 4 | Sweden | 7 |
| 5 | Australasia | 6 |
| 6 | British Isles | 5 |
| 7 | Great Britain | 4 |
| 8 | West Germany | 2 |
| 9 | =Czechoslovakia | 1 |
| | =Germany | 1 |
| | =Italy | 1 |
| | =South Africa | 1 |

The UK has been represented by the British Isles from 1900 to 1921, England from 1922 to 1928, and Great Britain since 1929. The combined Australia/New Zealand team took part as Australasia between 1905 and 1922. Australia first entered a separate team in 1923 and New Zealand in 1924. South Africa's sole win was gained when, for political reasons, India refused to meet them in the 1974 final.

## THE 10
# LATEST WINNERS OF THE SQUASH WORLD OPEN (MALE)

| YEAR* | PLAYER/COUNTRY |
|---|---|
| 1999 | Peter Nichol, Scotland |
| 1998 | Jonathon Power, Canada |
| 1997 | Rodney Eyles, Australia |
| 1996 | Jansher Khan, Pakistan |
| 1995 | Jansher Khan |
| 1994 | Jansher Khan |
| 1993 | Jansher Khan |
| 1992 | Jansher Khan |
| 1991 | Rodney Martin, Australia |
| 1990 | Jansher Khan |

* No championship in 2000

Source: Professional Squash Association

## TOP 10
# CAREER MONEY-WINNING WOMEN TENNIS PLAYERS

| | PLAYER/COUNTRY | WINNINGS ($)* |
|---|---|---|
| 1 | Steffi Graf, Germany | 21,895,277 |
| 2 | Martina Navratilova, US | 20,396,399 |
| 3 | Arantxa Sanchez-Vicario, Spain | 15,747,252 |
| 4 | Martina Hingis, Switzerland | 15,080,325 |
| 5 | Monica Seles, US | 12,891,708 |
| 6 | Lindsay Davenport, US | 11,934,628 |
| 7 | Jana Novotna, Czech Republic | 11,249,134 |
| 8 | Conchita Martinez, Spain | 9,335,263 |
| 9 | Chris Evert-Lloyd, US | 8,896,195 |
| 10 | Gabriela Sabatini, Argentina | 8,785,850 |

* To end of 2000 season

**GOLDEN GIRL**

*In 1995 the first player ever to win all four Grand Slam titles four times each, Steffi Graf is also the sport's highest-earning female player of all time.*

## TOP 10
# PLAYERS WITH THE MOST BADMINTON WORLD TITLES

| | PLAYER/COUNTRY | MALE/FEMALE | TITLES |
|---|---|---|---|
| 1 | Park Joo-bong, South Korea | M | 5 |
| 2 | =Han Aiping, China | F | 3 |
| | =Li Lingwei, China | F | 3 |
| | =Guan Weizhan, China | F | 3 |
| | =Lin Ying, China | F | 3 |
| 6 | =Tian Bingyi, China | M | 2 |
| | =Christian Hadinata, Indonesia | M | 2 |
| | =Lene Köppen, Denmark | F | 2 |
| | =Kim Moon-soo, South Korea | M | 2 |
| | =Chung Myung-hee, South Korea | F | 2 |
| | =Nora Perry, England | F | 2 |
| | =Yang Yang, China | M | 2 |
| | =Li Yongbo, China | M | 2 |

273

# Water Sports

**POWERING AHEAD**
*American powerboat racer Bill Seebold retired in 1997 after 46 years in the sport, during which he won 912 races and some 60 championships.*

## COLLEGES IN THE INTERCOLLEGIATE ROWING ASSOCIATION REGATTA*

| | COLLEGE | WINNING YEARS (FIRST/LAST) | WINS |
|---|---|---|---|
| 1 | Cornell | 1896–1982 | 24 |
| 2 | Navy | 1921–84 | 13 |
| 3 | California | 1928–2000 | 12 |
| 4 | Washington | 1923–97 | 11 |
| 5 | Pennsylvania | 1898–1989 | 9 |
| 6 = | Wisconsin | 1951–90 | 7 |
| = | Brown | 1979–95 | 7 |
| 8 | Syracuse | 1904–78 | 6 |
| 9 | Columbia | 1895–1929 | 4 |
| 10 | Princeton | 1985–98 | 3 |

*\* Men's varsity eight-oared shells event*

Source: *Intercollegiate Rowing Association Regatta*

The Intercollegiate Rowing Association Regatta, a contest between northeastern universities, has been held since 1895.

## POWERBOAT DRIVERS WITH THE MOST RACE WINS

| | DRIVER | COUNTRY | WINS |
|---|---|---|---|
| 1 | Bill Seebold | US | 912 |
| 2 | Jimbo McConnell | US | 217 |
| 3 | Chip Hanuer | US | 203 |
| 4 | Steve Curtis | UK | 185 |
| 5 | Mikeal Frode | Sweden | 152 |
| 6 | Neil Holmes | UK | 147 |
| 7 | Peter Bloomfield | UK | 126 |
| 8 | Renato Molinari | Italy | 113 |
| 9 | Cees Van der Valden | Netherlands | 98 |
| 10 | Bill Muncey | US | 96 |

Source: Raceboat International

## WINNERS OF THE MOST SURFING WORLD CHAMPIONSHIPS

| | SURFER/COUNTRY | WINS |
|---|---|---|
| 1 | Kelly Slater, US | 6 |
| 2 | Mark Richards, Australia | 4 |
| 3 | Tom Curren, US | 3 |
| 4 = | Tom Carroll, Australia | 2 |
| = | Damien Hardman, Australia | 2 |
| 6 = | Wayne Bartholemew, Australia | 1 |
| = | Sunny Garcia, US | 1 |
| = | Derek Ho, US | 1 |
| = | Barton Lynch, Australia | 1 |
| = | Martin Potter, UK | 1 |
| = | Shaun Tomson, South Africa | 1 |
| = | Peter Townend, Australia | 1 |
| = | Mark Occhilupo, Australia | 1 |

## WATERSKIERS WITH THE MOST WORLD CUP WINS

| | WATERSKIER/COUNTRY | MALE/FEMALE | SLALOM | JUMP | TOTAL |
|---|---|---|---|---|---|
| 1 | Andy Mapple, UK | M | 29 | - | 29 |
| 2 | Emma Sheers, Australia | F | 2 | 15 | 17 |
| 3 | Jaret Llewellyn, Canada | M | - | 16 | 16 |
| 4 | Toni Neville, Australia | F | 4 | 7 | 11 |
| 5 | Wade Cox, US | M | 10 | - | 10 |
| 6 = | Bruce Neville, Australia | M | - | 9 | 9 |
| = | Kristi Overton-Johnson (née Overton), US | F | 9 | - | 9 |
| 8 | Freddy Krueger, US | M | - | 8 | 8 |
| 9 | Scot Ellis, US | M | - | 7 | 7 |
| 10 = | Susi Graham, Canada | F | 6 | - | 6 |
| = | Carl Roberge, US | M | 1 | 5 | 6 |

Waterskiing was invented in 1922 by 18-year-old Ralph W. Samuelson of Lake City, Minnesota, US, using two 8-ft (2.4-m) planks and 100 ft (30 m) of sash cord. It grew in popularity, and the first international governing body, the World Water Ski Union, was established in 1946 in Geneva, Switzerland. Its successor, the International Water Ski Federation, organized the Water Ski World Cup, which by the year 2000 had expanded to include the Moomba World Cup, the US Masters, the US Open, the French Masters, the Recetto World Cup, the Austrian Masters, the Italian Masters, and the British Masters.

What sort of vehicles are used in the Iditarod Race?
*see p.277 for the answer*
A Dog sleds
B Hovercraft
C Land yachts

## TOP 10 ★
# OLYMPIC ROWING COUNTRIES

| COUNTRY | GOLD | MEDALS | | TOTAL |
| | | SILVER | BRONZE | |
|---|---|---|---|---|
| **1** US | 29 | 29 | 21 | 79 |
| **2** =East Germany | 33 | 7 | 8 | 48 |
| =Germany* | 21 | 13 | 14 | 48 |
| **4** Great Britain | 21 | 16 | 7 | 44 |
| **5** USSR# | 12 | 20 | 11 | 43 |
| **6** Italy | 14 | 13 | 10 | 37 |
| **7** =Canada | 8 | 12 | 13 | 33 |
| =France | 6 | 14 | 13 | 33 |
| **9** Romania | 15 | 10 | 7 | 32 |
| **10** Australia | 7 | 8 | 10 | 25 |

\* *Not including West/East Germany 1968–88*

# *Includes Unified Team of 1992; excludes Russia since then*

## TOP 10 ★
# FASTEST MEN'S 100-M FREESTYLE TIMES IN THE SUMMER OLYMPICS

| SWIMMER/COUNTRY | YEAR | TIME (SECONDS) |
|---|---|---|
| **1** Pieter van den Hoogenband, Netherlands | 2000 | 47.84 |
| **2** Pieter van den Hoogenband | 2000 | 48.30 |
| **3** Matt Biondi, US | 1988 | 48.63 |
| **4** Pieter van den Hoogenband | 2000 | 48.64 |
| **5** Alexander Popov, Russia | 2000 | 48.69 |
| **6** Gary Hall Jr., US | 2000 | 48.73 |
| **7** =Alexander Popov | 1996 | 48.74 |
| =Michael Klim, US | 2000 | 48.74 |
| **9** Michael Klim | 2000 | 48.80 |
| **10** Gary Hall Jr. | 1996 | 48.81 |

Gary Hall Jr., who makes two appearances in this list, in two Olympics, is a member of a family of swimmers. His grandfather, Charles Keating, was an All-America swimmer at the University of Cincinnati, his uncle was a member of the 1976 US Olympics team, and his father, Gary Hall Sr., won silver medals at the 1968 and 1972 Olympics and a bronze in 1976.

## TOP 10 ★
# OLYMPIC SWIMMING COUNTRIES

| COUNTRY | GOLD | MEDALS* | | TOTAL |
| | | SILVER | BRONZE | |
|---|---|---|---|---|
| **1** US | 192 | 138 | 104 | 434 |
| **2** Australia | 45 | 46 | 51 | 142 |
| **3** East Germany | 38 | 32 | 22 | 92 |
| **4** USSR# | 18 | 24 | 27 | 69 |
| **5** Germany+ | 12 | 23 | 30 | 65 |
| **6** Great Britain | 14 | 22 | 26 | 62 |
| **7** Hungary | 24 | 20 | 16 | 60 |
| **8** Japan | 15 | 20 | 14 | 49 |
| **9** Netherlands | 14 | 14 | 16 | 44 |
| **10** Canada | 7 | 13 | 19 | 39 |

\* *Excluding diving, water polo, and synchronized swimming*

# *Includes Unified Team of 1992; excludes Russia since then*

+ *Not including West/East Germany 1968–88*

**WATER BOY**

*At the 2000 Sydney Olympics, Australia's teenage swimming sensation, Ian Thorpe, added three gold and two silver medals to his country's impressive tally.*

**SWISS ROLL**
*The bobsled event has been part of the Winter Olympics since 1924. Switzerland has won more medals than any other country.*

## TOP 10 OLYMPIC BOBSLEDDING COUNTRIES
*(Country/medals)*

**1** Switzerland, 26 **2** US, 14 **3** East Germany, 13 **4** = Germany\*, 11; = Italy, 11
**6** West Germany, 6 **7** Great Britain, 4 **8** = Austria, 3; = Soviet Union#, 3
**10** = Canada, 2; = Belgium, 2

*\* Not including East/West Germany 1968–88   # Includes Unified Team of 1992; excludes Russia since then*

### TOP 10 ★
## MEN'S WORLD AND OLYMPIC FIGURE SKATING TITLES

| | SKATER/COUNTRY | YEARS | TITLES |
|---|---|---|---|
| 1 | Ulrich Salchow, Sweden | 1901–11 | 11 |
| 2 | Karl Schäfer, Austria | 1930–36 | 9 |
| 3 | Richard Button, US | 1948–52 | 7 |
| 4 | Gillis Grafstrom, Sweden | 1920–29 | 6 |
| 5 | =Hayes Alan Jenkins, US | 1953–56 | 5 |
| | =Scott Hamilton, US | 1981–84 | 5 |
| 7 | =Willy Bockl, Austria | 1925–28 | 4 |
| | =Kurt Browning, Canada | 1989–93 | 4 |
| | =David Jenkins, US | 1957–60 | 4 |
| | =Ondrej Nepela, Czechoslovakia | 1971–73 | 4 |

### TOP 10 ★
## FASTEST SPEED SKATERS\*

| | SKATER/COUNTRY/DATE | TIME IN SECONDS OVER 500 M |
|---|---|---|
| 1 | Jeremy Wotherspoon, Canada, Jan 29, 2000 | 34.63 |
| 2 | Michael Ireland, Canada, Mar 18, 2000 | 34.66 |
| 3 | Hiroyasu Shimizu, Japan, Feb 20, 1999 | 34.79 |
| 4 | Jan Bos, Netherlands, Feb 21, 1999 | 34.87 |
| 5 | Minetaka Sasabuchi, Japan, Jan 29, 2000 | 35.08 |
| 6 | =Syoji Kato, Japan, Mar 18, 2000 | 35.10 |
| | =Toyoki Takeda, Japan, Jan 29, 2000 | 35.10 |
| 8 | Junichi Inoue, Japan, Mar 19, 2000 | 35.13 |
| 9 | Patrick Bouchard, Canada, Jan 29, 2000 | 35.18 |
| 10 | Sylvain Bouchard, Canada, Mar 28, 1998 | 35.21 |

*\* All speeds attained at Calgary*

Source: *International Skating Union*

### TOP 10 ★
## SKIERS IN THE 2000/01 ALPINE WORLD CUP (FEMALE)

| | SKIER/COUNTRY | OVERALL POINTS\* |
|---|---|---|
| 1 | Martina Ertl, Germany | 346 |
| 2 | Janica Kostelic, Croatia | 239 |
| 3 | Michaela Dorfmeister, Austria | 186 |
| 4 | Sonja Nef, Switzerland | 166 |
| 5 | Anja Paerson, Sweden | 165 |
| 6 | Regine Cavagnoud, France | 144 |
| 7 | Christel Saioni, France | 135 |
| 8 | Brigitte Obermoser, Austria | 131 |
| 9 | Andrine Flemmen, Norway | 109 |
| 10 | Karen Putzer, Italy | 101 |

*\* Awarded for performances in slalom, giant slalom, super giant, downhill, and combination disciplines; as at November 30, 2000*

Source: *International Ski Federation*

### TOP 10 ★
## SKIERS IN THE 2000/01 ALPINE WORLD CUP (MALE)

| | SKIER/COUNTRY | OVERALL POINTS\* |
|---|---|---|
| 1 | Hermann Maier, Austria | 276 |
| 2 | Lasse Kjus, Norway | 246 |
| 3 | Stephan Eberharter, Austria | 240 |
| 4 | Michael Gruenigen, Switzerland | 168 |
| 5 | Heinz Schilchegger, Austria | 152 |
| 6 | Andreas Schifferer, Austria | 140 |
| 7 | Fredrik Nyberg, Sweden | 135 |
| 8 | Kjetil Andre Aamodt, Norway | 131 |
| 9 | Josef Strobl, Austria | 114 |
| 10 | Didier Cuche, Switzerland | 101 |

*\* Awarded for performances in slalom, giant slalom, super giant, downhill, and combination disciplines; as at November 30, 2000*

Source: *International Ski Federation*

**Did You Know?** British ski enthusiast Sir Arnold Lunn (1888–1974), credited with introducing the slalom event in 1923, was knighted in 1953 "for services to skiing."

## WOMEN'S WORLD AND OLYMPIC FIGURE SKATING TITLES

| | SKATER/COUNTRY | YEARS | TITLES |
|---|---|---|---|
| 1 | Sonja Henie, Norway | 1927–36 | 13* |
| 2 =| Carol Heiss, US | 1956–60 | 6 |
| = | Herma Plank-Szabo, Austria | 1922–26 | 6# |
| = | Katarina Witt, East Germany | 1984–88 | 6 |
| 5 =| Sjoukje Dijkstra, Holland | 1962–64 | 4 |
| = | Peggy Fleming, US | 1966–68 | 4 |
| = | Lily Kronberger, Hungary | 1908–11 | 4 |
| = | Michelle Kwan, US | 1996–2001 | 4 |
| 9 | Tenley Albright, US | 1953–56 | 3 |
| = | Meray Horvath, Hungary | 1912–14 | 3 |
| = | Anett Potzsch, East Gemany | 1978–80 | 3 |
| = | Beatrix Schuba, Austria | 1971–72 | 3 |
| = | Barbara Ann Scott, Canada | 1947–48 | 3 |
| = | Madge Syers, GB | 1906–08 | 3 |
| = | Kristi Yamaguchi, US | 1991–92 | 3 |

\* Irina Rodnina (USSR) also won 13 titles, but in pairs competitions, 1969–80

# Plus three further titles in pairs competitions

## OLYMPIC FIGURE-SKATING COUNTRIES

| | COUNTRY | GOLD | SILVER | BRONZE | TOTAL |
|---|---|---|---|---|---|
| 1 | US | 12 | 13 | 14 | 39 |
| 2 | Soviet Union* | 13 | 10 | 6 | 29 |
| 3 | Austria | 7 | 9 | 4 | 20 |
| 4 | Canada | 2 | 7 | 9 | 18 |
| 5 | GB | 5 | 3 | 7 | 15 |
| 6 | France | 2 | 2 | 7 | 11 |
| 7 =| Sweden | 5 | 3 | 2 | 10 |
| = | East Germany | 3 | 3 | 4 | 10 |
| 9 | Germany# | 4 | 4 | 1 | 9 |
| 10 =| Hungary | 0 | 2 | 4 | 6 |
| = | Norway | 3 | 2 | 1 | 6 |

\* Includes Unified Team of 1992; excludes Russia since then

# Not including East/West Germany 1968–88

Figure skating was part of the Summer Olympics in 1908 and 1920, becoming part of the Winter program in 1924.

## FASTEST WINNING TIMES OF THE IDITAROD DOG SLED RACE

| | WINNER | YEAR | DAY | TIME HR | MIN | SEC |
|---|---|---|---|---|---|---|
| 1 | Doug Swingley | 2000 | 9 | 0 | 58 | 6 |
| 2 | Doug Swingley | 1995 | 9 | 2 | 42 | 19 |
| 3 | Jeff King | 1996 | 9 | 5 | 43 | 19 |
| 4 | Jeff King | 1998 | 9 | 5 | 52 | 26 |
| 5 | Martin Buser | 1997 | 9 | 8 | 30 | 45 |
| 6 | Doug Swingley | 1999 | 9 | 14 | 31 | 7 |
| 7 | Doug Swingley | 2001 | 9 | 19 | 55 | 50 |
| 8 | Martin Buser | 1994 | 10 | 13 | 2 | 39 |
| 9 | Jeff King | 1993 | 10 | 15 | 38 | 15 |
| 10 | Martin Buser | 1992 | 10 | 19 | 17 | 15 |

Source: *Iditarod Trail Committee*

The race, which has been held annually since 1973, stretches from Anchorage to Nome, Alaska, the course following an old river mail route and covering 1,158 miles (1,864 km).

**TOP DOUG**

*Doug Swingley from Simms, Montana, is one of only two non-Alaskans (the other is Martin Buser) to win the grueling 1,158-mile (1,864-km) Anchorage-to-Nome Iditarod dog sled race.*

# Sports Trivia

## FASTEST WINNING TIMES FOR THE HAWAII IRONMAN

| | WINNER/COUNTRY | YEAR | TIME HR:MIN:SEC |
|---|---|---|---|
| 1 | Luc Van Lierde, Belgium | 1996 | 8:04:08 |
| 2 | Mark Allen, US | 1993 | 8:07:45 |
| 3 | Mark Allen | 1992 | 8:09:08 |
| 4 | Mark Allen | 1989 | 8:09:16 |
| 5 | Luc Van Lierde | 1999 | 8:17:17 |
| 6 | Mark Allen | 1991 | 8:18:32 |
| 7 | Greg Welch, Australia | 1994 | 8:20:27 |
| 8 | Mark Allen | 1995 | 8:20:34 |
| 9 | Peter Reid, Canada | 2000 | 8:21:01 |
| 10 | Peter Reid | 1998 | 8:24:20 |

This is perhaps one of the most grueling of all sporting contests, in which competitors engage in a 2.4-mile (3.86-km) swim, followed by a 112-mile (180-km) cycle race, ending with a full Marathon (26 miles 385 yards/42.195 km). The first Hawaii Ironman was held at Waikiki Beach in 1978, but since 1981 it has been at Kailua-Kona.

## COLLEGE SPORTS IN THE US*

| | SPORT | PARTICIPANTS, 1998–99 WOMEN | MEN | TOTAL |
|---|---|---|---|---|
| 1 | Football | – | 56,528 | 56,528 |
| 2 | Outdoor track | 18,220 | 20,401 | 38,621 |
| 3 | Soccer | 17,520 | 18,238 | 35,758 |
| 4 | Indoor track | 15,460 | 16,943 | 32,403 |
| 5 | Basketball | 14,365 | 15,710 | 30,075 |
| 6 | Baseball | – | 25,669 | 25,669 |
| 7 | Cross-country | 12,042 | 10,935 | 22,977 |
| 8 | Swimming/diving | 10,012 | 7,559 | 17,571 |
| 9 | Tennis | 8,492 | 7,729 | 16,221 |
| 10 | Softball | 14,943 | – | 14,943 |

* Based on participation in National Collegiate Athletic Association (NCAA) sports

Source: NCAA

In the period surveyed by the NCAA (1998–99), a total of 148,803 women and 211,273 men participated in college sports. These figures include "emerging," or non-championship sports, such as squash and women's ice hockey.

## PARTICIPATION ACTIVITIES IN THE US

| | ACTIVITY | PERCENTAGE CHANGE SINCE PREVIOUS YEAR | PARTICIPANTS* (1999) |
|---|---|---|---|
| 1 | Exercise walking | +4.1 | 80,800,000 |
| 2 | Swimming | -0.6 | 57,900,000 |
| 3 | Camping | +7.8 | 50,100,000 |
| 4 | Fishing | +7.1 | 46,700,000 |
| 5 | Exercising with equipment | -2.0 | 45,200,000 |
| 6 | Bicycle riding | -2.6 | 42,400,000 |
| 7 | Bowling | +3.9 | 41,600,000 |
| 8 | Billiards/pool | -0.4 | 32,100,000 |
| 9 | Basketball | -0.7 | 29,400,000 |
| 10 | Hiking | +3.3 | 28,100,000 |

* Participating more than once during the year

Source: National Sporting Goods Association

## ALL-AROUND CHAMPION COWBOYS

| | COWBOY | YEARS | WINS |
|---|---|---|---|
| 1 | Ty Murray | 1989–98 | 7 |
| 2 = | Tom Ferguson | 1974–79 | 6 |
| = | Larry Mahan | 1966–73 | 6 |
| 4 | Jim Shoulders | 1949–59 | 5 |
| 5 = | Joe Beaver | 1995–2000 | 3 |
| = | Lewis Feild | 1985–87 | 3 |
| = | Dean Oliver | 1963–65 | 3 |
| 8 = | Everett Bowman | 1935–37 | 2 |
| = | Louis Brooks | 1943–44 | 2 |
| = | Clay Carr | 1930–33 | 2 |
| = | Bill Linderman | 1950–53 | 2 |
| = | Phil Lyne | 1971–72 | 2 |
| = | Gerald Roberts | 1942–48 | 2 |
| = | Casey Tibbs | 1951–55 | 2 |
| = | Harry Tompkins | 1952–60 | 2 |

**ROUGH RIDE**

*Recognized as the "ultimate cowboy championship," the title of PRCA World Champion All-Around Cowboy is the most prestigious title in professional rodeo.*

## THE 10 LATEST WINNERS OF THE SPORTS ILLUSTRATED SPORTSMAN/SPORTSWOMAN OF THE YEAR AWARD

*(Year/winner/sport)*

❶ 2000 Tiger Woods, golf ❷ 1999 US Women's World Cup Squad, soccer ❸ 1998 Mark McGwire and Sammy Sosa, baseball ❹ 1997 Dean Smith, basketball coach ❺ 1996 Tiger Woods, golf ❻ 1995 Cal Ripken Jr., baseball ❼ 1994 Johan Olav Koss and Bonnie Blair, ice skating ❽ 1993 Don Shula, football coach ❾ 1992 Arthur Ashe, tennis ❿ 1991 Michael Jordan, basketball

**AUSTRALIAN RULES**
*The Victorian Football League was formed in 1896, changing its name in 1990 to the Australian Football League.*

## TOP 10 ★
# HIGHEST-EARNING SPORTSMEN

| SPORTSMAN | SPORT/TEAM | 2000 INCOME ($) |
|---|---|---|
| 1 Michael Schumacher, Germany | Motor racing, Ferrari | 59,000,000 |
| 2 Tiger Woods, US | Golf | 53,000,000 |
| 3 Mike Tyson, US | Boxing | 48,000,000 |
| 4 Michael Jordan, US | Basketball, Chicago Bulls | 37,000,000 |
| 5 Dale Earnhardt*, US | Stock car racing | 26,500,000 |
| 6 Grant Hill, US | Basketball, Detroit Pistons | 26,000,000 |
| 7 Shaquille O'Neal, US | Basketball, LA Lakers | 24,000,000 |
| 8 =Oscar De La Hoya, US | Boxing | 23,000,000 |
| =Lennox Lewis, UK | Boxing | 23,000,000 |
| 10 Kevin Garnett, US | Basketball, Minnesota Timberwolves | 21,000,000 |

*\* Killed February 18, 2001, during Daytona 500*
*Used by permission of Forbes magazine*

## TOP 10 ★
# SPORTING EVENTS WITH THE LARGEST TV AUDIENES IN THE US

| EVENT | DATE | RATING |
|---|---|---|
| 1 Super Bowl XVI | Jan 24, 1982 | 49.1 |
| 2 Super Bowl XVII | Jan 30, 1983 | 48.6 |
| 3 XVII Winter Olympics | Feb 23, 1994 | 48.5 |
| 4 Super Bowl XX | Jan 26, 1986 | 48.3 |
| 5 Super Bowl XII | Jan 15, 1978 | 47.2 |
| 6 Super Bowl XIII | Jan 21, 1979 | 47.1 |
| 7 =Super Bowl XVIII | Jan 22, 1984 | 46.4 |
| =Super Bowl XIX | Jan 20, 1985 | 46.4 |
| 9 Super Bowl XIV | Jan 20, 1980 | 46.3 |
| 10 Super Bowl XXX | Jan 28, 1996 | 46.0 |

*Source: Nielsen Media Research*

# TOP 10 AUSTRALIAN FOOTBALL LEAGUE TEAMS
*(Team/Grand Final wins)*

**1** = Carlton Blues, 16; = Essendon Bombers, 16
**3** Collingwood Magpies, 14 **4** Melbourne Demons, 12
**5** Richmond Tigers, 10 **6** Hawthorn Hawks, 9
**7** Fitzroy Lions, 8 **8** Geelong Cats, 6 **9** Kangaroos (North Melbourne), 4 **10** South Melbourne, 3

**Did You Know?** The first ever rodeo organized as a competition was held at Prescott, Arizona, on July 4, 1888. It was won by Juan Leivas, who won a silver trophy and the title "Best Cowboy."

# Index

**UK research assistants:**
Laurence Hill, Manuela Mackenzie

**Special US research:**
Dafydd Rees with help from Bonnie Fantasia, Linda Rees and Christiaan Rees

Thanks to the individuals, organizations, and publications listed below who kindly supplied information to enable me to prepare many of the lists.

Caroline Ash, Javier Beltram, Richard Braddish, Pete Compton, Kaylee Coxall, Luke Crampton, Sidney S. Culbert, François Curiel, Philip Eden, Steve Fielding, Christopher Forbes, Russell E. Gough, Monica Grady, Stan Greenberg, Duncan Hislop, Heidi Gyani, Andreas Hörstemeier, Tony Hutson, Alan Jeffreys, Larry Kilman, Robert Lamb, Jo LaVerde, Dr Benjamin Lucas, Chris Mead, Ian Morrison, William Nicholson, William O'Hara, Tony Pattison, Adrian Room, Leslie Roskind, Bill Rudman, Jacob Schwartz, Robert Senior, Lisa E. Smith, Mitchell Symons, Thomas Tranter, Lucy T. Verma, Tony Waltham

Academy of Motion Picture Arts and Sciences, ACNielsen MMS, Adherents.com, *Advertising Age, Airline Business,* Air Transport Intelligence, American Forests, American Institute of Stress, American Jewish Year Book Vol.100, American Society of Composers, Authors, and Publishers, Amnesty International, *Amusement Business, Art Newspaper,* Art Sales Index, Associated Press, Association of Tennis Professionals (ATP), Audit Bureau of Circulations Ltd, Australian Department of Immigration and Multicultural Affairs, Australian Football League (AFL), *Auto Express,* Beverage Marketing Corporation, *Billboard,* Booker Prize, Boston Athletics Association, *BP Amoco Statistical Review of World Energy 2000,* BPI, Breeders Cup, British Cave Research Association, British Columbia Vital Statistics Agency, British Home Office, British Library, British Museum (Natural History), Bureau of Federal Prisons, Business Ethics, Cannes Film Festival, Carbon Dioxide Information Analysis Center, Cat Fancier's Association, Center for Disease Control, Central Intelligence Agency, Central Statistics Office/An Príomh-Oifig Staidrimh, Ireland, *Chainstore Age,* Championship Auto Racing Teams (CART), Channel Swimming Association, Christian Research, Christie's, CIVC, *Classical Music,* Columbia University (Pulitzer Prizes), Competitive Media Reporting, Computer Industry Almanac, Inc, Country Music Association, Davis Cup, Death Penalty Information Center, De Beers, Deloitte & Touche, Duncan's American Radio, *The Economist, Editor & Publisher Year Book,* Electoral Reform Society, Energy Information Administration, Environmental Technology Center, Ernst & Young,

Euromonitor, Eurotoys, *FBI Uniform Crime Reports,* Federal Highway Administration, *Financial Times,* Fleetwood-Owen, *Flight International,* Food and Agriculture Organization of the United Nations, *Forbes, Fortune,* Global Reach, Gold Fields Mineral Services Ltd, *The Handbook of Private Schools,* Harley Medical Group, Hawaii Ironman, Hollywood Foreign Press Association (Golden Globe Awards), Honda UK, House of Commons Reference Library, Iditarod Trail Committee, Indianapolis Motor Speedway, Institute for Family Enterprise, Bryant College, Interbrand, Intercollegiate Rowing Association, International Amateur Athletic Association, International Associatiion of Ports and Harbors, International Atomic Energy Agency, International Civil Aviation Organization, International Cocoa Organization, International Coffee Organization, International Commission on Large Dams, International Council of Shopping Centers, International Federation of Red Cross and Red Cross Societies, International Game Fish Association, International Skating Union, International Ski Federation, International Table Tennis Federation, International Telecommunication Union, International Union for the Conservation of Nature, International Water Ski Federation, Inter-Parliamentary Union, Jockey Club, League of American Theaters and Producers, Lloyds Register of Shipping/MIPG/ PPMS, Magazine Publishers of America, Major League Baseball, Mazda UK, Meat and Livestock Commission, Metropolitan Museum of Art, Metropolitan Opera House, New York, Modern Language Association of America, Museum of Fine Arts, Boston, MRIB, *M Street,* NASA, National Academy of Popular Music, National Academy of Recording Arts and Sciences (NARAS), National Academy of Television Arts and Sciences (Emmy Awards), National Association of Broadcasters, National Association of College Bookstores, National Association of Consumer Agency Administration, National Association of Stock Car Auto Racing, Inc (NASCAR), National Basketball Association (NBA), National Book Foundation, National Center for Education Statistics, National Center for Health Statistics, National Center for Injury Prevention and Control, National Collegiate Athletic Association (NCAA), National Fire Protection Association, National Football League (NFL), National Gallery, Washington, DC, National Highway Traffic Safety Administration, National Hockey League (NHL), National Hockey League Players Association, National Hurricane Center, National Public Radio (NPR), National Retail Federation, National Sporting Goods Association, National Steeplechase Association, National Thoroughbred Racing Association, National Trotting Association, New South Wales Registry of Births, Deaths and Marriages, New York Drama Desk, Niagara Falls Museum, Nielsen Media Research, Nobel Foundation, NPD, Office for National Statistics,

UK, *Official Museum Directory,* Oxford University Press, PC Data Online, Peabody Awards, Pet Industry Joint Advisory Council, Phillips Group, Phobics Society, Popular Music Database, Public Library Association, Produktschap voor Gedistilleerde Dranken, Professional Golfers' Association (PGA), Professional Rodeo Cowboys Association (PRCA), Professional Squash Association, Public Broadcasting System (PBS), Publishers Information Bureau, *Publishers Weekly, Raceboat International, Railway Gazette International,* Recording Industry Association of America (RIAA), Research Director, 1999 PD Profile®, Royal Aeronautical Society, Ryder Cup, Salt Institute, Scott Polar Research Institute, *Screen Digest,* showbizdata, Siemens AG, W.H. Smith Ltd, Sotheby's, *Spaceflight,* Sports Business Research Network, *Sports Illustrated,* Stanford Institute for the Quantitative Study of Society, *Statistical Abstract of the United States, Steeplechase Times,* Stockholm International Peace Research Institute, *Stores, Supermarket News, Television Business International, Theatre World, Time, Top Gear,* Tour de France, Tourism Industries, International Trade Administration, Toyota UK, UCI Mountain Bike World Cup, UNESCO, UNICEF, United Nations, Universal Postal Union, US Agency for International Development, US Bureau of Economic Analysis, US Bureau of Engraving and Printing, US Bureau of Labor Statistics, US Census Bureau, US Committee for Refugees, US Consumer Product Safety Commission, US Department of Agriculture/Economic Research Service, US Department of Agriculture Forest Service, US Department of Justice, US Department of Transportation, US Geological Survey, US Immigration and Naturalization Service, US Mint, US National Park Service, US National Science Foundation, US Patent and Trademark Office, *Variety,* VH1, VideoScan, Inc, *Video Store,* Volkswagen UK, Ward's Automotive, *Wavelength,* Westminster Kennel Club, Women's International Squash Players Association, Women's National Basketball Association (WNBA), World Association of Newspapers, World Bank, World Cup Skateboarding, World Health Organization, World Intellectual Property Organization, World Motorbike Endurance Championship, World Resources Institute, World Science Fiction Society, World Superbike Championship, World Tourism Organization, Zenith International

**Index**
Patrica Coward

**DK Picture Librarians**
Melanie Simmonds

**Packager's acknowledgments:**
Cooling Brown would like to thank Carolyn MacKenzie for proof reading and Peter Cooling for technical support.

# Picture Credits

The publisher would like to thank the following for their kind permission to reproduce their photographs:

(Abbreviations key: t=top, b=bottom, r=right, l=left, c=centre)

**Advertising Archives:** 199tl.

**AKG London:** Marion Kalter 121; Tony Vaccaro 122tl.

**Allsport:** 279; Andrew Redington 266tr; Ben Radford 243l, 260; Clive Brunskill 242l, 245, 273; David Cannon 242c, 267; Doug Pensinger 242r, 263tr; Gary M Prior 246l; Jamie Squire 244; Michael Steele 262bl; Mike Powell 243r, 247bl, 251; Nathan Silow 247tr; Nick Wilson 275; Scott Barbour 255; Shaun Botterill 261, 276tl; Simon Bruty 5bc, 254; Stephen Dunn 253; Stu Forster 272; Tom Herbert 268-269.

**Apple Computer:** 212.

**Aviation Images:** Mark Wagner 239.

**Bite Communications Ltd:** 202tr.

**The Booker Prize for Fiction:** 99r, 111.

**Breitling SA:** 46c, 63b.

**Capital Pictures:** Phil Loftus 145.

**China Photo Library:** 96b.

**Christie's Images Ltd:** 99l, 108bl, 118tr, 119br, 123br, 176bl.

**Bruce Coleman Ltd:** Jeff Foott 34bl.

**Corbis:** 73tr; Bettmann 158br, 226; Bob Rowan/Progressive Image 195tr, 206bl; C Moore 93r; Daniel Lane 79l, 88tl; Earl Kowall 30r, 44l, 97br; Jack Fields 3, 77br; James Marshall 8l, 18l; Jay Dickman 215t; Jean-Pierre Lescourret 224l, 228; Jim Richardson 26bl; Kevin Fleming 45tl; Michael S Yamashita 155br, 229tl; Natalie Fobes 214bl; Paul A Souders 207tr; Peter Turnley 72l; Phililp James Corwin 71; Richard T Nowitz 22t; Robert Holmes 104tl; Sheldan Collins 103t, 194bl; Stephen Frink 35br; Trisha Rafferty/Eye Ubiquitous 198; Wayne Lawler/Ecoscene 21t.

**Brian Cosgrove:** 9r, 24-25.

**Eyewire:** 210l.

**Gables:** 52bl.

**Galaxy Picture Library:** D. Roddy/LPI 13tl; Gordan Garradd 10tr.

**Gettyimages Stone:** Antonia Reeve 102tl; Ron Sherman 98l, 105br; Will and Deni McIntyre 19tc; Yann Layma 78l, 85t.

**Ronald Grant Archive:** 181tr; "1992 Warner Bros/DC Comics 170br; "1998 Warner Bros/Brian Hamill 170tl; "1998 Universal/Dreamworks, photo Bruce Talamon 180bl; "1996 20th Century Fox 158-159; "1985 Amblin/Universal 161tl; "2000 Chan Kam Chuen/Columbia/Sony 163; "1996 Hollywood Pictures/Buena Vista 168tr; "2000 Jaap Buitendijk/Dreamworks/Universal 153r, 157br; "1999 K Wright/New Line 152c, 157tl; "1997 Keith Hamshire/Eon Productions, photo Keith Hamshire 168bl; "1961 Paramount 152r, 179; "1999 Warner Bros, photo Jason Boland 189; "1999 Ralph Nelson/Castle Rock/Warner Bros 153l, 173; "1998 Ron Phillips/Hollywood Pictures 152l, 175tr; "1975 United

Artists/Fantasy Films 164; "1997 Wallace Merie/20th Century Fox/Paramount 156bl; "1996 Warner Bros/Universal/Amblin 174; "1996 Working Title/Polygram 165.

**Hulton Getty:** 60tr.

**Kobal Collection:** ©1975 Universal (UIP) 159br; "1989 Columbia 160bl; "1993 Sam Goldwyn/Renaissance Films/BBC 154; "1995 New Line Cinema/Entertainment Film 169tr; ©1997 Columbia Tristar 171; ©2000 Arte France/Blind Spot/Dinovi 166; ©2000Bob Marshak/Universal 167; ©1994 Paramount UIP 161br.

**London Features International:** Jen Lowery 2.

**McLaren Cars Limited (www.mclarencars.com):** 227.

**The Museum of the Moving Image:** 177.

**NASA:** 10bl, 16; Finley Holiday Films 11t.

**Nordfoto:** Liselotte Sabroe 240.

**Panos Pictures:** Caroline Penn 104br.

**Amit Pashricha:** 211br.

**PetExcellence:** 277br.

**Photodisc:** 3, 47l, 51tr, 77l, 192; - 218-219, 220-221, 256-257, 258-259.

**Popperfoto:** 238bl; Reuter 217l.

**Redferns:** 132tr; Amanda Edwards 147; David Redfern 130br, 138bl; Ebet Roberts 134; Fin Costello 126c, 133br; Graham Salter 150; Harry Herd 131tl; JM International 136tr, 140; Michel Linssen 178; Mick Hutson 5c, 126l, 127r, 139r, 141, 148bl; Nicky J Sims 146; Paul Bergen 126r, 127l, 137r, 142, 149t; Richie Asron 151; Tom Hanley 143tr.

**Rex Features:** Bill Zygmant 125.

**Science Photo Library:** 48l; Frank Zullo 12bl; GJLP 49br; Hank Morgan 48tr; Hans-Ulrich Osterwalder 28tl; Laguna Design 27tr; Peter Thorne, Johnson Matthey 203br.

**Bill Seebold's Bud Light Racing Team:** Rick Stoff 274.

**Frank Spooner Pictures:** G Mingasson-Liaison 278; Regan/Liaison 172.

**Steiff Teddy Bears:** Paul & Rosemary Volpp 98l, 114.

**Still Pictures:** Fritz Polking 33cr.

**Swift Imagery, Swift Media:** 107.

**Sygma:** Corbis 235br.

**Kim Taylor:** 41br.

**Topham Picturepoint:** 57tc; Associated Press 237tl; Max Nash/SEF 56b; Tony Arruza 29t; Young Joon 65tr.

**Toyota (GB) PLC:** 229br.

**Jerry Young:** 37tr.

**All other images © Dorling Kindersley.**
**For further information see: www.dkimages.com**